THE
BEST OF
HUMAN EVENTS

Fifty Years of Conservative Thought and Action

Edited by
James C. Roberts

Huntington House Publishers

Huntington House Publishers
P.O. Box 53788
Lafayette, Louisiana 70505

Library of Congress Card Catalog Number 93-77299
ISBN 1-56384-018-9

Contents

Acknowledgments

Nearly a decade has passed since the idea of a HUMAN EVENTS anthology was conceived, and a host of people have provided invaluable assistance along the way. Pride of place in this list should go to Tom Winter and Allan Ryskind, the two chief editors of HUMAN EVENTS for over thirty years. Without their heroic efforts, there would have been no fortieth, much less fiftieth, anniversary of HUMAN EVENTS to celebrate.

Similarly, without their guidance and assistance in reviewing fifty years' worth of articles, there would be no book. For their friendship and support, I am deeply grateful.

Longtime HUMAN EVENTS employee Olin Miers also deserves special mention for his diligence and professionalism in typesetting the manuscript. Cleo Grant, loyal assistant to the HUMAN EVENTS editors, was also most helpful in doing the research and article retrieval needed. And, Marja Walker did a superb job in overseeing the scanning and correcting of the copy.

I'm also grateful to Tom Phillips, president of Phillips Publishing International, the new majority owner of HUMAN EVENTS, who inherited this book project and has given it his enthusiastic support. Thanks are due as well to Jeff Carneal, president of Phillips Publishing's subsidiary, Eagle Publishing, and to Mark Ziebarth, Eagle's vice president, for their support and assistance in bringing this project to fruition.

Many people at Huntington House Publishers have also played important roles in this effort. Foremost among them are Huntington House editor-in-chief, Mark Anthony, for his encouragement over a period of years and Renatti Dupont, who spent many long hours in preparing the manuscript for publication.

And finally, I want to thank my wife, Patti, for her steadfast support of this project—and many others—over the past eighteen years.

Introduction

During the weekend of 11–12 October 1986, President Ronald Reagan and his key defense and foreign policy lieutenants engaged in tense, marathon negotiations with their Soviet counterparts at Hofdi House in Reykjavik, Iceland. During these unprecedented talks (which were ultimately to founder on the question of the Strategic Defense Initiative), Reagan and Mikhail Gorbachev thrust and parried in a flurry of proposals and counterproposals to eliminate whole classes of nuclear weapons from the face of the earth. In the midst of the frenzy, Ronald Reagan paused and (according to columnists Rowland Evans and Robert Novak) asked his subordinates, "What will HUMAN EVENTS think of this?"

The question was a remarkable demonstration of the impact that HUMAN EVENTS ("The National Conservative Weekly") had on the thinking of the most powerful man in the world at that moment. The kind of relationship implied by Reagan's question has rarely been seen between any president and any publication. Even more remarkable, in the case of HUMAN EVENTS, the publication was one few Americans had even heard of.

The lack of renown is not a matter of concern to the present editors Tom Winter and Allan Ryskind. Like their predecessors, they have rigorously eschewed the limelight, preferring to let the publication speak for itself. And, HUMAN EVENTS' voice *has* been heard. Founded fifty years ago as a newsletter, it grew in the 1960s to tabloid size but rarely exceeded twenty pages in length. The subscription base has also remained modest over the years, rarely exceeding one hundred thousand.

The impact of HUMAN EVENTS, however, has been far greater than these figures would indicate. Its title inspired by the Declaration of Independence ("When in the course of human events . . ."), it can be argued that HUMAN EVENTS has been one of the most influential publications in the ensuing 218 years.

HUMAN EVENTS helped to launch the conservative movement and has been one of the mainstays of the movement for a half-century. HUMAN EVENTS' main constituency has been conservative activists, and its main contribution has been to get information to these activists informing them about what's happening in Washington and in cities and state capitals all around the nation. It has also had a significant impact on policy, especially on Republican presidents.

Week in, week out, year in, and year out for fifty years, HUMAN EVENTS has rallied the troops, resolutely opposing the latest liberal spasm, aggressively promoting conservative initiatives, smiting leading leftists, championing conservative leaders when appropriate, and chastising irresolute conservative leaders when called for, and, above all, standing steadfastly for principle in the face of constant pressures to compromise, cut a deal, or simply give up.

Over the decades, in federal, state, and national elections, in legislative battles, in the policies of presidential administrations, in matters great and small, HUMAN EVENTS has had an impact. There have been many defeats along the way, but also some great triumphs to savor—perhaps foremost among them being the inauguration of HUMAN EVENTS partisan Ronald Reagan as president of the United States in 1981 and ten years later seeing the collapse of the Soviet empire.

During five decades of publication, a host of authors have appeared in HUMAN EVENTS. Many of them—Gen. Douglas MacArthur, Herbert Hoover, Fulton Lewis, Jr., Victor Lasky, Lowell Thomas, William F. Buckley, Jr., Ronald Reagan, and Richard Nixon, to name a few—are household names. Many are less well known.

In this anthology, the editors of HUMAN EVENTS and I have selected only a few of the many thousands of articles published over fifty years in an effort to provide a sampling of the myriad issues and personalities featured in this singular publication. The authors are a disparate lot in many ways, but all share Richard Weaver's view that "ideas have consequences," the belief that principles matter, and a determination, as with Teddy Roosevelt's man in the arena, to become engaged in the great battles of the day.

When the history of this most bloody of all centuries is written, let it be recorded that the editors and writers of HUMAN EVENTS were there where and when it counted, resisting the forces of tyranny and barbarism, upholding the dignity of the individual, the central role of the family, the imperative of community, and the transcendent importance of faith.

JAMES C. ROBERTS

Ronald Reagan's videotaped remarks to the HUMAN EVENTS
50th Anniversary Gala Dinner in Washington, D.C., on 27 September 1994

Greetings fellow conservatives,

I'm delighted to join you tonight as you celebrate fifty years of HUMAN EVENTS. Five decades is certainly a milestone. I must admit, however, that when you get to be my age, you can't help but to put things into perspective. The truth of the matter is that I've got suits older than that.

Nevertheless, I am pleased to serve as tonight's Honorary Chairman, given the importance of this publication to the conservative movement. And because of the influence of HUMAN EVENTS, I'm impressed that many of America's most prominent conservatives have come to show their support.

HUMAN EVENTS has been spreading the revolutionary news of our crusade for as long as I can remember, and we all can attest to the power of the press. I've been reading it for over thirty-three years, and I know it was influencing conservative thought long before I came along. Nevertheless, HUMAN EVENTS has served a vitally important purpose all these years.

For decades, it has provided story after story of hard-hitting news on the front pages—stories on current issues, our future, and the direction of our nation. You have touched the minds and hearts of countless Americans by providing not only news and features but also wisdom about the human condition. With your help we won the war with the Evil Empire, and the Berlin Wall came crumbling down.

You and I had no doubt that, ultimately, the cause of political and economic freedom and, therefore, the spread of civilization would triumph. We knew then, as conservatives, it was necessary to be unwavering in our cause until all people are at last free to determine their own destiny. But the war to preserve our freedoms here at home continues. This is no trivial battle, and we must do everything in our power, despite the fact that we are under attack each and every day.

My friends, the nation once more hungers for our message. Our work is not yet done, and we must continue the crusade that began so many years ago. I feel confident that HUMAN EVENTS will be a powerful voice of freedom, and of hope, and of opportunity for the conservative movement.

Tonight, as you celebrate a true milestone, please know that my thoughts are with you. Thank you, and God bless you.

Chapter One | The Conservative Movement

Perhaps the greatest political phenomenon in postwar America has been the rise of the conservative movement. The creed of a few lonely politicians, intellectuals, and businessmen in the early 1950s, conservatism, it can be fairly said, is the dominant philosophy in America today. The articles in this chapter trace the growth of the conservative movement over the past three-and-a-half decades.

"HUMAN EVENTS and the Conservative Movement: Fifty Years Working Together" is a survey of the role HUMAN EVENTS has had in first helping to launch and then sustaining American conservatism over the past half century. The piece is by M. Stanton Evans, himself a major figure in the modern conservative revival (and a long-time contributor to HUMAN EVENTS) and was written for the fiftieth anniversary issue.

In "For Our Children's Children" (6 September 1950), Frank Chodorov, one of the founding fathers of the movement, laments the influence of Socialists on the college campus. He calls for corrective action, suggesting the founding of an organization that would instill an individualist, as opposed to a collectivist, outlook in the young.

The next year Chodorov's idea became a reality with the founding of the Intercollegiate Society of Individualists (later to be renamed the Intercollegiate Studies Institute). Over the succeeding years, ISI has given tens of thousands of college students an introduction to conservatism and ISI alumni now occupy key positions in Washington and throughout the nation.

William F. Buckley, Jr., who founded *National Review* in 1955, wrote his first postcollege articles for HUMAN EVENTS. In "Harvard Hogs the Headlines" (16 May 1951 issue), he presaged his famous book *God and Man at Yale*.

HUMAN EVENTS has, since its inception, pressed the Republican party to hew to a strong conservative philosophy. The editors have seen this as the principled thing to do of course, but also as the politically smart thing to do as well. In "The Middle of the Road—Where It Leads" (24 March 1956 issue), Richard Weaver, one of the foremost intellectual leaders of the conservative intellectual movement, writes of the dangers of the moderate approach to politics.

As the conservative movement grew, so did its literary output, and it wasn't long before conservatives had their very own bookclub. Anne Edwards chronicled "The Story of the Conservative Book Club" in the 20 May 1967, issue of HUMAN EVENTS.

HUMAN EVENTS and the Conservative Movement: Fifty Years Working Together

By M. Stanton Evans

(Mr. Evans, a former managing editor of HUMAN EVENTS *and now a contributing editor, graduated from Yale in 1955, magna cum laude and Phi Beta Kappa. In 1959, he left* HUMAN EVENTS *to become an editorial writer for the Indianapolis* News *and a year later was made editor of that publication. He returned to Washington in 1975 as a syndicated columnist and chairman of the American Conservative Union. In addition to his writing and commentating, he runs the Education and Research Institute and its National Journalism Center and is publisher of* Consumer's Research *magazine. He is the author of* Revolt on the Campus, The Liberal Establishment, The Politics of Surrender, The Law-Breakers, The Future of Conservatism, Clear and Present Dangers, *and* The Theme is Freedom.)*

The political game plan for conservatives of the modern era was written long ago by Archimedes: Give me a place to stand, and I can move the world.

Conservatives have also known for a considerable time the solid ground on which they should be standing: The age-old principles of the West, faith and freedom, limited government and the rule of law, the traditional precepts embodied in our Constitution. The principles were clear enough, and changeless. The problem was getting people to stand there: To convert these values into a platform that could redeem the confusions of our troubled epoch.

To make this transition from precept into practice has been the mission of HUMAN EVENTS since its beginning 50 years ago—at the height of New Deal-liberal rule, and a low point of conservative aspiration. In the intervening decades, the conservative cause has waxed in size and strength, with HUMAN EVENTS consistently in the forefront. The continuing growth is directly linked to the willingness of the conservative movement, and this journal, not just to do something, but to stand there.

That such resort to principle in point of fact has moved the world is evident most of all in the achievements of Ronald Reagan. As readers of this journal are perhaps aware, the career of Reagan and that of HUMAN EVENTS for many years were closely intertwined. He has been an inveterate reader of these pages, and HUMAN EVENTS in turn became a stalwart backer of Reagan's candidacies and programs.

Most notably, this journal supported the Reagan insurgent effort within the GOP in 1976, and his successful run in 1980. After his election, these pages brimmed with reports and comment backing all his major programs: Tax rate reductions and efforts to slow the growth of federal spending, deregulation, Supreme Court nominations, rebuilding America's defenses, support for anti-Communist forces around the globe, and a great deal else.

The affinity between President Reagan and HUMAN EVENTS was often a source of sardonic comment by "pragmatists" in the GOP and by many in the media. Lou Cannon wrote, for instance, that Reagan gave as much credence to something in HUMAN EVENTS as he did to an item in the New York *Times*—to Cannon a self-evident absurdity (to which Ed Meese replied: No, he gave *more* credence to HUMAN EVENTS, and with good reason, since its reports were much more factual).

What united our 40th President and this unusual publication was more than a shared belief in conservative values, though that was certainly apparent. It was the further belief that standing up for conservative precepts was a formula for *winning*—both in the internal political struggles of our nation, and in the far more deadly contest with our adversaries in the Kremlin. On both counts, the historical record shows that Reagan and the editors of this journal were correct, their "pragmatic" and liberal foes repeatedly mistaken.

What has happened in the decades since HUMAN EVENTS was founded, indeed, has been nothing short of a revolution, in which this journal played, and continues to play, a leading role. In the 1940s and early '50s, conservatism was disparaged as intellectually absurd and politically irrelevant. The critic Lionel Trilling conceded that there *were* no conservative ideas to speak of in our national discourse, a judgment fully endorsed by the academic and media sages of the time.

In explicitly political terms, it was generally believed that conservative ideas of limited government, lower taxes, and firmness in our dealings overseas were tickets to oblivion. An entire library of books was written to prove the point, suggesting that the Republican Party could survive only by transforming itself into a Wall Street version of the reigning Democrats.

Today such comments come over as musings from some other planet. The conservative viewpoint, once dismissed as hopelessly outmoded, is now in the ascendant intellectually, and has made astonishing advances in the world of voting politics. Liberal notions of big government on the home front and weakness overseas are thoroughly discredited, and liberal candidates who try to merchandise such nostrums to the public are in for serious trouble.

Much of this transformation in our thinking must be put down to hard experience. The liberal theories have been tried, and tried again, and been found wanting. It is difficult, indeed, to think of a policy area in which the social planners and accommodationists have succeeded; it is all too easy to name the ones where liberal panaceas turned out to be the source of agonizing problems.

Even so, policy failures don't analyze themselves. In order for the public to seek and get corrective action, there has to be a critique of the situation that points out the *causes* of the problem, devises necessary remedies, and energizes the forces that will put such remedies in motion. To supply these elements has been the role of the conservative movement in our politics—a movement that is today a powerful reality, but 50 years ago did not exist.

The rise of Reagan and the work of HUMAN EVENTS are merely different aspects of this development. The President came to notice in the middle 1960s as *the* political candidate of the conservative movement, and remained such during his years in office—though he also established a somewhat broader constituency along the way. HUMAN EVENTS, for its part, has been and is the newspaper of that movement, without which the political changes of the modern era would be difficult to imagine.

While there are many conservative journals and journalists that have played a laudable role in our political drama, HUMAN EVENTS takes pride of place in three respects: It is the senior conservative media outlet enjoying a history of continuous publication, it is situated in the nation's capital where the legislative battles are conducted, and it has labored indefatigably to inform and mobilize the cadres of the movement.

As a result, throughout this period of 50 years, HUMAN EVENTS has always been where the action is. It has spanned the history of political conservatism from the era of Hoover-Taft Old Guard Republicanism to the epoch of Reagan and Jack Kemp. And, more than simply "being there," it has actively helped to shape and direct the movement of ideas that has carried us from one political era to another. It hasn't merely grown in stature with the rising influence of conservatism; it has worked effectively to make that influence happen.

From the perspective of 1944, when HUMAN EVENTS was founded by Frank C. Hanighen, Henry Regnery, Gen. Robert Wood and others, conservative politics as it exists today would have been hard to envision. The journal itself in the early days was published from Hanighen's apartment, and the free-market, limited government views that it promoted were self-consciously heretical.

Even at that period, however, HUMAN EVENTS possessed a resource that would carry it through the darkest hours of liberal rule, and that it still possesses today: Its commitment to fundamental principle, and its willingness to test events and individuals by its unvarying standards. Despite occasional shifts in emphasis or packaging, the credenda of the publication today remain what they were in 1944—free markets and free people, affirmation of traditional values, defense of our just interests overseas.

In the early days, HUMAN EVENTS was closely aligned with the Taft wing of the Republican

Party. Its heroes were Taft himself, Styles Bridges of New Hampshire, Bill Knowland of California, and, the *bete noire* of the liberals, Joe McCarthy of Wisconsin.

Taft lost out to Eisenhower in 1952, of course, and McCarthy was dragged down by the liberal media, and censured by the Senate, two years later. Those were bleak times for conservative Republicans—and for HUMAN EVENTS. Undaunted, it continued to hold the conservative banner aloft, and to work for the development of a new and different kind of conservatism that could withstand the power of the media and Eastern GOP establishment that had done in Taft and Joe McCarthy.

Thus, HUMAN EVENTS was in the forefront of political developments in the early 1960s—which were, in retrospect, the formative period of the present era in our politics. It played host to the first conservative political action meetings—progenitors of the now well-established Conservative Political Action Conference, of which it is still a principal sponsor. It also started the first conservative journalism school, in its fashion the ancestor of National Journalism Center, which your servant has the honor to conduct.

More to the point, it was in this period that HUMAN EVENTS geared up its campaign to redeem the soul and straighten the backbone of the Republican Party—an enterprise that continues, in altered context, now.

The critique of "modern Republicanism" that had begun in the Eisenhower-Tom Dewey era, the battle against Nelson Rockefeller in the latter 1950s, and the sharpening partisan definition of the issues with the advent of the Kennedy Administration, all began to converge in the movement to nominate Sen. Barry Goldwater at the 1964 Republican convention.

HUMAN EVENTS had a leading role to play in that unfolding battle, not merely as an early and ardent supporter of the Arizona senator, but as a proponent of the kind of Republicanism that Goldwater represented and so well described in HUMAN EVENTS (Feb. 18, 1960). The publication correctly reported that the base of power within the GOP was shifting to the South and West, and that similar changes would occur in the nation's general voting patterns. It accurately foretold, in other words, the future contours of our politics.

Because of its convictions on this score, HUMAN EVENTS was quick to glimpse the possibilities inherent in the rise of Reagan, first as John Alden to Goldwater's Standish, thereafter as a major candidate himself. Thus, despite the altered circumstances from one era to another, the major themes and foremost figures of contemporary politics are fully visible in the pages of this journal, set in type three decades past.

Needless to say, HUMAN EVENTS has been equally steadfast in promoting conservative stands on a host of national issues. Among the substantive topics addressed repeatedly in these pages have been the need to put restraints on federal spending and the rising burden of taxation, reduce the heavy burden of federal regulation, bring a halt to busing and other social engineering schemes, and resist the further frenzies of the leftward counterculture on so-called "social issues" such as abortion, drugs, and prayer in the public schools.

In foreign affairs, HUMAN EVENTS has stood for a strong defense, opposed the clinical lunacy of "mutual assured destruction," called for an end to technology transfer to the USSR and other nations of the Communist bloc, warned against Communist penetration of this hemisphere, and urged support for U.S. allies such as the Republic of Vietnam, Free China, and anti-Communist nations in Africa, Latin America, and Asia.

Among Reagan foreign policy projects that HUMAN EVENTS consistently supported, against the browbeating of the liberal media and the faintheartedness of some inside the GOP, were his boldest Cold War initiatives: rebuilding our defenses, refusing to knuckle under to demands for peace-through-weakness, aiding insurgent anti-Communist forces in Afghanistan, Angola, and Nicaragua. Most important of all, perhaps, the President and his supporters here and elsewhere stood fast for the Strategic Defense Initiative, withstanding the clamor to surrender it to Gorbachev's demands in 1986.

In retrospect, it is obvious that these initiatives, taken together, won the Cold War for the West. Reasserting our latent strength, cutting off the lethal trade that sustained the Communist economies and helped them shadow our advances, then playing the trump card of SDI, were the keys to victory. Matched by frequent Reagan statements that accurately gauged the weakness of the Kremlin and corresponding virtues of our system, the cumulative impact of this global strategy forced the Soviets at last to fold their hand.

On the domestic front, given the spirit of the age, many HUMAN EVENTS crusades turned out to be losing battles. But there have been successes as well. Among the victories in which this journal played a major role, dating back to Nixon, have been defeat of the "family assistance plan" (a form of guaranteed annual income), the 1971 veto of the social-engineering child development bill, the blocking of soft-liners such as Theodore Sorensen and Morton Halperin from appointments to crucial national security posts, exposing the misrepresentations of liberal icons such as Geraldine Ferraro and the Clintons, passage of the Reagan tax rate reduction program, and many others. This last was an especially notable win, since it developed that Reagan first encountered the "supply side" theories espoused by Jack Kemp and others in these pages—in an article by Kemp.

One losing battle that turned out in many respects to be a victory was this journal's opposition to the Panama Canal treaties, as they first evolved under Gerald Ford and Henry Kissinger, and then took definitive form under Jimmy Carter. This was arguably the most powerful issue that Ronald Reagan surfaced in his near-miss campaign to unseat Ford in 1976—an undertaking that paved the way for Reagan's nomination and election four years later. HUMAN EVENTS was an ardent backer of the Reagan candidacy in both elections.

As the Kemp example suggests, HUMAN EVENTS has played another role as well—as a showcase and forum for new ideas and personalities. While wedded to unchanging principle, the publication has ever been ready to consider new approaches in the marketing and implementing of conservative policies. It was consequently among the first to give enthusiastic support to the "supply-side revolution." In like fashion, it has served as an outlet for young conservative writers—William F. Buckley, Jr., Richard Whalen and Kenneth Tomlinson all having published early efforts in these pages.

Among the legion of young conservative writers and activists who got their start with HUMAN EVENTS are William Schulz and Kenneth Tomlinson of the *Reader's Digest;* Kenneth Thompson, former press secretary to Sen. Steve Symms and editor with Radio Free Europe/ Radio Liberty; author David Franke; columnist Don Feder; editor and former talk-show host Cliff Kincaid; right-to-life lawyer James Bopp; columnist Steven Beckner; direct-mail expert Ann Stone, and author Lowell Ponte.

And, of course, numerous well-established conservatives have voiced their opinions here as well: Reagan, Goldwater, Senators Orrin Hatch, Jesse Helms, Sam Ervin and Phil Gramm; Representatives Philip Crane, Chris Cox, Bob Dornan and the late John Ashbrook; conservative writers such as Morrie Ryskind and John Chamberlain; and economists such as Milton Friedman and Paul Craig Roberts have all been published in HUMAN EVENTS. It would be hard, indeed, to think of a major conservative writer or spokesman who hasn't.

Because HUMAN EVENTS is so unabashedly conservative, its principal fame concerns its *advocacy:* It backed Reagan over Carter and Mondale, opposes the growth of government and increases in our taxes, urged a stronger posture in our dealings with the Soviets, etc. Most commentary about this journal—of which there has been considerable in the past few years— focuses on its point of view, the measures and candidates it favors, and the ones that it opposes. And such advocacy is, of course, an important feature of the publication.

Far more important, however, is the role implicit in the designation, *newspaper* of the conservative movement. The most valuable thing about HUMAN EVENTS is not the admirable opinions that it offers, which tend to be incidental to its weekly mission, but the *information* that it provides. Its conservative philosophy supplies the framework for the reportorial effort, but it is the reporting that makes it indispensable reading for conservatives, and for those who want to know about conservatism.

With the rise of the computer revolution, "information theory" is much in vogue. Society generally runs on information, which to be properly useful needs to be relevant, accurate and timely. That point has long been realized by business moguls and military strategists and intuitively grasped by most of us without the benefit of formal theory. If you don't know what is going on, and know it in time to take effective action, you are unlikely to accomplish very much in any sort of enterprise.

That common-sense conclusion has special relevance to the world of politics. Under a system of representative government, access to data about the conduct of people holding office is essential. And what is true of representative politics in general is even more so of a movement that seeks decisive change in the established order. That is why, in authoritarian countries, control of information is the *sine qua non* of retaining power, and developing alternative circuits of communications the first requirement of the revolutionary.

Such otherwise divergent upheavals as the French and American revolutions, for example, were instigated, and sustained, by energetic journalism. In seeking to foment his Marxist revolution, Lenin took as a first objective creation of a newspaper. By developing issues, conducting a critique of the existing system, and otherwise establishing a common fund of information for the cadres, such journals are essential catalysts of change.

In functional terms, this is the role that has been played by HUMAN EVENTS. It provides a constant flow of data about issues, candidates, the workings of government, political developments, opportunities and problems. This reportorial mission, in my view, is the most important aspect of the publication, and one that it performs in most exemplary manner.

Given the long-standing problems conservatives have had with the major media, this informational role is doubly significant. The liberal tilt of so many national news outlets has meant, for instance, that conservative candidates have been reported poorly or not at all, data supporting conservative positions have been given the shortest possible shrift, issues of interest to conservatives ignored or covered in one-sided fashion.

HUMAN EVENTS has provided a needed corrective to all this, in at least three different ways:

1. It has served as a kind of clearinghouse for conservative activists and sympathizers concerning who is who and what is what, the implications of intra-party battles, what is happening among conservatives themselves, critical events and developments in the political process. This function is of the utmost significance, both because of the information that it provides and because of the sense of common enterprise that it engenders.

This unifying effort has been especially notable in recent months, as media spokesmen and "pragmatists" in the Republican Party have raised a ruckus about the supposed depredations of the "Christian right." The object of this liberal outcry is plain enough—to drive a wedge between traditional Republicans and newly energized believers who have brought grass-roots conviction to the cause. HUMAN EVENTS has led the way in scotching this liberal-left maneuver, helping insure that traditional conservatives in the GOP and newly active members of the "religious right" are allies instead of adversaries.

2. It provides a needed antidote to the erroneous handling of major issues by the national media on everything from Reagan's "gaffes" to the decline of our defenses to the continued growth of social welfare spending. Such efforts at setting the record straight are of obvious importance to conservatives, but also to the well-being of our system generally: To the degree that the public is stuffed with error and disinformation on such matters (as it routinely is), representative government is going to malfunction.

3. Quite apart from correcting error, HUMAN EVENTS provides a constant flow of data about government and politics that otherwise doesn't get reported. If you want to know what is going on in Congress, inside the State Department or the White House staff, what really happened to the federal budget, or basic facts about the issues from SDI to health care, you *have* to read HUMAN EVENTS. In far too many cases, the coverage of such matters in the major media ranges from superficial to nonexistent.

Despite its relatively small staff, HUMAN EVENTS does a superlative job in all these areas. One reason it can do so is that its principal editors and writers have had considerable experience, both in the realm of conservative politics and in the world of Washington. Based on years of activity and effort, they have a multitude of sources and contacts who provide them with a vast amount of relevant information on a weekly basis.

The editors of this journal, Thomas Winter and Allan Ryskind, came on board in 1961 and 1959 respectively, and learned their trade from Mr. Hanighen and Publisher James Wick. They have thus had better than three decades to learn their business, and have learned it very well. The contents of these pages reflect knowledge of the issues, players, and institutional ways of government, drawing on contacts that range from conservative activists around the nation to congressional experts to specialists on every sort of issue.

While there are necessarily some overlaps, the editors have a general division of functions. Winter has been the "movement" political person, doubling as first vice chairman of the American Conservative Union and treasurer of the Conservative Victory Fund, first of the conservative PACs. Ryskind is the hard-driving reporter, foraging the Hill, the State Department and other agencies, for the latest in policy and legislative happenings.

The result is a weekly budget of news far more informative than much of what appears in the Washington *Post* or the New York *Times* or on the nightly TV newscasts.

Such reporting is crucial for those who understand that effective politics, conservative or otherwise, consists of much more than winning elections, important as that is. It is also necessary to insure that the people elected do what they say they will. Given the weaknesses of human nature, and the pressures to conform to the Washington pattern, this is a serious problem. HUMAN EVENTS is fully alert to it, and if Republican congressmen or senators stray too far from the conservative agenda, you—and they—are likely to read about it here.

In this respect and others, HUMAN EVENTS provides a continuing linkage between grass-roots conservatives and what is occurring in the nation's capital—and it is very much a two-way system of communications. Conservative activists need to know what is really going on in government, behind the facade of self-serving rhetoric and misleading media dispatches. Conversely, people in government need to be reminded of the grass-roots opinion that put them where they are.

From the beginning, sustaining HUMAN EVENTS financially was always a challenge. An independent and unapologetically conservative publication, it has never received the government benefits of not-for-profit groups and has remained committed to an editorial content unpalatable to most large advertisers.

But for 50 years, HUMAN EVENTS has continued its regular publication schedule with a relatively small and extremely committed staff. The newspaper has been kept going in large part due to the loyalty of its longtime readers and the generous response of a few like-minded corporations to its occasional fundraising appeals.

Looking toward the future in July 1993, Editors Winter and Ryskind announced that HUMAN EVENTS would be joining forces with Eagle Publishing, Inc., the newly established conservative political publishing subsidiary of the fast-growing Phillips Publishing International, Inc., headquartered in Potomac, Md. PPII President Thomas L. Phillips—a longtime conservative who had been active with Young Americans for Freedom and had been publisher of the conservative *Pink Sheet on the Left*—was enthusiastic about making HUMAN EVENTS more successful and influential than ever before.

Eagle Publishing—under the guidance of President Jeff Carneal—immediately helped rejuvenate HUMAN EVENTS, refurbishing its Washington, D.C., offices, installing new computers and production equipment, streamlining the format and adding new editorial and marketing talent. All involved are optimistic that HUMAN EVENTS will now be able to continue to lead the conservative movement for another 50 years.

Which leads us to our valedictory. The late Frank Chodorov, then a contributing editor of HUMAN EVENTS, once wrote that reversing the ideological direction of the country would be a 50-

year program, beginning with changes in the realm of ideas, which would gradually work their way into the world of politics. In this respect (as in others), he was quite prescient. It is taking 50 years, and then some, to get the work completed.

Over the past five decades, much has been accomplished by Human Events and the conservative movement of which it is a part; that is cause for much rejoicing. By the same token, however, there is much remaining to be done. Numerous problems at home and abroad that led to the founding of this publication are still out there, waiting to be addressed. Others that were not anticipated have only recently become apparent.

One of the problems that is just now beginning to be understood, and which makes the task of Human Events more urgent than ever, is the degree to which the liberal power structure in the nation's capital is impervious to changes in ideas *and* voting patterns. The institutional momentum of the bureaucracy and other components of the "permanent government," the locked-in nature of the spending process, the enormous leverage of the liberal pressure groups and media, keep left-wing policies in motion long after intellectual and popular support for them has vanished.

This massive institutional flaw will be corrected, if ever, only by focusing the light of full exposure on the process by which the system actually works, as opposed to the more straightforward model that we learn about in civics class, then bringing popular opinion to bear to get the necessary changes. Regardless of election outcomes, there can be no authentically conservative government until the people are shown the glaring difference between the platitudes of politics and the grim reality of government as it is practiced on a daily basis.

To achieve such institutional changes must be a top priority for conservatives in the coming decades—and, as usual, Human Events is well positioned to provide the necessary leadership, and information. It has the contacts, the know-how, familiarity with the players, and full awareness of the difficulty. And, just as important, it has an audience attuned to the problem, and able, through its energy and motivation, to work for necessary changes. To judge from the experience of half-a-century's striving, that combination can get the job done.

For Our Children's Children

By Frank Chodorov   *(From the 6 September 1950 issue)*

Whatever opposition to the trend toward complete socialization of American life we do have is aimed mainly at legislation, or at politicians who favor such legislation. If certain laws are enacted, or repealed, or if "our kind" of politician is elected—so goes the reasoning—then all will be well.

That kind of therapy comes from looking for quick results; it attacks the effects without looking to the cause. The laws, and the politicians who favor them, are the product of the mass-mind of America, and that mass-mind is the product of the ideas implanted in it long ago and carefully cultured through the years. Unless and until this mass-mind of America is re-educated to freedom the end product of Socialism is unavoidable. No program based on a policy of immediacy can prevent it.

The task of those who would stop our descent should not be the changing of laws but the inculcation of values which will make such laws impossible. That is a difficult chore, to be sure, but it is the only one capable of producing the desired result. It calls for a long-term project and, in the nature of things, those who undertake it cannot gather the fruits of their labors. Only our children's children will do the reaping, although some spiritual benefit accrues to those who enjoy fighting for principle.

It is exactly this kind of zeal that brought socialism to America. The advocates of that school of thought, 50 years ago, met with an aversion to political intervention far stronger than the current avidity for it. Nevertheless, they went at their seemingly impossible mission,

kept at it, and in less than three decades we had the New Deal. They did an effective job on the American mind.

The current and belated opposition to Socialism would do well to study the educational methods which preceded its advent; and to capture, if possible, the missionary fervor that brought success. The Socialists were fired by faith in the rightness of their doctrine, a faith which in turn rested on a "scientific" dogma. They had it on the authority of Karl Marx, who got it from the stars of history, that Socialism is the fated *modus vivendi* of mankind. There was nothing anybody could do to prevent it, and it would come without a lifting hand. Nevertheless, his followers undertook to hurry history along. They went to work on the American mind.

With admirable astuteness, they went to work particularly on the fertile mind of youth. They were amply rewarded. The college student took readily to their humanitarian and romantic slogans, and his inclination to precocity was satisfied by the pretensions of Socialism to scientific exactitude. "Workers of the world unite, you have nothing to lose but your chains" has all the qualities, including lack of sense, of a college yell; the plausibility of the "surplus value" theory easily raises it to an absolute in a mind unencumbered by experience.

Just how Socialism first came to the campus is unrecorded. It made its appearance early in the century. Perhaps some of the boys picked up the germ at a street corner meeting. They were bright boys, given to speculative ideas and endowed with the gift of articulation; also, they were boys who could make neither the fraternities nor the athletic teams. Their deflated egos were puffed up by a sense of martyrdom. They had a "cause."

After World War I the organization of these college Socialists into active, proselytizing groups took on a full head of steam. The success of the Bolsheviks gave impetus to the dogma of inevitability. Here was positive proof that Lenin was right; history can be pushed along. Henceforth, the policy of indoctrination was to be supplemented, if not superseded, by a program of action.

The immediacy of the millennium fired the imagination of venturesome youth, while their energy found an outlet in doing something about it. There was much to do. The underdog proletarian had to be aroused from his lethargy, even at the risk of a broken head on the picket line. There were speeches to be made, pamphlets to be distributed. Intercollegiate conventions required a lot of organizational skill, and one's *weltschmerz* was soothed in writing, debating and voting for resolutions covering every ill of mankind. And the spirit of solidarity was regularly revitalized at necking parties.

Long before the New Deal came upon us, thousands of these college-bred Socialists had taken their training into fields where it could be put to use: as labor leaders, ministers, teachers, lawyers, writers. They were opinion-makers. They worked themselves into positions of importance in these fields, and further entrenched themselves by hiring more recent graduates of the Socialist clubs. Contrary-minded graduates were carefully discriminated against. As heads of departments, our bright boys had the "academic freedom" to hire their own kind; as literary critics, they boosted their brand of books into bestsellers and gave short shrift to anything that sounded anti-socialistic.

When Franklin D. Roosevelt looked for help and advice in meeting the economic collapse, these quite articulate smart boys were the logical ones to turn to. They had established their reputations for wisdom in books and articles, on the rostrum and in the classroom. Their ideas had broken through the hard crust of American individualism. On the other hand, the American businessmen were useless in the circumstances, not only because they were bewildered by the turn of events but because it was assumed that they were at the bottom of all the trouble: the Socialists had proved that. The politicians did not invent the New Deal. They took to it naturally because it offered a grand opportunity to enhance political power, not because they understood or favored its underlying doctrine. The authors of this program were the graduates of the campus socialistic clubs. Popular acceptance of it was facilitated by the long, persistent struggle to reshape the American mind.

Today, the doctrinaire Socialist clubs on the campus (as distinguished from the Communist kind) would be excess baggage. It has done its work. Socialistic values have indeed become conservative and conservatism does not stir the adolescent. From his grade school days the American under 40 has had it hammered into him that society is everything, the individual merely a means; and he therefore takes to socialistic thought and legislation quite readily. He has been conditioned.

In that very fact lies the challenge to individualism. The formula of "something new and different," always attractive to the groping mind, is to be found in the very values that socialistic propaganda has so effectively submerged. The old is now the new. Hence, to start the mind of coming generations in the direction of freedom, it is only necessary that these old values be dug up out of the ash heap of the current culture, dusted off and presented to the revolutionary instinct in brand-new garb. Individualism must be offered as first-class radicalism—which it is, these days.

As for an effective *modus operandi*, where better to look for it than in the successful program of the Socialists? The Individualist Club (or, perhaps, the Freedom Club) must be planted on the campus. It would be welcome, just as its opposite was 40 years ago, and for the same reasons. Fortified with "extreme" values, its members would in short order establish themselves as the intellectual elite. They would attract to themselves the same restless, inquisitive type that took up with the Marxist promise; after all, freedom is a more impelling "cause" than collectivism. As an initial step in such a program, a lecture bureau should be established. Its business would be to book missionary lecturers on the campus, or near it. The faculties would undoubtedly resent the intrusion, but any opposition from this source would help the undertaking no end. It should be the business of the lecturers not only to introduce students to the doctrines of individualism, but also to destroy by logic, facts and ridicule the implicit and explicit collectivism in their textbooks, particularly in the field of economics. Such critical analyses of the "adopted" books would arouse resentment amounting to disgust.

The sophomore likes nothing better than to refute and confute his natural enemy, the professor, and if he is furnished with the ammunition he can be depended on to use it. Opposition breeds conviction.

In support of the lecturers, there should be a publication directed at the student mind. It should aim to present the pertinent news of the day factually but from the viewpoint of the individualist; it must be nonpartisan but definitely ideological. Its pages should be open to student participation and as soon as possible its editorial management should be turned over to the graduates of these radical clubs.

It is hardly possible here to go into the details of such a long-term project; nor is it necessary. The students would have something of value to contribute, particularly in the matter of organization.

The point to be considered now is whether there is in America a will for freedom of sufficient vigor to initiate the suggested campaign. Some investment will be required, though not as much as the Socialists put into their effort, because the response to freedom is more spontaneous; they got nowhere until they twisted this "bourgeois" concept into their ideology.

More than money, sincerity of purpose amounting to religious fervor is called for. The effort must be looked upon as a legacy for the future. With property confiscation on the increase, is there any other legacy a man can expect to leave to his grandchildren? See England!

Harvard Hogs the Headlines

By William F. Buckley, Jr.   *(From the 16 May 1951 issue)*

(Bill Buckley, who founded National Review *in 1955, began writing for* HUMAN EVENTS *with this article in the May 16, 1951, issue that presaged his book* God and Man at Yale.)*

As a Yale man, I think I have a legitimate gripe. Harvard saw the light of day 75 years before my alma mater, and has capitalized on this ever since. Yale has never lost the inferiority complex she got from Harvard's abortive arrival on the educational scene. This must be the explanation of why Harvard gets most of the credit for nourishing the new, irresistible, mid-century liberalism—collectivism.

Yale deserves just as much credit for it.

It's true that Harvard does things more flamboyantly. Most of this country's collectivists, admittedly, have been comforted and inspired, at one time or another, by the highly publicized speeches and writings of Alvin Hansen, Seymour Harris, Felix Frankfurter and the rest. Yale hasn't counterparts of such notoriety.

It is also true that Washington has been inundated over the past 15 years by precocious statists who received their enlightenment in Cambridge, and that these men have signally influenced national policy. Yale lags behind in the infiltration of the bureaucracy.

But Yale goes about her task differently. She doesn't make so many headlines, she doesn't contribute so much grist for Westbrook Pegler's columns, so many clerks for Supreme Court justices, or so many articles for the *New Republic*. But in a very real sense, Yale is more systematic. She goes about her task of collectivizing less ostentatiously. But let no one say that Yale is not pulling her oar, that she is shirking her responsibility to persuade her young men as to the merits of the Leviathan State.

Yale recognizes that the most important single springboard from which to launch collectivism is the basic economics course. Approximately half of her undergraduate enroll in "Elementary Economics" before leaving New Haven. And so it is here that much of the work can be done.

To that end, in the past five years, books by Samuelson (*Economics: An Introductory Analysis*), Bowman and Bach (*Economic Analysis and Public Policy*), Morgan (*Income and Employment*), and Tarshis (*The Elements of Economics*) have been used as basic texts.

Now all of these books profess respect for the institution and achievements of free enterprise, a tactic indispensable, at the present, to successful collectivizing. Socialism still has to be subtle. So it is only after calculated enthusiasm for our economic system that these text writers proceed to undermine the free market place. This approach is far more effective, in my opinion, than a hundred lectures at Harvard by Harold Laski. For he bore the label "socialist," and his straightforwardness put many of his students on their guard.

Not so with the text writers of Yale economics (whose approach is adopted by most of the instructors). For it is under the banner of "the preservation of capitalism" that they teach the unwary student to forsake every tenet of free enterprise.

For example: economic equilibrium cannot result from an unmolested free market, and capitalism, accordingly, must be modified. "To set the responsibility for attaining and maintaining full employment on the shoulders of individual consumers or individual businessmen, is absurd" (Morgan). Individualism "is giving way to changing concepts of what is meant by true equality of opportunity in economic affairs" (Bowman and Bach).

Since we've seen that the American economy has got to change, some of its traditional superstitions have got to go. There is no "right" of private property, and the freedom to engage in business for one's self "is *not* a basic freedom" (Morgan). And since there is no right of private property, the State must remedy the appalling inequality of income which "most Americans regard as inequitable" (Bowman and Bach).

Such income inequality, which seriously vitiates "maximum social well-being" (Tarshis) must and will be abolished by State intervention through taxation. This is a "generally accepted objective" of modern economics (Morgan).

Nor shall inheritance escape the egalitarian ax; everyone, after all, is "curious about the workings of an economic society that enables a few individuals to amass such large accumulations of wealth and power and to perpetuate them by inheritance" (Samuelson). So, by plugging loopholes and raising the rates, "there is no reason why we should not achieve at least the level of success of the British in increasing the productivity of death taxes" (Morgan).

Once the government has seen to equalization, it is only fair that it should also assume the burden of guaranteeing security to all its citizens. This is democracy at work, for "cradle-to-grave security has great popularity. If the private economy cannot supply it [which it cannot, the students are repeatedly told], naturally people will insist upon getting it artificially from governments" (Samuelson).

Thus we must have more and more social security, force separation wages, and a government guarantee of full employment (Morgan).

Unemployment can, of course, be offset by government spending—and it doesn't much matter how the government spends just so it spends: "Wise domestic investment is no more powerful than ultimately foolish investment" (Samuelson). Morgan quotes the god of all our enlightened economists, Lord Keynes, who wrote that "Pyramid buildings, earthquakes, and even wars may serve to increase wealth."

Those students who object to limitless government spending are quickly disabused of such reactionary objections. "The fear that increasing the public debt will make the nation go bankrupt is almost completely fallacious" (Bowman and Bach). "In the last analysis there is no problem, for the simple reason that the government controls the Federal Reserve Banks and can always compel them to buy government bonds" (Tarshis). Besides, the government "has complete power to issue new currency" (Samuelson).

So it goes, and the student is pretty well convinced, after the year's work, that he can at last visualize a program for fortifying free enterprise. He doesn't realize that this program involves destroying everything basic to the free economy—private property, production by private enterprise, production for profit and regulation by free competition.

Our economy is already mixed (i.e., the post office, education); we need only mix it some more. We can go as far as England—and even further, and still be a capitalistic nation, for even "when the British Labor Government completes the socialization program underway. . . some 80 per cent of national production will still be in private hands, only 20 per cent in the hands of the government" (Morgan).

There is not a deficiency in our society—social or even ethical—that remedial action by the *government* cannot cure. And we all know that there is no surer way to sensitize man's mind to collectivism than to teach him to turn instinctively to Government as the agent through which all good is accomplished.

In more advanced courses in economics, although they are not as important because the attendance is smaller, Yale sticks pretty close to the same line—the "mixed economy" line, which is really bearing fruit. The Department of Economics is slightly troubled by three or four oldtimers who keep ranting about such things as "limited government" (anarchists, the lot of them), "the gold standard" (does Tarshis put *them* in their place! He compares the gold standard to a limburger-cheese standard!), the threat of authoritarianism in the planned economy (these boys never *heard* of economic democracy), and other such archaisms.

But they're pretty old men. One has already retired. Another goes this year, and the other two within a few years. Their juniors know a good deal better than they.

To get back to Harvard: I'd pit the average Yale graduate of basic economics against the average Harvard man confident that my alma mater has turned out the more efficacious collectivist. For one thing, when the boy goes to Harvard, he is made aware, if not by George Sokolsky, then by his father, or uncle, that he is entering a hotbed of radicalism, with the result that many entering freshmen and graduating seniors are more critical of the theories passed on to them in the classroom.

But when a student goes to Yale, all of his friends and relations relax, because Old Yale is *so* conservative. The student falls for it, and readily swallows his economics lessons, and others, as the point of view of the right. If he is intellectually restless, he is more prone to move to the left than to the right, because so far as he knows, there is nothing to the right of Yale economics.

Occasionally, some Yale alumni do a little spade work, read some of the texts, get riled up and write in letters protesting the promulgation of socialist values. These few objectors can be easily dismissed as "fascists." They certainly are not typical Yale men—the kind who remain Yale men under all circumstances, who never fail to come to the aid of Yale when called upon.

Only this year the alumni have launched an endowment drive of $80 million to meet its annual deficit. Assuming that Yale men are committed to maintaining individualism in America, this drive is like asking them to furnish the rods with which the next generation shall whip them. But, I don't look at it this way. I prefer to think that Yale fundraising drives show evidence of genuine and disinterested altruism—typical of the man with the Yale degree.

Nevertheless, in this business of spreading socialist ideas, we do sit around and let Harvard hog the headlines.

The Middle of the Road—Where It Leads

By Richard M. Weaver *(From the 24 March 1956 issue)*

(Richard M. Weaver was the author of the well-known book, Ideas Have Consequences. *He was Professor of English at the University of Chicago and a member of the board of directors of the Foundation For American Principles and Traditions.)*

When you drive your car, do you drive in the middle of the road? This seems a silly question to ask because you don't, of course, if you want to stay alive and get somewhere.

But a lot of people have been sold on the idea that the middle of the road is the safest place in politics and on all sorts of controversial questions. They have been led to believe that in the middle position you are out of harm's way and you are more likely to be right than those who are on either side of a question. A little thought will show that this idea is borne not of wisdom but of confusion or fear or both.

Properly speaking, middle-of-the-roadism is not a political philosophy at all. It is rather the absence of a philosophy or an attempt to evade having a philosophy. All great movements in the past have grown out of and have depended upon some self-consistent view of man and society. They have presented a program embodying clear principles, and people have gotten behind the movements because they wanted the principles to triumph. In no case did they labor and fight to see the principles bartered away for a few concessions by the opposition. The great sacrifices of history have not been inspired by political trimming and unmanly compromise. Try imagining the figure that Washington would cut in history today if he had decided on a compromise settlement with the British.

Middle-of-the-road policies have a false attraction for some people because they keep them from having to think a position through. All they have to do is borrow a little from the parties on either side of them, add this up, and tell themselves that this is the "sound" position. But a position halfway between right and wrong is not a sound position. It only postpones and makes more difficult the eventual decision. And there are different views of man's destiny which can never be made compatible.

Middle-of-the-roadism is seldom anything more than short-sightedness. It is not an insight into political matters because it is wholly dependent upon what other parties say, or stand for. It takes its bearing from them. And far from being safe, it is just the spot to catch brickbats from both sides.

When you ask people why they have adopted a middle-of-the-road position, you nearly always discover that they fall into these two groups. The first group has been deceived into believing, as we have just noted, that you find the right by averaging right and wrong. If this were true, there would never be any use for intelligence and moral conviction.

The second group is usually fearful of taking a position which an enemy might characterize as "extreme" in spite of the fact that many ideas are attacked as extreme for no other reason than that they express clearcut principles. Nearly all advocates of principles have been attacked at one time or another as "extremists." But if the principles were sound, the leaders generally prevailed. It does take some intestinal fortitude to champion an idea that has powerful enemies.

But people who are frightened by this kind of criticism are usually afraid to stand up for any principle.

There is a third group of middle-of-the-roaders which is even less admirable than these two. These are the opportunists, the believers in pure expediency, who think that the best chance is to take a middle position and play off both sides against each other. Then while the parties on either side are fighting they try to run off with the bacon. These are the ones who believe that you cannot really stand for something and win an election. They are generally afraid of all ideas because their sole object is to get into office. They are politicians in the worst sense of the word. Everybody recognizes this type of political "leader."

History, however, shows that they are dead wrong even about the matter of winning. Occasionally dodging about in the middle of the road does lead to a temporary victory. But these are fleeting successes for the simple reason that you can't fool all of the people all the time. In their hearts people despise a trimmer and, as soon as they find him out, they leave him. The great causes that have triumphed and the leaders who have led them have never been found in the middle of the road. They have set their course by some ideal and have resisted all temptations, which have sometimes been many, to come halfway to the other side. And the parties that have played the game of compromise on vital issues have seen their glory and their power vanish. For proof of this, let's go to history.

A century ago this country had an important and powerful party called the Whigs. Its leader was the attractive Henry Clay and he had support from the best elements in all parts of the country. But his party made the fatal mistake of trying to straddle the fence on major issues. As a result, it was not Clay, "the Great Compromiser," who went to the White House, but the hard-hitting Andrew Jackson. By 1856 the Whig Party was dead. Stephen A. Douglas tried the same trick, looking for the middle of the road between issues that were in direct conflict. He lost to Abraham Lincoln, who had taken a definite stand on one side. Even when the Democratic Party has won, on issues that many do not approve of, it has done so in taking a decisive stand for something. Better an opponent whose position you are certain of than a supposed friend whose only interest is in dodging the crucial issues. Such has generally been the judgment of the American voters on those who were merely looking for the line of least resistance.

So much for the claim that the middle of the road is the path to success. Dodging issues and watering down solutions is not merely the way to failure; it is the way to extinction.

All great political parties owe their vitality to the importance of the things they stand for. And this is never truer than in periods of defeat which, in the normal alteration of political circumstances, must sometimes occur. A beaten party with a real issue has an excellent chance of coming back. A beaten party without an issue is a dead duck. And those parties which have tied their fortunes to some personality who happens to excite the masses are only setting a term to their effectiveness. When he goes, as he must, the wind is out of their sails. These considerations have a melancholy bearing upon the situation in our country today. There is one group, not clearly distinguished by a party name, but quite definite about what it wants and expects to bring about in this nation. Most accurately speaking, it is the party of collectivism. It works on various fronts and under various labels, but there need be no confusion about its objectives. It wants an America, new-modeled according to the Soviet Union.

There are two ideas in the philosophy of collectivism of which every American ought to be aware. One of them is a thoroughgoing materialism, which insists that man is merely a natural animal, which repudiates religion and all belief in the Divine Providence, and which maintains that happiness is purely a matter of gratifying this animal's appetites. The other idea is that the state is supreme and the individual nothing, that society should be managed down to the smallest details by a centralized authority, and that there is no higher power—no human tradition, no conscience, no precept of religion—by which this control can be criticized. An all-powerful state, designed along engineering lines to satisfy the physical wants of the masses, is their aim and goal, although often it is their method to admit only part of it at a time. In the writings of their prophets, Marx, Engels, Lenin and Stalin, however, it is revealed without any squeamishness.

There is a great segment of our population to the right of collectivism and morally committed to fight it. Strange as it may sound, however, a good many of its leaders have adopted the policy of appeasement. Instead of issuing a direct challenge, in terms of principle, they have tried to see how many concessions they could make without being accused of surrender. They have tried to see how closely they could approach the position of collectivism while still paying lip service to what they are supposed to be defending.

Logic and duty call for them to stand up for their side, not to fight the battle by retreating from it. They have sought a middle-of-the-road position between a militant collectivism and our tradition of freedom and individualism. Historical examples show that the next step is capitulation, or liquidation of the party which is so cowardly.

If this should come about, it will certainly be recorded by history that no people ever gave up so much for so little. We possess a great, beautiful, inspiring country. In our comparatively brief history we have created some traditions that any people would be proud to sustain; we have borne leaders and heroes to match those out of Plutarch; we have accomplished many things which by previous standards were thought impossible. We have combined equality with a method of rewarding success and distinction which has no parallel in history in its ability to produce social satisfaction and incentive to achievement.

Best of all, we have created a spirit of kindness and helpfulness which mitigates the lot of life's failures without trying absurdly to place them in the driver's seat. Every candid foreign observer is struck by this, and we feel intuitively that it is a very American thing. "Nowhere is cruelty more abhorred," Lord Bryce wrote admiringly of the America he saw. Now it is proposed to exchange this for the regimentation, the directives, the penalties, perhaps even the forced labor camps and executions of an alien and inhuman philosophy.

There is little doubt that the middle of the road today leads in this direction. The radicals know what they want; too many of the rest of us only temporize and hope.

Already a good many people are behaving as if their conscience hurt them over being American, so they give a little here and a little there in the hope of not being too offensive to the truculent enemy.

This is the reason that even the election of 1952 did not halt creeping socialism. Because no influential leader drew the line in terms of clear principle, the immense bureaucracy of the New Deal was allowed to consolidate itself further. This and that clamorous group has been able to extort state aid according to New Deal methods. All candid observers realize that the trend toward statism has not yet been reversed.

The need of the time is for a leadership willing to face the facts. Complacency toward what is happening is a betrayal of the America we have inherited. The kind of leader that people are willing to stay with, and to sacrifice personally for, is the kind that says, "I'm going to fight it out on this line if it takes all summer." Wavering and self-defeat through compromise where vital points are at stake never yet held a following. To win this struggle we have got to get on the right side of the road and keep it with resolution.

The Story of the Conservative Book Club

By Anne Edwards   *(From the 20 May 1967 issue)*

Just about everyone in New York publishing circles a few years ago had the same opinion: conservative books didn't sell. There was no market for them and any publisher who did take a chance on a conservative or staunchly anti-Communist book was almost certain to lose his shirt. That was the consensus—with one important exception, a publishing executive named Neil McCaffrey.

Neil had a dream. He wanted to start a conservative publishing House which would provide its authors with a full range of advertising and promotion services. He also had an idea about a conservative book club.

Through his work at Doubleday, where he had been in charge of several book clubs, and at Macmillan, for which he was a director of mail order advertising, he felt sure there was a market for good books on the Right. He could almost taste it.

But his sixth sense wasn't the only thing that told him there was a large conservative audience. He had tested the club idea some years before and the results had been positive. However, the conservatives he spoke to about the book club were too involved with other projects to give it much thought. Nor were they sure conservatism was big enough to sustain such an enterprise.

I had been working for Neil McCaffrey since 1961. As his secretary and gal Friday, I shared his dreams and his disappointments. He had a wonderful idea in the book club. All he needed was the right person to help him shape it into the kind of solid business proposition investors understood.

One day I introduced him to Stanley Goldstein, a brilliant young CPA and a sturdy convert to conservatism. Stan became very excited about Neil's project and helped put together an impressive prospectus. Armed with figures to make his plan plausible, Neil went hunting for capital. Before too long, two businessmen stepped forward and the dream soon became a reality.

The official birthday of the Conservative Book Club was April 1, 1964. Four people heard their footsteps echo through the rooms of a barn-like office in New Rochelle, N.Y. Why New Rochelle? It could have been any one of a half-dozen little Westchester County towns which lie just outside New York City, but New Rochelle was chosen because the principals found office space which was large enough to suit their immediate needs at a price they could afford to pay. The overhead in New York City would have been two or three times as high. Still, New Rochelle is convenient enough to the city to allow business luncheons in town or guest authors and publishers to travel out from the city without too much bother.

One of the first problems Neil had to deal with was that the name "Neil McCaffrey" would not be familiar to the thousands of conservatives he hoped to reach. Since conservatives want to know who is behind an organization before they join, it was clear that the club needed a list of well-known conservative sponsors. People like Sen. Barry Goldwater, William F. Buckley Jr., the late James L. Wick of HUMAN EVENTS, Sen. John Tower, Rep. John Ashbrook, Gen. Mark Clark—these men had faith in Neil, liked the concept of the Conservative Book Club and graciously agreed to lend their names to the venture.

The results of a test mailing, conducted before actual opening of the club, were interesting. Neil prepared three mailing packages designed to test certain variables and sent them to three sets of names, equal in number and derived from the same or similar sources. One mailing tested the name American Reading Society, the second the Conservative Book Club and the third the offer of a free book premium under the Conservative Book Club name.

First, he wanted to find out whether the word "conservative" helped or hurt the prospective book club. Second, he wanted to know whether the offer of a free book upon joining would make any significant difference in soliciting members.

Results showed that Conservative Book Club outpulled American Reading Society by 3 to 2 and that conservatives didn't need the lure of a free book to know a good thing when they saw it. (A good thing for us, too, because the club was on a tight budget.)

One of the first tasks was obtaining lists of conservatives so that the news of the club's formation could be passed along to them without delay. Some lists came from conservative organizations, many were purchased or rented from professional list brokers and others came from enthusiastic individuals who, hearing about CBC, sent lists of friends' addresses—sometimes including 50 or more names. The people who sent these free lists helped the struggling club more than they will ever know.

Mailings went out proclaiming the glad news and ads were run in various conservative publications. With steady work, the club's membership was raised to over 30,000 during the first year and a half. Today, CBC is responsible for the sale of some 15-20,000 conservative books a month.

As quickly as people joined and ordered books, the value of one of the original four employees became more and more evident. Marvin Nagourney, who had served as fulfillment manager for the Crowell-Collier book clubs, took over fulfillment operations for the club. As a result, CBC members receive their *Bulletins* and books as part of a steady routine designed and implemented through the experience Nagourney brought to the new company.

Marv's department handles everything from list maintenance to answering mail from members. One of Neil's strictest policies is that every letter received must be answered, and promptly. Needless to say, Marv is a very busy man. Before long, CBC recognized 31-year-old Nagourney's accomplishments with his appointment as vice president of the firm.

Publisher's Weekly is the major publishing trade journal and club editors study it closely for pre-publication announcements of books which might interest CBC members. They then request review copies of such books from the publisher, who usually sends a manuscript or galleys months before the book is actually released to the public.

Many publishers of such books now consider CBC a prime market and will often send unsolicited books to the club. In some cases, in fact, a publisher may send a manuscript to the club that he has not yet decided to publish. CBC approval of the manuscript might contribute significantly to the publisher's decision to bring out the book in question. In some cases, CBC members themselves recommend a book to the club's attention.

Because of Neil's contacts in the conservative movement, he has been able to enlist the services of many qualified people aside from the club editors to aid in the screening of proposed books. A book must have several favorable readings before it is chosen as a club selection. Books are judged on three main criteria: literary style, content, and the club's desire to offer a cross-section of subjects to its broad-based membership. The *CBC Bulletin* describes a selection in detail so that a member has the opportunity to reject any book he does not think will interest him. Books on political philosophy are popular with some members, while others like biographical works or fiction or anti-Communist documentation or political action.

The success of the Conservative Book Club laid the financial cornerstone for the second half of Neil McCaffrey's dream—in many ways the more important half.

On Nov. 1, 1965, Arlington House Publishers was born. Theodore Lit left Fulton Lewis Jr.'s staff in Washington, D.C., to become senior editor. Ted was joined shortly thereafter by Aaron Brown and Neal Freeman, a frequent contributor to *National Review* and other conservative publications.

Within a year of its founding, Arlington House had signed contracts with some 50 authors, both famous and unknown.

Since then Arlington House has published such diverse and needed books as *The Warren Revolution* by L. Brent Bozell, *Black and Conservative* by George Schuyler, *The Spirit of '76* by Holmes Alexander, *Wooden Nickles* by William Rickenbacker, *Spies, Dupes and Diplomats* by Ralph de Toledano, *Time Will Run Back* by Henry Hazlitt, *Hysteria 1964: The Fear Campaign Against Barry Goldwater* by Lionel Lokos, and F. Clifton White's *Suite 3505: The Story of the Draft Goldwater Movement*. Arlington House also reissued Victor Lasky's best-seller, *J.F.K.: The Man and the Myth*.

Although comparatively small and still young, Arlington House has already begun to make a difference in the publishing world. More and more book publishers are coming to the conclusion that there *is* a sizable market for conservative books.

HUMAN EVENTS Capitol Hill Editor Allan H. Ryskind interviews President Ronald Reagan in 1983.

Retired Lt. Col. Ollie North enjoys the 15 July 1989 headline of HUMAN EVENTS that reads, "Ollie North Deserves a Pardon."

Congressman Jack Kemp inscribed this photo to Cleo Grant, assistant to HUMAN EVENTS Editors Allan Ryskind (right) and Tom Winter. The publication was honored at a reception at the Georgetown home of Edward Dent in 1982. (Photo by Michael J. Pettypool/UNIPHOTO)

Celebrating HUMAN EVENTS' 50th Anniversary at a gala dinner at Washington's Mayflower Hotel, 27 September 1994, were Phillips Publishing International President Thomas L. Phillips (center), HUMAN EVENTS Editors Thomas S. Winter (left) and Allan H. Ryskind. (Photo by Marty LaVor)

Chapter Two

Domestic Policy

The articles in this chapter cover a variety of domestic policy questions of importance.

Completing the devastation wrought by liberal politicians was the judicial shredding of the Constitution at the hands of the Earl Warren Supreme Court. In "How the 'Warren Revolution' Has Changed America," Sen. Sam Ervin (D.-N.C.)—later to serve as chairman of the Senate Judiciary Committee—reviewed L. Brent Bozell's book on the Warren Court (21 January 1967).

By the 1990s, a consensus was emerging that the welfare system put in place by the Great Society was largely a failure, the unintended consequences of which were damaging the very people the system was designed to help. This consensus was confirmed in the 1992 presidential campaign when candidate Bill Clinton promised to "end welfare as we know it."

As Robert Carleson demonstrated in "The Real Answer to Welfare Reform" (8 April 1972) the essentials of welfare reform were apparent twenty years earlier. Carleson was the principal architect of then-Governor Ronald Reagan's successful welfare reform plan in California and later became U.S. Commissioner of Welfare in the Nixon administration.

"Mr. President, Why the Delay?" (5 May 1973) was a plaintive plea by HUMAN EVENTS for President Nixon to come clean about the Watergate mess.

The 1 May 1979 article by Francis J. McNamara ("Levi Imposes Severe Restrictions on FBI") targeted "reforms" that made it more difficult for the FBI to keep tabs on terrorist and criminal elements in the United States. In 1982, in part because of persistent pressure from HUMAN EVENTS, then-Attorney General William French Smith rescinded many of the Levi guidelines.

"U.S. Congress: The Last Plantation" (30 March 1985) by author and UPI correspondent Donald Lambro is a case study in Lord Acton's dictum that "power tends to corrupt and absolute power corrupts absolutely"—a situation that surely obtains on Capitol Hill where the Democrats have controlled the House of Representatives for fifty years.

In "An Energy Policy to Keep America Free" (13 February 1988), Donald P. Hodel, secretary of the Interior in the Reagan administration, contends that the best energy "policy" is no policy—that is, a policy that allows the free market to answer America's energy needs.

For the last decade the *cause celebre* of the nation's liberal elite has unquestionably been AIDS. Compared to mega-killers such as cancer and heart disease the number of AIDS deaths is small but among the ranks of the gay rights activists, artists, entertainers, and writers—all important constituencies in the Democratic party—the toll has been high. In "AIDS: The Chic Disease" (9 May 1992) *National Review* editor and syndicated columnist Jeffrey Hart notes the disproportionate attention given to AIDS because of the power of these powerful groups.

No politician in recent memory has been subjected to more ridicule and abuse than former vice president Dan Quayle. A speech delivered by Dan Quayle in 1992 particularly incensed the media elite because of its criticism of television's "Murphy Brown" and the program's seeming glorification of single motherhood as a preferred option. In "The Imperative of Moral Values" (20 June 1992), Quayle reiterated his devotion to family values, saying of the media elite, "I wear their scorn as a badge of honor." HUMAN EVENTS staunchly defended Quayle and his message, and within two years Bill Clinton himself admitted that on the question of family values Dan Quayle was right.

Although HUMAN EVENTS had been highly critical of George Bush's domestic record (predicting correctly that the president was courting electoral disaster), the publication supported Bush's re-election bid. The editors were largely skeptical about Ross Perot's populist platform and were scathingly critical of the platform of Democratic nominee Bill Clinton. HUMAN EVENTS predicted in "The Statists Take Over" (30 January 1993) that the programs of the "New Democrat" Bill Clinton would actually add up to a plan for an across-the-board expansion of the federal government's size and power.

Finally, in the wake of George Bush's defeat, a battle erupted within the GOP over the party's position on abortion. In "All Human Life Is Sacred" (3 April 1993) Dallas *Morning News* columnist William Murchison reminds readers that abortion is fundamentally a moral question.

How the "Warren Revolution" Has Changed America

By Senator Sam J. Ervin, Jr. (D.-N.C.)   (From the 21 January 1967 issue)

(Senator Ervin, a graduate of the University of North Carolina and Harvard Law School, was one of the Senate's leading constitutional experts. A practicing attorney for almost fifty years, he served on the North Carolina Superior Court [1937–1943] and the North Carolina Supreme Court [1948–1954] prior to his entrance to the U.S. Senate, where he sat on the Armed Services, Government Operations, and Judiciary Committees.)

Much is being written about the Warren Court. Most of it is too laudatory to be truthful. A new book has appeared which is too truthful to be laudatory. It is L. Brent Bozell's *The Warren Revolution*, which has just been issued by Arlington House.

The Warren Revolution is the first volume of a projected two-volume work dealing with the Supreme Court under Earl Warren. Bozell's main thesis is that for more than a decade the Warren Court has been engaged in Constitution-making and Constitution-amendment in violation of Article V, which vests the power to do these things solely in the Congress and the states in words so plain that no literate person can misunderstand their meaning. Bozell assures the reader that the second volume of the projected work will "ask whether the Warren Revolution is, on its merits, in the best interest of the American commonwealth and, if not, what weapons are available for the counterrevolution."

The author obviously accepts the sound conclusion that if we are to understand the institutions of today, we must know the events of yesterday which brought them into being. As a consequence, he prepared himself for the writing of this book by prodigious research in respect to the historical events which preceded, accompanied and followed the framing of the Constitution of the United States.

While he makes some inferences from these events which are strikingly original in nature, he sets forth the events themselves with such candor and clarity that the reader can evaluate the significance of the events himself and draw different inferences from them if he so chooses.

Bozell writes with complete forthrightness. Moreover, he expresses what he has to say in understandable and eloquent words.

For these reasons *The Warren Revolution* is an exceedingly readable, intriguing and illuminating book which will undoubtedly find an honored place on the bookshelves of those who still entertain the conviction that the American people are entitled to the government of laws which the Constitution was ordained to establish.

It certainly merits reading by those defenders of the Warren Court who assert that the court's deviations from plainly expressed constitutional principles prove that we have a "living Constitution." As Bozell notes, this question-begging assertion tends to prove exactly the contrary; i.e., that the Constitution is dead and that America is ruled by the personal notions of the judicial activists who sit on the Supreme Court bench.

The book will not commend itself to those who give the American people admonitions of this character:

"When the Supreme Court speaks, its decisions must be accepted as sacrosanct by the bench, the bar and the people of America even though they constitute encroachments on the constitutional domain of the President or the Congress, or tend to reduce the states to meaningless zeroes on the nation's map. Indeed, the bench, the bar and the people must do more than this. They must speak of the Supreme Court at all times with a reverence akin to that which inspired Moab to speak thus of Jehovah: 'Though He slay me, yet will I trust him.' "

Be this as it may, Bozell's writing of *The Warren Revolution* is warranted by Chief Justice Harlan F. Stone's assertion that "where the courts deal, as ours do, with great public questions, the only protection against unwise decisions, and even judicial usurpation, is careful scrutiny of their action and fearless comment upon it."

Let us put some things beyond cavil. The author does not question the good intentions of those Supreme Court justices who have been the architects of the Warren Revolution. Moreover, he expressly disclaims any present purpose to pass judgment on whether their deviations from the Constitution would be beneficial to the American people if they were possessed of the constitutional power to make them.

He only challenges most emphatically—and effectively—their constitutional power to make them.

He asserts, in substance, that the framers of the Constitution set forth in that instrument certain fixed principles of government; that they placed upon all judges and other public officials an oath-bound obligation to support those principles of government; that they provided that those principles could not be changed either in phraseology or in meaning except by a constitutional amendment adopted by the Congress and the states in the manner set out in Article V of the Constitution.

He also asserts, in substance, that the framers of the Constitution did these things to put these fixed principles of government beyond the reach of impatient legislators, autocratic executive officials, activist judges, temporary majorities and the shifting winds of public opinion.

In saying these things, Bozell states a position in harmony with that of Daniel Webster, who made some penetrating observations concerning public officers who substitute their good intentions for rules of law. As Webster said:

"Good intentions will always be pleaded for every assumption of authority. It is hardly too strong to say that the Constitution was made to guard the people against the dangers of good intentions. There are men in all ages who mean to govern well, but they mean to govern. They promise to be good masters, but they mean to be masters."

Bozell maintains that since the Constitution was written and adopted to express their purposes, it inescapably follows that those who interpret it must give effect to the intention of those who framed and adopted it.

In holding to this view, he espouses a principle of constitutional construction which found virtually universal acceptance in the United States before the advent of the Warren Court, and which was best expressed by Chief Justice John Marshall when he declared that "the enlightened patriots who framed our Constitution and the people who adopted it must be understood . . . to have intended what they said."

The author further declares, in essence, that under Article III of the Constitution and the acts of Congress implementing it, the Supreme Court is a court rather than a supreme organ of government and has no power whatever except the judicial power, which it exercises as a court of original jurisdiction by constitutional authority in a limited number of specified cases, and which it exercises as a court of appellate jurisdiction by the grace of Congress in all other cases.

Inasmuch as the judicial power simply authorizes a court to decide and pronounce judgment and carry it into effect between parties who bring a case before it for a decision, Bozell maintains that the Supreme Court has no power under the Constitution to issue fiats binding upon the legislative or executive departments of the federal government, or the states, or individuals when they are not parties to cases it decides.

Moreover, he points out that when it has to interpret a constitutional provision to determine a case before it, the Supreme Court merely has the power to interpret such provision; i.e., to ascertain its meaning, and not the power to amend the provision; i.e., to change its meaning.

In this, Bozell's concept of a court coincides with that of Chief Justice Edward Douglas White, who, describing how a court should exercise its judicial power, said: "The fundamental conception of a judicial body is that of one hedged about by precedents which are binding on the court without regard to the personality of its members."

Bozell selects some samples out of a multitude of available cases to show that the Warren Court has been able to take its journey and reach its destination because its activist members have thrown into their judicial garbage pail the doctrine of *stare decisis* (the rule that judges stand by and follow the decisions of their own court) and the fundamental principle of constitutional construction that effect must be given to the intention of the framers and the adopters of a constitutional provision. The rationale by which the Warren Court frees itself from the doctrine of *stare decisis* may be summarized as follows:

The Constitution must change to meet changing conditions. As its authorized interpreter, the Supreme Court has the power to make the Constitution conform to the views of the majority of its members. Since the doctrine of *stare decisis* might handicap the Supreme Court in making the Constitution conform to the views of a majority of its members, the Supreme Court is not bound by its own decisions on constitutional question.

In thus liberating themselves from the doctrine of *stare decisis*, the activist justices not only confuse the power to interpret and the power to amend, but they simultaneously reach the paradoxical conclusion that the 190 million other Americans and all the other officers, both federal and state, whom they put in office, are nevertheless bound by Supreme Court decisions on constitutional questions.

One of the cases selected by Bozell to disclose how the Warsen Court has repudiated the fundamental principle of constitutional construction is *Brown vs. Board of Education*, whose racial overtones have unfortunately obscured the havoc it wrought to constitutional government. In the *Brown* case Chief Justice Warren said: "In approaching this problem, we cannot turn the clock back to 1868 when the amendment was adopted or even to 1896 when *Plessy vs. Ferguson* was written." From a constitutional standpoint, this is an astounding statement.

The truth is that it was the duty of the court to turn the clock back to 1868 and ascertain and give effect to the intention of those who framed and ratified the 14th Amendment.

Had the Supreme Court performed this constitutional duty, it would have found and declared that the 14th Amendment not only did not require, but did not even countenance, the decision it rendered. This is so, notwithstanding the chief justice's assertion to the contrary, because nothing in our constitutional history is better authenticated than that those who framed and ratified the 14th Amendment did not intend that it should interfere in any way with the power of states to segregate pupils in their public schools on the basis of race.

Bozell selects the case of *Cooper vs Aaron* to describe the destination to which the Warren Court has journeyed. In this case, the Supreme Court said:

"It follows that the interpretation of the 14th Amendment enunciated by this court in the Brown case is the supreme law of the land, and Article VI of the Constitution makes it of binding effect on the states, 'anything in the Constitution or laws of any state to the contrary notwith-standing.' "

These words, which clearly reflect the position of the Warren Court in respect to its constitutional power, are wholly inconsistent with the Constitution in general and Article VI in particular.

There is not a word or syllable anywhere in the Constitution which sustains the position that a Supreme Court's interpretation of a constitutional provision constitutes the supreme law of the land. On the contrary, Article VI provides in unmistakable language that nothing consti-tutes the supreme law of the land except the Constitution, acts of Congress conforming to the Constitution and treaties made under the authority of the United States.

As appears by the *Cooper* case, however, the Warren Court now proclaims to the country that any decision it hands down on a constitutional question constitutes the supreme law of the land. If this means anything, it means that any decision by the Warren Court on a constitutional question which is inconsistent with the Constitution amends it, i.e., changes its meaning, just as effectively as an amendment adopted by the Congress and the states in accordance with Article V.

If this be true, as the Warren Court does affirm, the American people are no longer ruled by a Constitution. They are merely the subjects of a judicial oligarchy consisting of any five of the Supreme Court justices.

In making these things plain, Brent Bozell has rendered a service of transcendent impor-tance to all Americans who deem tyranny on the bench to be as objectionable as tyranny on the throne. They will await the second volume of his projected work with the hope that it will reveal some weapons "available for the counter-revolution."

The Real Answer to Welfare Reform

By Robert B. Carleson, California State Director of Social Welfare   *(From the 8 April 1972 issue)*

(In a special message to Congress last week, the President again vigorously urged both the House and the Senate to help enact his Family Assistance Plan–his multi-billion-dollar program that would double or triple the welfare costs. Why he continues to press for passage of this proposal is still somewhat of a mystery. But many apologists for the Administration, even those not particularly enamored with the President's plan, often respond to critics rather curtly. "Well," they ask, "what would you do to halt the welfare mess?"

We have answered that question on previous occasions, but briefly our reply boils down to this.

First of all, we would not compound the existing problem with the horrifying solution proposed by the President and the Moynihan-Ehrlichman-Richardson triumvirate. Secondly, we would urge Congress to turn control of the welfare situation back to the states. Is there any evidence that this solution would work? The answer is a resounding yes.

In California, the most populous state in the Union, Gov. Ronald Reagan has instituted a welfare reform program that has been a spectacular success. And he has managed to accomplish this miracle even within the framework of the present federal welfare system. How he has performed this astonishing feat is told in some detail below by Robert B. Carleson, the governor's astute director of social welfare.

If the President, his advisers and Congress are interested in real welfare reform, they should, in our opinion, draw up legislation that would encourage each state to adopt programs along the lines already enacted by the governor. The essential ingredient to a successful program of this sort is non-interference by the federal government, particularly the Department of Health, Education and Welfare.

Unlike the Family Assistance Plan [FAP], a visionary scheme whose basic purpose is not to reduce the relief rolls but to provide a guaranteed annual income for every family, the governor's plan has proved workable and extremely effective in holding down the welfare rolls. The question remaining is: Why does the Administration continue to ignore Gov. Reagan's successful reforms in welfare and push ahead with its untried, unproven and extremely costly venture?)

In August 1970 welfare in California was completely out of control, both in number of persons on the rolls and in total costs. Artificial freezes and cutbacks were being made in most state and county functions which were threatening the effectiveness of important and necessary programs because of the need to provide funds to meet welfare costs.

In 10 years time, during periods of great prosperity, California's welfare rolls had leaped from 600,000 to over 2.2 million persons. Welfare spending was in excess of $2.5 billion per year and all of the welfare and fiscal experts were predicting that, no matter what was done, the growth would continue and would require gigantic tax increases.

In California, welfare is administered at the county level and supervised by the state. Counties which in California had been the bulwark of support for a healthy home rule policy were one by one throwing up their hands and asking for state administration of welfare, until finally the California County Supervisors' Association itself took such a position. In addition, funds had been spread so thin that those who were truly in need of assistance were receiving insufficient grants to meet their needs while many who were non-needy were receiving assistance.

In testimony before the U.S. Senate Finance Committee on Feb. 1, 1972, Gov. Ronald Reagan said, "We didn't just become aware of this problem in 1970 but our earlier efforts to deal with it weren't too successful; perhaps because we relied on professional welfare experts to propose solutions and all too often they were more familiar with what they were sure they could not do, so the situation became worse instead of better.

"Finally, to avert a fiscal and human disaster, I asked several members of my administration, who had proven themselves in other state administrative posts, to form a task force and to devote full time for as long as it took to see if and how real reform of welfare could be developed and implemented."

The task force consisted of Ned Hutchinson, the governor's appointment secretary, the late Jerry Fielder, director of the State Department of Agriculture, John Mayfield, assistant director of the State Department of Conservation, and the author of this article. At that time I was serving as chief deputy director of the State Department of Public Works. The group was not publicized so that its effectiveness in getting facts and developing answers would not be blunted through controversy.

The task force organized itself into several sub-task forces headed by each of the principal members and was expanded, utilizing attorneys and fiscal experts to successfully conduct over 700 in-depth interviews with persons involved in the welfare system from top to bottom. Fielder met with federal officials in Washington as well as participated in the interview effort.

My role was to review in-depth state and federal laws and regulations and the organization of welfare administration. For assistance I called upon Mr. Ronald Zumbrun, a bright, successful attorney from the State Department of Public Works and Mr. John Svahn, a thorough and tenacious administrative analyst. We were assisted from time to time by fiscal experts from the State Department of Finance and others.

We found that many state and federal laws had been broadened, expanded and twisted by implementing regulations. We found that many "interpretations" of federal and state laws were being made by social work professionals who gained this knowledge on a word-of-mouth basis. Oftentimes opinions were not based on legal research.

In addition, we found that the welfare system, which originally had been primarily a system for providing social services to people, had now grown into a huge fiscal operation where 80 per cent of the money spent was in the form of unrestricted, direct money grants to welfare recipients. Expenditures for social services accounted for only about 20 per cent of the total welfare budget.

Welfare laws and regulations had been written assuming that professional social workers would utilize discretion in determining eligibility and the amount of the grant. However, federal and state courts had consistently been striking down this discretion and had been finding that if a person could be found eligible under the broad regulations, he had a right to be eligible and to receive the maximum grant. Therefore, welfare laws were laced with gaping loopholes.

Members of the task force found that in previous attempts to study the problem, committees and task forces had made reports based on consensus findings and opinions. This desire to submit recommendations which could be agreed upon by all had led to many good ideas being lost and a failure to accept necessarily drastic and controversial solutions. Therefore, the task force decided not to develop a formal report of recommendations but rather to turn all of the ideas, information, proposals and findings over to Gov. Reagan for his use and the use of his director of Social Welfare in developing comprehensive program for welfare reform. This effort was completed in December 1970.

In late December 1970 Gov. Reagan appointed Mr. James Hall, who was then his secretary of Business and Transportation, to coordinate all activities of state government relating to human relations as secretary of Human Relations. I was asked by the governor to serve as director of the State Department of Social Welfare. I appointed Zumbrun to the position of deputy director for Legal Affairs and Svahn to the position for deputy director for Administration. Charles Hobbs was retained as deputy director of Social Welfare.

This team then embarked on a comprehensive program of reorganization of the State Department of Social Welfare and instituted scores of administration changes. These changes were commenced in January 1971 and are continuing today.

A team of auditors had been brought in from the State Department of Finance at my request to review the effectiveness of the eligibility process at both the state and county levels. Their study indicated that the state was losing over $50 million a year through eligibility errors alone.

As a result of this study an eligibility audit program was developed in the department and assigned to the Fiscal Division. This program provided for the first time an audit of the eligibility system down through county and to the recipient. The reorganization is bringing in fiscal and administratively trained persons to operate the payment system process.

Another organizational change was to increase the number of attorneys in the department so that answers given to counties are based on legal research rather than on the "historic knowledge" of social work professionals. Several surplus middle and upper-level management positions in the social service categories were abolished and incumbents demoted. Although there were a significant number of demotions, because of vacancies caused by attrition, actual layoffs were not necessary.

Almost every action taken to reorganize the department and to reassign social work professionals met legal opposition from social workers' unions and from other organizations representing the welfare bureaucracy.

An attempt was made to destroy the new organization in the last hours of the considerations by the legislature of the state budget. This attempt was uncovered at the last possible moment and corrective legislation followed. The attempt, however, did serve to delay by one or two months reorganizational efforts.

In general, we have reversed the philosophy of the State Department of Social Welfare and have informed the counties we will expect their eligibility and grant processes to be accurate and fair and that there will be tighter audits. We have indicated also that we will back the counties when they take a firm position regarding the tight administration of welfare programs.

In addition, during January and February 1971 we worked to utilize the data, information and proposals developed by the task force to develop a comprehensive welfare reform program. These proposals were developed jointly by top new staff of the department, James Hall, members of the governor's Cabinet and the governor himself.

On March 3, 1971, Gov. Reagan delivered to the California Legislature the most comprehensive and detailed program for welfare reform that had ever been attempted in California or in any other state. The governor's message consisted of a book containing over 175 pages. The comprehensive reform program was comprised of over 70 major provisions with many sub-provisions and involved administrative changes, regulatory changes and proposed legislative changes. It indicated a potential annual savings of over $600 million per year in welfare spending in California.

By March 1971 many of the administrative and regulatory changes were under way and the focus of the battle shifted to the Democrat-controlled legislature. Resistance to reform came from various sectors—from welfare rights organizations, from social workers unions and from supporters of HR 1 who were dedicated to the proposition that only a complete federal takeover of welfare would be effective.

Much of the opposition we received from HR 1 supporters was brought about because of a fear that if welfare reform at the state level could succeed in California, chances of federalization of welfare would be destroyed. Opposition from this quarter oftentimes was subtle and is continuing to this day.

Shortly after the governor's welfare reform message, letters of support began pouring in from all over the state and Gov. Reagan appointed a representative citizens' committee from this group of supporters. The committee—headed by the chairman of the Board of Supervisors of Riverside County, Mr. Al McCandless—was a bipartisan group dedicated to welfare reform. The co-chairman was Neil Papiano, an attorney from Los Angeles, who was active in private sector welfare planning.

The committee developed over 120 local committees throughout California and the citizens' demand for welfare reform legislation began to be heard and felt in the legislature. After months of hearings, debates and delays, in late July 1971 Speaker of the Assembly Bob Moretti headed a team to negotiate personally with Reagan what was to become the Welfare Reform Act of 1971. Moretti's team consisted of State Sen. Anthony Beilenson and Assemblymen William Bagley, John Burton and Leo McCarthy. All of the legislative team members had actively opposed or criticized the governor's welfare program.

After a week's intensive negotiations between the teams headed personally by Gov. Reagan and Speaker Moretti, followed by 10 days of lengthy, heated further negotiations by the remainder of the negotiating teams, a compromise welfare reform act was agreed upon. An able, experienced and extremely expert negotiator, Gov. Ronald Reagan had been successful in getting 70 per cent of his legislative proposals enacted, an accomplishment which few thought possible.

The Welfare Reform Act consists of over 84 elements and many sub-elements. It was signed into law as an emergency measure on Aug. 13, 1971, and took effect Oct. 1, 1971. It has been subjected to court attacks and attacks by its nominal author, Sen. Beilenson, and other legislative negotiators who did not realize the extent to which they were agreeing to welfare reform until after the bill had been enacted. At that point they began receiving extreme heat and criticism from their supporters in social workers' unions, welfare rights organizations, etc.

Although there are over 84 elements in the bill, only 10 are in court and all of the sections that are in court are sections that were rewritten by the legislative staff during the final phase of negotiation. Welfare rights attorneys who are now bringing suits against the act were permitted to participate in the final drafting by legislative staff during intervals between meetings of the negotiators.

However, even with these attempts to water down or diminish legislative reforms, the act is a real success. Most of its sections are free of court challenge and the most significant sections will not begin to produce their full savings potential until later this fiscal year and next fiscal year.

The governor's welfare reform program started in January 1971 with administrative and regulatory changes. The rolls had been growing at the rate of approximately 40,000 persons per month. The legislative analyst had projected a continued and even accelerated growth, notwithstanding any changes that could be made at the state or county levels.

The rolls continued their upward climb through March 1971 when an abrupt reversal took place, with a large April drop in the number of persons on welfare in California. This was followed by an actual reduction in each month's welfare rolls for eight straight months.

In December the rolls remained steady and in January 1972 they dropped again shortly after the Welfare Reform Act was in operation. In December the governor noted that we had brought welfare under control in California and that we expect the welfare situation to stabilize. During January and February 1972 the rolls have remained relatively constant.

Because the success of Gov. Reagan's welfare reform program has caused embarrassment to those who opposed it and to those who are supporting HR 1 there seems to be a concerted effort by many people, including some legislators and county welfare directors, to discredit the effects of the governor's reforms.

The detractors are claiming that the drop in welfare in California was the result of a drop in unemployment rate and the result of a drop in the birth rate. The facts show otherwise.

Historically, over the last 10 years in California the welfare rolls, particularly the unemployed father rolls, have continued to go up every year even in times of prosperity when the unemployment rate was dropping. In fact, there were six years out of the last 10 years when the unemployment rate dropped but welfare rolls continued to expand explosively.

During 1971 the welfare rolls dropped for several months before the first measurable drop in the unemployment rate and the rolls dropped for approximately eight months before any significant drop in the unemployment rate. This would indicate that some of the reforms may have contributed to the reduction in the unemployment rate rather than the reverse being true.

We all recognize that there has been a gradual reduction in the birth rate. It is hard to believe, nevertheless, that anyone can seriously claim that the reduction in the birth rate was so sudden that it could have seen the rolls grow at the rate of 40,000 to 50,000 in one month and then an abrupt reversal in the next and succeeding months.

We did notice, however, a rather abrupt reduction in the average number of children per case. This followed the accomplishment of our new eligibility audit program. Today the welfare recipient in California knows there is a very good chance that the number of children reported by him will be checked and audited and the eligibility worker knows that his or her work will be audited. The task force had found during its study that a significant fraud and abuse factor was the over-reporting of the number of children in a family in order to receive a higher grant.

Whenever a change in welfare is made, there is usually a two- or three-month time lag before the effect is noticed. For example, administrative changes started in late January and February of 1971 and the first impact on the caseload was in April. This will be true also of the effect of the Welfare Reform Act. In any event, it will be impossible now or in the future to determine what individual elements of the reform program, either administrative or legislative, are contributing to the success, because so many of the reforms overlap and interrelate with each other, just as they were designed to do in such a comprehensive program.

The only way to keep score is to look at the actual case load vs. what they were projected to be and to look at the actual cost vs. what they were projected to be, and thirdly, to observe the increased benefits for the truly needy remaining on the rolls.

SCOREBOARD
February 1972

• 51,651 fewer persons on the rolls than were projected to be without reforms by even the most conservative estimates.

• 158,033 fewer recipients than on the rolls in March 1971. Seventy per cent of this figure represents reductions in the Aid to Families with Dependent Children category.

• $168 million less than would have been spent if rolls had continued to grow (fiscal year 1971-72, $388 million less).

• Increase in benefits to the truly needy—family of four from $221 to $280. Aged, blind and disabled a cost-of-living increase in December 1971.

California has demonstrated that even in the present system a state can and does have the flexibility to provide significant reforms if it is willing to take on the task and not merely to give up and shift the burden to the federal level.

In California we are demonstrating to the country that welfare can be reformed and that in large states, at least, the counties can and should be actively involved in the administration of welfare. Decisions regarding people and their needs should be made wherever possible by those closest to the people. Despite these successes, we still have a long way to go, both at the federal and state levels. Many changes should be made in the federal welfare law as recommended by Gov. Reagan in his testimony before the Senate Finance Committee.

One unexploited state reform, for example, indicates how much more can be saved as a result of the Welfare Reform Act of 1971. The State Department of Social Welfare established an Earnings Clearance System whereby a computer tape containing the Social Security numbers of all California's employable welfare recipients was processed through the state's employment service agency, matching these records with the reports of earnings submitted by employers for unemployment benefit purposes. After this computer operation, the earnings reported by employers by each person on welfare are sent to the counties to be checked against the earnings reported by the welfare recipient.

This process in no way violates anyone's privacy or involves making a contact with outside persons since the records checked are only records already held by public agencies. However, a welfare rights organization served by OEO-financed attorneys succeeded in getting a temporary restraining order halting this process, claiming that it violates federal regulation. No one should be hurt by this except those who are under-reporting their income and legal experts anticipate that the lawsuit will be resolved in favor of the state.

For a brief instant, however, we got a peak in the door. Counties reported that to the extent they were allowed to check before the court halted the operation, they found that in 48 per cent of the cases there was a significant discrepancy between the amount of income reported by the recipient and the income to the recipient reported by the employers. County welfare directors have estimated that in most of these cases recipients are receiving excessive aid or are not eligible at all.

We will not know what the real discrepancy percentage is unless and until we have an opportunity to review all the cases. However, in California one per cent error or fraud represents $20 million per year, therefore the savings potential is enormous from this single reform.

Many of the smaller states have not permitted their welfare systems to get out of control as California has done over the past 20 years and therefore may not be in need for as comprehensive a reform program as was necessary in California. However, we in the Reagan Administration firmly believe that the path to true welfare reform is not through a federalization of the program but is through active state and local reform efforts encouraged rather than discouraged by federal agencies, and through action by Congress to grant greater discretion to the states in the administration of federally assisted welfare programs.

Mr. President, Why the Delay?
Reagan Points the Way

(From the 5 May 1973 issue)

By the time these words are read the President, one hopes, will have finally begun the vigorous scouring of the White House that is absolutely necessary in the face of the continuing—indeed, burgeoning—Watergate scandal. Every moment he delays strengthens mightily the impression of many that the President himself is somehow deeply implicated in this sordid affair.

The dazzling, almost hourly revelations boggle the mind. Bugging. Burglary. Bribery. Hush money. Obstruction of justice. Forged documents to frame a former President. The burning of sensitive evidence by the FBI chief. And all condoned or committed at the highest levels of government.

How in Heaven's name did the Nixon Administration, this law-and-order Administration, become so neck-deep in this terrible business? How could Haldeman, Ehrlichman, Mitchell and Dean have permitted the presidency to be so tarnished? And why has the President done so very little to eradicate the Watergate blemish?

The President does need to find the White House staff guilty beyond a shadow of a doubt in order to move. It is enough to know that they permitted, covered up and turned a blind eye to the grossest kind of illegal operations. At the very least, the top White House staff should be formally suspended. Yet by the end of last week, in this most bizarre of cases, the President seemed to be making a concerted effort to spread a protective cloak about his key aides, all of whom have been embroiled in the Watergate disaster.

H. R. (Bob) Haldeman, the President's chief of staff, and John Ehrlichman, considered his top domestic policy adviser, were permitted to accompany the President to Meridian, Miss., to attend the dedication of the new John Stennis Training Center at the naval base there. This was the first time both men had been seen with the President since Nixon began his own investigation of charges that high-level White House aides had been involved in the Watergate incident.

Ironically, the President's show of support had come at a time when new reports were increasingly linking both names to the Watergate cover-up operations and soon after both men had hired criminal lawyer John J. Wilson to represent them in the Watergate case.

On Easter Sunday, the President had called his special counsel John Dean to wish him a "Happy Easter" and to assure him, "You're still my counsel." The support for Dean was even harder to comprehend. Whereas the charges against both Haldeman and Ehrlichman have been somewhat blurred, Dean has been specifically accused of approving the bugging and delivering hush money to the seven convicted Watergate conspirators.

Dean's response to the charges against him, made by Jeb Magruder; the second-ranking official at President Nixon's Re-election Committee who resigned last week as an assistant secretary of the Commerce Department, has been a 139-word note, conspicuous by its failure to flatly deny any of Magruder's accusations.

Why the President would choose to go out of his way to lend support to his White House staff, which, if nothing else, has served him miserably, is hard to understand.

Writing on the Watergate case last week, Pulitzer Prize winning-reporter Clark Mollenhoff, once a White House aide himself, noted:

"At this writing, there is no doubt that some White House aides took an active part in the planning and financing of the criminal acts of burglary and illegal wiretapping and eavesdropping. It is equally apparent that for 10 months they cleverly used the power of the President to obstruct justice by hiding their involvement in the original crimes.

"It was the power of President Nixon that made possible:

"1. The control over the huge cash funds at the Nixon re-election committee to be misused to pay 'hush' money to the seven defendants in the original Watergate case.

"2. The acquisition of raw FBI files by White House Counsel John Dean's office for use and misuse by both indicted and unindicted participants in the Watergate conspiracy.

"3. The misuse of this information by the White House officials to throw fear into such men as James W. McCord Jr., who appealed directly to Chief Federal Judge John J. Sirica because his lack of trust in the FBI, the prosecutors and other Justice Department channels.

"4. The hinted possibility that President Nixon's power of executive clemency would be available, as it was in the case of Teamster Boss James R. Hoffa, to cut the sentences short when the furor over Watergate subsided.

"The only real alternative explanations of the Watergate situation are that President Nixon was too trusting, was too much a captive of the White House staff or was too much involved with guilty knowledge of what was being done on his behalf.

"Only a precise knowledge of the conversations between the President and his two closest special assistants—H. R. (Bob) Haldeman and John Ehrlichman—can give us the ultimate answer to the questions on everyone's mind.

"President Nixon continues to place the barrier of 'executive privilege' on all conversations and communications with his top advisers. Only time will tell if Congress will permit that arbitrary secrecy claim to prevail in the face of the massive evidence of an obstruction of justice engineered from the White House.

"It is now apparent from the public admission of former Atty. Gen. John Mitchell, the equally reluctant admissions of former Special Counsel Charles Colson and the bellicose defensive comments of John Dean that the White House counsel's office was the instrumentality for obstructing justice."

Briefly, then, the President is doing his party and his country a grave disservice by failing to act swiftly on the Watergate issue and to clean out his top White House assistants. Even if a miracle should pass and none of them prove guilty of criminal wrongdoing, the White House cannot remain above suspicion when its aides are linked to new scandals hourly. And what scandals they are proving to be! Consider, for instance, just a few of the charges aired last week in the newspapers:

• L. Patrick Gray, who resigned as acting FBI director rather than damage the reputation of the agency (an honorable course that has not been followed by many others involved in the Watergate mess), has reportedly told friends that he destroyed documents taken from a central figure in the Watergate case without looking at them, after it was suggested at a White House meeting that the papers "should never see the light of day."

Gray, according to these reports, placed in his FBI "burn bag" files handed to him by John Dean at a White House meeting on June 28. The meeting was also attended by Ehrlichman. The files reportedly contained material relating to the Kennedy family and had been obtained by Watergate conspirator E. Howard Hunt, a former consultant to the White House. At the time the documents were handed over and destroyed, Hunt was under intensive FBI investigation and already heavily implicated in the Watergate affair. While Ehrlichman has denied any wrong doing, Gray has insisted that neither man informed him of what was in the Hunt files.

• Henry E. Peterson, the assistant attorney general now in charge of the Watergate probe, is said to have told Gray that Dean now contends that the Hunt files contained fake—that's right, *fake*—diplomatic cables, that Hunt had "fabricated State Department cables" indicating President Kennedy's complicity in Diem's assassination.

• A federal grand jury in New York City is looking into a reported promise from presidential aide Ehrlichman to aid fraud figure Robert L. Vesco in a bank deal in the Middle East. The Vesco case is also enmeshed in the Watergate scandals. Vesco, as the newspapers have reported, secretly dispatched $200,000 in cash to the Nixon campaign fund in April 1972, but this gift may be tied to the efforts of the New Jersey financier to get relief from a Securities and Exchange Commission (SEC) investigation begun in March 1971.

Among the disclosures made in the New York proceeding, according to an investigative report in the *Wall Street Journal*, are these:

• "On March 8, 1972, at his first discussion of campaign contributions with Maurice Stans, former secretary of commerce and the President's chief money raiser, Mr. Vesco complained he was being harassed by the SEC.

• "When Mr. Vesco offered to give as much as $500,000, Mr. Stans undertook to arrange for him to meet with John Mitchell, who had just resigned as attorney general to manage Mr. Nixon's campaign. A Stans aide guided Mr. Vesco upstairs to Mr. Mitchell's office.

• "Mr. Vesco sent word to Mr. Stans that he hoped the secret cash gift would result in some 'help' with his SEC troubles. Mr. Stans responded that Mr. Mitchell was 'handling' that side of the matter.

• "After a worn brown briefcase loosely packed with $200,000 in $100 bills was handed to Mr. Stans on April 10, 1972, Mr. Mitchell phoned Mr. Vesco's lawyer that it would be possible for the lawyer to meet with William Casey, then chairman of the SEC. That has already been told. What hasn't been pointed out is that although the attorney general had been asked to intercede with Chairman Casey as early as Feb. 11, 1972, he apparently failed to do so until May, after Mr. Vesco made his gift."

• Then we come to an even more bizarre episode. Los Angeles U.S. District Court Judge Matt Byrne, the judge in the Pentagon Papers trial, made public a secret memorandum last week saying that Watergate defendants E. Howard Hunt and Gordon Liddy burglarized the files of Daniel Ellsberg's psychiatrist and absconded with Ellsberg's psychiatric records.

But this, as, they say, only scratches the surface. Far more is expected to be divulged, as the Watergate scandal reactor continues to detonate.

Despite the President's somewhat erratic behavior in recent weeks, we fervently hope that he is not tied to this extraordinary case in any way. Yet he must act, quickly, decisively and in such a way that it is clear that he is free from all blame other than negligence. There are persistent rumors that he does have a game plan and that one of his wise counselors in his first term, Bryce Harlow, may figure prominently in any resultant shakeup. That indeed, is good news, if true. And the sooner the shakeup, the better.

Levi Imposes Restrictions on FBI
Will CP Fronts Be Probed?

By Francis J. McNamara   *(From the 1 May 1979 issue)*

(A longtime expert on security matters, Mr. McNamara is former executive secretary of the Subversive Activities Control Board and former director of the House Committee on Un-American Activities.)

The most obvious fact about the new guidelines for FBI domestic security investigations is that they are being carefully studied by Communist, terrorist and other subversive groups to see how they can best avoid or frustrate future FBI surveillance.

The same holds true of the National Lawyers Guild (NLG), the National Emergency Civil Liberties Committee, the Center for Constitutional Rights and other organizations composed of Communist and radical attorneys and established to protect and defend even those who hate the United States and its form of government so much that they will do anything to destroy it.

"Less Security for Americans, More Protection for Subversives," would be a fitting title for the guidelines.

The basic reason for this is found in Atty. Gen. Edward Levi's February 11 testimony before a House Judiciary subcommittee that the new guidelines (which went into effect April 5) "tie domestic security investigations closely to the violation of federal law . . . [T]he main thing, in my opinion, is that the purpose of the investigation must be the detection of unlawful conduct and not merely the monitoring of disfavored or troublesome activities and surely not of unpopular views."

The statement, first of all, is a typically ultra-liberal distortion of reality—a gross whitewash of the truly threatening activities (terrorism, foreign-directed communism, etc.) that have traditionally been the major subject of FBI investigations.

More important, it is a flat repudiation of the fact, *repeatedly upheld by the courts*, that the Federal Bureau of Investigation has a vital intelligence function in the domestic security field and that legitimate intelligence information is vastly different from criminal evidence.

That Levi is indefensibly downgrading the need for domestic intelligence is further evidenced by his testimony that the standards for a full FBI investigation now require both "a strong showing of criminal conduct" and an immediate cutoff "even if there is a clear threat of a violation of federal law if the threatened harm is *de minimus* or unlikely or remote in time."

This means, for example, that the FBI is barred from a full investigation of the Communist party because, though Congress and the courts have found that its ultimate aim is violent overthrow of the U.S., it is generally recognized that the possibility of its carrying out that crime is "remote in time."

The same is true of various other Communist groups. Their basic purpose, their *raison d'etre*—destruction of the United States—does not qualify them surveillance because none has a chance of accomplishing it in the foreseeable future.

Unless the FBI can come up with evidence they are plotting other major federal crimes and are likely to succeed in carrying them out in the near future, all will be immune to FBI investigation.

The guidelines authorize and set strict standards for three types of investigations—preliminary, limited and full. All are restricted to collecting data on individual and group activities involving force, violence, or violation of federal law. In addition, the force, violence or violation must have one of the following four purposes:

• The overthrowing of the United States or state government.

• Substantially interfering, in the United States, with the activities of a foreign government or its representatives.

• Substantially impairing the functioning of the United States or a state government, or interstate commerce, for the purpose of influencing U.S. policies or decisions.

• Depriving persons of their civil rights under the Constitution, laws or treaties of the United States.

No other security matters can be investigated. Typical Communist fronts, for example—outfits like the National Council of American-Soviet Friendship and some of the other most successful and dangerous fronts ever set up by the party in the United States—do not engage in the above activities and are therefore apparently immune to FBI investigation.

In this sense the guidelines betray a gross ignorance of basic Communist tactics on the part of Levi and the special Justice Department committee he appointed to prepare the guidelines.

The basic purpose of a Communist front is to promote the Communist position on some foreign or domestic policy issue through the devices of agitation and propaganda. Overwhelmingly, fronts are designed to operate within the law and do so—because this is how they can be most effective in regard to both their major and secondary purposes (recruiting new members to the party, raising money for it, etc.).

Communist theoreticians have always considered fronts as a vital, absolutely necessary support element. To a large degree, the success and security of a Communist party depends on the effectiveness of its front activity.

No government, therefore, can ever assess the internal danger it faces from a Communist party (and Moscow) unless it knows how many fronts that party is operating, whether they are national, regional, state or local in scope, their total membership and the extent of their influence on the non-Communist population.

The Constitution imposes on President Ford an obligation to keep himself informed about such matters along with others affecting the nation's internal security.

But the Levi-imposed FBI guidelines actually deny to the President a knowledge he must have to carry out his constitutional duty.

Informants cannot be employed, mail covers and wiretaps cannot be used in preliminary or limited investigations—though they are often the only way to obtain the evidence now needed to justify a full investigation. And even a full investigation must be halted any time it is failing to produce, as Levi testified, "specific and articulable facts" indicating one of the four above-mentioned transgressions.

Doubt is even expressed in the guidelines about the propriety of pretext inquiries, trash covers (inspections) and photography, all long-used, standard investigative techniques never condemned by the courts and some explicitly upheld by them (the guidelines neither approve nor bar these devices; apparently they are to be the subject of further deep thought).

• *No FBI "Preventive Action."* Prior to issuance of the guidelines on March 10, earlier drafts were released in December 1975 and on February 11. Both drafts had a section on "Preventive Action" which authorized the FBI to undertake "non-violent measures to obstruct or prevent the use of force or violence" in violation of certain federal laws or when "necessary to minimize the danger to life or property."

• *Wiretaps are unnecessarily restricted.* The Supreme Court has held that warrants are required for security wiretaps on domestic organizations. It defined a domestic organization, however, as one "which has no significant connection with a foreign power, its agents or agencies."

Under this decision [*Keith*], a warrant is not required for a tap on the Communist party because the Subversive Activities Control Board found that the party is "substantially directed, dominated and controlled by the Soviet Union." The Supreme Court itself upheld this finding. It is difficult to conceive of a more significant connection than direction, domination and control.

The FBI, without a warrant, could also have tapped various "peace" organizations of the Vietnam War era under this decision because they openly collaborated with Moscow and its World Peace Council, North Vietnam and other Communist powers. It could similarly tap other groups which are doing the same thing today.

• *Another wiretap restriction:* the guidelines provide that "whenever it becomes known that person(s) under surveillance are engaged in privileged conversation (e.g., with attorney), interception equipment shall be immediately shut off. . . ." This could result in the loss of important intelligence.

The fact is that Communist and radical attorneys in the NLG and similar groups have made a joke of the attorney-client relationship. Often in meetings and conversations with their clients they serve not as counsel, but as co-conspirators in their terrorist and other subversive acts.

Stephen Bingham, attorney and NLG member, has been a fugitive from justice since Aug. 21, 1971, the day he visited George Jackson in Soledad Prison and, a grand jury has charged, secretly gave him a 9 mm. pistol. Jackson, a revolutionary and lover of Angela Davis held on a charge of killing a guard in another prison, used the gun immediately after Bingham left in an attempted prison break. He, three guards, and two other inmates (who refused to take part in the break) were killed in the attempt. A "privileged" conversation?

The special Justice Department committee appointed by Levi to draw up the new guidelines has undermined the FBI's ability to insure the nation's domestic security and protect the lives and property of its citizens. It has also made the Ford Administration the weakest and softest in modern history when it comes to internal security matters.

Admittedly there have been abuses in some past FBI activities, though the media have tended to exaggerate and over-emphasize them while ignoring the bureau's accomplishments. Last December Levi warned the Church Committee that in efforts to prevent future abuse "if we are not careful, we will turn to solutions of the moment which a better reading of history might indicate are not the best solutions. . . . The importance is to the security and domestic tranquillity of the United States."

As HUMAN EVENTS pointed out last week in analyzing the Ford-Levi proposed foreign intelligence wiretap legislation, the attorney general has a habit of doing just what he tells others should not be done in the security area.

He has done it again with the new FBI guidelines—to the detriment of the nation's internal security.

U.S. Congress: The Last Plantation

By Donald Lambro   *(From the 30 March 1985 issue)*

(The following article is a chapter from Washington: City of Scandals, *published late in 1984 by Mr. Lambro. Copyright 1984 by Donald Lambro and Co., Inc. Reprinted with permission of Little, Brown and Co., Inc., 205 Lexington Ave., New York, N. Y. 10016.)*

"To do good is noble," Mark Twain once wrote. "To advise others to do good is also noble, and much less trouble." Congress has too frequently chosen to do the latter. Its legislative history has been one long unbroken legislative double standard. "Practice what you preach" is not a homily that Congress can honestly defend.

For nearly half a century Congress has been redressing America's most serious social and economic ills through major legislation that has resulted in difficult and sometimes turbulent social adjustments. Its prolific legal prescriptions have dealt with racial discrimination, unfair labor practices, worker health and safety, and the public's right to know how its government spends its money.

Yet throughout this historic legislative period, Congress has seen fit to exempt itself from virtually every piece of landmark legislation it has enacted.

The laws, rules, regulations, decrees and other social criteria Congress has imposed upon every American stops right at the doors of the Capitol. Inside, virtually undisturbed by these laws, there exists what has been cynically yet accurately called "the last plantation."

Consider just a few of the far-reaching laws that Congress has righteously—and in most cases correctly—applied to every member of our society, save itself:

- The Civil Rights Act of 1964
- The Equal Employment Opportunity Act of 1972
- The National Labor Relations Act of 1935
- The Fair Labor Standards Act of 1938
- The Equal Pay Act of 1963
- The Occupational Safety and Health Act of 1979
- The Minimum Wage Law of 1938
- The Freedom of Information Act
- The Privacy Act
- The Age Discrimination in Employment Act

In each of these and other pieces of legislation, Congress has inserted language which exempts legislators and their offices from the anti-discrimination, collective bargaining, worker safety, overtime protection, and other social safeguards it has decreed to be the law of the land.

When, for example, Congress enacted the Civil Rights Act of 1964 and the Equal Employment Opportunity Act of 1972, it outlawed discriminatory hiring practices. But lawmakers did not include themselves in such laws, despite the fact that at that time they belonged to one of the most lily-white institutions in America, where discrimination was practiced with virtual impunity. Indeed, black congressional aides were almost unheard of at that time, except in the rarest of instances.

Even as recently as 1978, a survey by the Black Legislative Assistants Staff Group, an ad hoc congressional employee group, could find only 33 blacks holding professional staff positions among the more than 3,200 employees who comprised the personal office staffs of senators.

A House study commission had determined in 1977 that blacks were often paid less than whites who possessed the same educational qualifications. Equally disturbing, a survey by *U.S. News & World Report* in March 1978 discovered that 27 out of the Senate's 100 members had no black employees in any position on their staff. Five of these lawmakers represented states with sizable black constituencies.

Incredibly, by 1983 the number of blacks holding non-clerical, professional staff positions has remained largely unchanged.

Minority employment practices in the House of Representatives are equally disgraceful. A 1983 survey I conducted showed that blacks held only 90, or 7.1 per cent, of the 1,266 highest professional positions on the personal office staffs of House members. But a total of 44, or nearly 50 per cent, of these aides worked for black members whose staffs are virtually all black.

Only 46 blacks were found occupying these three key positions—representing a bare 3.8 per cent out of the 1,209 top staff positions available among the more than 400 non-black House members I polled.

To put Congress' shocking racial record into sharper perspective, one need only understand that blacks make up 66 per cent of the workforce in Washington, D.C., and more than 10 per cent of the workforce nationally. While blacks are much in evidence throughout Congress as janitors, waitresses and cleaning women, and in other blue-collar positions, they are few and far between among professional positions on committee staffs or the personal Washington staffs of lawmakers.

Job discrimination in America? Why, it has been running rampant in Congress before, during and after the enactment of the landmark anti-discrimination laws of the 1960s and early 1970s. Yet few members of Congress will admit to what is being practiced within their own institution.

During the mid-1970s, a Joint Committee on Congressional Operations examined a sampling of employment requests from legislators. Their investigation uncovered 48 personnel requests that were blatantly discriminatory. Among other things, the job orders specified "whites only," "no blacks," "no Catholics," "attractive," and "young." The committee ordered that such personnel practices be halted, but it also made sure that the identities of the bigoted and sexist violators of Congress' anti-discrimination laws were never revealed.

Have personnel hiring preferences changed since then? Not much. Says one black House employee, "They [members] are much more subtle and careful about who they hire, but blacks are still the exception in the top jobs."

Affirmative action programs? That may be fine for the rest of the country, but not for Congress. "You have to know someone to get a job here," says a black House staffer to a Northwest congressman. "Like so much discrimination elsewhere, it's historical. Congress has never abided by its own anti-discrimination laws."

Similarly, the Equal Pay Act has resulted in hundreds of court cases in which major corporations have had to pay hundreds of millions of dollars in settlements to correct years of sex discrimination against women. Congress has exempted itself from the act's strictures. Yet women have long been discriminated against by Congress in pay, hiring and promotion practices.

Studies during the mid-1970s by the Capitol Hill Women's Political Caucus revealed that the median pay for female congressional staffers was $22,000, while the median for men was $28,000 for almost identical work. At the same time, a House study commission reported that men earning $30,500 outnumbered women 35 to 1.

A more recent study in 1982 by Congresswoman Lynn Martin of Illinois showed that pay practices have not changed very much. When Martin examined House staffers who were paid $40,000 or more a year, she found that 77 per cent of them were men and 23 per cent were women. Among those on the other end of the pay scale earning less than $20,000, 79 per cent were women, and only 21 per cent were men.

The Capitol Hill Women's Political Caucus undertook another study of pay discrimination toward women in Congress in 1980. The study showed that women in the House earned an average of 73 cents for every dollar earned by men. In the Senate, women earned 67 cents for every dollar earned by males. By 1983, those pay discrepancies had not changed significantly.

Elsewhere, the Fair Labor Standards Act and the National Labor Relations Act require that businesses must pay their employees the minimum wage and overtime. It also gives them the right to organize labor unions and bargain collectively. But no such privileges exist within Congress for its workers. Cooks, waitresses, doorkeepers, elevator operators, policemen, press gallery attendants and other congressional staffers are required to work overtime without pay whenever Congress decides to work late.

There is no recourse to a higher power for those who feel they are due additional compensation for extra hours worked. There is no fair labor standard practiced here. Congress is the sole authority over its personnel.

How about the right to bargain collectively? The mostly black and Hispanic restaurant workers in the Capitol complex have long sought the right to unionize, but powerful congressional leaders have denied them that freedom. Under the National Labor Relations Act, any employer who dared deny the right of workers to unionize would be held in contempt of court, fined, or perhaps even imprisoned, but not members of Congress.

Since its passage in 1970, the Occupational Safety and Health Act (OSHA) has certainly been one of Congress' most hated programs. Businesses have had to submit to unexpected inspections of their premises by OSHA agents, who have fined them for even the most minimal of safety infractions—from faulty electrical outlets to shaky stairway banisters to dirty restrooms. On the other hand, many congressional offices could never pass an OSHA inspection.

Employees are often crammed in desk-to-desk, sometimes in offices with no windows. There are poorly lit hallways, in some cases dangerously torn carpeting on building stairways, and other infractions that pose serious dangers to worker safety. Once again, lawmakers need never worry about being punished for such infractions of the nation's occupational safety laws.

The list of exemptions is as long as it is scandalous. The Freedom of Information Act gives the public the right to examine most government records, documents and other data. Congress also passed the Privacy Act to insure that there are safeguards on the files government maintains on its citizens. Again, Congress has exempted itself from these laws.

Social Security was certainly one of the worst of Congress' double standards. From the day the program was created in 1933, members of Congress and their employees were fully exempt from contributing to its support, but not from sharing in its benefits.

Congress stubbornly resisted demands that it integrate itself into Social Security until 1983, when new tax increases were enacted to save the system from impending bankruptcy. After years of ridicule and contempt for its two-faced position on Social Security, Congress finally agreed that lawmakers should also pay into the system.

On Jan. 1, 1984, members began for the first time to contribute to the system—paying the maximum tax of $2,400 per member. However, it was decided that all other congressional employees who were part of the congressional pension system as of Dec. 31, 1983, would remain exempt from paying Social Security taxes—though they, too, will one day receive at least the minimum retirement benefit in addition to their lucrative congressional pensions.

Thus, future increases in Social Security benefits and taxes, which congressional aides will help their legislators to write, understand and enact, will not affect most of the 30,000 congressional workers who are now grandfathered into this continuing exemption from the nation's second-largest federal tax.

Surely no better example of congressional prejudice exists than in the Federal Election Commission which Congress established in 1975 to regulate and monitor presidential and congressional campaigns. However, Congress made sure that when it comes to its own campaigns, the FEC was to stay out of its hair. FEC's history reveals that it has largely obeyed its narrowly drawn legislative mandate—generally avoiding any serious investigations into the campaign finances of congressional incumbents.

Congress' hypocrisy even extends to God.

In the early 1960s the Supreme Court banned organized prayer from our public schools. Many members of Congress defend the ruling and argue that prayer has no place in the schools because it violates the Constitution's separation of church and state.

Nonetheless, at the beginning of each daily session of the House and the Senate, a prayer is still given by an official chaplain, as it has for nearly 200 years. Somehow, the separation of church and state argument applies to our school kids but not to legislators. They are not at all bothered by the double standard of using taxpayers' money to hire full-time ministers of God to prepare and deliver a daily prayer for their souls.

As each house opens for business, members dutifully stand beside their desks and chairs, much like schoolchildren once did, their heads devoutly bowed, their eyes closed, participating in Congress' daily ritual of prayer.

The words "Let us pray," which begins each day in Congress, would probably be enough to get a public school teacher fired. Prayer in Congress, on the other hand, is not only practiced religiously (as it should be), but is fully and generously subsidized by the U.S. Treasury to the tune of over $142,700 a year.

Congress, in yet another double standard, prohibits federal officials who leave the executive branch from engaging in certain representational contacts with their former departments or agencies for a specific period of time. No such prohibition, however, is placed on former members of Congress. Many retirees become big-time, well-paid lobbyists who are frequently seen buttonholing lawmakers in Capitol corridors, attending committee hearings, and fully exploiting their continued access to the House and Senate floor.

"It is hypocrisy at its very worst," says Sen. Dennis DeConcini of Arizona, "when we in the Congress stand on the floor and orate about civil rights and equal opportunity employment at the same time we are not required to practice it ourselves. The double standard that runs through our government is deplorable. The time is long overdue that we put an end to this disparity and apply to ourselves the same laws we passed for the rest of the nation."

Since 1978, Sen. Patrick J. Leahy has been pushing a bill, co-sponsored by DeConcini, which would eliminate congressional exemptions from the government's major anti-discrimination and labor laws listed earlier in this chapter. Predictably, from the moment Leahy introduced his proposal, he encountered stiff, occasionally bitter opposition from his colleagues.

Yet Leahy's observations about Congress' disingenuous legislative deeds are deadly accurate in every respect. "This place is the last plantation in America," he told a near-empty chamber. "It is time that we in Congress begin to live by the same rules we have set for others. We should no longer allow such a double standard."

Unfortunately, the vast majority of Leahy's colleagues see no double standard at all. Many legislators insist that they cannot submit themselves to the same laws they enact for the rest of us because that would place their employment, pay and labor practices under the regulatory power of the executive branch, thus endangering the constitutional separation of powers doctrine.

Members of Congress insist that they must also remain flexible to operate and pay their personnel and hire their staffs as they deem best for their constituents and the orderly operation of Congress. There is a grain of merit to that argument. "But those special needs in no way justify congressional exemption from principles of fairness and equal opportunity," declared the *New Republic*. "A representative should not be able to claim *ex officio* immunity from charges of racism and sexism."

Sadly, the prospects of ending this congressional elitism do not appear bright. In 1976, Senators Lee Metcalf of Montana, Abraham Ribicoff of Connecticut and John Glenn of Ohio tried to implement some voluntary guidelines to remove the stain of hypocrisy from the Senate's legislating, only to run into unyielding opposition from Democratic leaders. Even when Massachusetts Sen. Edward Brooke, then the Senate's only black member, tried again with a similar proposal in 1978, he was forced to withdraw the measure when faced with a threatened filibuster.

"America may have witnessed the demise of the Great Southern Plantation System, a social, political and economic way of life whose last vestiges disappeared with the Civil War," says

Leahy. "But there is one last plantation that exists and flourishes today. This last plantation, sitting on the Hill in Washington, is the Congress which has shielded itself from the ravages of time and the effect of the laws it passes."

An Energy Policy to Keep America Free

By Donald P. Hodel   *(From the 13 February 1988 issue)*

America *must* take advantage of the domestic energy and mineral resources available to us. We do *not* have to choose between an improving environment and an adequate mineral and energy supply. We can do both, if we proceed in an orderly and careful manner. Our economic and national security depends on it.

The underpinning of our success in reshaping America's defense capability has been the nation's industrial might. That economic strength provides the power necessary to provide leadership in the free world.

At the base of our economic strength are our energy, minerals and agricultural resources. Unfortunately, the energy and minerals portion, crucial to this country, are not in good shape.

Energy is the lifeblood of our economy and of our standard of living. Much energy, particularly in the petroleum sector, is bought and sold in a world market, but we do not have a *free* world market. We are buying increasing amounts of our energy from unstable sources, especially the Middle East. We are approaching a period of time in the early 1990s where, it appears, we will exceed 50 per cent dependency on imports.

In a free world market, there would be nothing sacred about 50 per cent dependence upon imports. (We were, however, less dependent than that in 1973 when the Arab oil embargo hit.) The psychological effect of America's reaching that level of dependence may be to persuade those who are the leaders of OPEC, particularly the "hawks" of OPEC, that they are back in the driver's seat. As a result, they could believe they are in a position to dictate various policies to the United States or to raise prices dramatically, which would skew our economy.

We also cannot overlook the fact that, one year ago, the Soviet Union announced it would cut back its oil exports by 7 per cent, which just happened to coincide with the cutbacks announced shortly before by the OPEC nations. It was an obvious attempt to curry favor with OPEC, just as was its offer to escort tankers in the Persian Gulf.

In the meantime, what is happening in the United States?

• Congress currently is seeking to prevent exploration of certain areas of the federal Outer Continental Shelf (OCS), including some off the coast of California, Florida, Alaska and New England. There also is a proposal before Congress to close off even the chance to explore for potential gigantic oil or gas resources in a mere 8 per cent of the 19-million-acre Arctic National Wildlife Refuge (ANWR) in Alaska, created by Congress in 1980. *The United States cannot afford to blindfold itself to what its resources may be.*

• President Reagan created the Exclusive Economic Zone (EEZ) 200 miles out to sea, thereby allowing the U.S. to claim the potential energy and mineral resources from that part of the ocean. As mapping information comes in and is made available, commercial interests may well see opportunities to go out and mine the ocean floor.

However, Congress is contemplating legislation which would delay the earliest leasing of this promising frontier for at least seven years, maybe longer. This would delay the process of opening the door to create the incentive for people to make the investment to develop the techniques to find out what may be there for the sake of America.

• Presently, the southern California desert is the major potential source of rare earths in the U.S. Rare earths, among other things, may hold the key to the nation's effort to realize the benefits of superconductivity. Already large areas of this desert are in park and wilderness status, but Sen. Alan Cranston (D.-Calif.) has introduced a bill that would convert large additional areas into wilderness and park land and put it off-limits to any exploration or development for rare earths.

Thus, we are experiencing an effort to blindfold America, to tie our hands behind our backs, and to send a signal to our competitors in the energy and minerals industries or in the geopolitical sphere that says: "Go ahead and take advantage of us. We are incapable of taking care of ourselves."

For minerals, the U.S. is 100 per cent dependent upon imports of antimony graphite, manganese, and strontium, among others. We also are import-dependent for many platinum group metals.

The primary and often sole sources for many of these materials are the Soviet Union or southern African countries: South Africa, Zambia and Zaire. Minerals produced in Zambia and Zaire are refined in South Africa for transshipment.

U.S. imports from the Soviet Union of various vital minerals has been increasing since the passage of the comprehensive Anti-Apartheid Act of 1986, the act that barred their purchase (except for certain strategic materials) from South Africa. Pursuant to congressional directive, the Commerce Department conducted a study to see whether the act was having the effect of increasing our imports from the Soviet Bloc nations.

The Commerce Department reported, for example, that antimony imports from the Soviet Bloc are up 64 times; chromite imports are up eight times; and industrial diamond imports are up 66 times.

The Soviet Union can hardly be regarded as a secure source for these and similar items which are so important to our industrial might and our national security. How would we react if the Defense Department announced it had signed a contract with the Soviet Union as a source of supply of a critical component of a key weapon system because it was the lowest bidder? It does not make any greater sense to buy the materials which are essential to the production of that strategic or critical component to the weapon system from the Soviet Union.

We should be doing several things to make sure we can develop the energy and mineral resources necessary for a free America.

First, we should not make the situation worse by adding more obstacles in the form of taxes, regulations or prohibitions. We should not make it worse by removing key resource areas from both exploration and development. We need to encourage imagination, inventiveness and investment by the private sector. Those who have been prodded, poked, lectured, warned, regulated, and overtaxed by the federal government know that Washington does not have all the answers.

Second, we can improve the current situation by taking action to remove obstacles such as the windfall profits tax and natural gas price controls. We need to make selected areas in ANWR and in the federal OCS available for orderly, environmentally sensitive energy exploration and development.

Third, we need to continue to identify opportunities for the minerals industries, such as the EEZ. We can encourage American companies to be more aggressive in seeking export opportunities for this country. We can negotiate the removal of restrictions by other countries on American investments and exports.

Finally, we can seek substitutes. We know now that there are tremendous opportunities for advanced materials. Ongoing government research on the frontiers of science can complement the efforts of the private sector.

I believe there *are* energy and mineral resources to keep America free. However, there are some very difficult problems that we as a nation need to deal with if we seek to remain, as Abraham Lincoln once said, "the last best hope of Earth."

AIDS: The Chic Disease

By Jeffrey Hart   *(From the 9 May 1992 issue)*

Why is AIDS such a chic disease?

Hollywood stars throw AIDS benefit bashes. Magic Johnson became a sort of national hero when he proclaimed that he has the AIDS virus. A giant AIDS quilt is circulating around the country.

A survey taken last year showed that people identified AIDS as a greater threat to the nation than cancer by a margin of 3 to 1—whereas cancer is by far the greater killer.

Why do we hear so much more about AIDS than about heart disease, cancer, diabetes, pneumonia and other diseases that claim far more lives than AIDS?

During the fiscal year 1992, the federal government will spend approximately $2 billion on AIDS research, and also $2 billion on cancer research, yet cancer kills more people every six weeks than AIDS does in an entire year. (I am indebted for these and the following statistics to an article by Kimberly Coursen in the April issue of *Crisis* magazine.)

Cardiovascular disease is the No. 1 killer in this country. Yet in the current fiscal year, federal funding for research in that area will amount to only $844 million. The American public regards AIDS as a greater health threat than heart disease by an astonishing 23-to-1 margin.

The Magic Johnson case has been a bonanza to the AIDS cause, since it advanced the notion that AIDS can be transmitted heterosexually. Yet such a transmission amounts to only 6 per cent of all AIDS cases, and we have only Johnson's word on the point that he acquired the virus heterosexually.

On top of that, Magic Johnson's sexual behavior by his own admission was spectacular in quantity. I might observe that if you sky-dive often enough you might break your neck.

The heterosexual transmission of AIDS in fact is quite rare, despite propaganda suggesting otherwise. It seems to depend upon lesions produced by other diseases, such as syphilis, gonorrhea and herpes, to create an avenue for the transmission of the virus.

About 3 per cent of AIDS patients, including Arthur Ashe, have contracted the disease through contaminated blood transfusions, but this source has now been greatly reduced by better testing and processing methods.

The Magic Johnson case has been exploited to suggest that "straight" men and women are subject to AIDS infection, the motive I suppose being that this will facilitate more federal spending on AIDS research.

In fact, AIDS remains overwhelmingly a disease of intravenous drug users, homosexuals and their sexual partners.

And, in fact, you do not have to be Louis Pasteur to figure out how to stop the spread of AIDS. It would not take billions spent on research. All you have to do is to avoid specific forms of behavior—using dirty needles or engaging in high-risk sex.

We daily see TV ads warning against drunken driving, and there is a campaign against smoking as a main cause of lung cancer. We have learned that fatty foods are a cause of heart disease.

Why is there not a similar campaign against the practices that transmit AIDS?

It is true that in Africa the rate of heterosexual transmission of AIDS is much higher than in other continents, but that is because the public health level in Africa is so much lower. When the population is ravaged by a variety of other diseases that lower the immune system and cause sores and lesions, it is not surprising that AIDS is more easily transmitted.

There is no evidence that AIDS is being widely transmitted through casual heterosexual activity among American teenagers and college students. Yet public school systems and colleges, using AIDS as an excuse, have been deluging their students with free condoms. The sole result of the great condom blizzard has been to legitimize casual sex, scarcely the message that ought to be broadcast.

The myth that AIDS is about to burst into the general population does serve the cause of higher funding for AIDS. The myth is necessary for the fundraisers, because the normal majority of Americans frown upon the behavior that accounts for most AIDS cases. The majority must be conned into believing that it is threatened by AIDS, when in fact it is not.

Basic research into HIV would be good science, since the virus has fascinating characteristics, such as very rapid mutation. But crash public billions for AIDS is not called for. AIDS is not a general menace, and there is no indication that a cure is in sight.

(Copyright 1992, King Features)

The Imperative of Moral Values

By Vice President Dan Quayle   *(From the 20 June 1992 issue)*

(Vice President Quayle went on the "moral values" offensive again last week, stressing the need for strong families, religion and patriotism. He also sharply criticized promiscuity, the widescale use of abortion and the distribution of "sexual propaganda to third- and fourth-graders." Quayle also took on the homosexual lobby, by opposing gay parenting. The Vice President delivered his speech on June 9 before a highly receptive audience at the Southern Baptist Convention in Indianapolis. An excerpt of his speech follows.)

In some ways we're a nation of strangers. And, as a society grows, maybe that's inevitable. We cannot—as the sophisticated folks are always reminding us—"turn back the clock" to the America of Norman Rockwell and the small-town values he celebrated. And yet those values are still there.

They live in our thousands of Southern Baptist churches, and in other places of worship across America. They live in our communities, both large and small, where families get to know their neighbors, and where parents get to know their kids' teachers, the school bus driver, and the cop on the beat.

They live in every home where parents patiently pass their experience and their values along to their children. These values live because they are invaluable. They stand as our essential guide to a good and honest life.

Now change is a permanent part of life. As Americans, we do not fear change—we're always confident we can shape our own future for the better.

We believe that our destiny is not a matter of chance—it's a matter of choice. But this means choosing wisely. It means realizing that some of the changes in our culture in recent decades have not been for the better. Some of these changes seem to have undermined the values we cherish.

Changes Have Created a Cultural Divide

In fact, these changes have created a cultural divide in our country. It is so great a divide that it sometimes seems we have two cultures—the cultural elite, and the rest of us. Most of us look at these social changes and we say, "Yes, change is inevitable, and much of it is good. But some of it is not. Let us preserve the good and reject the bad." And, my friends, most of us believe we should not be afraid to continue to talk about values—to try to judge what is right and what is wrong.

Yet, as I discovered recently, to appeal to our country's enduring, basic moral values is to invite the scorn and laughter of the elite culture.

Talk about right and wrong, and they'll try to mock us in newsrooms, sitcom studios, and faculty lounges across America. But in the heart of America, in the homes and workplaces and churches, the message is heard.

A sense of moral, simple things, the simple gifts, and the simple truths that Americans have always sought to live by are more relevant than ever in our complex times.

Among the sophisticates, to talk about simple moral principles is considered an embarrassing "gaffe." I guess that means they're embarrassed about the views of the average American—because moral values are what the American people care most about. And that's why I say this about the scorn of the media elite: "I wear their scorn as a badge of honor."

My friends, we need to have a discussion among ourselves on the importance of moral values. It's time that we Americans speak out for what we believe in and what we stand for. It is time we Americans stand up for our values, stand up for America, and say that America is great because of our people and our values.

The cultural elite in Hollywood and elsewhere may have a lot of money; they may have a lot of influence. But we have the power of ideas, the power of our convictions, and the power of our beliefs. And we shall carry the day—because in their sense of morality, in their belief in personal responsibility, in their faithfulness, in their love of goodness and love of neighbor—the American people are far ahead of our country's self-appointed cultural elites.

Often those of us who talk of values, who defend the traditional family, who distinguish right from wrong, are accused of being intolerant. Let us be clear: we defend the rights of all Americans. We are for compassion and tolerance. We are, after all, commanded to love our neighbor. But we do not believe that being compassionate and tolerant means abandoning our standards of right or wrong, good or bad. We do not think tolerance requires abandoning our belief in the family.

No Tradition or Standards Respected by Cultural Elites

The cultural elites respect neither tradition nor standards. They believe that moral truths are relative and all "lifestyles" are equal. They seem to think the family is an arbitrary arrangement of people who decided to live under the same roof—that fathers are dispensable, and that parents need not be married or even of opposite sexes. They are wrong.

We believe the family is a sacred institution entrusted with the world's most important work. It is not only "nature's masterpiece," as someone once said—it is God's masterpiece.

We believe society is only as strong as the families who live and grow within it. And we believe that the family and family values need our support. In a time when those values are denigrated, I say it's time for us to join together and speak up for the family, family values, and the values and principles that make America great.

Many in the cultural elite sneer at the simple but hard virtues—modesty, fidelity, integrity. But when the tragic consequences of that moral cynicism become apparent, do they pause to rethink their views? No. Do they even acknowledge the consequences—an ever increasing rate of illegitimacy, youthful promiscuity, 1.6 million abortions every year? No. They deny that values have consequences.

Their response often compounds the problem—handing out condoms in the schools, or distributing sexual propaganda to third- and fourth-graders. Morally speaking, our children ask for bread and the cynics give them a stone. We believe our children were made for better lives than that—and that moral and spiritual integrity are the key to human fulfillment.

The elite's culture is a guilt-free culture. It avoids responsibility and flees consequences. If, as a result of one's own actions, a child is conceived, they have a simple solution—get rid of it.

Our solution, for those mothers who feel they cannot raise the child, is adoption. They treat God's greatest gift—new life—as an inconvenience to be discarded. We believe life is a beautiful gift to be loved and cared for—however "inconvenient." They believe in the right to dispose of life—we believe in the right to life.

You know, we who talk about values are accused of nostalgia for a time that once was. But those who imagine an America without clear moral values yearn for something that could never be. If America ever lost its moral vision, it would cease to be America.

To paraphrase my grandfather, I would say that America is good because America is free. But he understood that it works the other way around, too: that if America ceased to be good, it would cease to be free.

We would become a soulless and divided nation, a nation under siege instead of a nation under God. Our common vision of the good and just life is what keeps the "united" in "United States."

Moral Values Make a Nation Great

Moral values make a nation great—and they are the solid foundation of our lives as individuals and as families. They are not arbitrary. They are not "imposed." They are not handed down by politicians.

People like to caricature these values, as if they arose from narrow-minded, theological doctrines. But think about that word, "narrow-minded." "Do unto others as you would have them do unto you" . . . "Love thy neighbor" . . . "Walk humbly with thy God" . . . "Choose Life"—are those narrow-minded ideas?

The fact is that the great faiths of the world ask much the same thing of their followers. Far from being narrow or intolerant, such moral values represent the consensus of humanity about what makes for a good life and a good society. In the face of that consensus, moral cynicism is an easy out. Confronted with life's great moral issues, a sneer is not an answer.

And then there are people like yourselves, who don't just talk about values but seek to live by them. You know what it's like to bear the brunt of ridicule—as does anyone who has ever tried to stand up for a good cause. In raising up faithful children, in church work like maintaining homes for unwed mothers, in supporting the superb work of your Christian Life Commission, by honoring God in all things—you keep those values alive.

Simple, Plain Words to Live By

To the jaded, believers in traditional morality may seem to lead simple and plain lives, wanting only plain things. But I'm reminded of G. K. Chesterton's remark that "A plain word always covers an infinite mystery." Faith—fidelity—family—honor—duty—goodness—love. Such simple, plain words. But to anyone who tries to live by them—such infinite mysteries.

Speaking to your convention 10 years ago, Vice President George Bush described America as "a country born out of a spirit of renewal." And "Looking out on such a group as this one," our President told Southern Baptists, "I think the renewal is well begun."

Well begun, and yet only just begun. The decade since then has seen some tragic developments continue to unfold. Two good men have held the office of President—yet not even that is enough.

We have made superb appointments to the courts of our land—yet not even that is enough. Renewal, ultimately, is not primarily the work of government. It's our work, the work of our churches, the work of each person, responding each day to the hard questions of life and faith. It's the work of choosing wisely. Choosing to live in falsehood—or in fidelity. Choosing to follow man in his foolish ways—or the Son of Man who walked the way of love and mercy, full of grace and truth.

Let us choose the way of love and mercy, of grace and truth. Thank you for your commitment. Thank you for your support. Thank you for joining in the struggle for the restoration of values in this great country of ours, the United States of America. God bless each of you, and God bless America.

The Statists Take Over
Will they destroy ongoing economic recovery?

(From the 30 January 1993 issue)

The wretched excesses of the galas and the Hollywood hype are over, and William Jefferson Clinton now has to govern. But despite some obvious difficulties, it should be far easier than he has let on or his inaugural address would imply. For all his deficiencies—and we think there were many—President Bush has left the new chief executive a safe United States and a recovering economy.

America is now the lone superpower, Soviet communism no longer threatens the world, a democratic Germany is united, and, for the first time in recent memory, there is a chance—a small chance, but nevertheless it exists—for a peaceful settlement in the Middle East, thanks to Bush's courageous decision to humble Iraq militarily.

True enough, Saddam Hussein is still around, but he's far more a nuisance than a potent threat. And while a crisis of no small proportion exists in the Balkans, even that area of the globe doesn't directly threaten American security, and a peaceful agreement there is also not out of the question.

The economy, amazingly, has also turned around, too late to help George Bush, now ensconced in Houston, but a godsend for the 42nd President of the United States.

Larry Kudlow, the chief economist for Bear Stearns in New York, pointed out to us last week just how healthy the economy really is at the present time.

"There are a bunch of very promising indicators," he told us, "which show that the economy is already growing at a 3 to 4 per cent range when adjusted for inflation. Gross Domestic Product [GDP] was 3.4 per cent in the third quarter, and it's going to be at least that in the next. On top of all this, we have virtually no inflation and we have the lowest interest rate levels since the middle 1960s."

There are other "very promising" signs as well, he added. "If you look carefully, more than 30 states, including every large state except California, are showing much higher than expected revenues from payrolls, from income taxes and from sales taxes. In '89 and '90, those state revenues were collapsing, which hinted at the impending recession. But now those revenue flows are recovering."

Business profits are also soaring, he said, noting that "they're rising at a record rate right now—20 per cent over the last year. Corporate profits in 1992 have risen $75 billion over the year before and the balance sheet restructuring effort is now paying off. Interest expenses have come down, raw material expenses have come down, labor costs are in line with rising productivity rates—all are excellent indicators of recovery."

There's still another sign, he said. "People focus on car sales and car sales have recovered modestly, but American preferences are shifting and real action is now in the category called light trucks, as sales of jeeps, mini-vans, and trendy pickup trucks are having a tremendous climb, 20 per cent over the last 12 months. When you put car sales together with light truck sales, you see a real surge. In fact, automobile dealers which sell cars and light trucks experienced a 14 per cent increase in December '92 over December '91. And that's a splendid rise."

But conservatives, including us, we noted, had been criticizing Bush in all of 1992 for having burdened the economy with tax hikes and an enormous amount of regulation. How come things are turning around?

Kudlow explained that 1992 "was the first year in about the last four or five where government policies, for a change, did not increase the cost of doing business. Fortunately, in 1992, there were no tax hikes, there were no regulatory cost hikes, the credit crunch in the banking industry eased somewhat, and, in fact, the Bush Administration, through Vice President Dan Quayle, had lowered some of the regulatory burden on business.

"What has happened displays the resiliency of the private sector, which has now had a year of breathing room to recover from the shocks of earlier tax and regulatory cost burdens. Businesses have downsized, cut costs and generally accommodated."

"What concerns me," said Kudlow, "is that the Clintonites are misreading what has been happening. They are misdiagnosing the patient, and if they generate additional taxes and regulatory costs, they will take a recovering economy and push it back towards slow growth.

"The Clinton folks are talking about very narrow investment tax breaks and very stiff income tax hikes. On top of that, they are talking about adding consumption or value-added taxes, even an energy tax. All these things will do is retard and inhibit economic growth and job creation." In terms of the proposals they have had on the table for many months, he continued, the Clinton people appear to be proposing "an expanded version of the 1990 budget deal, an opinion that was reinforced after listening to the confirmation hearings of Clinton's pick for budget director, Leon Panetta, and Treasury secretary, Lloyd Bentsen.

"They're kidding themselves if they think raising marginal income taxes to 36 per cent on upper-income people and clamping a 10 per cent surtax on millionaires are going to raise much revenue. Those policies have been tried before. All that happens is that people start shifting their income away from taxable sources toward non-taxable assets.

"By taxing upper-income people, they are, in effect, killing the goose that lays the golden eggs, because the highest propensity to save and invest is at the upper-income areas. All that they will achieve is a reduction of economic growth, which will mean fewer jobs and lower revenues than would otherwise have been the case. I think it would be a great mistake to think you can raise taxes and reduce the deficit in the long run, and I thought we learned that lesson in the two years following the disastrous 1990 budget deal."

Clinton, in truth, has been dealt some high cards in the field of foreign and domestic policy, despite efforts by the media and the Clinton team to tell the nation otherwise. Important problems do exist, of course, ranging from crime-ridden inner cities to the size of the national debt, but Clinton could alleviate many of them by keeping the economic recovery rolling along with a pro-growth Republican agenda.

Unfortunately, however, as Kudlow suggests, "New Democrat" Clinton and his statist appointees look as if they're about to blow the decent hand left to him by George Bush.

All Human Life Is Sacred

By William Murchison   *(From the 3 April 1993 issue)*

Two wrongs don't make a right, our mothers used to inform us whenever, in childhood, our vindictive impulses threatened to get out of control. The solemn, civilized arithmetic holds up today. You don't shoot an abortionist in the back, as Michael Griffin, 31, of Pensacola, Fla., allegedly did in a ghastly incident that will reverberate for a while in our national consciousness.

If Florida ultimately executes Griffin, blame should attach not to the Florida justice system but to the prisoner, and to him only. No provocation justifies the cold-blooded murder of a defenseless man.

Yet, when all's said and done, an urgent question will remain: What about all the lives that continue to be extinguished in clinics such as Dr. Gunn serviced in his ceaseless perambulations?

If the life of an abortionist matters—and it does, profoundly—what about the lives an abortionist extinguishes in the way of business?

The "pro-choice" movement will not, I think, admit the equivalence of these questions. An admission would not serve the movement's purposes. Once you start equating the life of a 47-year-old doctor and the life of a 47-day-old "fetus," you run into major difficulties in defending abortion.

The operative word is "life"—one life lived outside the womb, the other inside it, by beings constructed alike, sharing the same complex, mysterious origin.

What about these lives? Is it so easy really to differentiate them—to say that, based on mere circumstance, one is valuable, the other beneath notice? And who decides? People with guns and surgical equipment? A fine argument, that, in a civilized society!—assuming that modern society still qualifies as civilized.

Those who, prior to his brutal murder, never heard of Dr. David Gunn—this is 99.9999 per cent of us—have no way of accurately appraising the value of his life. His dubious occupation aside, any abortion opponent has to concede Dr. Gunn the benefit of the doubt. He was human. He possessed an immortal soul.

From the pro-life standpoint, it was conceivable that, with prayer and time, he might have experienced conversion. Such things have happened before. And, oh, what a mighty witness he might then have offered! Has the Pensacola vigilante never heard the name of that erstwhile persecutor of Christians, St. Paul?

By contrast, the subjects of Dr. Gunn's ministrations—the developing human beings he, shall we say, terminated—enjoyed no such presuppositions of worth. They were—well, what? Blobs? Even thumb-sucking, breathing, stimulus-responding blobs?

No adult figure in their brief lives seems to have asked or, anyway, to have asked with interest, what about this one and that one? Who might he or she turn out to be—poet, preacher, plumber? Or just worthy citizen? A mother? A father? Forbear of someone extraordinary and world-changing? You can't know.

The presupposition of worth—that same presupposition to which abortionists are entitled—should benefit born and unborn alike. Not these days, though.

Abortion clinics are not in business to extend the benefit of the doubt, they are there to withhold it—in the same way the Pensacola vigilante withheld it.

Those who liken abortion clinics to the Nazi death camps are less extreme and impolite than the pro-choice movement would indignantly claim.

The camps were places of anonymous, impersonal death: nothing against this Jew or that one, save membership in a class marked down for destruction. Are unborn babies the new Jewry—a victim class all the easier to impose upon because silent and unseen?

Modern life's rock-bottom cheapness is not the work of the abortion movement, which postdates Auschwitz and Buchenwald by nearly three decades. The secularization of modern life and thought is the villain. Out of the secular ethic flows disregard for lives that, in the old religious dispensation, were deemed the gifts of God.

A gift of God had meaning, purpose, destiny; it was no accident of biology. Every day we see what happens in the new moral environment, where man, not God, is on top. What happens is, man plays God.

Chapter Three

Economic Policy

HUMAN EVENTS has been since its inception a staunch advocate of the free market economy as both the most efficient producer of goods and services and the only economic system consistent with a free society. In a corollary manner, the publication has argued the imperative of limited government—limited so as to maximize the freedom of the individual and the efficiency of the market.

The articles in this chapter provide interesting variations on these principles. The first, "The Path to Freedom" by Gen. Douglas MacArthur, will come as something of a surprise to the reader no doubt, because the general is remembered chiefly—and quite naturally—for his military achievements. As this 17 March 1958 article demonstrates, however, MacArthur had strong and well-reasoned views on economic matters. Subtitled "We Must Cut Taxes and Halt Inflation," the article is as germane to the 1990s as it was to the 1950s when it was written, and it reveals the general as something of a forerunner of "supply side" economics.

Henry Hazlitt, another great economist of the Austrian School, writes in prescient fashion of the coming demise of Keynesianism, the regnant economic orthodoxy of the preceding four decades, in "The Keynesians' Faith Is Oozing Away" (12 April 1969).

"Ludwig von Mises: Dean of Rational Economics," is a brief resume of the monumental work of the great Austrian School economist by Hans F. Sennholz, one of Mises' most prominent American disciples (11 April 1970).

"Needed: A Coalition Between Labor and the GOP" by Rep. Jack Kemp (R.-N.Y.), which appeared in the 22 September 1979 issue, has proved to be one of the more important articles published by HUMAN EVENTS. The piece was a reprint of a speech Kemp gave to the annual convention of the International Longshoremen's Association.

In the speech, Kemp assailed the Carter administration's no-growth philosophy and urged a program of federal tax cuts as a way to get the economy growing. The article caught the eye of Ronald Reagan who instantly recognized the logic of Kemp's plan and its appeal to working Americans.

Reagan enthusiastically adapted Kemp's tax cut idea and made it the centerpiece of his successful campaign for the presidency. Following his inauguration in 1981, President Reagan pushed successfully for enactment of the Kemp-Roth tax cut legislation. HUMAN EVENTS had signed on early in the Kemp-Roth cause and aggressively promoted the bill in its pages. And Kemp himself gives HUMAN EVENTS credit for being of crucial importance to the success of the effort.

The Path to Freedom
We Must Cut Taxes and Halt Inflation

By General Douglas A. MacArthur   *(From the 17 March 1958 issue)*

(Amid growing concern over the status of the U.S. economy–with consumers beset simultaneously by the problems of inflation and recession–America more and more seeks the counsel of its wisest citizens. Conceded to be foremost among these is General of the Army Douglas A. MacArthur–whose advice on economic matters was recently sought by Vice President Richard Nixon. In this article, adapted from his widely acclaimed speech to the stockholders of the Sperry Rand Corporation last year, the General, now Chairman of the Board of the Sperry Rand Corp., gives systematic expression to his views on the economic dangers that confront the United States.)

If businessmen were to be allowed a wish, I am sure it would be unanimously for lower taxes. The tax burden now is so oppressive as to be almost confiscatory of venture capital. Secretary of the Treasury Humphrey testified before a congressional committee: ". . . the present heavy tax burden will seriously hamper necessary economic growth"; and he added that "spending under existing Government programs will rise as fast as the increase in revenues resulting from economic growth unless Congress and the Administration alter and reduce these programs."

Taxes for 1956 came to a staggering total of more than $100 billion. This means that the cost of government consumes almost one-third of the national product. Government's appetite for taxes has grown steadily and inordinately. In 1885 the per capita tax take was $1.98. In 1917 it was $7.92. The fiscal year 1956 was the costliest of all: $446.36 per head for every one of us.

Such jet-propelled figures are difficult to comprehend. Much is hidden from direct view in the form of unseen nibbles at the paycheck after payment of the direct income tax. You never know you are paying because they appear as part of the purchase price of the items you buy. For example, you pay, in this indirect way:

Twenty per cent of the cost of your food; eight hundred dollars on a $3000 automobile; half the cost of a pack of cigarettes; nearly nine-tenths of the price of a bottle of whiskey.

Taxes have grown so rapidly in recent years that now they are the largest single item in the cost of living. Americans will pay for government this year more than they will spend on food, clothing, medical care and religious activities combined. There are 151 taxes on a loaf of bread, at least as many and maybe more on a pound of beefsteak, a box of soap, a can of beans.

If Government continues to wrest from the people the basis for future industries and businesses, our rapidly increasing population may eventually outgrow the number of jobs available and industrial labor will then face its greatest threat.

There seems to be no restraint in this lust for taxes. It began with the Federal Income Tax Law of 1914 which gave unlimited access to the people's wealth, and the power for the first time to levy taxes not for revenue only but for social purposes. Since then the sphere of Government has increased with a kind of explosive force. Thomas Jefferson's wise aphorism, "That government is best which governs least," has been tossed into the wastebasket with ridicule and sarcasm.

Whether we want it or not, we pay now for almost unlimited Government; a Government which limits our lives by dictating how we are fed and clothed and housed; how to provide for old age; how the national income, which is the product of our labor, shall be divided among us; how we shall buy and sell; how long and how hard and under what circumstances we shall work. There is only scorn for the one who dares to say, "The Government should not be infinite."

Our indebtedness is now estimated to be nearly $700 billion, a sum greater than the combined debt of all the other nations of the world. And it has been charged without challenge that our Government this year proposes to spend as much as all other governments put together.

How many of our leaders still hear the echo of Thomas Jefferson's voice when he warned, with reference to the future of this country: "I place economy among the most important virtues and public debt as the greatest of dangers to be feared. To preserve our independence, we must not let our leaders load us with perpetual debt. We must make our choice between economy with liberty, or profusion with servitude. The same prudence which in private life would forbid our paying our money, forbids it in the disposition of public money. We must endeavor to reduce the Government to the practice of rigid economy to avoid burdening the people and arming the Magistrate with a patronage of money which might be used to corrupt the principle of government.... The multiplication of public offices, increase of expense beyond income, growth of the public debt, are indications soliciting the employment of the pruning knife.... It is incumbent on every generation to pay its own debt as it goes."

How incomparably different in philosophy from Karl Marx, who said [in anticipation of Communist seizure of power]: "The surest way to overturn the social order is to debauch the currency." He referred, of course, to the process of inflation, induced by extreme taxation; the process of "planned economy"; the process of controlling economic conditions and thereby controlling the lives of individuals.

Chief John Marshall warned as early as 1819 that "the power to tax involves the power to destroy." And he might have added that the road to destruction is the road of socialism. Its evidences which we see and talk about so much—the collectors and dispensers of socialistically used funds, the planning committees and enforcement bodies, the services they presume to render and the pyramids they build, the votes they coerce to maintain control—all these expressions of socialism are but the offspring of excessive taxation. If we want economic liberty—want to be free to work most productively and to have what we produce—our concern must focus on the tax roots to shut off the revenue which nourishes the disease. To work at the other end and merely bemoan the detailed projects of socialism or damn the persons who happen to be manning those projects at the moment, or even to change political personnel, would be about as effective in stopping socialism as changing undertakers would be to stop death.

Excessive taxation produces results somewhat resembling the evils of slavery and serfdom in days of old. To illustrate: the Government takes in taxes over a third of the income of the average citizen each year. This means that he or she is required to work entirely for the Government from January 1 until May 10. This begins to resemble the Soviet forced labor system. It practically reduces the citizen for protracted periods to what amounts almost to involuntary servitude. It is indeed the modern, almost humanized, counterpart in the twentieth century of the abandoned slavery and serfdom of the preceding centuries. We will be fortunate if it does not finally reduce individuals to the universal status of robots.

The present tax structure is even now probably adequate eventually to socialize the United States. Our tax take is already greater than that of the admitted national socialistic countries, whether on this or the other side of the Iron Curtain. The effects may not yet be fully evident to the superficial eye, but the erosion of incentive, ingenuity and integrity that results will be as deadly as the hidden cancer is to life. It can in time change the basic character of this great Nation, as it has every other nation where it has become indelibly affixed.

In the last two decades our tax system has resulted in a creeping inflation which has devitalized the American dollar to 40 per cent of its previous purchasing power. If the present trend continues, the dollar may well sink to half its present value within another decade. Those who suffer most from such fiscal debasement are the men of small means—those living on fixed incomes, wages, annuities or pensions—especially the working man. But inflation does even more than debauch a nation's currency; it also debauches a nation's morale. It creates a false illusion of prosperity; it discourages thrift and honest effort; it encourages the kind of speculation that expects something for nothing. History shows how difficult it is for a nation to recover once it is in the sway of an irredeemably depreciating currency. The tendency is for prices to go higher and higher, the value of money to go lower and lower.

The inflationary forces which undermine the Western World of today are the same forces which were at work 1,700 years ago during the decline of the Roman Empire. Just as in Rome, our civilization is living beyond its means. It is living more and more for the moment, trying to anticipate today the pleasures of tomorrow. Why save, asks the citizen, if savings are likely to be expropriated through taxes and inflation? Why wait for the day when we can afford a house, or a car, or a TV set, if we can buy those things today on credit? It is no longer enough that our economy grows annually faster than the increase in population; the call is for twice this growth. Wages must rise faster than productivity, the standard of living faster than income.

If financial output has to be increased in one segment it must be correspondingly decreased in another. If defense spending has to go up, other spending, whether for housing, roads, schools, farm aid or social benefits, must be curtailed accordingly. This is only common sense. But, even though tax receipts have doubled during the postwar era, total public spending continues to exceed revenues. Promises continue to be made to expand all sectors of the economy at the same time. Some are 42 per cent larger than they were in 1953–54. Literally dozens of welfare projects little understood by the general public are hidden in the more than 1000 pages of the Budget, which has grown so big that nobody has any clear idea how much waste it actually contains.

The sum [of maximum estimates from the Government's agencies, bureaus, and departments], with some modification, becomes the Federal Budget, unless someone at the top lowers the estimates to correspond with the actual resources expected to be available. The problem of a balanced Budget, instead of being a mystic and untouchable phenomenon, is actually the commonest and most universal one in the world. It faces the head of every household every year of life. It is, simply: how much can be spent safely on living expenses? The question is not what can be luxuriously used, not even what may be actually necessary, but what can be obtained with the money available without injudicious borrowing.

It is exactly the same basic problem in government, with the vital difference that the money involved is not the spender's own but that of others collected by taxation. But what a monumental difference this makes! Instead of being frugal, one becomes lavish. Instead of being careful, one becomes reckless. Instead of being conservative, one becomes radical.

At best the [spending Budget] is but a guess, a speculative estimate with little or no controlling influences. How wrong it can be is testified to by the surpluses that have accumulated over the years. These surpluses, the overestimates in the national Budgets of actual needs, glut our warehouses from Coast to Coast. They are not limited to agricultural products but exist in practically every field and every commodity. A member of the Hoover Commission which studied the matter estimated to me that in the last decade perhaps $100 billion worth of surplus had accumulated. A large portion of this, he said, could probably never be gainfully used.

Our swollen Budgets constantly have been misrepresented to the public. Our Government has kept us in a perpetual state of fear—kept us in a continuous stampede of patriotic fervor—with the cry of grave national emergency. Always there has been some terrible evil at home or some monstrous foreign power that was going to gobble us up if we did not blindly rally behind it by furnishing the exorbitant funds demanded. Yet, in retrospect, these disasters seem never to have happened, seem never to have been quite real.

The painful truth is this: the Government produces nothing of itself. Whatever it spends for people it must previously take from the people in the form of taxes. Moreover, whenever the Government gives a service to people, it must at the same time take away from the people the right to provide and decide for themselves. And the amount which Government doles back to the people or spends to promote welfare is always only a fraction of what it takes away, because of the excessive cost of Governmental administration. It is the little people that pay the largest part of the bill.

Eighty-five per cent of all the billions of dollars paid in income taxes comes from the lowest rate—the 20 per cent paid by all persons with taxable income. Only 15 per cent is added by all the higher rates up to 91 per cent. Indeed, it has been suggested that one reason for the steep graduation of the income tax is to make the public think that people with high incomes pay most of the taxes. It is another illusion to think that excessive rates of a graduated income tax tend to redistribute the wealth. It merely prevents its accumulation and thereby blocks expansion of the Nation's economic strength. The very source of new and better jobs thus disappears. This is economic folly based on the false proposition that growth can be maintained through continuous inflation.

But even greater issues are involved than any I have yet mentioned. Some years ago, the late President Woodrow Wilson made the following statement: "The history of liberty is the history of the limitation of governmental power, not the increase of it."

The contest for ages has been to rescue liberty from the constantly expanding grasp of governmental power. The great patriots of the American Revolution revolted not so much against the actual taxes imposed upon them by a British King as against the concept of government behind the taxes: the concept that government had unlimited power to do what government thought proper. They had a deep suspicion that government, if permitted, would waste the labors of the people and ultimately curtail the power of the people, always under the pretense of taking care of the people. That is why they tried to bind the Government down with the modest restrictions of a Constitution, limiting the Government's powers to the performance of carefully specified responsibilities.

There are many who have lost faith in the early American ideal and believe in a form of socialistic, totalitarian rule, a sort of big-brother deity to run our lives for us. They no longer believe that free men can manage their own affairs. Their central thesis is to take your money away from you on the presumption that a handful of men, centered in government—largely bureaucratic, not elected—can spend the proceeds of your toil and labor to greater advantage than you who create the money.

Nowhere in the history of the human race is there justification for this reckless faith in political power. It is the oldest, most reactionary of all forms of social organization. It was tried out in ancient Babylon, ancient Greece and ancient Rome; in Mussolini's Italy, in Hitler's Germany, and in all Communist countries. Wherever and whenever it has been attempted, it has failed utterly to provide economic security, and has generally ended in national disaster. It embraces an essential idiocy, that individuals who, as private citizens, are not able to manage the disposition of their own earnings, become in public office supermen who can manage the affairs of the world.

The Soviets have tried to legislate the perfect society; and today the average Soviet citizen has little more freedom and less comfort than the inmates of American jails. The old American philosophy of government more effectively promoted the ideal of human freedom, with greater material abundance for more people, than any social system ever propounded; freedom to live under the minimum of restraint—freedom to make your own mistakes if you will. The fundamental and ultimate issue at stake, therefore, is not merely our money. It is liberty itself: the excessive taxation of an overgrown Government *versus* personal freedom; a least common denominator of mediocrity against the proven progress of pioneering individualism, the free enterprise system or the cult of blind conformity; the robot or the free man.

On September 12, 1952, Senator Robert Taft conferred at Morningside Heights with his successful convention rival for the nomination for the Presidency of the United States, General Eisenhower. They later issued a manifesto containing the following statement, [which sums the matter up in unmistakable language]:

"There is and has been one great fundamental issue . . . it is the issue of liberty against the creeping socialization in every domestic field. Liberty was the foundation of our Government, the reason for our growth, the basis of our happiness and the hope of our future. The greatest threat to liberty today is internal, from the constant growth of big government through the constantly increasing power and spending of the Federal Government. . . . The essential thing is to keep our expenditures . . . at a percentage of our total income which will not destroy our free economy at home and further inflate our debt and our currency."

Keynesians' Faith Is Oozing Away
Zealots still hold firm, but then some people never learn.

By Henry Hazlitt   *(From the 12 April 1969 issue)*

Oct. 26, 1968, marked a turning point in fashionable economic thought. The London *Economist* of that date carried an article on John Maynard Keynes. I recalled that at the end of his *General Theory of Employment, Interest and Money*, published in 1936, Keynes declaimed infamous passage on the hidden power of superannuated economic ideas: "Practical men, who believe themselves to be quite exempt from any intellectual influences, are usually the slaves of some defunct economist." And the *Economist* itself was then cruel enough to remark:

"The piquant situation is that Keynes himself is now a defunct economist."

The New York *Times* recognized that this remark was news. "In England, the land of his birth," announced the *Times* on November 6, "they have suddenly discovered that John Maynard Keynes is dead."

It could be argued, of course, that the article in the *Economist* may have indicated nothing more than a change of opinion on the part of the editors of that publication. Yet the New York *Times'* more sweeping conclusion is probably justified. For the *Economist* has long been a weather vane of fashionable economic thinking in England; for years its editorials have reflected the Keynesian ideology; and its public recantation reveals not only what has been happening inside the *Economist* but inside the whole British establishment.

Until that announcement some five months ago, the editors of the *Economist*, like the Keynesians in the universities, had ignored or derided any basic criticism of the patron saint of deficit spending.

When the present writer in 1959 wrote a book called *The Failure of the New Economics*, subtitled "An Analysis of the Keynesian Fallacies," the *Economist's* review dismissed it as "a dropsical pamphlet," and did not condescend to answer a single argument or factual statement in it.

The review, in fact, went on to express its low opinion not only of my own criticisms of Keynes but of everybody else's up to that time: "It is the more unfortunate that the only all-around reassessments [of Keynes] which have in fact been attempted . . . resemble nothing so much as the continuing Fundamentalist attacks on Darwin."

This amazing implication that all general criticisms of Keynes were ignorant or benighted was written when such criticisms had already been published by economists of world stature—including Jacques Rueff, F. A. Hayek, Ludwig von Mises, Jacob Viner, Frank Knight, Etienne Mantoux, Benjamin Anderson, Wilhelm Roepke, Arthur Burns and W. H. Hutt.

An anthology I edited in 1960, *The Critics of Keynesian Economics*, brought together 21 such "all-around reassessments"—all published before the *Economist's* stricture.

The refusal of the campus Keynesians to attempt any serious rebuttal of my own analysis could, of course, plausibly be attributed to the fact that I was only a journalist, and not a member of the academic union. But when, in 1963, Prof. W. H. Hutt, dean of the faculty of commerce at the University of Capetown, published his brilliant and penetrating volume, *Keynesianism—Retrospect and Prospect*, his criticisms met the same fate as mine. The Keynesians simply ignored their existence.

Yet while the Keynesians were ignoring these and other direct frontal attacks, their fortress was crumbling from within. They still, so to speak, kept up their regular church attendance, and preached the same sermons in the same esoteric vocabulary, but they were troubled by inner doubts. Their faith was oozing away.

There were, I suspect, two chief causes of this. Economic predictions based on Keynesian assumptions were constantly turning sour. Economic policies based on Keynesian assumptions were not producing the results expected from them. One could cite a long series of these disappointments, but I will content myself with the latest:

The Keynesians advocated the 10 per cent income-tax surcharge of 1968 in the belief that by itself it would "cool off" the economy and slow down the inflation. Yet in the calendar year 1968 consumer prices rose 4.7 per cent compared with a 3.1 per cent increase in 1967, and with an average annual increase of only 1.7 per cent in the 10-year period from 1957 to 1967. The price rise was as great in the six months after the tax increase as in the six months preceding it.

The weakness of Keynesian economics (which has today been rechristened "the New Economics") have become more and more obvious as the attempt has been made to apply it to economic policy. The New Economists, amply represented in the Kennedy and Johnson Administrations on the Council of Economic Advisers, confidently (not to say cockily) assumed that they could apply the new doctrines to "fine tune" the economy. The results have been disillusioning.

To apply the New Economics to fiscal policy it is first of all necessary to forecast what economic conditions are going to be if there is no change in fiscal policy. It is necessary that this forecast not only be correct but that it be made in time to prevent the feared depression or the feared inflation.

If a surplus or deficit is indicated, it is necessary to know how big it ought to be—to know the correct "dosage." The forecast must also be made early enough so that Congress will have time to take the appropriate action and so that the economic response to that action will not come too late.

In practice none of these requirements has been fulfilled. The forecasts have not been correct. They would have come too late even if they were correct. The proper dosage of deficit, assuming that there is such a proper dosage, has never been applied or even specified. Things have chronically gone wrong. For the fiscal year 1968 the government ran a mountainous deficit of $25 billion when even the canons of the new economics would have called for a surplus.

A detailed account of how and why the new economic theories and nostrums have gone astray can be found in George Terborgh's new book, *The New Economics* (Machinery and Allied Products Institute, Washington). After a careful examination of the actual record, Terborgh concludes that "so far as it goes it confirms the cynical assessment that the new economics is a one-way street to inflation."

But the New Economics failed not only because it is impossible to make sufficiently accurate economic forecasts far enough in advance, but because it is systematically wrong about what factors and changes produce higher or lower employment, higher or lower production, or higher or lower incomes and prices.

One of the alleged great "contributions" of Lord Keynes to economic science was to disregard changes in the quantity of money as an important factor in determining changes in economic activity, employment and prices. He threw all the emphasis on the relation between investment and government spending, on the one hand, and income, on the other.

People have a highly stable "propensity to consume," he contended, so that the amount they spend on consumption and the amount they save depends directly and dependably on the amount that people want to save and the amount that businessmen invest must be in balance. If businessmen do not invest enough, then the government must run a deficit to make up the difference.

Neither Keynes nor his disciples recognized the elementary point that if you want to increase the amount of "purchasing power," what is relevant is not whether or not there is a government budget deficit, but whether or not it is financed by the sale of government bonds to the public or by the printing of more money. It is the size of the increase in the stock of money that counts, not the size of the deficit.

In recent years the so-called "Chicago school," under the leadership of Prof. Milton Friedman, has been emphasizing this point and supporting it with formidable statistical documentation. The point was so completely overlooked in the Keynesian literature, however, that Friedman's contentions have been hailed as new and startling doctrine.

He himself has made no such claims for them. In a lecture in 1963, for example, he was saying: "The emphasis I have just been placing on the stock of money as the [inflationary] culprit is widely regarded as old-fashioned and out of date."

And he remarked at a later point in the same lecture: "One can go back one or two thousand years or more and find that every time there is inflation, two explanations are offered. One explanation is that the amount of money has increased. The other explanation is that something special has happened. . . ."

In brief, what the Chicago school has done has been to reinstate the classical quantity theory of money as the primary explanation of inflation and of changes in the price level, and to make it also the primary explanation of the quarterly, annual or other cyclical fluctuations in the economy. As such, it displaces the Keynesian explanation.

But perhaps the main reason for the decline of Keynesianism, among all but a comparative handful of hard-core zealots, has been the spreading recognition that the basic Keynesian remedy for unemployment, always and everywhere, has turned out to be plain inflation.

Keynes' *General Theory of Employment, Interest and Money* was published in 1936. In the 33 years since then the American budget has registered 27 annual deficits and only six surpluses. Consumer prices have risen 157 per cent. In other words, the purchasing power of the dollar has been degraded to less than 40 per cent of what it was in 1936. The British pound has been devalued twice. Practically all of the world's currencies have been devalued at least once. All of them without exception have lost purchasing power; all of them have depreciated.

The international monetary system set up at Bretton Woods in 1944, of which Keynes of Britain and Harry Dexter White of the United States were the two of chief architects, is in crisis. All the proposals to rescue it are proposals to permit and facilitate further inflation of individual currencies or of all currencies collectively—either to stop keeping the dollar even nominally convertible into gold, or to raise the price of gold, or to substitute paper "reserves" for gold reserves, or to remove any obligation of individual countries to maintain the value of their currencies in terms of gold, or the dollar, or other currencies.

Precisely how much of the inflation of the last 33 years, and how much of the pressure for still further inflation, can be blamed on the Keynesian ideology it would be impossible to say. But there is not the slightest doubt that the acceptance of Keynesian theories is responsible for a good deal of it—perhaps for the greater part of it.

Keynesianism has supplied the excuse and the rationale for the inflation of the last third of a century as well as the rationale for still further inflation. Keynesianism is still the doctrine of government economic planners everywhere. Though these planners now express perfunctory rears of further inflation, they still reveal much stronger fears of the unemployment they think would descend upon us if there were to be "too sudden" a halt to inflation. So they talk only of reducing the *rate* of inflation, say from 5 per cent to "only" 3 per cent a year.

In sum, Keynesianism, under that name, has definitely lost its former intellectual prestige. The majority of academic economists still pay lip service to it, but with more and more qualifications and less and less conviction. It is in the world of would-be practical men, in the world of the politicians and their appointed economic planners, that this defunct economic doctrine continues to rule, and as an unlabelled rationale for perpetual deficits and perpetual inflation, continues to work enormous harm.

Ludwig von Mises: Dean of Rational Economics

By Hans F. Sennholz   *(From the 11 April 1970 issue)*

(Prof. Hans Sennholz, a former student of Ludwig von Mises, was chairman of the Economics Department of Grove City College, Pennsylvania. The author of How Can Europe Survive?, *Dr. Sennholz has also written some 250 magazine articles.)*

When, in future centuries, historians search for the reasons for the phenomenal decline of Western civilization, few contemporary sources will be of any use. True, they offer colorful descriptions of the symptoms of this decline, but their explanations are usually infested with the very bacillus that is destroying our magnificent order. Future historians will be bewildered about our blindness and madness, our moral lethargy and decay.

"But were there no 20th Century philosophers" they will ask, "who recognized the ominous trend toward economic destruction, social disintegration, and political tyranny? Was there no prophet of the impending doom?"

We hope for their sake that they will discover the works of Ludwig von Mises who, since the beginning of this century, has been warning his contemporaries. Again and again he forewarned them about the growing popularity of ideologies of conflict and war, the rise of collectivism, and the sway of tyranny in the Western world. In fact, his writings, which will be so invaluable to future historians, are last-minute warnings to us, the living generation.

This is why the Foundation for Economic Education in Irvington-on-Hudson, New York, in conjunction with Arlington House in New Rochelle, N.Y., and Jonathan Cape Publishers in London, have again prepared new editions of some important Mises works.

Socialism, An Economic and Sociological Analysis (Jonathan Cape, 30 Bedford Square, London) was first published in 1922. Friedrich Hayek, one of Dr. Mises' most eminent students and disciples, recalls how *Socialism* overwhelmed him as a young student, awakened him in the midst of the Socialistic fashion of the day. Henry Hazlitt in his review, which appeared in the New York *Times* of Jan. 9, 1938, wrote:

"This is by far the ablest and most damaging answer to the Socialist philosophy since Boehm-Bawerk, another Austrian economist, also from the University of Vienna, published his memorable *Karl Marx and the Close of His System* in 1898.

"It is more than that. Boehm-Bawerk confined himself mainly to an examination of Marx's technical economics. Mises, apparently on the assumption that Boehm-Bawerk disposed so thoroughly of Marx's strictly economic analysis of capitalism that the work does not have to be done again, does not go over this ground, except by incidental reference. But he recognizes that socialism does not stand or fall with Marx's economic analysis; and therefore he devotes himself to the much wider task of examining all the arguments against capitalism or in favor of socialism from whatever source."

Mises' *Socialism* was revolutionary in its critique of the Socialist order. For the first time in the history of Marxism a scholar revealed its fundamental economic deficiency: its incapability of solving the problem of economic calculation.

Without the common denominator for economic calculation, which is the market price, a Socialist society cannot rationally allocate its labor, capital, land and other resources, and fairly distribute the yields of production. It would be unable to determine whether its production yields a social profit or social loss. It could not determine the contribution made and the reward earned by each worker.

In short, it could not rationally and economically compare the multiplicity of costs with the returns of production.

Prof. von Mises is not optimistic about our future. "Capitalism," he writes, "has raised the standard of life among the masses to a level which our ancestors could not have imagined. Interventionism and efforts to introduce socialism have been working now for some decades to shatter the foundations of the world economic system. We stand on the brink of a precipice which threatens to engulf our civilization. Opposition in principle to socialism there is none. . . ."

Mises' *Omnipotent Government, The Rise of the Total State and Total War* (Arlington House, New Rochelle, N.Y.), was first published in 1944 when 57 nations were locked in a total war that slew more than 15 million fighting men and countless women and children. It offers an ideological explanation of the international conflicts that caused both World Wars and continue to breed wars the world over.

Prof. von Mises illustrates his case with a review of the fall of Germany, from the collapse of classical liberalism to the rise of nationalism and socialism. But Germany merely constitutes an early example of the things to come—all of Western civilization is at stake.

Durable peace, Mises concludes, is only possible under perfect capitalism and laissez-faire government, a world of unhampered markets, free mobility of capital and labor, and equal treatment of everyone under one law. Government interference with business necessarily aims at autarky. But protectionism and autarky mean discrimination against foreign labor and capital and thus create international conflict.

The very ideas that breed bitter domestic conflict between classes and races also generate international conflict and war. "Progressives" at home and abroad aim at equality of income. But their own policies result in a perpetuation of the inequalities between classes and nations.

In Prof. Mises' own words: "The same considerations which push the masses within a country toward a policy of income equality drive the peoples of the comparatively overpopulated countries into an aggressive policy toward the comparatively underpopulated countries. They are not prepared to bear their relative poverty for all time to come simply because their ancestors were not keen enough to appropriate areas better endowed by nature.

"What the 'progressives' assert with regard to domestic affairs—that traditional ideas of liberty are only a fraud as far as the poor are concerned, and that true liberty means equality of income—the spokesmen of the 'have not' nations declare with regard to international relations."

At home and abroad they style themselves revolutionaries fighting for equal shares and proclaiming the right to take them by force if necessary. This is why our age is marked by perpetual conflict.

According to Prof. von Mises, "Government control of business engenders conflicts for which no peaceful solution can be found. It was easy to prevent unarmed men and commodities from crossing the borders; it is much more difficult to prevent armies from trying it. The Socialists and other statists were able to disregard or to silence the warning voices of the economists. They could not disregard or silence the roar of cannon and the detonation of bombs.

"All the oratory of the advocates of government omnipotence cannot annul the fact that there is but one system that makes for durable peace: a free market economy. Government control leads to economic nationalism and thus results in conflict."

The essay *Bureaucracy* (Arlington House, New Rochelle, N.Y.) was written and first published in 1944. Its main objective is an investigation of the contrast between bureaucratic management and business management. As such it is an invaluable contribution to the great historical debate between individualism and collectivism.

Prof. von Mises does not condemn or blame bureaucracy. He merely explains its meaning and discusses its proper spheres of application. In fact, in certain fields it may be the only possible method for the conduct of affairs. A police department, for instance, or the Marine Corps cannot be operated by profit management, as it cannot sell its services on the market. No matter how valuable and indispensable its achievements may be, they have no price on the market and therefore cannot be calculated in a profit-and-loss statement.

But whenever government endeavors to apply bureaucratic management to private business, the consequences are often disappointing. Social and political objectives usually supersede rational calculation of cost and yield, which fosters economic inefficiency and bureaucratic complacency. When economic production is completely bureaucratized, the individual is lost in a maze of regimentation and regulation. Youth especially is condemned to a listless life of subordination and obedience.

In the words of von Mises: "Government jobs offer no opportunity for the display of personal talents and gifts. Regimentation spells the doom of initiative. The young man has no illusions about his future. He knows what is in store for him. He will get a job with one of the innumerable bureaus, he will be but a cog in a huge machine, the working of which is more or less mechanical. The routine of a bureaucratic technique will cripple his mind and tie his hands. He will never be free to make decisions and to shape his own fate. He will never be a real man relying on his own strength. He shudders at the sight of the huge office buildings in which he will bury himself."

In 1957 Prof. von Mises added *Theory and History: An Interpretation of Social and Economic Evolution* (now Arlington House, New Rochelle, N.Y.) to his impressive list of scholarly publications. It is Mises' philosophical treatise that sums up his views on what man can know in his world. As man has always gone amiss in his attempts to bridge the gulf between mind and matter, he must adopt a dualistic approach—or methodological dualism.

According to von Mises, this dualism "merely takes into account the fact that we do not know how external events—physical, chemical and physiological—affect human thoughts, ideas and judgments of value. This ignorance splits the realm of knowledge into two separate fields, the realm of external events, commonly called nature, and the realm of human thought and action."

Ever conscious of this dualism and aware of the limitations of human knowledge, Prof. von Mises defends the sciences of human action against those philosophies and doctrines that would deny their very existence. In particular, he refutes the positivistic and panphysicalistic distortions of determinism, the doctrines of materialism, positivism and behaviorism, historicism and relativism.

Present-day ideologies, according to Prof. von Mises, are characterized by their summary rejection of individual freedom and private property in economic production. "Millions today enthusiastically support policies that aim at the substitution of planning by an authority for autonomous planning by each individual. They are longing for slavery.

"Of course, the champions of totalitarianism protest that what they want to abolish is 'only economic freedom' and that all 'other freedoms' will remain untouched. But freedom is indivisible. The distinction between an economic sphere of human life and activity and a non-economic sphere is the worst of their fallacies.

"If an omnipotent authority has the power to assign to every individual the tasks he has to perform, nothing that can be called freedom and autonomy is left to him. He has only the choice between strict obedience and death by starvation."

Even the most cursory review of Prof. von Mises' great writings would be incomplete without mention of his magnum opus, *Human Action, A Treatise on Economics* (Henry Regnery Co., Chicago). When it first appeared, his friend Henry Hazlitt wrote in *Newsweek* magazine (Sept. 19, 1949):

"I know of no other work, in fact, which conveys to the reader so clear an insight into the intimate interconnectedness of all economic phenomena. It makes us recognize why it is impossible to study or understand 'collective bargaining' or 'labor problems' in isolation; or to understand wages apart from prices or from interests rates or from profits and losses, or to understand any of these apart from all the rest, or the price of any one thing apart from the prices of other things. . . .

"*Human Action* is, in short, at once the most uncompromising and the most rigorously reasoned statement of the case for capitalism that has yet appeared. . . ."

Prof. von Mises' most recent essay, *The Historical Setting of the Austrian School of Economics* (Arlington House, 1969), finally, offers a brief review of the historical setting from which sprang not only rational economics but also statism and socialism that are sapping the foundations of Western civilization and well-being. This booklet and all other Mises books are required reading for everyone who cares about the future of man.

Needed: A Coalition between Labor and the GOP

by Representative Jack Kemp (R.-N.Y.)   *(From the 22 September 1979 issue)*

(Following is a speech by Rep. Kemp at the 44th Annual Convention of the International Longshoremen's Association [AFL-CIO], at Miami, Florida, July 16, 1979.)

I suppose many of you are wondering what a Republican is doing up here on this platform, rubbing elbows with Teddy Gleason and Al Barkan, and addressing a national convention of such a prestigious labor organization as the International Longshoremen's Association, AFL-CIO. Republicans, especially those who are labeled conservative, are generally about as welcome at a labor gathering as a hair in a biscuit. Republicans, after all, are supposed to be the party of Scrooge, the party of austerity and sacrifice, the party of big business, and the party that keeps pushing prosperity just around the corner.

It's true that ever since Herbert Hoover, a lot of Republicans have been advocating the economic equivalent of root canal work for American labor.

These Republicans have had a tough job, trying to convince workers that they would really be better off unemployed every now and then. You naturally don't pick up much of a labor constituency by arguing that raising tax rates to balance the budget and slowing down the economy to fight inflation is more important than making sure people have jobs. Not surprisingly, the American people haven't trusted Republicans with either house in Congress for nearly a quarter of a century. It's also true that many Republicans are beginning to recognize that this whole idea is foolish and counterproductive. If you're really concerned with balancing the budget, you can't do it by raising unemployment, because you lose revenue and have to spend a lot more on unemployment. There are some encouraging signs coming from my party. The House Republican leadership called for an immediate, massive, across-the-board tax cut last Friday to help avoid a recession. But I didn't come here to talk about Republicans and Democrats, or liberals and conservatives.

The issue facing this country, and especially its backbone, the working men and women, transcends all these political and ideological labels. The issue is whether we will have economic growth and opportunity, or contraction and unemployment. The issue is whether people will look forward to the future with hope and optimism, or despair at the prediction of Alfred Kahn, "that there is no way we can avoid a decline in our standard of living. All we can do is adapt to it."

Last week, the Administration and the Congressional Budget Office, which is the economic forecasting arm of the Congress, formally announced something that most of us already knew. We are in a recession, and a lot of working American men and women stand to lose their jobs. The Administration said it hopes that only 1.5 million people who now have jobs will lose them by next year. The CBO estimated that the figure could go as high as 2.3 million.

Three years ago, when he was running for President, Jimmy Carter made this promise: he said, I pledge that if I'm elected, we will never use unemployment and recession as a tool to fight inflation. We will never sacrifice anyone's job, his livelihood, for the sake of an economic game plan.

But today we have an economic game plan which proposes to do just that. The Administration is saying that it's not enough to raise taxes and balance the budget. People have to lose their jobs. To quote Barry Bosworth, who just resigned as head of the Council on Wage and Price Stability:

"The public should be told that balancing the budget by itself is not going to have any impact on wages or prices anywhere in the economy . . . Instead, if the restraints are really to have an impact on the rate of inflation, government expenditures must be reduced, and aggregate demand, production and employment must also be reduced. The result will be to throw a few million people out of work. To be sure, if enough of them are out of work, they will cease asking for wage increases. No one likes to say that, but that is what lies at the heart of the proposal for fiscal and monetary restraint."

The notion that we can fight inflation by employing fewer workers for lower wages to produce fewer goods tends to puzzle the factory and blue-collar workers in my district around Buffalo. By this definition, they have been fighting inflation since 1969. That's the last time they had a real wage increase after taxes and inflation, and they have had unemployment as high as 16 per cent. They may not all have gone to college to study economics, but it seems to them that when employment goes down and goods get scarcer, prices go up, not down.

But it's amazing how many people go along with this idea. The chief economist of the National Association of Manufacturers said recently in the Washington *Post* that recession is the only cure for inflation. "There's no other way to do it," he said. "We have to go through a painful period if we are going to stop inflation." The question is, painful for whom?

Why is no one any longer appalled that 12 per cent of the adult minority workers and 40 per cent of the black teenagers don't have jobs? It would be a big mistake for the Carter Administration or Congress to downplay the acute problem of minority unemployment in the name of fighting inflation.

For one thing, this unemployment is a major source of pressure to increase federal spending. But the overriding consideration is that to permit the waste of human potential is simply intolerable, even if it did cause inflation. But Margaret Bush Wilson is right: "Inflation is not caused by too many people working."

In fact, inflation is not caused by workers working, business doing business, consumers consuming or producers producing. To say that rising wages or prices cause inflation is like saying that wet streets cause rain. Inflation means prices are rising because there is too much money and too few goods. You can't solve inflation by producing less or controlling wages.

You may have heard or read in the newspapers that 23 members of Congress, all Republicans, as it turned out, filed a friend-of-the-court brief supporting the AFL-CIO in its challenge of the Administration's authority to enforce a 7 per cent limit on wages when inflation is running above 10 per cent.

You might ask what we had to gain by supporting a labor union on this issue. A lot of Republican businessmen, after all, go along with the wage and price guidelines—especially the wage guideline. And nobody thinks that by filing an obscure legal brief, we were going to get George Meany to change his voter registration. So why did these followers of Adam Smith do it?

Well, it was Adam Smith who said, "Whenever the law has attempted to regulate the wages of workmen, it has always been to lower them rather than to raise them."

Controlling particular wages or prices doesn't reduce inflation. If there is too much money in circulation, it just means that other prices or wages will rise, distort the market, and penalize those whose wages are controlled. Whenever we try to control all prices and wages, we just get widespread shortages and a big underground economy.

Telling workers to settle for 7 per cent while the government devalues the currency at 13 per cent is robbery. Republicans are quick to defend the profit incentive, but the wage incentive is no different. Take away either incentive and you ruin people's hopes and lives as you ruin the economy.

There is only one cause for inflation, and that is the government's policy toward the dollar. We didn't have inflation in this country for more than a century. The wholesale price index was exactly the same in 1930 as it was in 1800, because throughout that time, the government guaranteed a constant value for a dollar.

And in this century, when the government suspended its promise to maintain the dollar's value, there is still no evidence that inflation has anything to do with unemployment. Twice in the 1950s we had recessions without inflation. Three times now in the 1970s we have had recessions with inflation. In the 1920s and the mid-1960s we had unprecedented economic growth and employment without inflation. Between the last recessions, we have had strong economic growth with inflation.

Inflation and unemployment are two different problems. Inflation is caused when the government fails to maintain the value of its currency, and recession is caused when the government destroys incentives for employment, saving, investment and production.

We have been taxed into recession. The way our tax system is now, the more you work, the more you save, the more you invest—the higher your tax bracket. Or you can stand absolutely still, and the government will inflate you into a higher tax bracket. This is the main reason we are getting less employment, and production, and more inflation.

When you tax something, you get less of that thing. We are taxing work, saving, investment, enterprise and excellence, and we are getting less of each. When you subsidize something, you get more of that thing. We are subsidizing welfare, debt, unemployment and mediocrity, and getting more of each.

Slowing down the economy and employment and production actually increases inflation. If you have the same amount of money in circulation, but fewer goods, the price of goods has to rise. Whether we want to reduce inflation, balance the budget, or pay for social programs, we must have growth.

We haven't had a President since Jack Kennedy who understood that we either all move together as a country, or we don't move at all. Kennedy said, "A rising tide lifts all boats." Economic growth benefits everyone.

Ever since Kennedy, we have been afflicted with leaders who don't believe in the necessity of growth and opportunity, leaders who think life is a zero-sum game, where one group wins only if somebody else loses.

According to this view, there are only so many jobs in the world to go around. Only so much energy to go around, because the world will exhaust its resources some Wednesday afternoon. A fixed amount of prosperity, and a fixed amount of poverty. And they think it's the government's job to redistribute these fixed amounts so that the sum of the prosperity and the sum of poverty equal zero.

In this stagnant or contracting climate, politics becomes the art of pitting class against class. Rich against poor. White against black. Capital against labor. Sunbelt against Snowbelt. Old against young. Everybody has to become a special interest group and organize seven ways from Sunday just to protect himself. Opportunities become more attractive for lawyers and lobbyists and bureaucrats and accountants than for workers or businessmen. We have become so concerned with redistributing wealth that we have stopped producing it.

Redistribution is not the answer. I recall back in the 1972 presidential election, when George McGovern proposed what he called a "Demogrant." This plan would tax everyone earning more than $16,000 and give $1,000 to everyone earning less than $16,000 a year. At that time about 60 per cent of all Americans were earning less than $16,000 a year. But McGovern took a deep nosedive in the polls shortly after he announced this plan.

I remember reporters asking him after the election how he explained this, and he gave a very candid explanation. "I never realized," he said, "how many people there are in this country earning less than $16,000 who some day hope to earn more than $16,000."

I remember, too, a couple of weeks ago I was addressing a group of about 200 union factory workers in my district. I was talking about cutting tax rates to encourage new enterprises and create jobs. But I was talking specifically about abolishing the capital gains tax, as in West Germany.

When I had finished speaking, a young black worker stood up in the back and said, "Mr. Kemp, I agree with you. What can we do to help?" This surprised me, and I asked him whether he had any capital gains—a house to sell, or any stocks. He said, "No, but that's what I'm working toward." He had a goal: to buy a house, send his children to college, and watch his children have a better life than he did.

There is no reason to be embarrassed about calling it by its name—the American Dream. The American Dream was never that everyone be level with everyone else. The American Dream was that everyone had the opportunity to go as far or to climb as high as they could with their talents and their effort.

Redistribution is not the answer to our energy problems, either. The answer is not to ration a continual shortage. The answer is not to turn the thermostat up to 80 degrees in the summer and down to 60 in the winter, to swelter or shiver for the rest of the century. The answer is not to ration gasoline. The answer is not to outlaw driving one day a week. The answer is not to spend billions to subsidize Gulf Oil to produce a trickle of synthetic fuel at twice the price we pay for imported oil. The answer is not to turn our back on our neighbors in this hemisphere, and force Mexico to export illegal aliens and unemployment instead of natural gas. The answer is not to artificially control the production of natural gas, or tax away the production of oil with a huge excise tax.

The answer is production, and any other answer to our energy problems is the wrong answer. We aren't running out of energy anymore than we were in the 1850s when the United States was running low on whale oil. There are huge reserves of oil and natural gas in this country which are recoverable at or below the OPEC price for oil. And we haven't even begun to touch 90 per cent of known energy reserves in the world.

The issue is not rich versus poor, black versus white, capital versus labor, consumer versus producer, or conservative versus liberal. The issue is restoring that dream, getting this country moving again—not just for some, but for all. With economic growth, there is room for everyone to get ahead. Without it, the country tears itself apart competing for pieces of a smaller and smaller pie. And those pieces are getting smaller.

Let me read you a letter I received recently from a factory worker in Buffalo, who received a 6 per cent pay increase. He said, "I would like to show you the results of that increase."

Amount of monthly increase	$65.02
Federal tax increased	$37.58
State tax increased	$21.03
Social security tax increased	$7.87
Total increase	$66.48

"In other words, Mr. Kemp, the increase has cost me $1.46 a month."

In the meantime, his prices for food, shelter and necessities are going up by 13 per cent.

If you think this is an isolated example, take the case of a union which tried to stay ahead of inflation. I understand the Longshoremen negotiated a 30 per cent pay increase for 1978, 1979, and 1980. Back when you negotiated the package in 1977, the projected inflation for those three years was about 20 per cent.

Now the rise in prices is estimated to be 29.6 per cent. Because the government has caused inflation to be higher than anticipated in 1977, the longshoremen's pay increase will be only 0.4 per cent before taxes, in real terms. But a 30 per cent pay increase pushes you into higher tax brackets and raises federal taxes by more than 45 per cent. In real terms, you will lose more than 14 per cent as the result of a 30 per cent pay increase over three years.

This is the sort of thing that increases the likelihood of strikes and drives an ever-increasing wedge between the wages an employer pays and the wages a worker receives. It isn't capital's fault, and it isn't labor's fault. But they both suffer for it, and often blame each other.

The bottom line is this. Unless Congress and the President act immediately, at least eight million Americans will be without jobs for the next two years. The budget deficit will grow to at least $60 billion. It won't reduce inflation. There is no earthly excuse for permitting the third recession in ten years.

I stand before you as one half of that infamous tax-cutting team of Kemp and Roth. We have proposed an across-the-board 30 per cent cut in individual income tax rates over three years, and proposed to "inflation-proof" the tax code to prevent the tax increases caused by inflation. Kemp-Roth is not the only thing we can do to restore incentives.

We should liberalize depreciation rates, freeze social security taxes, and provide more incentives for American energy production. But the most direct thing we can do to immediately increase the amount of employment, saving and investment is to increase the reward or incentive for the next dollar earned by employment, saving, or investment. That means cutting tax rates. Everyone pays income taxes, whether on wages and salaries, interest, dividends, royalties, capital gains or pensions.

If we wait any longer, it will be too late for eight million unemployed Americans. It will be too late to balance the federal budget for many years. It will be too late to prevent an increase in inflation caused by a drop in production.

I am not interested in leading a tax revolt against the government or to cut worthwhile programs. What I am interested in is finding a way to pay for government, and right now that means avoiding a recession that will bankrupt us. I want to cut tax rates to restore incentives and get this country moving again. I want to reduce the wedge between labor and capital. I want to restore the dream of that factory worker who wants a better future for himself and his family.

It is time for Congress and the Carter Administration to stop haggling over how much to increase unemployment, how far to hold down wages, how to ration scarcity, and how far around the corner to push prosperity. It is time to get this country moving again.

Chapter Four

Education

The decline of education standards in the United States has been a matter of national concern for some time now, and the reasons for that decline have been detailed regularly in the pages of HUMAN EVENTS over the years.

The first article in this chapter is by William F. Buckley, Jr., "What Price Uniformity?" (11 June 1952). One of the first postcollege essays published by the young Bill Buckley, it takes Dr. James B. Conant, then-president of Harvard, to task for his attack on private schools.

In "MACOS: Pupils Brainwashed with Federal Funds" (10 May 1975), Joseph Baldacchino examines another pernicious element in U.S. education, "MAN: A Course of Study"—an appalling curriculum for 10-year-olds funded by the National Science Foundation.

William B. Ball, a former national chairman of the Federal Bar Association's Committee on Constitutional Law (and a man columnist James J. Kilpatrick called the Clarence Darrow of religious freedom), gives a wide-ranging analysis of the crisis in American education in an interview he gave to Joseph Baldacchino of HUMAN EVENTS ("Educational Freedom Drowning in Government," 21 April 1979).

Sally D. Reed's "U.S. Teachers Held Hostage by the NEA" (7 September 1985) examines the role in the decline of American education played by the National Education Association, the very organization supposedly dedicated to elevating educational standards.

Longtime school principal Howard Hurwitz, who has much experience in the field, makes "The Case Against Bilingual Education" (4 January 1986).

"Evolution: A Theory In Crisis" by M. Stanton Evans (24 May 1986) ponders the theory of evolution in the schools—namely that evolution has replaced creation-based explanations for life on earth because the former is supposedly based on fact; the latter on unverifiable religious beliefs. In fact, Evans points out, Darwin's theory of evolution must be accepted on faith because the observable geological and biological records provide almost no support for the theory.

"How To Make Sure Your Children Learn the Three R's" by J'Aime Adams (27 September 1986) gives excellent basic advice to parents who want their children to receive the essential educational basics the schools all too often do not provide.

And finally, in " 'Liberal History Lesson' Distorts 1st Amendment" (23 November 1991) Stan Evans explains that it is a fallacy to believe that our Founding Fathers wanted to create a wall of separation between the practices of civil government and the affirmations of religion.

What Price Uniformity

By William F. Buckley, Jr.   *(From the 11 June 1952 issue)*

The graduation ritual at the nation's private preparatory schools will be much the same as last year, and the year before. The Glee Club will sing, the valedictorian will talk about America in this troubled age, the football captain will be awarded a cup, the headmaster will amiably spoof the graduating class, and then commend its contributions to the school, and the visiting speaker will talk about great responsibilities.

And the whole show will be unabashedly public. Not everybody is invited, of course, but lots of people are—parents, alumni, benefactors, and the leading citizens of the town. All in all, a generous amount of fol-de-rol.

However, if James B. Conant, President of Harvard University, is right, the innocent appearing ceremony ought to go underground. There shouldn't be anything brassy to commemorate the intellectual puberty of a regiment of young men and women who, by virtue of their education in private schools, promise to introduce into our society "divisive" and undemocratic influences.

That's what they're going to do insisted Dr. Conant, in a speech before the American Association of School Administrators, last April. We can only achieve unity, he said, "if our public schools remain the primary vehicle for the education of our youth, and if as far as possible all the youth of a community attend the same school irrespective of family fortune or cultural background . . . there is some reason to fear lest a dual system of secondary education . . . come to threaten the democratic unity provided by our public schools."

Now the American people are not, as a general rule, given to talking back to educators, especially those who occupy such exalted posts as Dr. Conant's. We've been taught better. Education is good. More education is better. If education is good, it is because it teaches us things. More education teaches us more things. Hence, the more education, the more we know, the sounder our judgment, and the less we ought to be contradicted. Dr. Conant has had great gobs of education. His advice ought to be worth taking.

Still, some undisciplined folk are inclined to tell Dr. Conant to go take a ride on Charon's Ferry. They simply don't agree that private education is necessarily divisive and undemocratic, and they're not particularly interested in fostering the sort of unity Dr. Conant is probably interested in. In short, they want to know why Dr. Conant is attacking private education. What are the motives that conditioned his extraordinary attitude—especially since the record is clear that graduates of private schools, Dr. Conant included, have made and continue to make striking contributions to our society?

It doesn't help to read Dr. Conant's full statement, which treats mostly of the advantages of mixing the rich and the poor, the Catholics and the Jews, and the artists and the farmers. All of us agree that this is good, though perhaps rejecting Dr. Conant's intimations that this is the highest value of education; yet none of us has spotted any marked intolerance coming out of private schools—no more, for example, than what comes out of the public schools.

Nor are we convinced that there is less stratification within a public high school than in a private high school. So why should a man whose most casual asides shake the educational world come out and say such unfriendly things about the men and women who support private schools and send their children there?

The answer is that Dr. Conant, along with some powerful educational conferees, is out to fashion society in his own mold. This isn't a well-kept secret. It's not a secret at all. The most influential educators of our time—John Dewey, William Kilpatrick, George Counts, Harold Rugg, and the lot—have come right out and talked about what they're planning to do over the past thirty years.

They are out to build a New Social Order. And with a realism startling in a group of long-hairs, they have set about their job in the most effective way. They don't dissipate their efforts on such frivolities as national elections (though they do this incidentally); they work with far more fundamental social matter, the student. Through national educational associations, through teachers' colleges, and through textbooks and other literature, they reach out and influence the remotest classroom.

The chagrined and frustrated parent has very little luck opposing the advances of the New Social Order. Anytime a citizen feels like objecting to the orientation of the educational program of his local school, he collides with the iron curtain of academic freedom. "The consumer has no rights in the educational marketplace," Professor Henry Steele Commager puts it. Translated, this means that a parent has no right to seek reform regardless of the extent to which he disapproves of the net impact of the education of the local school. The educator, in short, has consolidated his position as the exclusive, irresponsible regent of education. *Le'cole*, he says—*c'est moi.*

Even with the academic freedom established, certain obstacles remain. There's not enough room in education for the New Social Order and religion. The New Order is philosophically wedded to the doctrine that the test of truth is its ability to win acceptance by the majority. Economically, the New Order is egalitarian, politically it is majoritarian; emotionally, it is infatuated with the State, the unchallengeable and irreproachable steward of every human being.

It clearly won't do, obviously, to foster within such schools a respect for an absolute, intractable, unbridable God, a Divine Intelligence who is utterly unconcerned with other people's versions of truth, and inattentive to majority opinion. It won't do to tolerate a competitor for the allegiance of man. The State prefers to secure monopoly for itself. It's intolerably divisive to have both God and the State scrapping for disciples on certain issues on which their views might differ.

Religion, then, must go. First of all, we must expose it as a not-very-serious intellectual and emotional avocation. (Viz., the famous 1945 Harvard Report's dismissal of religion: ". . . we did not feel justified in proposing religious instruction as part of the curriculum . . . whatever one's views, religion is not now for most colleges a practicable source of intellectual unity.")

Next, we must prove that to allow religion to be taught in public schools imminently commits us to uniting Church and State (viz., the *McCollum* decision of the Supreme Court). Having paved the way, we can rely on the results. If religion is given no place at all—or just token recognition—in the intellectual diet of the school, the growing generation will probably come to think of it as, to quote Cannon Bernard Iddings Bell, "an innocuous pastime, preferred by a few to golf or canasta."

THE FIGHT IS BEING WON! Academic freedom is entrenched. True, there have been a few setbacks, as for example, the "fascistic" episode in Pasadena, where the citizenry booted out its school superintendent, but considering the public chastisement extended to citizens involved, it's not likely that the incidence of this sort of uprising will increase.

But there remains an enemy. A Trojan Horse stands resolutely in the way of a uniform evolution towards the New Order. The private schools (outnumbered 10-1 by public schools) are still measurably independent, even though various conformist pressures are, of course, exerted by college administrators, who wield a decisive sanction—the power to refuse to matriculate the preparatory school's graduate. So long as these schools (and colleges) survive, the public education monolith is threatened.

The existence of these disruptive private schools clearly looms as a matter of the first urgency, and the question arises, how best to do away with them? The modern mind turns automatically to the State to do a job. Why not outlaw private schools? Dr. Conant is too realistic. The American mind is not yet conditioned to such heavy Federal action. Other means must be found to accomplish the same thing.

Private schools are supported by private money. So why not expropriate private money? This is the surest way to bankrupt the private school. The war of attrition is already succeeding. The private colleges are in a desperate shape. And they are masochists of the first order; they urge upon their students the evils of private property, and the glories of egalitarianism. Quite predictably, these students graduate to urge higher and higher taxation on their political representatives, who comply by absorbing a greater and greater percentage of individual income, thus making less and less of it available for the maintenance of private colleges. The next step, clearly, is for our government to rush in with various species of Federal grants to keep the schools from perishing.

But, if "public" money issued to support an educational institution, certain requirements must be fulfilled. No religious courses, of course, else you marry the Church to the State. And nothing too unkind about the State itself, as this would be churlish ingratitude. Nor may the school indulge itself in its own admissions policy. In short, the acceptance of Federal grants means the surrender of the school's independence.

Alongside an economic war against the private schools, a propaganda assault must be staged. The schools must be discredited. The movement to discredit them began, indirectly, a long time ago. The philosophers of egalitarianism and class hatred started to hack away at "private schools for young fobs." The psychological groundwork is laid, and the time is ripe for the direct onslaught. This time, not just against the people who support the schools, or the students who attend them, but against the institutions themselves. For they produce disunity and autocracy. They are a threat to our New Social Order.

SOME DAY, those Americans who believe in freedom are going to realize that they cannot indefinitely withstand the assaults of the State-lovers by restricting their defensive action to genteel parries. That is what we've been doing.

Way before Dr. Conant came out with his dirge about private schools, some responsible spokesman of freedom should have come out with a different observation about education. On the premise that every individual in our society ought to enjoy maximum freedom, which includes the freedom to superintend the education of his children, the suggestion ought to be made that every State rebate to the citizen who seeks private education budget that is earmarked for his public education. In short, we ought to adjust our thinking to devise ways and means of encouraging the *proliferation* of private schools, as the last, best bulwark against the monolith of the new, secular, statist social order.

MACOS: Pupils Brainwashed with Federal Funds

By Joseph Baldacchino   *(From the 10 May 1975 issue)*

Democratic Rep. James W. Symington of Missouri is making no secret these days of his desire to succeed his father, Stuart Symington (D.-Mo.), as a Missouri senator when the elder Symington retires next year. But if the people of that "Bible belt" state come to understand Rep. Symington's key role in defeating a recent amendment by Rep. John Conlan (R.-Ariz.) to the National Science Foundation authorization bill, he may experience difficulty getting himself elected dog catcher in Missouri, much less United States senator.

Conlan's amendment, which was rejected on a close 215-to-196 vote, was designed to prevent further use of NSF funds for the promotion or marketing of controversial courses in the nation's public schools—courses that manipulate unsuspecting school children into rejecting long-established moral values and even go so far as to rationalize infanticide, killing of the aged and wife-swapping.

What prompted the Conlan amendment was the National Science Foundation's spending of over $7 million to develop and promote a social studies course for 10-year-olds called "Man: A Course of Study," or MACOS.

After this course was developed by a group called the Educational Development Center, Inc. (EDC), at a cost to the taxpayers of over $6.5 million, it was considered so outrageously controversial that fully 50 commercial publishers refused to touch it. In order to make MACOS commercially available, therefore, the NSF entered into a dubious arrangement whereby it agreed to allow an offbeat publishing outfit known as Curriculum Development Associates, Inc. (CDA), an 80 per cent discount on royalties owed to the government.

The resulting savings—in effect, federal subsidies—enabled CDA to undercut prices to the nation's public school systems for more conventional, non-subsidized course alternatives published by the more reputable textbook firms. Much of these subsidies, moreover, have gone into a high pressure promotion campaign to persuade school administrators to adopt MACOS for use in their school systems.

Thanks in no small part to these federal subsidies, then, MACOS is now being used in an estimated 1,700 elementary schools, in nearly every state in the Union; and many parents do not even realize their children are being subjected to it.

Materials for MACOS, which include numerous books, films, records, pamphlets and other teaching aids, are full of references to adultery, cannibalism, infanticide, killing of old people, trial marriages, wife-swapping, murder and other behavior practiced by the Netsilik Eskimos studied as part of the course.

The idea, drummed into fifth-grade children day after day, is that such practices are considered all right by the Eskimo culture and, by extension, should be looked upon with tolerance by ours. And this is what bothers parents and other critics of this program. It is not that students should not be exposed to knowledge of other cultures, but there is some question as to whether children should be exposed to such harsh realities at this young stage of their development. In the view of many, this kind of material might better be reserved for college-level anthropology courses.

Even worse, if children are going to be exposed to this kind of behavior in other cultures, it should be made clear to them that such activities should by no means be considered acceptable or morally upstanding. Yet the purpose of MACOS, as its educator supporters readily admit, is precisely to get children to question this society's most cherished values.

The alarming result, as Susan Marshner demonstrates in a study to be published shortly by the Washington-based Heritage Foundation, is that children come to believe "that there are no moral absolutes. To say that it is not possible to use a set of moral values to arrive at answers to problems assumes the truth of situation ethics and relativism."

In short, MACOS teaches that nothing is sacred. Not the religious beliefs taught them by their parents. Not Western civilization. Not their country. Nothing, except perhaps the "anything-goes" beliefs of the course's leftist developers, Jerome S. Bruner and B. F. Skinner, whose book *Beyond Freedom and Dignity* showed in stark relief his affinity for changing human values through psychological conditioning.

Here are direct quotes from some of the written materials provided elementary and school children as part of their MACOS training:

• *Adultery and wife-swapping.* "Husbands have a very free hand in their married life and it is considered to be quite in order for them to have intercourse with any woman whenever there is an opportunity." (*The Netsilik Eskimos*, MACOS Vol. I, p. 117)

• "Two men who become song partners . . . are so **closely** bound together that they can exchange wives if they choose." (*A Journey to the Arctic*, MACOS Booklet 18, p. 38)

• *Cannibalism.* "The wife knew that the spirits had said her husband should eat her, but she was so exhausted that it made no impression on her. She did not care. It was only when he began to feel her, when it occurred to him to stick his fingers in her side to feel if there was flesh on her, that she suddenly felt a terrible fear; so she, who had never been afraid of dying, now tried to escape. With her feeble strength she ran for her life, and then it was as if Tuneq saw her only as a quarry that was about to escape him; he ran after her and stabbed her to death. After that, he lived on her, and he collected her bones in a heap over by the side of the platform for the purpose of fulfilling the taboo rule required of all who die." (*The Netsilik Eskimos*, Volume I, pp. 97-98)

• *Divorce and trial marriage.* "Divorce is common as long as there are no children, and there are women who go through seven or eight trial marriages before they finally settle down." (*The Netsilik Eskimos*, Volume I, p. 115)

• *Female infanticide.* "I talked to several Netsilik women in one camp about the children they had. One had borne 11 children—four boys and seven girls, of which four girls had been allowed to die at birth." (*A Journey to the Arctic*, MACOS Booklet 18, pp. 24-25)

• *Murder.* "As time went on, the old woman grew angry, for she too wanted a husband. She envied her daughter more and more, until one day when Kiviok was out hunting caribou, she killed her. She pulled the young smooth skin from her daughter's face and hand, and with it she covered her wrinkled, old face and her bony hands. When Kiviok returned, the mother went to greet him as her daughter always did." (*The Many Lives of Kiviok*, MACOS Booklet 25, pp. 11-12)

• *Senilicide.* "When we spoke of Eskimo murder, Father Henry told me about a man now at Committee Bay who had come to him one day, and, after the usual tea and silence, had said to him suddenly: 'I took the old woman out on the ice today.' It was his own mother that he had driven out and set down at sea to freeze to death.

"He was fond of her, he explained. He had always been kind to her. But she was too old, she was no longer good for anything; so blind, she couldn't even find the porch to crawl into the igloo. So, on a day of blizzard, the whole family agreeing, he had taken her out, and they had struck camp and gone off, leaving her to die." (*Old Kigtak*, MACOS Volume 7, p. 18)

The children are far from being passive observers in this program. On the contrary, they are required to grapple with some of the most difficult of moral questions. In addition, they are made to participate in psychological games involving surveillance of the actions of their fellow pupils and of their parents' conduct of family life.

MACOS has been denounced by the renowned New York clinical psychologist Dr. Rhoda Lorand, for 25 years a practitioner of psychotherapy for children and young adolescents and also a professor at Long Island University.

Said Dr. Lorand: "The program not only forces the children to be preoccupied with infanticide and senilicide as well as the gory details of animal slaughter, it also aims at making the children accepting of these practices. Further, the children are forced to identify with the customs through role-playing, even of Eskimo myths.

"In the enactment of one myth, a child about whom I was told was required to play the role of the elderly grandmother who clings to a boat which is about to leave her behind to die. Another child was assigned the role of her offspring who chops off the grandmother's fingers so that she cannot delay their departure."

Dr. Armand DiFrancesco, a family physician in Buffalo, N.Y., says MACOS has caused emotional traumas and psychological disturbances for several young children he has personally treated.

"I first became interested in this course of study when a young 12-year-old girl from a nearby city was referred to me because of severe anxiety, and insomnia, and school phobia, and who began to have sexual obsessive thoughts. In therapy, I have learned that this was brought about by the teachings and by the stories as recounted in the MACOS program.

"I subsequently had occasion to have two other cases of children who developed anxiety and conflicts as a result of some of the things that were taught in this program that were in conflict with some of their religious beliefs and teachings at home."

But as if MACOS were not doing enough harm, EDC is now moving forward under a new grant approved on January 10 of this year to promote and market a sequel to MACOS for high schools called "Exploring Human Nature."

Prior to receipt of the January 10 grant, EDC had already developed "Exploring Human Nature" at a cost to the government of nearly $2.5 million. The January 10 grant has nothing to do with developing the course. That has already been accomplished. This year's grant is strictly for use in developing and maintaining a high-powered system whose main purpose it will be to get MACOS, "Exploring Human Nature" and several other social-value-modification courses accepted by local school systems.

And what is the purpose of all this frantic organizing at taxpayers' expense? Why, to implement "Exploring Human Nature," MACOS, and related EDC curricula with NSF funding in a *minimum* of 1,900 additional classrooms in 500 school districts in 50 states. And this is to be accomplished by next year.

And adding insult to injury, the EDC promotion plan funded by this year's NSF grant actually requires each promotion team in the growing EDC educator network to apply for yearly NSF grants for their own activities for an indeterminate number of years into the future.

To understand the significance of this funding pyramid structure, it should be put in the perspective of recent educational developments in this country. In contrast to the early days of American public schooling when parents prescribed what the schools should teach and how, in recent years parents have been virtually shut out from decisions relating to the schools that teach their children.

As Dr. Onalee McGraw, coordinator for the National Coalition for Children, recently testified before a congressional subcommittee, the parents' "inherent right to decide how schools can best serve the educational needs of their children has been usurped by a highly powerful organization of educators and the National Education Association."

Members of this elitist group of educators, said Dr. McGraw, have widely stated that, in their view, parents are inadequate for child-raising. "They further view the home as an inadequate, unhealthy, and even pernicious source of character formation. They have thus established themselves as models for children's standards and behavior, in place of the children's own parents and relatives."

This belief has become orthodoxy among the educationist establishment in the United States today. And by using NSF funding for the promotion of their views, they are rapidly extending their grip into the various school districts nationwide. Only if Congress puts a stop to NSF funding of promotion activities for courses such as MACOS can this erosion of parental control of the public schools be slowed.

Educational Freedom 'Drowning in Government'

(From the 21 April 1979 issue)

In this wide-ranging interview, a noted constitutional lawyer discusses the secularization—and concurrent decline—of American public education, the bureaucratic threat to private alternatives, such solutions as tuition tax credits and educational vouchers, the dangers inherent in the proposed equal rights amendment, and how businessmen and others can successfully counter unwarranted government interference in their day-to-day existence. A graduate of Western Reserve University (1940) and the University of Notre Dame College of Law (1948), William B. Ball has achieved eminence as one of the nation's best-known and most successful constitutional lawyers. A partner in the Harrisburg, Pa., firm of Ball & Skelly, Ball has argued 13 separate appeals before the U.S. Supreme Court, including five in the last six years.

He has also argued important cases in the Supreme Courts of Montana, Iowa, Ohio, Wisconsin, Pennsylvania, Vermont and Massachusetts; Courts of Appeals of Oregon and Michigan; U. S. District Courts in Connecticut, Rhode Island, California, North Carolina, Pennsylvania and Indiana; and U.S. Courts of Appeal, 3rd Circuit and 7th Circuit.

A former national chairman of the Federal Bar Association's Committee on Constitutional Law, Ball has handled constitutional litigation on such wide-ranging issues as old age discrimination, environment and government regulation of business. But he is perhaps most renowned for his successful defense of religious and educational freedom, having won the famous Amish case in Wisconsin and the Dunkard in Ohio, among others.

For his prodigious efforts in the latter area, Ball has won acclaim from columnist James J. Kilpatrick, who called him "the Clarence Darrow of religious freedom," and Russell Kirk, who termed him "the most successful defender at law of church-related schools anywhere in the land." Mr. Ball gave the following exclusive interview to HUMAN EVENTS' *Joseph Baldacchino:*

Q. Mr. Ball, as a lawyer who has dealt with the subject as much or more than any other in the United States, do you believe that religious education is under assault in this country today?

A. Yes, I think there are considerable pressures being placed on both private education and private religions in a variety of ways. Of course, there's the economic assault—that of taxation and of inflation—but there are also governmental interventions at the federal and state levels which are a very definite threat to the future of private and private religious education. At the state level we've had in recent years an attempt upon the part of the state educational authorities to completely reverse the roles that are proper to state schools and private schools respectively; that is to say, state educational authorities have taken on the assumption that they are free to regulate private education—education which they didn't found and don't fund—and in some cases to subject it to plenary state controls. The end result is that they would seek to convert private education into simply another form of public education—a carbon copy of the public schools.

Q. Has this been a problem of long standing or is this relatively new?

A. I think it's relatively new. There have been statutes on the books of some states going a ways back, especially in some of the Western states where total control was placed in the government largely because of the absence of any kind of meaningful private educational voice. In some Southern states, the massive resistance statutes of the mid-1950s have been converted into vehicles for regulating private education. But for the most part, any aggressive use of these statutes and powers has only come about recently.

I should mention also that at the federal level we've had a whole series of intrusions lately as far as the religious schools are concerned—unemployment compensation, the attempt of the National Labor Relations Board to exercise its jurisdiction over the schools, activities of the Bureau of the Census and so on.

Q. I'd like to get into a number of these with you. One that you recently testified on in Washington was the proposed new Internal Revenue Service regulations that would eliminate tax exempt status and also the right to receive tax-deductible contributions from many of the private schools. Could you briefly summarize the testimony you have on that subject?

A. Yes, representing fundamentalist and Amish schools, I pointed out that these regulations are completely unworkable and grossly unconstitutional in terms of the religious liberties of those schools because it would impose on them recruiting requirements, for example, whereby they would ultimately have to select students not of the particular religion of the school but in conformity with the government's notion of what constitutes racial balance. They interfere with the religious liberty of the schools in many other ways: their freedom to select faculty, their internal programs—all are affected.

Q. For one thing the IRS in these regulations declares that they will ordinarily consider private schools that were founded or significantly expanded at a time of public-school deseg-regation in the same geographic area to be guilty of racial discrimination unless they meet a certain quota of minority enrollment. When such private schools don't meet the quota the IRS puts the burden of proof on them to prove that they are not discriminatory. And in most cases these schools will be required to carry out costly affirmative action programs. Now from your experience is it an accurate or fair assumption on IRS' part to consider these schools guilty of discrimination on the basis of such statistical criteria alone?

A. No, it's not at all. The IRS here has simply "opened on suspicion." They have taken it into their heads that the great numbers of private religious schools are racially discriminatory white havens, and the facts don't bear that out at all. But it isn't the business of government to find out one way or the other whether that is so.

Q. You've stated that the agency hasn't proper statutory authority from Congress for this proposal. As I understand it IRS bases its supposed authority on a court decision some years ago called *Green v. Connally*. Could you summarize first of all the thrust of that ruling and secondly state your opinion as to its importance as a precedent?

A. Well, in *Green v. Connally*, a number of Negro parents of children attending public schools in Mississippi brought a class action suit to stop the U.S. Treasury from according tax-exempt status and deductibility of contributions to private schools in Mississippi that were discriminating against Negro students. What was not involved in that case was any issue of religious private schools, and that's extremely significant because the decision is not a precedent with regard to those schools.

Q. Another aspect of the ruling in *Green* was the assumption that tax-exempt status and other tax privileges constitute a form of governmental assistance and that as recipients of this supposed government aid schools can be made to meet certain requirements laid down by the government. Is this a valid assumption—that tax exemption is a form of government assistance—or are the facts quite the opposite: that the tax-exempt status of religious institutions originated as a means of avoiding state interference in religion?

A. Well, the latter is plainly true. In the basic U.S. Supreme Court decision on religious tax exemption, which was *Walz v. Tax Commission*, the court was careful to point out that tax exemption is not a subsidy under a different name.

The Supreme Court said in that case that, when the government creates tax exemption, it is not transferring part of its revenue to churches but is abstaining from demanding that churches support the state. The church-state separation reasons for tax exemption are very, very strong, as the court makes clear in that decision.

Q. Another aspect of the *Green vs. Connally* decision was that the court went back to common law and stated that in order for an organization or school to receive tax exemption under the Internal Revenue Code it had to meet the definition of a charitable trust. The court went on to say that under the common law an institution that acted against recognized public policy did not meet this definition and that on this ground the IRS had the right to remove tax exemption. But if this premise is correct what would happen to an institution such as the United Negro College Fund? This organization raises funds to help send deserving black students to college but it does seem to focus its activities on assisting members of one particular race. Now if *Green v. Connally* were applied consistently would an organization like the United Negro College Fund get into difficulty even though it clearly performs a valuable service?

A. I'm not sure whether I'd want to base the answer strictly on the *Green v. Connally* decision, but on the general reasoning that there can be no tax exemption for a group or an institution which limits its interests to a particular minority, you would have to raise questions about that fund and a number of other activities which are tax exempt.

But when talking about religious institutions—religious educational institutions—we have to keep two other things in mind. One is the fact of religious liberty itself—that there is a religious liberty to observe fully one's religious mandate, even though that may mean that you operate on what would superficially be called a segregated basis. The second consideration is that a number of religious institutions—in fact, most such institutions—are themselves minority institutions. An Amish school is a minority school, and I don't believe that you can make that minority's rights subject to the requirements of other minorities.

Q. Another threat to the right of private schools to teach in accordance with their religious beliefs, as you mentioned at the outset, has been the attempt in some states to dictate what private schools should teach, what textbooks they should use, and so forth. I believe you are currently litigating cases along these lines in the states of North Carolina and Kentucky. Will you describe what is at issue in these cases?

A. Yes, at issue are contentions of the states that they have power—really plenary powers—with respect to private schools, and that the state is the best and wisest educator, and that it can dictate curriculum or what is taught, teacher certification requirements or who shall teach, and methodology—how subjects should be taught. And when you finish reading the sometimes extremely poorly worded but very, very broad regulations of states which are asserting that power, you realize that the private schools, apart from any question of religion, are to be nothing but carbon copies of the public schools. They'll have no individuality left.

Now you might ask me, well, are these state education boards and departments all that tough? Well, some are quite lenient. But what has been challenged in a number of these cases by very courageous people is not the benign exercise of the power, but the power itself. These people who have challenged these laws don't care whether the master is today benign and tomorrow severe. They don't believe they have a master who should have that power over them at all.

Q. Right but in addition I believe that at least in one of these cases and maybe several states have in fact been less than what one might call lenient. Wasn't it Kentucky that threatened to prosecute parents who sent their children to schools that didn't comply under threat of fines and possibly even prison sentences?

A. Yes, this has happened in Kentucky and in Ohio. Four years ago in Ohio the state simply went ahead and had a whole group of parents indicted by grand jury for the supposed crime of truancy, and these poor parents weren't guilty of any crime. The crime they were committing was having their children in a lovely little fundamentalist Christian school in Bradford, Ohio, where the children were learning well and performing beautifully, using nationally standardized achievement tests which are too advanced for the public schools to risk using. We were three years in court on that case, and the Supreme Court of Ohio unanimously held for the parents and declared all this terrible attempt to regulate this school to be unconstitutional.

Q. Now in Kentucky there was a similar situation, is that correct?

A. Yes, the Kentucky case originated upon the resolve of the state board of education that the parents of any children who were in so-called non-approved schools should be listed, and that compliance with the compulsory attendance laws should then be enforced. This meant that they were all going to be criminally prosecuted for truancy, and in one or two instances the local authorities went after pastors of church-schools under a statute alleging contributing to the delinquency of a minor, or words to that effect. That, of course, implied immorality. It's a terrible shame that people in a number of states have been lurched into by government and put to the travail of these court proceedings.

Q. In their defense of such policies these governments often state that they have a responsibility to guarantee that all of the children in the state receive an adequate education. In Kentucky for example they required that in order for a school to be accredited the teachers should meet certain educational standards. What is your view here?

A. When the public educational authorities have told the public and told the courts that all they're trying to do is ensure that all children get a good education, they have made the assumption that only through their standards can this good education be achieved. This is entirely incorrect. Public education today simply does not constitute a good model for American education to build upon or to imitate.

There is a justifiable national outcry against the low caliber of learning and achievement of children in many public schools. The fact is that many children are coming out of those schools simply not well educated. The failure to read, write, spell and handle English in the proper manner, the lack of ability to compute, the lack of knowledge of their country's geography and history and institutions, is an astonishing phenomenon of our day.

And when you consider that in some states 50 per cent of the entire state budget is devoted to public education, you wonder how it can be that there is this astonishing failure. When you see the growth of classroom violence and the involvement of children in vandalism, violence, sexual misconduct and so on, then you conclude that we had better look to other models if we're going to find good education.

Regarding schools that I have represented, I think proof is in the pudding. It's really ascertainable without the need for a vast socialized effort to regulate these schools that their children are achieving very well on good old standard national achievement tests. Their school buildings are modest but good environments for children to learn in. They are turning out virtuous children—children imbued with civic virtue and good traits.

Q. So you believe that in many instances schools which take approaches different from those approved by the public-school authorities may be the better for it?

A. Oh yes, very definitely.

Q. Are the public schools today truly neutral on matters of religion and moral values or have the courts made it difficult for schools to do this?

A. Well, there is a popular assumption, I believe—and I think it's still an assumption of the courts—that, since the Bible-reading decision, the public school is now a religiously neutral school. And that's based upon the idea that, if you eliminate very obviously religious exercises, such as prayers and Bible reading, and pretty well sterilize the social studies such as history and so on of religious advocacy, you have a neutral school. Then, when the objection is raised that the school which throws out the Bible can't be neutral, the stock answer given is that the Bible isn't thrown out: that it is there in literature along with all the great literature of the world and that, indeed, the public school is not a secular school.

But this is not true. The great error in that thinking is the fact that it reflects a secularist concept of religion. To find out whether religious belief is violated, you have to ask what is belief to the believer. That is the point that has been missed in a lot of discussion of religion in the public school.

So let's take a child who comes from a fundamentalist religious household. That child has been taught to consider that the Bible is the word of God. He comes into public school class and let's say there's a reference to the Bible and he says to his teacher, well, that's the word of God, isn't it? And children will do that kind of thing. The teacher then is going to have to respond in one of several possible ways.

The teacher can say, well, the Bible is wonderful literature. There's Shakespeare and the Bible and they're wonderful pieces of literature. But this to the fundamentalist is to contradict, materially contradict, the concept of the Bible as being a sacred instrument whose virtue doesn't lie in its being a piece of literature. Or secondly, the response will have to be that we don't say whether it's true, false or anything else; we can't pass any judgment on it.

But the fact of having to avoid that judgment, like the fact of having to avoid speaking about or preaching the word of God, implies—and especially to the child—a lack of importance. And home training will never make up for it. The child is in school for the real formative time of his day and of his month and year, and it's the principal influence in his life.

Q. So you're saying that in effect you don't believe that we can have a single publicly supported school system capable of treating everybody equally both believers and non-believers? Neutrality is in effect not really possible is that right?

A. Yes, I don't think neutrality is possible, not only for the reasons I gave you just now but for another reason, too. An awful lot of knowledge is intensively value related and really, the vacuum that's been left by the departure of Protestantism from the public school is a vacuum that has to be filled by other values.

It used to be when a child was in public school—and I can remember this when I was in public school many years ago—that if somebody stole something the teacher might say "That's a very bad thing to do." And if the question "Why?" was raised, the teacher might say, "Well, it's against the Ten Commandments," and there was a whole concept of sanctions, religious sanctions, that lay behind that value judgment. But now, if you look at public school curricula in the fields of health, for example, you find that there's a womb-to-tomb philosophy of life being offered, which necessarily is posited on anything but religious values.

Q. But if you went back to the old way it seems that secularists—believers in secular humanism or other non-theistic points of view—could equally have grounds to complain. So what do you think of this?

A. Well, I think that is true. Now this is not to say there aren't plenty of parents today who don't care, religiously. We talk a great deal about parental rights, but sometimes we have a rather imaginary parent in mind. There are a lot of parents today who aren't parents, and there are a lot of parents today who are irreligious.

But when you are speaking of those parents who do care very much about God and their relationship with their child—to God and to salvation—then you come to the necessity of assuring that the child is not forced into a publicly financed environment which is destructive of his religious views and those maintained by his parents.

The solutions are two-fold. One, that the *McCollum* decision of the 1940s ought to be overruled in order to allow a degree of accommodation for different religious faiths on the premises of public-school properties. That's one possible solution. The other is to free parents who desire their children to be raised in a religious-school environment of the economic handicap of having to pay a public-school tax while getting no tax break whatever to help educate their child in a religious school.

Q. You mention the *McCollum* decision. Could you elaborate on that?

A. Yes, the school district of Champaign, Ill., many years ago had provided a released time program which took place on the school premises at a regularly scheduled time. Under this program, which required little administrative effort on the part of the schools, a Jewish child, or a Catholic child, or a Lutheran child could attend a class or session where a rabbi, priest or minister would offer religious instruction or counseling to the child.

Now this was undoubtedly a useful program and enabled many a child to fully realize his religious liberty while still attending public school. The Supreme Court struck that down as constituting an establishment of religion, use of public funds to support religion. But some variant on that program is certainly one possibility that some have contemplated.

Q. Now the other suggestion you made was that somehow the law be changed to aid those parents who have strong religious reasons for wanting their children to get some other type of education than the one promoted in the public school system. Are you referring to such approaches as the voucher system or tuition tax credits?

A. Yes, some program such as tax credits. Yes.

Q. Okay that of course leads to another question: Isn't there a danger that in moving toward such a system you might open the door for the very kind of problems that you've encountered in certain states already namely the state making—as a condition of the voucher the tax credit or whatever—so many programmatic requirements that the schools turn out to be carbon copies of the public school system?

A. Yes, I think your point is very well taken. I think there's loose talk from some people on both sides of this controversy. Thus some who favor tax credits contend that the private school—even the religious private school—is really pretty much of a public and secular institution anyhow, and on that ground they assume that the school can be aided and they regard the tax credit as really direct aid to the school. Opponents, on the other hand, say the school is religious and, consequently, not aidable.

I think the true answer is this: There's a need and a right for parents to be able to educate their children with freedom, and this means in private schools, including religious private schools. But presently their capacity to enjoy these fundamental liberties is blocked by heavy taxation and by inflation. Hence, the rightness of tax relief as an accommodation of their liberties. That's precisely how I regard the tax break.

But, as you indicate, it should not be tax relief at any price. Not at the price of placing private education under state control. And that's going to happen if, to get the tax credit, you have to enroll your child in an eligible institution, which institution is defined as being approved, certified or licensed by the state board of education or department of education. That would simply open the way for vast enlargement of the state educational bureaucracies.

Q. I'd like to read a quote to you from a book by an author named John Fentress Gardener and see if you'd care to comment on it. In *The Experience of Knowledge*, Gardener writes that given that the 1st Amendment guarantees the right to freedom in the formation of belief and that education entails the essence of belief formation the spirit of the 1st Amendment requires us to realize that state power should keep hands off the schools as it does the churches. The state schools must eventually by due process and by many small steps and as a matter of harmonious evolution . . . be disestablished as state churches have been. Do you think there is validity in this or do you think he goes a little too far?

A. I think that's a good statement. I've not read the book and I'm only taking the quote you're giving me, but limiting myself first of all to private education, here I think there can be no state establishment in private education. I think the state ought to keep hands off the private schools; and except in the very, very narrow area I've described, I don't think the private school is the state's business.

I'd also point out that, for the protection of the public interest, there are always available laws respecting fraud, and of course our criminal laws with respect to violent conduct, treason, and conduct offensive to the public order. If someone is pretending to conduct a school, for example, but in fact is keeping kids in a garage or something, redress can be had in the anti-fraud statutes now available without having to impose upon schools and education a whole new body of regulation to meet the so-called need for public assurances.

But getting back to Gardener's statement, I think it's inevitable that, when a state runs a school and it cannot express theistic religious values, it's going to be expressing secularist religious values, either directly or by omission, and it's been doing it both ways in public schools.

Q. Do you think the voucher system would be more in line with what social justice ought to provide? People such as Milton Friedman the economist have proposed, as an alternative approach to public education, taking the total education budget and dividing that amount of expense among the number of students in the system. Each student would then get a voucher worth his share of the total education budget which he could spend to get an education as he or his parents see fit.

A. I think that's the ideal form of support for education—again, always being wary of the definition of the institution where the voucher can be expended.

Q. We've been concentrating so far on government over-regulation as it affects education and religious freedom but of course over-regulation in our society also affects many other groups. Small and medium-sized businesses for example have also been seriously harmed. Do the cases you have handled involving the church schools have any relevance to the broader question of government gone wild?

A. Yes, I think they have. One of the most interesting things about the religious school cases I've seen in the past three or four years has been what I feel is the striking relevance they bear to the broader question of freedom of the private sector. You mentioned, for example, small and medium businesses. I can think of many kinds of private endeavor other than religious schools in which the problems really are the same.

That is to say, we're drowning in government. Government is a non-creative thing, it produces no wealth, yet it's swelling in the country today. As a source of employment, as a source of careers, it's becoming a whole way of life.

It's a giant industry in our midst. And it's inevitable, then, that the private sector is finding itself in competition with what is becoming a monstrous thing on the national scene.

So you have small businessmen who are really in exactly the same position as the little preacher who is running a small religious school. He's faced with demands that he can't meet without great expense and inconvenience, and sometimes in direct violation of his liberties. He's faced with the constant problem of the benign administrator and the harsh administrator. He's faced with the question of not making waves or on the other hand deciding to stand up for his liberties. He also faces the blanket nature of regulatory material with its often vague language imposing limitless powers on people who are simply other citizens—namely, administrative officials.

But the example set by some of these church groups should remind us of the necessity for courage and the need for perceptiveness with respect to our liberties. I see a great deal of defeatism in the private sector today: a very pathetic compulsion to conform to regulation. You see this anxiety on the part of people to be, as they put it, "in full compliance."

Compliance with what? It's all too often compliance with something that isn't law at all. It's just the invention of an administrative agency; so these regulations and guidelines and directives and compliance requests and all the rest of it are all too often homemade laws—a phrase that keeps recurring to me. They're not the enactment of the legislature, but a product of the imagination of some individuals who happen to hold jobs as administrators.

Q. So you think that businessmen in many instances might be well advised to take a page from the notebook of some of these private educators and not hesitate, when they think they've been wronged by an administrative agency, to fight it out in court?

A. Yes, they should. They ought to always ask whether a regulation is in accordance with the statute. And then, if the statute is really bad, they ought to contest its constitutionality. We need an awful lot of counter-punch from the private sector. We have a lot of good public servants. They're fine people. But we have to keep in mind that they are servants and it's only a few of them who pretend to be Reichsmarshalls.

I hate to see citizens who man the hard-working, creative and economy-minded private sector of our society taking panic over these paper tigers, or going to exquisite pains not to make waves. These people are living as though they were already in the People's Republic and they just don't have to. And the more they live that way, the more they feed this system.

The great thing—and this can often be short of litigation—is to always ask, when a regulation is troublesome to you as a private-sector person, business or otherwise: "What's your authority for this requirement?"

U.S. Teachers Held Hostage by the NEA

By Sally D. Reed   *(From the 7 September 1985 issue)*

'Over the years, the National Education Association has consistently opposed every constructive attempt to improve the educating process and it is still doing so. . . . It has initiated policies which have demoralized teachers, made their jobs more difficult, and compromised the legitimate needs of all educators.'

The National Council for Better Education recently announced the results of a nationwide poll of classroom teachers—union and non-union—which we commissioned to ascertain whether the political positions espoused by the National Education Association (NEA) were in any way reflective of the views held by its 1.7-million-member constituency, and by all teachers in general.

The findings were based on a national survey of 1,007 randomly selected teachers conducted between June 14 and 17. Undertaken by professionally trained personnel, the interviews were supervised by Arthur J. Finkelstein and Associates, a well-established polling firm, and analyzed by The Dolan Report, Inc.

Union Hierarchy Out of Step with Teachers

The results, considered to be accurate within a range of plus or minus 3.1 per cent, showed beyond question that the NEA's union hierarchy is out of step with teachers, including its own members, on a wide range of issues; that the size of its membership has been due in large part to pressure and coercion; and that, contrary to the liberal-left tenor of the NEA, fully 76 per cent of American teachers consider themselves moderates or conservatives.

When asked why they joined the NEA, 16 per cent of member teachers responded that they were forced to join the union as a condition of employment.

Another 16 per cent cited something called "unification," an arrangement in widespread use since the early '70s under which anyone wanting to join the local teachers' organization must join the state and national organizations as well. Under "unification," even in right-to-work states, a teacher no longer has the option of joining just the small, local teachers' group.

Only 6 per cent of NEA members—fewer than one out of every 16 polled—said they joined because the NEA represented their views on the issues. By a better than 3-to-1 margin, moreover, the members of NEA made it clear that they do not appreciate having their dues money spent to promote political causes unrelated to education.

Thus, 3 per cent of the members polled said the NEA should use no membership dues to lobby Congress, while 74 per cent said such lobbying should be confined to educational issues alone. By contrast, only 23 per cent supported lobbying by the NEA on social and foreign policy issues.

Misrepresentation by the NEA

The NEA is in fact a well-oiled political machine which has greatly expanded its power since switching from a professional association to a full-fledged labor union in the late '60s. It has used this power to promote a leftist political agenda, often using forcibly extracted, compulsory dues for the purpose.

Perhaps most significantly, the NEA union leaders have managed to misrepresent themselves and their goals to the nation's teachers, causing educators, in turn, to misrepresent themselves to the American public.

The NEA told the public, as well as representatives of Congress in a 1983 telegram, that its 1.7 million teachers support federally funded abortion-on-demand. The organization has since reiterated this stand. Yet the recently conducted poll found that 57 per cent of NEA members *disapprove* of federal funding of abortions, while only 40 per cent approve of such a policy. An even larger number of NEA members—75 per cent—oppose the NEA's spending of their dues money to support that cause.

Why the disparity?

Well, one reason is that more than half of the union's members don't even know where the NEA stands on the issue. Thus, in answer to the recent survey, 27 per cent of the NEA members questioned responded "Don't know" to the question of where the union stands on federal abortion funding, while 29 per cent expressed the mistaken belief that the NEA opposes the policy. Only 44 per cent of NEA members answered correctly that the organization favors federal government funding of abortions.

Teachers Unfamiliar with Union Goals

This confusion, really, is the whole point. Too many teachers—NEA and prospective teachers—do not know what the NEA is all about.

In the case of the federally funded abortion issue, NEA officials present teachers with nebulous pronouncements about supporting "a woman's right to reproductive freedom." They don't tell the rank-and-file that they sent every member of the U.S. Senate a telegram which stated: "ON BEHALF OF NEA'S 1.7 MILLION MEMBERS, I URGE YOU TO OPPOSE S.J. RES. 3, A CONSTITUTIONAL AMENDMENT TO BAN ABORTIONS."

The NEA says teachers are bullish on busing. Wrong. Nearly 70 per cent of its members, as well as all teachers in general, oppose "forced busing to achieve racial balance in the schools."

NEA Backs, Members Oppose 'Gay Rights'

The NEA similarly takes an aggressive stand in favor of "gay rights." But a plurality of its members, and of all teachers, opposes this concept. And by an overwhelming 69 to 27 per cent margin, its members oppose the use of NEA dues to support gay rights.

The same pattern holds on other issues. NEA opposes allowing public schools to teach the biblical account of creation. But 60 per cent of its members favor allowing such teaching. NEA has also opposed U.S. support for the Contras in Nicaragua, but its members, by more than 2 to 1, oppose the use of NEA funds to lobby on the issue.

In typical form, NEA President Mary Hatwood Futrell dismissed the poll, claiming "she was not at all surprised by [Sally Reed's] latest attack."

As always, their strategy in such cases is consistent: If you don't like the message, attack the messenger.

The fact remains that the NEA union hierarchy is out of sync with teachers, with parents, and with tax-payers in general. And we believe that's wrong.

The obvious question this raises is: How has the NEA been able to run roughshod over the American school teacher? At least three important factors have contributed.

First, NEA policy is determined for the most part by a nine-member group of union leaders known as the Executive Committee, who represent not the rank-and-file teachers but the vocal, politically minded minority.

Second, most teachers are apolitical by nature, and the NEA leaders take full advantage of this fact. The same small number of people, almost invariably liberal activists, tend to run as delegates for the national convention year after year. The roughly 7,000 persons who attended the most recent convention comprised less than 0.5 per cent of the organization's total membership.

Small Group Adopts Controversial Resolutions

It is this small group that adopts the controversial resolutions that the NEA leadership passes off as reflecting the views of the entire membership. Before resolutions go to the convention floor for a vote, however, they must first be approved by an even more select group, the resolutions committee, which comprises less than 2 per cent of the convention delegates.

The delegates, who are not representative of the NEA'a broad membership, are usually reduced to voting *en bloc* for the resolutions approved in advance by the resolutions committee, whose membership tends to be even less representative of the NEA constituency.

The poll shows that most teachers do not join NEA for its political views. If they aren't forced to join or pressured into joining, teachers become members of the NEA to get benefit packages or buy low-cost group insurance, or for the promise of wage increases—a topic of considerable NEA hype.

Then, there is the coercion factor. NEA union officials claim that there is no compulsion to join, but the "agency shop" clause requires teachers in many states to pay a fee comparable to the dues paid *by union members* for the "privilege" of having the NEA bargain their rights for them. This is an old union tactic, which the NEA has learned to use to great advantage, and this helps to fund—and give weight to—its political agenda.

Another former member of NEA's executive staff, John Lloyd, told readers in an interview with the *Heritage Foundation's Education Update* (December 1984): "NEA does everything it can to squelch dissension. They consider it heresy to question within the organization."

Why Does NEA Misrepresent Teachers?

Why does the NEA still force teachers to join the organization, and then turn around and misrepresent them? The best answer, perhaps, is found in the words of the NEA faithful: past and present leaders who wield the most influence inside and outside the organization.

Stated Terry Herndon, NEA's outspoken executive director of 1980: "We want leaders and staff with sufficient clout that they may roam the halls of Congress and collect votes to re-order the priorities of the United States of America."

Other NEA voices echo in chorus:

George Fisher, 1970 NEA president, claimed that the union intends to control "who enters, who stays, and who leaves the profession. Once this is done, we can also control the teacher training institutions."

NEA President Helen Wise continued in 1974 with a goal "to reverse the national leadership in Washington . . . to build NEA's force over the next two years to the point where the presidential candidates will seek NEA endorsement."

Other than elect the President and "reorder the priorities of the United States," what do NEA union leaders really want?

Most apparent is the goal of total control over the nation's educating process, public and private.

Well, maybe public schools, you say—but private schools?

Resolutions F-1 and F-2 of the 1984-85 NEA Legislative Agenda call not only for the autonomy of teachers and control of the credentialing and accreditation processes, but also for the centralization of curriculum. But the NEA doesn't stop there.

In its Resolution S-1, the NEA eyes the credentialing and accreditation processes for "nonpublic school personnel"; in Resolution C-51, it calls for "immediate steps to become involved in college and university committees that control teacher education programs" with a view to ensuring that all prospective teachers are enrolled "in the NEA Student Program before participation in pre-professional experiences and student teaching." The resolution also states that "advisers of the NEA Student Program would be Association members."

So where would private school teachers get their training?

You guessed it: At the feet of the NEA.

NEA Goal: A Single Teachers' Union

Further on, under "New Business," the NEA president is authorized "to enter into discussions regarding the establishment of A SINGLE NATIONAL ORGANIZATION." This, coupled with Resolution I-2, would edge out any competing teacher associations.

These resolutions encompass all phases of the educating process—credentialing, accreditation, teacher preparation programs, inservice education—and would place them under the policymaking control of a centralized, nongovernment agency, which, of course, is to be the NEA.

Hence there would be no means for a teaching strategy or curriculum different from those endorsed by the NEA to find a way into either the teacher training institutions, which turn out public *and* private school teachers, or the public school classrooms themselves.

Circumvention of Parents and Communities

A second NEA goal seems to be to circumvent parents and local communities; specifically, to get children away from the influence of parents and under the influence of "trained professionals."

NEA's Resolution E-36 is perhaps the most significant of the entire 57-page legislative agenda: "The National Educational Association believes that communications between certified personnel and students must be legally privileged. It urges its affiliates to aid in seeking legislation that provides this privilege and protects both educators and students." Needless to say, this would legally bypass the parents in all communications between students and teachers, students and guidance counselors, students and school psychiatrists, or any other "certified personnel."

So just whom are students being "protected" from? Why, their parents!

The third, and, it would seem, the ultimate, goal of the NEA is the shaping of a "perfect" society—the primary vehicle of change being teachers who are trained to break down so-called outmoded ideas and patterns of behavior in favor of what the NEA considers more viable alternatives. This is being accomplished through a carefully structured program of what NEA literature terms "confluent education," which is described in the NEA publication *Values Education* as "rooted in the approaches and techniques of humanistic psychology and the human potential movement applied to education."

Other NEA publications outline a veritable compendium of values clarification/behavior modification strategies, most of which have little to do with intellectual learning or subject matter, and which are over and over referenced as humanistic learning strategies.

This, perhaps, would not be particularly alarming in itself—unless one happens to take a look at the two Manifestos, which declare bluntly that there is "no divine purpose or providence for the human species," that "traditional theism . . . is an unproved and outmoded faith" and that "religious institutions, their ritualistic forms, ecclesiastical methods . . . must be reconstituted as rapidly as experience allows."

The documents go on to belittle our form of government, to denounce competition and free enterprise as self-serving and responsible for the sort of intense nationalism that produced the Holocaust. They go on to explain how traditional religions, including the Judeo-Christian faith, have been an "obstacle to human progress."

The crux of the matter is this: The NEA has consolidated its gain tremendously in the past 15 years. It is a classic example of the public servants having become the public's masters.

Two years ago I established the National Council for Better Education—a group that would, hopefully, lead the charge in the reform of our public education system.

But every time I ran into a serious impediment to quality education and started to research its origin, I turned up the same answer: the NEA.

Over the years, the NEA has consistently opposed every constructive attempt to improve the educating process and it is still doing so. It has promoted programs and teaching strategies which are damaging to young learners; it has helped to structure and promote courses which undermine our form of government and pander to the enemies of freedom.

It has initiated policies which, in the end, have demoralized teachers, made their jobs more difficult, and compromised the legitimate needs of all educators.

It has helped to undermine parental authority, and thus the family unit; it has portrayed itself as representative of teacher views when such is not the case.

In short, the NEA has betrayed the public trust, and in the process created a negative attitude toward public school teachers and public education.

The NEA stranglehold on the public schools must be broken before any substantial reform can take place. This is why I commissioned the poll: to expose this insidious organization for what it is—the primary vehicle of the radical left to gain control of the American political process through its teachers.

The Case against Bilingual Education

By Howard Hurwitz   *(From the 4 January 1986 issue)*

(Dr. Hurwitz was appointed to the National Advisory Council on Bilingual Education, on the recommendation of President Reagan, in September 1984. He was reappointed by Education Secretary William Bennett. The views expressed in this article are his own and not that of the Council.)

The fallout following Education Secretary William J. Bennett's estimate of bilingual education as "a failure," after 20 years of federal intervention, is continuing. It is perceived as contamination of the turf carved out by Hispanic militants in the new Bilingual Education Act of 1984.

The language of the Act is sharp and to the point. Congress passed—and the President signed on Oct. 19, 1984—a law that fastens bilingual education on our schools with the tenacity of a rabbit trap. We are a nation of rabbits if we let a handful of self-serving Hispanic militants, who by no means speak for the diverse Hispanic community, capture our schools.

The Act states "that a primary means by which a child learns is through the use of such child's native language and cultural heritage; that, therefore, large numbers of children of limited English proficiency have educational needs which can be met by the use of bilingual education methods and techniques. . . ."

Anticipating that a secretary of education might somehow contrive to advance President Reagan's stated objective—use of English, not a foreign language—for instruction in subjects, the Act tightens the trap. "The Secretary shall not prescribe . . . any regulations further defining the terms defined . . . or any regulations restricting or expanding the definitions contained. . . ."

The Act is a political statement as far removed from the education interests of minority language students as Mars from Earth. From the first it was seen by militant, well-organized Hispanics (almost exclusively Puerto Rican and Mexican—*not* South American) as serving special purposes.

The effect of perpetuating Spanish language and culture through our schools is seen as insurance that politicians of Hispanic background will retain and expand their representation in areas where there are concentrations of voters of Hispanic origin. Atop the list of such enclaves are New York, Miami, southwestern Texas and southern California.

A dividend derived from the imposition of Spanish as the language of instruction for many years during a child's school life is the employment of Spanish-speaking teachers who might not otherwise have gained entry into school jobs.

Secretary Bennett's "media-hyped speech" (so styled by the bilingualists) to the Association for a Better New York, on September 26, was the occasion for catapulting Bennett to the top of the militant Hispanic hit list. An attorney for the National Association for Bilingual Education, James J. Lyons, was "shocked by the vehemence of the Secretary's attack" (Education Week, October 23). Lyons roared: "Since taking office, Mr. Bennett has traveled widely and talked loosely. . . . At best he is mixed up; at worst, he is malicious."

Lyons appeared before the National Advisory Council on Bilingual Education (NACBE) shortly after PL 98-511 (the new Bilingual Education Act) was enacted. "I wrote the law," he stated smugly to NACBE, meeting at the Department of Education.

Lyons, a lawyer, not an educator, is contemptuous of any alternative to the bilingual-bicultural education he espouses on behalf of his client. He assumed an air of indignation when he remarked that teachers of English-as-a-Second Language (ESL) "often fail to teach anything but English!"

Drawing upon a well of ignorance of methodology, Lyons states: "Prior to enactment of the federal Bilingual Education Act of 1968, language minority students who didn't know English were universally ignored."

The fact is that ESL has been used effectively as a means of teaching minority language students for a half-century. Curriculums are as detailed as for any subject, and teacher certification in ESL is required in almost all states.

My personal experience as an organizer of ESL classes extends over 30 years. I carried on with existing ESL classes (they existed before my arrival) at Seward Park High School (N.Y.), 1949-55. We taught hundreds of minority youths, mostly Chinese, many of whom emerged from ESL classes to participate in my history classes.

I never knew of a minority youngster who did not enter regular classes within a year and a half of starting the program.

At Seward and other schools, there were basic, intermediate and advanced ESL sections. It was easy to move them forward because we set up parallel classes permitting movement from group to group without upsetting the rest of the student's program.

Minority language students were programmed for three 40-minute periods a day. During other periods in an eight-period day, the foreign students were programmed for physical education, music, art, homemaking, typewriting and lunch. Some students were programmed for mathematics, since the language requirement is less than in history or science.

Of the 150,000 students now served in bilingual programs, Spanish is by far the predominant language of instruction. Dwarfed by Spanish are over a hundred different language minority populations funded by the Department of Education (ED). These include Vietnamese, Lao, Chinese, Hmong, French, Navajo, Haitian Creole, Arabic, Italian, Lakota, Portuguese, Cherokee, Russian, Zuni and Crow.

The Hispanic militants have dragooned other minorities into the bilingual program in the hope of moderating the sting that would be felt if the program were exclusively Spanish. So intense has their manipulation been that Indian tribes with no written language are now seeking federal funds to create a written language where none ever existed. Tribal kids will then be taught in their native language and tribal culture can be reinforced.

When I was principal of Long Island City High School (N.Y.), 1966-78, ESL was the method we used to teach minority language students from 40 countries.

Not surprisingly, we learned quickly that many of the minority youngsters read, wrote and spoke poorly in their native languages. The classes for natives were geared to improve basic skills in their native languages. It is most desirable for youngsters to retain fluency in two or more languages; but the primary mission with minority language children is to teach them English as quickly as possible.

Lyons, who spits when he utters "ESL," would have us believe that the Act "gives parents the right to decline placement of their children" in bilingual-bicultural programs. This is as close to reality as Mars to Earth. School authorities are awesome to minority parents who have no fluency in English.

The bilingual mandate is now a matter of law for the first time in the history of the 1968 Act, amended in 1974 and 1978, prior to the final coup in 1984. It was the eve of the 1984 election when PL 98-511 reached the President's desk. The night before, I received a telephone call from the Office of White House Personnel. I was asked to dictate over the phone a memorandum intended to dissuade the President from signing the bill.

At least two other NACBE members were called upon for such memos. The three of us have since been denounced in the pro-bilingual news releases as lacking "objectivity" and, therefore, undeserving of continued service on an Education Department (ED) advisory council.

Lyons, seeking to plug any loophole through which an alternative to bilingual education might be drawn, included in the Act a provision to increase the number of Council members to 20.

Since White House Personnel winnows applicants for advisory councils, the Lyons paws got clipped. I do not discern any remarkable change in the new Council's interest in new directions. Secretary Bennett, incidentally, reappointed me for a one-year (not three-year) term. The colleagues who most closely share my viewpoint have been appointed for three-year terms.

Bennett is now in the position of seeking to accomplish the President's objectives within the existing law. He has about the same chance of moving ESL to a position of equality with bilingual education as a pygmy of playing pro basketball.

As though the financial and legal restraints in the Act were not enough, Lori Orum of the National Council of La Raza, a Hispanic advocacy organization, warned: "Any school district has to be careful before going down the garden path with Mr. Bennett," because it will be struck instantly with a lawsuit if it seeks to curtail its bilingual-bicultural programs.

The pro-bilingual contingent has been assiduous and dishonest in its promotion of the program. From the first it has knowingly perverted the intent of the U.S. Supreme Court in *Lau v. Nichols* (414 U.S. 563, 1974). *Lau* was seized upon by bilingual fanatics as mandating instruction in the student's native language. Nothing could be further from the truth, or the intent of the justices.

The justices stated: "Teaching English to the students of Chinese ancestry who do not speak the language is one choice. Giving instructions to this group in Chinese is another. There may be others." The Court declined to impose its views on how minority language students might best be taught English.

When the Bilingual Act was first passed in 1968, the Congress had the simple but sound idea that it would be good to encourage acquisition of English by minority students. The stated goal of Title VII of the Elementary and Secondary Education Act of 1965 is to provide remedial instruction in English.

But, as Rep. James Scheuer (D.-N.Y.) noted during the debate on the Simpson-Mazzoli immigration bill, on June 19, 1984, ". . . its original purposes were perverted and politicized. I was an original sponsor of the Bilingual Education Act," the congressman recalled, "and history is perfectly clear—it was intended to be a pressure cooker exposure for the kids to learn English from foreign language homes."

As it turned out, the design of the pressure cooker has kept Spanish-surnamed—and not necessarily minority language children—under intense pressure to reinforce their native language and cultural heritage for as many as seven years.

The stranglehold sought by bilingualists has not gone unnoticed in the past decade. Former Secretary T.H. Bell sought, without the loud blast of Bennett, to undo quietly the bilingual knot tying Spanish-speaking kids to an unproved methodology.

In 1983, Bell transmitted to Congress amendments to the Bilingual Education Act. They would have broadened the range of instructional approaches. The proposals never saw the light of day. Earlier, Bell had sought to ease the Education Department's requirement that school districts institute bilingual programs. He got nowhere, and even this starting block was shattered by PL 98-511.

Although the controversy-soaked field seems to be covered by the Hispanic-manufactured tarpaulin, rain may yet penetrate to the grassroots. In recent years, several courts have indicated that bilingual education is not the only acceptable method of instruction.

In Colorado, the legislature passed the English Language Proficiency Act. This new legislation significantly increased the local option which permits flexibility in choosing the most appropriate educational method for serving minority language students.

In Rhode Island, where I testified as an "expert witness" before a legislative committee, there is now a law similar to that passed in Colorado.

Virginia has declared English the official language and went on to say "school boards shall have no obligation to teach the standard curriculum in a language other than English."

In the private sector, there is "U.S. English," an organization founded by former Sen. S. I. Hayakawa. It seeks passage of an amendment to the Constitution making English the official language in the United States.

Under-Secretary Gary L. Bauer said, shortly after Bennett's address that the Education Department would seek "to broaden the definition" of bilingual education to give districts more leeway in the amount of native-language instruction they provide limited English proficient (LEP) students. Soon thereafter, Bauer acknowledged, "My use of the word 'definition' might have been ill-phrased." He added that ED would obey the law and publicize other ways in which districts can perhaps lessen the amount of native-language instruction provided to LEP students.

In November 1985, Bennett announced that ED's Office for Civil Rights would offer some 400 school districts the opportunity of renegotiating agreements on bilingual education. This is by way of saying that federal funds will not be withdrawn if the districts show a new interest in alternative methods of instruction.

Tinkering with the Bilingual Education Act is, in my opinion, worthless. There is no longer any need, if indeed there ever was one, of federal intervention to teach English to minority language children.

Any school district that does not have the know-how by now should be closed down. Therefore, the time is now to abolish the Office of Bilingual Education and Minority Affairs (OBEMLA).

Bilingualists contend that the number of Hispanic-American youths who should be in bilingual programs is far greater than the present federal budget can accommodate. The current $170-million budget is regarded as grossly inadequate. The fact is that at no time has the OBEMLA budget paid more than a small fraction of the total cost of teaching English to minority language children. Nevertheless, school districts grasp at the federal bucks with the desperation of a drowning man reaching for a log.

The effect of total withdrawal of the feds from funding and guiding bilingual education will be to leave the problem with the states and school districts where it belongs.

This is the broad approach of the Reagan Administration to federal-state relations. State and local responsibility for education was once unquestioned. There is no provision for education in the Constitution. It is not mentioned. Education is left to the states, where it belongs.

Repeal of the Bilingual Education Act of 1984 should be a Bennett-led Administration goal. There can be no compromising with Hispanic militants whose political program would be ditched by meddling with their supreme creation.

Let the feds get out of bilingual ed once and for all. This would be one small step forward on a scarred moonscape.

Evolution: A Theory in Crisis

By M. Stanton Evans   *(From the 24 May 1986 issue)*

The recent decision of the U.S. Supreme Court to accept arguments on the Louisiana "creation science" case could prove to be a watershed event in the constitutional history of the United States, and in the intellectual history of the West.

At issue is a Louisiana statute requiring balanced treatment of Darwinian evolution and creationism in public school instruction on the origin and development of life. The law was overturned by a federal appeals court on the grounds that mandating creation-science if evolution is also taught is an intrusion of religion in the classroom. ". . . The act's intended effect," the court asserts, "is to discredit evolution by counterbalancing its teaching at every turn with the teaching of creation, a religious belief. The First Amendment . . . demands that no law be enacted favoring any religious belief or doctrine."

If permitted to stand, this decision would plant in legal concrete the current pervasive practice in the public schools: Darwinian evolution would be taught exclusively, on the grounds that it is "science." Creationism would be prohibited. The first is allegedly a matter of fact and evidence, thus permitted; the second a matter of faith and dogma, hence verboten.

Attorneys for Louisiana have argued against this view by marshaling data to show the scientific nature of the creationist position. Such teaching, they contend, can be conducted without reference to any species of religion. It is simply a matter of reviewing the evidence that the world, organic life and individual species came into being in a series of distinct, abrupt departures, rather than through the gradual, interconnected transitions beloved of Darwin and his adherents.

Another way of looking at the matter is to turn the argument around, examining the widespread belief—implicit in the appellate court decision—that Darwinian evolution is hard-nosed "science," as opposed to the gossamer speculations of religion. In point of fact, Darwinian evolution is in many respects the very antithesis of science. Its proponents hang on to the theory, not because of the available evidence, but in spite of it.

The extent to which this is now recognized to be the case is one of the most amazing, but least noticed, stories of our time. The factual record, the laws of probability and the recent trend of scientific discovery have been hostile to the Darwinian dogma—so much so that scholars as diverse as Fred Hoyle, Francis Crick and Stephen Jay Gould have felt compelled to abandon it.

The relevant data have been assembled in a remarkable new volume entitled *Evolution: A Theory in Crisis*, originally published in England and now available in the United States (Adler & Adler, Bethesda, Md.). The author is Dr. Michael Denton, a molecular biologist who approaches the subject strictly from a scientific, not a religious, standpoint. His conclusion is that the intellectual underpinnings of Darwinism have long since eroded away into oblivion.

Darwinian theory assumes that the universe and the life forms in it came into being through the workings of chance, with different species having arisen through an endless sequence of mutations conserved by "natural selection." By this random process, supposedly, life somehow arose from a "pre-biotic soup," then evolved upward from primitive to complicated versions, all linked together by a countless host of transitional species.

Reviewing evidence from paleontology, zoology, cladistics (the science of classifying species), genetics, and his own specialty of molecular biology, Denton argues that there is hardly an aspect of the Darwinian theory that is immune from devastating challenge:

1. First and foremost, in Denton's presentation, is the total absence of the "transitional forms" that would have had to exist in unimaginable profusion if the Darwinian theory were correct. There is virtually no sign of such transitions in the fossil record. Darwin himself was sensible to the problem, but thought that further examination in the years to come would bear him out. It hasn't.

2. A related point, affirmed by cladistics and by molecular biology, is the fundamental *discontinuity* among different forms of life. None appears to be a "transition" to another, but is very much itself, adapted precisely to its place and function. The mounting evidence on this score, Denton says, at most reveals "species to be related as sisters or cousins, but never as ancestors and descendants as required by evolution."

3. Quite apart from this evidence, Darwinians confront an insuperable difficulty in the very idea of "transitional forms" leading up to, say, the wing of a bird or the complex structure of the eye. Such an organ, once in existence, is exactly suited to its function, and integral to the adaptation of the bird or human being. But a "transitional" form of the organ, short of the completed version, would be of little value, and arguably would be a handicap.

4. Of all the discontinuities in nature, none is more profound than the gap between living and non-living matter, and that gap is even bigger than was once supposed. Current evolutionary theory presupposes that life somehow arose from the "soup" as energy from the sun, or someplace, forged a link between inorganic matter and primitive life forms. The problem with this view, as Denton explains at length, is that even the simplest life form is dauntingly complex, replete with all the awesome machinery of genetic coding, replication, transmission and storage of information, etc.

5. Underlying all of this is the fundamental incredibility of the notion that the universe, the multifarious distinctive organisms, and the mind-boggling complexity and sophistication of all living structures could have arisen purely through the random workings of chance, occurring not merely once but billions of times in the most fortuitous manner possible. Denton spells out the truly colossal mathematical odds against this, meaning belief in it is not a matter or rational deduction, but the reverse—a giant leap of evolutionist faith.

This is the merest inadequate summary of Denton's book, which deserves not only to be read as widely as possible, but to be pondered at length. What it tells us is that support of evolution is itself a species of religion, founded on the will to believe in Darwin. And if that be so, why should it be given pride of place in our nation's schools as "science"?

How to Make Sure Your Children Learn the Three R's

By J'Aime Adams   *(From the 27 September 1986 issue)*

"Never talk about education at a dinner party," a friend of mine insists. "You may talk about religion and politics, but never talk about education. It is a black hole. Everyone gets depressed when the subject is broached."

A slight exaggeration, perhaps, but a person would have to be blind not to realize that the public's perception of education is one of an institution in trouble.

For parents who want the best for their children and are dismayed by all that they are hearing or for the parents whose child is having great difficulty in school, there is little advice other than to take your child to the library, read to him, limit television, provide a learning atmosphere in the home and work closely with your school. None of this is wrong, of course, but neither is it very specific.

Very few parents know what to look for in a school, most lack confidence in assessing their child's work and nearly all parents feel that they are at a distinct disadvantage when questioning anything that goes on at school. All the talk about "working with your school" is just persiflage. The school holds all the cards.

On the basis of nearly 15 years of both classroom teaching and private tutoring, it is my belief that there are some very specific characteristics young children evidence while learning to read and write and that there are specific teaching techniques which work that both teachers and parents should know.

Generally, this article pertains to the elementary years, particularly first, second, and third grades and it contains much of the advice I have given parents over the years.

It is in these early years that patterns for the entire 12 years of schooling are set and it is my hope that this article will help parents evaluate what their children are getting in school and will equip them to work with their children more confidently at home if they feel there is a need to do so.

Before going into specifics of reading, writing and arithmetic, however, there are some facts parents should understand about good schools.

One of the most important characteristics of a good school is a quiet, dignified, daily routine. Beware of schools, public or private, where there is a big change in faculty or procedures every year.

It takes a good principal and a long time to develop a like-minded faculty that works together.

It takes all new teachers a year or two *at minimum* to settle into a program, to learn little tricks of classroom organization and discipline, to learn the most effective way to present material and to build up files for supplementing the curriculum.

Parents must understand that if the faculty is constantly changing, there is no possible way that the individual child's progress can be correctly monitored from year to year and his weaknesses addressed. *In this kind of changing atmosphere no school official is qualified to make informed assessments of a child's abilities.*

Secondly, it is not a good thing to be changing textbooks repeatedly. No textbook series is perfect. As the faculty uses a series, it learns the system's weaknesses and makes additions and adjustments in the curriculum. Again, this is a process that takes several years.

"Classroom enrichment"–a wonderfully impressive phrase–is another way in which orderly routine may be disrupted. Enrichment can mean almost anything–field trips, special speakers, role playing, cooking projects, films, etc. Parents should not be fooled by schools or teachers that boast of many enrichment projects.

Remember that on the elementary level, the purpose of school is to learn reading, writing and arithmetic. Those subjects are learned by practicing and doing them a lot. When your child is baking cookies in class, he may be having fun, but he is not learning to read.

American children today—even poor ones—are "enriched" to death. Nearly 16 years ago I was involved in a tutoring project for very poor black children. A District of Columbia social worker was head of the project and she gave us middle-class, do-gooder, white tutors some tough advice:

"Stick to reading and writing. You'll find these kids have been on every field trip imaginable—the zoo, the White House, the aquarium, the Children's Farm. They've had train rides, plane rides, horseback rides; they've been taken to the circus and to baseball games. If you really want to help them, just stick to reading and writing."

Young children get very excited by classroom interruptions and it takes time to calm them and get them back to work after extraordinary activities. Field trips and other such changes in routine should be used very sparingly, and should have specific relevance to subjects currently being studied.

Parents should also be aware of the fact that classroom discipline is much more difficult than it was 30 years ago. The media have covered well enough the drug problems that plague our high schools, but there are problems on the elementary level which, because they appear minor compared to drugs, get no attention.

A surprising number of children *of all classes* simply do not obey adults very well any more. It is often necessary to ask a child several times to do something before he complies. The child who has *formed the habit* of saying "please" and "thank you" is an oddity. A mother recently told me that her boys had been ridiculed in school for saying, "Yes ma'm" to the teacher."

It takes only one or two young trolls in the classroom to make even the experienced teacher's job very difficult. Time taken to settle little Attila and Genghis down is time taken away from teaching other children.

As families break up and more women enter the work force for various reasons, leaving children with baby-sitters and day-care centers, we can expect more students in the classroom whose behavior is not up to the standard needed to insure that public institutions will work smoothly. Manners and behavior, unfortunately for the schools, are taught best at home.

Educational problems cut across economic lines. Rich and poor children alike have difficulties these days. Because of these kinds of conditions outlined above, parents ought to involve themselves in their children's education and should take nothing for granted.

This is one reason I hope the burgeoning home schooling movement is allowed to flourish. For parents who can't afford private schooling or expensive tutors or who find that no progress is being made "working with the school," home schooling may be the only means of escaping a chaotic situation.

Reading

Most everyone concedes that children should learn to read by the phonetic method. This means that the child is taught that each letter or particular combination of letters represents a specific sound. In spite of the general agreement about phonics, however, most of the standard textbooks in use today still contain heavy doses of the so-called "look-say" approach. Open Court and Lippincott reading systems are two honorable exceptions.

While phonics is probably the single most important tool for learning to read, it is not an end in itself. Once a child knows the sounds of the letters, he can decipher most any word, *but he must be able, as well, to read smoothly and quickly enough for reading to become pleasurable, and this can only be accomplished by practice.*

Some few children—girls more often than boys—can read a story one time and remember every word thereafter; other children may need to read the story twice or three times or more before new words are imprinted on the visual memory and can be recalled at sight. In my own teaching I have always tried to make this point very clear to parents.

I tell them that when I am dissatisfied with the speed and ease with which a child reads any story, I will send the textbook home and expect the parents to let the child reread the story out loud a number of times until he gains a good pace. I have found parents cooperative and, in fact, overjoyed at being given a specific way in which to help their child.

At any rate, it is important to remember that for the beginning reader phonetics and speed-through-practice are the *twin* pillars of success. If the child reads too slowly, he loses the train of thought and reading becomes drudgery.

Perhaps this is the place to comment on an abysmal policy which exists in some schools and that is the policy of not allowing children to take their readers home. Reasons for this outrage on the part of the school system range from suggestions that parents and children are too irresponsible to bring the books back each day to fears that if parents work with children they may get ahead of their peers. I have heard both reasons.

The solution for the first excuse is easy enough. The schools should allow the parents to buy the books or rent them and there should always be a few extra copies of the texts in every class in case a child does forget his book. The second objection is mind-boggling. Why would any school object to a parent's helping his child move ahead? It merely takes responsibility and burden off the teacher and the school.

In discussing the pace at which children read, another important pedagogical principle comes to mind—the importance of daily *oral* reading for the beginning reader or the older child who is a poor reader.

The old "round-robin" method of reading which enabled the teacher to hear every child read out loud nearly every day has fallen into disrepute. Supposedly, the experts told us, round-robin was boring and oral reading inhibited comprehension, and so gradually even first-grade children were expected to do a good bit of silent reading.

Now the pendulum is perhaps beginning to swing backward, for no less an authority on reading than Harvard's Jeanne Chall has suggested that beginning silent reading too early may be a serious mistake (*Psychology Today*, February 1984).

Of course, the ultimate goal is for children to be able to read silently, but they must not be left to do a great deal of silent reading until it is certain they are reading correctly; otherwise, they will simply be practicing their errors.

It is my belief that elementary classes ought to be structured to give the teacher a large block of uninterrupted time and a small enough group so that she can realistically plan to hear most of the children read every day.

(I disagree with those critics of the school system who say that teachers' demands for small classes are just a way of creating jobs. *Individual attention goes up as the class size goes down and that is a fact.* Besides, another point which is important to consider is that children of all economic classes are nowhere near as well disciplined as they were 30 or 40 years ago and teachers have to work harder at maintaining order.)

But at all costs, if the parents suspect that the child is not reading orally every day and that no one is watching his pace, *it is imperative that he read at home to his parents.* (See box on "Tips for Working With a Beginning Reader or an Older Child Who Reads Poorly.")

Writing

It is the lack of daily monitoring in the primary grades which creates and perpetuates one of the most common "learning disabilities"—namely, the tendency for some children to print and read words backwards.

It is my observation that nearly every beginning reader reverses letters and numbers occasionally and left-handed children do it a great deal. To be sure, there are always a couple of practically perfect Mary Poppinses in every class who never make this kind of mistake, but most children do. The great majority of children who do this are evidencing not a "perceptual handicap" but rather a lack of experience in dealing with written language.

Why, then, do children write backwards? When a child begins to learn the alphabet and to print for the first time, he has no firmly fixed feeling for moving from left to right. If a child draws a dog, he may draw it facing left or facing right, but it is still a dog. A child approaches printing his letters the same way; it is still an "E" whether it faces left or right.

It is the job of the first-grade teachers to know this characteristic of little children and to make certain that no one is allowed to slip into the habit of reversing.

To accomplish this, the teacher must emphasize constantly the importance of left-to-right progression; she must make certain that every written assignment starts at the left side of the page. (Left-handed children frequently want to start on the right side of the page and move left.)

As the children write, the teacher must do a lot of walking among the desks—particularly in order to watch for any problems with the left-to-right progression. *She must never allow any reversal to go uncorrected.* That is a very important part of her job, for if a student is allowed to make these kinds of mistakes over and over without redoing them, by the end of the first grade a very bad habit will have been deeply imbedded.

On this point, a note of admonition to parents: If a child is bringing home papers with reversals on them, the parents must go over the papers and have the child correct the errors at home. It is also important to keep tabs on any work a child may be doing in a workbook at school to make certain his reversals are being corrected there as well.

The foundation for composition should be laid as soon as children begin to read words. Whatever a child is reading—even simple primary sentences—he should be writing on notebook paper as well. For the elementary-age child, composition hastens the acquisition of a sight vocabulary; it imprints spelling patterns on the memory; it is a superb reinforcement for the child who gets off to a slow start or for the older child who reads poorly; and more than any other activity done in school, it disciplines the mind and helps students to think.

The acquisition of a good writing foundation is severely hampered in elementary school by the overuse of workbooks and mimeographed pages. In the workbooks children are asked to circle the answer, fill in the missing word, select the correct answer from a choice of three, but rarely are they asked to read material, formulate an answer, and put it on paper.

Consider the following shocking statistic from *What Works*, a pamphlet released this year by the U.S. Department of Education:

"Just 5 per cent of students at age 17 have advanced reading skills and strategies that enable them to synthesize and restructure ideas. . . ."

Amidst all the circling, underlining, and filling-in, the child never gets the opportunity to "restructure" ideas on paper. American children cannot do this because for the most part they are never asked to.

If the schools pitched out the workbooks and embarked on a simple routine of answering questions in complete sentences about the material read or discussed in class, increasing the difficulty and sophistication of the assignments as the reading ability grows, we would have students in high school who were prepared for advanced work.

Another problem with workbooks is that they prevent students from forming the mechanical writing habits they should because everything is done for the student.

Youngsters just don't do enough work on notebook paper for good habits to be formed. Workbooks and mimeographed papers also prevent a feeling of routine in the classroom, the importance of which was discussed earlier in this article. Routine is very comforting for all of us and particularly for children, but take almost any first-grade workbook that goes along with the reading text and one will find that the child is frequently given something different to do other than writing nearly every day.

Monday he draws lines from pictures to words; Tuesday he fills in blanks; Wednesday he puts rhyming words in a list; Thursday he circles all the words that begin with the *sh* sound, which are sprinkled all over the page in odd positions (just dandy for learning left-to-right progression); Friday he draws a picture to show he understands the sentence.

How can a child feel he is gaining mastery of the writing process if his task is changing every day?

There is a strange idea that infects reading and writing pedagogy today and it is this: Children learn to read and write by studying cooking, cutting, pasting, role-playing and drawing. In every other area of achievement children are plunged into the task to be mastered.

If we want a child to swim, we put him in the water; if we want a pianist, we put the child on the keyboard. Only in writing do we teach something other than what we want the child to learn.

Teaching writing is very simple. On the first day children enter school, they should be given notebook paper on which they write their letters as they learn them, then words, then short dictated sentences, then longer sentences.

The writing tasks grow incrementally through the grades as the reading ability grows. But always the essence of teaching writing is facing the empty page and putting something on it.

For parents who realize that their children are not getting writing at school and who may want to work at home, there are several exercises that are very profitable if they are done every day.

Some good tasks for children are to have them read a story or passage and summarize it in their own words or answer questions on the material. Complete sentences should be insisted upon because at a very young age children can develop an ear for hearing whether a sentence is complete or not.

Another technique—an ancient one—is to have the child copy a short passage every day. It doesn't really matter what is copied (as long as the child isn't crucified with something dreadfully long). It could be a poem, a joke or any other item of interest to the child.

I have seen children with very low reading ability who were helped dramatically by means of these two techniques used on a daily basis. A colleague of mine also suggests that old-fashioned letter writing—virtually a lost art these days—is a pleasurable way to get children to write.

Mathematics

The foundation for success in arithmetic for the elementary student is the speed with which he can recall the answers to the addition, subtraction, multiplication and division tables, and the earlier the child can achieve memorization of the tables the better.

When "Johnny" is asked what 9 x 6 is and it takes him 15 seconds to come up with 54, he does not know his tables well enough. He should be able to give the answer instantly.

Without exception, every math teacher with whom I have spoken has pinpointed poor knowledge of the tables as the big problem for children not doing well.

Conversely, a child of average mathematical ability who does know the tables will be able to turn in a solid performance, working quickly and correctly, while the child with exceptional ability will be freed to progress in quantum jumps.

All this may seem obvious, but, in fact, a great number of students go through school never knowing the math facts very well. These days the problem is compounded by the increased use of calculators in elementary classes. Dr. Richard Berg, professor of physics at the University of Maryland, decries the use of calculators and computers before students have mastered the fundamentals of mathematics:

"We are getting kids on the college level who have grown up with calculators and computers and they don't catch crazy mistakes in simple arithmetic because they are used to letting the calculator do their thinking for them."

An interesting story was told to me by a teacher who helped organize a program in Fairfax County, Virginia, for children with high I.Q.'s. She knew a boy who was extraordinarily precocious in mathematics. After numerous conferences and interviews at several universities with prestigious math faculties, it was arranged for the boy to be privately tutored by one of the country's top mathematicians.

Much to everyone's amazement, the boy was required to do a great deal of elementary arithmetic right along with his advanced work. The professor's explanation was that he wanted the number relationships to be second nature to the boy and that only came from constant exercising of the memory through practice.

The majority of math textbooks are set up in such a way that the learning of the tables is dragged out for four years. The majority of first-grade math books do not go past adding and subtracting numbers up to 10. The second-grade books continue with adding and subtracting up to 20. Borrowing and carrying—depending on the text being used—frequently are not introduced until late second grade.

Then the whole slow, two-year process starts again in the third and fourth grade for the multiplication and division tables. In truth, most children can easily master all the addition and subtraction tables by the end of the first grade and all the multiplication tables by the end of the second *if that is the goal that the school sets for itself.*

I found in my classroom teaching that the textbooks designed for kindergarten and first grade moved at much too slow a pace.

In my private tutoring, we start five- and six-year-olds memorizing the addition and subtraction tables as soon as they can count correctly and identify numbers up to 20. We have consistently found that as soon as the child has picked up a little reading as well, we can by-pass the first and second-grade math books—since all they do is teach the addition and subtraction facts to 20—and start the students in a third-grade book.

There are all kinds of teaching aids for learning the tables on the market now, including old-fashioned flash cards. Anything that works is fine. If you have access to a duplicator machine, you might find it worthwhile to purchase *The Mad Minute*, published by the Addison-Wesley Publishing Co., Jacob Way, Redding, Mass. 01867. It is a brilliantly conceived book designed for classroom drill of the tables.

Most children find being drilled with a stopwatch great fun. A good drill for multiplication tables, for example, is to line up flash cards in order 0 x 9, 1 x 9, etc., up to 12 x 9 to see if the child can call off the answers in under 10 seconds. Let the child keep a record of his ever-increasing speed. The object is to keep working for a faster memory.

Again, it is the parents' responsibility to see that the child knows his tables by heart. Ten to 15 minutes' drill a day until the tables are learned will make an enormous difference in your child's attitude and performance in math. *Don't ask the school if it is time to do this; just do it.*

Perhaps it would be good to end a long article like this with a confession. As a beginning teacher I took great pride in the achievements of my students who entered school already very well prepared. These were those lucky children whose mothers were very interested in education and had already worked a great deal with them before starting school. Naturally, they did well in school from the very first day, and other children who had not had the benefit of such education-minded parents appeared slow by comparison. In my mind I had a totem pole of my class which went from dullest to smartest. Inexperienced teachers are always much more "expert" at discovering learning problems and declaring children unteachable than experienced ones—a fact parents would do well to keep in mind when dealing with their schools.

A milestone in my teaching was a speech I heard the late Eric Hoffer give in which he said that intelligence, talent and genius are very common and that it is only certain elitists who try to make us believe they are rare. America is great, he continued, because its political system has allowed the common man to work out his genius.

That speech and some guidance from older successful teachers who basically concurred with Hoffer changed my attitude about education and my abilities as a teacher improved with the change in attitude. Now I find myself incensed by suggestions that a child is learning disabled or just too slow to learn.

Parents and schools would do well to keep Hoffer's observation in mind and just presume that all children have good Yankee intelligence and can learn.

'Liberal History Lesson' Distorts 1st Amendment

By M. Stanton Evans   *(From the 23 November 1991 issue)*

My topic is the 1st Amendment and the reading of it given to us by the Supreme Court and indeed by almost all supposed authorities on this subject. That reading is essentially that the 1st Amendment was intended to create a wall of separation between the practices of civil government and the affirmations of religion.

The leading misconception involved in this kind of discussion, which is applied not only to 1st Amendment topics but to almost all topics where religion is concerned, is the idea that there is such a thing as a civil order that is not based on religious belief.

The fact of the matter is that every society, every culture, is based upon religious assumptions of one sort or another. Religious affirmations are answers to ultimate questions—such as, where did the world come from, why are we in the world, what does it mean to be a human being, how should human beings treat each other? The answers to all such questions are essentially religious in character.

If you remove one set of assumptions received from a particular religious tradition, you do not, therefore, have a social order that is not based on religious belief. You simply substitute one set of axioms for another.

The notion that it can be otherwise—that there is such a thing as a purely rationally deduced set of rules about human behavior or government—is chiefly an artifact of modernity. It is a notion that has arisen since the Renaissance, and more specifically since the Enlightenment: that the way to liberty, justice, democracy, progress, and other good things is to get rid of religious belief and to substitute a rationally constructed social order for the superstitions of religion.

For want of a better term, I call this way of viewing things the "liberal history lesson."

The treatment of American political history that is now conventional wisdom, embodied in the rulings of the Supreme Court on the 1st Amendment, and in most history books dealing with these topics, is a subdivision of this liberal history lesson. It is an effort to apply to the experience of the United States the assumptions that became conventional in the West at the time of the Enlightenment, and to rewrite that experience in the categories of liberal ideology. The basic idea is to treat the American Revolution as a cognate for the French Revolution—an explosion of anti-clerical sentiment aimed at secularizing every aspect of public life.

As it concerns the United States, all of this is totally historical. In fact, the American continent was settled primarily by people who were concerned about religious matters, who came here for religious reasons, and who brought with them religious assumptions about government that were products of centuries of Judeo-Christian experience and medieval practice, crystallized in early 17th Century England.

The period during which the early settlers came to these shores was when many of these issues were being fought out in England, culminating in the Parliament of 1628, and the people who came here brought with them very specific notions of church and civil government derived from that experience. The principal notion that is relevant here was their covenantal theology— the idea of the covenantal character of church government.

Essentially, it was the notion that authority in the church rose from the congregation and should not be imposed from the top down by the episcopacy. They left England primarily over that issue to come here and set up church and civil government based on these notions derived from Biblical teaching, mainly the Old Testament.

The idea of social contract, for instance, is usually portrayed in the liberal history lesson as something invented by John Locke in his *Treatise of Civil Government* in the latter part of the 17th Century.

In fact, social contract existed in the Western experience almost 70 years before this—in the Mayflower Compact of 1620.

When the Pilgrims arrived off the shores of this continent, they drew up a contract among themselves in which they stated that we do hereby "combine and covenant ourselves together into a civil body politic." So right there, based not upon secular theoretical considerations but on religious experience, you have the notion of social contract, articulated in the Mayflower Compact.

Ten years later, in October 1630, the Massachusetts Bay Company, which was a commercial corporation, held the first meeting of what became its General Court. The Massachusetts Bay Company was similar to corporations today in that it was governed by its directors, eight in number, who were the people entitled to vote on the affairs of the company. Nonetheless, when the first meeting of the General Court was held, 116 people were invited to vote, which is a source of great confusion to many liberal historians.

Why did the autocrats of Massachusetts Bay decide to do this? The answer was their covenantal theology. These were the members of the congregation; they were part of the covenant and entitled to vote in matters of church government, and matters of civil government as well.

Many other products of that early experience show the imprint of the religious beliefs of the original settlers. One of the earliest was the Massachusetts Body of Liberties in 1641, an embryonic version of the Bill of Rights, once again based upon religious principles. Likewise, in 1647, the first public schools were created on this continent by the authorities of Massachusetts Bay. This system was set up for the purpose of teaching young people—how to read the Bible.

This early experience continued in attenuated form up through the end of the 18th Century, attenuated primarily because of the proliferation of religious groups, not because of a loss of religious belief. Quite the contrary.

In the middle of the 18th Century, there occurred the so-called Great Awakening, an evangelistic phenomenon that brought many people into the fold of Christianity and re-energized others for whom Christian belief had been primarily a formal exercise. The result was that new religious sects and groups were formed and some that had been small increased in size. There was the tremendous growth of the Baptists and of the Methodist church. And as religious diversity increased, there was pressure upon the "established" character of religious practice in several of the states.

Contrary to the liberal history lesson, the world of the Founding Fathers was totally suffused with Biblical belief, expressed in innumerable ways in the civil practice of the time.

For example, in 1775, when the Revolutionary War was starting, nine of the 13 colonies had officially established churches, supported by tax revenues. As the proliferation of church groups continued through the latter part of the 18th Century, pressure mounted to disestablish a number of these churches.

Nonetheless, at the time of the Constitutional Convention, three states still had established churches—Massachusetts, New Hampshire and Connecticut. Even in the states that had disestablished—the Anglican Church in some parts of the South or the Congregational Church in other areas—there remained a system of official sanction and support for religious belief, principally the requirement that one profess a certain kind of doctrine in order to hold public office.

These practices persisted well after adoption of the 1st Amendment. The established church in Massachusetts was not abolished until 1833. In New Hampshire, a requirement that one had to be not simply a Christian, but a Protestant to be a member of the legislature persisted until 1877. In New Jersey, Roman Catholics were not permitted to hold office until 1844. In Maryland, one had to be a Christian to hold public office, a stipulation that lasted until 1826. In North Carolina, the stipulation until 1835 was that one had to be Protestant, and until 1868 to be a Christian, to hold office.

The state of Vermont, which broke away from New Hampshire in 1791, was considered theologically one of the most liberal of the states. Nonetheless, this was the oath you had to take in Vermont in order to assume office:

"I do believe in one God, the Creator and Governor of the universe, the Rewarder of the good and the Punisher of the wicked. And I do acknowledge the Scriptures of the Old and New Testaments to be given by divine inspiration and own and profess the Protestant religion."

That was the oath that had to be taken in one of the more *liberal* states at the time the 1st Amendment was being put on the books.

The case of Virginia is one most frequently cited in such discussions. By the standards of the day, Virginia was also a very liberal state. This was a result of the fact that the Anglican Church had been the established church in Virginia.

When the Presbyterians and then the Baptists grew in strength, it created a three-way tug of war for political influences, pushing the state toward disestablishment of the Anglicans, which came about in the 1780s. The bill for disestablishment that finally passed was presented by James Madison in the Virginia legislature on Oct. 31, 1785. This bill and the associated commentary by Madison are frequently mentioned in the literature as showing the secularizing impulse behind the 1st Amendment.

The Supreme Court and the others involved in this discussion never mention, however, that on the same day Madison presented his bill for religious freedom, which was to disestablish a specific sect, he also presented a bill to punish those who broke the Sabbath. This bill spelled out the penalties that would be imposed upon those who broke the Sabbath by conducting other than household duties. It was put forward on the very same day that the bill for disestablishment was offered. This is not referred to because it doesn't fit the secularizing model of the liberal history lesson.

Many practices that existed at the state level also existed at the federal level, first in the Continental Congress and thereafter in the new Congress under the Constitution.

The Continental Congress had chaplains, and it had prayers. In 1780 it authorized the printing of a Bible, after first ensuring that the text was orthodox. It provided money for the Christian education of Indians. It passed the Northwest Ordinance for governing the territory north and west of the Ohio River, stating that it was doing this among other reasons, for purposes of promoting "religion and morality." It stipulated that in the sale of lands in the Northwest Territory, Lot N29 in each parcel of land "be given perpetually for the purposes of religion."

In the new Congress under the Constitution, most of this was re-enacted. The chaplains were re-established. Prayers were conducted. Days of thanksgiving were voted. Money was appropriated for the Christian education of the Indians. All were practices totally contrary to anything you would guess from reading Supreme Court decisions or the conventional liberal history on this subject.

How is all of this—religious affirmation by the several states, established churches, religious requirements for public office, prayers, chaplains, religious education of the Indians—to be reconciled with the reading of the 1st Amendment given to us by the Supreme Court, which says in essence that no tax money may be used for any authentic religious purpose? How can you reconcile the history just recited with the adoption of such an amendment? The answer, of course, is that you cannot; and the reason for this is that the real history of the 1st Amendment is very different from what the liberal history lesson would have us believe.

There were specific reasons for the adoption of the 1st Amendment, fully available in the records for anybody who cares to look at them. This has a lot to do with the politics and the concerns at the time about the impact of the new Constitution.

There was a great deal of agitation by Patrick Henry and others to the effect that this new government would swallow up the rights of the states. Henry, Richard Henry Lee, and others therefore said there needed to be a Bill of Rights, which would guarantee the freedom of the citizens and the states. In large measure, this was a stratagem to prevent adoption of the Constitution, and it became a very effective weapon in the ratification struggle.

Madison, who was promoting adoption of the Constitution, had originally said a Bill of Rights was unnecessary, and he had some good arguments. He said in essence that this was a government of enumerated powers. It had authority to do only those things granted to it, and no authority to do the things not granted to it, and therefore a Bill of Rights would not be needed.

However, Henry succeeded in generating so much opposition that Madison changed his position and said, in effect, "All right, I'll concede your point. Let's compromise on a formula whereby we go ahead and ratify the Constitution, and then adopt a Bill of Rights as soon as the new Congress convenes." That was his campaign pledge when he ran for Congress in Virginia. When Madison switched in favor of a Bill of Rights, he took away the principal issue against him, and got elected to the House of Representatives.

There he presented his proposals for a Bill of Rights in fulfillment of his campaign pledge. It is very interesting to go back and read the reasons given by Madison for presenting the Bill of Rights and his interpretation of what became the 1st Amendment.

For example, he was challenged by Roger Sherman and others about the very argument he himself had made—that this was a government of enumerated powers, so why was this Bill of Rights necessary? Madison said: "Whether the words are necessary or not [referring to what became the 1st Amendment] he did not mean to say, but they had been required by some of the state conventions who seemed to entertain an opinion . . . that . . . [Congress might] make laws of such a nature as might infringe the rights of conscience and establish a national religion." And therefore, he was presenting them for the consideration of the Congress.

He added that "If the word 'national' were introduced it would point the amendment directly toward the object it was intended to prevent," which was the prospect of federal interference with the religious (and other) practices of the states.

As it happened, the actual language of the Amendment voted by the House was not proposed by Madison, but by Fisher Ames of Massachusetts, a state with an established church. It is interesting to note that the language that finally emerged from Congress was adopted by a conference committee, including on the House side Roger Sherman, and Oliver Ellsworth from the Senate.

The important thing about Sherman and Ellsworth was that both were from Connecticut, another state with an established church. In fact, in Connecticut at the time a law existed that you could be fined 50 shillings if you didn't go to church on Sunday.

Sherman and Ellsworth, who not only represented Connecticut but were believing Calvinists, would hardly have gone into a conference committee and voted for an amendment nullifying Connecticut law about religion. In the light of all this, the language of the 1st Amendment as it came out of that conference committee should be fairly clear: "Congress shall make no law respecting an establishment of religion." Now what does that mean? It means that the national legislature shall make no law having anything to do with, concerning the subject of, respecting an, establishment of religion. That is: Congress cannot pass a law creating a national established religion; and Congress cannot pass a law interfering with the established churches or other religious practices in the states.

That language, which had been debated through the late summer of 1789, was passed by the House of Representatives on Sept. 24, 1789. On the very next day (this must be considered in the context of what the Supreme Court now says this language means), the very same House of Representatives passed by about a 2-to-1 margin a resolution calling for a *national day of prayer and thanksgiving*. The day after it passed the 1st Amendment, here is the language the House adopted:

"We acknowledge with grateful hearts the many signal favors of Almighty God, especially by affording them an opportunity peacefully to establish a constitutional government for their safety and happiness."

They therefore called upon President Washington to issue a proclamation designating a national day of prayer and thanksgiving. This was Washington's response:

"It is the duty of all nations to acknowledge the providence of Almighty God, to obey His will, to be grateful for His benefits and humbly to implore His protection and favor. . . . That great and glorious Being who is the beneficent author of all the good that was, that is, or that ever will be, that we may then unite in rendering unto Him our sincere and humble thanks for His kind care and protection of the people. . . ."

Such was language officially adopted, first by the Congress and then in a proclamation by George Washington, contemporaneous with adoption of the 1st Amendment.

It seems to be reasonably clear that two things were encompassed by the 1st Amendment. The first was to protect the existing religious practices of the states, including established churches, religious requirements for public office, and so forth, from federal interference. The second was to permit even the federal government to give general support to religion, which continued without stint in all the various ways described a century and more after adoption of the 1st Amendment.

Let me read by way of conclusion the sentiments of Thomas Jefferson, the person most cited on this subject next to Madison by the Court and by the liberal historians (though Jefferson was not a member of either the Constitutional Convention or the first Congress). Here is what Jefferson said in his second inaugural address:

"In matters of religion, I have considered that its free exercise is placed by the Constitution independent of the powers of the general government. I have therefore undertaken on no occasion to prescribe the religious exercises suited to it. But have left them as the Constitution found them, under the direction or discipline of state or church authorities acknowledged by the several religious societies."

Jefferson also wrote a few years later to a Presbyterian clergyman who asked why he had not issued thanksgiving proclamations (of the early Presidents, Jefferson was the only one who did not). Here is what Jefferson answered:

"I consider the government of the United States as interdicted from intermeddling with religious institutions, their doctrines, discipline, or exercises.

"This results from the provision that no law shall be made respecting the establishment or free exercise of religion, but from that also which reserves to the states the power not delegated to the United States. Certainly no power to prescribe any religious exercise or to assume authority and religious discipline has been delegated to the general government. It must thus rest with the states as far as it can be in any human authority."

The inexorable conclusion is that there was no wall of separation between religious affirmation and civil government in the several states, nor could the 1st Amendment conceivably have been intended to create one.

Chapter Five

Foreign Policy

HUMAN EVENTS in its early years was basically isolationist, a position with an old and honorable pedigree in the United States reaching back to George Washington's admonition to avoid "entangling alliances" with foreign powers. Once the United States entered World War II, of course, the publication rallied to the cause, although it continued to dissent on the way in which the war was conducted.

Herbert Hoover is remembered chiefly—and unfairly—as the architect of the Depression. Almost forgotten today are his great humanitarian efforts—efforts that were largely responsible for preventing massive starvation in Europe following World War I. In "The Case for the Children," published in the 17 May 1944 issue of HUMAN EVENTS, Hoover outlined a relief policy for Europe at the end of World War II.

Norman Thomas, the Socialist party's candidate for president in 1944, differed totally from HUMAN EVENTS' free market approach but he shared the publication's isolationist viewpoint. In the "Foreign Policy Planks of the Major Parties," published in the 26 July 1944 issue, he expressed well-founded skepticism about the utopian postwar order lovingly envisioned by the liberal internationalists.

HUMAN EVENTS' isolationist policy underwent a dramatic shift in the immediate postwar period as a result of the emergence of the Soviet Union as a world power with global designs. The publication came to the view that international communism poses a direct and lethal threat to the peace and security of the world and that the Soviet Union as the chief purveyor of this insidious ideology must be forcefully opposed, whatever the cost.

An event that severely jolted HUMAN EVENTS was the loss of China to the Communists in 1949. "Appeasement in China: Where It Leads" (17 November 1958) is a perceptive analysis of why China was lost, by Gen. Albert Wedemeyer, one of the key U.S. officers on the scene at the time.

With the inauguration of Richard Nixon as president in 1969, HUMAN EVENTS (which had supported Nixon's nomination and election in 1968) expected a dramatic improvement in the conduct of American foreign policy. These hopes were largely dashed, however, with the advent of detente and the policy of accommodation with the Soviets adopted by Nixon. The chief architect of detente was Henry Kissinger, first Nixon's national security adviser and later secretary of state.

"The Trouble with Henry Kissinger" by M. Stanton Evans (8 September 1973) sums up HUMAN EVENTS' many misgivings with Kissinger's world view.

In "U. S. Foreign Policy Needs a Forward Strategy" (21 February 1981) by Allan Ryskind, the HUMAN EVENTS editor argues that the United States must replace its static, defensive approach for dealing with the Soviets with an aggressive strategy that puts the United States on the offensive.

One of the most influential articles published by HUMAN EVENTS was "The Sandinista Government Should Be Overthrown" (20 March 1982). According to the Washington *Post's* Lou Cannon and others, this piece had a major impact on President Reagan's thinking and was a key catalyst in his tenaciously maintained policy of aiding the Nicaraguan freedom fighters, or Contras.

From the inception of Iraq's invasion of Kuwait in August of 1990 HUMAN EVENTS was a steadfast supporter of George Bush's declaration that the invasion "will not stand." Although the paper differed with some of the details of the president's policy—and although editor Allan Ryskind had a son in the Eighty-second Airborne Division, which was dispatched to the gulf—HUMAN EVENTS never wavered on this position.

Upon the conclusion of the Persian Gulf War, HUMAN EVENTS paid a well-deserved tribute to President Bush for his decisive victory in "Hail to the Chief" (9 March 1991).

The Case for the Children

By Herbert Hoover   *(From the 17 May 1944 issue)*

I welcome the opportunity to restate for readers of HUMAN EVENTS the problem of food for the occupied democracies of Europe. It behooves us to get our thinking straight on this subject.

On September 15, 1939, two weeks after the invasion of Poland, the Polish Ambassador approached me with an official request from his Government that I should organize and direct operations for feeding children and certain restricted categories in Polish territory occupied by the Nazi armies. *With the approval of the Department of State* this work was initiated and carried on *under agreements negotiated with the British and German Governments*, within the limits of the *funds furnished by the Polish Government*, up to the time of the Nazi invasion of Soviet Russia. This successful operation is often overlooked in discussing the possibility of relief for the other occupied territories.

In May, 1940, when Belgium was invaded and occupied, I received a similar official request from the Belgian Ambassador, confirmed a few days later by his Government.

I cite these instances to dispose of the criticism that those Americans who have worked for relief are officious and meddlesome. They have worked only in response to the formally official requests of interested Governments. They have declined to participate in enterprises without such formal governmental requests.

Governments of these and other occupied countries have appealed earnestly and repeatedly to the British and American Governments to permit them to send food through the blockade *under adequate safeguards*. Such appeals have been uniformly rejected as *contrary to British policy*. There is no justification for such unilateral decision. The survival of our allies is more than a matter of British policy. It is—or should be—a matter of *allied policy*, to be settled only after full consultation among the allied governments.

II

We Americans are playing our full part in this war and we too have a right to make our voice heard. The Government of the occupied democracies have at least an equal claim. In view of their sacrifices we have no right to ignore them. These Governments are as anxious as we are to win the war; only thus can the enemy be driven from their countries. Certainly they would not urge child feeding if it would aid the enemy or prolong the war. They are just as much a part of the United Nations group as we are.

What right have Britain and America to usurp all power in deciding this matter?

To be fair we must recall that the British decision that there should be no relief was taken shortly after Dunkirk, at a time when Britain stood alone and her military position was precarious. It was perhaps asking a good deal to expect statesmanlike and humanitarian decisions at such a time. But with equal fairness we may recall that there has been a vast change in conditions since then and that there has been ample time to reconsider the facts in agreement with this country and the other allies.

Our own Administration has unquestioningly deferred to the British Government in this matter for four years. Indeed during this time anyone who raised his voice in favor of relief had to be prepared for denunciation as anti-British.

Yet there are in Britain large elements of respectable people who advocate relief and there have been impressive debates in the House of Commons in which the Government's policy on relief has been criticized in far stronger terms than any used on this side of the Atlantic. In Britain they retain, even in time of war, the democratic right to criticize the action of Government. The long list of prominent Americans who disapprove the relief policy of the British and American Governments effectively disposes of the charge that advocates of relief are anti-British.

III

Opposition to relief usually takes the form of saying that nothing can be done without weakening the war effort. This overlooks the fact that there is one important relief operation not only permitted but supported by the British and American Governments. Since 1941 Greece has been fed. She is still being fed. Unfortunately neither Britain nor America can claim credit for inaugurating this work.

It is too often forgotten that in 1941 the Turkish Government, moved by a compassion lacking in avowedly Christian capitals, shipped food to the starving Greeks *in defiance of the British blockade.* It was not politically expedient to antagonize the Turks, so decency won out. Making the best of things, Britain and America have contributed financially to keeping the work going and our Department of State has repeatedly certified that the food reaches the Greeks, that the Nazis have not benefited, and that there has been no weakening of the war effort.

The arguments advanced by the Department of State in defense of Greek relief are precisely those they have rejected when I advanced them on behalf of other occupied countries.

Until we reconsider the whole subject our course will stand in shameful contrast to the statesmanlike and compassionate behavior of the Turks.

There is some inadequate comfort to be found in the fact that the national will is more enlightened than the action of the Government. Thousands of American leaders in every field have demanded that our Government exert itself in behalf of starving children. The Federal Council of the Churches of Christ in America, the Catholic Archbishops and Bishops, the Rabbinical Assembly of America, and organized labor have all supported the demand for child feeding. Churches, lodges, clubs, societies, and organizations of every kind have passed resolutions.

Half a million or more people have written letters urging the Administration to take action. And in response to this popular movement the elected representatives of the people have taken impressive action.

On February 15 the Senate, *by unanimous vote*, urged the Administration to take steps to send food to the starving children of Europe (S. R. 100).

On April 17, the House of Representatives, *by unanimous action*, made the same request (H. R. 221).

IV

Of course the Executive is not obliged to act upon congressional advice, but it is almost unthinkable that, in a democracy, a request of this character, adopted unanimously, should be ignored, as this one has been. These resolutions represent the culminating expression of the popular will. They were adopted only after exhaustive hearings and full consideration. It remains to be seen whether the Administration will act now to avert further suffering or will continue in cynical contempt of national feeling.

We can at least be gratified that Congress has recognized a great moral and humanitarian issue and has done its part worthily.

Aside from humanity, common sense and self-interest demand that we try to save the freedom-loving peoples of Europe. If a better world order is to be maintained, it must be by those sharing our ideals. If there is no change in our attitude Germany will emerge from the war strong and healthy, while our friends and allies will be weakened by starvation, subnormal in mind and body. If we plan to establish democracy as the ruling system in the world, it is elementary common sense to save from destruction those people who have demonstrated their capacity for democratic government. If we let them perish, we may find ourselves alone in the event of another war.

There is no justification for our present course in expediency or morals. On the contrary both humanitarianism and political expediency dictate a supreme effort to save at least the children of our allies from starvation.

(Editor's note: Herbert Hoover, former president of the United States, is undoubtedly the world's outstanding authority on the subject of organized relief work. His service in this capacity includes Chairmanship of the American Relief Commission in London, 1914–15; Chairmanship of the Commission for Relief in Belgium, 1915–19; Chairmanship of the Interlude Food Council during the last war; and Chairmanship of the American Relief Administration and the European Relief Council thereafter. Mr. Hoover has from the outset been active in the work of the present Temporary Council on Food for Europe's Children.)

Foreign Policy Planks of the Major Parties

By Norman Thomas   *(From the 26 July 1944 issue)*

Once more the Republican and Democratic parties have accomplished the task of writing virtually interchangeable platform. Insofar as their positive plans are concerned, Dewey and Roosevelt could swap platforms and the voters would not recognize the difference. A campaign which promises to be bitter will be waged on personalities, "the record," and failure to renominate Henry Wallace, rather than on the platforms.

This general observation is peculiarly pertinent to the sections dealing with peace and the post-war organizations. On either platform the next President could justify any program between the extremes of frank isolation and a superstate, both of which eventualities are about equally unlikely.

Against a background of considerable theological training in explaining the sacred books of both Mark and Marx, I have carefully examined both platforms and find these minor differences worth passing notice:

II

The Republicans are more specifically concerned that the Peace treaties shall be "just" (an amiably vague adjective!) and that "the organized cooperation of the nations should concern itself with basic causes of world disorder."

The Democrats covet this matter by pledging support to the Atlantic Charter and the Four Freedoms but, perhaps significantly, limit their application to the "United Nations and other peace-loving [*sic*] nations"—a limitation not to be found in the Charter itself. The Democrats are a shade more emphatic in endowing their international organization "with power to employ armed forces when necessary to prevent aggression and preserve peace." But like the Republicans, they are careful to bless themselves with the word "sovereign" and to make it clear that armed forces are to be national. The Democratic convention shouted down an amendment in favor of an international air force.

The Republicans are specific in promising to "keep the American people informed" (not consulted) "concerning all agreements with foreign nations" and to adhere to the constitutional provisions for ratifying treaties or agreements. The Democrats make no parallel promises.

Both parties favor unrestricted Jewish immigration into Palestine, but both are silent on American hospitality to refugees. Thus, in a country where there are almost no Arab but many Jewish voters, they satisfy our consciences and appease all groups, including anti-Semites who are entirely willing that Jews should go to Jerusalem. The Republicans merely ask a "free and democratic commonwealth in Palestine," but the Democrats also want it to be "Jewish." Neither says how many American boys should stand ready to die if the Arabs object.

Neither Governor Dewey nor President Roosevelt pointed up these minor differences in his acceptance speech, nor did either introduce new differences. The President did not follow the lead of the Democratic keynoter, Governor Kerr of Oklahoma, in blaming Republican "isolationists" for sinking more ships than the Japanese sank at Pearl Harbor. This bit of demagoguery, peculiarly blatant even for a political convention, referred to the results of the Washington Conference for Limitation of Armaments in 1921, which old Democrats not only supported but at their 1924 convention criticized for not going far enough. It will be interesting to see if Governor Kerr correctly interpreted his party's brand of internationalism by this bit of jingoism.

It is obvious that nothing in this record of minor and dubious differences between the old parties justifies the expense of an election. Indeed, many voices hail the unity of the parties in this field as a definite advantage as the war nears an end. So it would be, if it were in fact an evidence and statement of national unity on fairly specific and adequate bases for peace. It is nothing of the sort. It is instead an evasion of differences of opinion calculated to prevent discussion of the great issues upon which the prevention of a Third World War depends—issues upon which the latent differences of American opinion are very sharp. The present verbal unity settles nothing; it blocks the road to a democratic mandate on peace; it clears the way, at least temporarily, for the President's "great design," which apparently has Governor Dewey's general approval. At least, all his recent statements have been in line with it.

III

And that, to one who believes as firmly as I do that the "great design" is an invitation to World War III, is a major failure in the democratic process pregnant with disaster for our country and mankind.

This "great design" contemplates a revived League of Nations completely dominated by a cartel or alliance of imperial powers: the U.S.A., Great Britain, and the USSR. China will be a nominal fourth. But actually China, probably rive by evil war, will be too weak to count very much for a considerable time. There are no signs that Stalin will begin the practice of forgiving an enemy—for example, Chiang Kai-shek, the only man who ever got the better of him—or that Churchill will initiate the dissolution of the British Empire by restoring Hong Kong to its rightful nationality.

The workability of the "great design" rests upon two assumptions, both contrary to all that we know from history, logic, and psychology. They are:

1) That machinery to enforce peace is far more important than the kind of peace that is to be enforced;

2) That it will be possible in a world of big and little sovereign states and their dependent colonies successfully to maintain the dominance of an alliance of three great powers, whose conflicting interests and ideologies are already apparent in the midst of a life-or-death struggle against a common German enemy. (Japan is not yet their common enemy.)

At Cairo the President apparently underwrote recovery and maintenance of the French, Dutch, and British Empires in the Far East with American blood and treasure; at Tehran, the Balkanization of Europe by Moscow and London, with himself as a kind of acrobat balancing on the Stalin-Churchill see-saw for power. His alliance has less holiness to commend it than the post-Napoleonic Holy Alliance of brief but unhappy memory. It will be challenged by the resentments of those excluded and torn by rival interests.

IV

For years I predicted that our entry into the Second World War would be by way of Asia, through Japan. I now predict that an entrance into a far more fatal Third World War will be by way of Asia through the revolt of colored nations and races. Sooner or later the USSR, probably the greatest of all powers, is bound to forget its present alliance and to aid native revolt against white—predominantly British—supremacy. If we fight again with and for Britain (and our own share in the fool's gold of imperialism), it will be a terrible and unsuccessful war. That war, or long sustained preparation for it, will doom our democracy.

I could also argue the impossibility of maintaining competitive armaments among sovereign states with conflicting interests and, at the same time, securing united action for crushing an "aggressor" nation. Roosevelt's League will fail more disastrously than Wilson's, which would not have been saved by American membership in it.

I believe that an increasingly secure peace can be established if the peoples of the victor nations will insist on commencing organized and inclusive cooperation, economic and political, on the basis of self-government for all and the end of imperial exploitation. But if we Americans cannot or will not enter that road, better a thousand times a comparative and friendly isolation than any triple alliance imperialism, masked by a phony and vindictive "internationalism."

Appeasement in China: Where It Leads
An Inside Account by a Top Expert on Asia

By General Albert C. Wedemeyer   *(From the 17 November 1958 issue)*

(General Albert C. Wedemeyer served as commander of U.S. forces in the China Theater during the years 1944-46, and also as Chief of Staff to Generalissimo Chiang Kai-shek. The famous "Wedemeyer Report"–his 1947 survey of Chinese and Korean affairs, delivered to President Truman–opposed the sellout of those vital areas to Communist Governments under the direction of Moscow. It was covered up until inquiring Senate investigators forced its disclosure.

This article is adapted from the new book, Wedemeyer Reports. *The contents are copyrighted by Gen. Wedemeyer, and reprinted by permission of the publisher.)*

On October 27, 1944, while lying in my bunk at Kandy, Ceylon, I received my order from General Marshall to hold myself in readiness to depart for China. I had been deeply immersed in my duties in India, where I had been Deputy Supreme Commander under Lord Louis

Mountbatten, so my new double assignment as Commander of US troops in China and Chief of Staff to Generalissimo Chiang Kai-shek came as a bombshell.

I knew that I faced a problem akin to "untangling a can of worms," which was General Dan Sultan's description of what faced me. As I flew into China over the Hump at 21,000-foot altitude, I reviewed what I knew of the situation. There was, as I had been told by Sultan and others, the dissension caused by the long-standing antagonism between General Joseph Stilwell, the overall US Commander in the China-Burma theater, and General Claire Chennault, the creator of the famous Flying Tigers, who was in charge of the Fourteenth Air Force in China. But this, I had already conjectured to my aide, Captain William McAfee, was only the immediate cause of the difficulties. The fundamental reason for Stilwell's recall and my sudden promotion to a job I was loath to take (China was known as graveyard for American officials) was "Vinegar Joe's" extreme antagonism to Chiang Kai-shek.

I recalled the description of Chiang ("coolie class," prone to "tantrums," "incompetent") as I had heard it from Stilwell's own vehement lips in Marshall's office in Washington. I recalled, too, his hard words about Chennault's "intrigues." As General Marshall's strategic "planner," I was not disposed to doubt my chief's high opinion of Stilwell at the time. Since then I had heard a good deal more about Stilwell's difficulties with both Chennault and the Generalissimo. When I visited with Chennault on my first evening in Kunming after dropping down through the rain and overcast on the inner side of the Hump, the old Flying Tiger's objectivity contrasted strongly with my memory of Stilwell's diatribes against anyone sharing authority with him.

I had already met Chiang Kai-shek on a war-time flight around the world in 1943. Now, on the occasion of my first official call on the Generalissimo after I had assumed the China command, I was impressed all over again by this small, graceful, fine-boned man with black, piercing eyes and an engaging smile.

As I learned more about Chiang, I realized that his course in holding out against the Japanese from 1937 to 1944 expressed a spirit even more gallant than Churchill's famous "blood, sweat and tears" speech after Dunkirk. Chiang had all along been fighting a war on four fronts: against the Japanese; against Russia in the person of the Chinese Communists; against the centrifugal forces in China, represented by former war lords or semi-independent provincial governors and generals; and against the "Western imperialists," meaning in particular the British, whom, thanks to their strategy of self-interest, he had no reason to trust. Chiang's greatness and weakness lay in the fact that he never lost sight of the original objective of the Kuomintang, namely, the unification and independence of China. Paradoxically, it was the Communists who benefited by the fact that the political unity of China was conserved by Chiang Kai-shek.

Naturally, the Generalissimo, knowing that he could do little to win the war as long as aid from America had been reduced to a trickle, hoped to refrain from provoking the Japanese to advance any further in Chinese territory. This led to the false charge (made by John Davies and others) that a *modus vivendi* had been worked out between the Nationalists and Japan. General Stilwell's reports to Marshall did nothing to combat the charge. When I went to the American Embassy in Chungking to pay my respects to Ambassador Gauss, who was shortly to be replaced by the colorful Pat Hurley, I was shocked to hear him say: "We should pull up the plug and let the whole Chinese Government go down the drain."

Such an attitude, which had been sedulously fostered by Stilwell's four State Department political advisers, John Davies, John Service, Raymond Ludden and John Emerson, all of whom I inherited, became more and more incomprehensible to me the longer I stayed in China. Although I locked up the papers relating to the relief of Stilwell in a file called "Oklahoma" (named after Pat Hurley's native state), where they remained unread until after the war, I soon discovered that no Chinese Communist forces had ever fought in any major engagement against the Japanese. The Communists, wrongly called "agrarians" and "Jeffersonians," simply played the role of jackal or hyena against the wounded and suffering Chinese elephant who would not submit to his enemy.

In discussing communism with Mao Tse-tung and Chou En-lai I raised the point of their prior loyalty to the Soviet Union. Chou En-lai, who quoted Lenin and Marx in a most un-agrarian way, replied that the Chinese Communists—or "liberators"—could not be separated from the socialist mother state nor could they operate without the aid of both the international proletariat and the Soviet Union. My meeting with Mao and Chou En-lai gave the lie to reports that the Chinese Communists were simply agrarian reformers interested in the welfare of the people.

Stilwell had a reputation for being a fine fighting man. Obviously he could inspire troops. I do not doubt that he loved the Chinese soldier or that he was a capable division commander. But despite his criticism of Chiang for not prosecuting the war against Japan with unity and vigor, Stilwell himself had no concept for bringing about a coordinated, decisive effort against the Japanese.

Today, reading through the reports sent to me and to the State Department by Davies, Service, Emerson and Ludden, it seems obvious that not only that their sympathies lay with the Chinese Communists, but also that they were either consciously or unwittingly disseminating exaggerated or false, Communist inspired, reports concerning the Nationalist Government. These reports were designed to stir up all manner of Sino-American distrust—as, for instance, when John Davies sent me long accounts of rumors or unsubstantiated reports that the Generalissimo was collaborating with the Japanese.

John Davies had not been content to press for aid to the Communists. In one of his secret reports, dated December 12, 1944, he went so far as to recommend that the US cut off supplies to the Nationalist armies unless they ceased fighting to contain Communist forces.

At Hurley's insistence, Davies was recalled by the State Department. Subsequently he was transferred to Moscow, where (as Pat said to me) one could hope that "John would experience at first hand the chicanery as well as the tyranny of communism."

Our basic attitude toward China, after Pearl Harbor, was one of a completely unrealistic impatience. We chivvied and harassed Chiang Kai-shek for not doing more to "ease pressure on the United States and the British Commonwealth in the Pacific." No word of recognition of the gallant fight which China had waged against Japan all alone during four and a half years, during the greater part of which period both England and the United States continued to sell the sinews of war to Japan. No word to China that henceforth, having been attacked ourselves, we would come to her aid. To complete the picture, after the US Navy's defeat of the Japanese at Leyte Gulf and Stalin's promise in October, 1944, that 60 Soviet divisions would be available for operations against Japan three months after Germany's defeat, the British-American Joint Chiefs of Staff lost all interest in China's war effort.

I knew that a civil war in China would destroy the economic and political equilibrium in the Far East. It was my hope in expressing this view to General Marshall that President Truman and Stalin would jointly agree to avoid interference in the internal affairs of China. Realizing that my Government would not give Chiang the logistical and arms aid he must have to take over Manchuria, and also that the Chinese Nationalist Government unaided would not have the strength to re-establish its authority over North China if it also attempted to occupy Manchuria, I suggested to the Generalissimo that the Chinese Government propose a temporary five-power guardianship over Manchuria by the United States, Great Britain, France, China and the Soviet Union. At the same time I recommended to Chiang that he would be wise to send his best administrators as well as military leaders to North China, south of the Great Wall, to insure that his control there would be firmly established.

Chiang did not accept my recommendations, and, in any event, my advice would surely have been ignored in Washington. We were still in the sunset period of the "Trust Uncle Joe" epoch. Having rushed into the war for the kill only eight days before Japan's surrender (very much as Mussolini had attacked the prostrate body of France in 1940), the Red Army met practically no enemy resistance and was soon in complete control of Manchuria. The Russians immediately proceeded to dismantle all removable industrial equipment and destroyed most of the rest. It seemed strange that they should destroy installations that their own Chinese Communist forces might use. I came to the conclusion that the reason for their seemingly illogical behavior was that the Kremlin leaders never dreamed the United States would be so supine as to permit them to remain in Manchuria or enable the Chinese Communists to take it over.

I was needled by Communist-sympathizing American and other correspondents concerning the help I was giving the Nationalists, under cover of my directive to arrange for the repatriation of the Japanese. But to me it seemed that we had a moral obligation to give China the necessary political, military and economic support to insure that Soviet Russia would not be able with impunity to ignore her pledges in the treaty we had practically compelled China to sign. Moreover, it was obviously in our national interest to keep China from becoming a Soviet satellite. Hence my effort to contain the Communists by interpreting vague and contradictory instructions in the most elastic fashion possible.

Meanwhile the Kremlin was not only denying the Chinese Nationalists access to Manchuria, but it was also busy supplying the Chinese Communist party with surrendered Japanese arms and equipment. I asked the War Department to send seven American divisions to China in order to create a barrier through North China and Manchuria against Soviet Russia. The Joint Chiefs replied that the divisions were not available. However, two Marine Corps divisions were sent out. I disposed them from Peiping to the sea, including the Shantung Peninsula within their area of protection.

During a brief visit to Washington I was directed by President Truman and the Joint Chiefs of Staff to write a report on China. The President and General Marshall felt that I should refrain from coming to definite conclusions, and asked for several alternative lines of action. Accordingly, I could do no more than make my views of the situation clear, while refraining from stating that only one course could preserve American interests, namely, unequivocal assistance to our ally, the Chinese Nationalist Government. Neither then, nor before, nor subsequently, did I receive a clear-cut directive from Washington.

In December, 1945, I received word from General Marshall that he had been requested by President Truman to serve as a special envoy to China and would arrive in Shanghai shortly. I met the General and accompanied him to the Cathay Hotel in Shanghai. He was unpacking his effects while we discussed plans for his first call on the Generalissimo. He showed me a copy of his directive from the President, which requested him to bring the Nationalists and the Communists together in a coalition Government. I told General Marshall that he would never be able to effect a working agreement between the Communists and Nationalists, since the Nationalists, who still had most of the power, were determined not to relinquish one iota of it, while the Communists for their part were equally determined to seize all power, with the aid of the Soviet Union.

General Marshall reacted angrily and said, "I am going to accomplish my mission and you are going to help me."

That night I was in a quandary. I recalled that at the Casablanca Conference, Marshall had said: "You will be doing me a disservice if you do not always give me the benefit of your thinking." (This was after I had come out strongly in opposition to the doctrine of Unconditional Surrender.) I wondered what had happened to cause Marshall to assume his present aloofness, almost hostility, because I had spoken my mind frankly and freely. Although General Marshall later recommended my appointment as Ambassador to China, I felt certain that his concept of what American policy should be was not mine. As with Pat Hurley the year before, I knew there was no possibility of an accommodation between Nationalists and Chinese Communists.

Because of Communist pressure I was eventually turned down for the Ambassadorship.

Taking issue with Marshall and State Department policy in my memorandum for Forrestal, I went on to say that Chiang could make progress toward the unification of China "if he had realistic American aid—not measured by bulk but by the wisdom with which it is applied and offered."

I should still esteem Marshall as one of the great men of our generation if he had ever acknowledged his fatal mistake in China, namely, maintaining that the Nationalists and Communists were simply two factions contending for power and that he was therefore justified in embargoing all arms and ammunition supplies to China in 1946-47 in order to force Chiang to come to terms with the Communists. (In defending the Marshall position, Dean Acheson was either misinformed or was deliberately misleading Congress when he cited "our military observers on the spot" as authority for his statement that Chiang had lost no battles for lack of arms and ammunition.)

Marshall's mistake carried over into the period of my last mission to the Orient in 1947. I was told to write my own directive for the mission, but I fear that this was merely a "cover" for Washington skulduggery. My subsequent recommendations—that the United States, through the offices of the United Nations, give material aid to Chiang for post-war rehabilitation, and that a guardianship be instituted over Manchuria to keep it from being "drawn into the Soviet orbit"—were ignored. My report was simply buried until, in due time, it was exhumed by Senate Committee investigators who had become alarmed at the imminent loss of China to the Communists.

The State Department's "let the dust settle" policy rendered inevitable the Communist conquest of China. The Chinese people are realists. They became so disheartened and demoralized by our attitude that they finally ceased to resist the Communists. What reason could there be for continuing to oppose them if even America wanted China to come to terms with them?

The Trouble with Henry Kissinger

By M. Stanton Evans   *(From the 8 September 1973 issue)*

Appointment of Dr. Henry Kissinger as secretary of state is a climactic event which is in one sense fitting, in another profoundly disturbing. Where Kissinger is concerned, the double focus is not unusual.

The move is fitting in that Kissinger has been the *de facto* arbiter of American foreign policy for the past four years while Secretary of State William Rogers by all accounts fulfilled a largely secondary and ceremonial role. Kissinger's new position will bring the formal structure of our government in line with the realities of the situation, ending possible confrontation about who is generating policy for America and who is responsible for the results—a modest gain for procedural clarity.

The move is disturbing in that Kissinger's power will be enhanced by it and there is every reason to wish that his power be curtailed. Kissinger is the country's chief promoter of *detente* with the Communists, and as such has played a major role in befuddling popular and official understanding on the nature of the Cold War conflict. As secretary of state *and* national security adviser to the President rolled into one, he will be able to spread befuddlement on a truly awesome scale.

Enhancing the likelihood of this development is the fact that President Nixon obviously views Kissinger as a major asset to be deployed in combating bad publicity over Watergate. **The official line is that we should put the Watergate travail in perspective by contemplating the "success" of the Kissinger foreign policy, a stance which clearly suggests that more of the same will be forthcoming. The success of Kissinger's efforts is, indeed, a kind of universal axiom, but what exactly makes them so successful is never made quite clear.**

We are informed by *Time*, for example, that the truce in Vietnam is the crowning accomplishment in a series of "greatest achievements in foreign policy" by Kissinger-Nixon. This is in line with Kissinger's own prior statements in which he said the Paris peace agreement was a workable compact which would bring about a reduction of North Vietnamese forces in South Vietnam. Today that agreement lies in shambles as the Communists press their aggression all over Indochina and the flow of Hanoi's forces to the South continues, as Kissinger argued it would not.

The Peking Move

Kissinger's attainments are equally problematical in a second major area of Asian policy—the rapprochement with Peking. Any benefits to the United States from this departure, beyond the ancient liturgy of beneficial "contact," have yet to manifest themselves. On the negative side of the ledger there is a policy of studied negligence toward the question of Peking's heroin trade, a diplomatic freeze toward our allies on Taiwan, and the ouster of Free China from the United Nations—another outcome directly contrary to Kissinger's assurances.

More generally, it has been in obedience to Kissinger's convoluted notions of *detente* that the United States has embarked on trade agreements with the Communists which have weakened our economy, as in the grain deal, and strengthened the enemy, as in the construction of a $1-billion truck factory for the Soviets on the Kama River. The calamitous details of the grain transaction are only now beginning to surface, while the truck deal is still surrounded by a wall of government secrecy. Again, any solid benefit to America from all this has yet to be demonstrated.

Is Trade Helping?

The usual line concerning such matters is that trade and aid from America will encourage the Soviets to pursue a more reasonable course in their internal and external policies, but there is little to indicate that any such effect has been achieved. Internal repression against Soviet Jews and against intellectuals like Zhores Medvedev, Aleksandr Solzhenitsyn, and Andrei Sakharov, indeed, has taken the unusual step of warning the West against providing technology to the Kremlin, on the grounds that commerce of this type will strengthen the aggressive dictatorship in Moscow.

From Kissinger's standpoint, of course, it is the external behavior of the Soviets which counts, and it has been widely reported that the general accommodation with the Kremlin was aimed at enlisting Soviet help in cooling down the conflict in Vietnam. The success of this stratagem may be inferred from the fact that Moscow's Hungarian and Polish stooges on the control commission have devoted their energies to covering up for repeated violations of the peace accord committed by the North Vietnamese.

Even more important to the question of American security, Kissinger was the godfather of the SALT agreements which embrace and institutionalize the peculiar theories of the disarmament lobby Nixon was supposedly going to dislodge, explicitly disowning the idea of defending America's civilian population from enemy attack. (See "The Greatest Story Never Told," HUMAN EVENTS, July 28, 1973.) The esoteric fantasies of Robert McNamara, Jerome Wiesner and other disarmament buffs on the Kennedy-Johnson years have been endorsed in full by the Nixon strategists.

Quizzed about such matters, Kissinger and his proponents reply that he is doing the best he can for hard-nosed anti-communism amid impossible circumstances. The "doves" are rampant in Congress, the American people indifferent to vital questions on defense and foreign policy. What can one do? The measures promoted by Kissinger are the most that can be obtained in default of sensible public attitudes. That explanation has persuaded certain hawks and conservatives, who come away believing Kissinger shares their own distress and is battling valiantly against enormous odds. It is, however, unconvincing.

Why, after all, is the American public indifferent? Why is it unwilling to support a strong defense arsenal—or continued strategic support to anti-Communist elements in Indochina? One obvious answer is that the public has been led to believe that the Cold War is adjourned, that Brezhnev and Chou En-lai are decent fellows, and that the era of *detente* is full upon us—precisely the notions that Henry Kissinger has made it his business to propagate in every corner of the globe. He is himself the source of the confusions he invokes to justify his conduct.

'Limited War' Advocate

Such confusions are not surprising. Kissinger throughout his career has been in and of the liberal community—sponsored and promoted by the liberal-establishmentarian Council on Foreign Relations, protege and foreign policy tutor to Nelson Rockefeller, friend of Schlesinger, Wiesner, Bundy, etc. He was a major force in exploiting the "missile gap" delusion of the '50s and early '60s and a withering critic of John Foster Dulles. His principal fame accrued through his advocacy of "limited war" in which sanctuary was conceded to the enemy and certain zones and targets declared off-limits in deference to an alleged "stalemate" which did not in fact exist. Vietnam, of course, was such a war.

How does it happen that a man of Kissinger's background and ideas has become the sovereign master of American foreign policy under a supposedly conservative Republican administration? The answer may be found in Kissinger's taste for ambiguity and contradiction, both in his formal writings and in his policy recommendations.

Kissinger has an unusual faculty for couching accommodation proposals in the language of *realpolitik*, and a gift for pressing subtle procedural distinctions which make his views seem "different" when in substance there is little to choose between them and the maunderings of the most abandoned dove.

Metternich Example

From his writings and recent press statements it is plain that Kissinger revels in such contradiction and pursues it deliberately. Like his subject Metternich, he has a yen for appearing to do one thing, while actually doing another. This is indeed a favorite explanation of Kissinger policies: We bomb Vietnam in order to get out (to doves), we accommodate Red China to save Free China (to hawks), we sign the SALT accord *because* our defense arsenal is in parlous shape, and so on.

It is possible to read through the 2,000-plus pages of Kissinger's books and find oneself nodding in agreement with ingenious points scored off the more soft-minded liberals. Kissinger is always and everywhere "realistic," "tough," unsentimental—a tone appealing to Cold War hardliners. Yet his toughness is almost always technical and retrospective; seldom does it affect the substance of what we should be doing now. His method is to accept the major themes of liberal policy—missile gap, stalemate, no-win strategies, summit conferences, arms control, *detente*—but to quibble exhaustively about the details.

That this tendency would appeal to President Nixon is apparent. It is eminently suited to the political exigencies with which a "centrist" administration believes itself to be confronted. Policies framed in such a manner can be impartially justified to liberals and conservatives, depending on the particular aspect of the matter that is stressed. In terms of domestic politics, the Kissinger approach effectively marshals conservative reasons in behalf of liberal policies. So long as conservatives are content with that performance, it will continue to be acclaimed a universal success.

U.S. Foreign Policy Needs a Forward Strategy
Why Castro Should Be Rendered Harmless

By Allan H. Ryskind   *(From the 21 February 1981 issue)*

(The following is the text of a speech HUMAN EVENTS Capitol Hill Editor Allan H. Ryskind delivered February 2 at Hillsdale College for the Center for Constructive Alternative's seminar on "Washington's New Leadership: Will It Make a Difference?")

The general theme at this seminar, as I understand it, is: Can the new Administration make a difference, can it change things for the better? My response, as a fairly longtime observer of the Washington scene, is that it would be difficult for things to get worse. Double-digit inflation, high unemployment, high interest rates, low productivity and a runaway budget suggest that the Reagan Administration assuming it is fully determined to slash tax rates and apply a tourniquet to our hemorrhaging budget, will at least diminish the intensity of the pain.

But what about the area of foreign policy, the main topic of my speech tonight? Here, again, I believe, it would be difficult for the Reagan Administration to make things worse. Under the late—and some would say unlamented, I would say unlamented—Administration, the United States and that portion of the world that is still eager to resist communism suffered enormous setbacks.

The Communists of North Vietnam, who stormed over the South in the spring of 1975, managed to nearly consolidate their hold on the entire Indochina peninsula, having installed their puppet in Cambodia in January 1979. A few weeks after the fall of Phnom Penh, several thousands of miles away in the pivotal Persian Gulf area, the shah felt impelled to flee his country, leaving Iran to the tender mercies of a fanatical anti-American Shiite Moslem, the Ayatollah Khomeini.

How critical was the loss of the shah? Former Secretary of State Henry Kissinger, with whom many of us on the right don't always agree, has made an eloquent response. "In my own experience," he said, "the shah never failed to stand by us." With the demise of the shah's regime, an unfriendly power now borders the Strait of Hormuz, through which passes 70 per cent of the imported oil consumed by Western Europe and 90 per cent of that used by Japan. The new Iran, unlike the old, is a deadly enemy of both Israel and Egypt, a supporter of such pro-Soviet terrorist regimes as Libya and a foe of the West in general.

The facilities which were used in Iran to monitor the Soviets' strategic missile test range are no longer available to us. What may be even more dangerous to the West's survival is that the political earthquake that shattered Iran has already had unpleasant consequences for the major oil-producing nation in the gulf, Saudi Arabia. The loss of Iran, in short, has placed the West in the greatest peril.

I wish this were the only sad news I had to relate. But 1979, unlike the words of a singer identified with the Reagan era, was, alas, a very bad year. More foreign policy catastrophes were to come. In December 1979, the Soviets engaged in a massive invasion of Afghanistan. It was the first time since the conquest of Eastern Europe that Soviet soldiers were dispatched en masse beyond the borders of their post-World War II empire.

The Afghan rebels, we are told, are giving the Soviets a rough time, but, in speaking to knowledgeable Afghans who have left their oppressed nation, one is led to believe that the rebels cannot last forever without far more help than they are presently being given by outside sources.

By moving into Afghanistan, Soviet armies now threaten both Pakistan and Iran, and, indeed, the entire Gulf region. With a Sovietized Ethiopia and Yemen threatening Saudi Arabia from the west and the south and a Sovietized Afghanistan menacing Iran and Pakistan from the east, the oil lifeline of the West is facing a powerful Soviet pincer movement that hardly warrants optimism on our part.

In the Middle East and Asia, then, there were stunning setbacks for the West. But we also suffered a major blow in our own back yard: Central America. The President would not admit it, but the Soviets and the Cubans had managed to acquire a new nation in our hemisphere in July 1979. Once considered a pro-Western ally and the key to control of the region, Nicaragua was overrun by the Sandinistas, with the United States paving the way through an arms embargo on the Somoza government.

The Sandinistas were spawned by the Cubans, trained by them and virtually controlled by them. When Nicaragua fell, they established a Cuban-style political apparatus that was effective right down to the block level; they invited Cubans in as military advisers and teachers; and they were soon signing agreements with Moscow.

While the Sandinista rulers have repeatedly denied exporting revolution, so flagrant has been their involvement in El Salvador that even our extremely liberal ambassador there, Robert White [since fired], was moved to denounce the Nicaraguan intervention. Castroism under President Carter had been spreading so swiftly throughout the Central American-Caribbean region that the Communist parties in the area recently remarked that "In Central America, the revolution feels itself stronger than in any other years in history."

Aside from absorbing these staggering losses, the United States, in the eyes of President Carter's own key military appointees, had slipped behind the Soviet Union in our strategic capabilities. Just last year, Gen. Richard Ellis, head of the Strategic Air Command, whose mission is to deter Soviet aggression with our nuclear arsenal, told a House Defense Appropriations subcommittee:

"Our calculations show that there was indeed essential equivalence in 1977 and early 1978. Since then it has eroded to the point where we must say essential equivalence does not exist."

Why have these catastrophic reversals taken place? If you believe, as some have contended, that personnel is policy, then there is no mystery as to why the West has suffered such enormous setbacks. I cannot think of any administration in our history which placed into critical governmental positions so many people who espoused defeatism, pacifism, radicalism or anti-Americanism.

From Sam Brown, who headed Action, and controlled the Peace Corps, to Andrew Young, who set our Third World policy at the United Nations, to even Secretary of State Edmund Muskie, the Carter Administration was wallowing in strange characters preaching astonishing doctrine.

There is an old but inelegant saying that "the fish stinks from the head." And President Carter, unfortunately, was largely responsible for the tenor of our foreign policy. A tip-off as to the disaster that was to follow when he assumed office came when he tried—unsuccessfully, it turns out—to install Theodore Sorensen as chief of the Central Intelligence Agency.

A former speech-writer for President Kennedy, Sorensen had become a partisan of the Democratic left in this country. He was an early booster of George McGovern, a supporter of "massive" defense cuts and an advocate of unilateral disarmament. Equally revealing is that the man Carter picked to head the CIA—the agency upon which the President must depend for making crucial foreign policy and defense decisions—was a conscientious objector. His Nebraska draft records show that he was classified "I-AO, a conscientious objector available for non-combatant military service only" when he initially registered. He also had that classification during the Korean War.

Sorensen has never repudiated his "conscientious objector" beliefs, and, indeed, defended them before his Senate confirmation hearings in 1977. He did insist, however, to many a skeptical solon, that "my preference for personal non-violence" would not inhibit his advice to the President on military policy.

Sorensen withdrew his name from nomination the first day of the hearings because it was obvious he could not be confirmed. But for the President to have purposely chosen a conscientious objector to rule over our major intelligence-gathering agency clearly signaled that this country was about to embrace a very soft foreign policy. Nor was the Sorensen selection particularly out of "synch" with the rest of the Carter appointments.

Sam Brown, Carter's choice to head Action, had led the anti-war movement in the United States. But he was not just anti-war, but pro the enemy, pro the Vietcong and the North Vietnamese battalions. On Sept. 25, 1977, after he was already the chief of Action, the agency which governed the Peace Corps, Brown participated in a "celebration and welcome" to honor the arrival of the Vietnamese Communist delegation to the United Nations and joined in applauding Vietnamese Deputy Foreign Minister Ngo Dien who heatedly condemned the "U.S. imperialists."

How much a speech-writer can influence a President is debatable, but the fact that President Carter chose Hendrik Hertzberg to script his major addresses because they seemed to think alike is not only interesting but a bit scary as well. Hertzberg emerged as the President's favorite ghost in 1979. Just two years earlier—when he began employment at the White House—he was listed on the masthead of *Win*, a publication of the radical-pacifist War Resisters League.

Not only was Hertzberg on the editorial masthead—until it was revealed in the press—but he was a frequent enough contributor. One of his more startling articles was featured in the Aug. 1, 1974, edition. Titled "It's Time to Start Worrying About the Bomb Again," the article was highly supportive of a proposal by then Sen. Harold Hughes, the Iowa Democrat, who announced that if he were ever elected President, the American people must know that he would never, under any circumstances, use nuclear weapons.

Hertzberg himself suggested that it might be a dandy idea for the U.S. to unilaterally destroy our entire atomic arsenal. Such a plan, he said, "could be undertaken openly, and television crews, foreign diplomats and representatives of international organizations would be invited to observe the dismantling of our warheads. The initial reaction everywhere would be stupefaction, giving way, I imagine, to a dramatic improvement in the world's moral and political climate."

I do agree with Hertzberg on at least one point: The world would, indeed, be "stupefied" if we carried out his program. But how the world would be better off after we had instantly handed the Soviet empire complete military mastery over every country on earth leaves me somewhat mystified.

Is it not somewhat remarkable that the man who was scripting the President's speeches believed we should unilaterally destroy our nuclear weapons, even if it meant our own annihilation, and that he embraced the theory that Hanoi's victory over a relatively free South Vietnam was "something honorable in the human spirit"?

But this only scratches the surface of the kind of men who surrounded the President. Whom did the President install as our chief arms negotiator for the SALT II talks? Paul Warnke. And what was Mr. Warnke's claim to fame? He served as the principal adviser to Sen. George McGovern on national security issues during the 1972 campaign.

Analyzing the McGovern position on defense, Dr. William Kintner, a highly respected American defense expert, stressed that the dramatic defense cuts planned by McGovern amounted to "a fiscal formula for unilateral disarmament. This could only satisfy the Soviet Union, upon whose benign sentiments we and our allies would then depend, because the McGovern budget would give them no choice."

Warnke's preference for "unilateral" initiatives was evidenced in the Spring 1975 issue of *Foreign Policy*, where Warnke proceeded to blame the arms race on the United States.

"As its only living superpower model," stated Warnke in doleful tones, "our words and our actions are admirably calculated to inspire the Soviet Union to spend its substance on military manpower and weaponry. . . ."

"The chances are good . . . that highly advertised restraint on our part will be reciprocated. The Soviet Union, it may be said again, has only one superpower model to follow. To date, the superpower aping has meant the antithesis of restraint."

Unforgivably, in my humble opinion, Warnke blamed us for provoking the Soviet Union for engaging in the most massive military buildup in history, even though the record will show that the U.S. defense budgets experience dramatic declines during the Nixon and Ford years. Ever since the Cuban missile crisis, furthermore, the United States has deliberately pursued a unilateral disarmament policy designed to permit the Soviets to match our strategic might, to assure them that we have no aggressive intentions.

Warnke, however, is apparently someone who favors a policy fashioned to give the Soviets, not parity, but *strategic superiority*. At the very least, he is not disturbed by the possibility. Testifying before the Senate on the 1972 SALT I agreement, Warnke said the ceilings on "both land-based and sea-based missiles should not be the cause for any concern on our part. They do give the Soviets an apparently large mathematical edge. . . . We should not be concerned about any attempts that the Soviet Union might take to add additional, useless numbers to their already far more than adequate supply."

When Warnke was under fire before being confirmed by a rather narrow margin by the Senate, President Carter continued to express "complete confidence" in him. He stated: "His views are well considered by me. . . . I have accepted them. . . . I believe Mr. Warnke's proposals are sound."

Is Warnke's nuclear weapons philosophy so different from Hertzberg's? Is it any wonder that with Warnke as our chief negotiator for SALT II, Lt. Gen. Edward Rowny, the Joint Chiefs' representative at the talks, ended up denouncing the treaty we concluded? Is it any wonder that the Senate refused to ratify it, believing it was not in our own interest to do so?

Andrew Young, of course, also played a strategic role in shaping our foreign policy. You may recall his statements with a few shudders. I know I do. But when he resigned under pressure in the summer of 1979, the Liberal Establishment, while faulting him for misleading the secretary of state, hailed his supposed statesmanship, with the Washington *Post* insisting that "he made some truly outsized contributions to American diplomacy." Did he really?

Young saw himself as the spokesman for the downtrodden, but his legacy at the U.N. was not as a champion of the oppressed, but as a spear carrier for the oppressor. Contrary to the liberal myth, his voice was not raised on behalf of the moderates, the peace-makers and the poor, but on behalf of leftist, totalitarian regimes and revolutionaries.

His record on their behalf is close to perfect. When the Cubans arrived in Angola, intent on supporting the minority Communist-dominated MPLA and crushing the majority opposition, Young contended that Castro's forces "were essentially opposing racism, and driving the South Africans out." As he was being considered for the U.N. post by the Senate Foreign Relations panel, Young appeared on CBS-TV where he said, ". . . [T]here's a sense in which the Cubans bring a certain stability and order to Angola. . . ."

Young played a disastrous role in shaping our foreign policy. He sent out the dangerous signal around the world that the U.S. is the friend of revolutionary Marxists, not their enemy. And many would contend that this is why the Cubans, the Ethiopians, the South Yemenis, the Patriotic Front, the Vietnamese, the Sandinistas, et al., were having such an easy time in pursuing their imperialistic ventures.

Though Young couched his rhetoric in the most provocative and outrageous terms, the basic thrust of his views were, to a great extent, policy. With Young at the helm, the U.S. did support the MPLA in Angola, did back the Marxist left in both Africa and Latin America, did withdraw our backing of the shah and purposely undermined Somoza.

The picture would not be complete without at least mentioning the two secretaries of state during the Carter years, Cyrus Vance and Edmund Muskie. Vance was, perhaps, the weakest secretary of state in modern times. Apparently traumatized by his initial support of the no-win war in Vietnam, he became a do-nothing secretary of state, who customarily endorsed Andrew Young's policies and offered no resistance of any note to either Soviet or Cuban adventurism. He quit his post because he couldn't go along with a decision by the Administration to use very limited force to liberate our hostages.

When the Soviets invaded Afghanistan and President Carter made the decision to impose the grain embargo, shelve SALT II and squeeze the Soviets in other ways as well, Vance refused to be strongly identified with the toughening response from the White House.

I attended the White House press briefing when Brzezinski and other top Administration officials explained the need for these anti-Soviet measures. Vance was conspicuously absent. The next day, when the State Department had a special briefing on the Administration decision, Hodding Carter III, the press spokesman, was the man in charge, with Vance again conspicuously absent. When I asked Carter where Vance was, he said he was in the building but didn't have the time to brief the reporters. Whether out of conviction or otherwise, he had decided not to be closely identified with the Administration's tentative efforts to apply a stronger policy toward Moscow.

His replacement, Edmund Muskie, had been considered a dove when he was in the U.S. Senate, and this belief was underscored by the little-known remarks that he delivered to the Beth Jacob Brotherhood Donor Dinner in Pikesville, Md., on Jan. 30, 1980, about a month after the Afghanistan invasion.

Amazing as it might seem, Muskie, while claiming he supported President Carter's hardened attitude toward Moscow, issued a virtual brief on behalf of the Soviets. Aside from trying to "stabilize the region" and fearing that the United States might "intervene militarily" in neighboring Iran, the Soviets, said Muskie, "may well have misunderstood recent American actions as aggressive in nature."

With this kind of thinking permeating the Administration from top to bottom, you can see why I believe that it would be difficult for the Reagan Administration to do worse.

Having said all this, having detailed the gory aspects of the Carter foreign policy, and outlined the defeatist and near-pacifist thinking of its philosophers, I am still not certain, despite the wonderfully refreshing statements about the Soviets that are emanating from the President and the secretary of state, that the new Administration will do immeasurably better.

I say this because, during the entire post-World War II era, every administration—whether Republican or Democratic, whether soft line or hard line—has lost ground to the Soviet empire and/or communism. Under President Truman, Eastern Europe and China disappeared behind a Communist curtain. Under President Eisenhower, the Soviets—by our refusal to do anything to challenge the Russians when the Hungarian revolution broke out—consolidated their hold over Eastern Europe. And they breached the Monroe Doctrine when they established a major beachhead in this hemisphere in 1959 with Castro's assumption of power in Cuba.

Under Presidents Kennedy and Johnson, Indochina began slipping into the Soviet sphere of influence and the United States, through the disarmament philosophy of Robert McNamara, saw its strategic nuclear superiority vis-a-vis the Soviets begin to erode rapidly.

Under Presidents Nixon and Ford, Hanoi expanded its grip on Southeast Asia, the Cubans began spreading their soldiers into Africa and we continued to fall behind the Soviets militarily. In addition, detente opened the way for the Soviets to receive a massive infusion of sophisticated technology from the West, much of which they used to build up their nuclear and conventional forces. The Carter years, as I have suggested, greatly accelerated our retreat from the world and the growth of Soviet power.

So what should be done? What is desperately needed, in the eyes of many Kremlinologists, is a forward strategy. For too long we have decided to retreat to events, never to take the lead. In the opinion of a growing number of students of Soviet power, we must greatly increase the pressure upon the Soviet Union and its satellites. We must not only retain the grain embargo, but we must expand it to include our high-grade technology. The Afghan rebels, as the recent Islamic conference in Saudi Arabia makes clear, are in deep, deep trouble, so it is incumbent upon us to furnish them with as many critical weapons as they can handle.

We must totally reverse our policy toward Angola, giving Jonas Savimbi the kind of backing a friend of the West and an enemy of Soviet-Cuban imperialism deserves.

But I would also contend that we scrap the Brzezinski Doctrine and reestablish the Monroe Doctrine.

We should be determined to get at the source of our troubles in this hemisphere, Fidel Castro.

As Moscow's cat's-paw, the Cubans have handsomely extended Soviet influence throughout Africa and the Middle East. They have conquered Angola and are conniving against Saudi Arabia from their havens in Ethiopia and Yemen. Through arms and training, they have helped to bring about the Communist conquest of Nicaragua and have frequently appeared on the brink of toppling El Salvador as well. Cubans are literally swarming throughout the Caribbean.

There is no question as to their impact. As Martin J. Scheina, analyst for Cuban affairs, the Defense Intelligence Agency, said in congressional hearings last year: "... Cuba's support for radical governments and revolutionary movements increased notably during 1979. . . . Cuba has nurtured the Sandinistas for two decades. As their activities gained impetus in 1978, this low-profile assistance dramatically changed. It is very doubtful that the Sandinistas could have achieved victory without Cuban support."

Our new ambassador to the United Nations, Jeane Kirkpatrick, has made some ominous observations about the Cuban threat. "In the past four years," she has written in a recent *Commentary* article, "the Soviet Union has become a major military power within the Western Hemisphere. In Cuba, the Soviets have full access to the naval facilities at Cienfuegos, nuclear submarines, airstrips that can accommodate Backfire bombers. From these, Soviet naval reconnaissance have on several occasions flown missions off the east coast of North America. They also have electronic-surveillance facilities that monitor American telephone and cable traffic and a network of intelligence activities under direct Soviet control. And, of course, a Soviet combat brigade.

"During the same four-year period the Soviets have continued to finance, train and staff a Cuban military establishment which has by now become a significant instrument of Soviet expansion in Africa, the Middle East, and South Asia as well as throughout the Caribbean and Central and South America. Today Cuba possesses a small navy; a sizable number of supersonic aircraft—including IL-14's and mg 21's and 23's—that can be quickly armed with nuclear weapons; modern transport planes capable of airlifting Cuban troops anywhere in the area; a huge army; and an estimated 144 SAM/anti-aircraft missile sites."

What the Reagan Administration should do, in the opinion of various geo-strategists, is amputate this cat's-paw. It would be tantamount to eliminating a bishop or a knight in our global chess game with the Russians. In one fell swoop, much of Africa and most of this hemisphere would be freed from any immediate Communist threat. A defeat of this magnitude could also shatter the illusions of so many that communism, whatever its defects, is somehow inevitable and must be accommodated. I do not say the Soviet empire would crumble because of it, but it might give us all in the West a little breathing room.

Many would argue that this is too drastic an action, that communism will someday collapse of its own dead weight. Perhaps. But I am unaware of a country that has come under full Communist rule in recent history that has managed to wriggle out from under such rule. Thus there are many who would strongly suggest that the Reagan Administration begin to focus its attention on how to render the imperialist Cuban government harmless.

Unless we are prepared to press ahead with such a forward strategy, many would argue, the Reagan Administration may not fare much better than the Soviet imperialism.

The Sandinista Government Should Be Overthrown

(From the 20 March 1982 issue)

The Administration is finally headed down the right track on Central America. For the first time since the release last year of the White Paper on El Salvador, it is beginning to lay out for the American public the reason why this nation needs to salvage Central America from Soviet-Cuban penetration.

There will never be any substantial backing for covert—or overt—aid to individual nations and/or anti-Communist forces in this hemisphere unless the American people realize the enormous extent of Soviet-Cuban subversion and the great threat it represents to America's security. Beginning with the slide show on Nicaragua at the State Department last week, the Administration appears to have initiated a heavy educational campaign along these lines.

The liberals and the media—along with the Sandinistas—have shown a certain consternation about this campaign. They fear it may foreshadow an effort to overthrow the Marxist-Leninist rulers in Nicaragua. We hope that it foreshadows just such an attempt.

The Communists must finally come to understand that this country is no longer going to pursue a "static" foreign policy, but one that will roll back hostile forces, particularly in our own backyard. The way to peace in El Salvador is through the toppling of the increasingly unpopular Marxist-Leninists in Nicaragua, which has become a central, privileged sanctuary for the Salvadoran guerrillas.

Trembling at the prospect that the U.S. might pursue a much-needed forward strategy, the Washington *Post* insisted last week that the President "foreswear an intent" to unseat the Sandinistas in order to "honor the traditional hemispheric ideal of nonintervention. . . ." But just who the hell does the Post think is intervening? The U.S. government, assuming that it is now backing covert actions against the Sandinistas, is perfectly justified in doing so because it is the Sandinistas who have decided to become pawns of Moscow and Havana.

It is the Sandinistas who have decided to threaten the hemispheric peace by expanding its army to 70,000 soldiers—the largest army in Central America—equipping itself with Soviet weaponry, constructing four major airfields configured to accommodate heavy jet attack aircraft and acting as a central supplier of the Marxist-Leninist guerrillas in El Salvador.

The U.S. must act against the Sandinista government—preferably in concert with other Latin nations, but alone, if necessary—in its own self-defense. To allow the Nicaraguans to continue on their own merry way is an invitation to a foreign policy disaster.

Nicaragua is not yet Cuba. But if we fail to oust the present rulers fairly quickly, it is bound to become another strong, Soviet-controlled base, complete with a Russian combat brigade. The truth is if this nation cannot summon the will to dislodge the rulers of a hostile, offensively postured country—which is a fraction of our size and population and has yet to solidify control over its own people—we might as well toss in the towel to Brezhnev right now.

There is proof aplenty concerning Nicaragua's untoward provocations and aggressiveness. The State Department, employing the government's premier photo interpreter, John T. Hughes, the same man who interpreted the photographs that showed the Soviets had introduced missiles into Cuba, graphically illustrated the major military buildup of the Nicaraguans last week.

Moreover, it is absolutely clear that the Nicaraguans have been lying through their teeth by insisting that they are not supporting the Salvadoran guerrillas with arms and training. Because much of the information is "sensitive," the U.S. government has not been able to release as much material as it has wanted to in this regard.

Still, the charges against Nicaragua are obviously accurate. When the intelligence community gave extensive briefings on this matter to the House Permanent Select Committee on Intelligence in early March, Rep. Edward P. Boland (D.-Mass.), the panel's chairman and a very liberal Democrat, issued this statement on committee stationary:

"The Committee has received a briefing concerning the situation in El Salvador, with particular emphasis on the question of foreign support for the insurgency. The insurgents are well-trained, well-equipped with modern weapons and supplies, and rely on the use of sites in Nicaragua for command and control and for logistical support. The intelligence supporting these judgments provided to the Committee is convincing.

"There is further persuasive evidence that the Sandinista government of Nicaragua is helping train insurgents and is transferring arms and financial support from and through Nicaragua to the insurgents. They are further providing the insurgents bases of operation in Nicaragua. Cuban involvement—especially in providing arms—is also evident.

"What this says is that, contrary to the repeated denials of Nicaraguan officials, that country is thoroughly involved in supporting the Salvadoran insurgency. That support is such as to greatly aid the insurgents in their struggle with government forces in El Salvador."

Sen. Barry Goldwater (R.-Ariz.), chairman of the Senate Intelligence Committee, issued this statement following a February 25 briefing by intelligence officials:

"In a recent ABC interview, the Nicaraguan ambassador to the U.S., Francisco Fiallos, said that his country 'does not send weapons and is not going to send weapons to El Salvador.'

"On Thursday, February 25, CIA Director William Casey and other representatives of the intelligence community briefed members of the Senate Intelligence Committee in executive session on developments in Central America. The briefing, which lasted several hours, addressed the military situation in El Salvador, the structure and composition of guerrilla forces there, and the degree of external support to the insurgents in El Salvador, especially that provided by the Sandinistas in Nicaragua.

"The briefing left no doubt that there is active involvement by Sandinista government officials in support of the Salvadoran guerrilla movement. This support includes arrangements for the use of Nicaraguan territory for the movement of arms and munitions to guerrillas in El Salvador, the continuing passage of guerrillas in and out of Nicaragua for advanced training in sabotage and other terrorist tactics, and the presence of high-level guerrilla headquarters elements in Nicaragua. There is strong evidence of a great surge in the delivery of arms, ammunition and related materials from Nicaragua to El Salvador.

"Speaking as chairman of the Committee, I must stress the sensitive nature of the intelligence provided us. The details must remain secret. But the American people deserve to know that the officials charged with developing and implementing U.S. policy in this area are doing so on the basis of solid information."

What is essential now is to follow through, to increase our covert and overt activities and, finally, to bring the Sandinista government down.

Hail to the Chief!

(From the 9 March 1991 issue)

Conservatives have never had a big crush on George Bush. But the overwhelming majority of them, along with the nation at large, were lustily singing the President's praises last week over the rout of Saddam Hussein and the liberation of Kuwait.

The Persian Gulf War has been Bush's finest hour, and is likely to have favorable historical consequences for the United States and much of the rest of the world.

For the moment—and it is a heckuva moment—Bush has become the Mother of All World Statesmen.

Joint Chiefs of Staff Chairman Colin Powell was recently asked what were the differences between the Bush Administration and the Reagan Administration. Powell's response: "Bush was bolder." Considering all that President Reagan did, we seriously disagree. But in the case of the gulf crisis, Bush was as bold—and as wise—as they come.

From the moment Saddam invaded Kuwait and threatened the entire gulf region, the President doggedly pursued a policy almost flawless in its vision and execution.

With his stunning victory, he has unified the nation, laid to rest much of the Vietnam syndrome and enormously elevated the stock of the U.S. military. Patriotism, as can be seen from the flags and yellow ribbons that engulf our cities and towns nationwide, is in full flower.

And the war has forever put to rest the liberal taunt: just what *did* the Defense Department do with all that money it received during the Reagan defense buildup?

Well, now we know. It purchased this nation a high-tech, military machine that, contrary to all those "60 Minutes" exposes, performed so marvelously that the U.S. defeated a country with the fourth-largest military force in the world, and did so *with fewer than 100 American combat casualties*. Surely this is an extraordinary achievement that will be studied in the military textbooks for years to come.

We're still not enamored of America's becoming the planet's policeman, but with this overwhelming victory, a relatively peaceful world seems far more likely for at least the near future. Terrorist Third World nations are not apt to "pull a Saddam" anytime soon.

Viewing the ruins of their military machine in Iraq and Kuwait, the Soviets, even should the hardliners totally prevail, are likely to pause for a long time before deciding to strike militarily at vital U.S. interests.

Because of George Bush, in short, the U.S., and most of the rest of the globe, can breathe more easily.

Yet the obstacles to this brilliant victory seemed enormous when it began.

Who could have believed that any American President could have taken a group of wildly disparate nations, including those frequently bitterly hostile to U.S. interests, weave them into a coalition, and then have them embrace, or at least not fatally undermine, the decision to force the Iraqis out of Kuwait?

But President Bush did precisely that. Surely, some of us thought, many of the countries in this fragile "alliance" might jump ship before we had successfully implemented our war aims. Iran's neutrality, for instance, was key to an early win, since it has 50 million citizens, includes a 700-mile border with Iraq and could have joined with Saddam to battle the "Christian" West and the Arab "betrayers" of Islam.

But even after Saddam returned the land he had gained from the Iraq-Iran war, and tapped enormously favorable sentiment with his Scud attacks against Israel, Iran's leaders stuck with the line that Saddam was at fault, stayed out of the war and kept embargo violations to a minimum.

And how could we trust the Soviets not to stab us in the back? Well, it turned out we couldn't. But the President and Secretary of State James Baker persuaded Moscow to support those 12 United Nations resolutions—including the call for an economic embargo and the use of force, if necessary, to free Kuwait—before the 11th-hour Soviet attempt to rescue Saddam and his military from a coalition defeat. Moscow's efforts at sabotage came too late.

The President also had to reckon with another crucial threat: the possibility that, once the fighting began, the Arab world would be "set aflame," with radical elements likely to topple Mideast and North African countries siding with America against Iraq. Arab demonstrations on behalf of Saddam were impressive, and, at times, it looked as if the pro-Iraqi Palestinians in Jordan would overthrow King Hussein—an event that could have had a shattering effect on moderate Arabs in the region.

King Hussein held on, but, more importantly, not a single Arab country friendly to our policy collapsed under the strain of pro-Saddam sentiment in the streets.

Moreover, the Arab nations with troops on the ground in Saudi Arabia, including Egypt and Syria, were willing to engage militarily against their brothers from Iraq, a fact that suggests Arab moderates might eventually prevail in this region after all.

Keeping this volatile coalition stable, making certain it would stick together until the Iraqis were ejected from Kuwait, was a monumental task, but the President proved quite up to it.

Equally stunning was George Bush's capacity to build a winning coalition at home. The President's decision to contain Saddam by imposing the embargo and stationing troops in Saudi Arabia had widespread support.

But taking the country into war was not so easy. Removing Saddam from Kuwait was certainly considered a just pursuit, but there was a huge amount of resistance on the Hill to rushing into a war, especially because a number of military experts kept warning about the enormous number of American casualties that would result.

Many of these experts, some of whom had served in the Reagan Administration (such as former Navy Secretary James Webb), could not be considered "doves" or "pacifists," and they were saying that this war was likely to be long and bloody. Some of the most conservative estimates indicated casualties would be "in the thousands." And Joint Chiefs Chairman Colin Powell, in perhaps his only major blunder, lent credence to the figures when he publicly mocked the air war strategists, and talked up the ground campaign.

The President moved quickly to defuse these fears, however, and Rep. Les Aspin (D.-Wis.), chairman of the House Armed Services panel, issued a critical report on January 8 that did much to convince lawmakers the air war was the Administration's strategy of choice, and that casualties were likely to be "moderate." Four days later, both houses of Congress had been convinced by the President that sanctions were not likely to work and that he should have the authority to root out the Iraqi military presence from Kuwait by force.

From the beginning, HUMAN EVENTS backed the President's decision to check Saddam's aggression, but we were among those who argued that a land war should not be fought if huge U.S. casualties would result. They never materialized, and that blessed fact, along with Saddam's decisive defeat, has made this war outcome an enormous triumph, justly celebrated, and historic in its implications.

There are numerous people who should receive great credit for the war's outcome, including Schwarzkopf and Powell, Baker and Cheney, Scowcroft and Gates. And, of course, our American soldiers, and the men who made those wonderful high-tech toys, deserve the highest of tributes.

But if it hadn't been for George Bush, who with exceptional skill built the international and domestic coalitions needed to eject Saddam militarily from Kuwait, the extraordinary victory the American-led forces achieved in the gulf war last week quite possibly never would have been achieved. He deserves to bask in the glory of his truly wondrous accomplishment.

Chapter Six

Defense

HUMAN EVENTS has always been an advocate of a strong national defense and a harsh critic of the misguided policies that contributed to the undermining of America's defense capability.

"Do Unilateral Disarmers Influence Defense Policy?" by Allan Ryskind (10 August 1963) lays bare the fatuousness of the Mutual Assured Destruction policy or MAD doctrine.

"SALT Plan Threatens U.S." (27 May 1972) dissects the flawed Strategic Arms Limitation Talks treaty in an analysis that has proved to be all too correct.

Frank Barnett's "Why the U.S. Should Pursue 'Star Wars' " (8 November 1986) makes the case for President Reagan's Strategic Defense Initiative, while a front-page HUMAN EVENTS article "Time Is Right to Scrap the ABM Treaty" (21 February 1987) urges the removal of the legal impediments to the deployment of an ABM system.

Do Unilateral Disarmers Influence Defense Policy?

By Allan H. Ryskind   *(From the 10 August 1963 issue)*

Something new in "unthink" has been going around the New Frontier for some time now. It's called disarmament. This is not disarmament in the framework of carefully negotiated treaties, ironclad inspections, and a genuine effort to reduce the effects of a catastrophic arms race.

A different type of disarmament is in the making: There is a deliberate, determined and massive effort by our highest government authorities to dismantle America's nuclear superiority over its deadly enemy the Soviet Union.

We are attempting to gut our nuclear superiority through *unilateral* disarmament steps which include a refusal to produce and deploy certain new weapons and an effort to abolish existing ones. These authorities are willing to take—*and have taken*—such measures for the purpose of grossly appeasing the Communists.

These "unilateralists" have infiltrated every government agency dealing with defense matters. They advocate that we take "calculated risks" and "gamble" with our defense policies in order not to "provoke" Moscow. They not only urge the United States to stop striving for nuclear superiority over the Soviets; they have publicly proclaimed their desire that the Soviet Union increase its own formidable nuclear capabilities.

The Harriman-Khrushchev proposed test-ban treaty fits neatly into the philosophy of those willing to take "calculated risks" with our defenses. While the test-ban will freeze American plans to set off nuclear shots in the atmosphere, for example, it will not prevent the Soviets from testing in this element. The plan is so full of loopholes that the Soviets, as Dr. Edward Teller has warned, could safely set off sneak, undetectable nuclear air bursts which would enable them to perfect their partially deployed anti-missile defense system. And who feels the Soviets, if they have the chance, will not cheat?

McNamara Hopes for Stronger USSR Defenses

Foremost among the "unilateralists," I believe, is the man legally in charge of bolstering America's defense establishment: Defense Secretary Robert Strange McNamara. In a Dec. 1, 1962, interview with Stewart Alsop in the *Saturday Evening Post*, Secretary McNamara suggested the incredible proposition that the United States would actually be better off if the Soviet Union could *increase* its already devastating nuclear warfare capabilities! According to Alsop—a fond admirer of Mr. McNamara—America's own defense secretary actually lamented the fact that Soviet Russia's nuclear forces today were so "soft" and vulnerable that the United States could wipe out Russia's warfare capabilities in one, sure, swift blow. Instead, said the incredible McNamara, he hoped the U.S.S.R. would soon be able to achieve what America presumably already has: a "sure second-strike" capability, and says Alsop, the secretary meant, "the sooner, the better."

If the Soviet Union ever developed a "sure second-strike" capability, its nuclear strength would be increased several fold. For a nation with a "sure second-strike" potential has its missile-bomber system so well protected—"hardened" in defense terminology—that it can absorb a massive atomic attack and still wreak devastating, unacceptable damage upon the enemy.

What could be the possible logic of the secretary? McNamara apparently reasons that in time of increased world tension, when war seems possible or probable, the Soviets might feel under terrible pressures to launch a massive sneak attack upon the United States—to bring their vulnerable missile and bomber force into play before America could annihilate this warfare capability with that one, sure, swift blow. Thus, says the secretary, the Soviet Union should develop a sure "second-strike" potential. For a nation which can still retaliate in a devastating manner after receiving the first punch would have "no rational basis on which to launch a pre-emptive attack."

It cannot be denied, of course, that the Soviet Union might launch a sneak attack against the United States if nuclear war seems inevitable. But what is highly intriguing is McNamara's unfathomable logic that as the Soviet Union grows militarily stronger in relation to America, the chance of surprise attack from Nikita—we will bury you—Khrushchev diminishes.

What is almost beyond credulity is that America's *defense secretary decidedly opposes a United States military capacity to wipe out the enemy's major and effective nuclear forces in the first blow!*

Defense Secretary McNamara says he wants a "more stable balance of terror" in the world—in short, nuclear stalemate between the United States and Russia. What the secretary is saying, of course, is that he is not at all pleased with the *imbalance* of terror which now favors the United States.

Nor should it be any wonder that a defense secretary who wants the Soviets to increase their nuclear fire power in relation to the United States has not developed a single new weapon system since he has entered office.

If McNamara's thoughts seem utterly irrational, they appear like a fresh breeze of logic compared to the cerebrations of Paul H. Nitze. Mr. Nitze, I remind the reader, is not someone stuck away in some Pentagon file. He is, in fact, currently serving as assistant secretary of defense for international security affairs. By all accounts, he is a highly influential planner helping to determine our defense policies.

His philosophy on defense was expressed April 28, 1960, to some 500 business and professional people at Asilomar on California's Monterey Peninsula. At this seminar, Nitze, like clear superiority over the Soviets was no longer a desirable defense posture. His reasoning was curiously close to that of his present boss. But Mr. Nitze went even further than his boss in outlining a radical defense policy for the United States. Nitze proposed that America should take ". . . a series of unilateral actions designed to produce a reciprocal action on the part of our allies and also on the part of our enemies" to slow down the arms race. The United States, said Nitze, should "scrap" its "fixed based" missile and bomber bases (part of a Class A power); the United States should put its Strategic Air Command, headquartered in Omaha, Neb., and considered the prime American defense system against the Soviets, under a "NATO command"; and, finally, that the United States should inform the United Nations "that NATO will turn over *ultimate power of decision on the use of these systems to the General Assembly of the United Nations. . . ."* (Emphasis added.)

Alas, Mr. Nitze and Mr. McNamara are not the only officials with preposterous views on defense matters. Consider, also, Dr. Hans Bethe. Dr. Bethe has been a key adviser to the President for some time. At Cornell University, Jan. 5, 1962, Dr. Bethe suggested the United States should begin to ease tensions with the Soviets. We could do this, he explained, by abandoning our "long range bombers" and even some of our missiles. Such weapons, said Bethe, might be provocative to the Soviets and so they should be withdrawn.

In this topsy-turvy world of unthink—where defense planners rejoice over the strength of the enemy—one must also mention Dr. Jerome B. Wiesner, the President's chief scientific adviser. Carl Kaysen, a key "disarmament" strategist who works under McGeorge Bundy, the President's special assistant, told this reporter that Wiesner was one of the most influential planners in this area. The 47-year-old soft-spoken, pipe-smoking professor from the Massachusetts Institute of Technology, wields enormous powers over critical agencies relating to America's defenses. The Pentagon, the Atomic Energy Commission, the National Science Foundation are only a few such governmental bodies that come under his personal supervision. Wiesner, according to one high Pentagon source, has a decisive influence upon Robert S. McNamara's own defense theories.

Wiesner: We Should Take 'Calculated Risks'

According to a personality profile of Wiesner in the *Saturday Review* (Dec. 10, 1960), the MIT professor "looks upon arms control as almost a crusade." He desires, according to the article, to put "peace explorers in the White House, in the State Department, in the Pentagon, in the Atomic Energy Commission" and "elsewhere at key points." While Wiesner believes any arms agreement with the Soviets may carry calculated risks, the professor also stresses that "science must develop such an overwhelming case in support of the soundness of the calculated risk philosophy that the fearful politician will have nothing left to hide behind."

In other words, we should take calculated risks in reaching a disarmament agreement with a nation which has vowed it will exterminate us!

Such, then, are some of the leading disarmament theoreticians and practitioners on the New Frontier. What is highly disturbing to many military men is the common, pernicious thought threaded through their philosophies; that as the Soviet Union achieves nuclear parity with the United States that as its defenses get increasingly better, the chance for war grows increasingly dim. What, truly, could be more insane? Would Sonny Liston have felt better if Floyd Patterson had had a better defense and a stronger right arm?

On the absurd theory that America would be better off if the Soviets begin matching our nuclear power, we should erect a national monument to Julius and Ethel Rosenberg for supplying the Soviets our atomic secrets!

Is it true, however, that the disarmament theorists have influenced our defense strategy? The available evidence suggests that this is, indeed the case.

It now develops, in fact, that our present defense policies were initiated when President-elect Kennedy sent two professional disarmers—Walt Whitman Rostow (now State Department Planning Counselor) and Jerome Wiesner—to the Pugwash Conference in Moscow in November, 1960. The two went to discover the possibilities of disarmament with the Soviet Union.

There can be little doubt today that this conference blueprinted subsequent New Frontier moves to scrap production of "provocative" long range bombers, to yank medium-range ballistic missiles from Turkey and Italy and to refuse to deploy an anti-missile defense system.

On March 30, 1961, the Chicago *Sun-Times* revealed this astounding story through its crackerjack reporter, Thomas B. Ross. The substance of what Ross wrote (which first appeared nationally in HUMAN EVENTS, April 14, 1962) bears repeating in part:

Ross claimed that President Kennedy's defense message of 1961 was actually sown in hush-hush talks between Rostow and Soviet Deputy Foreign Minister Vasily V. Kuznetsov. Kuznetsov, according to Ross, complained that in order to achieve any progress in relieving tensions between East and West, the United States should abolish its provocative weapons, specifically manned bombers and missiles which ring the Soviet Union. Rostow, said Ross, then wrote a confidential memorandum to Kennedy suggesting we scrap these provocative weapons and build up, instead, a defense composed of allegedly invulnerable missiles, such as the Polaris, and non-nuclear forces. According to Ross, Rostow's advice "reverberated" in Kennedy's first defense message. The White House meetings, where the final defense message went through a threshing process, were "directed," said Ross, by Theodore Sorensen, the President's special counsel *who was a conscientious objector during the Korean War. (!!!)*

Among the weapons deleted from the budget that year (and each year subsequently) were the B-70 superbomber and the anti-missile missile. Each of these weapons—including the purely defensive Nike-Zeus anti-missile missile—were labeled provocative weapons for varying reasons.

Rostow Memorandum Shapes American Policies

The substance of the Ross story—never denied despite its countless repetitions in news media and before Congress—has clearly been the operating policy of the United States.

Certainly it must be rated more than coincidence that Rostow's reported advice has been carried out in detail: We have stopped production of the B-70 and all other manned bombers; despite numerous successful test firings, we have refused to deploy a Nike-Zeus anti-missile defense system; Polaris submarines are replacing our overseas bombers and missiles. The Ross story, once felt to be sheer hallucination, must now be regarded as hard fact. Nor is it difficult to believe that our "unilateralists"—with their weird disarmament theories—have feverishly worked toward abolishing such "provocative" weapons. If the United States, as the unilateralists believe, would be better off if the Soviets began matching our nuclear power, then why is it so difficult to believe that we have slowed down the arms race unilaterally to allow the Soviets a chance to "catch up"?

The diehard skeptic may still doubt that the Rostow-Wiesner mission framed our defense policies. But what certainly can be proved beyond the shadow of a liberal's doubt is that the "unilateralists" have heavily favored the disarmament steps outlined in the Ross story. Mr. Nitze, Dr. Wiesner and Dr. Bethe, as we have seen, have publicly expressed their opinions that we should relegate to the junkyard our long range bombers and missiles overseas. Few question they are headed in that direction today.

The arguments against deploying an anti-missile missile in the United States is immersed in technical detail, intraservice rivalry and politics. But the one, clear and decisive fact that emerges is that the unilateral disarmers have energetically worked to see it killed off permanently. The chief military reporter for the pro-New Frontier Washington *Post* (John G. Norris) enlightened the public on this score Jan. 20. Wrote Norris: "President Kennedy has taken a calculated risk in deferring any missile defense of American cities and defense centers until the late 1960s."

While Norris stressed that some military men think this is a sound "gamble" (!!!), he also related:

"Some of President Kennedy's advisers, moreover, argue that building an urban missile defense system would be 'provocative' in that Russia would have to follow suit and the arms race would be accelerated."

We know that the man who champions the "calculated risk" philosophy, Dr. Wiesner, also firmly opposes our deploying an urban defense system. He told this to Soviet and American scientists gathered at the Pugwash disarmament conference both he and Rostow attended. Said the good doctor in his Nov. 29, 1960, speech: "It is important to note that a missile deterrent system would be unbalanced by the development of a highly effective anti-missile defense system and if it appears possible to develop one, the agreements should explicitly prohibit the development and deployment of such systems."

Refusing to heed Wiesner, however, the Soviet's earlier this year began to "unbalance" the defense picture by deploying one fully operational anti-missile installation near Leningrad. Wiesner refused to be provoked. In the June 23 *Saturday Evening Post*, New York *Herald-Tribune* reporters Earl Ubell and Stuart H. Loory publicly revealed Wiesner's role in getting Kennedy this year to shelve deployment of our successfully tested Nike-Zeus missile. The authors report that "Wiesner had advised the President, 'Don't deploy Nike-Zeus. . . . Keep it in research and development.'"

Still, people will ask: How can you say we're disarming? What, for example, is wrong with gradually substituting Polaris-bearing submarines in the North Atlantic and Mediterranean, as we are doing and as the Rostow memo suggests, for long range bombers and missiles based overseas? Isn't the Polaris a super-sleek, modern, "invulnerable" weapon?

The Polaris-bearing subs are, indeed, superb weapons in our atomic arsenal. But the evidence suggests that Polaris subs should be supplemental to, not a substitute for, land-based missiles and bombers overseas.

It is agreed upon by most military men that the only weapons which could definitely dig out Soviet offensive missiles in hardened sites are the powerful nuclear warheads which today only long range bombers—not missiles, least of all Polaris missiles—are capable of delivering.

When it comes to invulnerability, this point should be added. On April 17 of this year the Defense Department admitted the Soviet Union's anti-missile installation near Leningrad was capable of shooting down nuclear-tipped intermediate range Polaris missiles.

SALT Plan Threatens U.S.

(From the 27 May 1972 issue)

President Nixon, who vowed in 1968 to provide America with "clear-cut military superiority" over the Soviet Union, is in Moscow this week pleading with the Kremlin's leaders to sign an agreement that is likely to freeze the United States into a posture of nuclear inferiority. That's the informed word from specialists in the military field who have been privy to the disarmament discussions going on at the Strategic Arms Limitation Talks (SALT) and who are familiar with the agreements we are offering the Russians.

According to these sources, here's what the Nixon SALT package—all but agreed to by the Soviets—will accomplish: It will give the Soviets a permanent lead in the total number of offensive ballistic missiles—both land- and sea-based—and it will provide the USSR with an extraordinary opportunity to soar ahead of us in the number of deliverable warheads.

The agreement will be divided into two parts: a permanent draft treaty requiring Senate passage, which covers only anti-ballistic missile systems (ABM); and an executive agreement to be initiated by Nixon and the Soviet leaders covering offensive missiles, land-based and sea-based, for a duration of five years.

The executive agreement reportedly consists of these specifics:

• The United States, which now has 41 nuclear submarines, has agreed to freeze its submarine fleet at existing levels. Incredibly, however, the understanding permits the Soviet Union to construct at least 60 nuclear submarines (Yankee-class), equipped with at least 960 offensive missiles.

Under this agreement, the Soviets will be allowed to surpass the United States in both the number of nuclear subs and sea-based offensive missiles by approximately 50 per cent. Currently, sea-based missile deployment represents the only remaining U.S. lead over the Soviet Union in the entire missile field.

The Soviets have 25 operational subs already, with 17 more under construction. But the Nixon package generously permits the Soviets to build an additional 18 or more modern nuclear submarines, the only condition being that they would have to scrap some 200 older land-based offensive missiles, the SS-7s and SS-8s.

• The executive agreement would also generously permit the Soviet Union to have close to a three-to-two advantage over us in land-based intercontinental ballistic missiles. Assuming the Soviets choose to convert their older, land-based missiles into submarines, for instance, the Nixon plan would still allow the Soviets to have 1,400 land-based ICBMs, while the United States' land-based offensive missile force would be fixed at its present, 1,054 level. If the Soviets by some whim choose not to cash in their SS-7s and 8s for subs, their lead in land-based offensive missiles would increase by approximately 200 more.

• Furthermore, the United States is prohibited from replacing its Minuteman and Titan fleets with larger missiles, while the Soviet Union has no such restriction with respect to its already huge SS-9. The Soviets have recently been testing a far bigger successor to the SS-9.

• Informed sources also point out that under the conditions of this compact, the Soviet Union would have the ability to catch up to the United States and eventually surpass it in the number of deliverable warheads.

The Soviets now have more missiles than we do, some of which, particularly the SS-9s, pack a far greater wallop than ours. But because we are ahead of them in warhead technology, our missiles can deliver approximately as many warheads as theirs can—2,500.

Since the proposed SALT agreement fundamentally freezes the existing number of offensive missiles on both sides, the Soviets, assuming they can match our current warhead technology, which most experts do assume, will be able to achieve the capacity to rain at least five times as many warheads upon the United States as we will be able to unleash upon the Soviet Union.

Nor does this exhaust the tremendous concessions we are about to make to the Soviets at the summit. Though the Pentagon has insisted all along that we must erect several ABM sites to protect our land-based missiles from the threat of those massive Soviet SS-9 missiles, the draft treaty—which would be permanent—would force us to dismantle two out of three Safeguard sites already authorized by Congress. The Soviets, however, are not required to eliminate a single SS-9, which leads one to wonder why we ever maintained they were a threat in the first place.

Aside from requiring no on-site inspection nor restricting the production of bombers, the treaty significantly fails to even touch upon the Soviet Intermediate Range Ballistic Missiles (IRBMs) now menacing the whole of Western Europe.

Indeed, many experts believe that the proposed package—as it has been outlined to lawmakers and government personnel in Washington last week—is an outright gift to the Soviet Union, bestowing upon this Communist colossus nuclear superiority for years and years to come. In one stroke the United States would permanently remove the nuclear umbrella of protection it has extended to our allies and bring our own survival into grave question as well.

In a little-noticed speech delivered in October 1969, late Secretary of State Dean Acheson suggested that SALT could actually turn into a "Munich."

"One can easily see," he emphasized, "the advantage to the Soviet Union and the lethal danger to the United States in an agreement that would bind the open and public American society to nuclear parity with the Soviet Union without opening the closed and secret Soviet society to far more inspection and oversight than it has ever been willing to grant in 20 years of discussion of the subject."

The chances for real success in the discussions, Acheson stated, "must be almost infinitesimal, yet the lure of them to negotiators and the danger of falling into their own bear trap is substantial. Until Communist society becomes more civilized and reliable, the risks of improvident agreement, like those of continuous Russian roulette, are uninsurable, and perhaps greater than those created by no agreement at all."

The risks seem even greater, Acheson maintained, when we add another consideration: "Currently the Soviet Union greatly surpasses Western Europe in intermediate range ballistic missiles and conventional forces. The threat that this superior power might impose Soviet demands on Western Europe, as it has on Eastern Europe, has been offset by the provisions of the North Atlantic Treaty and the presence in Europe of substantial United States conventional forces as a practical guarantee of U.S. strategic nuclear support.

"If, however, Soviet and American intercontinental nuclear power were neutralized by agreement to maintain parity, leaving Soviet intermediate-range and conventional power unchangeable, the balance of power in Europe would be so openly and notoriously upset that the imbalance might be as great and could be as decisive as it was after Munich. Not that war would be inevitable, but Soviet domination *would* be if American intervention should be foreclosed."

In Acheson's view, a nuclear Munich would have been struck if we even opted for parity with the Soviets. But in Washington last week, military experts were suggesting that we were offering the Soviets a disarmament treaty far more disadvantageous to the United States than anything Acheson ever dreamed of.

Why the U.S. Should Pursue 'Star Wars'

By Frank R. Barnett   *(From the 8 November 1986 issue)*

(This article is excerpted from The Intelligent Layperson's Guide to "Star Wars," *published by the National Strategy Information Center, Inc. Mr. Barnett, founder and president of the National Strategy Information Center, has been actively involved for many years in promoting national security education to political groups across the political spectrum and in furthering the cause of the Atlantic Alliance.)*

It is popular to argue there might be more prudent gambles than SDI, such as more persistent tries at arms control. Yet, arms control is scarcely an untested hazard. We have played at the arms limitation table now for more than 60 years, first against Nazi Germany and Japan, then against the Soviet Empire. For the most part, we gained little more than euphoria from being seen in the Peace Casino, while our adversaries went home to convert "lawful" winnings into larger stockpiles of more advanced weapons.

Arms control agreements have been so ineptly crafted, or so poorly enforced by the West, that the Soviet military threat has demonstrably increased in the wake of the ABM, Outer Space, and SALT I and II treaties.

Moreover, history is replete with evidence that "treaties" between nations with incompatible moral and legal premises do not usually benefit that society which is reluctant to resort to conspiracy and deceit.

Between 1983 and 1985, five presidential reports to Congress have detailed the means by which the USSR has evaded the aim of nearly half the arms control pledges it has signed since the end of World War II.

Not a few Americans and Europeans predicate new peace proposals on their confidence that Moscow—despite both deployment patterns and military doctrine to the contrary—*really* adheres to the wisdom of Mutual Assured Destruction.

Soviets Don't Embrace Orthodoxy of MAD

One trouble with this analysis is the flawed premise: the Soviets have never embraced the orthodoxy of MAD; they have always been stubborn heretics from the McNamara dogma, unwilling to concede that Mother Russia must be delivered as a passive hostage to American warheads.

No number of patronizing tutorials from American arms control enthusiasts seems likely to deflect Soviet strategy from its historic commitment to a ferocious defense. Those whose ancestors survived the invasions of Napoleon and Hitler are psychologically able to allocate resources to the defense of the homeland on a scale unimaginable to us.

For more than two decades, the Kremlin has applied awesome energy to achieve both (a) damage-limitation to Soviet industrial plant and (b) assured survival for the *Nomenklatura*, the elite who manage the political, military, internal security and economic consortia of the USSR. Since the Politburo presides over a vast defensive enterprise of its own, we need not be overly concerned that its members will become paranoid over a U.S. program with parallel aims.

What should alarm us more is the Russian definition of what, to us, seems an innocuous term: "damage limitation." In Soviet military doctrine, the efficient (and acceptable) way to limit damage to one's own cities and people is to destroy enemy missiles before they are launched.

While American think-tanks debate "How much is enough?", the Russians suffer no such indecision. What is "enough"—in modern nuclear weapons as in the awesome mass of Stalin's World War II artillery—is not only "more than the opponent," but conspicuously enough more to overawe, intimidate, preempt and annihilate.

We Cease Building, Russians Continue

President Carter's secretary of defense, Dr. Harold Brown, rebutted the notion that there is a direct correlation between American initiative and Soviet response with regard to offensive weapons production. Secretary Brown observed that when we build, they build; but when we cease building they continue to build. The Kremlin's programs in defense are likewise grounded in Soviet strategy and gather momentum from Soviet priorities, not from Western example.

In short, forbearance on our part will deter neither Moscow's production of SS-18's nor its advanced research on war lasers and particle beams. We have inside evidence for this evaluation.

Thirty émigré scientists from the USSR wrote an open letter to the American people in June 1986. Based on their experience, they asserted that, since the late 1960s, the Soviet Union has devoted more of its resources to strategic defense than has the United States. Moreover, added the former Soviet scientists, Communist leaders will continue to work on their own version of "Star Wars," either overtly or covertly, and with high priority, no matter what they say or what they sign, or what the U.S. does.

SDI in Harmony With Deepest Values

The "nuclear freeze" movement in Europe and America, together with opposition to our current strategy by Catholic and Methodist bishops, indicates that the old consensus in favor of "defense through reprisal" is coming unraveled.

Most of our European partners were against the neutron weapon. Nobody in NATO likes chemical arsenals. Our nuclear warheads are smaller and cleaner than the Kremlin's. We have no aggressive doctrine of war-fighting. We don't plan to preempt. Thus, in terms of culture as well as strategy, the goals of the SDI are more harmonious with the deepest values of our society than is the relentless perfection of offensive megatons required to undergird the strategy of MAD.

Hence, knowing that Moscow has been in vigorous pursuit of strategic defense for nearly 20 years—as usual behind a cloak of disinformation—is more than a sufficient motive for Washington to engage in SDI.

SDI Could Warn Of Soviet 'Breakouts'

At minimum, our research effort should lead to early warnings of potential Soviet "breakouts" and provide safeguards against technological ambush. Moreover, even if SDI does not produce a 100 per cent effective missile barrier, the concentrated pursuit of novel defensive technologies is likely to offer unforeseen options to future Presidents who, absent the SDI, would find themselves in a strategic straitjacket.

Chance often favors those with enlarged freedom of choice. To expand that choice, we are asked to place a practical wager on the proven genius of U.S. scientific laboratories and aerospace firms which, in turn, are improving the odds by enlisting crack research and engineering talent from Germany, Britain, Japan, France and Israel.

No wonder Moscow's propaganda seeks to nullify a judicious bet on such an aggregate of ingenuity and industrial competence.

Rhetoric aside, as of now there are two quite different force deployments to back up two quite different theories on how to prevent nuclear war, or at least greatly limit the damage to one's own side.

Soviet heavy missiles, very accurate, are deployed in support of the doctrine that the best strategy is to destroy an enemy's missiles before they can be launched. U.S. Fighter, less accurate, missiles are deployed to underpin the doctrine that the best strategy is to demonstrate unequivocally that the enemy's cities will be destroyed even if he has fired first—thus deterring war in the first place. Now President Reagan advances a *tertium quid:* the best strategy is to deploy a defensive system which, if the enemy launches offensive missiles, will destroy them in flight.

Note the psychological and moral distinctions between Soviet military doctrine and the concept of "Star Wars."

To destroy American missiles before they leave their silos would necessitate a surprise first strike by Moscow. That improbable "bolt from the blue" could be a coldblooded act of decapitation. However, a more likely possibility exists—an "unwanted" Soviet launch, prompted by misplaced fear.

A first strike could be based on the Politburo's *assumption* that Washington "might" be thinking of mounting its own attack on the USSR.

The anti-missile shields of "Star Wars," by way of contrast, would not lead to holocaust through a wrong assumption. Only after Soviet missiles were actually in flight would they be attacked. In other words, SDI defense would not be triggered by what Washington *thought* Moscow's intentions *might* be; the force of the shields would only be invoked against the unmistakable fact of Soviet missiles under way.

SDI doesn't upset a "safe" status quo; rather, it shifts the context from a track on which we are losing to a playing field on which, eventually, both sides (and mankind as a whole) can win by competing to build better defenses instead of more lethal warheads.

Finally, unlike the posture required by MAD, the SDI would devalue the worth of Soviet missile stockpiles, reduce the potential for a successful first strike and provide protection should deterrence fail.

Star Wars is not the antithesis of the current strategy of deterrence. If it works, in successive stages the SDI would first enhance, then complement, and lastly modify deterrence; almost certainly it would never abolish it.

Thus, while we debate the wisdom of the SDI gamble, we must not forget that our security in the foreseeable future must still rest largely on deterrence. Whether the hopes of the SDI materialize or wither by the year 2000, there is an imperative and continuing need to modernize, disperse, and protect our retaliatory forces at least for the next decades.

To some, MAD is a pragmatic, lesser evil; to others, the doctrine is immoral and intolerable; but, until a reliable Star Wars apparatus is actually in place, the first defense priority is to ensure that the Kremlin will always know it can never escape the mutuality of destruction, even with a surprise first strike.

It is a paradox that many who oppose SDI simultaneously criticize the Reagan Administration for having no national strategy. Yet the SDI could lead to the most revolutionary and pervasive change in strategy since 1917-18, when defense dominated the battlefield, only to be superseded by the primacy of the offense in the following seven decades.

Moreover, if SDI technology generates "spinoffs" applicable to conventional war-fighting, strategy may be profoundly altered at the theater level as well as in the nature and methods of global deterrence.

SDI a Decisive Change in Strategy

Thus, the SDI is not only a quest for novel defensive weapons, but a decisive change in strategy; and history suggests that, once creators have been animated by such a challenge, the technological means to support a new strategy will follow. Of course strategic defense is still an uncertain venture; but serendipity often smiles on those who risk exploration of multiple pathways. Some may lead to a *cul de sac*, but others may open on to a mountain pass invisible from the placid meadows below.

It is also a paradox that many of those prepared to parade against nuclear weapons seem disinclined to mobilize the scientific laboratory, in addition to the picket line, to reduce the danger of atomic holocaust.

Time Is Right to Scrap the ABM Treaty

(From the 21 February 1987 issue)

President Reagan has the opportunity to strike a major blow on behalf of the security of this country by announcing that the U.S. plans to withdraw from the AntiBallistic Missile (ABM) treaty and push full-speed ahead with the Strategic Defense Initiative (SDI).

That would not only be a bold maneuver, but it is the growing consensus of a number of his strongest "Star Wars" supporters in Congress, including Rep. Jim Courter (R.-N.J.) and Sen. Malcolm Wallop (R.-Wyo.).

The move toward deployment would ensure his place in history, and almost certainly knock the Iran/Contra "scandal" off the front pages. Instead of being referred to as a "lame duck" or "disengaged," the President would be riding high again, inspiring his friends and confounding his foes.

Sure, there is bound to be a wild hullabaloo raised by the Left, but the President, we venture to say, would emerge as the clear winner, with a stunning issue for the GOP in 1988 if the Democratic Party chooses to go in opposition.

The polls are all on the President's side. The respected firm of Penn & Schoen Associates, which has done work for Sen. Teddy Kennedy (D.-Mass.) and Walter Mondale, came up with this startling response from those it surveyed last year: *81 per cent* of the American people favored SDI research and development, and *78 per cent* supported deployment.

The CBS/New York *Times* survey, following the Reagan-Gorbachev meeting in Reykjavik, found that close to 70 per cent of the American people wanted to go ahead with SDI, even if the Soviets agreed to a big reduction in nuclear weapons if "Star Wars" were killed.

The Lou Harris poll worded its question in the least helpful way for the pro-SDI position, asking: "If you had to choose right now between eliminating all strategic nuclear missiles or proceed with Star Wars development which would you prefer?" The response: 55 per cent said "Proceed with Star Wars."

Maybe the Democrats want to go down in history as the party which destroyed a highly popular idea that can protect millions of Americans from nuclear devastation, but we don't think so. And if they should be so foolish as to try, the Republicans should come back with a bang in next year's elections.

So far, however, the President appears unwilling to break out of the 1972 ABM treaty, the dramatic signal that would conclusively demonstrate that his Administration seriously intends to deploy a nuclear shield. (Indeed, we are legally prohibited from *ever* erecting a strategic defense system unless we withdraw.)

Judging from the reports of last week, both Defense Secretary Caspar Weinberger and the President have a different approach. They want to creep—rather than rush—toward eventual deployment by first making a fight over the "interpretation" of the ABM treaty.

Minutes of a White House meeting of senior Administration arms control advisers show that Weinberger recommended formal acceptance of the "broad" interpretation, so that the U.S. could engage in various tests considered essential for SDI development. The President also wanted to "go ahead" with Weinberger's controversial view.

But what SDI's strongest supporters in Congress are saying is that if the Administration is going to spill its blood (and the broad view on testing is a blood-spiller), then it should do so, instead, over the core issue, the one that is certain to win over the public: The need to protect ourselves against the Soviet atomic arsenal. And there's only one way this can be achieved: withdrawing from the ABM treaty, the move the Administration will have to make in order to legally erect a full-blown anti-missile system.

Why not bleed for something substantial, it is being asked, rather than for a murky legalism, which, even if the Administration prevails, still doesn't allow the U.S. to deploy an effective defensive shield?

Senate Democrats, led by the chairman of the Armed Services Committee, Sam Nunn (Ga.), have already bluntly informed the President that the "broad interpretation" by the executive branch would invite a Democratic rebellion.

In a stiff letter to the President, Sen. Nunn said any formal adoption of the broad interpretation "would put immense pressure on SDI funding and in my opinion would cause much deeper SDI cuts than would otherwise occur. . . ."

"Finally," he added, "I am concerned that absent due consultation, a unilateral executive branch decision to disregard the interpretation of the treaty, which the Senate believed it had approved when the accord was ratified in 1972, would provoke a constitutional crisis of profound dimensions."

Nunn appears to be acting out of partisan motives pandering to his party's doves. But he also may be correct (even though the way he has raised the issue is certain to impede the SDI program). Former Secretary of State Henry Kissinger, under whom the treaty was negotiated, said on "Meet the Press" last week that "In 1972, as I recall it, and I have not looked at the documents, the American position strongly advocated what is also today called the narrow interpretation. . . . When the treaty was submitted to the United States Congress, the United States supported it with interpreting it in the narrow way."

Many of the senior members of the U.S. team that negotiated the treaty for President Nixon have opposed or not defended the broad interpretation, and Paul Nitze, the Administration's key arms control adviser who helped negotiate the ABM treaty, is said to have supported the narrow interpretation in mid-September 1985, just two weeks before the State Department's legal adviser, Abraham Sofaer, ruled that the "broad interpretation" was the correct view.

The "broad" view *may* be correct, in fact, but why should the issue be framed around Nunn's concerns? The issue to be debated is not whether President Reagan is violating a solemn treaty, but whether it is sound policy to construct a credible defense against the Soviet nuclear arsenal.

Rep. Jim Courter made that point well in a February 9 letter to the President. As Courter stated in part:

"It should be apparent to all concerned that the current debate over the 'narrow' and 'broad' interpretations of the ABM treaty of 1972 threatens to spiral out of control, thus endangering the prospects for phased deployment of SDI systems. We must not lose sight of our ultimate goal, which is not victory in an arcane legalistic debate but the actual deployment of defenses for the American people and our allies. Actions by your Administration in the near future should further this strategic objective.

"The impediments presented by the ABM treaty should be tackled directly in an unambiguous fashion. I'm thinking, of course, about actual withdrawal from the ABM treaty as provided for in Article XV:

" 'Each Party shall, in exercising its national sovereignty, have the right to withdraw from this Treaty if it decides that extraordinary events related to the subject matter of this Treaty have jeopardized its supreme interests. It shall give notice of its decision to the other Party six months prior to withdrawal from the Treaty. Such notice shall include a statement of the extraordinary events the notifying party regards as having jeopardized its supreme interests.' "

Even Nunn has suggested he might buy this option. Asked by Sam Donaldson on "This Week With David Brinkley" if we shouldn't just "withdraw from the treaty. There's a provision for that," Nunn responded: "Well, if you're going to take a treaty and stand it on its head by reinterpretation, then it seems to me that you ought to ask the question, why not just give six month's notice, which the treaty permits in the supreme national interest, and tell the Soviets you're going to abrogate it?

"Now I don't counsel that now. I think that, too, would require a lot of consultation with allies and so forth. But I do believe that is the honorable way to go about it."

It is not only honorable; it *is* in the "supreme national interest." The notion that we must abide by any of the strategic arms limitations agreements with the Soviets when they have massively violated them is ludicrous on its face.

As Defense Secretary Weinberger recently noted: "Take, for example, the Soviets' deployment of the SS-25 intercontinental ballistic missile; SALT II allows only one new type of ICBM, and yet Moscow is going forward with two new types of missiles—the SS-X-24 and SS-25.

"The SS-25 is a completely new missile, not a modification of the older SS-13 as the Soviets claim. And even if one accepted the Soviet assertion that the SS-25 is simply a modernization of the SS-134, the SS-25 would *still* be a violation, since it has *twice* the throw-weight or payload of the SS-13, or 20 *times* the allowed increase.

"In short, there is no doubt that even one SS-25 was a major violation of SALT II. And how many have the Soviets deployed? Seventy-two—72 separate violations. And yet we still hear that there have been no *major* violations!"

Fundamental Soviet violations of the ABM treaty have also been thoroughly exposed. Indeed, as Rep. Jack Kemp (R.-N.Y.) stressed in a letter to Sen. Nunn, the Soviets have a "growing breakout capability to erect a nationwide defense. . . . They have deployed dense rings of ABM defenses around Moscow. Their air-defense capabilities dwarf our own. They are mass producing the components necessary for a full-scale strategic defense system. Indeed, Soviet actions and their persistent cheating call into question what in fact remains of the ABM treaty."

Evidence of Soviet cheating aside, there is nothing inherently provocative or immoral about constructing a defensive shield to protect our own citizens from a possible nuclear assault. Why doesn't the President get on with it?

Chapter Seven

Communism

As noted in Chapter 5, HUMAN EVENTS' isolationist posture changed dramatically following World War II as a result of the advent of the international Communist challenge. The articles in this chapter examine many of the aspects of this challenge.

"For Yalta, Read Munich" by Felix Morley (21 February 1945) is a scathing indictment of the agreement that consigned much of Eastern Europe to Soviet subjugation.

"Heraclitus and Hollywood" is an insider's account of the Soviet attempt to infiltrate Hollywood, written by Morrie Ryskind, the Pulitzer Prize-winning playwright and a key figure in the Screen Writers Guild during the 1940s and 1950s (26 August 1953).

Many statesmen were initially taken in by "good old Joe" Stalin, but, in 1944, at the height of the U.S. alliance with Moscow, William Henry Chamberlin penned an article that with great prescience forecast Stalin's postwar expansionist plans, "Russia Moves West." This analysis was fleshed out in 1946 in a book, *Blueprint for World Conquest*, published by HUMAN EVENTS. In the introduction, reprinted here, Chamberlin detailed Moscow's plans to subvert nations around the world using indigenous Communist parties.

In 1957, two years before Fidel Castro took power in Cuba, Frank Hanighen, a founding editor of HUMAN EVENTS, wrote a remarkably perceptive article on Castro's Communist background ("Cuban Revolt," 17 August 1957).

In "Hitler, Mussolini, Peron—All Were Welfare Staters" (16 November 1963 issue), James L. Wick, the long-time publisher of HUMAN EVENTS, explained that even those considered dictators of the "right" are essentially Socialist in nature.

During the Vietnam War, famed conservative radio commentator Fulton Lewis, Jr., revealed how the American Communist party was active in the "antiwar" movement in the United States ("How the Communists Have Built Up Anti-U.S. Propaganda on Viet Nam," 22 May 1965), and Reed Irvine, the founder of Accuracy in Media, detailed Lee Harvey Oswald's addiction to Marxism ("The Assassination of John F. Kennedy: The Reasons Why," 24 July 1971).

Richard Nixon's key role in exposing the treasonous activities of Communist agent Alger Hiss made Nixon a hero to conservatives—a status he retained with many for the remaining forty-six years of his life. "Lessons of the Alger Hiss Case" (15 March 1986) is an edited version of a speech Nixon delivered in New York City to the Pumpkin Papers Irregulars, a group of conservatives that meets annually.

For almost forty years the conservative movement was in the forefront of the struggle against communism. When Ronald Reagan became president, he implemented the "forward strategy" advocated by HUMAN EVENTS—taking the battle aggressively to the Soviets.

As communism was beginning to crumble, HUMAN EVENTS editor Allan H. Ryskind spent a week in the Soviet Union and wrote of the changes underway in "Through the Glasnost Semi-Darkly" (25 June 1988).

Upon the demise of Soviet communism in 1991, HUMAN EVENTS saluted the resolute spirit of conservatives during the long struggle in "Conservative Movement Should Take Well-Deserved Bow" (7 September 1991).

For Yalta, Read Munich

By Felix Morley   *(From the 21 February 1945 issue)*

It is scarcely possible that some of our newspaper editors actually believe what they have been writing about the conference of the "Big Three" at Yalta. The minimization of Stalin's diplomatic triumph there; the effort to find the concessions supposedly made by him are just too forced. As one illustration, the Philadelphia *Evening Bulletin* of February 14 devotes its lead editorial to the subject of "Soviet Cooperation" and, groping for supporting evidence says:

"On the boundary issue he [Stalin] has assented to deviations from the Curzon Line in favor of the Poles, to the extent of from three to five miles in some regions."

This is the reasoning of Cloud Cuckoo Land. Rather more than one-third of the total area of Poland, as heretofore recognized in London and Washington, is to be annexed outright by Russia. And an important American newspaper finds it a significant "concession" that Stalin is willing to let a few villages in this area remain under a henceforth satellite Polish government.

When the policy of appeasement is carried to such lengths, in a press which is still free to draw conclusions bearing some relationship to actual facts, one must look for psychological explanation. It may be found in the uncertainty of purpose in which our foreign policy is enmeshed. While the war continues it is the natural desire of commentators to avoid admission that this confusion as to objectives is as complete as is unfortunately the case.

Judging from the little that has as yet been revealed on the recent conference in the Crimea, it was an outstanding diplomatic victory for Stalin. And, as we learn of the arrangements still kept secret, it is improbable that the scope of this Russian triumph will be diminished.

At any settlement reached by three men with partially divergent objectives, the will of the clearest and least inhibited thinker is likely to prove dominant. Stalin's current success is in part due to the tremendous concentration of physical power which lies under his autocratic direction. It is in part due to his evidently outstanding personal ability. Beyond these factors, however, is the Russian actors insistence on never regarding hostilities as a rational end in themselves, but always as a means towards the development of a clearly-visualized political and social policy.

It is the absence of any similar clarity of purpose which fatally handicaps the diplomacy of both Churchill and Roosevelt. They think in terms of the "unconditional surrender" of opposing nations instead of, like Stalin, concentrating on the future development of a civilization in which the Nation-State is only a temporary and incomplete political expression.

The cloudiness of most Anglo-Saxon thinking on this subject is increased by our tendency to acclaim as our objective in war certain inherited ideals which the process of war is itself certain to destroy. There is the deepest pathos in recalling now such definitions as those made by Mr. Churchill, in the House of Commons, on September 3, 1939: "It is a war . . . to establish, on impregnable rocks, the rights of the individual, and it is a war to establish and revive the stature of man."

Stalin has no such humanitarian objective, which is indeed the very opposite of everything for which Communism stands. His unfaltering ambition has been to augment and consolidate the power of the Russian Socialist State, for a time in full cooperation with the Germans and

Japanese, more lately in a titanic struggle against the German National Socialists. Stalin's ambitions have been helped, as those of the Democracies have been hindered by the sad fact that war means not revival but suppression of "the stature of man." The longer and harder the war, the more pronounced the subordination of the rights of the individual to the necessities of the State.

There is a tendency to condemn as cynicism any consideration of the collapse of Anglo-Saxon idealism as contrasted with the parallel success of Russia's pragmatic policies. Much more cynical, however, is such attempted deception as the inclusion in the Yalta Declaration of a solemn affirmation of "faith in the principles of the Atlantic Charter." This assertion is refuted in the parts of the document dictated by Stalin.

The second principle of the Atlantic Charter, as offered in August, 1941, stated that the President of the United States and the Prime Minister of Great Britain "desire to see no territorial changes that do not accord with the freely expressed wishes of the peoples concerned."

The third principle states that "they respect the rights of all peoples to choose the form of government under which they will live; and they wish to see sovereign rights and self-government restored to those who have been forcibly deprived of them."

Yet, in the Yalta Declaration, only a few lines after paying lip-service to the Atlanta Charter, "the three heads of Government" casually annexed one-third of Poland to Russia without a mention of the rights or wishes of the Poles affected. And this is followed with the further ukase that "Poland must receive substantial accessions of [purely German] territory in the north and west."

The idea underlying this arrangement is that the puppet Polish government, in order to retain what is annexed to it from Germany, will have to rely on Russian support, and therefore most permanently accept direction of its policy by Moscow. This is clever political manipulation—but it is not an expression of the principles of the Atlantic Charter.

One may be sure that neither Mr. Churchill nor Mr. Roosevelt enjoys the spiritual humiliation involved for them in this new partitioning of Poland. They must realize that history will record it in terms far less flattering than those of current journalism. And the conscience of Winston Churchill, who attacked Neville Chamberlain so bitterly at the time of the Munich Agreement, should be particularly tender. One recalls Mr. Churchill's eloquent words at that time:

"All is over. Silent, mournful, abandoned, broken, Czechoslovakia recedes into the darkness. She has suffered in every respect by her association with the Western democracies. . . ."

For Czechoslovakia, read Poland. For Munich, read Yalta.

There is no question that Russia has earned and richly deserves the triumph which Stalin achieved at Yalta. Moreover, the Soviet attitude has throughout been free from any semblance of hypocrisy. For all who cared to read, notice of intention has been continuously served in advance from Moscow and, once given, has been adhered to.

Over a year has now elapsed since the Supreme Soviet revised the malleable Russian Constitution so as to give each of the constituent Republics authority to establish its own armies and "the right to enter into direct relations with foreign states, conclude agreements with them and exchange diplomatic and consular representatives."

In advocating this supremely significant alteration in Russian political structure, Vyacheslav Molotov, People's Commissar of Foreign Affairs, frankly announced that it will "reveal still more fully the historic meaning of the existence of the Soviet Union to the Peoples of the East and West." The purpose of this step, taken shortly after Tehran, becomes more apparent after Yalta.

The Russian system of federated and satellite Soviet States is unlikely to stop its westward expansion with Poland, or its eastward development at the borders of Inner Mongolia. With the capture of Budapest the outward push from Asia gathers a momentum unparalleled since the Turks stormed up the Danube in the 16th Century. But the Mohammedan conquests had no such physical power behind them, and no such fertile soil ahead, as has Russia today.

The Yalta Declaration reaffirmed not only the Atlantic Charter but also "unity of purpose of action" as "a sacred obligation . . . to all the peoples of the world." Unity of action on the military plane, for the overthrow of Hitler, is assured. But unity of purpose has clarification of purpose as a prerequisite. And of "the three heads of Government" who met at Tehran and Yalta, Stalin alone has so far been able to make his political purpose clear, and to make it stick.

Heraclitus and Hollywood
or The Greek Who Had Two Words for It

By Morrie Ryskind   *(From the 26 August 1953 issue)*

I am a fellow notoriously frugal in handing out praise. When I watch a rookie third baseman save an early-season game with a brilliant double play, I give due credit; but I do not immediately label him the greatest infielder I ever saw. I am content to wait a few games and see how he handles a bunt and whether he hits in the clutch before I begin comparing him to Heinie Groh.

True enough, this parsimony in distributing honors has gained me the unenviable reputation of a churl. But if I don't give many awards, I cherish the notion that those I do part with are highly regarded. And the time has come to loosen up with an Oscar: this year's laurel wreath, suitably engraved, goes to a surprise entry—Heraclitus.

There were many competitors, drawn from the many fields I am interested in, and the choice was not easy. Indeed, to show you the catholicity of my tastes, the man who came down to the wire head and head with Heraclitus only to be nosed out in a photo-finish was Jockey Willie Shoemaker. I was present at Hollywood Park that unforgettable day when Wee Willie established a track record by winning six out of the eight races. When I say unforgettable, I mean it: I established something of a track record myself that day by betting Shoemaker only twice— in the two races he lost. That made me the only man in the park who never saw the cashier's window.

Indeed, there has been some malicious gossip hinting that the sixteen dollars I dropped decisively influenced my judgment. This I dismiss as the typical character-assassination technique of the ADA. Those who know me well know that I was losing eight races a day before I ever heard of Shoemaker.

I defy the slurs and slanderers. This year's award was based solely on two words: everything flows. And who said that? Well, five to eight it wasn't Willie Shoemaker.

No, it was Heraclitus who laid it on the line 2,400 years ago—long before Shoemaker was born. "Everything flows," he said. "The world is in a constant state of flux, and there'll be some changes made." Look around you, brother! Did anybody ever say it better or truer? If this isn't flux, what is?

Now I make no pretensions to being an intellectual, and it's some 35 years since I studied either Greek or philosophy. And yet I think of Heraclitus every time my Eastern friends write me asking if things have changed at all in Hollywood—changed, that is, as far as the movie colony's attitude toward Communism is concerned. They recall vividly the Hollywood of 1947, when hundreds of movie stars, directors, producers and writers formed the famous Committee for the First Amendment; contributed thousands of dollars to buy newspaper space and radio time to denounce the infamous inquisition of the House Un-American Activities Committee; and sent to Washington a galaxy-studded plane, containing at least a billion dollars worth of movie flesh, to beard the legislative lions in their den.

Led by Mr. and Mrs. Humphrey Bogart and reinforced at the capital by Senators Claude Pepper and Glen Taylor, the cinema intellectuals marched en mass into a famous Washington hotel, threw a cocktail party for the press, posed for pictures and thundered "J'accuse" at the witch-hunters. It was an awe-inspiring spectacle that rose to a fitting climax when that eminent authority on civil liberties, Mr. Danny Kaye, made an impassioned defense of the First Amendment—which, it turned out, he had unfortunately confused with the Eighteenth Amendment. They tell me Mr. Kaye was never funnier.

But that was 1947, and this is 1953. The Great Hollywood Liberal who testified in 1947 that he saw no reason why he shouldn't hire a Communist (and, boy, *did* he hire 'em!) is now making weekly speeches on the Red Menace in Kiwanis luncheons. That same precious cargo of high-priced talent that fellow-traveled to Washington is now (with the exception of those who have since been identified as C. P. members) applauding publicly the Hollywood hearings of the Un-American Activities Committee. And the Producers' Association—that hard-headed group of financial tycoons who climbed into bed with the Commies to defend the virginity of the screen from its would-be-violators (a procedure I once irreverently termed "saving the girls by sleeping with the madam")—is today on record that it will not hire anybody who refuses to answer the $64 question.

Enter the MPA

So far, so good. The change would tend to prove, it may be argued, that even the Hollywood Intelligentsia are educable. But that is a thesis I am unwilling to endorse. Not yet, anyhow. I wish the converts well, but I want to see how they act in the clutch before I pin any medals on them. After all, Heraclitus had to wait a helluva longer time before receiving the Ryskind Award.

I grow a little nauseated too, when I hear some of the Johnny-come-lately boys explain to their thrilled admirers how they cleaned up their guilds and drove the Huns out of Hollywood. They won this war about the same way Russia won the Japanese War, and all good readers of *Pravda* know about *that*. And further, the self-anointed saviors proclaim, they did it without using the methods of McCarthy or the equally intolerable tactics of the MPA.

The MPA, in case you don't know, is an organization made up of Hollywood's premature anti-Communists. (The official title, grandiose I concede, is the Motion Picture Alliance for the Preservation of American Ideals.) Back in the late '30s, it became clear to a good many of us that there was a determined effort being made by the Commies to take over the movie guilds and unions. At that time, most of us were not too aware politically; but we got sick and tired of watching the obvious shenanigans of the Kremlinites. They palpably didn't give a damn about anything unless it fitted their zigzagging line. They would yell for one point on Monday and vote solidly against it on Tuesday. (They would stall the voting at meetings by parliamentary tactics, of which we knew little; they would move "point of order," "question," "out of order" and submit amendments to amendments until the average member, baffled and bewildered, had gone home. Then would come that quick survey which showed them they had a majority—and wham! the vote.) I needn't stress the point—the tactics I saw in the Screen Writers Guild were used by every Commie group in every guild and union in the country.

It was a rugged time for us premature anti-Communists. In our own guilds, we had to fight not only the cunning of the Sovieteers but the derision of the Liberals and the apathy of the vast majority. And the toughest of these was apathy. We grew hardened to the superciliousness of the intelligentsia, and we could take the eye-gouging of the Reds, but the apathy of the good decent citizen who didn't know the score was the thing that almost broke our hearts and backs.

And, besides the dirty work in the guilds, there were the scores of fronts. There were the Hollywood League Against War and Fascism, the Hollywood Anti-Nazi League (what decent man wouldn't join this organization, even if he were to be slightly puzzled when it disbanded right after the Soviet-Nazi pact?), the Hollywood This and the Hollywood That. Good God, how the money rolled in!

It was the late—and great—James K. McGuinness who said, "We're sitting ducks because we aren't organized as the Commies are. Let's get together and even this scrap up."

So early in 1944 we organized the MPA to fight Communism and said so out loud. There were about five hundred of us: writers, directors, actors, producers (we had enough famous names to get the story printed nationally) and, overwhelmingly, labor. The labor boys were engaged in a death-battle with the Commie movement and they knew it; so the heads of the studio drivers, the prop men, the plasterers, the cement finishers, the teamsters, the grips and the others all came. Within a week or so, our ranks had swelled to 750 (it's over 1,500 today, and I mean dues payers).

Carriers of Poisoned Spears

And then the Commies let loose the poison gas. It was during the war, so "Hitler's Friends Organize" ran the screaming headline in the *People's World*. "Red-baiters, pro-fascists, anti-labor, anti-Semites," yelled the Commies, and, given that music cue, no true Hollywood Liberal could resist joining in the chorus. Katherine Hepburn denounced us in a speech at Gilmore Stadium; John Gunther flew in to Hollywood, had dinner with the Proper People, got the lowdown on us, and shortly after issued his findings. Elmer Rice, consulting his ouija board, castigated us in the *Saturday Review* and added one more charge against us: that of Jim Crowism, probably based on the obvious fact that we didn't see eye to eye with Paul Robeson.

True, we didn't have many Negroes in our midst, but we had as many as the Screen Writers Guild, the Directors and the Producers Association. The simple fact is that, except in the acting field, there are few Negroes in Hollywood. But you might have thought that the fact that our members were made up overwhelmingly of labor men might stop even a Liberal like Rice from echoing the Commie charges. Just as the fact that a number of my co-religionists were on the executive board of the Alliance with me might, to a man of ordinary intelligence, convey the impression that the Alliance couldn't be anti-Semitic.

But when you deal with the Intelligentsia, you are dealing with people of no ordinary intelligence. When, in an answer to Rice's attack which the *Review* graciously permitted me to make, I listed the names of fourteen labor leaders who had joined the alliance and pointed out that there were many Jewish members, Elmer had the Perfect Rebuttal: he simply reiterated his charges and added, "Mr. Ryskind seems unaware that there are anti-Semitic Jews, anti-labor union leaders and writers who are traitors to the literary craft." The clear implication was that I was guilty on two counts and possibly, if you accept guilt by association, on all three. God had spoken and it was hardly in order for me to point out that there were excellent playwrights who were political idiots. (I should like to add one more quote from Rice: ". . . it seems to me incredible that anyone can take seriously the charge that American motion pictures show even the slightest trace of Communist influence." If the more than 300 movie names that have been identified since have changed Mr. Rice's opinion, I have read no article by him to that effect.)

One of the ex-Communists told me recently something of the tactics they used at the time. "When the MPA was formed," he said, "we were scared stiff. We had meetings every night debating strategy. Finally, we decided to use anti-Semitism as our main target. Then, we hoped to get the Screen Writer's Guild, where we had the Liberals in our pocket, to line up the other guilds."

And with that, they started. The cells in each studio got on the job—with excellent results. Thus, if Producer A was Jewish, Comrade X, a writer, in discussing the cast, would mention that B (an MPA member) was a fine actor and would fit the role but they oughtn't give an anti-Semite a part in these times. The startled producer, who had known B for years, would ask what he meant. Then X, reluctantly and in strict confidence, would confide something that he said B had told him about Jews. Angered, the producer would usually blurt out that B would never work for him again. And, in spite of the confidence, you couldn't blame him if he managed to inform his co-religionists of what B had done. "We didn't have to say another word after the first time," said the ex-Red. But B never knew what hit him. After a while, his agent would suggest that there might be more jobs if he dropped his MPA membership and joined one of the more Liberal organizations that the Right People belonged to.

By the time the smears had been repeated and enlarged upon, there was no doubt in the mind of any decent intellectual that we were financed by Hitler and Mussolini. And you could come to the same conclusion by reading the "right" magazines. Of course, the readers of the *Nation* and the *New Republic* were the first to know. But those who perused the calm, dispassionate dispatches of some of the press associations and magazines like *Time* were not too slow in gathering the shameful truth.

(One jolly little paranoiac enjoyed himself writing poison-pen letters in which he charged that the heads of the MPA made most of their money by peddling meat in the black market. The letters had quite a vogue, even reaching New York, until a detective traced them to their source for us—and the author, to save an industry scandal, was quietly dropped by his studio. He was lucky at that: in one of his notes he charged that Sam Wood, the famous director who was our president at the time, was making pro-Hitler speeches and urging people not to buy war bonds. When Sam discovered who the writer was, he was literally sat on by some of the huskier men in our fold to prevent him from rushing over and handling the matter himself. Sam was in his 60s, but in excellent physical condition—and we felt we couldn't afford a charge of mayhem on top of everything else.)

The Hollywood Intelligentsia

During those early hectic days, the attitude of the businessmen who controlled the industry was "A plague on both your houses." They frankly didn't give a hoot about who was a Communist and who was a fascist. All they knew was that all this talk was hurting the industry. And who had started the talk? We had. The other boys were "protecting" the good name of the industry. Besides, they argued knowingly, did we really believe that certain men like _____, _____, and ____, getting thousands of dollars a week, were Communists? Preposterous!

By the end of 1946, however, most of them had been sucked into various fronts and had become Liberals. This was a brand new role, and they were enjoying it to the hilt. For the first time in their lives, they were being treated as intellectuals and not as mere money-grabbers. By simply joining an organization—and making a suitable contribution—they could sit at dinner with the Hollywood Intelligentsia and listen to discussions on Art (the Russian Ballet), Literature (Howard Fast's latest book), World Affairs (how Stalin is cooperating with Roosevelt and to Hell with the MPA). New horizons opened to them and they realized how drab their previous lives had been. They began to produce "significant" pictures: the Warner's did "Mission to Moscow" and Sam Goldwyn made an epic on life in the Soviet fatherland as Lillian Hellman saw it. And all the producers suddenly began to talk like Paul Hoffman.

So when it became apparent in 1947 that the industry was to be openly "lynched" by the Un-American Activities Committee and that a good many of the MPA boys were going to repeat before Congress the "vicious lies" they had been circulating locally, the producers prepared themselves. Just before we of the MPA left for Washington, a group of us met with two of the attorneys for the industry. Their attitude was that we had hurt the industry enough and they hoped we would be friendly.

We replied that when we testified we would be under oath, and could hardly be expected to pull any punches. And, we went on to say, we thought that sweeping dirt under the rug was never effective. We suggested that, even at that late date, the industry could gain the plaudits of the country by getting on our side. But we were told coldly that there were such things as Civil Liberties and that freedom of thought was an American tradition. At the same time, we were informed, in a nice way, of course, that the industry knew how to protect itself against its enemies. I do not say any threat was uttered; I do say that I gathered from the remarks that some of us might be expendable—which shows you the kind of nasty mind I have.

Anyhow, we went on to Washington to testify against the Unfriendly Ten. The press lined up almost solidly against us, but somehow the people lined up solidly with us. The reaction was swift. Attendance dropped frightfully at theaters where the more Hollywood names were being starred. There were some organized boycotts, but the big drop came from the average, unorganized American. He just didn't like it when the famous $64 question wasn't answered.

As public reaction became clearer and clearer, the industry heads met and did a first-class switcheroo. They forgot all about Civil Liberties and hastened to assure the public that they were through with the Unfriendly Ten and anybody else who didn't answer the legitimate questions of a sacred Congressional Committee. Mr. Bogart wrote an open letter, telling how he had been misled into joining the First Amendment tour. In the Screen Writers' Guild there was a counterrevolution. In the ensuing election, the Liberals ousted some of the more notorious Stalinists they had defended so long, and elected a new board. True, the new board was just as anti-MPA as ever, but it at least was conscious that communism was not much better.

And that, my friends, is how the liberals won the war and saved Hollywood.

Of course, it's true that Jim McGuinness, one of our best leaders, came home to find out he had been demoted—after 18 years—by his studio; and that the Liberal Producer who saw no reason for not hiring Commies was shortly thereafter made head of the same studio; and that, not too long afterward, Jim consented to a settlement of his contract. These are coincidences, and life is full of them.

And I know a writer, generally considered a good craftsman and one who worked as often as he pleased. Against his doctor's advice, he went to Washington with the other MPA boys to testify against the Commies. Curiously enough, since that time he has not seen the inside of a studio. I hear he can't write anymore, and that I'm in no position to dispute. I suspect he should have listened to his doctor and stayed in bed.

The Rat's Den

But every war has its innocent casualties. One thing is certain: the Commies are on the run in Hollywood and are no longer getting huge sums for the party. The Fronts don't flourish and what Reds there are remain silent.

I would say that a great part of this is due to Roy Brewer, now president of the MPA, who is the local head of the I.A.T.S.E., the powerful theatrical and movie union. And I suspect Roy's power comes more from his position as labor leader than from his place in the Alliance. Roy met the Commies head on the labor front and whaled the everlasting tar out of them. At any rate, when Roy talks, the producers listen—and probably wish they had listened years ago.

So, in the main, everything, with the few minor exceptions noted, is hunky-dory these days. The attacks on the MPA abate—at least the most virulent form. We're all on the same side now, and a few Liberals have even renewed a nodding acquaintance with me.

But somehow, in spite of everything, I keep my guard up. Maybe, after 15 years in Coventry, I don't know how to act with people. And maybe I've read too much. For, in addition to Heraclitus, I recall an old French saying to the effect that the more things change the more they remain the same.

Anyway, I'll watch a few more games.

Blueprint for World Conquest
Introduction

By William Henry Chamberlin

THE REPRINTING OF THESE DOCUMENTS which set forth with complete authority and with remarkable detail the technique by means of which Communism hopes to conquer the world is a great and badly needed public service. The threat of Communism, which is now primarily a fifth column agency of Soviet infiltration and expansion, to the peace and the world is infinitely greater than it was in 1920 or 1928, when these blueprints of international conspiracy were composed.

It is obvious that any government whose leaders are animated by this philosophy could only be super-militarist in character. If war is inevitable, and this proposition is advanced over and over again, it would be sheer imbecility not to make every conceivable political, economic, military and psychological preparation to win.

And here one finds the perfect clue to Soviet policy before World War II, during world War II, and since World War II.

Now, the balance of international force has changed appreciably in favor of the Soviet Union. Despite heavy losses in manpower and industrial equipment, the Soviet Union is an unchallenged member of the Big Three. It is far and away the strongest land Power in Europe and in Asia, in terms of area, population, natural resources, armaments and trained military forces.

Events have already shown that it proposes to use its new strength without the slightest regard for its own voluntarily assumed treaty obligations or for the idealistic phrases which were inserted into the Charter of the United Nations. The Soviet diplomatic record is a shambles of broken treaties and obligations. The non-aggression treaties which the Soviet Government concluded, at its own initiative, with Poland, Finland, Latvia, Lithuania and Estonia were all treated as scraps of paper at the first convenient opportunity.

The non-aggression treaty with Japan was broken as soon as the Soviet Government saw an opportunity to gain cheap spoils in Manchuria and Korea after Japan's collapse was assured. Soviet promises at Yalta to insure "free and unfettered elections" in Poland have already been dishonored over and over again by the institution in occupied Poland of a government whose key figures (Bierut, Gomolka, Radkiewicz, Berman) are not only Communists, but indoctrinated and trained Moscow agents. Equally obvious is the disregard, in Romania, Bulgaria and Yugoslavia, of the Yalta promise that the Soviet Union, the United States and Great Britain will jointly assist the peoples in liberated States "to form interim governmental authorities broadly representative of all democratic elements in the population and pledged to the earliest possible establishment through free elections of governments responsive to the will of the people."

Public opinion is sometimes curiously illogical in its reactions. There was undoubtedly more apprehension of the threat of Communism after the First World War, when Russia was quite helpless to undertake major military operations outside its own borders, than there is now, when the Soviet Union is one of the world's great military powers.

This is partly the result of the hangover of the propaganda during the war, when all unfavorable references to the Soviet system and philosophy were officially discouraged. There has also been a big softening-up campaign, launched from Communist and near-Communist sources and designed to induce the American people to take an ostrich attitude toward the plain facts of Soviet aggression and expansion in defiance of treaty obligations and the principles of the Atlantic Charter, of which the Soviet Union is a co-signatory.

Curiously enough this campaign is often spearheaded by individuals who formerly insisted that appeasement of or compromise with Hitler and the Japanese militarists was at once futile and dishonorable. They now devote their energies to trying to prove that appeasement of the Soviet dictatorship, sacrifice of one free people after another to its expansionist claims, is both honorable and enlightened.

In the atmosphere of ignorant unreality which dominates much thinking and speaking about Russia, it is extremely valuable to place before thoughtful Americans a summary of the philosophy which dominates the thinking of Stalin and other Soviet leaders. There can be no question as to the authority and authenticity of the documents reprinted here.[1]

One is a statement of the resolutions and theoretical instructions drawn up at the Second Congress of the Communist International, held in Moscow from July 17 until August 7, 1920.

The others contain similar material, prepared at the Sixth Congress of the International in Moscow in 1928.

We have the testimony of the veteran Communist, D.Z. Manuilsky, who represented the Ukranian Soviet Republic at the San Francisco Conference and at the opening session of U.N. in London, that "not one important document of big international significance was issued by the Communist International without the most active participation of Comrade Stalin in its composition."[2]

The fact that the Communist International formally dissolved itself in the spring of 1943 does not affect the validity of the working program of revolutionary action which Stalin helped to prepare. In the first place, there is no evidence that Communist parties outside of Russia have ceased to keep time by the Kremlin clock since the International was outwardly disbanded. In the second place, Stalin is a single, not a dual, personality. The doctrines which he actively participated in formulating, as a leader of the Communist International, inevitably affect his thinking and his actions as the dictatorial chief of a powerful State.

The truth of the matter is that Stalin is just as much committed to the ultimate objective of world revolution through the overthrow of all "capitalist" States as was Trotsky. Apart from the personal rivalry between these two heirs of Lenin, the difference was not as to the end, but as to the means by which this end could best be achieved.

Trotsky, the theorist, the agitator, the doctrinaire, clung to the old-fashioned, orthodox method of trying to stir up working-class revolutions in countries outside of Russia.

Stalin, more practical, more cynical, more opportunist, drew certain lessons from the failure of the Communist International to win any important victories during the first years of its existence. So he concentrated his attention on building up Russia as a mighty, totalitarian, militarist State which could impose Soviet political and economic changes on weaker neighbors at the first convenient opportunity. At the same time he kept a tight rein on Communist parties throughout the world as useful agencies of volunteer propaganda and espionage in normal times, as potential fifth column auxiliaries prepared to commit treason and sabotage when the day of advancing world conquest should arrive.

The belief that Stalin has renounced interest in revolution outside of Russia can be disproved by his own words. His book *Leninism*, while it is drier and less lurid in style, is just as much a "must" for Soviet youth as Hitler's *Mein Kampf* was for the Nazi younger generation in Germany. And this is what Stalin wrote in the 1933 edition of *Leninism:*

"The victory of socialism in one country is not an end in itself; it must be looked upon as a support, as a means for hastening the proletarian victory in every other land. For the victory of the revolution in one country (in Russia, for the nonce) is not only the result of the unequal development and the progressive decay of imperialism; it is likewise the beginning and the continuation of the world revolution."[3]

Equally revealing is Stalin's official explanation of the reason for maintaining in Russia the terrorist political police, formerly known as the GPU, more recently as the NKVD [later the KGB]. Talking to a French Workers delegation in 1927, he said:

"From the point of view of the internal situation, the revolution is so firm and unshakable that we could do without the GPU. But the trouble is that the enemies at home are not isolated individuals. They are connected in a thousand ways with the capitalists of all countries who support them by every means and in every way. We are a country surrounded by capitalist states. The internal enemies of our revolution are the agents of the capitalists of *all* countries."[4] [Italics in the original.]

What does this mean? It means that in Stalin's mind there is irreconcilable hostility between the Soviet Union and the "capitalist" world. It means that Russia can never know security so long as "capitalist" (i.e., democratic) States continue to exist.

A man publicly committed to such ideas would only be acting logically if he set as his aim the elimination of the "capitalist" States which he regards as irreconcilably hostile. And here

Stalin's ambitions are clearly reflected in the course of events during and since the Second World War. Twelve formerly independent States in Eastern Europe (Poland, Latvia, Lithuania, Estonia, Finland, Czechoslovakia, Yugoslavia, Bulgaria, Romania, Hungary, Austria, Albania) have been brought under some form of Soviet control. The type of this control varies from the outright annexation which has been imposed on the Baltic States and Eastern Poland to the more indirect, remote control system which prevails in Finland and Czechoslovakia, Austria and Hungary. In between these two extremes are the puppet regimes, with all strings pulled from Moscow, which have been set up in Poland and Romania, Bulgaria and Yugoslavia. Soviet troops are also in occupation of a large part of Germany and of the Danish island of Bornholm, key to the southern approach to Sweden.

Winston Churchill once referred to Soviet foreign policy as "a riddle wrapped in a mystery inside an enigma." This same idea must have frequently occurred to puzzled and well-meaning Americans as they surveyed the yawning gap between what they would like to believe about their wartime ally, the Soviet Union, and the actions and policies of the Soviet Government.

Many of the unruly pieces in the jigsaw puzzle of Soviet foreign policy fall neatly into place as one follows attentively the short-range and long-range strategy outlined in these pronouncements of the high councils of the Communist faith. Why take U.N. seriously if wars between "capitalist" and Communist States are predestined and unavoidable? Why expect treaties and promises to be observed when deceit and camouflage are recommended as essential elements in the technique of Communist propaganda? For the same reason, why take seriously the professions of innocence of the numerous Communist "front" organizations which exist in America and other countries?

A valuable feature of these documents is their extreme frankness. There is no beating about the bush, no suggestion that Communists are just well-meaning, liberal social reformers. The 21 conditions[5] which the Second Congress of the Communist International laid down for parties desiring to affiliate with this organization represent the most complete school for treason which could very well be imagined.

Communist parties are instructed "to create everywhere a parallel illegal apparatus," to combine "legal" and "illegal" work. Misguided Americans who, in the name of a false conception of civil liberty, maintain that Communists should be eligible for commissions in the armed forces should consider the implications of Condition 4, which reads literally as follows:

"Persistent and systematic propaganda and agitation must be carried on in the army, where Communist groups should be formed in every military organization. Wherever owing to repressive legislation agitation becomes impossible, it is necessary to carry on such agitation illegally. But refusal to carry on or participate in such work should be considered equal to treason to the revolutionary cause, and incompatible with affiliation to the Third International."

Those who believe that the Soviet Government is genuinely interested in seeing U.N. function effectively may be referred to Condition 6:

"Every party desirous of affiliating to the Third International should renounce not only avowed social patriotism, but also the falsehood and the hypocrisy of social pacifism: it should systematically demonstrate to the workers that without a revolutionary overthrow of capitalism no international arbitration, no talk of disarmament, no democratic reorganization of the League of Nations will be capable of saving mankind from new imperialist wars."

Is it surprising that some trade-unions and "cultural" organizations in which Communist tactics of infiltration have been successful should invariably take sides with Russia and against America when one reads the ninth of the 21 conditions:

"Every party desirous of belonging to the Communist International should be bound to carry on systematic and persistent Communist work in the labor unions, co-operatives and other organizations of working masses. It is necessary to form Communist nuclei within these organizations, which by persistent and lasting work should win over labor unions to communism."

Condition 14 is illuminating as to the obligation of the Communist to fight for Russia against his own country in the event of any conflict:

"Each party desirous of affiliating to the Communist International should be obliged to render every possible assistance to the Soviet Republics in their struggle against all counter-revolutionary forces. The Communist parties should carry on a precise and definite propaganda to induce the workers to refuse to transport any kind of military equipment intended for fighting against the Soviet Republics, and should also by legal or illegal means carry on a propaganda amongst the troops sent against the workers' republics, etc."

Very often the wording of these Communist resolutions is a preview of events which were to occur in the future. Stirring up revolution in China and India was recognized as "one of the most important questions before the Second Congress of the Third International." How is this objective to be realized? A tortuous and complicated strategy is outlined in the following excerpts from the resolution on this question:

"It is the duty of the Communist International to support the revolutionary movement in the colonies and in the backward countries. . . . The Communist International must establish temporary relations and even unions with the revolutionary movements in the colonies and backward countries, without however amalgamating with them, but preserving the independent character of the proletarian movement even though it be still in its embryonic state. . . .

"The revolution in the colonies is not going to be a Communist revolution in its first stages. But if from the outset the leadership is in the hands of a Communist vanguard, the revolutionary masses will not be led astray, but may go ahead through the successive periods of development of revolutionary experience. . . ."[6]

The phraseology is dry and complex. But the meaning is clear. Communists are to enter nationalist movements, like the Chinese Kuomintang, the Indian National Congress, etc., go along with these movements in their struggle against "foreign imperialism," but retain their independent organization, so that they may seize the reins of power at the first convenient opportunity.

This is a precise blueprint of the strategy which Chinese Communists, constantly coached by their Soviet advisers, followed in China during the '20s. Because Chiang Kai-shek frustrated their maneuver and drove them out of the Kuomintang in the decisive year, 1927, the Generalissimo has been the object of the unrelenting hatred and vilification of Communists and fellow travelers all over the world. However much one may hope for Chinese unity and cessation of civil strife, it remains to be seen what use the Chinese Communists will make of the offices which they will presumably hold if a coalition government is finally organized in China.

When Winston Churchill's predominantly Conservative Government gave way to a Labor Cabinet in Great Britain last summer some naive commentators believed that a honeymoon era in Soviet-British relations was in prospect. But democratic socialism is one of the principal hates of dictatorial Communism. Democratic socialist parties were outlawed in Russia under the Soviet regime. Their members were killed, sent to concentration camps or driven into exile. Two of the most prominent Polish Social Democrats, Henryk Ehrlich and Viktor Alter, were shot after the first Soviet occupation of Poland. The sharp exchanges which have marked some of the meetings of the British Foreign Minister Ernest Bevin, with Molotov, Vishinsky and other Soviet representatives were foreshadowed in the following vituperative references to moderate Socialists and labor leaders in the resolutions of the Sixth Congress of the Communist International:

"A cynically commercial, and imperialistic, secular form of subjecting the proletariat to the ideological influence of the bourgeoisie is represented by contemporary 'socialist' reformism. Taking its main gospel from the tablets of imperialist politics, its model today is the deliberately anti-socialist and openly counter-revolutionary 'American Federation of Labor.' The 'ideological' dictatorship of the servile American trade union bureaucracy, which in its turn expresses the 'ideological' dictatorship of the American dollar, has become, through the medium of British reformism and His Majesty's Socialists of the British Labor Party, the most important constituent in the theory and practice of intentional Social Democracy. . . .

". . . Social Democracy has utterly and completely betrayed Marxism, having traversed the road from revisionism to complete liberal bourgeois reformism and avowed social-imperialism:

it has substituted in place of the Marxian theory of the contradiction of capitalism, the bourgeois theory of its harmonious development; it has pigeonholed the theory of crisis and of the pauperization of the proletariat; it has turned the flaming and menacing theory of class struggle into prosaic advocacy of class peace . . . in place of the theory of the inevitability of war under capitalism it has substituted the bourgeois deceit of pacifism. . . . It has replaced revolution by evolution, the destruction of the bourgeois State by its active upbuilding. . . ."[7]

In this diatribe, as in much Communist polemical literature, it is noteworthy that there are two unforgivable sins. One is belief in the possibility of permanent peace under "capitalism." The other is to suggest that social grievances can be redressed and social tensions relaxed by a process of orderly and peaceful progress within the framework of a democratic political system.

No thoughtful person, after reading *Mein Kampf*, with its frequent insistence on the necessity of war, could have felt that world peace would be very secure once the author of this work had become master of the most powerful military and industrial State in Europe. For just the same reasons the outlook for future world peace is not improved by the fact that the dictatorial leaders of one of the world's three most powerful States are so deeply indoctrinated with the ideas that war and violent revolution are inescapable phases of the historical process.

We learn from these official documents that profound deceit and hypocrisy are required of Communists as a duty to the cause. The frequent repudiation by Communists of their membership in the party, the familiar trick, in America, of forming organizations under Communist control with innocent sounding labels—"liberal," "constitutional liberties," "democratic," "progressive," "anti-fascist," etc.—acquire new significance in the light of the following instructions to Communists throughout the world. These are quoted verbatim:

". . . It is especially necessary to carry on illegal work in the army, navy and police. . . .

"On the other hand, it is also necessary in all cases without exception not to limit oneself to illegal work, but to carry on also legal work overcoming all difficulties, founding a legal press and legal organizations under the most diverse circumstances, and in case of need, frequently changing names. . . .

". . . the Communist parties must create a new type of periodical press for extensive circulation among the workmen: 1) Legal publications, in which the Communists *without calling themselves such and without mentioning their connection with the party*, would learn to utilize the slightest possibility allowed by the laws as the Bolsheviki did at the time of the Tzar, after 1905." [Italics in the original.]

"2) Illegal sheets, although of the smallest dimensions and irregularly published, but reproduced in most of the printing offices by workmen (in secret, or if the movement has grown stronger, by means of a revolutionary seizure of the printing offices), and giving the proletariat undiluted revolutionary information and the revolutionary slogans."[8]

This is followed by a glint of unconscious humor in the shape of the statement:

"Without involving the masses in the revolutionary struggle for a free Communist press the preparation for the dictatorship of the proletariat is impossible."[9]

In other words, the masses are to be incited, in the name of freedom of the Communist press, to set up a regime in which there will be no freedom for any kind of press.

It is quite obvious from our American experience that the instructions about creating camouflaged organs of opinion, directed in the Communist spirit without admitting any connection with the Communist Party, has been followed on a very wide scale. It is equally obvious that individuals who have been taught to lie and cheat to conceal their true opinions, to practice hypocrisy as a matter of party discipline, are excellently conditioned for espionage and fifth column work.

The most important function of Communist parties outside of Russia is this fifth column activity, which varies from country to country, depending on the strength of the Communist movement and the immediate needs of Soviet foreign policy. In those countries and regions which have been annexed by the Soviet Union or which are politically controlled from Moscow

(Latvia, Lithuania, Estonia, Poland, Yugoslavia, Bulgaria, Romania, etc.) the Communists, especially those who have gone through long indoctrination training in special schools in Moscow, supply the key men in the local puppet regimes.

In lands where the Communists possess a strong mass following, but do not yet feel able to take over power (France, for instance) they constantly put pressure on the government to follow a pro-Soviet line in foreign policy. How strictly the Communist deputies in any parliament or congress are controlled by the party organization may be judged from the wording of Condition 11 laid down for parties which desire to join the Communist International:

"Parties desirous of joining the Third Intentional shall be bound to inspect the personnel of their parliamentary factions, to remove all unreliable elements therefrom, to control such factions, not only verbally but in reality, to subordinate them to the Central Committee of the party, and to demand from each Communist representative in parliament to subject his entire activity to the interests of real revolutionary propaganda, and agitation."[10]

Finally there remain countries like the United States and Great Britain, Canada and Australia, Sweden and Switzerland, where deep-rooted traditions of democracy and liberty and a relatively high standard of living have greatly restricted the appeal of Communism. In such countries the Communists are not numerous enough to elect many representatives to national and local legislative bodies. But they are by no means useless to their Moscow masters. Because of their tight discipline and their experience in conspiratorial technique, they wield an influence out of all proportion to their numbers. A few Communists, knowing what they want and working closely together, can often infiltrate into key positions in a trade-union, a so-called cultural organization, a government agency.

Any doubt as to the close association of the Soviet regime with revolutionary movements in other countries, with insurgent colonial movements, should be cleared up by the following statements in the resolutions of the Sixth Congress of the Communist International:

". . . the U.S.S.R. inevitably becomes the base of the world movement of all oppressed classes, *the center of international revolution* the greatest factor in world history. In the U.S.S.R., the world proletariat for the first time acquires a country that is really its own, and for the colonial movements the U.S.S.R. becomes a powerful center of attraction. . . ." (Italics in the original.)

"In the event of the imperialist States declaring war upon and attacking the U.S.S.R., the international proletariat must retaliate by organizing bold and determined mass action and struggle for the overthrow of the imperialist governments with the slogan of: Dictatorship of the proletariat and alliance with the U.S.S.R. . . .

"Thus, the development of the contradictions within modern world economy, the development of the general capitalist crisis, and the imperialist military attack upon the Soviet Union inevitably lead to a mighty revolutionary outbreak which must overwhelm capitalism in a number of the so-called civilized countries, unleash the victorious revolution in the colonies, broaden the base of the proletarian dictatorship to an enormous degree and thus, with tremendous strides, bring nearer the final world victory of Socialism."[11]

There are many more interesting and illuminating passages in these authoritative blueprints of the Communist scheme for world conquest. A technique of subversion is outlined for every nation, for every class, for every type of political situation.

Inasmuch as the philosophy outlined in these documents dominates the thinking of the rulers of one of the strongest military Powers in the world, American readers should become familiar with it. They can find here the explanation of many Soviet methods and actions which would seem ill-advised, even irrational, on the part of a regime which was sincerely anxious to cultivate international peace and good-will.

The publication of these documents will doubtless excite in Communist and fellow-traveler circles the familiar outcries, "red baiter," "Russophobe," "Russia-hater" with which these circles try to stifle any serious and objective discussion of the Soviet regime and its foreign policies. But at least another familiar phrase about "sowing suspicion" can scarcely find much application in this case. For the documents were originally published under the imprimatur of the highest Communist authority. They are not the speculations of a "suspicious" foreign observer, but the considered judgments of Lenin, Trotsky, Zinoviev, Bukharin, Stalin, Manuilsky and other Soviet Communist leaders, alive and dead.

One may hope that this fantastic scheme of world conquest through revolution will be abandoned. But until there is convincing proof that the Soviet Government has given up the desire to expand aggressively beyond its proper frontiers (and so far there has unfortunately been no such proof), the only sensible attitude of the United States and other democratic countries toward the blueprint of organized subversion which is outlined in these documents is to maintain the eternal vigilance that in this age, perhaps more than ever, is the price of liberty.

Endnotes

1. The Theses and Statutes of the Communist Intentional, as adopted by the Second World Congress, July 17 to August 7, 1920; Constitution and Rules of the Communist International, as adopted by the Sixth World Congress, September 1, 1928; The Program of the Communist International, as adopted by the Sixth World Congress, September 1, 1928.

2. See Stalin, a publication in Russian of reminiscences and laudatory tributes, issued by OGIZ, the Soviet State Publishing House, p. 93.

3. J. Stalin, *Leninism* (London: Allen & Unwin, 1933), I, 212.

4. Ibid., II, 91.

5. Pp. 65 ff.

6. Pp. 124-125, 130.

7. Pp. 225, 227.

8. Pp. 54, 55, 56.

9. P. 56.

10. P. 69.

11. Pp. 222, 223.

Cuban Revolt

By Frank Hanighen   *(From the 17 August 1957 issue)*

Many on the hill are beginning to say now: "We ought to be worrying more about the Communist menace in Latin America, on our very doorstep, than about communism in the far away Middle East." What's really behind the revolt led by Fidel Castro against the Cuban Government, billed by the New York *Times* and the liberal press as a simple rebellion against dictatorship, comes into clearer focus from the following statement, obtained exclusively by the staff of HUMAN EVENTS from the former U.S. Ambassador to Cuba, Spruille Braden. This retired American diplomat has long qualified as an expert not only in Cuba but also on all Latin America: having served in other posts south of the border, he has in recent years won recognition as a critical observer of the workings of the Communist apparatus in the Caribbean and South America.

Mr. Braden says of the Fidel Castro, leader of the fledging Cuban revolt, that, according to official documents he has seen, "He is a fellow-traveler, if not a member of the Communist Party and has been so for a long time. He was a ring leader in a bloody uprising in Bogota,

Columbia in April, 1948, which occurred just at the time when the Pan American Conference was being held in the capital, with no less a person than Secretary of State George C. Marshall present. The uprising was engineered and staged by the Communists, and the Colombian Government and Columbia press subsequently published documentary evidence of Fidel Castro's role as a leader in the rioting which virtually gutted the Colombian capital. The appearance of this Cuban at the head of the recent uprising in his own country stamps the insurrection as another part of the developing Communist pattern of such subversion throughout Latin America—although a member of thoroughly decent and patriotic Cubans have been mislead into the Fidel Castro movement."

Hitler, Mussolini, Peron—All Were Welfare Staters

Except for their obnoxious racist and militaristic policies, their demagogic anti-business and welfarist programs would have made them the idols of many U.S. liberals.

By James L. Wick   *(From the 16 November 1963 issue)*

Louisiana's Huey Long—perhaps the ace of aces among all the demagogues who have crossed the American scene—once said that if fascism comes to the U.S.A., it will come disguised as anti-fascism. With equal accuracy, he might have said that if socialism or communism comes it will arrive sponsored by persons and committees claiming to be anti-Socialist or anti-Communist.

The principal difference between fascism and socialism is in the psychological approach. Fascists call themselves anti-Socialists, thereby lulling the owners of property into a passive acceptance of fascism by capitalizing upon their fear of socialism. Once in power, however, Fascists feed large doses of socialism into the economy "to keep the masses satisfied."

Americans have been told so much about the anti-Semitic and race-supremacy traits of Hitler and Mussolini that they have missed the welfare statism so central to Fascist rule. They have overlooked the fact that fascism, like socialism, is the half-way house to communism.

Peron might have won an enthusiastic following among U.S. liberals but for his personal admiration for Mussolini and his worship of the Nazi military system.

Under Peron, the labor bosses got what they wanted: government pressures upon all workers to get into unions, followed by huge pay increases, job security, bigger and earlier pensions and other fringe benefits. Up with the welfare state, down with incentives, productivity and the like.

In return for lavish favors, the nation's labor leaders became the mainstay of Peron's support.

Fascism is government control of property whose ownership is left—nominally—in the private hands. Control affords to the government the opportunity to confer enormous favors upon those it likes and to wreak terrible vengeance upon those it dislikes.

Despite their pretense to the contrary, Hitler and Mussolini were Socialists. Hitler chose for his party the name "The National Socialist German Workers Party." He did so, because first, ideologically he was a Socialist—a fanatical advocate of the government-planned economy; and secondly, his aim was to wean Socialists and Communists away from the parties bearing those labels. At the same time, he told anti-Socialists and anti-Communists that his heart was with them; he was resorting to these devices only to fool the Socialist and Communist masses. As so often happens, however, the conservatives were the ones who were fooled.

In the economic sphere, Hitler simply intensified the controls over businesses inherited from Bismarck. This program harmonized with his socialistic beliefs but he also recognized the political potential. Fear of how the controls would be administered forced businessmen to seek his good will; those who resisted were put out of business.

Hitler left the ownership titles to industrial properties in private hands, but he assumed the right to make the vital decisions that are the essential attributes of full ownership.

Item: By decree, Hitler held down prices, telling the public he issued the order to prevent inflation—which his price controls were causing.

Item: Hitler allocated government orders to those firms which played ball with him. Because of Hitler's huge expenditures for militarism and welfarism, government was directly or indirectly the biggest customer by far for nearly all industries.

Item: Subject to wage and price controls, Hitler allowed earnings to be as large as managerial efficiency could make them. But he required that the earnings above 6 per cent be invested in government bonds. Some investors were thus lulled into a false security; others recognized the fraud but felt helpless to do anything about it.

The attention of America was so riveted upon Hitler's goose-stepping pageantry and upon the Nazi claims of Aryan supremacy that these anti-business characteristics and the many welfarist programs he introduced or expanded were overlooked.

The astonishing truth is that but for Hitler's anti-Semitism and militarism he might have become the idol of America's liberals—the "planners"—instead of their pet hate.

Big government liberals would not have been outraged by the diminution of freedom that accompanies government controls; on the contrary, they would have snorted: "You can't make an omelet without breaking eggs"—the same sentence with which they explained away Stalin's liquidation of millions of resisting kulaks.

Conservatives in Germany were victimized by the cliché—so often used by American liberals—that the way to stop communism is to give the masses small doses of socialism; otherwise the Communists will take over and give the masses total socialism.

Hitler (who was a great imitator of Communistic techniques) had no trouble making a deal with Stalin when he thought it helpful. The day the Hitler-Stalin pact was signed, anti-Communist, anti-Soviet and anti-Stalin propaganda ceased in Germany. Anti-Nazi and anti-Hitler propaganda ceased in Russia.

Mussolini

Because Mussolini repelled Americans by his enormous arrogance, few Americans noted the many New Deal measure he promulgated. Mussolini began his adult life as a dedicated Socialist. He defected when he recognized the opportunity created by the hysterical fear of socialism among the upper and middle classes. He promised frightened businessmen that he would preserve the private ownership system by giving the masses enough—but only enough— socialism to keep them from revolting.

American Socialists immediately denounced Mussolini's socialism—to which Il Duce gave the name fascism as a means of fooling the public. Norman Thomas insisted that "democratic socialism"—the name given to his own brand—was something entirely different from Mussolini's. Under "democratic socialism," the people would be allowed to go into the polling booth and— American Socialists would guarantee—the ballot would be secret. If the ballot is secret, they argue, how could anyone assert that the will of the people will not prevail?

The liberal assumption is that if the people vote as they really wish, it will be socialism. By socialism, they mean a system under which the government would provide the people with everything the Socialists think they ought to have.

The Socialists want a much larger portion of the national income siphoned to "the public sector of the economy"—meaning to the government—so bureaucrats can decide what is good for the masses to have.

The private sector of the economy should be given less income because the people, when left to themselves, refuse to spend their money as the intellectuals—playing God—would spend it for them.

Social security benefits in Italy were small before Mussolini. They were increased under fascism until the social security and unemployment benefit taxes collected from employers and employees equaled about 30 per cent of their pay.

Mussolini sought to increase his popularity with the masses by putting the unemployed to work on great public works projects which were always monumental, but often of little economic value.

One of Mussolini's decrees which U.S. labor unions now demand made it almost impossible for employers to fire employees except by the payment of long severance pay. Even with this proviso, permission to fire had to be obtained; the bureaucracy, having promised full employment, usually refused permission to dismiss.

If an Italian firm could not sustain the huge government-required costs, the government invited an application for help. The aid might take the form of government orders, government loans or government purchases of some of the firm's common or preferred stock. In some cases, a complete government take-over might occur. How high or low was the take-over price depended entirely upon bureaucratic whim. Pro-Mussolini firms were often surprised at government generosity—and they passed the word along.

In such an atmosphere, dishonest and depraved industrialists thrive; the honest and the conscientious are frozen out.

Whenever Mussolini felt his popularity with the workers declining, he would add a "paid holiday." After two decades of Mussolini, Italy had more paid holidays than any other industrial country.

Those who did not live through the periods of Fascist rule cannot understand the fanatical devotion to fascism that existed among millions of the unthinking. Hitler, Mussolini and Peron were idolized by the gullible in their countries. The reasons are not hard to understand. Here is what was delivered by fascism whether Hitler's, Mussolini's or Peron's:

(1) Wage rates were raised—regardless of productivity.

(2) Higher pensions were decreed and at an earlier age. The nation's capacity to support persons no longer productive bore no relationship to the size of the pensions.

(3) The number of persons holding soft jobs on the government pay-roll was built up.

(4) Workers were required to become union members as a means of subjecting them to union discipline.

(5) Union leaders were brought into the ruler's inner circle.

Some of these items increase costs; others increase government power. Many of them promise something for nothing, appealing to the infantile mind. Because of their anti-business nature, they had a special appeal to the "intellectuals." All of the items make perfect weapons for demagogues.

Peron

Latin America is the victim of its heritage—as the English-speaking America is exalted by hers.

The Spaniards sent their soldiers to the New World to conquer the natives and to get the gold with which the conquerors could return to the Old World and lead a life of ease. In contrast, the United States and Canada were settled by immigrants prepared for a life of hardship; they expected nothing except what they might earn. The Spaniards came to get something for nothing; the North American immigrants came to build themselves log cabin homes in the wilderness. They were thinking less of themselves than of their children and grandchildren.

Argentina is the South American country with a climate most like the U.S.A. Its natural resources are immense. By all the laws of economics, its standard of living should be as high as that of the United States.

The Peron period began in 1943-44. Like a number of other non-European countries, Argentina was essentially a neutral country during World War II. Its formal declaration of war was intended only to get a seat at the peace table.

Argentina made record-breaking profits from the sale of meat, grain and raw materials to the warring countries. She could have emerged from the war and post-war periods with a far greater increase in productivity than any country in the world. Instead, Argentina (and other non-warring countries controlled by shortsighted demagogues) emerged with as great poverty and as wild inflation as the countries which had suffered the most devastation.

The invaded countries like Germany, which suffered almost complete paralysis, have by now multiplied the size of their prewar production plants while the demagogue ruled countries in Latin America have emerged poverty-stricken.

To stop inflation, Peron, calling himself the enemy of the reactionaries, instituted price controls. This was the way, said Peron, to stop inflation—the inflation he himself was causing.

When the government treasury began running low, Peron began nationalizing foreign-owned industries. He had the normal Socialist-Fascist passion for nationalization, but he also had a secondary motive; to get his hands on the substantial profits being made by the well-run foreign-owned enterprises. Unfortunately, in most cases as soon as the government took possession, the profits turned to losses.

In the late Thirties, Franklin D. Roosevelt encouraged South American nationalization of U.S.-owned properties by declaring that American investors deserved what they got; their record, he said, was one of "exploitation" below the Rio Grande. From then on, our State Department merely went through the motions of making formal protests, after which it accepted the promise of the nationalizing governments that the owners would be compensated for the "fair" value of the enterprise.

The "fair" value, as adjudicated, invariably turned out to be mere fraction of actual value. In addition, the compensation was to be paid over a long period of time—in fast depreciating native currency.

Peron came to power in Argentina in 1943-44 as a result of a military coup. He met Evita Duarte, a third-rate blond radio actress who was mildly attractive and sexually promiscuous. Being herself illegitimate, she hated "respectable" people, especially those of the upper classes. Knowing she could get nowhere in her own right, she became Peron's mistress, then his wife, hoping thereby to climb the social ladder.

Evita had enormous energy and a calculating brain which understood the psychology of "masses." She realized the way to power for her husband was through control of labor, control of charity, promises of welfare. The Argentinian masses became easy victims; they had never been indoctrinated with the old-fashioned "Puritan ethic" virtues of getting the good things of life by their own efforts.

One of Evita's objectives was to get all workers into labor unions. Once a worker has been forced into a labor union, his thoughts, his acts, his politics can be controlled by the union leaders.

The laboring masses soon discovered that the way to get more was through Evita. But not as individuals, no matter how many. Non-union workers got no consideration.

To get what laboring men wanted—and sometimes much more—the credentials needed were simple. Come, led by pro-Peron leaders. Come, by the tens of thousands. Dictators loved pageantry. Come, prepared to idolize Peron and Evita.

The rewards often amazed the most optimistic.

For bargaining purposes telephone workers once asked for a 70 per cent increase. To their surprise, Evita gave them the entire 70 per cent.

On one occasion, the labor leaders, bringing their masses, asked for a 40 per cent raise, hoping for 20 per cent. The enthusiasm of the mob so delighted Evita that she ordered their employers to give them 50 per cent.

In another moment of ecstasy, the mob being even more worshipful than usual, Evita ordered employers to add a month's pay as a Christmas present to their workers.

Decrees came along requiring large severance payments for laid-off workers. But—learning from Mussolini and Hitler—even when business firms were willing to make the severance payments, the department of labor's decision was quite likely to be an order not to reduce the number employed.

Evita's method of getting the support of union leaders was to grant their demands, no matter how extreme. The way for an Argentine labor leader to gain popularity with his workers was to play ball with the Perons. In that case, he could get everything he asked for. The more extreme a union leader's demands, the greater his popularity with his members.

Evita's secret was obvious: Prove that the government was the source of all good things: wage increases, fringe benefits, increased pensions, etc.

However, the net result was that instead of being the servant of the people, the Argentine government became the master of the people.

Yes, the ballot was secret; the votes were honestly counted; everyone could vote. These three conditions fulfill the proof required by liberals that a country is a democracy. But where the government is all-powerful, as most liberals believe it should be, then—as the people of Argentina discovered—the ballots must be cast for candidates approved by the government which can withhold as well as bestow.

In Argentina, union members were technically allowed a full and free choice of their labor leaders. However, Peron-approved leaders had no reason to worry since there was such a vast difference in what the members would get if they chose the Peron-endorsed labor leaders as against the Peron-opposed candidates.

How much was in their paychecks depended not upon their own efforts but upon what the Perons decreed.

In Argentina, the outward trappings of democracy were maintained in both political and economic spheres. Why not? Every voter knew that there was only one choice—unless he was willing to starve for principle—and that was to choose the candidates who had the favor of *Juan and Evita*.

There is no chance that the United States would accept a dictatorship based upon Hitler's racism and Prussian-type militarism or Mussolini's swashbuckling braggadocio. These elements are repugnant to the overwhelming majority of Americans.

But Hitler and Mussolini had one characteristic in common with ADA liberals. They believed "the good things of life" should come by government decrees and decisions. By using this technique, they could tell the people how much they—out of love for the people—had done for them.

Communists, Fascists and New Frontiersmen all want the people to feel a personal dependence upon their rulers for their happiness and welfare.

Once the people feel that way, they will vote for those who promise the biggest government benefits.

One speech of Hitler's made nearly 30 years ago received little attention in America. It should have been printed on every front page. Its theme was contained in the following paragraph:

"We shall banish want; we shall banish fear. The essence of National Socialism is human welfare. National Socialism is the revolution of the common man. Rooted in a fuller life for every German from childhood to old age, National Socialism means a new day of abundance at home and a better world order abroad."

How the Communists Have Built Up
Anti-US Propaganda on Viet Nam

By Fulton Lewis, Jr.   *(From the 22 May 1965 issue)*

Rep. H. Allen Smith of California has received letters by the bushel demanding the withdrawal of U.S. troops from South Viet Nam.

The congressman was, quite frankly, confused: public opinion polls have consistently shown that an overwhelming majority of Americans favor a get-tough policy toward the North Vietnamese invaders.

Smith, a former FBI agent, began to investigate the mail that he and other members of Congress had received—mail that often ran 100-1 in favor of surrender. From sources at the Justice Department, the California Republican learned that leaders of the Communist Party, U.S.A., had for more than a year made Viet Nam agitation their main task. In a meticulously documented speech last week, Smith disclosed the top-secret activities of party leaders.

1. Party boss Gus Hall in March, 1954, dispatched to district leaders throughout the country a directive entitled "The United States and Viet Nam Developments." Party members were urged to send telegrams to President Johnson protesting against American "aggression," to organize protest meetings and picket lines, and to enlist the support of non-Communist leftists in their activities.

2. Viet Nam was the principle topic at a meeting of Communist leaders in June, 1964. Here veteran Communist Margrit Pittman laid down the party line on Viet Nam and instructed her comrades to use telegrams, resolutions meetings, marches and demonstrations in demanding American withdrawal.

3. The incident that moves the Communist campaign into high gear was the American action at the Gulf of Tonkin last August. Addressing her chief lieutenants, the party's southern California district leader, Dorothy Healey, called for 50,000 letters condemning the "dirty aggression" of American servicemen. National headquarters in New York distributed new orders calling for massive protests.

4. At a meeting of party leaders in November, public relations director Arnold Johnson reported on the Vietnamese campaign. Party activity was stepped up. New directives were mailed to party leaders. Infiltration of union and religious groups was suggested.

5. Following a precedent set during the Gulf of Tonkin confrontation, party leaders were quick to assail the United States when North Vietnamese military targets were first attacked on February 7. Party boss Hall declared the air strike "an act of brutal aggression which horrifies the world." Party members were again ordered to flood Washington with letters and telegrams.

6. At a meeting of party officials in mid-February, National Labor Secretary Carl Winter reported on the success of the Communist campaign. President Johnson, he said, was beginning to feel the pressure of peace advocates.

7. Communist party "spokesmen" began to fan out across the country, lecturing college groups on American "aggression." Party theoretician Herbert Aptheker addressed numerous demonstrations, moving east from Los Angeles through St. Louis to New York.

8. Communist party officials played a major role in the April 17 march on Washington sponsored by the Students for a Democratic Society. Participants in the march included Arnold Johnson and southern regional director George Myers. At a meeting of the party's National Committee in late April, Johnson disclosed that party members from every section of the country had participated in the march.

9. Major demonstrations in support of the march took place in Chicago, San Francisco and Los Angeles, with party members playing important roles. The party-controlled W. E. B. Du Bois Clubs increased their agitation.

10. Chief Red Gus Hall, in a meeting of the party's national committee late last month, commented favorably on the Communist drive, but urged members not to let up. He again called for a united front of the Communist and non-Communist left to press for a reversal of U.S. policy.

The Assassination of John F. Kennedy: The Reasons Why

Reviewed by Reed J. Irvine   *(From the 24 July 1971 issue)*

If this book (*The Assassination of John F. Kennedy: The Reasons Why*, by Albert H. Newman, Clarkson N. Potter, Inc.) had been published five or six years ago, we might have been spared much of the speculation about whether or not Lee Harvey Oswald was really the murderer of President Kennedy. In spite of the very strong evidence of Oswald's guilt, and in spite of the unequivocal findings of the Warren Commission, there has been considerable reluctance both here and abroad to accept the Warren Commission conclusion that the killer was Oswald and Oswald alone.

One strong reason for these doubts was the failure of the Warren Commission to establish a convincing motive for Oswald's actions. Any reader of murder mysteries knows that the establishment of motive is a key factor in determining the identity of the guilty party. The Warren Commission made a stab at assigning a motive for Oswald's deed, but the result was far from convincing.

The commission thought that his motivation could he found in his maladjustment to his environment, his hatred for American society, his desire to be a great man and his commitment to communism. No effort was made to spell out how any of these factors could have explained his decision to kill the President.

There are many maladjusted people in the world, but few of them become assassins. Oswald's commitment to communism certainly had a bearing on his behavior, but the commission failed to show why this should have been so.

If Oswald had been a right-wing fanatic, his crime would have been explained as a political act, inspired by what many people labeled "the climate of hate" that was supposed to have prevailed in Dallas. It came as a surprise to many people, including Chief Justice Warren, to learn that it was a man of the left, not the right, that fired those fatal shots in Dallas.

Arthur Krock posed the bothersome question that cried out for an answer: "Why did the man who first attempted to kill Gen. Walker, a passionate advocate of the far right in political philosophy, choose for his next target President Kennedy, an advocate of a political philosophy somewhat to the left of center?"

This is the question that Albert Newman answers in his carefully researched and imaginatively written book. Newman painstakingly unravels the mystery of Oswald's peculiar conduct from the time he returned from his self-imposed exile in the Soviet Union in June 1962 until he was killed by Jack Ruby on Nov. 24, 1963.

Newman shows that after his unhappy sojourn in Russia, Oswald returned home disillusioned with Soviet-style communism. However, he remained a Marxist, a faith that he had acquired at an early age, solely through reading. It is interesting to note that he was first propelled in this direction by a pamphlet on the Rosenberg case that some unknown agitator had handed him when he was only 13 years old. The chain of events set off by that chance encounter culminated in the tragedy of Dallas, a fact that might be pondered by those who defend the wisdom of exposing immature students to all strains of thought.

Very soon after returning to the United States, Oswald discovered the Trotskyite brand of Marxism. He tried to join the Trotskyite party, the Socialist Workers party. He subscribed to that party's publication, *The Militant*, and he came to share its ardent admiration for Fidel Castro. *The Militant* devoted a great deal of space to Castro and his speeches. Also, Newman shows that Oswald owned a shortwave radio that was able to pick up Radio Havana. His habits suggested that he listened to Radio Havana regularly. The Warren Commission was so unconcerned with the kind of ideas that Oswald was feeding upon that they did not even bother to note that the radio had a short-wave band.

Newman shows, quite persuasively, that Oswald's decision to try to kill Gen. Edwin Walker was triggered by statements Walker made about the desirability of U.S. action against Castro. In addition, the Communist press that he was reading had pinned the "fascist" label on Walker.

Newman hypothesizes that Oswald planned to kill Walker and make his escape to Cuba, where he expected to receive a hero's welcome for having eliminated America's leading "fascist." He accumulated evidence that would demonstrate that he was Walker's slayer in a scrapbook, evidently intending to take it with him to Cuba. He destroyed the book after his attack on Walker was unsuccessful, but he saved some of the photographs.

What those who have difficulty reconciling the attack on Kennedy with the attack on Walker forget is that John F. Kennedy was also an object of Castro's violent hatred.

The Cuban missile crisis occurred shortly after Oswald returned to the U.S. Castro was humiliated by the removal of the missiles, and Radio Havana blared forth abuse of the United States and its President. The Communist press, including *The Militant*, was also loaded with denunciations of John Kennedy.

Newman points out that Oswald once told a friend that he could tell what the Communist papers wanted him to do by reading between the lines. A copy of *The Militant* that was found among Oswald's possessions printed a Castro speech that contained these lines: "With the rifle and the work tool, the work tool and the rifle, with these both we must bring about our victory."

Did expert rifleman Oswald read between the lines and interpret this as a message that he should use his rifle to eliminate Castro's No. 1 enemy in the United States, John F. Kennedy? The chance to do so was presented to him when the presidential motorcade was routed past the building in which Oswald worked. He made a quick decision to perform what he considered to be a service to his hero Castro, even at the risk of his own life.

Unlike all earlier presidential assassins, Oswald fled from the scene of the crime undetected, but Newman shows that he apparently did not harbor any hope of fleeing the country. He believes that after killing the President, Oswald determined to kill Gen. Walker as well. He tries to show that he was heading for the Walker residence when police officer J.D. Tippit spotted him. It was Tippit rather than Walker that became his victim.

Newman has combined a painstaking sifting of all the known facts about Oswald and his actions with deductive reasoning designed to fit his actions into a rational pattern. What he comes up with makes a lot of sense. The hypotheses cannot be proven, but there can be no doubt after reading this book that Oswald was motivated to kill John F. Kennedy because he thought that in doing so he would be helping the Castro Communist cause.

The book is a valuable contribution, not only for the light it sheds on the slaying of President Kennedy, but for its demonstration of the impact that ideas have on conduct.

The Lessons of the Alger Hiss Case

By Richard M. Nixon   *(From the 15 March 1986 issue)*

(The following are excerpts from the speech made by former President Nixon before the annual meeting of the Pumpkin Papers Irregulars on Oct. 31, 1985, at the Princeton Club, New York City.)

After reading [CIA Director] Bill Casey's remarkable address to the Pumpkin Papers Irregulars last year, I wrote to him that I had thought that I knew everything about the Alger Hiss case, but that he had dug up fascinating information that I was not aware of.

What I would like to do tonight is to share with you some personal observations indicating how I saw the events at that time, how the case affected my career, and the lessons of the case for the future.

I have often been asked for my opinion as to what was the single most important physical piece of evidence which broke the case.

Various books have emphasized the importance of the old Woodstock typewriter on which Mrs. Hiss typed the secret State Department documents; the 1929 Ford roadster which Hiss claimed he had "given, loaned, or sold" to Chambers; the Bokhara rug, a gift from Col. Bykov—the chief Soviet espionage agent in the United States—which Chambers had delivered to Hiss; the prothonotary warbler, a rare and beautiful bird, which Hiss and Whittaker Chambers—both ardent amateur ornithologists—referred to in their testimony.

All of these items played a role in convicting Hiss of perjury. But the indispensable physical piece of which set in motion the chain of events which led to his conviction was none of these. It was Chambers' teeth.

It is necessary at this point to reconstruct briefly the events which led up to Hiss' finally admitting that he knew Chambers. On Aug. 3, 1948, Chambers had testified that Hiss was a member of a Communist cell in Washington. On August 5, Hiss had categorically denied it. He went further and said that he had "Never met a man by the name of Whittaker Chambers." When shown a picture of Chambers, he observed that it was not an unusual face, and that "it might look like you, Mr. Chairman," referring to Congressman Karl Mundt.

This was Hiss' first major mistake. We could not prove that Hiss was a Communist; it was one man's word against another's. But I felt strongly that we could find out whether Chambers knew Hiss through third-party evidence. The way to do that was to examine Chambers intensively on what he knew about Hiss.

For almost three hours on August 7, I bombarded Chambers with questions covering everything I could think of which one man should know about another if they knew each other. The answers came back one after another unequivocally and in the most minute detail on such items as Hiss' hobbies, his pet cocker spaniel dog, the interiors and exteriors of the houses in which he had lived, his tastes in food, clothing, etc.

When I asked whether Hiss had a car, Chambers' answer was particularly descriptive. He described a 1929 Ford roadster, black and dilapidated, which had windshield wipers that had to be worked by hand.

On August 16, we went down the same list of questions with Hiss and with hardly any exceptions, we got the same answers. Hiss defensively charged that the committee was trying to build a web around him, but after our intensive probing he finally testified that he had known a freelance writer by the name of George Crosley who might have known the facts about him which Chambers had testified to.

We now had to find out whether Chambers and Crosley were the same man. We decided that it was time to have the two confront each other and get a positive identification if possible. This led to the most crucial hearing of the entire Hiss case. It occurred in the most unlikely place—Room 1400 of the Commodore Hotel in New York City.

The room was nondescript except for the ironic fact that there were Audubon prints on the walls. Hiss arrived first and after about 10 minutes of questioning on collateral issues, I asked one of our staff investigators, Lou Russell, to bring Chambers in. I then asked both Hiss and Chambers to stand and said, "Mr. Hiss, the man standing here is Whittaker Chambers. I ask you now if you have ever known this man before."

"May I ask him to speak?" said Hiss. "Will you ask him to say something?" I asked Chambers to state his name and business.

Chambers responded, "My name is Whittaker Chambers."

Hiss walked toward Chambers until he was no more than a foot away and peered down into his mouth. He said, "Would you mind opening your mouth wider?" Chambers repeated,

"My name is Whittaker Chambers." Hiss, speaking more loudly, demanded again, "I said, will you open your mouth? You know what I am referring to, Mr. Nixon. Will you go on talking?" Chambers continued, "I am senior editor of *Time* magazine." Hiss then said, "May I ask whether his voice when he testified before was comparable to this?" "His voice?" I asked.

"Or did he talk a little more in a lower key?" Hiss continued. One of us observed that the voice was about the same now as we had heard before. Hiss was not satisfied and asked, "Would you ask him to talk a little more?"

I handed the *Time* magazine editor a copy of *Newsweek* which was on the table and asked him to read from it.

After Chambers had read a few paragraphs, Hiss interrupted, "The voice sounds a little less resonant than the voice that I recall of the man I knew as George Crosley. The teeth look to me that either they have been improved upon or that there has been considerable dental work done since I knew George Crosley which was some years ago. I believe that I am not prepared without further checking to take an absolute oath that he must be George Crosley."

I asked Chambers if he had any work done on his teeth since 1934. He replied that he had had some extractions and some bridge work done in the front of his mouth.

Hiss then said, "Could you ask him the name of the dentist who performed the work?" By this time, I could hardly keep a straight face but I decided to play the game out. "What is the name?" Chambers replied, "Dr. Hitchcock, Westminister, Maryland."

Hiss was still not satisfied. He said, "I would like to find out from Dr. Hitchcock if what he has just said is true because I am relying partly—one of my main recollections of Crosley was the poor condition of his teeth."

By this time, we had had enough and I said, "Before we leave the teeth, Mr. Hiss, do you feel that you would have to have the dentist tell you just what he did to the teeth before you could tell us anything about this man?" Hiss realized that he had overplayed the hand and after a long silence he changed the subject.

Our chief investigator, Bob Stripling, gave him the *coup de grace*. He said, "Now here is a person you knew for several months at least. You knew him so well that he was a guest in your home, that you gave him an old Ford car and permitted him to use or you leased him your apartment and the one thing that you have to check on is this denture. There is nothing else about this man's features which you could definitely say that this is the man I knew as George Crosley, that you have to rely entirely on this denture for your position?"

He still refused to take an oath that Chambers was Crosley. "He may have had his face lifted," he protested. After some more sparring, he finally threw in the towel and said that he was prepared to identify Chambers as George Crosley. Stripling observed, "You are willing to wave the dentures?"

Then Hiss made his second big mistake. He walked over to Chambers and shook his fist at him and said, "May I say for the record at this point that I would like to invite Mr. Whittaker Chambers to make these statements out of the presence of this committee, without their being privileged for suit for libel. I challenge you to do it, and I hope you will do it damned quickly."

The critical factor in breaking the case, however, was the charade about Chambers' teeth. Before that, along with other members of the committee, I had a nagging doubt that Chambers might have made a study of Hiss' life and concocted the story about him because of some grudge or because as Hiss had implied he was either a pathological liar or mentally and emotionally unstable.

But now, while we still were not sure that Chambers had told the truth about everything and particularly about Hiss's being a member of the Communist party, we knew that Hiss had lied about not knowing Chambers. He had, in effect, been bitten by Chambers' teeth. It was a self-inflicted wound.

Whom should Hiss blame most for his conviction? Chambers, the committee, [prosecutor] Tom Murphy—all are prime candidates.

After Hiss claimed that he knew Chambers, although under another name, he was damaged, but not fatally. No criminal charges had been leveled against him, and without further developments the case would have faded away. Three unlikely people were responsible for keeping the case alive: Hiss himself, the editor of the Washington *Post*, and Hiss' lawyer.

Hiss did himself in by challenging Chambers to make his charges in public. On August 27, when Chambers appeared on "Meet the Press," Ed Folliard—a reporter for the Washington *Post*—pressed Chambers to do just that. Chambers categorically stated, "Hiss was a Communist and may still be."

Three weeks passed without Hiss' backing up his threat to bring a lawsuit in the event that Chambers made his charge publicly away from the privilege of a congressional hearing. The Washington *Post* editorialized that Hiss, in effect, should put up or shut up. Hiss could ignore attacks by his enemies, but not from his friends. He sued Chambers for libel.

Hiss' lawyer took Chambers' deposition. He pressed Chambers over and over again to produce some documentary evidence to back up his charge that Hiss was a Communist. Chambers declined to do so. He told me later that at that point he was reluctant to reveal the fact that Hiss and other members of the ring were engaged in espionage. Hiss' lawyers then deposed Esther Chambers. They cross-examined her so ruthlessly that Chambers later told me that they had made her cry.

It was then that he became convinced that Hiss and his lawyers were determined to destroy him and that he had no choice but to produce the papers and microfilms which would clearly demonstrate that Hiss as well as he had been involved in espionage.

He went to New York and retrieved the typewritten papers, some notes in Hiss' handwriting, and the rolls of microfilm which he had given to his wife's nephew, Levine, 10 years ago as "life insurance" in the event that the Communists harassed him after he left the party in 1938.

To the amazement and consternation of Hiss' attorneys, Chambers produced the typewritten papers and the handwritten notes at the deposition hearing. The papers were turned over to a representative of the Justice Department, who swore everybody to silence with the risk of criminal prosecution for contempt of court if they talked publicly about the papers.

Two weeks later, I saw a United Press dispatch in a Washington newspaper indicating that the Justice Department was ready to drop the Hiss/Chambers case for lack of evidence.

It was then that Bob Stripling and I drove up to the Chambers farm. We showed him the dispatch. He looked out the window and shook his head without saying a word for at least a minute. Then he turned to us and said, "This is what I have been afraid of." He related the fact that he had turned over documentary evidence in the deposition hearing and that he could not tell us what was in the documents except to say that they were a real "bombshell."

I asked him if the assistant attorney general, Alex Campbell, had these documents. He replied, "No, I have another bombshell in case they try to suppress this one." Without knowing what he had, I said, "You keep that bombshell. Don't give it to anyone except the committee."

When we returned to Washington, I signed a subpoena *duces tecum* for all evidence that Chambers had and the next night Chambers led our investigators into his now famous pumpkin patch and gave them the rolls of microfilm which he had hidden there.

The key point is that there would never have been any pumpkin papers and Hiss would never have been convicted had it not been for the actions he, the Washington *Post*, and his lawyers took in his behalf. Again, it was a self-inflicted wound.

*   *   *   *   *

Let me tell you now how the Hiss case affected my political career. The year 1985 is an anniversary year—the 40th anniversary of the end of World War II and the founding of the United Nations. It also happens to be the 25th anniversary of the closest presidential election in United States history.

Of almost 70 million votes cast, a shift of 12,000 in Illinois and one other smaller state would have changed the result. A friend of mine was postmorteming the election a few days later. He expressed the view that much of the media antipathy directed against me during the campaign was due to my role in the Hiss case. He went on to say, "If it had not been for the Hiss case, I think you might have been elected." I replied that without the Hiss case, I would probably not have been nominated.

In the 1952 campaign, domestic communism was a major issue. Eisenhower recognized that this was the case, but he did not want to address the issue himself and did not want to leave it to Joe McCarthy, who had earned his undying enmity because of his attacks on Eisenhower's idol, George Marshall. He told me, "One of the reasons I picked you was that you got Hiss and got him fairly." He urged me in the campaign to talk about the Hiss case because a lot of people thought McCarthy had gotten Hiss.

Ironically, without the Hiss case I might not have run for governor of California. It was a very close call, with California party leaders urging me to run and many of my best friends and family urging me not to do so.

A letter I received from Whittaker Chambers in February 1961 probably tipped the scales on the side of running. As I read that letter today, I am profoundly impressed by the simple, understated eloquence which characterized Chambers' writing and his speech as well.

I reread this letter just before making my final decision eight months later. I followed his advice; I ran, I lost, and I was out of the 1964 race. I made a comeback in 1968. If I had not run for governor in 1962, I very possibly would have run for President in 1964 and would have lost, because no one was going to beat Lyndon Johnson that year. I would have had no chance to be nominated and elected in 1968.

My association with the Hiss case and with Whittaker Chambers had a profound effect in shaping my attitude toward the war in Vietnam. Bob Taft opposed the war in Korea. Chambers liked Taft better than Eisenhower, but when I asked him about Taft's criticism he shook his head and said, "He is wrong. What people do not understand is that for the Communists, the war in Korea is not a war about Korea, it is a war about Japan."

I tried to analyze the war in Vietnam in the same way. From my vantage point, the war in Vietnam was not just about Vietnam but about Cambodia, Laos, Indonesia, Angola, Ethiopia and Nicaragua. It is fashionable to deride the domino theory today, but any sophisticated observer of foreign policy recognizes that on the world scene, when one domino falls, others do not fall immediately nor even adjacently.

We are recovering from the Vietnam syndrome, but the specter of no more Vietnams even today is being raised by those who oppose a strong U.S. role in Central America or other areas of the world where the Communists are engaged in direct or indirect aggression. The American defeat in Vietnam did not just affect Vietnam. It encouraged our enemies, it discouraged our friends, but most damaging of all, it weakened the spirit and will of Americans to play a responsible role in the world scene.

What are some of the major lessons of the Hiss case? What is most important is to recognize the breadth and depth of Soviet espionage activities in the United States.

Some of Hiss' supporters scoffed at the documents and microfilms that Chambers turned over to the committee and to the courts. They contended that they were really unimportant and were not damaging to U.S. security.

They failed to take into account the testimony before the committee of John Peurifoy, who was the State Department's assistant for security. He pointed out that anyone who had access to the pumpkin papers, which were photo-static copies of State Department cables, would have been able to break the State Department's code.

That meant that the Russians were probably able to read all messages using that code in the period before World War II when the Soviet Union was allied with Nazi Germany. Of course, some might observe that the way the State Department leaks today, they would not need to break our code to find out what was going on.

The critics also overlook the fact that the papers and microfilms that Chambers turned over were his last haul—as he put it, his "insurance" if the Communists threatened him after he had defected. He testified that at least 70 other times he had collected a similar amount from Hiss and had delivered them to his Soviet contact.

Another point that the critics fail to recognize is that Hiss was only one of Chambers' contacts. He testified that his sources who provided documents for him included four in the State Department, two in the Bureau of Standards, one in the Picatinny Arsenal, one in the Aberdeen Proving Grounds, and contacts in the Electric Boat Co., Remington Rand, and Illinois Steel Co.

And they also fail to recognize that Chambers is only one of several couriers who collected documents and turned them over to Soviet agents.

Another major lesson of the Hiss case is that it provides a vivid example of the mistake often made in the media and in intellectual circles generally in confusing style and substance.

Most of the media covering the Hiss case were obsessed with style. Although he was a *Time* senior editor, Chambers was poorly dressed, pudgy, undistinguished in appearance and in background. Hiss, in contrast, was a striking representative of the fashionable Eastern Establishment—a graduate of Harvard Law School, clerk to a Supreme Court justice, an aide to Franklin Roosevelt at Yalta, and one of the major organizers of the United Nations conference in San Francisco. He had impeccable social and intellectual qualifications. An indication of this was the list of names he submitted of people who would vouch for his character—officials ranging from Adlai Stevenson to John Foster Dulles. He, in effect, pled innocence by association.

All of this had an enormous impact on the media. They were so dazzled by Hiss' background and by his brilliant conduct on the witness stand when he first appeared on August 5 that they failed to see that beneath the unimpressive exterior, Chambers was a stronger, more intelligent man than Hiss.

*   *   *   *   *

When he first testified on Aug. 3, 1948, Chambers said that he told his wife that when he left the party in 1938, he thought that he was leaving the winning side, but that "he would rather die on the losing side than to live under communism."

I have just returned from an around-the-world trip which took me to many countries I had visited 32 years ago on a similar trip when I was Vice President. On the first trip, many non-Communist educators, labor leaders, and members of the media honestly felt that the Communist model of the Soviet Union or China might be the best and fastest way to economic progress for newly independent countries in the Third World.

That is not the case today. Why? Sixty-five years ago a starry-eyed newspaper reporter, Lincoln Steffens, returned from the Soviet Union and wrote, "I have been over into the future and it works." Today, the world has seen that future and it doesn't work.

*   *   *   *   *

The most moving moment of any hearing I have ever attended as a member of the House or Senate came at the end of a long, seven-hour day, Aug. 25, 1948. It was the first televised congressional hearing. I regret, incidentally, that it was not the last.

Hiss had testified for almost five hours. Chambers had testified for over two hours. As he neared the end of his testimony, I asked Chambers, "Can you search your memory now to see what motive you can have for accusing Mr. Hiss of being a Communist at the present time?"

Chambers responded, "What motive I can have?"

I elaborated, "Yes, is there any grudge you have against Mr. Hiss over anything he has done to you?"

Chambers replied, "The story has spread that in testifying against Mr. Hiss I am working out some old grudge or motives of revenge or hatred. I do not hate Mr. Hiss. We were close friends, but we are caught in a tragedy of history. Mr. Hiss represents the concealed enemy against which we are all fighting and I am fighting. I have testified against him with remorse and pity, but in a moment of history in which this nation now stands, so help me God, I cannot do otherwise."

Chambers is dead. Alger Hiss still lives. But history will record that Chambers was on the right side and you in this room can help make sure that he was also on the winning side.

Through the Glasnost Semi-Darkly

By Allan H. Ryskind   *(From the 25 June 1988 issue)*

(Mr. Ryskind's article is largely based on his week-long stay in the Soviet Union earlier this year, though it contains information and anecdotes that surfaced later. The trip was sponsored by the bipartisan American Council of Young Political Leaders [ACYPL], and included 30 "alumni" of previous ACYPL-sponsored Russian trips and a number of wives.

The delegation leaders included Co-chairmen Hodding Carter, the well-known journalist, and Rep. Donald Sundquist [R.-Tenn.]; Vice-chairmen Arthur B. Culvahouse, counsel to the President, and Rep. Steny Hoyer [D.-Md.], who heads the Helsinki Commission; and Secretaries Randal Teague, a senior adviser to Jack Kemp's 1988 presidential campaign, and R. Spencer Oliver, chief counsel, House Foreign Affairs Committee.)

There *is* change in the Soviet Union. *Glasnost*, or openness, *does* exist to a remarkable extent. *Perestroika*, or economic restructuring, is a critical new phase in this Socialist nation. *New thinking*—should it take hold—could prove to be the key to a revived, less hostile and less repressive society. Certainly this is what the Soviets are hinting will be the result as they prepare for their historic Party Conference, and this is obviously the grand hope for the optimists in the West.

Yet just how deep-seated all of these reforms will become remains a huge, unanswered mystery. And even if the changes turn out to be more than superficial, not just an elaborate trick to lull the West to sleep while refortifying the Evil Empire, the United States would be foolish in the extreme to relax its guard.

If the Soviets are "softening," as some believe, why shouldn't they be pressed even *harder* by the West, until they are finally forced to yield their global conquests and let the rest of the world live in peace?

Upon returning to the Soviet Union after 14 years, I have developed the unoriginal hunch that the Russians are on the run. They have failed in their effort to subdue Afghanistan, and appear on the verge of a calamitous defeat. They are losing out in Angola, and may even be prepared to abandon their colony to Jonas Savimbi's pro-Western UNITA resistance if the State Department doesn't sell Savimbi out first.

A U.S. Embassy official told me that the Soviets are now saying—for the first time—that they don't think they can ever overwhelm Savimbi's forces, because the South Africans are determined not to let him go under (though the Soviet assessment could well be wrong). And there are signs—some faint, some strong—that they are willing to cut deals favorable to the West in other parts of the globe as well.

Soviet satellites are sending out major distress signals, with Vietnam and Ethiopia facing starvation or still suffering from its ravages. Eastern Europe is in an endless state of ferment, and Poland constantly looks as if it's on the brink of breaking away completely from the Soviet empire.

And there is massive turmoil inside the heart of the Soviet Union itself, with sustained violence and protests erupting in Armenia, Azerbaijan, the Baltic states, Central Asia and other areas over explosive ethnic divisions.

Economically, the USSR is still a Third World country—a nuclear-armed Bangladesh, as some are tagging it—where rickets is widespread, measles a common childhood disease, and typhoid nearly 30 times the rate in this country. Between the 1960s and the 1980s, the death rate rose steadily, with the longevity of newborn males declining from 66 years to 62, "unprecedented in a developed nation," explains Murray Feshback, an expert on Soviet demographics.

And the Soviets remain deeply concerned about the rebuilding of America's military, with special venom directed toward the development of the Strategic Defense Initiative, which was furiously battered as a "first strike" weapon in English over Radio Moscow—a message that came in loud and clear over the radios in our hotel rooms.

But just how far the Soviets are willing to go to convince the West that a more reasonable, potentially less aggressive USSR is under way—aside from executing a few significant but tactical retreats and exuding a general *bonhomie*—is difficult to assess.

Harsh Self-Criticism

Certainly, they have opened the door to harsh, internal criticism. A Moscow play going on while we were there, *The Dictatorship of Conscience*, finds Lenin in the dock, questioned as to what went wrong with socialism. In a comedy skit, a Russian says two plus two equals seven. A second says, "Comrade, that's the Old Thinking, you can now say six." "Well," says the first, "why not five?" "Ah," says the second, "that's too close to four."

The U.S. ambassador, Jack Matlock, a small, compact, balding foreign service officer, who gives quite a good impression to visitors, despite the fact that he ran afoul of conservatives when he served on the National Security Council, has far more access to top Soviet officials than previous ambassadors. He is frequently on Soviet TV, has frank exchanges with Soviet officials and has even lectured at their war college.

Astonishingly though, Feshback, who—in a celebrated *Atlantic Monthly* article—said the Soviets were in a terrible, ruinous state of decline because of acute alcoholism, lack of medical care, pollution and the lowering of the average male's lifespan, recently spoke at the U.S. ambassador's residence at Spaso House, where he was warmly greeted and listened to attentively by Soviet specialists.

Pravda, the official Communist party organ, has carried some stunning criticisms of Soviet practices, including an article by academician Tatyan Zaslavskaya, which excoriated the bureaucracy for failing to compile adequate data so policymakers could judge the health of their nation.

"Data," claimed the author, "are not published on the prevalence of crime, the frequency of suicide, the level of alcohol and drug abuse or the ecological situation in various cities and regions, although these phenomena are traditional subjects of statistics in economically developed countries. . . . And why are data on disease distribution among the population canceled?"

Artists, composers and writers have begun to take on the Communist party approved unions that the intellectual and artistic class have had to belong to to make a decent living. One musician, for instance, boldly told some of us that he despised the head of the union, composer Tikhon Khrenikov, contending it had become fundamentally corrupt under his leadership, and that those musicians the union chieftain favored would manage to get their works purchased by the government, even though many of these works were never performed.

Under *glasnost* and *perestroika*, he hoped that sort of thing would change, insisting he had already found ways to peddle his fare without having to get union approval. He even thought his union official might be ousted in the new era, though Khrenikov—who has been in command since 1948—has been hanging on with fierce tenacity.

Underground publications have been flourishing, but even *official* publications are filled with controversy and debate, and previously banned works, such as Boris Pasternak's *Doctor Zhivago* and even George Orwell's searing indictment of Soviet tyranny, *Nineteen Eighty-Four*, have been or are about to be printed in the USSR. . . .

Damning Stalin and Stalinism in the most brutal terms is now something of a yawner. But the extent to which the Soviets appear willing to specify his horrendous crimes is still extraordinary to those who recall how limited the criticism had been in previous years.

His paranoia, his purges, his lust for bloodletting—all of this seems to be fair game for books, articles and plays. The March issue of the monthly *Voprosy Istorii*, put out by the USSR Academy of Sciences, carries a letter by demographer V.P. Danilov confirming that Stalin was responsible for the deliberate starvation of millions in Ukraine through the forced collectivization program. Without question, says Danilov, this was "Stalin's most horrible crime, a catastrophe that has reverberated throughout the entire subsequent history of the Soviet countryside."

And *Literaturnaya Gazeta* is now hinting that another of Stalin's most heinous crimes—the physical liquidation of 15,000 Polish officers, triggered by the Hitler-Stalin pact—may soon be exposed. This would be still another shocking admission for Soviet citizens to digest.

Stalin's most famous victims, like Bukharin, are steadily being rehabilitated, and virtually all of his major policies—from forced collectivization, to the liquidation of party and army leaders, to his conduct of World War II—have been severely condemned or sharply questioned in the Soviet Union's most important journals. . . .

More remarkable, however, is that even the Infallible Lenin, the ideological and political founder of the Soviet Union, the man whose writings have been regarded as sacred texts, has begun to come under some astonishing criticism. In some respects, this dramatic turn can be likened to the improbable event that fundamentalists would begin to seriously fault the teachings of Jesus Christ.

In *Sovetskaya Kultura* in April, for instance, historian Nikolai P. Popov implies that by concentrating excessive power in the hands of the Communist party, Lenin had paved the way for Stalin's creation of "the perfect totalitarian state." And in the most recent issue of the monthly *Novy Mir*, Vasily Selyunin strongly suggests that Lenin's initial decision to abolish private property and his building of a repressive secret police apparatus under Felix Dzerzhinsky set the stage for Stalin's brutal forced labor system.

The Old Guard that desperately wants to halt these explosive revelations and condemnations of the past would seem to have a powerful point. For the more the Soviets focus on their grievous mistakes, the closer they hold up Stalin's reign of terror to a merciless light, the more they permit a public questioning of Lenin himself, the more the whole foundation of communism is likely to seem suspect in the eyes of every Russian, including party members, both young and old.

The Soviet Union is likely to remain a powerful adversary for years to come, but it is difficult to believe that these brutal revelations and assessments aren't sowing the seeds of its ideological and possibly physical destruction. . . .

When I went to the Soviet Union in the fall of 1974, I came away in a furious frame of mind, largely because I felt, save in very special one-on-one encounters, that you could never carry on serious conversations with Soviet officials about either the present or the past. So many of their spokesmen came on like coarse propagandists, harshly critical of the United States and boasting that socialism, i.e., communism, would sweep the world.

As a result, the article I wrote was so unflattering that *Pravda* assailed me as a "dinosaur"— a sobriquet I wear quite proudly, I have to admit. Getting under the Soviet skin has turned out to be one of the more pleasurable aspects of my journalistic endeavors.

I had gone in the era of Détente I, but the Soviets, while initially polite at the various sessions we attended, were eager enough to say they intended to impose their grim way of governing upon the world. They rhetorically postured themselves in a combative mode, stressed their ideology was "irreconcilable" with the West's, proudly proclaimed their desire to pursue wars of national liberation and even demanded that we alter our economic structure before there could be a genuine peace.

Since we were then in that supposed period of détente, the White House's Mort Allin asked a group of Soviet journalists, do you think the United States is solely to blame for the Cold War? "Oh, no," came the instant response, only momentarily leading us to believe they would blame themselves as well, "this was the contribution of Churchill also." How about the Soviet conquest of Eastern Europe? I shot back. Wasn't that a "contribution" to the Cold War also? The Soviets "liberated" Eastern Europe, we were informed.

As part of our going-away presents in 1974, the Soviets provided us with an English-language propaganda booklet, *Soviet Youth*. With a certain degree of gall, they furnished the delegation with this mini-book at our final, farewell meal, supposedly in the spirit of "friendship." The booklet was brimful of support for Soviet-inspired wars of national liberation all over the globe, ostensibly being waged against American "imperialism." Some goodbye gift!

Why do we deal with such people? I wondered. Why are we shoveling all this technology to the Soviets—as we were under Détente I—when they are massively violating the Vietnam "peace" agreement, boasting of their intent to promote liberation wars, and can't even tell the simplest truth about anything at all? What a miserable bunch of goons, I thought to myself.

The tone of things had, indeed changed 14 years later. At the sessions with such Communist party bigwigs as Anatoly Dobrynin, the longtime ambassador to the United States who is now chief of the critical International Affairs Department, the ubiquitous Georgi Arbatov, chief of the U.S.A.-Canada Studies Institute, and even the seemingly ageless Andrei Gromyko, the line had considerably softened.

Indeed, Dobrynin, a master of his craft, was jovial, avuncular, even conciliatory. He suggested the Soviets were willing to compromise on a whole range of issues, including Afghanistan, the number of Russian combat soldiers in the Warsaw Pact, and even aid to Communist liberation movements. He pledged that his country would never revive the Stalin terror, promised additional domestic and human rights reforms, including a major accommodation of religious believers.

Arbatov, too, seemed eager to adopt a more conciliatory attitude than the last time I had met him, when he was actively applauding wars of national liberation, and urging us to radically change our economic system. "We're more interested in conventional arms [reductions] than you are," he insisted at one point, undoubtedly in an effort to soothe those who think the INF treaty will leave the Soviets in a commanding military position in Europe. Conventional weapons, he went on, "cost a lot." Soviet military doctrine, which seems threatening to the West, might be modified, he hinted, and he conceded that the controversial Krasoynarsk radar was a "violation" of the ABM treaty, albeit just a "technical" one.

His tie askew and shirt open at the neck, Andrei Kokoshin, deputy director of the Arbatov institute, came on strongly as a new-style—actually *American* style—Soviet. Resembling Alan Arkin with a Kissingerian accent, he frequently wisecracked and joked his way through exchanges admitting that the Soviets had made some "mistakes" that fueled the Cold War (though he never said precisely what these mistakes were, and added that he thought the West had made many more).

Kokoshin told me that he thought Soviet support of national liberation wars—a topic I constantly raised with the Russians—was coming to an end, because colonialism (Western-style colonialism) was also ending. And that the real problem for both the United States and the Soviets was going to be how to "cure poverty" in these Third World countries (never quite realizing how foolish he sounded, since the Soviet economic and political model is precisely what has brought such devastating poverty to those nations).

At *Pravda*, the talks also reeked of candor and conciliation, with the editors so conspicuously disagreeing among themselves, you almost felt as if they had been ordered to "perform a bit of *glasnost*" for the Americans. The editors said they now had lively discussions before publishing a story, willingly retracted errors (a no-no in the old days) and delved into previously forbidden topics.

Clearly their overall mood had shifted remarkably from 1974, when you felt that you were fundamentally talking to robotic propaganda machines. The Soviets may not have any intention of militarily disarming themselves, but there is a certain rhetorical disarmament going on. And they're doing a clever job of it.

I was prepared to find my gorge rising anew in these ideological encounters, but, I confess, their softer, more seemingly reasonable approach left me less hostile, left me wondering if this is just another flat-out hoodwinking of the West, or whether Gorbachev, because he feels Russia really *is* on the ropes, believes that the Soviets have to sheathe their bear claws for awhile, and is willing to make some truly significant concessions. . . .

Why Not Victory?

While the West should welcome the forces that the reforms have unleashed, Gorbachev's Russia must still be viewed as a lethal enemy, but an enemy that is clearly vulnerable and in a state of ideological retreat. Hence, the West must not relax its anti-Communist vigil, but seize the offensive, pushing the Soviet ruling elite into making even more revolutionary concessions. We should be unrelenting in our efforts to press the advantage. Why should we settle for Détente II, when total victory, or at least a sizable win, is potentially within our grasp?

For the West to become "friendly" with the Soviets, softer tactics and even some significant retreats on their part should not be enough. We've gone through scores of big and little "thaws" in the past, only to find ourselves facing a more powerful enemy down the road. This time we should demand a Soviet surrender on an array of fronts.

What one senses from the Soviets is that they seem to be saying to us, we're going to be nice fellows now, so leave us alone, but meanwhile give us your credits and technology, rebuild our economy and allow us to become as productive as you are in the West.

Our response should be firm. Nothing of major substance this time around until the internal reforms encompass freedom for courageous men like, Grigoryants, who should be allowed to directly challenge the Soviet system. Nothing of note until you have yielded your illicit conquests and no longer pose a threat to the West's survival.

Those "free and unfettered" elections for Poland and the rest of Eastern Europe—solemnly pledged at Yalta—must be implemented, East and West Germany must become united under democratic rule, the Third World satellites must be decolonized. We cannot, we must tell them, be satisfied until you have atoned for your past atrocities. We can't let you off the hook just because of a few nicely executed retreats in foreign and domestic policies.

For Gorbachev, Lenin is still the idol, still the model for communism. But Lenin established the one-party, totalitarian system that governs the Soviets today, complete with the secret police and the severe repression of all Western-style freedoms, severe even with the reforms.

The core philosophy of Marx and Lenin, upon which the entire Soviet system rests, is still fueled by the malignant doctrine of class struggle, which virtually demands Soviet support of revolutionary violence against even liberal democratic regimes abroad.

The West, in short, would be foolish to begin even thinking about easing the pressure until the Soviets repudiate the ideological underpinning of their regime, a revolutionary, aggressive, violent doctrine, unsoftened by tenets associated with Western ideals and religious faith. Surely we should refuse to rest until the Soviet system has finally gone the way of the tsars.

Conservative Movement Should Take Well Deserved Bow

(From the 7 September 1991 issue)

Ding-dong, the wicked Red witch is finally dead. In the wake of the failed 72-hour coup, the Soviet Union, and indeed, Soviet communism were disintegrating before the eyes of the entire world. You could see it on CNN live.

The Soviet center could no longer hold. The 15 individual Republics that once comprised the USSR were busting loose from Moscow, many of them set on becoming independent countries. The Soviet Communist party was rapidly losing significance, with Russian Republic President Boris Yeltsin intent on uprooting CP officials from every corner of power.

"The signs of the fall of communism were everywhere here in the country of its political birth," reported the Washington *Post's* superb Moscow correspondent, David Remnick.

With a nudge from Yeltsin, Gorbachev, who had amazingly embraced the party even *after* its leaders had attempted to oust him by force and violence, realized he would have to crack down if he were to retain even a semblance of credibility.

So he (1) resigned as the CP's general secretary; (2) issued orders barring the party from operating cell organizations in the KGB and the military; and (3) ordered the government to seize all party property. Police were seen sealing the Central Committee building in Moscow and even the Smolny Institute in Leningrad, which had been Vladimir Lenin's revolutionary head-quarters. Even with this *volt-face*, it was unclear whether Gorbachev could survive.

Under Yeltsin's orders, *Pravda*, the official propaganda organ of the party, stopped publishing for the first time since 1917, and the Russian president banned five other CP publications as well.

Eighty per cent of the military's high command was going to be changed, while the KGB was also undergoing radical surgery. Across the unraveling empire, Soviet icons—including the sainted Lenin and the founder the KGB, Feliz Dzershinsky—were being destroyed by the people in the streets. So traumatic were events for old-line Communists that a number of top Soviet party officials were literally committing suicide.

With communism having been vanquished in Eastern Europe and now collapsing in the heart of the Soviet Union, could the despotic Red remnants in such outposts as Cuba, Afghanistan, Indochina and China continue to hold out? Fidel Castro could hardly be slumbering peacefully these days, especially since the new Soviet ambassador to the U.S., Viktor Komplektov, told CNN's Bernard Shaw that Yeltsin wants all foreign aid subsidies to be ended.

What has happened in the last two glorious weeks in the USSR is not only a stunning reversal of fortunes for the founders of communism and their acolytes and apologists world-wide. It is also a cause for special celebration among American conservatives who brought about the pivotal historical event that led to Soviet communism's demise: the election of Ronald Reagan in 1980.

Unlike the days of Gerald Ford and Jimmy Carter, when the Soviets were blithely gobbling up countries in Indochina, East Asia, Africa and Central America, Ronald Reagan not only halted communism's seemingly endless advances, but achieved what no other President had done before him: *He significantly rolled back the Soviet empire.*

Under President Reagan, we purchased an indisputably smarter, better paid, better trained and better armed military than we had for decades. Through Defense Secretary Caspar Weinberger and two of his key aides, Richard Perle and Stephen Bryan, we choked off critical technology that had previously flowed to the Soviets.

And we were willing to use force in a prudent way. One Soviet surrogate government in Grenada was forcibly ejected by American troops, while the Afghan freedom fighters, equipped with American-supplied Stingers, were chasing Soviet soldiers from their homeland.

Under the "Reagan Doctrine," two more Soviet puppet states—Nicaragua and Angola—were also pressed hard by American-armed guerrillas. As a result of both economic and military pressures exerted by Reagan, Nicaragua's Sandinistas were eventually forced to hold an election that removed them from the presidency. Having accepted elections because of a similar squeeze, the ruling Communist party in Angola is likely to meet the fate of the Sandinistas.

Through his determination to supply arms to anti-Communist insurgent forces, rebuild our military with Stealth's, B-1 bombers, advanced missiles and a 600-ship Navy, place Pershing IIs and cruise missiles into Europe and push for a weapons system that obviously still frightens the Soviets—the Strategic Defense Initiative—Ronald Reagan clearly forced the Soviets to change direction under Gorbachev.

Sensing he was willing to cry "Uncle" in his economic and military battle against the West, Reagan seized the initiative by agreeing to work with the new Soviet leader—even against the advice of a number of anti-Communists—to allow him to stage a major global retreat. With relatively little loss of blood, that retreat has ended in the rout of communism worldwide.

U.S. Liberals are now desperately scrambling to rewrite history, to inform us that communism would have fallen even sooner without the anti-Communist "belligerence" of the Reagan presidency. The only trouble with this theory is that Soviet-backed regimes were sprouting like mushrooms on three separate continents until the 1980 elections.

During Jimmy Carter's Administration, when we were no longer supposed to have an "inordinate fear of communism," the USSR continued its massive conventional and nuclear buildup, sparked a major disinformation campaign against the United States globally, enabled the Sandinistas to waltz off with Nicaragua and brazenly—and brutally—invaded Afghanistan.

Fidel Castro was king in our neck of the woods, spreading communism and chaos throughout the Western Hemisphere with a huge assist from Moscow.

All this was reversed when Reagan became President. Having skirmished with the Communists in Hollywood, Reagan believed in victory over communism, a philosophy most conspicuously enunciated publicly in 1964 by another product of the Conservative Movement, Barry Goldwater. Reagan, Goldwater's political heir, rejected the Democratic strategies of both containment and then appeasement. He wanted to roll back the tide of communism, and did.

While the left tends to ignore resistance to communism as a factor in its defeat, many other editorialists, especially in the pages of the *Wall Street Journal*, tend to credit Socialists, liberal anti-Communists, neo-conservatives, labor union leaders and almost every anti-Communist entity *but* the Conservative Movement for communism's demise.

HUMAN EVENTS would be the last to deny that a number of these neo-conservatives played critical and splendid roles in the anti-Communist crusade. Yet the truth is that most of these folks—many of whom we have affection for and admire—put their faith far too long in a Democratic party that was divided against itself and had been incapable of putting together a coherent defense and foreign policy since the days of Harry Truman.

Many of these anti-Communists worshipped at the feet of Hubert Humphrey, who was invariably falling for international leftists like Fidel Castro and the Dominican Republic's Juan Bosch, and who was a great expounder, as one would expect from a former Americans for Democratic Action chairman, of unilater disarmament measures. Others were champions of Jack Kennedy, who gave us a no-win war in Vietnam, the Bay of Pigs, and a vulnerable defense posture designed by Robert McNamara to "entice" the Soviets to disarm.

The AFL-CIO, led by George Meany, effectively combated the Communist labor movement both at home and abroad. But the same labor movement so cheered by anti-Communist liberals year after year poured its energies into electing liberal Democrats to the presidency and channeling union wealth into the campaigns of such far-left Democratic lawmakers as George McGovern (S.D.), Howard Metzenbaum (Ohio), Alan Cranston (Calif.), Teddy Kennedy (Mass.), Frank Church (Idaho) and Chris Dodd (Conn.), politicians who frequently paralyzed America's ability to implement a strong, anti-Communist defense and foreign policy. Here at home, the unions labored to put into elected office those who dreadfully weakened our national defenses, and turned their backs on conservative politicians eager for a strong America.

For too many years, anti-Communist liberals were indiscriminately wedded to a party of weakness and appeasement, a party that was betraying their own strongly held beliefs. As a result, communism continued to advance.

Not until the election of Ronald Reagan, who welcomed them aboard his Administration, were these liberal anti-Communists and "neo-cons" able to achieve their goal of the defeat of communism. Not until they became, so to speak, the hired hands of the Conservative Movement—a movement they had scorned for so much of their lives—were they able to prove so effective.

There should be no misunderstanding here. Those anti-Communist, liberal and "Hubert Humphrey" Democrats who joined the Reagan Administration—the Richard Perles, the Jeane Kirkpatricks, the Elliott Abramses, the Constantine Mengeses, the Max Kampelmans—all performed exceptionally well, and each contributed enormously to the success of the Reagan

Administration's anti-Communist foreign policy. Without their assistance, the Reagan effort to roll back the Soviet empire would have been far less effective.

Still and all, the record should be set straight. The Conservative Movement, the kind of people who read HUMAN EVENTS and *National Review*, who set up the Heritage Foundation and adore Phyllis Schlafly—the very people who fought so long and hard in the trenches for Barry Goldwater and Ronald Reagan to lead the country—should take a well-deserved bow. Without that movement, those Democrats who boarded the GOP during the Reagan campaign and after his election would never have had an effective forum and the Soviet Union, we dare say, would still be breathing heavily down our necks.

A Salute to HUMAN EVENTS' Founding Fathers

If HUMAN EVENTS' founding editors were alive today, they would be hugely pleased with the collapse of the Soviet enterprise. When this publication was founded in 1944, there were few places one could discover the aims of Stalin's USSR or the ruthlessness of his regimes.

This, after all, was a time when America and Russia were still allies in the war against Nazi Germany, when the American Communist party was riding high and when Soviet moles had penetrated the highest echelons of our government.

During the early and mid-1940s, Hubert Humphrey, a rising liberal political star in Minnesota, was playing "footsie" with the Communists in the Democratic Farmer-Labor party (though he would eventually turn on them), pleading the Soviet case for the annexation of Eastern Europe and even condemning the concept of "containing" the Soviet Union as "un-American."

Many statesmen and politicians were initially fooled by "good old Joe" Stalin, but HUMAN EVENTS' writers had seen behind the facade, and none more clearly than journalist and historian William Henry Chamberlin. In his essay, "Russia Moves West," penned in October 1944, Chamberlin wrote that of all the belligerent powers, the Soviet Union "seems to stand the best prospect of realizing its war aims."

Among those aims, he said, was the incorporation of Eastern Europe, including Poland, Hungary, Yugoslavia, Romania and Bulgaria. Through the Red Army and the secret police, he added, the Soviets would be able to impose their will.

In 1946, HUMAN EVENTS published the book, *Blueprint For World Conquest*, which revealed the Soviet rules for joining the Communist International, the Soviet organization which issued instructions to Communist party organizations worldwide, telling their members how to subvert the country they were living in.

In his introduction, Chamberlin pointed out that these Soviet documents set forth "with complete authority and with remarkable detail the technique by means of which communism hopes to conquer the world. . . ." The Communist threat to world peace, he went on, "is infinitely greater than it was in 1920 or in 1928 when these blueprints of international conspiracy were composed."

Over the years, HUMAN EVENTS turned the spotlight on the Soviet Union's skullduggery, and the actions of its friends and allies in the United States as well. Two years before Fidel Castro came to power, for instance, founding editor Frank Hanighen wrote an eye-opening piece on Fidel's Communist background.

HUMAN EVENTS' founding fathers, in short, deserve a salute for their endeavors, and we only wish that they were around to enjoy the triumph over the enemy they so early realized was a major threat to America's well-being.

Chapter Eight

Politics

The editors of HUMAN EVENTS have never been content to simply report the news. Rather they have also been news makers, directly and aggressively involved in the great partisan and policy struggles of the day.

This has always been true of HUMAN EVENTS as "The New Ruling Class" by Edna Lonigan illustrates (30 March 1949). Miss Lonigan's article is a remarkable attack on the New Deal, the Fair Deal, and Harry Truman.

"My Former Friends . . ." by George Morgenstern (8 October 1952) is a lament for Sen. Robert A. Taft's presidential bid, which HUMAN EVENTS had supported.

The editors of HUMAN EVENTS and Barry Goldwater became friends and allies almost immediately upon the Arizonan's election to the Senate in 1952, and HUMAN EVENTS became Goldwater's earliest and most ardent media supporter.

In Goldwater's first by-lined article in HUMAN EVENTS, "Future of Republicanism" (28 January 1959), the senator reflects on the defeat the GOP had suffered at the polls the preceding year and ponders how to handle the challenge posed by organized labor.

For the next four years, HUMAN EVENTS would be in the forefront of the effort to nominate Goldwater for president. The effort was beginning to see results three years later as the article "Over 9,000 Attend Draft Goldwater Rally" (20 July 1963) proves.

One of the other key people in the draft Goldwater effort was Phyllis Schlafly whose book *A Choice, Not an Echo* provided the rallying call of the effort. Following Goldwater's defeat there was an effort by liberals—especially the Rockefeller wing—to recapture the party. In her article "The Future of Republicanism: Liberals' Raid on the GOP" (11 May 1968), Mrs. Schlafly again rallies conservatives to battle.

In its 24 January 1970 assessment of Nixon's first year as president, "Nixon After One Year," however, HUMAN EVENTS had concluded that the promise of a new conservative era was being frittered away by an administration that "appears confused and at cross purposes with itself" (24 January 1970).

A scant two years later the disillusionment had deepened to the point that the editors of HUMAN EVENTS could not support the renomination of Nixon. Instead, they led the way in a protest effort to nominate Rep. John Ashbrook of Ohio as the Republican candidate for president. In "The Importance of Ashbrook's Candidacy" (5 February 1972), the publication makes the case for Ashbrook.

The Ashbrook effort failed in the narrow sense, of course, as Richard Nixon was renominated, but it did have an immediate impact on the administration's personnel policies and on the GOP platform. In the long run, however, the Ashbrook candidacy proved to be important because it salvaged the integrity of the conservative movement, demonstrating that principle was more important than personality. This realization was to stand conservatives in good stead in the rough years to come.

Following Nixon's renomination, HUMAN EVENTS rallied to his side, confronted with the odious alternative: George McGovern.

After Nixon's resignation and Gerald Ford's elevation to the presidency, HUMAN EVENTS was in the vanguard of the draft Reagan effort. Following Ford's narrow defeat of Reagan at the GOP convention in 1976, however, the publication was again confronted with a lesser-of-two-evils choice and faced with the Carter-Mondale prospect cast "A Reluctant Vote for Gerald Ford" (30 October 1976).

We return to the depressing Carter theme four years later in "Jimmy Carter: Four Years of Failure" by Bentley Elliott, later to become chief speechwriter for Carter's successor, Ronald Reagan (19 July 1980).

"George Bush is *Not* the Conservatives' Leader" (22 June 1991) is a rebuttal to a column by Irving Kristol in the *Wall Street Journal*. In the column, Mr. Kristol relates his impression formed at a just-held conference sponsored by *National Review* that most of the conservative leaders present had fallen into line behind Mr. Bush as the *de facto* leader of the conservative movement.

This contention came as a great surprise to HUMAN EVENTS' editors, who had been sharply dissenting from a growing list of objectionable Bush policies and programs. These grievances were essentially the same ones laid down by Patrick Buchanan a few months later when he challenged President Bush for the Republican presidential nomination.

In late 1991, very disillusioned with the record of President Bush, the editors of HUMAN EVENTS became early, enthusiastic backers of columnist Pat Buchanan's challenge to Bush in the GOP primaries. Although it was ultimately unsuccessful, Buchanan's candidacy had an energizing impact on the dispirited conservative movement and his prime-time speech—"The War for the Soul of America" (23 May 1992)—was a highlight of the Republican National Convention.

Finally, Dennis Dunn takes a look at one of the most popular issue of current politics in "Term Limits Will Put New Life in Political Process" (25 July 1992).

The New Ruling Class

By Edna Lonigan   *(From the 30 March 1949 issue)*

The United States has passed through several political crises since 1929, but strangest of all is the crisis that began with the national conventions last June. Since then we have had a succession of popular moods each sweeping the whole country, yet followed almost immediately by a quite different mood.

The incredible election, itself a reversal of mood, was accepted by the nation with an outpouring of good will toward a President who was obviously a plain homespun American, a cracker barrel politician not afraid of the hustings. Despite a few tall promises it was not believed that Truman would do anything to undermine our form of government. The years of bitter social strife seemed to be over.

The black mood followed quickly, when the President submitted his annual messages, and it became evident that he had learned nothing and forgotten nothing. Now the black has been replaced by a grim gray mood, a realization that even the self-styled "Fair Dealers" are unhappy, and may yet decide to plunge us into war to keep their power.

Do these violent psychological fluctuations merely reflect the instability of the crowd, "vain as a leaf upon the stream"? Are they the responses of a politically sophisticated people to forces too alien for them to analyze in terms of their historical understanding?

The second question points the answer. We are confronted with a development that Americans do not have the experience to envisage, something for which our language does not even have a name. Opponents of Statism have divided their forces in separate battles directed against the New Deal, Fascism, and Communism. We have failed to recognize the common factor in all these issues. The political problem of our day is the emergence, beneath all the Left Wing governments, of rule by the "palace guard." This small elite within the bureaucracy knows all the Machiavellian arts of power, and skillfully uses the pretext of mass welfare to establish itself in absolute control.

We were right, in November, in regarding President Truman as a cracker barrel politician, out of the old West. We were also right, in January, in thinking that the Administration had abandoned our Constitution. What we missed was the connecting link; the fact that the "palace guard" controls Truman, as it controlled Roosevelt, and that its only policy is maintenance of its own power. Harry Hopkins and other shining lights of the Roosevelt elite are gone, but they were not important as individuals. The elite is a new *class*, trained in handling the high voltage wires of absolute power. When one topples, another is ready to take its place. The forces that support this group must be defeated, if we wish to return to Constitutional government.

Nineteenth Century Left Wing movements were dominated by an ideal, a belief that economic life could be made over so that those who did the hard work of the world would have more wealth and more ease. That movement is dead. There is no Left Wing party in power now. There are loyal Left Wing leaders in prominent, if not important, positions, but actual control of the government has moved to the power-minded.

James Burnham, in *The Managerial Revolution*, pointed out that by 1940 Socialism had everywhere ceased to be proletarian Socialism, and had become government by "the managers." He showed that industrial workers had gained full political power in many countries after 1918, only to see that power everywhere slip from their grasp. The workers do not have the talent, training or inclination to be a ruling class.

The Left Wing party has everywhere changed to the *leadership party*, in which a sophisticated elite emerges and keeps its mass followers in line with subsidies, propaganda and plebiscites. This change in Socialist party character, from the membership party to the leadership party, is the most important political fact of the Twentieth Century.

Lenin won over his political rivals because he had a disciplined body of picked men, who acted as an officer class, and regimented the masses as a body of raw conscripts. Mussolini and Hitler also saw that the masses, once regimented, could be organized behind any ideology.

Many have failed to see the underlying significance of these developments. They wanted, for sentimental reasons, to believe that the Left Wing movement was a success but had been diverted from its goals by men of violence. Many did not want to admit that the rise of the leadership party, where the members are not citizens but ciphers, has been the logical outcome of Left Wing political theory itself.

Left Wing governments failed because they were unworkable. Like the Weimar Republic, they weakened the moral power of government by refusing to let people govern themselves. They wasted the capital of the nation by restricting, hampering and penalizing private enterprise. They built vast unproductive bureaucracies, paralleled by vast armies of unemployed. The moderate Socialist leaders had neither the courage to return to liberty, nor the ruthlessness to go on to confiscation of wages, regimented "defense" production, and compulsory labor. And so the Left Wing governments came everywhere under the domination of men who know that to hold *concentrated* power one must abandon all scruples.

The goal of the new elite is the same in every country. They advise one program of "welfare" after another, but, however their "planned economies" may seem to differ, they all centralize power.

The role of the Leader, while important in the beginning, is easily exaggerated. The Leader is the symbol to which the people's emotions are attached, the charismatic "savior," whom Max Weber foresaw so clearly a generation ago. The elite strip the people of their possessions while the Leader holds them enthralled. So completely is the Leader's function that of a symbol that he can continue to head the government long after he is physically broken, as Roosevelt proved.

The governing elite must be conspiratorial, because it is doing the exact opposite of what the Leader says. Every governmental utterance must be designed to delude. The elite must be secretive, because it must constantly change its tactics to keep the people deceived, and to confuse its adversaries. The elite must be dynamic, to seize quickly all the new means of power, before people realize what is happening.

When it assumes power, the leadership party's program is pacific and takes the form of the domestic Welfare State. But first in Germany, then in Russia and Japan, now here in America, we see the effort to build the World Welfare State, scattering its largesse and spreading its tentacles over the world. Of course this brings opposition, and then the Welfare State becomes the Garrison State, in which the people are induced to surrender what remains of their wealth to the elite, for protection against "The Enemy." But whatever the stage of the development, government by the elite is a return to Absolutism. When the elite manages a dominant share of the nation's resources, the voters' representatives cannot exercise the power of the purse, and therefore they cannot keep the executive subordinate to Law. The Constitution functions only when the people keep their own money, and dole it out through their own representatives to an executive which takes orders. It is necessary for a new elite to keep up the forms of government by law so that citizens will not be aroused.

But in time a new danger arises, from rival leaders with their own would-be elites, and then the cloak of legalism is thrown off, and the elite in power uses force to make its rivals conform. We are close to that stage, in this country, today.

The early New Dealers were mostly Left Wing dreamers. As their projects failed, the power these romantics lost was picked up by the ruthless. Today our government takes at least 25 per cent of our earnings. Ten years of the productive life of the average American is committed to his political managers. Is this confiscation producing peace, prosperity or ease of mind?

At the moment our elite is financing a world Neo-Socialist elite which is opposing a Neo-Communist elite for control of the world. Whether "we" win, or the Neo-Communists take over by penetration, or new factions arise, is anybody's guess. In any event the American experiment will be a thing of the past. It cannot survive as a yardstick to measure the performance of the State economy.

There are still 20 million or more Americans who believe the American experiment is the last best hope of earth, that the only way to contain Communism, at home or abroad, is to maintain this Republic. Can these disunited citizens control a domestic elite which is unscrupulous, conspiratorial and dynamic, which is wrapped in the symbols of an old social idealism, and supported by millions of uninformed voters and billions of our money?

If all the people who are opposed to Neo-Communism, to Neo-Socialism and to New Dealism were to realize that they are all fighting one thing, the rule of the elite, they could join forces, find a common policy, and take back the sovereign power while there is still time.

The issue is control of the national income. If we surrender our earnings to government, we can get nothing but rule by an elite. Only government by the ruthless is tough enough to hold this enormous power. So the aim of those who believe in liberty must be to reduce the share of the national income which the elite is permitted to manage. The strategy for defense of the Constitutional or limited government is to block *all* efforts to give our money to the elite. They always have "good" reasons for asking us to give up our earnings. But the Welfare State can never provide welfare. And when people begin to doubt the welfare slogans, patriotism becomes the last refuge of the power-mad.

"My Former Friends . . ."

By George Morgenstern   *(From the 8 October 1952 issue)*

(Historical note: The following address, appraising the progress of the presidential campaign which he was not chosen to make, was delivered by William Elphinstone before a rally at Bad Axe, Michigan. Elphinstone's addresses in pursuit of the Presidential nomination were published by HUMAN EVENTS *in the issues of 4 June and 2 July 1952.)*

It is demonstrable through all experience that rationality never governs in American politics. Therefore, I am forced to predict that General Eisenhower will limp home triumphantly aboard his warhorse. The nomination of General Eisenhower made no sense whatsoever. The inevitable logic confronting the Convention dictated the nomination of another man, namely Senator Taft. Three times Mr. Taft had picked his party off the floor following defeat and put it together again. Morally and intellectually he was its unchallenged leader, and in himself personified the values which the party was supposed to represent. Miss Dorothy Thompson was never more cogent than when, in expressing the outlook of Taft's followers, she quoted a carpenter who urged her to support Taft, and described in his terms what those values were:

"We are the people who pay our taxes even when we hate what the government does with them; who regard it as a disgrace to expect our fellow citizens to support us; who believe we should get what we earn but earn what we get; whose sons are the first to volunteer in America's wars and who expect if we get in them to win them; and who know darn well nobody is ever going to protect America but Americans. We are the vanishing Americans, pushed around by big business, big labor, big government and big military. And if we lose this election we are finished. Eisenhower won't win it for us even if he wins. He'll win it for another branch of the same people who are running the country now."

This was the viewpoint that sought expression through Senator Taft, and the Senator was equipped to give it expression. He was informed on the issues and the arguments, and was capable of addressing himself to them with the remorseless efficiency of a buzz saw. In contradistinction, General Eisenhower, as is by now apparent, was entirely uninformed about anything and was competent only to catch his feet in his suspenders every time he opened his mouth.

Yet, sight unseen, and even in advance of any personal profession of party attachment, the General's candidacy was espoused by an unlikely set of New Deal newspapers and syndicated columnists, all declaring the sudden conviction that the nation's well-being demanded that the two-party system be preserved through a change of Administration. It seems obvious that this dedication was inspired by only two considerations: that the General's sponsors really wanted precisely what Washington had been giving them, especially as concerns foreign policy, and that inasmuch as they feared that Senator Taft would not only beat the Democrat but would change all this, it was imperative to beat him for the nomination.

Here, in pursuance of the immutable law that irrationality must prevail under all political circumstances, enters the first reason why Eisenhower has to win. He is bound to attain a Republican victory for the paradoxical reason that thereby he will assure the perpetuation of the New Deal creed.

The second reason why Eisenhower is bound to win is that his sponsors misbranded him and sold him to the party under false grade labeling. They represented him as capable of appealing to and reconciling the most diverse elements, as witness the supposed success of his Atlantic treaty mission—indeed a dubious claim.

Eisenhower's remote control managers also attributed to him, through some mystic alchemy of personality, a gift of projecting conviction and sincerity, which, it was said, would sweep the nation like a prairie fire. He was supposed to possess a gift of gab which made the most humdrum copybook maxim shine like an inspiration of rare and refreshing novelty. In truth, having at first said, "If the people want me, they will know where to find me," the General was compelled to take off after them in the most importunate fashion even to gain for himself the nomination. Since then his discourse on government has had all of the persuasion of a schoolboy come ill prepared to recitation. The polished Stevenson is miles ahead on points, but I prefer to believe that, like the ill-starred Sugar Ray Robinson, he will yet knock himself out by his own exertions.

These spurious attributions of peculiar virtue cannot be abandoned without some reference to the most colossal confidence game of all, perpetrated in the General's behalf. I refer to the great convention fight for the "fair play" amendment, dedicated to the proposition that foul play was the most assured means of permanently disposing of Mr. Taft. This controversy centered on the custody of delegates from certain Republican rotten boroughs of the South.

Any moralities (however slight) involved in the adherence of these delegations in the convention might have predisposed toward the view that the faithful professionals, savoring at last a favoring wind in a post office year, should have been allowed to ding to their preference for Senator Taft. This position, however, was disputed on the ground that large infusions of new blood had altered the character of the Republican Party (South) in favor of General Eisenhower.

In this connection, I cite the post-convention testimony of the *Times-Picayune* of New Orleans, that "there are only 1,443 registered Republicans in New Orleans and maybe 2,500 in the whole state." This newspaper confirms that any votes for Eisenhower "will be Democratic and not Republican votes."

Similarly, the contention was advanced by those who called themselves "Texas Republicans for Eisenhower" that, among the issues involved in seating them at the Convention, were these: "Whether the Republican Party can go to the public with clean hands in November and ask the voters to throw out the degraded and debauched Democratic administration; whether Texas and other southern states can ever have a two-party system, (and) whether new voters and dissatisfied Democrats will be allowed to join the Republican party."

The outcome was that the regular Democrats, in state convention, decided to urge all Democrats to vote for Eisenhower and Nixon, so that Texas effectively becomes a one-party state, with that party in possession of both party labels. We are presented with the anomaly that "the degraded and debauched Democratic administration" is to be thrown out by degraded and debauched Democrats. Thus there is more than a little to the contention of the Taft camp that the question in Texas and other southern states was "whether the voters of one party are to be allowed to nominate their own candidates and candidates of the opposing party."

We come now to the cream of the jest. This was the assertion that the nomination of General Eisenhower, *ipso facto*, would result in a reconstitution and rebirth of the Republican Party, in which that element conveniently named the Old Guard would suffer expulsion and disgrace. This thesis dodged the plain logic that the Eisenhower nomination was engineered by those very forces which were entitled to be known as the Old Guard. Eisenhower could not possibly have emerged had it not been for the agency of Governor Dewey and his associates representing the forces of Wall Street and internationalism, which had successfully dominated the party since 1940. If men who had failed to control the party through four successive campaigns were to be known as the Old Guard, what are we to call those who had been in the driver's seat through those repeated calamities?

In any event, a clamor arose from the minaret of Times Square to drive into outer darkness all who had favored the aspirations of Senator Taft. A "Republican revolution" would "have been successfully accomplished" only when the Old Guard should no longer "retain a significant voice in the top councils of the party." The "anachronistic voices of reaction on domestic policy" must not be tolerated. The "Roosevelt revolution" must be acknowledged, and its "reforms" must be stamped "permanently into the pattern of American life."

Although unconditional surrender could scarcely require more than this, there were additional special conditions. One was that the Republican party confess that "if ever there was a truly moral war the Korean war is it." The other was that Senator McCarthy be disavowed by name; that he and Senator Jenner, because of their *lese majeste* in giving an accurate description of the stupidity of General Marshall, be denied a ride on the nonexistent coattails of the Eisenhower battle jacket.

These conditions, brashly asserted in the first flush of victory, were justified, in the words of the *Washington Post,* on the grounds that "disgruntled Taftites" had nowhere else to go. The august Mr. Lippmann warned Eisenhower to be firm: "Otherwise . . . the Old Guard will sit out this defeat as they have so many others." Eighteen days later, Mr. Lippmann sounded a more ominous note: "If the Republicans are defeated for the sixth time, and defeated under Eisenhower and after the fight that took place at the convention, their party may fall completely into the hands of its irreconcilable and ruthless factions."

Although, like a good boy, General Eisenhower did most of what he was told, his "crusade" limped to such an apparent degree that, by August 9, the *New York Times* editorially advised him to appease dissident elements of the party for campaign purposes, without any intention of humoring them after election, but again specified that he have no truck with "the extremists"— i.e., the McCarthys and the Jenners.

On September 9 disaster struck Times Square. Senator McCarthy won renomination in Wisconsin by a record vote, polling 100,000 more than the combined vote of seven contenders on both Republican and Democratic tickets. On September 11, Mr. Arthur Krock of the *Times* urged the need for "re-examination" of the Eisenhower campaign tactics. On September 12, Senator Taft yielded to General Eisenhower's frantic importunities and declared a readiness to help salvage what he could with his despised professional aid. Senator McCarthy promised modestly to assist.

As a man of honor, jockeyed into an uncomfortable position, Senator Taft could do no less. His earnest plea to his followers to support Eisenhower was unlikely to prevail with all of them, for they thought the wrong man was running. Nor was Senator McCarthy's good will likely to benefit a man who had inferentially refused to touch him with a 10-foot pole. To cap this series of ironies, the *New York Times* and its Mr. Krock, on the very morning of McCarthy's unprecedented victory, conceded in response to a criticism of Governor Stevenson that it had originally plumped for Eisenhower to head off Taft and the "calamitous" consequences of a Taft victory to its cherished foreign policy, but that had Mr. Stevenson been in the running at the time it would have been equally satisfied with him.

Eisenhower's candidacy has been governed by miscalculation and illogic from beginning to end. Anything thus blessed is certain to be rewarded according to the ancient rule that that which makes no sense will be crowned with success, and that which makes the least sense will be most certain of fulfillment. I submit that Eisenhower makes less sense than Stevenson, he makes less sense than Truman, he even makes less sense than Roosevelt. Anyone so endowed is in!

You may say, my former friends, that in these predictions I am insincere. Perhaps I am.

Future of Republicanism
A Conservative's Fighting Faith

By Senator Barry Goldwater (R.-Ariz.)   *(From the 28 January 1959 issue)*

Vice President Richard M. Nixon should plant the Republican flag somewhere to the right of the political center and run for the Presidency in 1960 as the candidate of America's conservative majority.

I do not take too seriously a number of newspaper reports that Nixon has been siding with the "liberals" in the Republican party on the matter of party organization of the Senate or on the Budget question. Of course, he might be trying to pacify them, pointing out to them the poor position they have adopted in breaking away from the party that has elected them. I think that the Vice President is fundamentally a conservative and I hope he makes that clear to the people of the country.

Many commentators say it will be either Nixon or Nelson Rockefeller for the GOP nomination in 1960. I think that Rockefeller has yet to make a name for himself politically. He has only been in the state house in Albany a few weeks. In the gubernatorial election in New York in November, there were no debates on issues. It was just a popularity contest.

I think we should try to stop this pattern of popularity contests replacing real, honest-to-goodness political contests. We are descending to the Hollywood type of election in which we chose men without even knowing what their political philosophy is. That's what happened in New York.

Judging him politically by the kind of campaign he waged in New York for Governor, I have this thought to offer about Rockefeller. If he should be nominated by the GOP in 1960 for the Presidential race, he would be running on the same platform as the Democrat nominee, who is certain to be a New Dealer. And if we Republicans continue this trend toward "me-tooism," we're through as a party.

There are a number of good issues in the Republican arsenal, which reflect the traditional outlook of the party. Economy in Government is one of these, and I think we Republicans should look forward to paring down sharply the bloated expenditures of today's Federal Government. For example, there is one specific law I would very much like to see amended, and that is the Agriculture Act. I would begin the job this year and whittle it down over a period of five or six years, until we are on a cost-support basis where we can take care of the farmer who suffers financial loss because of such things as vagaries of the weather.

Despite the variety of strong issues from which we have to choose, our party went down to defeat in 1958. I think the lesson of our defeat last November lies in this: the Republican party did not cut a public image sufficiently different from that cut by the Democrat party to warrant Democrats voting Republicans, or even to warrant Republicans voting Republican. We did not state our policies and principles and then battle it out along that line. If we had, we could have attracted the independent voters, the disillusioned voters who had been staying away from the polls and the discontented conservative Democrats (who are much more numerous than many commentators imagine).

The Republican party, in my opinion, has to occupy a position to the right. The left is already thoroughly peopled by so-called "liberals" of many varieties, and they—at least in the North—are mostly tied in with the Democrat party. I feel that if Republicans will do as I did—talk openly in favor of conservatism and what it means today—then we can build a strong party.

In my campaign for re-election in the state of Arizona last year, I appealed, not to "liberal" Democrats, but to *conservative* Democrats. I commiserated with the latter in their plight, wherein the "liberals"—I prefer to call them "radicals"—had taken over control of the Democrat party reins. I urged them to find a hospitable home by voting Republican—for me, and for the GOP ticket. Although the Democrats have had a much larger registration than the Republicans in Arizona, both last year and traditionally, I won by over 35,000 votes out of a total 280,000 cast.

This shows what can be done. I believe that there are many more conservatives in this country than radicals. But the conservatives have not followed the proper political course in trying to attract these right-wingers. I think, for its political health, the country needs a strong "liberal" party and a strong conservative party, not two parties reflecting only one philosophy.

As for the labor issue: I have frankly criticized the misuse of power and union dues by the labor leaders, and the latter have openly tried to defeat me (although I by no means oppose the existence and growth of trade unionism). Yet, in my election last November, I made my greatest voting gains, compared with my election in 1952, in the more industrial, heavily unionized areas of Arizona. I believe that candidates who follow my course, provided they use modern political methods to get out their vote, will not suffer from anything they say in criticism of the labor oligarchy.

I notice that some Republicans are blaming the presence of right-to-work propositions on state ballots last fall for Republican defeats in congressional races. I see no convincing evidence of this, and in fact I note a lot of evidence to the contrary. Before last fall's elections there were 18 states that had right-to-work referenda were defeated in November, there were obvious reasons why they failed.

The fact is that last fall Kansas passed right-to-work by a healthy majority. Partisans of such a law began to form a well-organized movement to that end at least two years prior to the balloting. They debated the matter in the public forum and put over a clear and convincing case. They successfully discredited many mendacious statements about the effect of the right-to-work laws. In the end, the largest industrial area of the state (Wichita) came up with a majority for the law. The secret was obvious: the right-to-work forces had good precinct organization and they made a good case to the public through publicity channels. And conservatives—in Wichita, for instance—came out openly for the reform and waged a dogged fight for it. These right-to-work supporters included many business leaders.

I am aware, of course, that in the state of Ohio a number of good Republicans went down to defeat, together with the proposal for right-to-work. I have not made a study of that situation; but I note one aspect of it. In 1950, the labor bosses openly challenged the late Senator Taft's bid for reelection because he had a few years previously presumed to curtail their dictatorial rights by gaining passage for the famous Taft-Hartley Act. But this challenge to their respected Senator aroused the people of Ohio; Ohioans organized, precinct by precinct, and created a special organization of labor leaders called Labor's League for Taft. Hundreds of local labor leaders came out openly and called for support of "Mr. Republican." Taft won by a huge majority. None of these steps, however, were taken in Ohio in last fall's election. I think that Republicans who profess to be afraid of the right-to-work issue had better study the Ohio situation, both in 1950 and 1958, more closely.

The issue of voluntary vs. compulsory unionism is one of the most important subjects before the Nation today. No political figure can shrink from taking a stand on it. My belief is that eventually compulsory unionism will be banned in every state in the Union, that right-to-work laws will be on the statute books from Maine to California. I believe this because what is involved is a basic human right, which will someday have to be legally recognized and protected.

As I have often emphasized in the past, right-to-work laws do not threaten the existence of trade unions. The facts show that unions have made greater increases in their membership in states having right-to-work laws than in states without them. Right-to-work laws do increase the power of rank-and-file members to call corrupt and radical labor bosses to account. The business agents have to heed the wishes of the rank and file, and cleaner union administration is promoted.

It is an interesting fact that, although many businessmen support the right-to-work (some big business firms oppose it), business as such gets no immediate or direct benefit from such laws. After the laws are on the books, however, the business climate tends to improve and businessmen do not have to operate in an atmosphere dominated by dictatorial labor bosses. They can rely on a more independent attitude of rank-and-file union members to hold high union officials in check.

Indeed, I think that American businessmen should receive a tribute for their role in the right-to-work movement. Twenty years ago many businessmen opposed the existence of any unions at all in their localities. Now they recognize the right of unions to form and to bargain collectively. But they are also smart enough to realize that responsible union performance depends on free men, on union members who need not fear the tyranny of union bosses, on independent rank-and-filers whose Power to check the bosses results in a better social and business climate. I think that this represents a new look among businessmen, represents real "progressive conservatism," and is an important development in the history of the country.

All that I have written here about the labor issue has important bearing on politics and the political future of conservatives. In 1955 I made a survey for the Republican National Committee on the condition of the party. In it, I predicted what happened to the Republicans in 1958. I pointed out that a vacuum had been created in political organizations, since civil service legislation and the expansion of Federal civil service coverage had been greatly extended and had dried up political patronage. The Democrat party turned to the labor unions to fill up this gap. The Democrat-minded Political Action Committee and COPE provided the political workers and grass-roots organization; but, I pointed out in 1955, the Republicans had nothing comparable.

Today, the situation has deteriorated so greatly that we face two alternatives: (1) either Congress effectively bans all union political activity; or (2) the Republicans roll up their sleeves and form their own grass-roots political action groups to counteract the union attack which in large part defeated them last fall. I recently posed these alternatives to the AFL-CIO and suggested that we talk it over, but the offer was rejected; so it looks to me as if the second alternative is imperative. Conservatives must now create in every state the precinct-by-precinct organization which is necessary for victory in 1960. But first there must be a statement of principle and evidence of leadership.

Over 9,000 Attend Draft Goldwater Rally

(From the 20 July 1963 issue)

More than 9,200 Goldwater fans jammed Washington, D.C.'s National Guard Armory July 4 to hear conservative speakers denounce the New Frontier and boost Sen. Barry Goldwater for the GOP nomination next year. Representatives from 44 states were present; the bigger-than-expected crowd came out to cheer the Arizona Senator in spite of the traditional fireworks display at the Washington Monument, holiday festivities and an unseasonably pleasant day.

Featured speakers included Sen. John G. Tower (R.-Tex.), Carl T. Curtis (R.-Neb.), Rep. John Ashbrook (R.-Ohio) and Arizona's GOP governor, Paul Fannin. In addition, a 27-year-old Cuban Bay of Pigs veteran, Dr. Enrique Llaca, lashed out at the JFK Administration for failing to help bring about a free Cuba.

Peter O'Donnell, Jr., chairman of the National Draft Goldwater Committee, kicked off the large rally by saying, "This evening marks the first step toward our goal—to put Goldwater in and Kennedy out!"

The crowd responded with singing, cheering and thunderous chants of "We want Barry." O'Donnell, noting the New York, Pennsylvania and Massachusetts contingents, said: "This is proof positive that Kennedy does not have the big states signed, sealed and delivered, no matter what the corrupt big-city machine politicians tell the Kennedys!"

Gov. Paul Fannin, a boyhood friend of Goldwater and the man who placed his name in nomination at the 1960 GOP convention, declared Goldwater to be "the last best hope of truly effective leadership for freedom's cause in this Nation and throughout the world."

Nebraska's Curtis attacked liberals as a "motley combination of starry-eyed theorists, lame ducks who go before the people once too often, spoilsmen and family members. . . ."

Sen. Tower, in the closing address, said that Goldwater would be a truly national candidate: "Sen. Goldwater would not be a regional candidate, not a pressure group candidate—but a candidate for all the people. No other candidate of either party can command the intense loyalty and effort of so large a segment of the American citizenry."

The Future of Republicanism
Liberals' Raid on the GOP

By Phyllis Schlafly   *(From the 11 May 1968 issue)*

"Rockefeller will either win the Republican nomination or make the party adopt his liberal platform as he did in 1960."

"The two major political parties are as much alike as Tweedledum and Tweedledee; George Wallace's third party is our only hope for a change."

"I'm not going to work for the Republican party until I know who the candidates are going to be."

These three comments are widely heard today among conservatives. They represent an erroneous view of the Republican party and a lack of understanding of practical politics.

The New York kingmakers and their liberal allies are hoping conservatives will fall for these arguments. The kingmakers try to purge conservatives from the party every chance they get, and their constant hope is that conservatives by the hundreds of thousands will take a walk from the Republican party so as to leave the liberals in full control.

The kingmakers know that a third party can never succeed in its first national election. Even Theodore Roosevelt, running as a popular ex-President with all the contacts and support which his magnetic personality commanded, could not defeat the two-party system. Conservatives will fall into the kingmakers' trap if they adopt a "no-win" attitude about the Republican party and decline to exercise the control that their majority merits.

Not only the big majority of Republicans, but a substantial majority of most Americans, have certain objectives in common:

- to restore law and order to our cities;
- to win the "no-win" war in Viet Nam and end the policies which bring on more Viet Nams;
- to clean up the rampant corruption in Washington and end the coddling of security risks and influence peddlers;
- to protect our homes from a nuclear attack and from suicidal disarmament;
- to restore local self-government and fiscal sanity.

There are many roads which lead to these objectives, but the one which takes us there most quickly is political action through control of the Republican Party. There is no other method which has a practical chance of success in the foreseeable future.

The New York kingmakers and their liberal allies also have their well-defined, but seldom articulated, objectives. These are: (1) the perpetuation of the "America Last" foreign policy which results in gigantic spending for unnecessary wars, foreign giveaways, soft loans, and the strengthening of Communist governments through such aid as below-cost sales of farm products; and (2) the concentration of control at the federal level which results in galloping inflation, high taxes, high interest rates, and gigantic spending to buy the people's vote with their own money and to provide payola to insiders and machine politicians through contracts such as TFX. Why are these the goals of the kingmakers? Because big government spending means big power and big profits to those on the inside.

The kingmakers and the bipartisan liberals have realized for several decades that the key to continued big federal spending is control of the Republican party. Then they can relax and say: "We have our man on both tickets. It doesn't matter which one wins."

The kingmakers work unceasingly for this objective. No college Young Republican unit, no local women's Republican club, no state central committee is too minor to be exempt from their money and behind-the-scenes pressure. This is the clique which crammed Wendell Willkie, a Democratic precinct committeeman, and Tom Dewey, a me-too campaigner, down the throats of the Republican party, and is now trying to repeat with Nelson Rockefeller.

Every weapon was hurled against Robert Taft and against Barry Goldwater because the bi-partisan liberals knew those men would cut federal spending substantially and thus eliminate payola to the kingmakers and their confederates.

Some 1968 tactics of the New York kingmakers in their campaign to capture the Republican nomination for Rockefeller are already apparent. A principal device is the gathering of men of impressive financial and social prestige. They were a little late this year in getting together, but they can now be identified and exposed.

They include:

• Thomas S. Gates, chairman of the Morgan Guaranty Trust Co. and also known as the man who installed Harold Stassen as president of the University of Pennsylvania in 1948 in order to keep him available for the Republican nomination.

• Douglas Dillon, investment banker and secretary of the treasury for Kennedy and Johnson.

• Henry J. Heinz II, chairman of H. J. Heinz Co., who paid all the bills for the 1957 Bilderberger meeting at St. Simon's Island, Ga. (described exclusively in *A Choice Not an Echo*), a gathering of liberal U.S. and foreign figures interested in international affairs. (The group, which meets once or twice a year, is named for a hotel in the Netherlands where the first meeting was held in 1954 under the sponsorship of Prince Bernhard.)

• Eugene Black, former president of the World Bank, who also attended the St. Simon's meeting.

• John A. McCone, who was director of the CIA at the time of the Cuban missile crisis, one of the worst U.S. intelligence failures in history.

• John Hay Whitney, former publisher of the pseudo-Republican New York *Herald Tribune*, the original sponsor of Windy Wendell Willkie (the only Democratic precinct committeeman ever to be given the highest office of the Republican party).

• Walter N. Thayer, president of Whitney Communications Corp.

• J. Irwin Miller, chairman of Cummins Engine Co., and Stanley Marcus, president of Neiman-Marcus, both of whom supported LBJ in 1964.

Falling in line behind this impressive display of financial strength are *five* former chairmen of the Republican National Committee, including Thruston Morton, who has been traveling the country saying we cannot win in Viet Nam, but must trade with Communist countries.

The public opinion poll has been one of the principal weapons of the kingmakers ever since 1944 when the Gallup Poll sold Tom Dewey to the Republican party. Most of the polls are based in the East and, funny thing, their results seem always to favor the candidates of the New York establishment and to discredit candidates *not* backed by the New York establishment.

On March 22 newspapers reported that Nelson Rockefeller declined to run for the Republican nomination for President. That is not exactly correct. He declined to run in the primaries, and decided instead to run in the polls.

Rockefeller took soundings around the country, realized he is not in the "mainstream" of Republican thinking, and decided it would be far easier to win with the pollsters than with the voters. So, with his backers claiming the polls had shown a great "reservoir of support" for him, Rocky waited until the final filing deadline for every state primary had passed before making his April 30 announcement of his candidacy.

The trick of the polls as a political weapon is the way the questions are worded. Ask a loaded question, and you get a loaded answer. Like computers, the output can only be as accurate as the input is honest.

In January 1968 the Harris Poll put out a report headlined "Survey Shows Reagan Is Losing Strength Fast." The lead sentence said: "Gov. Ronald Reagan of California appears to be in weaker shape with the voters than he was . . . last August." Now let us look at the input which produced the verdict that Reagan is slipping.

Those polled were asked whether they "agree," "disagree," or are "not sure" about the following loaded statements: "Reagan's background as an actor is not the kind of experience needed to become President." "Reagan is an opportunist, having switched from lifelong liberal to right-wing conservative." "Reagan lacked integrity in discussing his staff members' personal problems."

With questions like that, it is a wonder that Harris reported any support at all for Reagan! There were some friendly questions, too, but they could not possibly compensate for the loaded negative questions.

Now, let's take this tactic of the polls and turn the cutting edge against the candidates of the Eastern Establishment. Here are some questions that have *never* been asked by the Gallup or Harris polls:

(1) "Richard Nixon and Ronald Reagan both volunteered for military service and served our country in uniform during World War II. Nelson Rockefeller and George Romney, although of military age and obviously very healthy, did not choose to fight for their country. Do you think a man should be elected President who declined the opportunity to serve his country in uniform in wartime?"

(2) "Although racial violence during the summer of 1967 erupted in more than 100 cities, cost many lives and millions of dollars of damage, Gov. Nelson Rockefeller apparently sees some good in this. He told the AP on Aug. 23, 1967, that racial rioting is 'a sign of progress.' Do you agree, disagree, or are you not sure?"

(3) "When a race riot erupted in Detroit in the summer of 1967, Gov. Romney refused to allow police and National Guardsmen to use guns with ammunition to protect lives and property in Michigan. Do you approve, disapprove, or have no opinion?"

(4) "The New York *Times* reported on Jan. 16, 1967, that Nelson Rockefeller has made an alliance with the Cyrus Eatons to promote trade with the same Communist countries which are shipping supplies to Viet Nam to kill American boys. How will this affect Rockefeller's presidential chances: much, moderately, or slightly?"

These are four questions which you can be sure will *never* be asked by the Gallup, Harris, or Roper polls. As long as the pollsters are asking the questions which build up candidates of the New York establishment and belittle candidates opposed by the kingmakers, their results are predictable. Is it any wonder that Rockefeller would rather run in the polls than in the primaries?

There is no denying that the kingmakers start with the advantage of big money, big power, big press, and a big bag of campaign tricks and smears perfected in many campaigns. But we have an asset worth more than all that—*the big majority of the Republican party*. No amount of money or power or publicity can take that away from us—unless conservatives are foolish enough to adopt a defeatist, "no-win" attitude toward controlling the Republican party.

There are many proofs that the Republican party is steadfastly conservative, in spite of all the power and ploys of the New York kingmakers. For example, the Republican National Convention in 1964 chose the conservative presidential candidate over the liberal by the largest majority in any contested Republican convention of modern times. This exposed Javits, Case and Scott, et al., as a small minority, completely outside the mainstream of Republican opinion.

The American Conservative Union, of which Congressman John Ashbrook is chairman, recently published a remarkable document called "The D.M.V. Report" which gives chapter-and-verse documentation proving that the majority of Republicans in Congress vote conservative.

In other words, in spite of all the political, economic and social pressures, in spite of the clever propaganda of the liberal press, in spite of the carrot-and-stick tactics of the Kennedy-Johnson Administration with its enormous power to bribe and to blackmail, most Republicans in Congress during the last seven years still voted conservative.

Any realistic appraisal of congressional voting records must lead us to echo a patriotic American slogan: "Don't give up the ship"—but send another 100 Republican congressmen to Washington to join ranks with the stalwarts who are already on Capitol Hill.

Are you tired of high taxes and of inflation caused by federal deficits?

Then consider the comparative record of Republicans and Democrats on fiscal policy. In this century, 1900 through 1968, Republicans held the White House for 33 years and the Democrats 36 years. Here is the record.

Republicans increased your personal taxes only once, the Democrats increased your taxes 13 times. Republicans reduced your taxes six times, Democrats reduced them four times. Republicans balanced the federal budget 21 years out of 33, the Democrats balanced the budget six years out of 35. Republicans had deficits 12 out of 33 years, the Democrats had deficits 30 out of 36 years. The cumulative deficits under Republicans amount to $22 billion, under the Democrats $314 billion.

This is not merely a difference of degree. This represents a fundamental difference in policy and in performance.

Some conservatives point to the Eisenhower Administration as an excuse for saying "a plague on both your houses" to the two major parties. No one can deny that the Eisenhower Administration failed to clean out the State Department and was wrong on Castro, Hungary and Earl Warren.

But let us not forget the plus side of the ledger. During the Eisenhower Administration no American boy was killed in any foreign war. On the other hand, four of the last five Democratic Presidents have led us into foreign wars.

In 1916 Woodrow Wilson won re-election on the slogan, "He kept us out of war." Within a few months he had the United States involved in World War I.

In 1940 Franklin Roosevelt won re-election with this famous promise: "Mothers and fathers, I give you one more assurance. I have said this before, but I shall say it again and again and again. Your boys are not going to be sent into any foreign wars." This line was put into Roosevelt's speech by ghost-writer Robert Sherwood, and today even the Roosevelt lovers no longer try to defend it. The historical fact is that Roosevelt, in the words of his own secretary of war, Henry Stimson, tried to "maneuver them [the Japanese] into the position of firing the first shot without allowing too much danger to ourselves."

On June 1, 1950, Harry Truman said: "We are closer to peace now than at any time in the last five years." Within a month, he had us involved in the Korean War.

In 1964 the Democrats sponsored those infamous television spots which showed the little girl picking daisies being incinerated in a mushroom cloud. These spots were deliberately designed to mislead the voters into believing that Barry Goldwater was a trigger-happy warmonger. We now know that, at the same time Lyndon Johnson was promising peace, he was committing American boys to fight the same type of land war in Asia, with privileged sanctuaries for the enemy, which had cost us so many lives in Korea.

We are never so close to war as when the Democrats are promising peace. Yet the American voters have been deceived again and again and again. One would think that by now the voters would know that the surest key to peace is to elect a Republican President.

Likewise, on the great issue of an adequate defense, the difference between the Eisenhower-Nixon Administration and the Kennedy-Johnson Administration is the difference between defense and disarmament. It may well be the difference between survival and surrender to nuclear blackmail because of the shocking way former Secretary of Defense Robert McNamara scrapped and canceled many of the strategic weapons our country desperately needs.

Every nuclear weapon defending America today was built or ordered under the Eisenhower Administration.

It is not enough to have the issues on our side; it is not enough to have attractive candidates and ample financing. It is also necessary to have control of the Republican party. The road to control of the Republican party is a long and tiresome one. It means night after night at meetings, and endless hours of thankless work; it takes money and persistence; it brings controversies and disappointments. There are no short cuts.

Some who have wearied at the task are casting a hopeful eye on the man who comes riding the third-party horse, promising to leapfrog the problems. They point to the rise of third parties in the 19th Century. They failed to reckon with the practical obstacles which have been erected since that time, making the success of a third party a hundred times more difficult than winning conservative control of the Republican party.

State laws are rigged for the purpose of keeping the U.S. a two-party nation. Not only is it very hard for a third party to get on the ballot in most states, but, as a practical matter, third-party votes are often not counted after they are cast. There can be no fair election for any party which cannot supply poll watchers in every precinct.

It has been said that $1 of political contributions early in the campaign is worth $10 given during the last couple of weeks. The same is true of political volunteers. One volunteer *before* Miami is worth 10 after the convention. The work done *now* and the decisions made in the primaries and state conventions will determine who controls the Republican party.

If all the conservatives who are standing around waiting to see if the nominees in Miami will be worthy of their support, would instead go to work for control of the Republican party, they could have any nominee they want. And they could elect him, too. What is needed is the grassroots determination that the conservative majority shall not be outwitted and defeated by the liberal minority.

Nixon After One Year
Conservatives Worried

(From the 24 January 1970 issue)

Richard Nixon has been at the nation's helm for a full year. How has he fared? What has he accomplished of note? Is his Administration liberal, middle-of-the-road, or conservative?

The answers to these questions, unfortunately, remain irritatingly vague. To be sure, conservatives, while vexed, are not totally pessimistic; life in the United States appears better than when the President initially took up residence at 1600 Pennsylvania Avenue. When LBJ retired to the ranch, he had, quite bluntly, brought the country to grief. The war in Viet Nam appeared unending with no honorable way out. Rioting rocked the campuses and the cities were going up in flames. Racial turbulence was at an all-time high. The Johnson Administration, stubbornly pushing a guns-and-butter policy, had unleashed a torrent of inflation.

When the country finally cried "Uncle," Nixon was handed the task of cleaning up the Augean Stables. But while making him President, the electorate had also made it difficult for Nixon to govern effectively. For the new President was inaugurated with only a minority of the popular vote and faced a Congress dominated by the opposing party. The Senate, especially after the death of Republican leader Everett Dirksen, proved particularly obstreperous and succeeded—with the help of liberal Republicans—in hampering the President's efforts in bolstering our defenses and combating crime and inflation.

Despite all these obstacles, however, the President has managed, at least for the short run, to change some things for the better; troubles still bedevil the land, but the country seems to have breathed a partial sigh of relief. One wakes up in the morning without the terrible thought, "Well, what does the President have in store for us today?"

The Vietnamization formula may yet prove a chimera, but it is difficult to deny that it has temporarily defused the war issue and with a bit of luck the formula could extricate us from Viet Nam with honor. The comparative quiet of the campuses and streets from previous years has coincided with the changing of the guard and some of this tranquillity can be traced to the fact that John Mitchell, unlike the fatuous Ramsey Clark, is in dead earnest about prosecuting revolutionaries like the SDS and the Black Panthers and criminals like the Mafia.

Inflation still threatens to engulf the economy, but the President has made a far more strenuous effort at balancing the budget than did his predecessor. For this, we think the public owes the President a debt of gratitude.

When all this is said, however, there remains for most conservatives, including ourselves, a genuine unease about the Nixon Administration.

Judging from Nixon's campaign pledges, the philosophy of men like Strom Thurmond and John Tower, who were instrumental in his nomination, and the political predilections of the voters who made him President, we think we had a right to expect policies that were perceptibly conservative. With all the varying political vectors at work, we did not believe Nixon could suddenly change the country's course 180 degrees. And, as we said in our 1968 endorsement editorial, "We are certain we will have our battles with him in the future."

But we did expect that the Administration, recognizing the forces that had put it in office and the rightward trend in the country, would take on a conservative coloration. We are disappointed that after 12 months in office it has not done so.

We don't accuse the Nixon Administration of being truly liberal, or even blindly middle-of-the-road. More often than not, it appears confused and at cross-purposes with itself. Too frequently it seems as if the President has no real philosophy, that his entire goal is to tranquilize the electorate rather than to lead it in a certain direction. When the conservatives get uppity, Spiro Agnew comes to the fore with all his hard-line rhetoric. But as the liberals become incensed, Agnew fades offstage and the spotlight suddenly focuses on Robert Finch, who has been patiently waiting in the wings with his latest liberal spectacular.

Defense Secretary Melvin Laird then steps forward in a wondrous garb that makes him look half hawk, half dove. One day Laird can be heard fiercely bellowing like Mars and issuing ringing declarations about how the Soviets are surpassing us in nuclear weaponry; but the next day he will just as avidly announce heavy cuts in military spending and talk about beating missiles into plowshares.

The President can be seen embracing the views of liberal leprechaun Daniel Moynihan one morning and then that afternoon side with the conservative Arthur Burns. Nixon condemns the anti-poverty program as a waste, but then pushes for its extension for at least two years. He permits Atty. Gen. Mitchell to lobby for the Whitten anti-schoolbusing amendment in the House, but when it passes, lo and behold, he benches Mitchell and suits up Finch, who sinks it in the Senate. Etc., etc.

All this makes for excellent entertainment, but is it policy? Certainly it is not conservative policy. And rather than please all elements, four years of such gyrations could end up antagonizing almost everyone.

The thrust of this constant shifting and blurring of issues is to confound the conservatives, leaving them puzzled and uncertain—and, if our mail is any indication, increasingly angry. Maybe the President is planning to march us down a moderately rightward path, but we honestly don't know for sure.

Take, for instance, President Nixon's foreign and military policies. He has consistently stated or implied that the United States should not permit South Viet Nam to be conquered by Communist aggression. And the Vietnamization formula of equipping South Vietnamese soldiers with sophisticated equipment and solid training may, indeed, be the correct plan to prevent a Red takeover while reducing American involvement.

Yet it is still not entirely clear whether Vietnamization is a policy for saving South Viet Nam or a cover for a precipitous withdrawal of U.S. troops.

Some who have talked privately with the President, including GOP National Chairman Rogers Morton, convey the impression that all our combat forces will be withdrawn or inoperative within the next year, no matter whether Vietnamization is working or not. Secretaries Melvin Laird and William Rogers have strongly suggested that the chief American goal is to get out rather than to save South Viet Nam.

What is the truth of the matter? We frankly confess our ignorance, another case where the President has left us dangling.

In his last major speech of the 1968 campaign, Nixon's topic was the "security gap" which he charged had developed while the Pentagon was under the reign of Robert S. McNamara. Nixon argued convincingly that the policy of a Republican Administration would be to rebuild the American nuclear arsenal to the point of clear superiority—a word he used repeatedly. Yet in his first press conference after taking office, the President repudiated the use of the word "superiority," replacing it with "sufficiency" on the grounds that continued use of the former word could be provocative.

While this could be just a case of semantics, the President has initiated no new strategic weapons program—the ABM Safeguard being only a modified form of the Johnson Administration's Sentinel plan. At a time when the Soviet Union has engaged in a crash effort to overtake us militarily and, according to U.S. officials, has actually speeded ahead of us in long-range missiles, Defense Secretary Laird seriously tells the public on TV's "Face the Nation" show that we are drastically cutting our military budget so we can spend more money on health, education and welfare!

Whether Laird is being intentionally devious is uncertain, but it is impossible for conservatives to defend such a policy.

The SALT disarmament discussions are also a cause for concern, for the President has dispatched to those meetings some of the very same people who adhered to McNamara's disarmament policies.

The President also promised a shake-up in the State Department, but so far the only shake-up we are aware of is what happened to Otto Otepka, the security expert who was shaken both up and out of the department by Secretary of State William P. Rogers. The Administration, furthermore, appears intensely interested in establishing trade relations with Red China. Perhaps, as we have been told from time to time, this is a move to sow friction between Mao and the Kremlin gang, but again this is uncertain. And the question arises: If we can trade with Peking, why won't the President take steps to re-open trade with an anti-Communist friend like Rhodesia?

President Nixon's domestic policies appear even more puzzling. During the campaign he repeatedly condemned the growth of the federal government. He stressed that during a Nixon Administration there would be a much greater emphasis on eradicating our social ills by working—not through the federal government—but through private industry, local government and voluntary organizations.

"The choice we face today," he maintained at one point, "very simply is this: do we continue down a road that leads to big government and little people, or do we take a new road, one that taps the energies of the greatest engine of productivity the world has ever seen—the engine of American industry and American private enterprise? . . . Private enterprise, far more efficiently than the government, can provide the jobs, train the unemployed, build the homes, offer the new opportunities which will produce progress—not promises—in solving the problems of America."

At still another time: "The reason we must spend less at the federal level, of course, is the state of the economy. We cannot possibly stabilize the country if we do not stabilize prices. . . . But we can't bring inflation into line if we continue excessive increases in federal spending."

And once again: "Perhaps the current Administration's greatest failure has been its disinclination or inability to take on the hardest job in government—the setting of priorities. As a result, the aggregate size of the federal budget has risen to unacceptable levels. The problem is, as always, to separate the necessary from the merely desirable, to do the former and stockpile the latter, and ruthlessly eliminate the inefficient and unnecessary. . . . It is clear that *every* federal activity is—and must be—a candidate for expenditure control, and that every existing federal function must be reassessed or else we will bankrupt America."

Nixon also maintained: "What we do *not* need now is another round of unachievable promises of unavailable federal funds."

Yet it seems to us that the President ignored most of his own rhetoric during the first year. Instead of ruthlessly examining existing domestic legislation and eliminating the unnecessary, he kept all the Kennedy-Johnson programs, called for increased funding of them in some instances and even dreamed up a new welfare scheme which he acknowledges will cost more than the existing welfare set-up.

True enough, the President made some sincere efforts to trim funds for existing projects, but there was no effort—no effort at all—to roll back the bureaucracy. Indeed, some observers might conclude there was an effort to *entrench* established programs.

The President, the vice president and the House Republicans campaigned against the scandal-ridden, riot-fomenting, anti-poverty program. Many of the Democrats, particularly from the South, have been equally irritated with OEO. But instead of abolishing it—which he could have done with relative ease—the President called for funding it at a $2-billion-a-year level, agreed to extend its life for at least two additional years and raise the rank of the OEO director to Cabinet-level status!

When House Republicans, Southern Democrats and even liberal Democrats like Edith Green demanded some moderate revisions, the new OEO director stubbornly refused to bend an inch in their direction. Surely this is not ruthlessly eliminating the inefficient and unnecessary. Foreign aid, model cities, food stamps, aid to the arts, and a thousand and one other projects are all still with us. And new ones, like the SST and the welfare plan, are in store.

In the midst of what he claims is an economic crisis, the President called for a doubling of expenditures on the arts, and he has already pushed through Congress a $300-million increase in food stamps. President Nixon's welfare reform proposals—which the Administration was pushing last week—would increase the present outlay in federal tax dollars from $5 billion to nearly $10 billion. While many agree that a new welfare approach should be tried, the real criticism of the President is that he is campaigning for this mammoth new program in the middle of an economic crisis and before it has even been tested on an experimental basis. Furthermore, he has made no pledge to ruthlessly retrench other welfare-connected programs—save for the AFDC—as his new proposal is phased in. How does he expect conservatives to embrace such an approach to domestic legislation?

As a result of his less than frugal spending policies, it is really no wonder that the surtax had to be continued or that the 7 per cent investment credit for business had to be repealed. Nor is it any wonder that the federal budget—despite some rigged bookkeeping devices—continues to operate at an enormous deficit.

Don't misunderstand us. There are some bright sides to this Administration. The President's court appointments—and not just those picked for the Supreme Court—have consistently been on the conservative side. Mr. Mitchell in the Justice Department is doing what conservatives expected of him: cracking down on crime. The President, moreover, has been willing to place conservatives in top positions.

Harry Dent, the former aide to Strom Thurmond, is at the White House; so is Presidential Counselor Bryce Harlow. Mr. Nixon's old friend Arthur Burns now captains the Federal Reserve Board. The Defense Department has made important use of men from the hawkish Hoover Institute and men like Fred Buzhardt, a toughminded military expert, has the ear of Mel Laird. Conservatives are well positioned in various other departments as well. The "unleashing" of Spiro Agnew has also helped to establish an opinion climate which makes it much easier for conservative ideas to be accepted. Still, we remain concerned about the action and lack of action on both the foreign and domestic front.

The President has much more room to maneuver in a conservative direction than he has done. Despite the fact that he is a "minority" President, the country—judging by the combined Nixon-Wallace vote in 1968—is veering sharply toward starboard. The amazing popularity of

Spiro Agnew is another good indication. But the President, we believe, has conspicuously failed to translate this powerful conservative sentiment into significant conservative proposals and actions. And he has catered to the whims of the liberals far, far in excess of what is warranted by their numbers and their real power.

Those who know the President tell us that despite all this, Richard Nixon has every intention of trying to reposition America to the right. We hope for the sake of the country that this is the case, but we must admit to harboring a significant number of doubts.

The Importance of Ashbrook's Candidacy

(From the 5 February 1972 issue)

In the wake of the revelations concerning the massive deficits piled up by the Nixon Administration, new spending proposals in the State of the Union message and fresh concessions offered the Communists in Paris, the Ashbrook challenge to the President in the primaries becomes even more imperative.

There is no question in our minds that the Ashbrook bid represents a grand opportunity for conservatives and that if the Ohio congressman pulls well in the primaries—even if he does not win the GOP nomination—the Administration will have to respond to conservative concerns far more than it has up to now.

The Ashbrook candidacy is progressing fairly smoothly at this point in terms of popular support, but there are still some conservatives, including many of those who could greatly help the campaign financially, who wonder whether the time and the money spent in this effort will result in anything worthwhile.

We fervently believe that Rep. Ashbrook can accomplish solid achievements for the conservative wing of the GOP. Indeed, even though a vote has not yet been cast, the Ashbrook candidacy has paid off in concrete concessions from the White House.

Here are just a few of the things the Administration has been doing to appease the conservatives—things it was not doing before the Ashbrook threat became a reality.

Item 1: Just days after the papers leaked word that the Ohioan would probably run, the President, in mid-December, vetoed the wildly radical child development legislation. That legislation would have cost, even according to its proponents, at least $10 billion a year and could have radically altered the life of the family.

Those who were consulted in the framing of the veto message have reluctantly admitted that the Ashbrook threat was instrumental in getting the President to veto the measure on substantive grounds, thus probably killing its revival in the near future.

Ripon Society officials, many of whom lobbied for the legislation, also acknowledged that conservative pressure was a key to the President's firm veto. In that veto message, furthermore, the President also boldly struck down the Democratic-proposed legal services program, a program that contained no safeguards against abuses by professional supporters of radical causes.

Item 2: Shortly after the Ashbrook candidacy was formally announced, the President in a TV interview with CBS correspondent Dan Rather helped undermine mounting efforts by liberals to dump Vice President Spiro Agnew from the ticket at the Republican convention in San Diego. Nixon warmly praised the Vice President and when asked if Agnew should be his running mate, Nixon answered: "My view is that one should not break up a winning combination."

Columnists Evans and Novak, no enthusiasts for the Vice President, reported what most sharp political observers in Washington now know: "By the time Rather popped the question, Mr. Nixon was keenly sensitive to the sudden right-wing challenge headed by Rep. John Ashbrook of Ohio. The result: An embrace so warm that it surprised most Nixon political intimates and may have drastically reduced the President's flexibility to dump Agnew. . . ."

"The President's surprisingly strong endorsement of Agnew must be seen in the light of two long-time Nixon characteristics: First, his habit of making calculating gestures of appeasements to the Republican right when it grows restive; second, his habit of throwing a protective arm around political allies under hard attack for having done his bidding."

According to these columnists, whose sources of information inside the White House are exceptional, it was Ashbrook's plunge into the presidential sweepstakes that helped force Nixon's hand. "Thus it may be," they wrote, "that John Ashbrook's forlorn splinter candidacy has accomplished far more than anyone dreamed possible."

Item 3: The President's fresh interest in defense can be partly attributed to the Ashbrook race. Columnist Kevin Phillips, who is close to Atty. Gen. John Mitchell, soon to be Nixon's campaign manager for 1972, has written in his recent newsletter: "Everything you hear about new defense items in the fiscal 1973 budget is true. Partly in response to conservative pressure, the Administration is definitely taking a harder line. Spring will see groups like the Chamber of Commerce, the American Security Council and the Melvin Laird-linked American Enterprise Institute beating the defense-preparedness drums."

Defense spending has not been jacked up enough, according to conservatives, nor has Agnew's position on the GOP ticket been made firmly secure. Nevertheless, the Administration has tipped its hat to the Ashbrook bid in a very important way. We do not believe it is any accident, moreover, that the Administration has bowed to the conservatives in some of the precise areas where Rep. Ashbrook has displayed major concern.

While the White House has hardly turned conservative or returned to the campaign promises of 1968, the lesson to be learned from the Ashbrook bid so far is that steady, solid pressure from conservatives has paid off—and not just in rhetoric alone. Ashbrook and his supporters, of course, can hardly be satisfied with the bones that have been tossed their way, and pressure must be maintained to ensure that the Administration doesn't backslide on what it has already given.

Thus conservatives should realize they have it in their power to force the Nixon Administration to the right. Indeed, if the Administration has been willing to nod now and then toward conservatives for the purpose of undermining the Ashbrook candidacy—still in comparative infancy—the nod should turn into a deep, reverent bow if the Ohioan pulls a sizable vote in the forthcoming primaries.

The essential fact for conservatives to remember is that the President bends to pressure. Generally speaking, he has buckled under to the liberal-left because, with the powerful aid of the media, it has placed remorseless, public pressures on the White House. Having remained mostly mute during the past three years, major conservative spokesmen have failed to offer any countervailing pressures, thus virtually assuring the Administration's leftward drift.

The Ashbrook race, however, changes this. Countervailing pressure now exists. For the first time, the President really feels threatened by the right, and he has already made some belated efforts to appease it. How far he goes in conciliating conservatives, however, may very well be determined by the size of the vote John Ashbrook receives in the upcoming primaries.

Ashbrook's success could work wonders. Not only would it certainly pull the Administration to the right, but it would unquestionably shift the Congress to starboard as well.

A sizable vote at the grassroots could doom, for instance, the Administration's Family Assistance Plan, likely to be voted on by the Senate sometime around the date of the New Hampshire and Florida contests. The Administration might timidly back off its welfare reform program in the face of a solid Ashbrook vote. Certainly many senators and congressmen up for re-election in 1972 would have second thoughts about supporting it.

Yet John Ashbrook will not receive the necessary votes to accomplish this unless he gets considerably more financial support than he has so far.

A Reluctant Vote for Gerald Ford

(From the 30 October 1976 issue)

This election year is a "bummer" for conservatives, and we can understand why there are those who want to go fishing, write in Ronald Reagan's name or cast a protest vote for Tom Anderson, Roger MacBride or even Lester Maddox. With so many Democrats echoing Reagan and with Milton Friedman acquiring a Nobel Prize, the mood of the country seems perfect for the election of a solid, conservative President. But that is not to be. Come January either Jerry Ford or Jimmy Carter will be running the country.

And while we're not happy with either of these fellows, we urge a reluctant vote for Ford. On foreign policy, we confess, there doesn't seem much to choose between the two. Jerry Ford in the Oval Office means four more years of Kissinger—or, at the least Kissingerism—which, in turn, almost certainly means a SALT II agreement that gives the Soviets a break in strategic arms; the end of U.S. sovereignty over the Panama Canal Zone; the breaking of our Mutual Defense Treaty with Taiwan; further pressures on such conservative, anti-Communist regimes as Chile, Rhodesia and South Africa; and a generally softish diplomacy.

But is Carter better? We can't decipher any hopeful signals. Despite some of his hard-line rhetoric once in awhile, he, too, favors detente, continued trade with the Communists; at least $5 to $7 billion in defense cuts; the delay—and perhaps elimination—of the B-1 bomber; a pullout of our troops in South Korea; and even greater pressure on Chile, Rhodesia and South Africa than even Ford and Kissinger are applying.

In certain areas, his pronouncements have been even more dovish than Administration policy. Though the U.S. tried to arm the anti-Communist factions in Angola before it fell to the Soviet-Cuban dominated MPLA, Carter scored Ford and Kissinger for their efforts to help these pro-Western elements, demagogically accusing them of trying to start another Vietnam.

To its credit, the Administration waged a successful campaign to prevent the Italian Communist party from gaining a foothold in the Italian government. Carter, on the other hand, has looked with favor on coalition governments in Eastern Europe. In an ominous statement in the May 10, 1976, European edition of *Newsweek*, Carter gave us perhaps a glimpse of how much further he would carry detente by saying:

"I think it is shortsighted of us to deal openly with Brezhnev and leaders of the Soviet Union and refuse to understand and become acquainted with leaders in a NATO country who are Communist. I believe we should support strongly the democratic forces in Italy, but still we should not close the doors to Communist leaders in Italy for friendship with us.

"It may be that we would be better off having an Italian government that might be comprised at least partially of Communists, tied in with the Western world than driven into the Soviet orbit irrevocably."

There is a remote chance, we concede, that Carter could turn out to be somewhat better than Ford in foreign policy, but that "hope" lies with his temperament, not with his rhetoric or his advisers. While he has campaigned on a platform of love, it is now apparent to all but his most devoted admirers that he is a mean, vindictive sort of person—but that might be useful in dealing with the Soviets.

If the Soviets double-cross Carter the way they did Kissinger in Angola, for instance, there is the possibility that he would let his combative nature overrule his inclinations for detente. But this is mere speculation. Overall, we think neither candidate is likely to reverse U.S. foreign policy and get tough with the Russians.

On the domestic front, however, we see a world of difference. Here we really feel more positive toward President Ford, despite his past mistakes.

Carter, in our view, is a dedicated liberal Democrat, who willingly wants to take this country down a path toward socialism. While some contend he shouldn't be held accountable for the

Democratic platform—even though his issues man, Stuart Eizenstat, had a significant hand in shaping it—Carter can be held strictly accountable for his own statements.

And what has Carter personally endorsed? The list is almost endless. He has championed a "comprehensive" national health insurance program; a guaranteed annual income plan; "an expansionary fiscal and monetary policy"; The Humphrey-Hawkins "Full Employment Act of 1976" (though he admittedly has some reservations about the original plan); billions of dollars in new education programs; expansion of the mass transportation system; federal construction of "high-quality, accessible child-care facilities"; increased revenue sharing; billions of dollars for "counter-cyclical" assistance to the cities, and dozens of other measures that the Office of Management and Budget and others have estimated would cost between $100 billion and $200 billion a year.

Taking the conservative estimate, Carter would increase the budget by a full 25 per cent. If the $200 billion figure is correct, the Carter programs would swell the budget by half its present size.

So far as regulating the economy is concerned, Naderism would reach full flower under his Administration. Carter calls for "standby wage and price controls which the President could apply selectively," opposes efforts "to deregulate the price of old oil," supports "restrictions on the right of a single company to own all phases of production and distribution of oil" and calls for "standby rationing procedures."

He would "hold fast" against efforts to lower clean air requirements, urges federal land-use planning, calls for "strengthening" the Occupational Safety and Health Act (OSHA) and champions the creation of the Consumer Protection Agency, another Naderite cause.

In the first Ford-Carter debate, Carter had a chance to publicly alter his position on these vast spending and regulatory proposals, but he deliberately refused to do so—instead suggesting he would try to implement them as quickly as feasible.

Not only is he single-minded in his desire for big-spend government proposals, he seems equally committed to wrenching the funds to pay for them out of new and higher taxes. Carter repeatedly talks of tax reform, but what he means is more taxes. He first suggested he would raise taxes on everyone above the median family income—about $14,000-a-year—but then retreated under fire, saying he would "shift the burden of taxes . . . onto the rich, the big corporations and the special interest groups."

Since even *Time* magazine has noted that the U.S. has fared badly in terms of new industrial investment per capita in recent years, with only Luxembourg and Great Britain ranking lower among the 20 top industrialized countries, what Carter proposes to do is to kill the corporate goose that has been providing jobs for American labor. Carter's plans could collapse the American economy in much the same way that the Labor party in Great Britain has collapsed that nation's economy, and, indeed, the recent stock market tumble is seen as a reaction to Carter economics.

Ford, on the other hand, running on a Reaganized platform, is promising tax cuts and a check on federal spending. Equally important, he is not promising any vast, new spending schemes, and, if elected, will not have to satisfy any of the special interest groups Carter would be indebted to.

Unlike Carter, who is surrounded with such Keynesian economists as Lawrence Klein, Ford is following the advice of such free-market champions as William Simon and Alan Greenspan. Significant also, is the fact that Ford is interested in placing those with a pro-free market bias in the dozens of federal regulatory agencies that now exist.

There are those who say that, given the flawed conservative credentials of Ford and the liberalism of Carter, the more principled position in this election is to vote for one of the conservative candidates running on a third-party ticket, even while recognizing that no one of these candidates can possibly win or even have a telling impact on the election. Some also argue that the election of Carter—while bad in the short run—would finish off the GOP, thus paving the way for a major new conservative party, or alternatively, turn the GOP once again into a principled, conservative opposition vehicle.

These positions are certainly defensible and there are many conservatives we admire who think along these lines. They have just not convinced us.

We believe it is far more likely that if Carter is elected, with the Democrats assured of control of Congress and no more Ford vetoes, the Carter Administration will push through so much major legislation that, by the time conservatives can regroup and finally take power, it will be much harder to turn the country around—if it can be done at all.

We don't believe Ford has the determination or the skill to halt the growth of government, but it is difficult to imagine that he would race this country toward socialism as quickly as Carter.

Obviously it is hardly exciting for us to advocate the half-a-loaf approach, but the lessons of history—which conservatives must heed—teach us that major government programs are extremely difficult to roll back. The Brookings Institution has just issued a study to that effect.

In the last 40 years, government has grown bigger and bigger under each succeeding President. Lyndon Johnson left office in near disgrace in 1968, his Great Society considered a failure by even liberal Democrats. Yet none of Johnson's programs has been repealed. Despite the several Conservative party governments in post-war England, that country is more weighed down by Socialistic programs today than at any time in the recent past. What happens is that once a fresh government program is passed, it builds up a constituency which even the most courageous of lawmakers and Presidents find difficult to resist.

Why, then, should we make the conservative task in the future that much more arduous by electing Jimmy Carter today? That is why we—albeit reluctantly—are going to vote for Gerald Ford.

Jimmy Carter: Four Years of Failure

By Bently T. Elliott   *(From the 19 July 1980 issue)*

Four years ago, an unfamiliar Georgia politician with little understanding of Washington or the world, and with only a mediocre record as governor of his state, approached the podium at the Democratic National Convention in New York's Madison Square Garden. The first thing people noticed about him was his smile. At times, he would turn it on and off, jerking his face from sunny to serious with seemingly instantaneous speed. But mostly, he never stopped smiling, and grinning, and beaming with all his mountainous teeth, and stretched skin and piercing eyes.

When Jimmy Carter spoke and told Americans why he wanted to be their President, his voice was not strident, but soft and reassuring. Here was a man who would keep America strong, and promote private enterprise, and fight inflation, and reduce unemployment, and lift up the poor, and treat women like equals. All that for openers.

And then he offered much, much more, for as we were to be constantly reminded, this was no ordinary man. He was tough and determined, but also deeply religious and compassionate; he would heal America's wounds; he would bind us together; he would be a man of morality, of honesty, and of trust. In a word, he would be *Mr. Everything* . . . and you could depend on it.

We are reliving it all again, as Jimmy Carter has once again begun his amazing road show.

While few should be persuaded by this year's verbal overkill, let us touch on some of the points that might just be forgotten in all the rush and excitement while the campaign is under way.

For example, under this President, America may, for the first time in its history, actually experience triple double digits all in the same year—double-digit inflation, double-digit interest rates, and double-digit unemployment.

Under this President, the IRS has been transformed into an Internal Ravenous Service that only loves a taxpayer for his booty. When the books are closed on the four Carter budgets, the record will show that the man who solemnly promised never to increase taxes on working Americans has raised taxes higher and faster than any other American peacetime President. The four-year total could amount to approximately $270 billion, which is equivalent to a colossal increase of nearly 75 per cent.

Under this President, who does deserve credit for supporting the deregulation of the transportation industry, the federal government, nevertheless, has significantly increased regulation of virtually every other industry by systematically sticking its nose into more and more businesses across America.

Finally, it seems ironic, but under this President, with his wide, reassuring smile, America has suffered its first foreign policy with no teeth. Mr. Carter has tried so hard in so many ways to convince the world of his desire for peace—at almost any price—that many people now believe he is a pacifist.

It is this commitment that carries potentially the greatest and most tragic irony of all: Mr. Carter, the supreme peacemaker, is making this world a far more dangerous place.

Mr. Carter's failures in domestic and foreign policy are deep and undeniable. He has failed for two fundamental reasons. The first is ideological. Certainly not all Americans today consider themselves conservatives. But more and more are sickened by the steady hemorrhaging of their personal liberties. They are also increasingly united in opposition to the welfare state, and they are genuinely concerned about our unwillingness—or perhaps, our inability—to contest Soviet expansion.

The second reason for Mr. Carter's failure is his overpowering ambition. He has an almost desperate need "to win," which has made him act with a ruthlessness that violates the strict code of ethics on which he himself campaigned in 1976, and which leaves him exposed to what many believe are serious charges of corruption.

Finally, it is this same thirst for power that makes him such an easy touch for the powerful, big government constituencies willing to barter their political support for an expansion of social spending at the expense of forgotten taxpayers and a stronger national defense.

Mr. Carter's behavior and rhetoric have seemed contradictory, and have often confused many Americans, but his goals have been consistent. On the principal theme of his 1976 campaign—personal integrity and trust—his Administration has been caught in one awkward lie after another. And despite conservative rhetoric, his underlying liberalism has constantly been reinforced by a dependency on big government constituencies which are out of sync with the majority of the American people.

The Peter Bourne Affair

On July 19, 1978, the Washington *Post* reported that Dr. Peter O. Bourne, special assistant to the President and director of the White House Office of Drug Abuse Policy, had prescribed a dangerous controlled substance, Quaalude, for his administrative assistant, making the prescription out to a phony name. The action, which Bourne did not deny, was in clear violation of the law.

Nevertheless, the White House first tried to permit Bourne to take a leave of absence while continuing to draw his $51,000-a-year salary. Only when the political fall-out became intense was Bourne coaxed to resign, but even then Jimmy Carter's Justice Department failed to press charges. One enraged career Justice Department attorney complained to columnist Michael Novak: "Here is a President who can lecture lawyers about equal justice for the downtrodden and the big shots . . . but his own drug adviser—a federal official—escapes without even a federal investigation. If a President wants to crack down on big shots, he can begin right in his own office."

In many ways, Jimmy Carter is the ultimate yes man. He has supported everything from the ludicrous $50 rebate to the Consumer "Protection" Agency, labor law "reform," increases in the minimum wage, more public service jobs, more welfare, more quotas, more farm subsidies, more grants to buy more votes, the creation of giant bureaucracies to push new federal initiatives in energy, education and family life, and through it all, higher taxes on everyone, and lower taxes for no one.

But it is not enough to describe his policies as merely those typical of traditional liberals with big hearts. For Carter, above all, is a man driven by a towering ego fed by what close associates admit is a deep feeling of insecurity.

The flip side of this tremendous insecurity is the ruthless arrogance with which he strikes out at anyone challenging him or his Administration's policies. The consequences have been terribly destructive for our economy in two ways.

First, America has rarely known a President so mean, so vindictive, so given to demagoguery, and thus, so divisive as Mr. Carter. He has personally called LBJ a "liar," cancer-stricken Hubert Humphrey a "loser," Edward Kennedy a "demagogue," and now Ronald Reagan the same. Arthur Schlesinger Jr. has observed: ". . . but, pray five times a day as Mr. Carter may, he remains a smiler with a knife. No President has used the resources of incumbency with such cynical aplomb. . . ."

The second destructive consequence of the President's arrogance is that it nearly always results in less freedom for the American people and more power for Jimmy Carter and his army of bureaucrats. And why not? For how else can this national healer cure what he knows ails our economy—and us? Thus, no matter who has supposedly committed which wrong, the painful cure or punishment is always the same—higher taxes.

This was true when he attacked: All those fat cats who supposedly spend their lives slurping their way through tax-deductible "three martini lunches"; the "millionaires" who are reaping insufficiently taxed capital gains; all the companies ripping off the public with their "unearned, excessive" profits, and, finally, the American public itself which he blamed for making inflation worse by spending rather than saving those little dollars whose values his policies were doing so much to destroy.

The first priority for this President is, and has always been, to push for higher taxation. Rep. Dave Stockman (R.-Mich.) once remarked that Mr. Carter's main message is don't produce, don't save, don't invest, just pay more taxes. Indeed, paying more taxes to finance his federal budget of runaway "restraint" has been the one, central, unchanging feature of the President's domestic program. While it is true that he has earned the reputation for flip-flopping on at least one major issue each week, on the question of raising taxes, election-year maneuvering aside, the President has manifested all the faithfulness of the finest family dog.

Mr. Carter has proposed the largest increase in taxes ever put forward in our nation, and that includes the World War II taxes of the Roosevelt Administration.

For example, few Americans remember anything about the President's first energy address, except that he was wearing a cardigan sweater and sitting in front of a crackling fire. Actually, that program proposed increasing taxes on crude oil, on gasoline, on the industrial use of oil and natural gas, and on so-called gas guzzlers. Columnist Nicholas Von Hoffman called it "the most massive and minute peacetime intervention in business, industry and private life since the New Deal." Mr. Carter's recent $227-billion excise tax on oil, the infamous "windfall profits tax" is the single largest tax in American history. The President signed it with glee, even though he would have preferred an even larger one.

Mr. Carter signed a $225-billion Social Security tax increase on Dec. 21, 1977, calling it one of his greatest accomplishments to date.

Mr. Carter also sought to raise taxes by proposing the elimination of a whole variety of business and personal tax deductions, including those for business meals; first-class airfare; state sales, personal property and gasoline taxes; and for medical and casualty expenses unless they exceed 10 per cent of a person's income—i.e., unless they are, as the Republican National Committee put it, "about to ruin a person financially."

But as bad as all this seems, it is little more than petty cash compared to what Mr. Carter is planning next. For fiscal 1981, he is pushing a $96-billion tax increase, the largest one-year increase in American history. Indeed, it is so large it equals the size of the *entire* federal budget just 20 years ago, and, if enacted, it will amount to an almost unbelievable increase of approximately $1,000 per taxpayer. Apparently the President really is determined to balance the budget—even if it takes every cent we have.

And if he is reelected, he is going to make it possible for every taxpayer to ante up even better than $1,000 each year. In the four years between FY 1981 and FY 1985, he proposes tax increases of nearly half-a-trillion dollars!

The bottom line then is this. In four years, Jimmy Carter has worked to kill initiatives, whether big, small, general, specific, Republican or Democratic that would have: reduced taxes by holding them to a fixed percentage of the gross national product; reduced individual tax rates; indexed tax rates; reduced taxes on savings; reduced taxes on investment; reduced taxes on capital gains; and reduced inheritance taxes on family businesses. In light of his implacable resistance to tax reduction, one can only marvel at this audacious comment Mr. Carter made on Oct. 3, 1979: "We've been successful in reducing income taxes since I've been in office. I think next year, for instance, the income tax reductions that we've already initiated will amount to about $40 billion."

Upon taking office, Mr. Carter announced a 30 per cent reduction in the size of the White House staff, a figure he apparently pulled out of the air. Within two months, the staff had grown by 30 per cent. He also approved an immediate 25 per cent pay raise for his staff, but then had the huge increase announced to the public as "a savings." And during his first three months in office, he proposed more presidential commissions and advisory panels than Presidents Ford and Nixon established in their two Administrations combined.

Item: Just this last February, as the rate of inflation was rocketing toward 20 per cent, Mr. Carter described his fiscal 1980 budget with obvious pride, saying: "We have had a tightly restrained budget." Even as he was speaking, economists had already projected that this budget would increase by nearly 15 per cent, a rate exceeded only once (1967) in the past 25 years.

Item: According to current projections, in just the four years of the Carter presidency, the total size of the federal budget will have increased at least 52 per cent above the level it had taken all our previous history to reach! This is restraint?

Thus, when Mr. Carter's name enters the history books alongside those of other post-war Presidents, it is already certain what his principal economic legacies will be: Record inflation, record interest rates, record taxes, record deficits, and, quite possibly, record unemployment. Add them all up and they equal record pain. But pain within the private economy finds its precise counterpoint in the sweeping new powers being amassed by the federal government.

Regulation

Mr. Carter has approved increases for regulatory budgets averaging 54 per cent over his four years. He blessed OSHA, the chief federal harassment agency, with an increase of nearly 75 per cent. Murray L. Weidenbaum, a leading regulatory expert, estimates the annual cost of federal regulation to business alone is now equivalent to almost $500 for every living American.

Energy: Mr. Carter's entire approach to one of the greatest challenges facing the free world can be summed up by these two remarks he made on Oct. 14, 1979: "Our No. 1 reliance on correcting the energy problem is conservation. . . . As a last resort we'll have to have some additional energy supplies." It boggles the mind to hear the leader of the greatest nation in the world refer to the idea of increasing production—which, after all, is the very lifeblood of our future economic growth—as a "last resort."

Despite estimates that the U.S. has enough undiscovered oil to be totally self-sufficient for 75 years, not to mention huge supplies of other forms of energy, the President has locked out some 300 million acres to any exploration or development; slapped the biggest tax in history on the only industry with the know-how to increase oil and gas production; sat by as environmental agencies prevented the mining of coal and hysterical anti-nuclear zealots obstructed the development of safe nuclear power.

Carter did move boldly, however, to create a bureaucratic boondoggle, the Department of Energy. Its chief accomplishments to date include dramatically increasing the size of its staff and budget; losing 126,000 pieces of mail a year; being cited as the main cause of the nation's long gas lines in the summer of 1979; being chastised by Congress for its "abysmal record in saving energy," but requesting, nevertheless, a 17 per cent increase in its own travel budget, presumably so it can travel to more places to give more speeches on the need for more Americans to conserve more energy . . . by traveling less.

Education: On Oct. 17, 1979, Mr. Carter signed into law the creation of another new, tremendously expensive bureaucracy, the Department of Education. This action represents a massive shift in emphasis by the federal government from supporting local school districts to establishing and implementing a national educational policy. Just one day later, Mr. Carter was endorsed for reelection by the powerful teacher's lobby, the National Education Association. No connection there, of course. Certainly not.

Welfare: Despite his 1976 promise to include strong work requirements as a central part of any welfare reform, Mr. Carter's first welfare proposal contained *no* work requirement. But this "reform," which, luckily, did not pass, would have greatly increased welfare spending and permitted some 50 million Americans to qualify eventually for welfare assistance.

Speaking of families, to "strengthen" them, Mr. Carter organized a White House Conference on Families. But he allowed it to become so stacked with liberals that it proceeded to throw the traditional definition of families out the window and then recommended national health insurance; an expansion of welfare; publicly funded abortions; government-guaranteed jobs; support for homosexual rights; and even one recommendation that urged the "highest priority" be given to developing and implementing new government programs dealing with "all types of intimate relations."

From his declaration in May 1977 that Americans "are now free of that inordinate fear of communism," to his kiss and warm embrace of Communist party boss Brezhnev at the signing of the SALT treaty in June 1979, to his admission that the invasion of Afghanistan had opened his eyes to the Soviets' real intentions, Mr. Carter's foreign policy has been one of uninterrupted, disastrous weakness.

Mr. Carter has not just neglected our military forces, he has virtually decimated them by canceling, postponing, or delaying virtually every strategic weapons program scheduled under the Ford five-year defense plan. Not surprisingly, he has tried to mislead the country with Pavlovian reassurances that our defense is still "second to none." But as Gov. Reagan has remarked, we are second to one—the Soviets—and only to one because they are the only ones competing. Former President Ford recently lashed out at Mr. Carter's distortions by noting:

"The record shows President Carter in the 1976 Presidential campaign promised to reduce defense spending by $17 billion. Unfortunately, he lived up to those naive promises. . . . The Carter Administration reduced my proposed defense budgets for 1979 through 1983 by $57 billion. . . . Carter slashed our strategic program $24 billion, general purposes forces were cut $25 billion, and research and development was reduced by $10 billion. . . ."

The Administration is quick to reassure that despite certain quantitative deficiencies, the U.S. still can hold its own thanks to superior technology. But the man who knows, Dr. William Perry, Pentagon official in charge of Research and Development, has publicly admitted: "We've been losing our technological advantage year by year."

But Mr. Carter has gone even further down the road of unilateral disarmament. He has been willing to honor the terms of the SALT II treaty even though a majority of his own party was prepared to reject it because it was so lopsided in favor of the Soviets, and because the Kremlin's record of blatantly cheating on past treaties has been so thoroughly exposed. Gen. Edward Rowney, Joint Chiefs of Staff representative to the SALT talks, resigned in protest over the conduct and outcome of the negotiations. He told the Armed Services Committee that the pact was "detrimental to our national security" and that the U.S. had made too many concessions "in our zeal to reach an agreement."

Early in his Administration, Mr. Carter pursued normalization of relations with Cuba and Vietnam, while attempting to pull U.S. forces out of Korea. He abruptly abandoned our long-standing defense treaty with the Republic of China on Taiwan—America's most loyal ally in Asia—without gaining anything in return from Communist China. He supported economic sanctions against pro-Western Zimbabwe-Rhodesia despite strong congressional and public sentiment that they should be lifted. Now we must deal with Robert Mugabe, an avowed Marxist.

Carter abandoned the shah of Iran at the height of his crisis ("I've never panicked in a crisis."), and he has constantly raised the expectations of radical elements in Arab states by trying to deal the Soviets into the Mid-East negotiations, by pressuring Israel to make more and more concessions, and by supporting the infamous United Nations vote condemning Israel—a vote he later shrugged off as merely "an error."

Jeffrey St. John has written that the Carter Administration's policy in the Caribbean has allowed ". . . Havana and Moscow to gain one foothold after another, while giving away the Panama Canal and supporting a policy in Central America that has destabilized pro-U.S. Nicaragua, El Salvador and Guatemala.

"If the latter goes the way of Marxist Nicaragua and anti-U.S. Panama, the Soviets and Cuba will not have much trouble pushing oil-rich Mexico into a Marxist posture. With Russia controlling all of Central America and the Caribbean becoming a Marxist-Leninist lake, the U.S. could become a hostage in its own backyard."

Mr. Carter claims the Soviet invasion of Afghanistan made him street-wise, but as Sen. Gordon Humphrey (R.-N.H.) noted: "He seemed to overlook the fact that Soviet-supported terrorism paved the way for the coup which toppled the pro-American Afghan regime in the first place. In fact, Americans should ask why the Soviet advances in the Horn of Africa, the stationing of combat troops in Cuba, Soviet support of South Yemen, and Soviet and Cuban terrorism and subversion throughout Latin America and Africa, all failed to bring Mr. Carter to his senses years ago."

Nor has Mr. Carter met Soviet aggression with any meaningful response. The unacceptable Soviet troops in Cuba were accepted within a week. The crisis of Afghanistan was followed by his request to cut the defense budget. Yet his long-awaited military aid package to Pakistan has still not materialized.

When Brezhnev warned the United States not to interfere in Iran, Mr. Carter ordered the *U.S.S. Constellation* to sail from the Philippines to the Persian Gulf to show the flag. But then he backed down and left the carrier to mirror perfectly his own indecision by sailing around in circles in the Indian Ocean. When Saudi Arabia requested an urgent show of American support, he sent F-15s, but unarmed. Then, of course, there was the horribly bungled, tragic rescue mission in Iran. In classic Carter style, he called it "an incomplete success."

If Mr. Carter tries, as he undoubtedly will, to portray his presidency as any kind of success, he will be attempting the second greatest deception of his career. His first being: "I will never lie to you."

Syndicated columnist Joseph Sobran surveys the Carter record and wonders: "Can any other mortal clean up after him?" My answer is no. Indeed, the ultimate irony of the Carter presidency might just be that only a miraculous act of divine intervention can now permit America to rise above the mess this one man has made.

George Bush Is *Not* the Conservatives' Leader

(From the 22 June 1991 issue)

We were surprised, to say the least, by Irving Kristol's June 3 piece in the *Wall Street Journal* headlined, "The Conservatives Find a Leader." For those who may not have read the article, our new captain is said to be none other than George Bush.

Many of us rubbed our eyes in amazement at the news. Kristol wrote that he had recently been to a conference sponsored by William Buckley's *National Review*, where some two dozen conservatives were in attendance. Foreign policy, he reported, was simply not discussed.

The issue of abortion was "mentioned in passing, but sparked no controversy," and conservatives, while generally anti-abortion, are now, he said, willing to accept a Republican candidate who only advocates an end to public financing of abortion—the same position, incidentally, held by Jimmy Carter when he was in command of the Oval Office.

All those attending, Kristol went on, were upset with Bush's breaking of his "no new taxes" pledge, and strongly disapproved of the 1990 budget agreement, but the budget deal was not a pact "in which nothing was gained. Indeed, something worthwhile was gained, namely severe restrictions on congressional spending over the next several years."

Kristol ended his column by saying, "In sum, President Bush is now the leader of the conservative movement within the Republican party. He is not their leader of choice, but he is their leader."

Whether Kristol accurately reflected the consensus of those present is not precisely clear, since some of those who attended tell us the conservatives there *were* looking for a fresh leader and that Bush wasn't it. Nevertheless, some of the gathered captains of the movement undoubtedly created the impression that Kristol conveyed.

But that impression should not be allowed to stand. For George Bush, whatever his virtues, is *not* the leader of the conservative movement; nor should he be considered as such by anyone who considers himself a member of the tribe.

Take a look at that budget pact, for instance, that Kristol argues some conservatives are beginning to have a few positive feelings about.

The President, as we've noted before, did not just slightly "bend" his no-tax pledge when he signed off on that budget deal; he shattered it beyond recognition. Before the "compromise," taxes were expected to rise more than $400 billion between 1990 and 1995. Under this brilliantly crafted deficit reduction plan, taxes are to go up yet another $160 billion.

Worse still, the legislation actually *raised* marginal tax rates—which Bush also pledged he wouldn't raise—and then, amazingly, virtually ruled out *future* tax cuts, including the President's own capital gains tax cut, which he had repeatedly stressed was essential for restoring this country's economic health!

Conservatives are supposed to be satisfied with this record, to believe that the man who presided over this disaster is our leader? Give us a break.

True enough, as some recall, Ronald Reagan also raised taxes during his eight years in office, but Reagan began by giving the nation a major tax cut, and then taking back a portion of it. George Bush, whose most publicized promise in the 1988 campaign was "no new taxes," has given us only . . . new taxes.

Under this "deficit reduction" package, spending, contrary to a perception left by Kristol, was not brought under control. Not a single domestic spending program was eliminated in this agreement; virtually all domestic spending programs, including congressional salaries, were to rise.

The Office of Management and Budget, Dick Darman's little shop of horrors, informed us just last week that total federal spending in 1991 will climb nearly $159 billion over last year's outlays. The deficit, says OMB, will be nearly $100 billion more. For this, we should be thankful?

The U.S. arsenal that devastated Iraq's military and has broken the spirit of the Soviets—the arsenal produced by Ronald Reagan, incidentally, not by George Bush—is being shredded under White House leadership. Indeed, military spending as a percentage of GNP will soon be at pre-Pearl Harbor levels.

But domestic spending—which conservatives used to abhor—is reaching heavenward under the Bush Administration. As the Heritage Foundation's Scott Hodge recently noted, "Mr. Bush's first term will see domestic spending increasing an inflation-adjusted average of $29 billion a year—outspending Presidents John F. Kennedy, Lyndon Johnson, Richard Nixon, Jimmy Carter and Ronald Reagan.

"In inflation-adjusted dollars, Mr. Bush's domestic spending spree will be . . . a staggering five times greater than President Reagan's."

With the spending approved by last year's budget agreement, says Hodge, "the federal government now consumes 25 per cent of Gross National Product, the highest level since 1946 and up from 22.3 per cent in 1989."

Those highly touted "spending caps," Hodge relates, "have been set so high for the first five years of the five-year budget agreement that spending is assured of soaring. For another thing, current entitlement programs generally are exempt from spending limits."

And nothing, he adds, prevents Congress from removing or revising the caps in the future, just as the supposedly "tough" limits imposed by the once-famous Gramm-Rudman-Hollings deficit reduction measure were radically relaxed when they began to bite.

Hodge has laid out his case against the Bush budget deal in Heritage Foundation background papers, the pages of the *Wall Street Journal* and other publications. Not a word of dissent, however, has emerged from the OMB. Indeed, Hodge is so sure of his figures he taunted the OMB's director just last week: "I defy Darman to prove me wrong." So far, Darman isn't talking.

Dissatisfaction with Bush abounds in other areas. The President, as economics writer Warren Brookes and others have detailed, is also imposing enormous burdens on business through such regulatory programs as the Clean Air Act, the Americans with Disabilities Act and so forth. As a result, says Dr. Richard Rahn of the Chamber of Commerce, "the economy may incur additional compliance cost expenditures of over $200 billion in 1991 and again in 1992."

There are other millstones weighing down the economy, including the S&L bailout, soaring state taxes, the need to replenish federal bank reserves and the added expenses for the ongoing—and seemingly endless—operations in the Persian Gulf. Most of these economic burdens are not the fault of the President, but the truth is he has virtually abandoned a pro-growth agenda that would relieve these burdens.

When the House passed a capital gains tax cut in 1989 and a majority of the Senate wanted to embrace it, the White House caved in to Senate leader George Mitchell's demands that no cut should pass. When Sen. Patrick Moynihan (D.-N.Y.) pressed this year for a reduction in Social Security taxes, the White House dispatched Dan Quayle to the Senate, where he stood poised to block the proposal if his vote were needed. By so vigorously opposing Moynihan, the White House also sank the chances of the Wallop-De-Lay pro-growth plan that ingeniously outfoxed the anti-tax cut provisions in the 1990 budget deal.

How has Bush's performance been on social issues? He has been loyal to his pro-life supporters, but in other areas he disappoints. He has been soft on the pro-gay agenda, having even invited members of prominent gay activist groups to the White House.

He has championed the National Endowment for the Arts, which has become a multi-million dollar cornucopia for deviant artists celebrating homosexuality, obscenity and blasphemy. When the Southern Baptist Convention recently excoriated the NEA, the President responded by praising its chairman, John Frohnmayer, "for doing a good job."

Bush's Pentagon has welcomed legislation now moving through Congress that promotes women in combat, and his education secretary, Lamar Alexander, is pressing for a form of Sovietized schooling, where schools would be open year round, from dawn (6 a.m.) to dusk (6 p.m.), where every "child would have his or her own computer and workstation" and where children as young as "three months old" would be permanently parked.

Readers of our publication on a consistent basis know that we are not unremitting critics of the Bush Administration. We think he performed heroically in checking Saddam Hussein's aggression, he has generally been good in picking conservatives for the courts, and he is, clearly, better than just about any Democrat you could name.

But our leader? Our champion? The man we think defines conservatism? Barry Goldwater and Ronald Reagan were the political standard bearers for the conservative movement in the recent past; today, no one has emerged to replace them. Certainly not George Bush.

Sorry, Irving, the fellows you talked to gave you a bum steer.

The War for the Soul of America

By Patrick J. Buchanan   *(From the 23 May 1992 issue)*

(Following is the commencement address delivered by GOP presidential candidate Buchanan before the graduates of Liberty University, Lynchburg, Va., on May 9.)

Last Monday in Los Angeles I went to Koreatown to visit the devastated zone. As I came upon a shop, gutted and burned, a man came up beside me. This was my business, he said; he then told me what happened:

On Thursday afternoon, 24 hours after the riot began, no police were around. And the mob came. The man was on the roof watching when the firebombs came through his front window. "I couldn't do anything," he said. So he ran.

My whole life was here in this laundry, he told me. I started it 12 years ago; I built it up to 19 workers; now it's all gone. I came to America in 1968, I am an American citizen. But I have no insurance, and only $2,000 left in the bank. What am I going to do?

"I don't know," I said; and the Korean man began to cry.

L.A.: Evil Exultant And Triumphant

That evening I watched on television as some of those who had been in the thick of the rioting laughed in exultation and triumph at how the Koreans had gotten what they deserved.

Theirs was the authentic laughter of the barbarian from time immemorial, after some church or synagogue is burned or looted, after they have brutalized and beaten. From Brown Shirts to Red Guards, the mocking laughter is always the same. Friends, make no mistake: what we saw in Los Angeles was evil exultant and triumphant and we no longer saw it as through a glass darkly, but face to face.

In Los Angeles, government failed in its first duty, to protect the property and lives of its citizens. And those who lacked the courage to move against that mob, or to condemn its evil deeds unequivocally, are guilty of moral appeasement.

A year ago I stood on Constitution Avenue in Washington, D.C., as Gen. Schwarzkopf led the armies of Desert Storm in the victory parade. It was a moving sight. As I told a friend, this is what it must have been like reviewing the Roman legions as they marched in triumph after yet another victory in Gaul or Spain.

The analogy holds. As America's imperial troops guard frontiers all over the world, our own frontiers are open, and the barbarian is inside the gates. And you do not deal with the Vandals and Visigoths who are pillaging your cities by expanding the Head Start and food stamp programs.

Marlin Fitzwater has been mocked for saying Great Society programs caused the riots. But in the ashes of Los Angeles we do see the burnout of the Great Society idea.

It is folly to think you can engender character in men and women by taking away from them their duty and responsibility as parents and citizens, to feed, clothe, house, educate and nurture their own children, and obey society's laws like everyone else.

But where did the mob come from?

Well, it came out of public schools from which God and the Ten Commandments and the Bible were long ago expelled. It came out of corner drugstores where pornography is everywhere on the magazine racks. It came out of movie theaters and away from TV sets where macho violence is romanticized. It came out of rock concerts where rap music celebrates raw lust and cop-killing. It came out of churches that long ago gave themselves up to social action, and it came out of families that never existed.

If they didn't know any better, perhaps they were never taught any better. When the Rodney King verdict came down, and the rage boiled, these young men had no answer within themselves to the questions: Why not? Why not riot, loot and burn? Why not settle scores with the Koreans? Why not lynch somebody—and get even for Rodney King?

For decades, secularists have preached a New Age gospel, with its governing axiom: There are no absolute values in the universe; there are no fixed and objective standards of right and wrong. There is no God. It all begins here and it ends here. Every man lives by his own moral code. Do your own thing. And the mob took them at their word, and did its own thing.

For 30 years we have watched; one by one, as the conscience-forming and character-forming institutions—family, home, school and church—collapsed. When the mob came out into the street, it discovered that society's external defenses as well—the police—were gone. So, for 48 hours, the city was theirs.

While we conservatives and traditionalists were fighting and winning the Cold War against communism, we were losing the cultural war for the soul of America. And we can see our defeat in the smoking ruins of Los Angeles, in the laughter of the mob, in the moral absolution already being granted the lynchers and the looters.

In the wake of Los Angeles, everyone has a "solution" to the "problem."

And these solutions come from earnest and well-intentioned men and women. But, invariably, they advance economic or political ideas to solve what are at root moral questions.

Social programs and enterprise zones may be excellent ideas, but they are not relevant to the crisis at hand. They are not going to stop a mob on a rampage; they are not going to convert evil men into good men. They do not reach the human heart.

As in the '60s, so, today, we are told that the root cause of the riots is poverty and joblessness. But there was far greater poverty and unemployment in the 1930s than today, and there was racial segregation in every sphere of American life. Yet we did not lynch one another in the streets, or burn our cities down in the Great Depression.

In my meeting with police in their inner-city compound, I asked a captain how large his department was. We have 7,800 officers in the LAPD, he said. And how many gang members are out there? I asked. A hundred thousand on file, he said. But how many are active now? I pressed. A hundred thousand, he said again.

That is the equivalent of six-and-a-half U.S. Army divisions. Then the captain showed me the pamphlet being passed around the streets, calling on the Crips and Bloods and other gangs to join together, wait for the troops to depart, and start killing cops.

Can anyone believe this Lost Generation, steeped in drugs, crime, immorality and hate, is going to be converted to decency by an offer of jobs at the minimum wage?

"Of all the dispositions and habits which lead to prosperity, religion and morality are indispensable supports," George Washington said in his Farewell Address. "In vain would that man seek the tribute of patriotism, who should labor to subvert these great pillars of human happiness."

Yet, relentlessly, for 30 years, the adversary culture, with its implacable hostility to Judeo-Christian teaching, has subverted those pillars. From the public classroom to the TV screen, from the movie theater to the museum.

Look at the works that ignited the controversy over the National Endowment for the Arts. Almost all were desecrations of Christian images.

Andres Serrano submerged a crucifix in a vat of his own urine. Robert Mapplethorpe twisted a statue of the Mother of God into a bloody tie rack. In a book called *Queer City*, a poet depicted Jesus in an act of perversion with a six-year-old boy. A "serious" work of art, said John Frohnmayer. If art is the mirror of the soul, what is the state of the souls of such men?

There is a religious war going on for the soul of America. And just as the Commandments that lay down the law of God have been expelled from our schools, so the lessons of history that undergird these truths are being erased.

Arnold and Hale Ignored by Schools

In high school history texts, Benedict Arnold's treason at West Point, a betrayal that broke the heart of his commander in chief, is being dropped. So, too, is the story of Nathan Hale, the boy-patriot who spied on the British army and went to the gallows with the defiant cry, "I regret I have but one life to give for my country!"

If a country forgets where it came from, how will its people know who they are?

Will America one day become like that poor old man with Alzheimer's abandoned in the stadium, who did not even know where he came from, or to what family he belonged? The battle over our schools is part of a war to separate parents from children, one generation from another, and all Americans from their heritage.

A few years ago, Jesse Jackson led the Stanford red in a parade across the Palo Alto campus chanting, "Hey, hey, ho, ho, Western culture's got to go!" Faced with such a powerful and compelling argument, Stanford capitulated and junked its Western Civilization requirement.

On the 500th anniversary of the discovery of America we hear Columbus vilified as a racist and practitioner of genocide. The name of Custer National Battlefield must be changed, lest the descendants of Sitting Bull and Crazy Horse be offended. In some schools, they teach that our Constitution was plagiarized from the Iroquois, that Western science was stolen from sub-Saharan Africa.

When I was a boy, I remember how we all laughed at how, in Stalin's "Workers' Paradise," people were indoctrinated to believe all great inventions, from the automobile to the airplane, had been made by Russians. In 1992, we emulate such idiocies in our own elite universities.

We see the assault on Western culture, too, in our changed holidays. Easter, which commemorates the Resurrection of Christ, now takes a back seat to Earth Day. Christmas is winter break. Washington's Birthday disappears into President's Day, when we can all reflect on the greatness of Millard Fillmore, Chester A. Arthur and Jimmy Carter. The statues of Confederate soldiers must be removed from town squares, because Dixie's cause was not moral.

Slavery versus freedom, that's all it was about, they tell us. But go up to Gettysburg, as I did last summer. Park your car behind the center of the Union Line; look across that mile-long field, and visualize 15,000 men and boys forming up at the tree line. Then see them walking across into the murderous fire of cannon and gun, knowing they would never get back, or ever see home again.

Nine of 10 never even owned a slave. They were fighting for the things for which men have always fought: family, faith, friends and country. For the ashes of their fathers and the temples of their gods.

American History: Glory and Greatness

America is the greatest country on Earth—our history is one of glory and greatness, of tragedy and hope. We must not let them take it away. But, to appease the unappeasable, everything must be changed. Even the name of the Washington Redskins must be altered; and the tomahawk chop of the Atlanta Braves discontinued.

Maybe the Irish should demand they stop calling those big black police vans Paddy Wagons. After all, the vehicles were so named for my ancestors who used to receive regular rides in them.

The war for the soul of America will only be won with basic truths, and the basic truths Western civilization has discovered are simple and straightforward. They are spelled out explicitly in the Old and New Testaments, and implicitly in our great literature and art.

The challenge and duty facing this generation, who have the gift of an education rooted in Christian truths and Judeo-Christian values, is to show your countrymen the way to recapture America's culture and our country—from the new barbarism.

But out of that riot in Los Angeles also come stories of hope.

When I visited the police and Army compound, an officer of the 18th Cavalry who had come to save the city handed me a medallion. On it were inscribed the words *Velox and Mortifer*. After six years of studying Latin under the Jesuits, I still had to ask him what they meant. "Swift and Deadly, Mr. Buchanan" he said, laughing. "It's right there on the coin." And so it was.

Then the officer introduced me to two of his troopers who could not have been 20 years old, and told them to recount their story.

They had come into Los Angeles late in the second day; and they came up a dark street where the mob had looted and burned every building but one, a convalescent home for the aged. The mob was heading into the home to ransack the apartments of the men and women inside.

When the troopers arrived, M-16s at the ready, the mob threatened and cursed, but retreated. It had met the one thing that could stop it: Force, rooted in justice, backed by courage.

"Greater love than this hath no man than that he lay down his life for his friend." So the Good Book tells us. Here were 19-year-old boys ready to lay down their lives to stop a mob from molesting innocent people they did not even know.

And as they took back the streets of Los Angeles, block by block, so we must take back our cities, and take back our culture and take back our country.

God bless Liberty University and God Bless America.

Term Limits Will Put New Life into Political Process

By Dennis Dunn   *(From the 25 July 1992 issue)*

House Speaker Tom Foley won another election last November 5. His margin of victory was by far the tightest in many years—a rather uncomfortable 54 per cent to 46 per cent. Not that his name was actually on the ballot, you understand, but the ferocious intensity with which Foley campaigned against Washington State's Initiative 553 last fall gave one the impression the 13-term congressman was fighting for his very political life. And, indeed, he was.

The lessons learned from that battle are important for conservatives everywhere—especially those in the 15 states in which term limitation proposals are likely to be on the ballot this year.

The controversial 1991 ballot issue in Washington State was the first term limits measure in the nation seeking to make tenure in Congress *retroactive*, and had it passed (and withstood the certain court tests) it would have forced Foley and all his House colleagues from the Evergreen State out on the street (or at least out of the public trough) by 1994 at the latest.

Washington voters were being asked to go it alone, so to speak: to strip themselves of all clout and seniority in the halls of Congress, without any other state in the country losing theirs. *That* was the Achilles' heel of Initiative 553, and—in the end—that was its great vulnerability, which allowed a veteran campaigner like Foley to chop its head off just before it could strike him down.

Strong Support of State's Voters

Amazingly, just two weeks before the election, various polls showed the term limits initiative favored by anywhere from 65 per cent to 70 per cent of the state's voters—a reading not far from the results of October's *Wall Street Journal*/NBC News poll which showed Americans backing the idea of term limits by 75 per cent to 21 per cent nationwide. Voters earning less than $20,000 a year supported term limits by 77 per cent to 16 per cent. Both Democrats and blacks gave term limits 71 per cent support. Women favored term limits even more strongly than men. So how did 553 manage to lose?

The campaign against it was an extraordinarily clever ambush engineered by Speaker Foley and the entire Democratic power structure in Washington State.

Ten days before voters were to go to the polls, Democratic Gov. Booth Gardner called a press conference to announce he would not be seeking a third term next year—and then proceeded to launch a vicious broadside at the term-limits ballot measure.

Next, Rep. Al Swift (D.-Wash.) announced he would retire from public life after running for just one more term in 1992, and then he launched a mighty blast at the initiative.

During the final few days of the campaign, Speaker Foley presented himself for interviews to virtually every major newspaper and TV station in the state. According to Sherry Bockwinkel, a liberal-Democrat and state campaign director for the reform proposal, pro-553 forces were offered "rebuttal time" to the Foley blitz by only three of Washington's dozen-plus television stations. Several others had scheduled programs or interviews with the proponents of the initiative, but canceled them at the last minute during the final weekend before the election.

The campaign against 553 was one of the shrewdest I have ever seen. It played at all times to the emotions of fear and self-interest. The measure was alleged *not* to be "home-grown." It was being "promoted" and "financed" by "outsiders." It was "an attempt by extreme right-wing activists to hijack the initiative process of the state," charged Foley. (Forget about the quarter of a million Washingtonians—100,000 more than necessary—who had signed the initiative in the first place just to get it on the ballot!)

In one self-serving attack after another during the final 72 hours before the voters went to the polls, the silverhaired, silver-tongued speaker of the House kept up a constant drumfire of criticism aimed at sabotaging the ballot measure: "It's a rather arrogant insult to the electorate to suggest that they should have their right to vote limited. . . . The basic thrust of this is small 'd' anti-democratic, anti-people, don't let the voters vote, stop them before they vote again."

And in one incredible example of sterling disingenuousness, Foley stated, "I'm not trying to shake out California as a threat, but . . . by next year, one out of every eight representatives in the U.S. House will be from California."

In desperation, Foley & Co. conjured up one phantasmagorical nightmare after another depicting the harm that would befall the state if 553 became law. Everything from the wealthy oil barons drilling off Washington's coastlines once again, to the "thirsty, power-hungry Southwest" states "diverting" the waters of the Columbia River, to the Bonneville Power Administration raising Northwesterners' cheap power rates.

The TV clips used against the Washington initiative were almost exactly the same ones used two years ago in California by the forces that tried unsuccessfully to defeat *that* state's term-limits proposal. Even the same hapless seabird covered with oil sludge was included. Opposition radio spots reinforced that image by talking about "supertankers zig-zagging through the fog in Puget Sound."

Knowing that the presence on the same ballot of Initiative 119 (the euthanasia "Death with Dignity" measure) would draw senior citizens to the polls in record numbers (which it did), the opponents of 553 carried their brazenness to the point of declaring that passage of term limits in the state might jeopardize the Social Security benefits of Washingtonians! This, supposedly, was the hidden agenda of the "rightwing" sponsors of 553!

Perhaps the most sinister and effective piece of anti-553 propaganda to appear in print was the editorial run by the state's largest newspaper, the Seattle *Times*. Written by former Associate Editor Richard W. Larsen, who retired from journalism on Jan. 1, 1992, and entitled "Californians Love Term Limits in Washington," the politically lurid text pulled no punches.

Two sentences will serve as illustration enough: "Washington would be stripped of the strength it's held in Congress for more than three decades . . . the strength that allowed it to frustrate Californians' agenda of greed. . . .

"In California, in the offices of politicians, the headquarters of developers, the ultraright political clubs of Orange County and elsewhere, they've probably begun to chill the champagne for the victory party."

"Chill" was the key word, all right, and just enough voters got "cold feet" at the last minute to scuttle the one ballot measure in the entire country that had the capacity to put the Big Chill into the hearts of the career politicians in the U.S. Congress.

Seattle *Times* Writer Longtime Foley Friend

Incidentally, it should not go unnoted that although many Washington voters are aware that Larsen was the principal political writer at the Seattle *Times* for nearly 20 years, I suspect most have forgotten (or never knew) that back in the '60s, during Tom Foley's first two terms in Washington, D.C., Larsen was his chief of staff. They are longtime friends and political allies.

While Gov. Gardner and Congressmen Foley, Swift, Norm Dicks, et al., were the "spear carriers" leading the charge against the measure, the executive director of the "NO on 553" campaign was a fellow named Mark Brown. Brown was not just your average citizen getting involved to protest a ballot issue he didn't like. He happens to be the official paid lobbyist for the Washington Federation of State Employees, AFL-CIO.

Based on information contained in the October 15 and December 10 filings made by the "NO on 553" Committee with the Washington State Public Disclosure Commission, the anti-limitation campaign was clearly a classic textbook study of how Big Business and Big Labor team up (over and over) to protect the incumbent political power structure.

We expect it of Big Labor, but I never cease to wonder at the way Big Business continues to feed the mouths that always return to bite it (again and again).

Consider the following, partial, alphabetical list of major contributors against the term-limitation initiative:

Anheuser-Busch ($5,000); Association of Trial Lawyers of America ($10,000); Boeing Co. ($10,000); Boeing Aerospace Machinists ($5,000); Burlington Northern Railroad ($10,000); Centel Corp. ($2,500); Consolidated Rail Corp. ($5,000); CSX Corp. ($5,000); Kaiser Aluminum ($15,000); Norfolk Southern Railroad ($5,000); Phillip Morris ($25,000); Raytheon Co. ($5,000); Southern Pacific Transportation ($5,000); TRW Corp. ($5,000); Union Pacific Railroad ($5,000); Washington Education Association P.U.L.S.E. ($7,000); Washington Federation of State Employees ($13,600); Washington Public Employees Action Committee ($2,500); Washington State Labor Council ($24,500); Washington State Trial Lawyers Association ($2,750); Washington Teamsters ($5,000); and Weyerhaeuser Corp. ($2,500).

It is not surprising, given their political leanings, that even the national electronic media got involved financially in trying to defeat term limits in Washington. The National Association of Broadcasters gave $500, and National Cable Network sent $5,000.

A cursory look at the list of contributors to the "NO on 553" Committee reveals another major group of donors: namely, Democrats. Clearly the organized Democratic Party, nationally and at all political levels, felt very much threatened by Initiative 553. The Washington State PDC filings contain literally dozens of contributions reported from various Democratic Party committees and incumbents—district, county, state and national.

A few of the larger, more interesting ones are: the Washington State House Democratic Caucus ($1,500); the House Democratic Campaign Committee (Washington, D.C.) ($3,000); the DNC (Democratic National Committee) Services Corp. ($3,000); the DCCC (Democratic Central Campaign Committee) of Washington, D.C. ($1,902); and the House Leadership Fund (Potomac, Md.) ($5,000).

It is intriguing to speculate as to what part Speaker Foley may have had in arranging for those contributions, or in channeling other contributions through those various funds and committees.

Out-of-State Demos Also Contribute

Whereas not a single Republican Party committee or member of Congress donated to the campaign against 553, no fewer than eight Democratic congressmen from *outside* the Evergreen State so feared the long-term impact of a successful 553 passage on their plans for career incumbency that they deemed it appropriate to take funds from their re-election campaign treasuries and spend them trying to influence the outcome of a local ballot issue in that far-away "other Washington."

Perhaps the voting constituents of those eight Democrats would appreciate knowing their identity and how much they contributed against term limitation. Here they are—courtesy of the Washington State Public Disclosure Commission.

Committee to Re-Elect Jack Brooks (Tex.), $1,000; Citizens for Downey (N.Y.), $250; John Bryant Campaign Fund (Tex.), $1,000; Fazio for Congress (Calif.), $500; Manton for Congress (N.Y.), $500; New Mexicans for Bill Richardson, $250; Larry Smith for Congress (Fla.), $250; and Solarz for Congress (N.Y.), $1,000.

Not surprisingly, the campaign against 553 was also supported by the so-called "good government" groups as well. In the summer of 1991, opponents had initially sought to kill the initiative by filing a lawsuit to knock it off the fall ballot. That legal effort, though ultimately unsuccessful, was co-sponsored by the Washington State League of Women Voters, the Washington Environmental Council, and the Washington State Grange. Sponsorship of the lawsuit by the Grange (not to mention their subsequent $500 gift to the "NO on 553" Committee) was particularly galling to many Grange members. They had been polled earlier in the summer for their views on the term-limits initiative, and their statewide membership had voted strongly in favor.

The League of Women Voters also became deeply involved in helping Foley and Brown. According to Bockwinkel, not only did the league furnish the "NO on 553" campaign with speakers for numerous TV and radio debates and talk shows, but it also reimbursed those speakers their expenses and provided the "NO" Committee with "office furniture, countless computer hours, countless volunteer hours, and a part-time paid staffer." Nowhere in his mandatory reports to the Washington PDC does Brown list any of these very substantial in-kind contributions.

Then there's the matter of Brown's own salary. His expenditure reports, signed by him and filed with the PDC, show only $4,600 worth of "staff and administrative support" supplied by the Washington Federation of State Employees. Are we expected to believe that Brown—the official paid lobbyist for the W.F.S.E., AFL-CIO, and a man who devoted four full months to the anti-553 campaign—is salaried at less than $14,000 a year?

Such gross under-reporting pales, however, when compared to the total *omission* from Brown's expenditure reports of the TV ad "buys." If the "NO on 553" campaign did *not* pay for those TV ads, then who did? By law, whoever did foot the bill had to be reported by Brown as an in-kind contributor—but wasn't. Bockwinkel tells me she may file with the PDC some formal complaints on behalf of the Washington LIMIT campaign. She is also giving serious consideration to filing a suit against either the W.F.S.E. or the League of Women Voters—or both.

One of the strongest attacks Foley & Co. made against 553 was that it was being promoted and financed by "outsiders." In one sense, the charge had some basis, because the initiative's biggest contributor (by far) was the Citizens for Congressional Reform Committee (CCRC) based in Washington, D.C. However, it is important to understand that CCRC raised funds in all 50 states for reform measures like 553 and had—as of last summer—over 7,000 individual citizen contributors from Washington State alone!

How many "individual citizen contributions" did the "NO on 553" Committee receive? According to Brown's PDC filings, only 19, totaling a mere $3,020 out of the $364,321 in contributions reported.

A study of the PDC file reveals with crystal clarity that the assault on 553 was financed largely from outside the state, and directed largely from Washington, D.C. It is not unlikely that Speaker Foley and DNC Chairman Ron Brown were jointly instrumental in planning, financing, and implementing the entire successful effort.

A woman named Linda Marson was flown in from Washington, D.C., for five weeks to work with Mark Brown. She was well-compensated for her time, to the tune of $5,000 plus expenses. The Democratic political consulting firm of Greenberg-Lake, located in the Nation's Capital, was paid nearly $20,000 for multiple pollings done on Washington State voters.

One of the most fascinating facts contained in the "NO" Committee reports is that nearly half of the money paid to Greenberg-Lake was for "After Campaign Polling" and "focus groups" run during the *10 days following the defeat of the initiative.*

Perhaps equally intriguing, for the future political battles it suggests, is the expenditure item showing that Mark Brown, on Nov. 14, 1991—nine days after the election—flew to Washington, D.C., at a cost of $1,352, to attend the following day what he candidly describes as a "House Democratic Caucus Retreat on Term Limits."

New Term Limits Scheduled For Ballots

This autumn, the "war" will break out again on many more fronts. Bockwinkel announced on July 2 that Washington State's *new* Term Limits Initiative, #573, collected well over 200,000 signatures to qualify it for this November's ballot. A similar measure will be presented simultaneously to the electorate in at least 12 other states. The "retroactive" tenure clause has been eliminated this time, and the outlook for passage is considered excellent in Washington State.

There is no doubt in this writer's mind that, if Initiative 553 had been tied to a U.S. constitutional amendment imposing term limits on the members of Congress from all 50 states simultaneously, it would have passed by a wide margin. Perhaps the drafters of those other state initiatives will have chosen a more softball approach to the issue, along the lines of Colorado in 1990, where voters imposed term limits on *their* congressmen—but not to take effect for 10 to 12 years. "To take effect in the year 2000" sounds like a good number.

It is also equally clear to me that unless the federal Constitution is amended to impose *congressional* term limits, just as it was amended to impose *presidential* term limits, America's future will one day be in serious jeopardy. Many people believe that may already be the case. Grassroots support for term limits is deep, nationwide, and cuts across all partisan and ideological lines. *Term limits will not be a panacea, but they will help get our country back on the right track.*

As the concept spreads like wildfire throughout the land, it will breathe new life, new hope, and put new blood back into our political system. More candidates will run, more people will vote, more incumbents will fall, and all of that will be healthy for America.

Our people know something has gone terribly wrong in Washington, D.C. They know that the crises our country faces today in the areas of crime, drugs, education, and public health are far more serious than they were 20 or 30 years ago. Even 10 years ago. Even five.

They can see that all those trillions of their tax dollars spent, and all those additional trillions of federal deficit dollars spent, have not succeeded in reversing any of the frightening trends. Americans are becoming frustrated, angry, fearful—and determined. Determined to take back control of their own government *before political incumbency becomes totally institutionalized.*

The career politicians have obviously failed us. As entrenched incumbents, they've simply become—over time—too fat, too smug, too arrogant, and too out-of-touch.

Before we can have a citizen legislature or Congress, however, we have to be able to convince good people, good citizens, outstanding individuals who have accomplished something noteworthy in their private lives, *to abandon temporarily those private lives and to run for public office.* That involves huge personal sacrifices for anyone who has been successful in the private sector.

How do we get quality people today even to consider running for public office? People who will regard such service as a duty to their country and a short-term sacrifice rather than as a super ego-trip? It certainly doesn't help convince them when we have to explain why some 96 per cent of all incumbent congressmen who seek re-election are successful. A paltry 4 per cent chance of winning, you say? With such long odds, and with such heavy personal sacrifices involved, the usual response nowadays is, "Who needs it?"

Potential Voters Don't Think It Matters

Add to that the fact that in 1990, one incumbent congressman out of every four didn't have any opponent at all, and it gets easier to understand why so many believe the citizen Congress has all but gone the way of the dodo bird. No wonder voter apathy is at an all time high! Only 36 per cent of the eligible population in the country even bothered to vote in the last presidential election, let alone the last congressional election. Millions of potential voters simply don't think it matters anymore.

The problem isn't just that Lord Acton was right, that "political power tends to corrupt, and absolute power corrupts absolutely"; it isn't just that man's basic nature is frail and flawed and prone to be self-serving; it's simply that most elected politicians—in pursuit of votes and their own self-interest—support nearly every welfare program and local pork-barrel project that comes down the pike. It's called constituent service, I believe.

Sadly, few members of the Congress seem able or willing to focus on the larger picture and vote in accordance with what's best for their country, instead of what's "best" for their state or congressional district—or themselves.

Nearly everyone agrees that our political system is not working well. And, if not "broken," it is at least stagnating—right along with our economy. Let me suggest that what America desperately needs at this critical juncture in her history is an infusion (or perhaps *trans*fusion is a better word) of new competition, new faces, and new ideas. Congressional and legislative term limits constitute one major reform that will guarantee more competition between political candidates and between political ideas. It is clearly an idea whose time has come.

Jeffrey Carneal is the president of Eagle Publishing—a subsidiary of Phillips Publishing International and the parent company of HUMAN EVENTS.

Ambassador Jeane Kirkpatrick has been a favorite of HUMAN EVENTS since the early Reagan years.

Phyllis Schlafly, the "first lady of American conservatism," has written for HUMAN EVENTS since the early days of the Goldwater movement.

Famed conservative columnist and editor William F. Buckley, Jr., wrote his first post-college articles for HUMAN EVENTS— including a piece that prefigured his famous book *God and Man at Yale*.

Chapter Nine

On the Left

Washington, D.C., is the headquarters of literally hundreds of political and quasi-political organizations representing causes of every conceivable variety.

In this chapter, HUMAN EVENTS takes a jaundiced view of four organizations: the League of Women Voters, the National Council of Churches, the Institute for Policy Studies, and the American Civil Liberties Union.

Terry Catchpole's 3 July 1965 article "The League of Women Voters: Its Partisan Slip is Showing" examines the liberal leanings of this supposedly nonpartisan organization.

Allan Brownfeld's "The National Council of Churches: Advocate for the World's Militant Left" (7 February 1981) lays bare the divisive, leftist agenda of an organization supposedly founded to unify Christians of many denominations.

Cliff Kincaid, an associate editor of HUMAN EVENTS, in "The IPS and the Media: Unholy Alliance" (9 April 1983) exposes the media's coverup of the Marxist orientation of the Institute for Policy Studies.

"Where Does the ACLU Stand on the Issues?" (16 July 1988) by William A. Donohue had a major impact on the presidential campaign of that year. The Democratic nominee, Michael Dukakis, had said that he was proud to be a member of the organization, prompting Donohue to take a look at the group's stands on the issues. The resulting article, detailing many of the ACLU's controversial policy statements—such as advocating removal of tax-exempt status of churches and synagogues, and its support for repeal of child pornography laws—made Dukakis' affiliation with the organization a major liability. The Bush campaign hammered Dukakis relentlessly on the issue and it is commonly believed to have contributed to Dukakis' sharp drop in the polls.

The League of Women Voters: Its Partisan Slip is Showing

By Terry Catchpole   *(From the 3 July 1965 issue)*

(For a long time the League of Women Voters has presented itself as a non-partisan organization, but the author gives some cogent reasons why he feels this isn't the case. The League is already in the process of asking its members to make recommendations on candidates and policies for next year. Yet the chances are, as this article indicates, those who control the League won't even listen to what the members have to say. We suggest you pass it on to your friends, particularly those friends of yours in the League. It might be an eye-opener.)

The League of Women Voters of the United States claims only 135,000 members throughout the nation. The organization does not go headline hunting, but prefers to work behind the scenes for legislation it champions; when it does speak out it is usually on the local level. Yet, the League is strong and effective enough to cause Sen. George Aiken (R.-Vt.) to remark: "Only 135,000 of them? I thought there were millions."

The LWV claims to be non-partisan and the educational material it publishes supposedly presents "both sides" of an issue. This policy is based on Article II of its bylaws: "The purpose of the League of Women Voters of the United States shall be to promote political responsibility of citizens in government. The League may take action on governmental measures and policies in the public interests. It shall not support or oppose any political party or candidate."

Yet the League's policies are so definitely liberal and consistently left-of-center that Rep. James Utt (R.-Calif.) says, "in my opinion the League of Women Voters is nothing but the 'ladies auxiliary' of the Americans for Democratic Action (ADA)."

While this leftist attitude is obvious in everything which the National League does, it is not always this way on the local level. There are many women who join the League because they do want to be informed voters and want to work with their elected officials; these LWV members work hard to keep their local Leagues on a more moderate-conservative path. Unfortunately, these members are not strong enough in number to break the iron grasp which the national League holds on major policy decisions.

The National League supplies a questionnaire to all local Leagues for them to give to area congressional and senatorial candidates. As one Republican congressman from the East remarked, "My main objection to the League of Women Voters is the loaded questionnaires which they distribute to candidates. The questions they ask are so worded that they demand a certain type of answer; these answers are then printed in the League's election information as being my position on the subject, when it is only my reply to their loaded questions."

The customary policy in these questionnaires is to use the tactic of pre-supposition. The writers of the questions will assume something is desirable—such as federal government welfare programs, for example—and then ask how the candidate thinks this program can be improved. They do not ask whether or not there should be a welfare program in the first place; thus the candidate who responds that we should not improve it but abolish it or cut it down, is put in a bad light.

The questionnaires also give an example of the National League's domination of its member Leagues: The local cannot alter in any way the questionnaires written by the National for congressional candidates.

The deceptive technique of pre-supposition is perfectly exemplified in a question asked contestants for state representatives by the Manchester (N.H.) local League. The question read: "There are existing programs for improved mental health and educational services in the state for which there is insufficient revenue. How do you think these programs should be financed? Do you think existing programs are adequate to meet future state needs? Please explain."

This query, with its flat statement of assumption in the first sentence, brought interesting responses from candidates. One Republican, an incumbent in the state legislature, replied "I do not know where you get the information that there is insufficient revenue. Serving in Concord, I know there is enough revenue to handle the mental health and education services."

A liberal Democrat answered, "If revenue is insufficient, your question is still ambiguous. Do mental health and education belong to the same category or the same question? . . . . Your assumptions are not necessarily correct. They put words in the candidates mouth that are not his."

A surprising reply indeed from a Democrat, but one which shows that the League's trickery on its questionnaires is beginning to unnerve even those they are trying to help.

Similar in technique to the questionnaires are the "candidate's nights" which the League sponsors to provide contestants for elective office a forum to air their views. These programs are moderated by a League member and, although the public is invited, a majority of the audience usually turns out to be ladies of the League.

Because of the League's use of loaded questions, many congressmen and senators refuse to answer the questionnaires or attend the candidates nights and the local Leagues sometimes play this up.

GOP officials say a candidate in the West a few years ago refused to answer the League's questions and was rewarded a few days later with a large newspaper advertisement, sponsored by the League, which asked: "WHAT HAS HE GOT TO HIDE?"

But it is on the question of the positions it takes on national and international issues, and the dictatorial conduct of the LWV National Board in the selecting, wording and nature of the positions, that the League is most reprehensible in its tactics.

The "National Program" of the LWV—the list of their current stands on issues—is composed of two general sections: the "Current Agenda," which contains a list of specific "governmental issues chosen by the Convention for concerted action," and the "Continuing Responsibilities," which are broadly stated "positions on national issues to which the League has given sustained attention and on which it may continue to act."

One needs look no further than the League's "National Program—1964-1965," adopted at its convention last April, to see that charges of League liberalism are well founded.

Perhaps no better example can be found than the League's stand on the United Nations. The Current Agenda says simply that the LWV will give its "support of U.S. policies which strengthen the U.N. system and its ability to keep the peace." But this support goes much further.

Not only does the League urge uncritical support of the United Nations, but "greater use of the World Court." To this end, it seeks repeal of the tried and trusted Connally Amendment, which, sanely enough, prevents the United States from being hauled up before the World Court without U.S. consent.

Total support is also given the U.N.'s technical agencies, especially the left-leaning UNESCO, which not so long ago published a booklet which asserted "It was the Communist party which showed the peoples of Russia the true way to free themselves from social national oppression."

In fact, the League is such a supporter of the United Nations that it regrets United States participation in such anti-Communist and military regional organizations as the North Atlantic Treaty Organization. In 1947, a brochure admitted that the league "reluctantly supported U.S. membership in NATO."

The League is also opposed to "constitutional change that would limit the existing powers of the Executive and the Congress over foreign relations." This position brought it into sharp opposition to the Bricker Amendment, which was devised to prevent the President from making a treaty which would violate our Constitution.

Just how does the League, a nonpartisan group, it says, arrive at such a series of positions, so definitely partisan? Easy: the National Board makes all the decisions.

Under normal circumstances, the local Leagues supposedly "study" the topics on which the League will take a position. But who carefully selects the literature the local members will read? The National Board.

The "Current Agenda" for '64-'65, for example, shows the League is interested in the "Development of Human Resources," a broad category which, presumably, will eventually lead to positions on poverty, civil rights and other connected legislation.

In a bibliography on "Human Resources" provided local members by the national headquarters in Washington, D.C., is a list of "suggested readings" for the ladies all across the land. In this list are 93 different readings—books, studies, magazine articles purporting to present "all sides" of the subject.

Of these 93, less than 10 could be classed as conservative writings, while the remainder are overwhelmingly liberal. The literature which the National League itself publishes is no better.

The League pamphlet entitled "Prospects for Education and Employment" explains why poor children cannot read with this nifty bit of non-think:

"A child from the slums is not surrounded by the toys, books, magazines and breathing space of most middle-class homes. . . . Often he has never taken even a short trip beyond his immediate neighborhood. Yet he is expected to learn to read from books about well-dressed children who sleep in their own beds in suburbia and travel miles to see Grandma. Not too surprisingly children of the poor frequently do not learn to read well in the early grades. . . ."

The line of reasoning here is that children will only become interested in learning to read if they read about things similar to their environment. How, then, would the League like to explain the fact that millions of children have become literate by reading about King Arthur and Peter Rabbit without ever having donned an armored breastplate or been tossed into a briar patch?

In this manner of selection of suggested reading and the wording of its own pamphlets, the National League of Women Voters can quite easily control the thinking of local members and the direction of their work on different projects.

The unfortunate thing about this is that many women join the League because they want to be "informed and active" participants in government.

The outcome of this "education" is that when local League members sit down with congressmen to present their view, they discover they do not know the entire story behind the program involved; as Rep. Passman said about foreign aid, "they have no understanding of the true facts."

The National Board's domination of the entire League is exercised throughout the process of selecting, wording and passing the "National Program." It is a procedure which holds out to the local members the feeling that, somehow, they are involved; at each step of the way, however, it is the National Board which makes the final decisions.

One woman, a veteran of many years in the League, concluded that "The National Board commands, controls, and directs to the point at which the individual unit leagues become instruments toward an objective which they themselves have had little part in determining."

The local members have absolutely no way of finding out why these decisions were made; the recourse they have to alter a Board decision on the program is so filled with parliamentary roadblocks that changes, understandably, are seldom made.

The selection of a National Program begins in August of the year before a National Convention (held biennially in even-numbered years).

By November all proposals are in and Board members begin evaluation. All this may seem "democratic," but at the January meeting the Board arbitrarily works out a "Proposed Program" for adoption at the national convention.

The Board then sends its own non-democratically selected program to the local Leagues for two to three weeks' study. The Leagues then make recommendations.

When the recommendations are in, notes a League pamphlet, "the Board evaluates these comments and *may* revise the Proposed Program" (emphasis added). The Board may revise, but can just as easily ignore. At the League of Women Voters' national convention, which normally takes place in late April, the Board's Proposed Program is finally brought up for floor debate.

The only items that can be considered for addition to the Proposed Program at this time are those which were suggested by local members four and a half months before the convention. And these suggestions cannot be adopted unless they are accepted by a whopping three-fifths of the convention! The Board's own Proposed Program, however, becomes official policy when only a majority of the convention delegates endorse it.

The question of how the National Board finally decides what position to take on what issues in the Proposed Program revolves around that mystical word often used by the League, "consensus" (LBJ's?). While the local members send in their suggestions and the delegates vote on the Program at the convention, it is the National Board members who arbitrarily decide where there "is a wide area of agreement among the membership" and selects the final program which is placed before the convention—with little fear of defeat.

The National Board can also take a position on controversial issues under a nebulous "Continuing Responsibility" clause in the LWV bylaws. Under this clause, the Board "has the responsibility of interpreting the legislative and administrative situation and League readiness for action," even though a piece of legislation may never have been studied or discussed by the League members.

The 16 members of the National Board are nominated by the powerful Nominating Committee. And the convention delegates usually buy the entire proposed slate. (Of course, there is always the provision that alternative nominations can be made from the floor requiring only the candidate's approval. But the time involved in organizing, selecting a candidate and rounding up support makes the possibility of electing anyone from the floor extremely difficult. Indeed, it has happened only once in the League's 45-year history.)

This standing Nominating Committee is composed of just five persons. *Two must be from the National Board and are appointed by it*. The other three are elected. Thus, the two Board members on the Nominating Committee can completely control it if only one of the three elected committee officials sides with them.

In discussing the League of Women Voters with Republicans of Capitol Hill, the author was told by some that the best way to change the LWV from a liberal, Democrat-oriented organization to a more moderate, truly nonpartisan one, would be for conservative Republican women to get in and change it.

Simple and nice as it sounds, it is not easily done, mainly because of the above-described nomination-election procedures.

The League is always boasting, however, about how well both Republican and Democratic women can work together toward common goals within the organization. The LWV encourages its members to actively participate in their own political parties (National officers cannot, however), but the League itself, remember, is non-partisan and encompasses both parties and they all work lovingly side by side, Republicans and Democrats.

How accurate are these "working together" statements? If the League is a fair, representative, democratic organization, its National Board should reflect the politics of the nation as a whole.

A check was made of the party registration of each present National Board member with the individual's local county or election board.

What was found was that of the 16 Board members, two are registered Republicans, *ten* are registered Democrats, and the other four are unregistered, but except for the president, active Democrats.

It would be safe to assume that the 13 Democrats find it very easy "working together" with the two Republicans on the National Board.

Perhaps, however, we shouldn't expect much other than a liberal bias from the League, considering its origins.

The woman who first conceived the idea of the League of Women Voters, and served as a guiding spirit in its early days, was Mrs. Carrie Chapman Catt. Mrs. Catt was president of the National American Women's Suffrage Association from 1915 until her death in 1947; at the NAWSA convention in 1919, with the right-to-vote for women secured, she proposed the formation of a new organization to educate women on politics and get them active in government. And the League of Women Voters was born.

During her long and active political life, Mrs. Catt found herself keeping some strange company on the far left. During the time of the Spanish Civil War in the late '30s she was associated with the Coordinating Committee to Lift the Embargo, later identified by the House Committee on Un-American Activities as "one of the numerous Communist-front enterprises which were organized around the Communists' agitation over the Spanish Civil War."

Mrs. Catt was also listed in the Feb. 10, 1944, issue of the *Daily Worker* as a sponsor of the Committee of Women of the National Council of American-Soviet Friendship, another Red front. Earlier, in 1942, she had joined a committee to petition on behalf of notorious West Coast pro-Communist labor leader Harry Bridges.

Local Leagues have had their own flirtations with the far left in the past. In 1938 the New York City League opposed a bill which would have barred from public school teaching any person who believed in the violent overthrow of the U.S. government; in 1954, the LWV of Illinois voiced opposition to a similar bill in that state. Defeat of both these pieces of legislation was a *cause celebre* for the Communists.

While direct association with the Communist left is rare in League history, its continuous championing of blind liberalism has led it to some uncomfortable moments. But if these links are uncommon, playing footsie with notable non-Communist leftists is not.

In 1947 the LWV set up a Carrie Chapman Catt Memorial Fund (CCC Fund) to serve as an "educational" subsidiary of the organization, to publish pamphlets and other material. In its early years the CCC Fund was heavily financed by donations from the Fund for the Republic, the pro-disarmament, anti-military "think" group which now masquerades under the title "Center for the Study of Democratic Institutions."

Two other groups which the League of Women Voters has been associated with in the past are the Women's Joint Congressional Committee and the Program Information Exchange. Both of these bodies were composed of member organizations—such as the LWV—and their purpose in both cases was to disseminate legislative information and "educational" materials supporting federal government welfare legislation and other liberal schemes.

As for what other organizations the League is working with now, members of its Washington staff say only that they will work with "groups whose goals are the same as ours." This does, of course, invariably mean left-wing groups such as the United Nations Association (formerly American Association for the U.N.) and the American Civil Liberties Union.

On numerous occasions the League has worked closely with organized labor, including the AFL-CIO's Committee on Political Education and other Democrat-biased union adjuncts.

It is, then, on both the educational and active levels of the League that it is markedly left-of-center. It is definitely not a "non-partisan" organization working only toward "informed and active participation of citizens in government." It is a liberal pressure group that misleads its members and ignores their opinions on issues.

The National Council of Churches: Advocate for the World's Militant Left

By Allan C. Brownfeld   *(From the 7 February 1981 issue)*

Ostensibly a religious body established to promulgate Christianity, the National Council of Churches is, instead, a deeply political organization which has, from its beginnings as the Federal Council of Churches early in this century, deeply involved itself in a series of political crusades.

At the present time it is committed to the elimination of the free enterprise system and its replacement with a government-controlled economy. It is opposed to all efforts to maintain American national strength. It has given aid and comfort to the enemies of freedom and, through its affiliation with the World Council of Churches, has contributed funds to terrorist organizations. Its stands on criminal justice, abortion and school prayer are typical of the permissive, secular attitudes toward these subjects and are contrary to what most American church members believe to be a Christian approach.

This may sound like a harsh and one-sided indictment. The evidence, however, confirms its validity. More and more concerned churchmen and others have been speaking out in recent days about the negative role being played by organized religion.

Excesses of Political Activism

Even some liberal clergymen are becoming concerned about the excesses of political activism on the part of some of the churches. Prof. Martin Marty, a University of Chicago theologian, states that "The advocates of revolutionary socialism, whether they ground their advocacy in Christian millenialism, in mixed Christian and Marxism 'liberation theology,' or in simple secular philosophies of history cannot point—or at least have not pointed to my satisfaction—to post-revolutionary resolutions that allow for true intellectual and religious freedom.

"They complain about 'repressive tolerance' in our own current society without letting us point to the 'repressive intolerance' of Socialist regimes everywhere. They may say that I am demonstrating the provincialism of a Westerner with a full stomach when I cherish religious freedom without noting that other economic systems bring fuller stomachs. They have not shown that such systems are all that provident. And they slide past the murder of perhaps 7 million under Maoism or of too many millions to count under the Stalinist system (which none of them any longer favors or even likes to hear brought up), and past the persecution that most post-revolutionary socialisms enact.

"To be told that such systems tolerate 'religious freedom,' because some of them allow churches to remain open so long as church people do not criticize the regime, is to leave us no further along than we would be under right-wing regimes in, say, Korea or Chile."

More and more, both the National and World Council of Churches are carriers of "liberation theology," as are some elements of the Roman Catholic Church, particularly in Latin America.

Capitalism Oppressive, Socialism 'Liberating'

Writing in the liberal journal, *Christianity and Crisis* (March 19, 1979), Prof. Peter Berger argues that "Since the 1960s there has been a widespread identification of Christian morality, if not Christianity as such, with the political agenda of the left. The concept of 'liberation' has come to serve as the *idee-clef* of this identification. . . .

"Thus we are told that capitalism is intrinsically exploitative and oppressive, that socialism by contrast is intrinsically 'liberating,' that America is the most violent nation on earth, that racism is endemic to Western culture and so on. These and comparable statements of facts. . . . And the most important criticism to be made of the new Christian leftism is *not* that it promulgates false norms, *not* that it is *based on demonstrable misconceptions of empirical reality*. Put differently: What is most wrong about 'liberation theology' is neither its biblical exegesis nor its ethics but its sociology."

In 1980 the National Council of Churches adopted a resolution stating, "It is becoming increasingly recognized that massive armaments buildup diverts resources away from human needs, does *not* provide national security and endangers the survival of civilization. . . . It is our hope that the day will come when the world will be freed of nuclear and other military weapons."

This statement came at a time when the Soviet Union had invaded Afghanistan and when it was known to all that during the 1970s, Soviet defense outlays steadily increased while those of the U.S. declined. The dollar value of Soviet military expenditures now exceeds U.S. military spending by 25 to 50 per cent.

The NCC resolution, however, said not a word about either this massive Soviet buildup or the invasion of Afghanistan. It called, instead, for what clearly amounts to unilateral disarmament on the part of the U.S. In its resolution, after all, it was addressing Washington—not Moscow.

In its 1980 resolutions, the NCC also called upon Congress "to reject the President's request for appropriations and legislation to institute registration for the Selective Service." This resolution stated that "national security rests on the development of international economic and political cooperation, the peaceful settlement of disputes, and the determination to abolish war . . . the significant unresolved societal issues of racism, sexism and economic discrimination are exacerbated in and by the military . . . the proposal by the President to institute registration for Selective Service is evidence of recurring and increasing reliance on military responses to world problems."

On Nov. 6, 1980, the NCC adopted a lengthy policy statement on the Middle East in which it called upon Israel to include the Palestine Liberation Organization in Middle East negotiations. According to the NCC, the PLO "functions as the only organized voice of the Palestinian people and appears to be the only body able to negotiate a settlement on their behalf." The NCC does not insist that the PLO cease all terrorist activities before being admitted to negotiations but mildly suggests that "Further, each party should refrain from all hostile acts against the other." Thus, terrorist murders of women and children are placed on an equal basis with government efforts to resist terrorism.

Support for the PLO is wholly consistent with past support by the NCC of such terrorist groups as the Patriotic Front in Rhodesia, SWAPO in South West Africa, FRELIMO in Mozambique, and the Sandinistas in Nicaragua.

Opposes Voluntary School Prayer

In the June 1980 issue of its publication, *Mark Up*, the National Council of Churches declares its opposition to voluntary prayer in the public schools, noting that it "would open the door to violation of the separation of church and state by permitting the exercise of religious practices in public schools."

While seeing fit to criticize El Salvador, Israel, the registration for the Selective Service, military spending and school prayer, the National Council of Churches had nothing to say about the holding of U.S. hostages in Iran, the Soviet invasion of Afghanistan, or the brutality being inflicted upon the people of Vietnam and Cambodia by the Communist regimes in those countries.

Unfortunately, the National Council of Churches' opposition to U.S. military preparedness, its harsh criticism of friendly governments, and total indifference toward the harshest violators of human rights in the world, such as the USSR, is not new. Neither is its advocacy of partisan political issues, such as its support for the Equal Rights Amendment, or its advocacy of congressional spending for some programs, such as food stamps, but opposition to other programs, such as registration for the Selective Service.

In 1980, the National Council of Churches is what it has been almost since its creation, a vocal advocate of a particular political agenda. It has dangerously confused politics and religion and has spoken in the name of millions of American Protestants who reject its political perspective.

Dr. Ernest Lefever of the Ethics and Public Policy Center at Georgetown University states that "It is dangerous for any Christian body to identify itself fully with any specific political cause or order, whether the prevailing one or a challenge to it. In identifying with a secular power or agency, the church runs the risk of losing its critical distance and of subverting its prophetic function, its capacity to judge all movements and systems by universal Christian standards. It is thus just as foolish . . . for the church to endorse socialism as it is to support Franco's Fascist Spain. Christians can and should support justice, freedom, the rule of law and respect for the human person."

To understand the very negative force which the National Council of Churches is at the present time, it is essential to understand its history and to review the path it has taken on the road to radical political activism.

The Federal Council of Churches was officially organized in December 1908. In his study of the National Council, *The Holy Alliance* (Arlington House, 1975), Prof. C. Gregg Singer of Catawba College writes, "Even before it was formally organized, the conference on inter-church relations of 1905 had actually revealed the fundamental purpose of this ecumenical gathering in bringing political issues before its attention. Particularly, was it concerned with the problem of the misrule of Leopold II of Belgium in the Congo. This report of one of its commissions became involved with the temperance and immigration issues on the home front. Thus, even before it was formally organized, it was clear that the Federal Council of Churches was to be an ecclesiastical pressure group in national and international political, social and economic affairs."

The original document, Prof. Singer argues, "clearly reveals the 'Christian socialism' of Walter Rauschenbusch, who was a member of the conference that created the federal Council. . . . Although the document proposals seem mild in the light of contemporary economic and social legislation, they contain the seeds of strict governmental regulation of all of life in the name of the Gospel. Their theological basis was the social gospel of Rauschenbusch, George Herron and Harry F. Ward."

Collectivist 'Liberation Theology' Adopted

The National Council of Churches has turned its back upon the traditional Christian belief in individualism and has adopted, instead, the "liberation theology" of collectivism. One of its key goals, as a result, is the substitution for our free enterprise system of a form of socialism which it has not as yet defined. Its efforts in this regard have become more outspoken each year.

Just as the National Council has provided aid and comfort to terrorists and has attempted to replace our system of free enterprise with a government-controlled economy, so it has vigorously opposed efforts to strengthen the nation's defense.

Writing in the New York *Times*, March 25, 1979, Kenneth Briggs, that newspaper's specialist on religious affairs, noted that "The drive among American churches for international disarmament is taking the place in church life that once was occupied by civil rights and the antiwar movement of the 1960s and early 1970s. . . . Disarmament is becoming the most prominent social issue for the decade ahead."

Communist Arms Buildup Ignored

The National Council of Churches, the World Council, groups such as the Sojourners and individuals such as William Sloane Coffin, if they are sincere in their advocacy of arms limitation, have chosen the wrong target. It is the Soviet Union, not the U.S., which has been engaged in a massive arms buildup in recent years. Moscow has sustained steady real increases in military outlays for 15 years while the U.S. has maintained a steady pace in decreasing real military expenditures. In the early 1970s our paths crossed. Since then, the Soviets continued to climb and we continued to descend.

While pronouncements from the NCC would lead the public to believe that the U.S. was pursuing an aggressive international posture, the fact is that in real dollars, the 1980 fiscal year budget request for defense was less than the U.S. defense budget of 1965. The long-term decline in U.S. defense spending has resulted in smaller forces and in the purchase of fewer weapons.

While the U.S. falls further behind the Soviet Union, the National Council of Churches uses all of the resources at its disposal to resist all efforts at restoring U.S. military strength.

The National Council of Churches and the World Council of which it is a part have been militant in opposing the U.S. commitment in Vietnam, in fomenting terrorist actions in Rhodesia, Angola, Mozambique and South Africa and in Latin America—but have hardly said a word of criticism over the years of the most serious violators of human rights in today's world, the Communist states such as the USSR, the People's Republic of China, Vietnam and Cambodia.

At the very moment when a brutal totalitarian state was being imposed upon Vietnam, the NCC said little in behalf of the victims but, instead, embraced their oppressors. The NCC declared its opposition to a U.S. veto of Vietnamese membership in the U.N., stating that "The healing of the many wounds of war . . . can best take place once Vietnam has become a full participant in the family of nations." It also asked the U.S. to establish relations with the Communist government of Vietnam and, beyond that, to provide that tyrannical regime with economic assistance. It contributed hundreds of thousands of dollars on its own to that Communist regime for "relief."

At the very moment it was embracing the Vietnamese Communists in November 1976, the NCC expressed concern about "flagrant violations of human rights to which the African majority is being subjected" in South Africa and Rhodesia. While calling for recognition of the Communist regime in Vietnam, it passed a resolution urging the U.S. government to "refrain from recognizing the Transkei," a newly independent state in southern Africa.

The 18-day Nairobi assembly of the World Council of Churches, held in 1975, is instructive with regard to the political complexion of this movement.

When the WCC meeting came to making a statement about meddling in Angola, it pointed a finger of blame only at South Africa. Similarly, the council criticized attacks on human rights in Asian and Latin American nations, but failed to attack repression of liberties in either the Soviet Union or the nations of Black Africa. In fact, the delegates were forced to face the question of Soviet repression principally by a Nairobi-based Christian newspaper, *Target*, which printed a smuggled plea to the World Council from Moscow priest Gleb Yakunin and layman Lev Regelson. The two complained that the WCC had made no protest when "the Russian Orthodox Church was half destroyed" in the early 1960s, and pleaded for a crusade against persecution of Christians in the Soviet Union.

The political complexion and orientation of the WCC was demonstrated clearly in the Nairobi meeting when Michael Manley, prime minister of Jamaica, told the assembly that churchmen today must help destroy the capitalist system. "In the name of capitalism," he said, "all of the most dangerous instincts of man have been elevated to the status of behavioral laws." According to United Press International, this anti-capitalist declaration "received prolonged applause" from the nearly 800 delegates.

Despite the overwhelming evidence of its political approach, the World Council continues to be defended by leaders of the National Council of Churches. Dr. Cynthia Wedel, an NCC leader and one of six presidents of the WCC, recently declared that there are no Communists in the Council. Mrs. Wedel, who served as president of the NCC, was hardly unaware of the fact that Metropolitan Nikodim, who serves with her, is, in fact, an identified agent of the KGB. She said: "There are no Communists in the council, only Christians that happen to live in Communist lands."

The fact is that delegates from Communist countries to the various World Council meetings beginning with New Delhi in 1961, have been identified as members of the secret police. Janos Peter, who represented the Hungarian Reformed Church in Evanston, Ill., in 1954, came back to the U.N. as a delegate of the Hungarian government. Alexander Solzhenitsyn has said this of the "approved" clergymen of the state-controlled Russian Orthodox Church: ". . . the church . . . ruled dictatorially by atheists . . . a sight never before seen in two millennia!"

*   *   *   *   *

During the 1980 presidential election there was much criticism of the role played by fundamentalist religious groups such as the Moral Majority. They were accused of confusing religion and politics and to those who have long been concerned about the role played by the NCC and other activist church bodies in the political arena these remain serious questions to be explored.

It cannot be proper, for example, for clergymen to be hailed for politicizing religion in one direction and condemned for doing it from a different point of view. To do so is simply to quarrel with the nature of their politics, not the validity of their using the church for such an enterprise. In the end, it is a corruption of religion to say that it either mandates unilateral disarmament or the recognition of Taiwan.

Yet, for leaders of the NCC to criticize the political role played during the 1980 campaign by conservative clergymen is strange indeed. No group, the NCC declared, can legitimately claim to represent the "Christian vote" to the exclusion of others. The Rev. William Sloane Coffin, a long-time apologist for the most oppressive regimes in the world and an advocate of U.S. disarmament, was especially harsh on the fundamentalist clergymen. He criticized the way they used the Bible: "I would agree that the Bible contains all the answers, at least all the significant ones. The Bible is something like a mirror; if an ass peers in, you can't expect an apostle to peer out."

The president of the NCC, Dr. William Howard, and the past president, Dr. William P. Thompson, joined the group launched by television producer Norman Lear, People for the American Way. Dr. Thompson, who is the chief executive officer of the United Presbyterian Church, said: "We are trying to communicate to the American people that the Christian community understands that people must make up their own minds about political issues."

The irony of those who have been in the forefront of left-wing political activism expressing outrage over being challenged by conservative religious organizations and, in effect, denying fundamentalist clergymen the right to do the very thing they have been doing themselves for so many years was not lost upon the American people.

In a free society every organization has the right to express its viewpoint, however mistaken that view may be. The political posture of the National Council of Churches is clear.

It is opposed to free enterprise, opposed to a strong national defense, and supportive of terrorism in the Third World. It is indifferent to the violations of human rights in Communist countries. Does the National Council, ostensibly a religious body, have the right to transform itself into a radical political activist group and maintain its tax exemption? Does it have the right to misrepresent the views of millions of American Protestants who do not share its radical perspective? These are more difficult questions.

What is involved is not the National Council's right to express its radical views—which is beyond question—but its right to do so in the name of church members who disagree with those views, and to be subsidized by all American taxpayers in doing so.

Many strange things have been done historically in the name of God, from heresy trials to massive religious persecutions to burning at the stake. The substitution of radical politics for Christianity by the National Council of Churches at the present time is another in a long line of corruptions of the Gospel of Jesus Christ. American Protestants, in whose name the National Council acts, have a responsibility to examine the NCC record, only a small portion of which has been alluded to in this report, and decide whether or not they want this organization to represent them in the future. All Americans have a responsibility to consider this record and determine whether or not a group such as the NCC is entitled to remain tax exempt.

The IPS and the Media: Unholy Alliance

The liberal media have publicized the connections that some conservative journalists have with the controversial Unification Church of Sun Myung Moon. But liberal-left journalists have disguised their links to a more controversial organization, the Institute for Policy Studies. The IPS has supported CIA defector Philip Agee and Communist regimes such as Cuba and North Vietnam.

By Cliff Kincaid   *(From the 9 April 1983 issue)*

(Mr. Kincaid was an associate editor of HUMAN EVENTS. This article was underwritten by the Fund for Objective News Reporting.)

The question of which conservative journalists are "associating" with the Unification Church of Sun Myung Moon has become something of a hot topic in the Nation's Capital.

The Washington *Times*, the Washington, D.C., newspaper launched in May 1982 by businesses related to the Moon organization, stands at the center of the controversy. Despite the fact that the majority of its top editors and reporters are not disciples of Moon, and despite the fact that the newspaper was promised journalistic independence, critics of Moon have alleged that conservative journalists who write, work for, or contribute to the *Times* are somehow promoting Moon's "doctrines." Even those conservatives whose syndicated columns are carried by the *Times* have been denounced as "Moonie columnists."

But the controversy surrounding the *Times* is unusual in one major respect because many members of the news media, including some critics of the *Times*, have themselves associated with a controversial organization that has maintained links to *unfriendly* foreign governments.

This organization, the Institute for Policy Studies (IPS), was the subject of an article by Joshua Muravchik that appeared in the April 28, 1961, New York *Times Magazine*.

The IPS was formed in 1963 by Richard J. Barnet and Marcus Raskin, who both served in the Kennedy Administration, and it is has grown to the point that it operates on a budget estimated at more than $2 million a year. This money, obtained from nonfederal sources such as foundations, is used to underwrite the "scholars and activists" who work at the Institute as fellows, associate fellows, visiting and guest fellows, research and staff associates, administrators, and members of the "Washington School" faculty.

On defense and foreign policy issues, Muravchik pointed out, some of those associated with IPS have voiced support for Communist regimes such as Cuba and North Vietnam and revolutionary movements in Africa, Central America and the Middle East.

In addition, Muravick noted, the IPS facilitated CIA defector Philip Agee's travels in Europe, sponsored the controversial figure, Orlando Letelier, a Chilean Marxist with close ties to Cuba, and played a key role in the effort to restrict the operations of American intelligence agencies.

On domestic issues, Muravchik said that in 1978, at the request of 56 members of Congress, the IPS prepared a study of the federal budget that proposed a number of Socialist economic measures and a cut in the military budget by nearly 50 per cent. (Fifty-two members requested a similar study in 1982.)

But the Muravchik article, while noting that the IPS was seeking to strengthen its ties with Congress, the Democratic party and organized labor, failed to explore in detail the IPS's considerable influence in the national news media.

Yet the IPS 1979-1980 annual report, the latest available, boasted of such influence. The report stated that IPS fellows have appeared on the NBC "Today Show," ABC's "Good Morning America," "Bill Moyers Presents" on the Public Broadcasting Service (PBS), and "a range of national television documentaries." The report added that commentaries by IPS fellows "are heard regularly over National Public Radio and through local radio interviews and broadcasts."

The annual report also pointed out that "IPS fellows and associates" have written for *Christianity and Crisis*, *The Nation*, the New York *Times*, the Boston *Globe*, the Washington *Post*, *Mother Jones*, the *New Yorker*, *In These Times*, the Baltimore *Sun* and other publications.

In fact, however, as this investigation will demonstrate, the annual report *understated* the degree of influence and access that the IPS enjoys with the national news media.

The Cover Up

Herbert Aptheker, a leading theoretician of the Moscow-funded U.S. Communist party, once wrote, "There are precious few positive and stimulating products coming out of Washington these days; a large proportion are being issued by the non-profit Institute for Policy Studies."

As a non-profit, tax-exempt group, the IPS said in its annual report, "The Institute endorses no institutional political line: it serves no political interest and no political party." IPS described itself as "a source of radical scholarship, posing fundamental questions, providing conceptual thought for engaging the world around us."

Not surprisingly, the journalists who have been associated with the IPS echo this line.

For instance, Karen DeYoung, the Washington *Post* foreign editor who teaches at the IPS "Washington School" and received $1,000 for one class, told me, "The organization itself doesn't stand for an ideology."

Frank Mankiewicz, the president of taxpayer-funded National Public Radio, who taught some classes at the "Washington School" but doesn't remember if he was paid for them, told me, "I really don't know the institutional position of IPS." He added that "I'm not even sure they've put out documents on behalf of their position. . . ."

Scott Armstrong, the *Post* investigative reporter and coauthor of *The Brethren*, who has also taught at the "Washington School," said about the IPS: "I'm not sure how it's structured."

Curiously, one relevant fact about IPS which provides some important insight into its "political line"—its publication of the self-described "independent socialist newspaper," *In These Times*—was not mentioned in its annual report. Also not mentioned was the fact that *In These Times* cosponsored a June 1980 "Marxist Union Conference."

It was in December 1978 that *In These Times* became a "project" of the IPS, announcing that since its "inception" it had enjoyed a "close relationship" with the fellows of the Institute. Near the end of June 1982, without any fanfare, *In These Times* assumed a new publisher—Mid-America Publishing Co. Fellows of the IPS continue to write for the publication, however, and it appears that the "close relationship" continues.

Apparently, the official IPS connection, though unacknowledged in the annual report, became too controversial. It is known, for example, that not too long after Ronald Reagan took office, *In These Times* Editor James Weinstein sent out an hysterical fund-raising letter in an envelope that bore the ominous statement, "They're Out to Destroy Us. . . ." The envelope was marked "postage paid" by the IPS.

The Secret of Success

When IPS fellows appear on television programs, or when they are mentioned in magazine articles, the liberal media never refer to them as Socialists, let alone pro-Marxists or Marxists.

When *Newsweek's* David C. Martin, for instance, wrote a May 18, 1981, article on the anti-defense spending views of IPS co-founder Richard J. Barnet and former Jimmy Carter speechwriter James Fallows, he referred to IPS as a "liberal" group.

Even worse, the New York *Times* op-ed page, which was edited until June 1982 by Charlotte Curtis, wouldn't even identify IPS as "liberal," preferring to label it as just a "research organization."

To further confuse matters, on Dec. 18, 1981, the *Times* published an op-ed piece by an IPS "visiting fellow" on the media's misapplication of political labels such as "extremist," a term that could be applied to the IPS.

Entitled "Winging It in Politics," the author of the piece argued that the Communist-backed terrorists in El Salvador were not extremists, but were "landless peasants and destitute laborers taking up arms against repressive economic and political conditions."

The real extremists in the world today, the author continued, were those "in power" in the U.S. who had given us "the genocidal war in Indochina."

The *Times* identified the author of the piece as Michael Parenti, the author of several books and a "visiting fellow" at the IPS, an "independent research organization."

To say the least, the tone of the column led me to suspect that the *Times* had not accurately identified Michael Parenti. And sure enough, in a telephone conversation, he identified himself not as an "independent researcher," but as "a Socialist—a democratic Socialist."

He refused to comment—in fact he hung up the phone—when I asked him about a report in the Communist party newspaper, *Daily World*, that he had appeared at a conference of Marxist scholars held in October 1980 at Hostos Community College in New York. The *Daily World* reported that "Michael Parenti of the Institute for Policy Studies" had spoken about "the mythology of anticommunism," which was referred to as "the 'great scare' technique, and how it is used to build up armament spending."

The *Daily World* reported that Parenti "debunked the myth of pluralism which states that the U.S. is democratic because it is a multi-party system. He pointed out how the political process is, in fact, dominated and controlled by one class."

Parenti wrote an article for *The National* of April 11, 1981, explaining the latter point. Even though we have "a diffuse array of groups situated in such varied places as the Pentagon, the scientific and academic establishments, the large corporations, the media and in Congress," he said, ". . . all of them work in perfect orchestration to increase the military budget and propagate the imperialist, interventionist interest of the ruling class."

He went on to identify himself not as "a Socialist—a democratic Socialist," but as a "Marxist." He said, "we as Marxists pledge our lives and our sacred honor" to the "struggle" to expose "the myths of the ruling class," including the "imperialist myth" of the "Giant Red Menace."

The case of Michael Parenti—a self-proclaimed Marxist who criticizes the media for false labeling, while being falsely labeled himself—illustrates the curious relationship that exists between the IPS and the media.

Going to School at IPS

For a couple of years now, the IPS "Washington School" has offered courses on a variety of subjects, including the media, sex and politics, feminism, socialism, human rights, religion, national security, natural resources, the Congress, civil rights, the Third World and the Soviet Union. The courses are intended to attract congressional aides, government employees and assorted political activists.

A number of journalists have participated in these courses, either as instructors or guest lecturers. Perhaps the best known of these is veteran radical journalist I. F. Stone, a long-time associate of the IPS who told a national television audience on the CBS program, "60 Minutes," that Ronald Reagan was a nice man who "scares the hell out of me" and that Libyan dictator Col. Qaddafi was a provocative "flea" who should be met with "patience, restraint, good sense and humor."

Stone told a National Press Club audience on June 18, 1981, that "disinformation" was a "very paranoid term about the press" and that "the chief source of disinformation is the [U.S.] government, particularly the State Department. . . ."

An assistant to I. F. Stone in the 1960s, Peter Osnos served as national news editor at the Washington *Post* and is now its London correspondent.

During the summer of 1980, Osnos was a guest lecturer at an IPS "Washington School" course on "foreign reporting" taught by Karen DeYoung, who is now the *Post's* foreign editor, and who was then deputy foreign editor.

Osnos, a former Moscow correspondent for the *Post*, admitted under questioning by members of the class that he was ignorant about the ultimate intentions and goals of the Soviet Union. He said, "I've given up trying to decide why they do what they do because they're aggressive or because they're scared." Osnos concluded that the Soviets were "just bullies."

In March 1979, Osnos visited Cuba and couldn't find evidence of Moscow's control of that island. He reported in the *Post* on March 11, 1979, that ". . . despite the enormous Soviet influence on Cuba's foreign policy, the Kremlin is not in charge here."

He also reported that there was "apparently genuine rapport" between Castro and the Cuban people. But a little more than a year later hundreds of thousands of Cubans fled the island, complaining about economic and political repression.

Karen DeYoung told that class, attended and taperecorded by this reporter, that "most journalists now, most Western journalists at least, are very eager to seek out guerrilla groups, leftist groups, because you assume they must be the good guys." DeYoung herself demonstrated the truth of that remark when she wrote a series of stories datelined "At a Sandinista Training Camp," during the Cuban-backed revolution in Nicaragua.

At that time, she reported that despite claims by Nicaraguan President Anastasio Somoza that the Sandinistas were Communist terrorists, the Sandinistas said they were committed to the establishment of a "pluralistic democracy," not a "new Cuba."

During this eight-week class we were treated to a steady stream of left-wing journalists as guest lecturers, including Eric Roulea of the French newspaper *Le Monde*, who was described as one who "sort of sides with radical elements of the Arab world"; Peter Pringle, who was then with the London *Sunday Times*; William Shawcross, author of the book, *Sideshow*, which tries to blame the U.S. for contributing to the Communist genocide in Cambodia; and Elizabeth Becker, who continues to cover events in Southeast Asia for the *Post* and who now serves as a "visiting scholar" at IPS.

Letelier and the Media

Perhaps the most controversial figure ever associated with the IPS was Orlando Letelier, the former top official of the Marxist Salvador Allende regime in Chile who was identified as both an associate fellow of IPS and a director of the IPS international branch, the Transnational Institute, which is based in Amsterdam, The Netherlands. Letelier began working for IPS after Allende was overthrown by a popular military coup in 1973.

Letelier was thought to have been opposing the new military regime in Chile because he wanted to restore "human rights" in his native land. But he was exposed by papers found in his briefcase after his murder in 1976 to have been secretly promoting Communist goals, with the assistance of Cuba.

The papers contained a letter addressed to Letelier datelined, "Havana, May 8, 1975," which showed that Letelier had received a $5,000 payment and a promise of another $1,000 a month "from here" to support his activities. The letter was signed by Tati Allende, who was living in Cuba and married to Luis Fernandez Ona, identified by U.S. intelligence as a top official of the Cuban intelligence service, the DGI.

Another important item in the Letelier briefcase was an address book, revealing that Letelier had contacts with Soviet and Cuban officials in Washington and New York, some of them identified by U.S. intelligence as Communist intelligence operatives, as well as a large number of prominent journalists.

One journalist for whom both home and office phone numbers were listed was Laurence Stern, who served as national news editor at the *Post*.

Stern emerged into the spotlight of left-wing activities when he was identified as a "participant" in the 1974 founding conference of the Center for National Security Studies (CNSS), the anti-CIA organization once headed by Robert Borosage, the current executive director of the IPS.

When Stern died in 1979, a large, well-dressed, dark-skinned man appeared, shook hands with Washington *Post* Executive Editor Ben Bradlee and others attending the funeral and declared:

"I am from Cuba. I am a Marxist-Leninist. I am human. Larry Stern was one of my friends, one of my best friends. I loved him."

The speaker was Teofilo Acosta, a first secretary at the Cuban Interests Section (Castro's embassy) in Washington, and one of the many Communist-bloc contacts that Letelier had listed in his address book. A defector from the Cuban intelligence service, the DGI, has identified Acosta as a Cuban intelligence agent.

But there was no uproar in our major media about Laurence Stern's Cuban connection. And it's the curious failure of the major media to cover such stories that is the subject of *The Spike*, the novel about Communist disinformation activities written by the noted journalists, Robert Moss and Arnaud de Borchgrave.

The Alternative Press, Philip Agee and IPS

De Borchgrave said that Agee "has his connections in this country" and "gets his information into [the] alternative press—*Mother Jones*, *Village Voice*, *Soho News*, and *The Progressive* magazine—and worms its way through the establishment or mainstream press."

Adam Hochschild, a contributing editor to *Mother Jones*, and Erwin Knoll, editor of *The Progressive*, dismissed de Borchgrave's charges. But the truth is that all of the publications cited by de Borchgrave, along with others such as *The Nation*, the *Guardian* and, of course *In These Times*, have been closely associated with the IPS, which, by its own admission, has facilitated Agee's anti-CIA activities in Europe.

An IPS "fact sheet," put together in response to Muravchik's New York *Times* magazine article, acknowledged the charge that the IPS had made some "efforts on behalf of Agee," but claimed they were "negligible."

The "fact sheet" explained, "When Agee was booted out of England after a Star Chamber proceeding in which no charges were filed and no evidence presented, IPS's Amsterdam Center provided him a place to stay while he figured out where he would live. *We would make the same decision again*." (Emphasis added.)

Yet even the Washington *Post* reported that Agee, who has said "I aspire to be a Communist and a revolutionary," was kicked out of Britain because he was accused of disseminating material harmful to British security and maintaining "regular contacts with foreign spies," especially Cuban agents.

Mother Jones, a magazine named after "pioneer socialist" Mary Harris "Mother" Jones, is published by the tax-exempt Foundation for National Progress, which stated in its 1976 financial report that it was established on the West Coast to carry out the "charitable and educational activities" of the IPS.

Perhaps the most effective outlet for the IPS is the Pacific News Service (PNS), an "alternative news agency" that began as a project of the Bay Area Institute, an organization established with the help of IPS money in 1970. IPS co-founder Richard J. Barnet serves as a "contributing editor" of PNS.

The PNS supplies about 30 stories a month to more than 200 subscribers. These have included newspapers such as *In These Times* and the *Guardian*, as well as major newspapers such as the Cleveland *Plain Dealer*, the Atlanta *Journal*, the Boston *Globe*, the Chicago *Tribune*, the Los Angeles *Times* and the San Francisco *Examiner*.

Perhaps the most important outlet for the PNS, which is marketed nationally by the Des Moines Register and Tribune Syndicate, is the Washington *Post*. According to Sandy Close, an editor at PNS, *Post* Executive Editor Bradlee made the decision several years ago to purchase a subscription to PNS stories.

The New York *Times* doesn't subscribe to PNS, Close told me, but Charlotte Curtis, the recent editor of the *Times* op-ed page, is a "strong advocate" nonetheless. Curtis still serves as an "associate editor" at the *Times*.

Liberation News Service, IPS and the Post

But one of the oldest alternative news services, the Liberation News Service (LNS), recently disbanded operations. An openly pro-Marxist organization, LNS officials spent their final days "selling off printing presses, desks and chairs, along with the posters of Lenin, Malcolm X and Che that decorate their loft," according to *In These Times*.

In his very revealing book, *A Trumpet to Arms: Alternative Media in America*, David Armstrong said that the LNS had "worldwide contacts among Western radical groups and Third World guerrilla forces." It began, he said, as a radical news service for underground and college media. Its name was proposed by Ray Mungo, a past editor of a campus newspaper in Boston, who was "inspired by what he saw as the dedication of the NLF [National Liberation Front] to the liberation of their homeland."

"The news service was financed by hook and by crook," Armstrong reported. "According to Mungo, some of LNS's equipment was 'liberated,' and many of the LNS's bills went unpaid. Friends at the Washington *Post* helped to develop LNS photographs on the sly, while typesetting equipment at the Institute for Policy Studies—Washington's leftist think tank—was commandeered for setting copy. In earlier days, LNS shared a house with the underground *Washington Free Press* and Students for a Democratic Society. Staffers occasionally lunched with I. F. Stone, who took a paternal interest in the news service."

Although the LNS is now defunct, many of the news organizations associated with the IPS continue to carry on its work by sponsoring reporters who actually seek out and report on revolutionary movements and governments around the world.

• Wilfred Burchett, who reported the Korean and Vietnam wars from the Communist side, was a correspondent for the *Guardian* before breaking with that paper over its reluctance to back Hanoi's invasion of Cambodia. Despite Burchett's long record of service to the cause of Communist "journalism," he then went to work for the IPS newspaper, *In These Times*.

• The *Guardian* itself carried reports from El Salvador's guerrillas written by Robert Armstrong, who is now with NACLA.

• Laurence Johnson, a free-lance writer, was working for both PNS and *Mother Jones* when he was apprehended and kicked out of Colombia, accused by authorities there of serving as "an international liaison agent" of the terrorists. A few years ago Johnson traveled to the Philippines, where he searched out Communist guerrillas opposed to the regime of Ferdinand E. Marcos.

• Chris Koch, who worked on projects for National Public Radio, began his career with the Pacifica Radio station in New York and in that capacity traveled to North Vietnam in 1965 with a delegation that reportedly included Michael Myerson, the current head of the Communist-controlled U.S. Peace Council. Koch's stories about the war were regarded as favorable to the Communist Vietnamese.

• Lionel Martin, who was an occasional correspondent, a stringer, for the Washington *Post* in 1977, served as a correspondent for the *Guardian*, and actually worked for the Castro regime in Havana.

Media Criticism, IPS Style

At the "Washington School" class on "foreign reporting" taught by the *Post's* Karen DeYoung, participants were not given homework, but were given suggestions about what to read as background. DeYoung suggested *The First Casualty*, a book about war correspondents by Phillip Knightley, and some articles from the *Columbia Journalism Review* (*CJR*), a publication usually described as "prestigious" and the bible of today's journalism students.

The recommended *CJR* articles included "Iran," written by Edward W. Said, a PLO sympathizer, which appeared in the March/April 1980 *CJR*. In this article, written during the Iranian crisis, when Americans were being held hostage by pro-Marxist fanatics in Teheran, Said argued that the media had been too critical of the Iranians. There were exceptions to this anti-Iranian coverage, Said acknowledged, including one op-ed piece by Fred Halliday in the Boston *Globe*. Halliday just happened to be a "fellow" of the IPS Transnational Institute.

The other article recommended by DeYoung was "The Greatest Story Ever Told," written by Garry Wills, which appeared in the January/February 1980 *CJR*. In this article, Wills criticized the media for glorifying that year's visit to the United States by Pope John Paul II. The *CJR* described Wills as a syndicated columnist and author, but didn't mention that he was a member of the IPS board of trustees.

The White Paper Controversy

The IPS connection to the newspapers and publications already named in this report may help explain why themes and story ideas pursued by the alternative press get picked up by the major media, which expose them to millions of ordinary Americans. Although such a trend is noticeable in coverage of several domestic and foreign policy issues, the campaign to discredit the State Department White Paper on El Salvador, the Feb. 23,1981, document that exposed Soviet-bloc arms smuggling to the Salvadoran guerrillas, is an important case study.

Even before the White Paper was officially released, when it was the subject of leaks and speculation in the press, CIA defector Philip Agee held a news conference in West Germany to claim that some of the captured guerrilla documents on which it was based were probably forgeries manufactured by the CIA. After Agee finally got his hands on the White Paper, he produced a 46-page critique of the document, which included his charge that some of the captured materials were, indeed, forgeries. This critique was released in Washington, D.C., by Agee's associates.

By that time, however, John Dinges had already written an article for Pacific News Service claiming that the U.S. government's documentation of arms shipments to the guerrillas was faulty. The Dinges story, according to PNS Editor Sandy Close, appeared in 30 major newspapers in the U.S.

The anti-White Paper campaign was also joined by Alexander Cockburn and James Ridgeway in the *Village Voice*, James Petras and ex-CIA employe Ralph McGehee in *The Nation*, Roger Burbach of NACLA in *Mother Jones*, and Jeffrey Stein in *The Progressive*.

Eventually the *Wall Street Journal* and the Washington *Post* published attacks on the White Paper, with reporters for these two newspapers admitting that they had seen some of the above-mentioned stories, as well as the Agee critique. Peter Osnos of the *Post* who was then national news editor, admitted at the time that a call from Jeffrey Stein urging an examination of the White Paper promoted him to assign reporter Robert Kaiser (with assistance from Karen DeYoung) to do just that.

After HUMAN EVENTS exposed the fact that the *Post* and the *Journal* (reporter Jonathan Kwitny) had used the Agee critique as a confidential source, and after Arnaud de Borchgrave charged in a New York *Times* column that Agee's critique was prepared with Cuban help, John Dinges prepared another story for PNS trying to obscure Agee's role in the anti-White Paper campaign.

Ignoring Agee's own claim that his critique formed the basis of the articles in the *Post* and *Journal*, Dinges noted that his own criticism of the White Paper had been distributed by PNS before the Agee critique was even released. "I wrote it with no help from Agee or the KGB or the Cubans or any other creatures from the conspiracy seekers' menagerie of villains," he said. Therefore, Dinges tried to argue, the fact that similar criticism of the White Paper appeared in the Agee critique, his own article, as well as the *Post* and the *Journal*, meant only that some of the "same discrepancies" had been discovered.

Yet, as Reed Irvine pointed out, Dinges made only a few feeble criticisms of the White Paper. The Agee critique, on the other hand, included scores of criticisms, 14 of which were echoed in the *Journal* article and 11 of which were echoed in the *Post*. "The articles in the *Post* and the *Journal* clearly owed a lot to Agee and little to Dinges," Irvine pointed out.

Moreover, a HUMAN EVENTS comparison of the Agee critique with the *Journal* and *Post* stories showed striking parallels. In one case, both Agee and *Journal* reporter Jonathan Kwitny made the same clumsy mistake.

Incredibly, on Jan. 7, 1982, months after Agee's role in the White Paper controversy had been completely exposed (though the *Post* has not yet acknowledged the fact that it used Agee as a source), Jack Anderson charged in his column that the White Paper had been "shown to have relied on highly questionable and probably forged documents"—the same line that had been pushed by Agee himself! Anderson ignored the fact that the criticisms of the White Paper, including those made by Agee, were all answered by the State Department.

Philip Agee and the Media

On some occasions, Philip Agee has been able to make his views known directly to the American people. For example, he starred in the series "On Company Business," an attack on the CIA, which was aired by the Public Broadcasting Service (PBS) in 1980.

Like Agee, associates of the IPS have also been able to present their views directly to the American people by way of public broadcasting. IPS fellow Saul Landau, for example, helped produce the anti-nuclear film, "Paul Jacobs and the Nuclear Gang," which aired on public television in 1979. He has said that his latest film, "Target Nicaragua," which attacks the U.S. for allegedly assisting the Nicaragua freedom fighters, may also be shown on public television.

Last year public broadcasting aired a film, "From the Ashes . . . Nicaragua Today," directed by Helena Solberg-Ladd, a member of the "Washington School" faculty at the IPS. The film was a glorification of Marxist rule in Nicaragua.

But just as the relevant facts about Philip Agee are withheld from the selection audience, the nature of the IPS connection is not explained to those who view the Landau and Solberg-Ladd films on public television.

Where Does the ACLU Stand on the Issues?

By William A. Donohue   *(From the 16 July 1988 issue)*

The subject of civil liberties is fast developing into a major campaign issue as presidential candidates George Bush and Michael Dukakis line up on opposing sides. In the middle of the controversy is the American Civil Liberties Union, which has long been considered the nation's leading civil rights organization.

Dukakis, who boasts he is a "card carrying" member of the Union, is thought to be generally supportive of the ACLU's positions. Bush has recently opened fire on the group's record. The issue has been raised in the Bush camp that Dukakis, because of his affiliation, is likely to appoint ACLU-minded judges to the bench.

But just where does the ACLU stand on critical issues? The organization has put out a policy guide, approved by the ACLU's board of directors, which constitutes the official voice of the Union. When an affiliate goes to court, for instance, it uses the policy guide as a basis for its actions. The policy guide includes 270 separate issues the ACLU has endorsed.

The following I.Q. test is culled from the ACLU's most recent policy guide and provides a basis for further discussion about the wisdom of its policies.

1. Do you believe that all laws banning the sale and distribution of hard core pornography, including child pornography, should be declared unconstitutional? The ACLU does.

The Union says it opposes "any restraint on the right to create, publish or distribute materials to adults, or the right of adults to choose the materials they read or view, on the basis of obscenity, pornography or indecency." And then adds that: "Laws which punish the distribution or exposure of such materials to minors violate the First Amendment . . ." (Policy No. 4)

The ACLU says it does not support child pornography and maintains that it is perfectly fine for the police to prosecute those who harm children. But it defiantly defends those who profit from child pornography. Indeed the ACLU's passion for defending the sale and distribution of child pornography led it to argue before the U.S. Supreme Court that child pornography is a form of free speech, protected by the 1st Amendment.

Fortunately for the children, the high court rejected the ACLU's claims. Child pornography, it was decided, was not what James Madison had in mind when he wrote the 1st Amendment allowing free speech. The ACLU, it should be noted, receives funding from the Playboy Foundation.

2. Do you believe that the film classification system, which designates movies G, PG, PG-13, R and X, constitutes censorship and should be eliminated? The ACLU does. The ACLU doesn't like the "restrictive impact on the marketplace of ideas" because of such a system, and says that ". . . experience has shown that ratings inevitably have serious chilling effects on freedom of expression." (Policy No. 18)

Since its founding in 1920, the ACLU has repeatedly asserted that it defends the right of Americans to be free from government censorship, claiming that what private groups do is not a 1st Amendment consideration. Not true. It openly rejects even non-governmental, non-censorship systems which merely identify for prospective viewers (many of whom are parents) what the level of maturity is of various movies.

The ACLU is particularly disturbed by the R and X ratings, contending that such labels discourage further production of these movies! It is upset that hotels and airlines "frequently refuse to accept X-rated films." Children, of course, frequently board planes, and their parents hardly expect them to be subjected to "Deep Throat" while flying the friendly skies. The ACLU actually maintains that the rating system, "through its X and R ratings, interferes with the autonomy of the family. These ratings deprive parents of the right to determine what films their children may see." The policy speaks for itself.

3. Do you believe that a voucher system, or a policy allowing for tuition tax credits, is unconstitutional and should be forbidden? The ACLU does. (Policy No. 80, sections c and e)

There have been many reports on the status of the public schools in the 1980s and none has been glowing. The urban poor, many of whom are black and Hispanic, have been ill-served, as virtually everyone agrees. One would think that an organization that proclaims its support for minorities would be leading the fight to enable the disadvantaged to reject those schools they find unsatisfactory.

Moreover, it is rather strange to see an organization that never tires of boasting of its commitment to free choice (the ACLU is relentless in its defense of a woman's right to choose abortion, for example), leading the fight to deny parents the right to choose which schools they want their children to attend. But no, the ACLU's politics dictate that freedom of choice, in this case, be overruled.

4. Do you believe that the display of a Christmas Creche or Menorah on public property is unconstitutional and should be forbidden, even if paid for with private funds? The ACLU does. (Policy No. 81, section 5)

Every December an ACLU affiliate files suit in a federal district court seeking to deny Christians and Jews the right to publicly express their religious beliefs. The same organization, which says that if people don't like to see pornography openly displayed by street vendors "they can avert their eyes," refuses to adopt the same logic when applied to a Nativity scene or Menorah. In these cases, nothing less than censorship will do.

Similarly, the ACLU will defend the freedom of any student to print obscenities in a school newspaper, but will not come to the defense of those who wish to sing "Silent Night" in the classroom. In fact it will try to stop them. This is a classic example of its moral priorities.

5. Do you believe that the words "under God" in the Pledge of Allegiance are unconstitutional and should be forbidden? The ACLU does. (Policy No. 84, section a)

There are some people who feel that religious objectors should not be required to say the Pledge of Allegiance. The ACLU goes well beyond that position by literally stating that "The insertion of the words 'under God' into the pledge of allegiance is a violation of the constitutional principle of separation of church and state."

There are some officials in the ACLU who actually brag about their refusal to say the Pledge. Gara LaMarche, executive director of the Texas affiliate, has written that "The Pledge of Allegiance is not the essence of the Constitution. Not pledging is." To LaMarche, not pledging is more American than doing so because dissent is a Constitutional right. But rights entail responsibilities (though that is not something the ACLU likes to stress), and the essence of pledging is to affirm one's duty to country, not to affirm one's right to be a cad.

6. Do you believe that churches and synagogues should be denied their tax-exempt status? The ACLU does. (Policy No. 92, section a)

The ACLU is in court right now trying to deny the Roman Catholic Church its tax-exempt status. The problem? The Catholic Church preaches against abortion, and the way the ACLU sees it, that's a violation of its tax-exempt status. But the Catholic Church also preaches against murder, stealing, and adultery. So what? Aren't religious institutions entitled to freely express themselves on matters of morality?

Come to think of it, why hasn't the ACLU filed suit against Rev. Jesse Jackson for taking up a collection for his presidential campaign in the black churches of Chicago? The founder of the ACLU, Roger Baldwin, once told me that the Union's decision to strip churches and synagogues of their tax-exempt status was "very foolish." It's more than that: It's downright hostile to the freedoms traditionally understood to be both Constitutional and supportive of democratic society.

7. Do you believe that all drugs should be legalized, including crack and angel dust? The ACLU does. (Policy No. 210)

Survey data show that most Americans do not want to legalize drugs. Of those who do, few are in favor of legalizing every drug. There are some drugs, like crack and angel dust, that are so disabling and convulsive in their effect that almost no one wants them legalized. Furthermore, advocates of legalization usually specify that only certain people (e.g., those who have been "medically certified") should be able to obtain drugs. Finally, most proponents of legalization admit that their position is born of exasperation with present policies, and is not derived from a school of liberty that includes the right to self-abuse.

The ACLU differs in every respect. It wants all drugs legalized, stating that "the introduction of substances into one's own body" is a civil liberty. It is not against "reasonable regulatory restraints" but does not demand that any "reasonable regulatory restraints" be levied before crack is legalized. And most revealing of all is the ACLU's philosophical belief that liberty includes the right to self-abuse, even when it is certain that drug addicts cannot help but infringe on the rights of others by engaging in uncontrollably violent and deviant behavior and by burdening the taxpayers with enormous bills for their medical and welfare expenses.

8. Do you believe that prostitution should be legalized, including street solicitation? The ACLU does. The Union bluntly "supports the decriminalization of prostitution and opposes state regulation of prostitution. The ACLU also condemns the abuse of vagrancy or loitering laws or licensing or regulatory schemes to harass and arrest those who may be engaged in solicitation for prostitution." (Policy No. 211)

There is very little public support for legalization of prostitution. And with good reason: urban areas are already plagued with so many serious social problems that the idea of giving sanction to them is mad. It is an American phenomenon that where prostitutes congregate they act as a magnet for deviants and degenerate of all kinds. Drug addicts and muggers are drawn to these areas, making entire neighborhoods unsafe for families and consumers.

Legalization would spare no neighborhood, as prostitutes, assisted by ACLU lawyers, would demand that the police observe their "civil liberties" by allowing them free rein. And in all likelihood, prostitutes would not target those communities where civil libertarian lawyers live, leaving them immune, once again, from the consequences of their ideas.

9. Do you believe that curfew ordinances for juveniles are unconstitutional? The ACLU does. (Policy No. 206)

Communities do not indiscriminately order kids off the street at night. In the rare case that curfews are employed at all, it is because a series of unusual events are seen to merit preventive action on the part of the police. For example, in 1981, after scores of black children were found missing or dead, Atlanta Mayor Maynard Jackson approved a law that ordered children off the streets after 9 p.m. According to the logic of the ACLU, Mayor Jackson was not acting in the best of interests of the children—he was flatly violating their constitutional rights.

Once again, the Union's obsession with rights has blinded it from realizing that there are some occasions where the exercise of rights leads not to liberation, but to the loss of freedom. In this case, it was life itself that stood to be lost.

10. Do you believe that sobriety road checks are unconstitutional and should be forbidden? The ACLU does. (Policy No. 217)

In an attempt to apprehend drunk drivers, before they injure themselves or someone else, the police in many states have conducted road checks, usually at bridges or toll booths where traffic is required to stop anyway. Here again, the ACLU has its blinders on to legitimate public safety concerns. No one doubts that it is intrusive for the police to stop and check drivers for driving under the influence of alcohol. But the intrusion is minimal and, considering what is at stake, highly justified. The ACLU is even against the administration of a breathalyzer test, used as a spot check, to detect drunk drivers. (Policy No. 260)

11. Do you believe that school officials should be denied the right to search the lockers of high school students for drugs? The ACLU does. (Policy No. 76)

In this day and age of drug abuse, there has been tremendous public outcry in favor of cracking down on drug users. In particular, the public favors greater scrutiny of high school students. But the ACLU objects. It wants principals to secure a search warrant before student lockers can be checked for drugs, pretending, as it does, that a school locker is a sacred vestibule of privacy, off-limits to school authorities. That the purpose of the search is to seize illegal matter, and that the location is that of a school—not a private home—is of little interest to the ACLU. All that matters is that student lockers be given constitutional protection.

12. Do you believe that all prisoners should have the right to vote, regardless of the nature of their offense, and that they should be allowed out of prison to vote at their last place of residence prior to confinement? The ACLU does. (Policy No. 241, section b-5)

Convicted felons do not, and should not, have the same rights as others. They forfeited some of their rights when they chose to violate the rights of innocent people. If the people's representatives deem it wise to pass laws that deny citizenship rights to those who have yielded citizen responsibilities, that is as it should be. The ACLU not only wants to restore the right to vote to all prisoners, regardless of the offense, it wants them to be allowed to vote at their last place of residence!

13. Do you believe that all criminals, except those guilty of such crimes as murder or treason, should be given a suspended sentence with probation and sent back to the community from which they came? The ACLU does. (Policy No. 242)

This is one of the more incredible policies of the ACLU. Aside from "the most serious offenses, such as murder or treason," no one should go to prison. The ACLU recommends that a fine should always be the preferred form of penalty, though it is not clear what the appropriate fine might be for rape. The Union suggests that "re-integrating the offender into the community" is the most appropriate correctional approach, meaning that those who prey on others should not be removed from the neighborhood of their victims.

There is no way to understand the mind-set that is at work here other than knowing how the ACLU feels about prisons in general. "Imprisonment is harsh," the policy reads, and that is why the ACLU prefers probation. According to the ACLU, "probation maximizes the liberty of the individual while at the same time vindicating the authority of the law and effectively protecting the public from further violations of law." But the purpose of punishment is not to maximize the liberty of criminals, it is to minimize their liberties so as to maximize the liberties of the innocent. And it is hard to know how the law is vindicated by treating muggers as if they were jaywalkers.

14. Do you believe that all military personnel should be granted an honorable discharge,

including those found guilty of dishonorable behavior? The ACLU does. (Policy No. 253, section 8)

That's right. This is the official policy of the ACLU: "All service personnel should receive one form of discharge, with no qualifications." The reason? "Dishonorable, general and bad-conduct discharges do not serve any reasonable military need and impose a heavy and unnecessary stigma upon the military ex-convict which follows the person throughout his or her civilian life and which seriously affects future employment opportunities."

Does this mean that those guilty of treason, desertion, insubordination—even rape, robbery and murder—should be given an honorable discharge? Yes it does. Does this mean that all such persons would qualify for veterans' benefits? Yes it does. Does this mean that the ACLU believes that those who betray their country are entitled to exactly the same rewards as those who earned the Purple Heart? Yes it does. Does this mean that if a serviceman commits sabotage that his crime should be expunged from his records? Yes it does: "No notation of convictions for crimes committed in service should be made on the discharge form." Flat statement—those are the words of the ACLU.

15. Do you believe that health professionals should not be allowed to trace for AIDS, and that doctors should be prohibited from notifying unsuspecting persons that they might be infected with the deadly disease? The ACLU does. (Policy No. 268, sections A-6 and B-5)

The ACLU is so wedded to the gay rights movement that it cannot objectively pass judgment on the issue of AIDS. It has resisted every conceivable effort to warn unsuspecting spouses that they might be infected with the deadly disease. Janlori Goldman, an official of the ACLU's Project on Privacy and Technology, has admitted where her bias lies: "The benefits of confidentiality outweigh the possibility that somebody may be injured." "May be injured" is ACLU-speak for die.

According to the ACLU, the emergence of AIDS "as a major threat to public health has serious implications for civil liberties such as control over one's body, freedom of association and the right of privacy of one's medical records." Nowhere in ACLU policy is there the slightest hint that promiscuous behavior is linked to AIDS, or that sexual restraint ought to be practiced. In fact it says that "judgments about AIDS often become entangled with *perceived issues of personal morality*, particularly regarding sexual conduct and intravenous use of illicit drugs, as the virus linked to AIDS seems to be transmitted predominantly, though not exclusively, through those two means." (My emphasis) The ACLU cannot even summon the moral courage to say that promiscuous sodomy and heroin use is wrong; it's just a perception that some people have.

16. Do you believe that homosexuals have a Constitutional right to a) marry, b) operate bathhouses, c) become foster parents, d) become a Big Brother, and e) engage in street solicitation? The ACLU does. (Policy No. 264 and lawsuits)

The ACLU wants to eliminate every law that distinguishes between heterosexuals and homosexuals, allowing of no exceptions. It wants the law to recognize same-sex "marriages" so that homosexuals may qualify for the same tax advantages that married men and women have. It wants employers to extend to homosexual couples the same privileges they provide married couples.

It wants foster care agencies to rewrite their policies to accommodate the interests of the gay rights lobby. It wants to force voluntary associations to accede to homosexual demands. It wants to give homosexuals the right to solicit sex on the street and then be permitted to go to a bathhouse, the very spot where AIDS was spread in the first place. In short, it wants to replace the mores of society with the mores of the ACLU.

17. Do you believe that the existence of metal detectors in airports is unconstitutional and should be forbidden? The ACLU does, insisting that the "current practice of searching the persons and belongings of *all* individuals, simply because they wish to board an airplane, is completely inconsistent with . . . 4th Amendment principles." (Policy No. 270)

According to the mentality of the ACLU, anyone who has boarded a plane in recent years has had his Constitutional rights stripped from him by merely walking through metal detectors. That's right. The danger that terrorists pose is subordinate to walking through a metal detector. Better run the risk of being hijacked to Cuba than to have a security agent take a peek at the insides of our luggage.

What is even more remarkable about this policy is the ACLU's inability to appreciate why the public favors keeping the detectors: "Perhaps the most troublesome aspect of the airport search question is the readiness with which most people, civil libertarians included, have accepted and indeed welcomed such procedures." No, the most troublesome aspect of the airport search question is the ACLU's readiness to sacrifice public safety to the idol of civil liberties.

18. Do you believe that workfare, and policies which require able-bodied adults to work as a condition for receiving welfare, are unconstitutional and should be forbidden? The ACLU does. (Policy No. 318)

Over the past decade, a consensus has grown among public policy analysts that welfare recipients ought to be required to work, if at all possible. The Reagan Administration and both houses of Congress are in favor of some kind of workfare provision, and the sentiment in the liberal media has also been receptive to this idea. Indeed one would be hard pressed to find any responsible organization that denies the merits of workfare. But look no more, for the ACLU is on record opposing any work requirement as a condition for receiving public assistance. Once again, the ACLU's fixation on rights is so total that it loses all interest in concomitant responsibilities.

It is often said that although the ACLU frequently takes extremist positions, it is nonetheless vital to the country that it continue its work in defending individual rights against governmental constraints. But this view suggests that a commitment to civil liberties must mean a commitment to extremism, for that is what the ACLU is all about—extremism.

To be sure, anyone who believes in freedom must necessarily believe in the rights of the individual. But are there not lines to be drawn? Aren't there other values that count in a free society, such as civility, community and public safety? No one would say that because law and order is necessary to a free society, we must necessarily approve of everything done in its name. Why then is it acceptable to say that respect for civil liberties means respect for everything done in its name?

The ACLU has been around since 1920, and over the past 68 years it has done many things that all Americans can be proud of, things which have helped to keep us free. Unfortunately, the good deeds of the ACLU have too often been overshadowed by its extremism, especially in recent years. It has yet to learn, as Madison once said, that "liberty may be endangered by the abuses of liberty as well as by the abuses of power."

Chapter Ten

Personalities

The articles in this chapter are portraits of individuals who for good or ill have had a significant impact on American politics.

The first piece is an obituary for James L. Wick (1874–1964), the president and publisher of HUMAN EVENTS from 1954 to 1964 and one of the towering figures of the conservative movement. It appeared in the issue of 24 November 1964.

The chapter continues with a not-too-flattering portrayal (25 August 1960) of President Lyndon B. Johnson by renowned columnist and commentator James J. Kilpatrick ("Lyndon Johnson: Counterfeit Confederate").

"Barry Goldwater of Arizona" by Edwin McDowell (14 September 1963) is the story of the man Jim Wick and Frank Hanighen and their colleagues at HUMAN EVENTS touted for president for years before his nomination in 1964.

"Herbert Hoover: 1875-1964" is a eulogy of the much misunderstood and maligned former president by Eugene Lyons, then a senior editor of *The Reader's Digest*, which appeared in the 31 October 1964 issue of HUMAN EVENTS.

"The Rise and Stand of George Corley Wallace" (27 January 1968) examines the phenomenon of the Alabama bantam who kept American politics convulsed for much of the period from 1968 to 1972. It was written by Victor Gold, who later served as press secretary to Vice President Spiro Agnew.

"The Odyssey of Whittaker Chambers" (14 March 1970) is the story of another noble yet tragic figure. It was written by William S. Schlamm, former assistant to *Time* magazine's Henry Luce.

The fall of Agnew, a bitter shock to conservatives who had great hopes for him, is the subject of "Conservatives Lose a Hero" (20 October 1973).

Since the 1950s *McCarthyism* has become the favorite term of abuse of the liberals. In liberal parlance the word referred to the gratuitous smearing of someone as a Communist—a tactic supposedly practiced by the Right with devastating effect on the reputations of thousands of good, decent people. In "History's Vindication of Joe McCarthy" (16 May 1987), published to commemorate the thirtieth anniversary of McCarthy's death, M. Stanton Evans corrects the record about McCarthy, documenting how on most of the charges in dispute the senator has been proved correct.

William J. Casey, a true American patriot and a hero of the Reagan administration, is lovingly portrayed by his nephew Lawrence W. Casey in the 15 August 1987 issue ("William Casey: Forty Years in Defense of Freedom").

Vice President Gore's supposed expertise in the environmental field is ripped to shreds in Julian Simon's "Gore's Environmental Ignorance" (1 August 1992).

After Herbert Romerstein first fingered late author I. F. Stone as a KGB agent, the forces of the Left tried valiantly to deny the charge. They could not do so, however, as Romerstein points out in "I. F. Stone Was Indeed a KGB Agent" (15 August 1992).

In "Prepping Anita for Sainthood" (31 October 1992) L. Brent Bozell has some fun at the expense of Anita Hill, Justice Clarence Thomas' flawed accuser. Bozell is the founder and president of the Media Research Center.

James L. Wick, President of Human Events (1897-1964)

(From 21 November 1964 issue)

The founder of Human Events, Frank Hanighen who edited this publication for 20 years, died suddenly in January of a heart attack. And now, not quite 10 months later, the president of Human Events, Jim Wick, has died of cancer. Fortunately in pouring their sweat and genius into this publication, these towering figures in the conservative movement provided Human Events with a firm foundation upon which it can and will grow.

Though this is the century of the computer, Jim Wick's contributions to Human Events cannot be statistically measured. But, some things should be stated. At the request of Frank Hanighen, he came to Human Events in 1954 to take over the business side. And, with the unflagging zeal of a Hercules performing his seven labors, Jim Wick went to work.

The publication had only 9,000 paid subscribers at that time, but in short order Jim Wick had the circulation climbing. In 10 years, he had increased it sixteen-fold and had given conservatism a powerful national forum. At one time Human Events had been a four-page weekly newsletter, but now it is 16 pages, carrying 21 prominent news columnists plus original news and features.

It goes out to over 140,000 subscribers, in every state of the union and in many foreign countries. The publication has also become a practical school for aspiring young journalists. Many who have come to work at Human Events have moved on to become editors, editorial writers and reporters for such papers as the Dallas *Morning News*, the Indianapolis *News*, and other influential metropolitan dailies.

Few, outside his close friends, his wife and the staff, knew how much time he devoted to making Human Events the thriving publication it is. He arose, normally, long before any self-respecting rooster would think of rousing himself from slumber. To the consternation of his employees, the boss was always there to greet them at work in the mornings, having quite probably arisen at 4 a.m., and arrived at work around 5 or 6.

The truth is, when most of the staff was straggling in bleary-eyed at 7:30 or 8, Jim Wick was contemplating what he would have for lunch. One positively marveled at his energies. After starting the day by reading 10 or 11 morning newspapers, he would begin a furious round of dictating correspondence, memos and articles. He literally wore out his secretaries. There would, of course, be staff conferences and businessmen and subscribers to see—all sandwiched in before high noon.

Afternoons, he might be enplaning to some place like San Francisco or New York to attend a conference of newspaper editors or of advertisers. Throughout his life he had been a man in perpetual motion, having found time to have been a reporter, lecturer, author, political adviser, businessman, promoter, publisher, court stenographer and Heaven knows what else.

Even in the last weeks of his life Jim Wick refused to slow down. Hospitalized and in considerable pain, he tried to carry out his work. Though the nurses and doctors looked askance, he demanded his daily newspapers, wire baskets, pencils, paper clips and his long red crayons. These crayons were famous among the staff, for he would use them to write memos and mark copy. When he particularly liked a piece of copy, he would grade it in crayon with an "A" followed by three red plus marks. We on the staff looked forward to those A triple pluses.

Jim Wick is no longer alive, but affectionate memories of him still linger. These memories will linger for a long, long time.

James L. Wick, president of HUMAN EVENTS, died of cancer on November 6.

Mr. Wick was born in Bowdle, South Dakota, May 11, 1897, and went to South High School in Minneapolis. He embarked on a lifelong career in the newspaper field shortly after graduating *cum laude* from the University of Minnesota in 1925. His first jobs were as a reporter for the Stoughton (Wis.) *Daily Courier-Hub*, and then the Grand Rapids (Mich.) *Press*.

In 1927 he became publisher of the Niles (Ohio) *Times*, a post he held for 10 years. In 1936, while keeping up his newspaper management interests, he went to New York City, and in 1937 founded the National Committee for Art Appreciation.

Three years later he became bureau chief of the Research Institute of America. During the 1940 elections he served as national defense specialist for the Republican National Committee.

In 1941 Mr. Wick traveled as a correspondent through Great Britain, Spain and Portugal. The next year he returned to New York and until 1945 was editor of the Prentice-Hall newsletter, "What's Happening in Washington?" From August to November of 1944 he was also a member of Gov. Thomas Dewey's research staff in the presidential campaign.

For the next eight years Mr. Wick was a free-lance writer and lecturer traveling widely throughout the United States.

On the basis of his experiences in the 1940, '44, and '48 campaigns he wrote a book entitled, *How NOT to Run for President*, published in 1952.

Also in that year he organized the first of three editors tours abroad. The newsmen on this trip interviewed Adenauer, Figl, Tito, Eden, Venizelos, Ben-Gurion, Mossadegh, Pope Pius XII, de Gaulle and Pleven. Denied permission to enter the Soviet Union to interview Stalin, Mr. Wick and several others on the tour sent the Russian premier a four-question telegram. On April 2, 1952, the day Mr. Wick returned to New York City, he received a cabled answer from Stalin which included the statement that the Soviet leader did not think World War II was any closer then than it was in the late 1940s. The cable to Mr. Wick received headlines throughout the United States and in many foreign countries.

In 1953 Mr. Wick led a tour of 10 American editors which gained admission to the Soviet Union just before Stalin's death. The editors were unable to interview the premier because of his illness. A tour of 16 American editors followed in 1954 and this time the editors were admitted to Czechoslovakia, Poland, the Soviet Union, Hungary and Rumania.

From information gathered on these tours Mr. Wick wrote a series of articles on Russia which was syndicated by the North American Newspaper Alliance.

He was general manager of the *Freeman* magazine during 1953.

In 1954 Frank Hanighen asked Jim Wick to come to Washington and become executive publisher of HUMAN EVENTS. Because Mr. Hanighen was worried over his health he and Mr. Wick had worked out an arrangement for a smooth transfer of ownership, and when Mr. Hanighen died earlier this year, Mr. Wick became president of HUMAN EVENTS. He worked 12 hours a day, seven days a week on both the editorial and business sides of the newspaper. His brother, Milton Wick, now assumes the post of president and will continue the publication with the same conservative political philosophy.

Besides his post as president of HUMAN EVENTS, Mr. Wick during his lifetime had holdings in over 30 newspapers, including the Rome, Italy, *Daily American*. At his death he was chairman of the board of the Roanoke Rapids (N.C.) *Daily Herald*, the Bogalusa (La.) *Daily News* and the New Iberia (La.) *Daily Iberian*—all part of the Wick Newspaper chain.

He was a member of the American Statistical Association, the American Economics Association, the Academy of Political Science, the American Political Science Association, the American Newspaper Publishers Association, the American Legion, the American History Association and Delta Sigma Rho.

He belonged to the National Press Club, the Capitol Hill Club and the Overseas Press Club.

He is survived by his widow, Dodee (nee Ekstrom), a former actress in the New York legitimate theater, his brothers Milton of Scottsdale, Arizona, and Stanley, a Presbyterian missionary in Guatemala, and his sisters, Mrs. F. M. Olsen of Minneapolis, Minn., and Mrs. Paul Castle of Marshall, Minn.

A memorial service was held in Washington, Monday, November 9. The Rev. David P. Kahlenberg of St. Paul's Lutheran Church officiated.

Among the honorary pallbearers were:

Rep. Bruce Alger, Mr. Fred Allman, Mr. Richard H. Amberg, Mr. Rudolph Anderson, the Hon. T. Coleman Andrews, Mr. Robert Bauman, Mrs. Rutherford Bingham, Mr. Lemuel R. Boulware, Mr. Constantine Brown, Rep. Donald Bruce, Mr. William Casey, Mr. Frank de Ganahl, Sen. Everett McKinley Dirksen, the Hon. Charles Edison, Mr. R. C. Foresman, Mr. Walter Greaza, Corinne Griffith, Mr. W. T. Hackett, Mr. Don Hall, Mr. Bernard F. Hanighen, Mr. Walter Harnischfeger, Mr. Henry Hazlitt, Mr. A. G. Heinsohn Jr.

Also, Mr. David W. Howe, Sen. Roman Hruska, the Hon. Walter Judd, Mr. Walter Knott, Mr. Ray Koken, Mr. Fulton Lewis Jr., Mrs. J. Vernon Luck, Mr. W. F. MacQueen, Mr. T. H. Madden, Mr. Lou Major, Mr. Jack Mangan, Dean Clarence Manion, Mr. Walter Mickelson, Mr. Roger Milliken, Adm. Ben Moreell, CEC, USN (Ret.), Sen. Karl Mundt, the Hon. Samuel B. Pettengill, Mr. John G. Pew, Mr. Mandel Redish, Mr. Henry Regnery, Dr. Emerson P. Schmidt, Mr. John Scott, Mr. Rudolph Scott, Mr. William Stephens, Mr. Bascum D. Talley Jr., Mr. Louis K. Timolat, Sen. Strom Thurmond, Mr. Samuel Veitch, Mr. Stanley Wilder, Mr. M. A. Wolcott, Gen. Robert E. Wood.

Additional services and interment were in Minneapolis, Minn., Wednesday, November 11.

Lyndon Johnson: Counterfeit Confederate

By James Jackson Kilpatrick   *(From the 25 August 1960 issue)*

(Mr. Kilpatrick was editor of the Richmond, Va., News Leader.)

The band broke into Dixie the night they nominated Lyndon out in L.A., but there wasn't much singing back home in the South. To the party professionals assembled in the Sports Arena, it seemed a consummate stroke; they wet their pencils and began calculating the electoral vote. Senator Johnson's name would guarantee the ticket: Texas, they said, means 24; plus 8 from Oklahoma makes 32, plus 8 from Arkansas is 40, plus 10 from Louisiana is 50, plus 8 from Mississippi and 11 from Alabama and 10 from Florida makes 79 . . . By the time they finished, they were up to 146, and the election was in the bag.

And there is this to be said for the reasoning of the professionals: on paper it looked very good. The ticket needed some balance. In Mr. Kennedy, the party had a Presidential nominee who was young, liberal, Catholic, a Northerner. And how were these assets, or liabilities as the case may be, to be supplemented? Why, obviously enough, by awarding the Vice Presidential nomination to a man with a touch of gray, a man with a reputation of moderate conservatism, a Protestant, a Southerner, in brief, by tapping Senator Lyndon Baines Johnson, 52, the pride of the Pedernales River. To be sure, some of the far-left liberals might be offended, but where did they have to go? A handful of labor leaders would object; they could be soothed. The South's electoral votes were vital; LBJ could bring them in.

Well, it may be so; it may be so. But I venture the opinion, for whatever it may be worth, that in putting this Counterfeit Confederate on the ticket, Mr. Kennedy and his advisors have blundered. If Mr. Kennedy sweeps the South, it will not be because of Lyndon, but in spite of him; for the Senator from Texas, however he may be respected on the Senate floor, is neither liked nor admired below the Potomac. In the South of 1960, as in the South of 1870, a carpetbagger may be bad, but a scalawag is worse.

Why this resentment? When it comes to elected officials, the South is a sophisticated region; its politics, to borrow from Artemus Ward, are of an exceedin' accommodatin' character. With a bland and tolerant eye, the South embraces the humbug, the demagogue, the cornball; nowhere on earth are the deals and stratagems of legislative in-fighting savored with greater enjoyment than in the capitols at Jackson, Baton Rouge and Richmond. Early in his life, if he gives a hoot about such things, the Southerner learns that politics is a body contact sport, not to be played by those whose tender sensibilities are easily bruised. The ordinary voter asks very little of the men he puts in office.

But he asks, in the big things, a certain loyalty. It is a requirement that goes beyond party and transcends personalities and political issues. There died in Virginia this spring a state legislator, a liberal with a great mind and a great heart, who had fought Harry Byrd in season and out for 30 years. He was loved by thousands of Virginians who never would have voted for him because they saw in this man—his name was Robert Whitehead—a man with an abiding loyalty to his people and to his political principles. You knew where Robert stood. He was critical of the South, but he was proud of it too, and he never compromised a conviction.

Lyndon Johnson is not seen in this way. If he had built a reputation over a period of many years as a "Southern liberal," in the pattern of Alabama's Hill and Sparkman, there would not have been nearly the reaction that erupted last winter at his role in leading the fight for a further civil rights bill. If it had been established that he believed deeply and profoundly both in the need for this legislation and in some constitutional justification for it, his loyalty to personal principle would have won a measure of respect.

No such record, and no such dedication, were in evidence. "South is Betrayed Again by Johnson for the Sake of His Own Ambitions," cried the Augusta *Herald*. "He is despised by the people he has betrayed," said the Shreveport *Journal*. "A political charlatan," said the Nashville *Banner*. "The Southern Benedict Arnold," said the Jacksonville *Times-Union*. In South Carolina, the Columbia *State* termed him "the Texas Yankee." In Virginia, the Richmond *Times-Dispatch* bitterly assailed him as "just another office-hungry Senator." In Birmingham, *South* magazine called him a "political polygamist."

The deeper hurts came in the weeks that followed. Bit by the Presidential bug, Lyndon turned his back upon the South. Before a cock could crow thrice, this son of Confederate Texas was denying every identification with his Dixie brothers. A Southerner? Not he. He was a one-hundred-per cent American, and if some regional label were required, why, he was a Westerner, podner. Look at the chaps and cowboy boots. The cartoonists had a field day. His campaign literature had a fine mesquite flavor: "The Johnson home was in the rocky frontier country of Texas on the banks of the Pedernales River. The stone houses where his grandparents fought off Commanche raids still stand in Johnson City today."

This feeling that Johnson is ashamed to be seen in public with a Southerner, as Antony said of the wound inflicted by Brutus, is perhaps the most unkind cut of all, but the antipathy of many Southerners for Senator Johnson rests on other considerations also. There was, for example, the incident of H. R. 3. We do not forget such things.

This occurred in August of 1958. It will be recalled that the Supreme Court was under fire at the time for a series of opinions in which the court had extended the powers of the central government at the expense of the powers of the States. Among these opinions was the court's ruling in the Steve Nelson case, asserting that the Smith Act had pre-empted on behalf of the Congress all power to enact legislation in the field of subversion against the United States. The effect was to invalidate the anti-subversion laws of more than 40 States.

Virginia's Congressman Howard W. Smith, author of the Smith Act, knew that his act never had been intended to do any such thing. He therefore introduced a bill, known as H. R. 3, to put the State and Federal relationship back in better balance. The bill was no more than a guide to judicial construction; it said simply that Congress was not to be presumed to have pre-empted a legislative field unless Congress specifically asserted such an intention. Over the noisy opposition of such liberals as New York's Emanuel Celler, H. R. 3 sailed through the House by an astonishingly wide margin.

On the Senate side, a careful count indicated that a companion Senate bill, S-654, would pass by 46 to 39. States righters had reckoned without Lyndon. The majority leader never performed with greater brilliance than he performed that August 21. He talked Florida's Senator Smathers into pairing his vote for the bill with the vote of Oklahoma's absent Senator Monroney against the bill. He persuaded Senator Young of North Dakota, Senator Frear of Delaware, and Senator Kerr of Oklahoma, all supporters of the bill, to take a walk down the corridors when the bell sounded for a roll call vote. He induced Senator Lausche of Ohio—against the Ohioan's own better judgment, as he ruefully confessed the next day—to switch his vote. And while the roll call actually was in progress, he saw to it that Republican Senator Bennett of Utah was high-pressured into voting against the bill in order to prevent a tie that might have embarrassed the Vice President.

In the end a vote that had been expected to go 46-39 in favor of the bill wound up 41-40 against the bill, and a statement of sound governmental policy went by the boards. Florida's two Senators did not vote. Every other Senator from the Deep South or the Old South went down the line for the bill: Hill, Sparkman, McClellan, Fulbright, Russell, Talmadge, Ellender, Long, Eastland, Stennis, Ervin, Jordan, Johnston, Thurmond, Byrd, and Robertson. Even Gore of Tennessee voted for it. But not Lyndon Johnson.

Now, if there is one thing made clear by the Index of key votes compiled by Americans for Constitutional Action, it is that the impression of "Southern conservatism" has a good deal of fiction mixed in with the fact. The ACA's analysis of 77 key Senate roll calls over a five year period discloses a good deal of liberalism in the nine States of the late Confederacy.

Johnson was recorded on 71 of the ACA's 77 key votes; he took a conservative position precisely seven times: In 1956, he voted to exempt natural gas producers from Federal regulation. In 1957 he voted against a fairly fantastic proposal by Wayne Morse to authorize 200,000 public housing units a year; he also voted against a civil rights amendment proposing to vest wide powers in the Attorney General to bring suits on behalf of Negro complainants. (He is committed, by his pledge to the Democratic national platform, to support this "Title III" amendment now.) In 1958, he voted against a move by Senator Kennedy to liberalize unemployment compensation benefits, against an unwise effort by Douglas to cut income and excise taxes, and against Senator McNamara's $2 billion school construction bill. In 1959, he voted in favor of retaining an anti-Communist oath in the National Defense Education Act. Those seven votes are the sum total of the conservative votes cast by Senator Johnson 1955-59, in terms of the ACA rating.

What of his 64 other recorded votes in this period? Eight roll calls raised questions of private ownership as opposed to government ownership; Johnson took a conservative position on none of these. Eight roll calls raised questions of individual liberty as opposed to government coercion; Johnson took a conservative position on none of these. Ten roll calls raised questions of policy against communism; Johnson took a conservative position on one of these, the anti-Communist oath noted above.

Where do we find Lyndon Johnson in this period? With the exception of two votes already mentioned, against especially extravagant programs of school construction and public housing, the Senator from Texas plumped for every significant spending and subsidy scheme that reached the floor. He supported lavish spending for local sewage works, aid to depressed areas, high crop supports, subsidies for fishing vessels, and subsidies for dry-docks (even Kennedy opposed him on this last one). His affirmative vote represented the difference between passing and killing Hubert Humphrey's $400 million scheme for a Federal Youth Conservation Corps. He voted for

Federal construction of the Hells Canyon dam; he voted to override the 1959 veto of an omnibus public works bill; he refused last year to accept a cut of even $100 million in a $1.3 billion bill for foreign military aid. He was entirely agreeable to having American tax funds poured into communist dominated satellites.

Johnson's votes in the field of labor are especially notable. Between June 13 and June 17, 1958, five significant roll calls were taken on amendments proposed to the Labor-Management Reporting and Disclosure Act. One of these would have permitted the States to exercise jurisdiction in the "no man's land" that is created when the National Labor Relations Board declines to act; Johnson refused to accept even this small degree of States' rights. Two other amendments, both sponsored by Senator Knowland, would have protected a union member's right of secret ballot; Johnson opposed both of them. A fourth amendment was intended to prevent the use of union dues for political purposes unrelated to collective bargaining; Johnson voted nay. The fifth was designed to give employers some protection against the brutally unfair device of secondary boycotts and hot cargo coercion; again Johnson voted nay.

The following spring, April 22-24, 1959, the same questions came up again. Johnson was nothing if not consistent. He voted against McClellan's "Bill of Rights" amendment; he voted against a "no man's land" provision; he voted against an extension of the secondary boycott ban to unions not covered by Taft-Hartley. This record would seem to demonstrate sufficient penance, in labor's eyes, for the mortal sin Johnson committed in voting for the Taft-Hartley Act 13 years ago, but the Senator's old conservative image comes back to the banquet halls like Banquo's ghost. "We worked night and day in Los Angeles to get Kennedy nominated," said Reuben Soderstrom, president of the Illinois AFL-CIO, "but the Democrats made chumps of us and gave us Johnson anyway. There isn't a labor official in the country who feels good about the Johnson thing."

Brother Soderstrom, there aren't too many Southerners who feel good about the Johnson thing either. The week after the Los Angeles convention, a remarkable form letter came to newspaper offices across the country, the literary labor of one of the Senator's fans in Houston. This gentleman proposed that groups of 30 persons be formed, each of whom would deposit a nickel in a mite box labeled "Late Blooming Judas," with a message inside to LBJ: "Judas had his 30 pieces of silver. Here are yours." In Charleston, S. C., Tom Waring of the *News Courier* termed Johnson's nomination "a masterful stroke of political fraud." In August, Roy V. Harris of the *Courier*, a choleric fellow in his calmer moments, fairly outdid himself: "There is no force on earth sufficient to make me swallow John Kennedy, Lyndon Johnson and the damnable platform which they are trying to ram down our throats." In Mississippi, where Congressman John Bell Williams had remarked in February that he believed more Southerners would vote for Adam Clayton Powell than for Lyndon Johnson, rebellious forces headed by Governor Ross Barnett prepared to carry the State for uncommitted electors.

Love that Lyndon? Not down South. And it was down South that the Senator was expected to charm the Byrds from the trees. In the light of recent Presidential history, it is difficult to understand the professionals' faith in such a gambit. The beloved Alben Barkley was put on the ticket in 1948: the electors of Alabama, Louisiana, Mississippi, South Carolina, and one maverick from Tennessee went for the States' Rights ticket anyhow. In 1952, Sparkman of Alabama was the sop, and in 1956, Kefauver of bordering Tennessee was the putative appeal; each time, Florida, Kentucky, Louisiana, Oklahoma, Tennessee, Texas and Virginia went Republican.

What of November? Things are different this year. Nixon is no Eisenhower, but Kennedy, at the same time, has liabilities that Adlai Stevenson never had to cope with. The movement toward independent electors is not nearly as well organized, *so far*, as the States' Rights movement of 1948. Many Democratic officeholders, such as Virginia's Governor Almond, are publicly supporting the national ticket; they haven't had a judgeship for eight years, and they hunger for the old days of Presidential patronage. If the Los Angeles convention had put Symington on the ticket, or Washington's affable Senator Jackson, or almost anyone but Humphrey, the South probably would have returned, grumbling, to the Democratic fold.

It is an ironic commentary on the illogical character of Southern politics that the convention chose instead the man least likely to help the ticket where the ticket needs help the most. For Lyndon is known as the Southerner who turned his back on the South, and the South, ever sensitive to deliberate slight, may yet turn its back on Lyndon.

Barry Goldwater of Arizona

By Edwin McDowell   *(From the 14 September 1963 issue)*

(Mr. McDowell was an editorial writer for the Arizona Republic.*)*

The crowd was on its feet applauding, whistling and cheering as the erect, bronzed figure made his way slowly toward the microphone. Enthusiastic delegates from Hawaii stopped him long enough to adorn his neck with a colorful lei. Well-wishers reached out to shake his hand as he neared the speaker's rostrum. The ovation grew louder and louder until it cascaded throughout the Presidential Room of the Statler-Hilton and threatened to spill out onto 16th Street.

It was still a long 12 months until the National Convention at San Francisco in July 1964. But to the more than 600 registrants from 45 states in Washington, D.C., for the Sixth HUMAN EVENTS Political Action Conference, there was no doubt who deserved the GOP presidential nomination: Arizona's Sen. Barry Goldwater.

In fact, Barry Goldwater long had been the almost unanimous choice of both Republican and conservatives for the presidency. Now suddenly, through the summer of 1963, it was becoming apparent, from polls and from the deep, enthusiastic support that the Goldwater name generated from one end of the nation to the other—that Mr. Conservative's widening political appeal was winning him the backing of voters who only short months before were content to accept the liberal description of conservatives as political anachronisms.

"The liberal approach to the problems that beset us both at home and abroad has been given every conceivable chance," Goldwater told the delegates. "It has been tried, and tried, and tried, over and over and over again. And it has never worked."

Since he came to the Senate in an upset victory in 1952, on what he unabashedly claims were Dwight Eisenhower's coattails, the 54-year-old Goldwater has never deviated from his mission to "make the word conservative a respectable word."

No one has ever worked harder on behalf of any cause. For the past half-dozen years Barry Goldwater has tirelessly traveled from Atlantic to Pacific, from the Mexican to Canadian borders, delivering his message, sometimes speaking on both coasts the same day. By commercial airplane or flying his own twin-engine Beechcraft Bonanza, by rented auto or in his Corvette Sting-Ray, he has traveled to massive rallies in Madison Square Garden or in Detroit's Masonic Temple, to informal coffee-klatches in Maine and Utah and to all Democratic gatherings in the heartland of Dixie, where no real live Republican official ever before had set foot.

His book, *The Conscience of a Conservative*, has, unbelievably, sold *more than 1 million copies* (and has been described as "the best-selling book of political philosophy in our century"). And Goldwater himself spent several days at Yale in 1962 under sponsorship of the Chubb Fellowship (which brings prominent persons in public life to Eli), explaining his beloved conservative philosophy.

Undeniably, the Goldwater charisma continues to attract converts to conservatism. In an informal poll conducted by M. Stanton Evans, editor of the Indianapolis *News*, students—asked to name the individuals or publications that were most effective in crystallizing their political views—pointed to Barry Goldwater and his book.

Back to the Store in '64'

Even those who most vigorously oppose Goldwater's "quaint, antediluvian" views are impressed with his refusal to take himself seriously. In fact, Goldwater has been able to obtain a hearing even from those whose disagreement with his personal views runs from mild to pathological. Williams S. White, the eminently fair and intellectually honest syndicated columnist, wrote in *Harper's*, "Here in Goldwater, is an absolutely honest politician." James Reston, writing in the New York conservative, said of Goldwater: "He is an honest conservative. He is attractive personally."

The New York *Herald Tribune* in 1960, before it became the fountainhead for the Rockefeller 1964 thrust, said admiringly, "The Goldwater formula is simple: be honest."

Most surprising of all, perhaps, was the assessment of Goldwater by Karl E. Meyer, editorial writer for the rabidly anti-Goldwater Washington *Post*. Writing in *The Progressive* in April 1961, Meyer spoke of the "stoutness and general decency of his character." Goldwater, Meyer said, "*cares* about principles . . . fights cleanly and has usually shown a scrupulous regard for the rules of the game." He is "a decent, upright and thoroughly attractive politician."

And so he is. True, in the past, liberals could afford to be tolerant of the Arizona anomaly, for there seemed little or no chance that his philosophy would ever appeal to more than an insignificant few in either party. Now that Goldwater has, almost single-handedly, shifted the Republican party from the left side of the road to the solid terrain of the right, it is unlikely that they will remain tolerant.

No man ever has been more a product of his environment than is Barry Morris Goldwater.

Few men have ever taken more or given as much in return to their native states as has the Arizona junior senator. And no politician has ever been more genuinely in love with the state he represents than is Mr. Conservative. Years before he joined the U.S. Senate, businessman Goldwater was to write of his native state:

"Arizona is a state of mind, some say. To others, it is a state of reality—but to all people it is a state of Beauty in all its many facets. Sometimes hers is the beauty of dark clouds and rain. Sometimes the beauty of her people and her history. Then again the light touch of moonlight adds softness to the contrasted brilliance of her sun."

The Goldwater Family: Pioneers, Patriots, Builders

When Michael (Big Mike) Goldwasser left his home in Konin, a province of Prussia after the third partition of Poland, he had no thought of emigrating to America. But after taking up residence briefly in Germany, Paris, and London (long enough to marry Sara Nathan and Anglicize his name to Goldwater), he gave in to younger brother Joseph's importunity and set out to seek his fortune in the American West.

The Goldwater brothers arrived in San Francisco in 1852, during the height of the gold rush. They quickly decided there was more money to be made peddling merchandise to prospectors rather than panning for gold, as almost the entire population of California seemed to be doing. The immigrant merchants didn't strike it rich, but within two years they had scraped together enough money to open the first Goldwater establishment in the brawling frontier town of Sonora.

Gunpowder and Calico

The first Goldwater store in Arizona was opened at La Paz, on the Colorado River. In 1860, the brothers moved six miles downstream where they constructed a new store on the river bank and laid out the settlement of Ehrenberg (named after a friend, a German-born mining engineer, who had been murdered by outlaws or Indians). The store doubled as city hall, jail and the territory's first post office. (Finding no other official on hand, Big Mike swore himself in as postmaster.)

The Goldwaters helped lay out the wagon route from Ehrenberg to Prescott, the territorial capital. Countless times they hauled merchandise to military posts in the interior. And often they were harassed by Indians.

In 1870 the brothers sold their Erhenberg store, opened a store in the infant city of Phoenix, sold it four years later, and decided to try their luck in Prescott. By the time Big Mike retired to California, 11 years later, the Prescott store was acclaimed the finest in all Arizona.

Two Brothers

There is some question about the authenticity of the tale that Baron Goldwater (Barry's father) came to Phoenix after playing a showdown hand of casino with brother Morris to determine who would open a Goldwater store in the bustling young city. Nevertheless, Baron departed for Phoenix in 1895.

It was Morris Goldwater who, by example and by teaching, was to leave an indelible mark on nephew Barry. Arizona Territory was under control of the Republican administration when Morris set out to organize the Democrats in the early 1900's. And organize them he did: he served as mayor of Prescott for more than 20 years; he served as vice president of the 1910 Constitutional Convention; he was president of the 20th Territorial Council; and he served as the official and unofficial spokesman for the conservative Jeffersonian Democrats.

Baron Goldwater, on the other hand, was far more reserved, far more fastidious than his brother. Twelve years after his arrival in Phoenix he married Josephine Williams, a Chicago nurse who struck out for Arizona when doctors told her she had tuberculosis and might live only a short time. The doctors were wrong. "But I didn't know it then," Josephine Goldwater remembered, "so I bought a ticket on the Santa Fe and headed West." The ticket took her as far as Ash Fork, Ariz.

Planes, Radios, Cameras

Josephine Williams and Baron Goldwater married on New Year's Day, 1907. Exactly two years later, to the day, Barry Morris Goldwater was born—three years before the Arizona Territory became the 48th state. A Phoenix newspaperman predicted that the new arrival "promises to add luster to a family name already distinguished in the annals of Arizona."

The children of Baron and Josephine Goldwater—Barry, Bob and Carolyn—led normal active lives. Barry, always searching for new outlets for his unbridled energy, taught himself to play the saxophone, clarinet and mandolin. Then he discovered an exciting new invention, radio. Hanging around Early Neilson's shop on North Central, he and some friends built and operated amateur station 6BBH, which later became the present-day 5,000-watt KOY. Together they built a two-tube, 10-watt transmitter, and Barry went on the air with his own station, 6BPI.

Flying was still a relatively, risky business in 1930, yet Goldwater's compulsion always to be doing something new led him to take flying lessons. "I was up at 5 o'clock those mornings," he recalled. "I'd beat it out to the field, take my lessons and get back to the store in time for work. Mum (his nickname for his mother) never asked me what I was doing up at that hour and I didn't tell her. I found out later she thought it had something to do with a girl." Since then Maj. Gen. Goldwater has piloted more than 75 different aircraft, including 16 jets.

It was during the time that Goldwater first became interested in photography. During the 1930's his photographs of Arizona were exhibited in salons all over the world and throughout the U.S. He was elected to associate membership in the Royal Photography Society of London.

Unfortunately, little of the indefatigable Goldwater energy in those days was devoted to studies. Therefore his father decided not to allow him to return to Phoenix Union High School, where he had served as president of the freshman class, but where he came dangerously close to flunking. Baron Goldwater decided to enroll his son in Staunton (Va.) Military Academy, where he felt the rigorous discipline and rigid academic reputation would straighten out his eldest boy. When he graduated, Barry was awarded the Kable Medal as the outstanding all-around cadet.

The following fall Goldwater journeyed 100 miles southeast of his Phoenix home to enroll at the University of Arizona at Tucson. Sporting a 1929 Chrysler roadster, he wasn't long in making a name for himself. He was first string center on the freshman football team. He pledged Sigma Chi fraternity. He was elected class president for the second semester. He became chairman of the freshman Stadium Fund committee, in which capacity he proved his merits as a fund raiser for construction of the U of A football stadium. And, like most college kids of his era, he partied his way through "Button Up Your Overcoat," "Crazy Rhythm," "Diga Diga Doo," "Makin' Whoopee!" and "Sweet Sue—Just You."

Life was good to the freshman from the prominent Arizona family. Then one March evening in 1929 the bottom fell out of the fun-loving Goldwater's pleasurable life: Baron Goldwater had died of a heart attack. Barry, at age 20, was now the man of the Goldwater household. He no longer could enjoy the luxury of college.

Barry Goldwater did not step immediately into his father's well-polished shoes in the family store. He started, instead, as a junior clerk. "He's one boss's son who really worked in every department in the store," confided Mrs. Sugar Burlingham, a Goldwater employee for 39 years. "He was always one of us; you'd never know he was the boss's son."

A Beloved Employer

When the store initiated a 5-day work week for all employees in 1951, Barry—whom detractors accuse of wanton disregard for his fellow man—said, "The tempo of today's working and living makes a 5-day week imperative to maintain human rights."

"He was one of the best loved men there was," said Kathleen Wuersch, who recently retired after 37 years with the store. "He gave me inspiration to work up, to keep at it. Even as a young boy he inspired people. There was just something about him.

"Oftentimes girls came to Arizona with sick husbands, went to work in the store, and when Barry heard about their troubles he helped them out with their doctor bills. He was that kind of person—one in a million."

The stores merged with Associated Dry Goods Corp. of New York in 1962. Barry retains the title of chairman of the board, although there no longer is a board of directors, and brother Bob remains president—a title he assumed in 1953 when Barry left for Washington.

Late in 1932 Barry was introduced to Margaret ("Peggy") Johnson, a Muncie, Ind., girl whose father was a founder and vice president of Borg-Warner Corp. The Arizonan was persistent. After what he describes as "a cross-country courtship" which took him to Michigan, Washington and Indiana, he proposed on New Year's Eve—in a phone booth. They were married on Sept. 22, 1934, in Grace Episcopal Church in Muncie amid the good wishes of relatives and friends.

Goldwater Wins Senate Seat Against Overwhelming Odds

A few months before America's official entry into World War II, 31-year-old reserve officer Goldwater signed for a year's active duty with the Army Air Corps and was assigned to nearby Luke Field. He suffered from a stigmatism and from knees badly battered from football. But he was valuable enough to the quickening defense effort to teach pilots the art of aerial gunnery and to author the widely used wartime manual on fixed gunnery. Still, Goldwater wanted to fly. And it wasn't long before he hit on a workable scheme:

Riding as a passenger in the rear cockpit of airplanes, Goldwater used his photography talents to take pictures of pilots as they flew by in other planes. Instead of selling the pictures, he traded them for flight instruction, and became so proficient that when he later demanded an opportunity to qualify for Service Pilot wings, he passed without difficulty. Soon afterwards he passed the test for a full pilot's rating.

In 1942, Capt. Goldwater volunteered for the lone flight of single-engine fighter planes (P-47's) across the North Atlantic. Later he flew cargo across the Hump from India to China. When the war ended, Lt. Col. Goldwater remained in the reserve, becoming the first federally recognized officer in the Arizona National Guard when it was organized in 1946.

Public Service Calls

Barry returned to his family and to the store after the war. The older, more mature businessman had developed other interests, and soon obtained his first taste of public life. Arizona, in 1946, became the second state to pass a right-to-work law. And Goldwater headed the retailers' portion of the campaign.

The following year he became general chairman of the Community Chest campaign which raised, at that time, the largest sum ever collected on behalf of the city's chest activities. He served on the Arizona Interstate Stream Commission and as a member of the Interior Department's advisory commission on Indian Affairs. He was a director of the Phoenix Art Museum and the Museum of Northern Arizona. And he served as director of the Boy Scouts.

Through it all, Goldwater had managed to stay aloof from partisan politics. The trouble was, so did most other leading citizens of Phoenix, with the result that Arizona's capital city was a wide-open town: a patronage-ruled city hall, gambling and prostitution flourished and contracts were awarded on the basis of political cronyism.

In 1949, however, a group of prominent Phoenicians decided to form a council-manager charter government. And Goldwater, Phoenix's Man of the Year, was inveigled into running by his longtime friend and former North Central Athletic Club member, Harry Rosenzweig.

Barry wrote brother Bob and Bill Saufley, another Goldwater executive, of his decision, saying, "I don't think a man can live with himself when he asks others to do his dirty work for him. I couldn't criticize the government of this city when I myself refused to help. I don't know if we can win but if we do then I know Phoenix will have two years of damned good government that I hope will set a pattern for the coming years and the coming generations."

The 40-year-old-businessman not only led the ticket, carrying every precinct, but he polled three times as many votes as his nearest rival. He was elected vice-chairman of the council, and, with his help, the new group managed to give Phoenix the kind of government it had not known for years, so good that in 1950, Phoenix was one of 11 cities named "All-Americans City," because of the progress it made in city government.

The following year Howard Pyle, a popular Arizona radio announcer, announced his decision to run for governor. Barry Goldwater agreed to serve as his campaign manager.

Barnstorming by Plane

All during that summer, candidate and campaign manager hopped, skipped and jumped from city to town in Goldwater's red, white and blue Beechcraft, running up more than 22,000 miles together. When the returns were in, Pyle had won by almost 3,000 votes—a tribute to his tireless campaign and his tireless campaign manager. Almost overnight, the Republican party found itself alive and kicking.

Barry Goldwater knew what he was up against in his race for the U.S. Senate in 1952. Ernest McFarland, a rustic, slow-spoken glad-hander, not only was a popular figure in Arizona but was also Senate majority leader under Truman. Furthermore, the Democrats were unveiling their big guns—Speaker Sam Rayburn (Tex.) and Vice President Alben Barkley (who made TV plugs)—in support of McFarland, who seemed little concerned about Goldwater. His strategy seemed to be to ignore the upstart businessman. But Goldwater had no intention of being ignored, or of ignoring McFarland.

Goldwater tore into McFarland's earlier claim that he was one of the four most powerful men in the United States. One by one, the challenger enumerated examples of Democratic mink coats and freezers, and asked if the incumbent, as one of the four most powerful Americans, claimed 25 per cent of the corruption.

He lashed out at McFarland for describing the Korean War as "a cheap war." "I challenge the junior senator from Arizona," Goldwater exclaimed; "to find a single mother or father who counts our casualties as cheap—who'll be willing to exchange the life of one American boy for that of nine Communists or nine hundred Red Communists, or nine million Communists."

As his campaign gathered momentum, Goldwater preached appeals to conservatism, for economy in government, for peace with honor in Korea at each whistle stop—or, in this case, at each country airport. Throughout the state, Goldwater workers installed 200 sets of Burma-Shave like signs which taunted:

"Mac is for Harry / Harry's all through. / You be for Barry / 'Cause Barry's for you.— *Goldwater for senator.*"

When the tumult and the shouting ended, Goldwater defeated McFarland by 7,000 votes—36,000 fewer than Eisenhower defeated Stevenson by in Arizona.

Although Goldwater has often said he was "the greatest coat-tail rider in history," the fact is he ran an outstanding race against overwhelming odds.

Corruption, Murder

Once in Congress, the Arizonan wasted little time establishing a conservative image. Four months after taking his oath of office, Goldwater delivered his first major speech, speaking out against the futility of price controls. His first major debate (over foreign aid) was with veteran Sen. Walter George (D.-Ga.).

He readily struck up a friendship with Robert Taft, who personally appointed Goldwater to the Labor and Public Welfare Committee—a post where Goldwater became acquainted with another freshman senator who was on the committee, John F. Kennedy of Massachusetts.

Except for his involvement almost seven years earlier in Arizona's successful effort to pass a right-to-work law, Goldwater had little experience with labor problems.

But he proved eager to learn and, in addition, proved to be a good listener. What he heard in sworn testimony before the Labor Committee both shocked and dismayed him. Tales of corruption within the hierarchy of powerful unions . . . stories of intimidation . . . of beatings . . . even of murder . . . quickly made Goldwater realize that something was dangerously wrong when any one group in America could obtain so much power and could use it to flaunt law and order.

Goldwater loosed his first major blast at the officials of organized labor in a 1955 speech to the Republican National Committee School. In it, he hit out at compulsory political "contributions" for purposes of electing Democrats. He rapped organized labor's undue influence in Congress. And he enumerated—and graphically illustrated—acts of violence perpetrated by unions during strikes.

After that Goldwater was a marked man, and he did nothing to finch from organized labor's hostility. His particular *bete noire* was Walter Reuther, whose United Auto Workers had perpetrated numerous acts of violence and coercion during the lengthy Kohler strike in Wisconsin. Reuther, Goldwater declared at one point, "is more dangerous to America than the Sputniks, or anything Russia might do." Reuther quickly fired back that Goldwater was "this country's number one political fanatic, its number one anti-labor baiter, its number one peddler of class hatred."

The feud continued cross-country from Detroit to Washington. All the while the nation looked on, fascinated. It had been a long time since anyone had taken on Walter Reuther or any other powerful labor leader. As the Rackets Committee uncovered widespread corruption and coercive tactics in organized labor's ranks, Goldwater's warnings were remembered. People began asking questions. And soon letters began finding their way onto his desk from union members who offered to talk if they and their families could be assured of protection from the reprisals certain to follow.

Not unexpectedly, organized labor singled out Goldwater as its archenemy. In 1956 the AFL-CIO gave him a "zero" rating for some 20 important issues on which it claimed he voted "wrong" from the union point of view. In February 1958, organized labor officially named Goldwater as the senator it would most like to beat in an election.

COPE Loses Battle

Just before Goldwater's overwhelming re-election in 1958, Fulton Lewis Jr. warned that the Arizonan faced a "fight to the death" from organized labor. A Chicago *Tribune* reporter, after an on-the-spot investigation in Arizona, reported that an estimated $500,000 was being wielded by COPE in cash, time and services, in an effort to defeat Goldwater. Two COPE officials were convicted of distributing unidentified campaign literature in Arizona which sought to link Goldwater with communism.

But the Arizona senator continued making speeches . . . continued hammering away at the theme that the working man was being exploited by his bosses . . . continued charging that organized labor had too much power . . . that it was tyrannical bosses, not rank-and-file workers, he was against.

His crusade began to have results, especially when a *Saturday Evening Post* article described him as the freshman with "more leadership potential" than any other Republican in the Senate during the past 10 years.

Civil Rights Record

Organized labor is not alone in trying to pillory Goldwater. It is now frankly acknowledged that he is the major politician who appeals most to the South; therefore, liberals, looking ahead to the 1964 presidential election, have attempted to depict him as a segregationist.

The fact is that few men in public life have expressed their sympathy for Negroes—verbally and through actions—more often than Goldwater. As a member of the Phoenix City Council, politician Goldwater voted to desegregate the restaurant at Sky Harbor Airport. As chief of staff of the Arizona Air National Guard, Col. Goldwater handed down an order that segregation was henceforth to be banned in their air guard.

And in both 1951 and 1952, private citizen Goldwater donated $200 to the legal defense fund of the Maricopa County (Phoenix) NAACP in an effort to speed integration of public schools. He remained a member of the NAACP until 1956, and is today a member of the Urban League, also dedicated to aiding the Negro cause.

"My firm conviction," Goldwater wrote to a Southern editor earlier this year, "is that desegregation should be conducted at the state level without federal intervention. Therefore I felt that by contributing to the local group [NAACP] as a private citizen, I was helping its chances of resolving the problem."

It is true that Goldwater opposes federal intervention, including the proposed "public accommodations" law. Yet during debate over this year's civil rights bill, Goldwater was quoted in a front page New York *Times* story as saying it was unquestionably "morally wrong" to deny Negroes equal access to public accommodations. Nevertheless, he said, an attempt to correct this moral evil by law "will not solve anything"; such a law would only "upset individual rights and states' rights."

Barry's brother Bob, president of the Goldwater stores, recently commented, "Barry has always been very much for the Negro. He and I grew up here in Phoenix, played football and baseball with them. We had a lot of Negro friends, and hope we still do." He then proceeded to point out that the Goldwater stores employed 17 Negroes, several in jobs of supervisory nature, out of a total of some 400 employees. This amounts to slightly better than 4 per cent in an area where Negroes comprise only about 1/2 of 1 per cent of the Phoenix-area population—a figure far more liberal than quotas demanded by the NAACP during recent nationwide protest marches and demonstrations.

Barry's boyhood friend, Harry Rosenzweig, said, "When citizens in our town felt it was time to end segregation in the schools, the Catholic leader of that effort—a man far from Barry in political matters—received a generous check from Goldwater to help that effort."

States Must Interpret

In *The Conscience of a Conservative*, Goldwater said:

"I have great respect for the Supreme Court as an institution, but I cannot believe that I display that respect by submitting abjectly to abuses of power by the court, and by condoning its unconstitutional abuses of power by the court, and by condoning its unconstitutional trespass into the legislative sphere of government. The Congress and the states, equally with the Supreme Court, are obliged to interpret and comply with the Constitution according to their own lights. I therefore support all effort by the states, excluding violence, of course, to preserve their rightful powers over education."

Herbert Hoover: 1874-1964

By Eugene Lyons   *(From the 31 October 1964 issue)*

Over 15 years ago I wrote a short biography of Herbert Hoover which I called *Our Unknown President*. I was alluding, of course, to what seemed to me the tragic failure of the American people to comprehend the human being behind the masks.

The falsest and cruelest of these masks had been deliberately fabricated by partisan malice. For some 15 years hordes of propagandists labored zealously on the myth of a monster who "caused" a depression and then "did nothing" to alleviate its horrors.

In utter contempt of fact and logic, they brainwashed the country and especially the new generation that had little personal memory of Hoover's epic humanitarian achievements before he came to the White House—into accepting him as a symbol of the very things he most abhorred: fascism, reaction, depression, complacency in the face of human suffering.

Another mask had been imposed by his own introverted nature, by his essential shyness and distaste for personal ballyhoo. Uniquely among political leaders, Hoover was compelled by his innermost character to build walls between his private and his public personalities.

He succeeded in concealing, as he wrote at the time, "the warm, whimsical and tender Hoover known to his intimates, the very human and deeply humane Quaker behind the solemn facade."

Unhappily, this native mask greatly facilitated the job of ungallant and dirty-minded little men in big places who were fashioning the grotesque myth. For one thing, had the people had a better understanding of the real man, they would not so readily have surrendered their common sense by accepting the propaganda hoax.

For another, Hoover was inhibited by his sensibilities from putting up a robust and effective self-defense. He would not, indeed could not, descend to the level of demagogic mudgunning, and so left a clear field for mischievous vilification.

But even before my book came off the press its title began to lose some of its validity. Around 1947 it became evident that Hoover's long ordeal by abuse was drawing to an end.

With the passing of the New Deal era more and more Americans were becoming ashamed of its self-righteous immorality and its zeal for attacking critics. And the public rehabilitation of our 31st President proceeded with dramatic swiftness.

The speed and completeness of the collapse of the ugly myth is a remarkable episode in our national history. Republican politicians who had long sought to disown Hoover were suddenly treating him as one of the party's important assets. Even the so-called liberal press turned deferential. Those who continued to distrust Hoover's views were moved by his moral stature.

In the renewed esteem for the man, in the revived pride in his greatness, there was a strong element of remorse. The country recognized that in persecuting Hoover it had dishonored itself, and to this day the injustice visited upon him weights on the national conscience. It was naturally assumed, in the years of his eclipse, that Hoover was "embittered." The assumption was false. He was saddened and profoundly hurt, but calm and tolerant. Upon the mudgunners he looked not in hatred but in pity.

His humility was inborn, Quakerish, but too genuine to be alloyed with false modesty. In the midst of his ordeal he knew, with an engineer's knowledge of reality, that time inevitably would straighten out the record.

It was this that helped him to remain equable under the hail of insults. He stood where he had always stood, for it was not in him to make compromises. He did not catch up with the people—the people were streaming back to him, shamefaced and penitent, after their hectic wanderings.

Fortunately for himself and his friends, the inevitable change came while he was still alive. Fortunately for the country, it came while his amazing abilities and energies were undiminished, so that he could carry out more great enterprises in benevolence and public service.

The fact that popular admiration and affection for Hoover continued to grow attested, I think, to the core of simple decency at the heart of America. His life adds up to a classic triumph of integrity.

The one thing that his partisans and detractors always agreed upon was that Hoover was "no politician." The implication was not that he was deficient in sound political judgment, but that he lacked dexterity in selling himself and his policies to the crowd, in playing on mass emotion.

There simply was not enough flexibility, not enough gift for cutting moral corners, in his make-up. Ideas to him were not externals to be adjusted to current fashions. The professionals in the political game could never feel at their ease with this stern amateur and his moral imperatives.

Normally great men are less heroic to their intimates than to the public at large. Hoover was the supreme exception. Twenty years ago I wrote that "Hoover has a multitude of enemies but no ex-friends." Nothing has happened since then to change this. Not one of the men and women who worked closely with him, through all the decades of his immense and varied activities, ever turned against him.

Their devotion to him came close to adoration and had in it, too, an element of protectiveness, as if he needed to be shielded against the pettiness and connivings of lesser men.

The country senses the wholeness, the genuineness of Herbert Hoover. It saw in him, as in a mirror, the best in its own character and history. He was the instrument of America's most humane and disinterested impulses in relation to the rest of mankind—a personification of charity joined with efficiency that is somehow peculiarly American.

Herbert Hoover was a great monolithic figure. Rarely has such a capacious intelligence as his been combined with such a great heart and robust spirit. In paying homage to him now we, his countrymen, pay homage to ourselves. For his career was deep-rooted in the American soil and integral with our national heritage.

The Rise and Stand of George Corley Wallace

By Victor Gold (*From the 27 January 1968 issue*)

From the outset of his remarkable political career, George Corley Wallace always looked one election down the road.

As James E. (Big Jim) Folsom's south Alabama campaign manager in 1954, then Circuit Judge Wallace laid the red day groundwork for his own gubernatorial race four years later. Though defeated in 1958 by John Patterson, Wallace immediately launched his 1962 campaign for governor before Patterson was even sworn into office. Finally winning the governorship in '62, Wallace within four months converted the front walk of the University of Alabama's Foster Auditorium into a national springboard that sent him winging into the 1964 presidential primaries, which in turn . . .

Small wonder that the question in Alabama today, despite the recent recurrence of Lurleen Wallace's illness, is not *what* makes George Wallace run, but where and when he intends to stop running. And the answer, according to Alabamians most familiar with his rise from statewide obscurity to national prominence, is nowhere short of the White House—in 1972.

To be sure, George Wallace, a political realist, knows that even if the latest of long hot summers of racial violence has enhanced his political appeal beyond the Mason-Dixon line, this year the best a Wallace third-party candidacy can do (or worst, as the case may be) will be to gum up the country's electoral machinery and perhaps exert a modicum of political leverage on the major parties and candidates.

But then again, what sophisticate or oddsmaker a few years ago would have predicted that come 1968 a former governor of Alabama, operating out of the branchheads rather than the mainstream of American political life, would accomplish even that?

Moreover, having learned his trade in a state where politics is the art not so much of the possible as the *impossible*, Wallace also knows that voracious ambition is not fed on realism alone. After all, if he had been an undiluted realist he might still be an Alabama circuit judge.

Indeed, the record shows that bucking the Establishment and the odds has been a Wallace penchant from his undergraduate political days at the University of Alabama, when he was a non-affiliated country boy challenging the big city boys' fraternity machine for control of student government, right down to the movement in early 1966 when he decided to run his wife for governor, although, as he concedes, "Nobody in this state but me thought she could get elected . . ." (including, we are left to surmise, the prospective candidate herself).

But the gamble of gambles, the calculated risk that gave him an unprecedented grip on political power in Alabama and made possible his current bit to "Stand Up for America" as a presidential candidate, occurred that bright Tuscaloosa afternoon in May 1963, when then Gov. Wallace burst across national television screens in charismatic confrontation with then Deputy Atty. Gen. Nicholas Katzenbach and two would-be Negro matriculants at the University of Alabama.

It is typical of Wallace's anomalous career that his "stand at the schoolhouse door," though viewed by millions, remains one of the more obscure political events of our time, obfuscated in equal part by Wallaceites and anti-Wallaceites.

Questions are raised: What were the circumstances surrounding the Justice Department's aerial surveillance of the campus and Atty. Gen. Robert Kennedy's contacts with state and university officials in the days preceding the confrontation? Was the entire affair a choreographed, pre-arranged political charade, as charged in 1966 by Lurleen Wallace's Republican opponent, James Martin? Or was Wallace indeed manning the parapets of constitutional principle?

Did Wallace "back down" from a pledge to go to jail, if necessary, to make his constitutional point? Or did he, although finally stepping aside, leave Katzenbach with knees aquiver, as was reported at the time by one Alabama political commentator?

In Alabama, almost five years after the event, these questions still trigger fierce and windy arguments—disputes so colored by current political passions that it remains for the passage of time alone to provide light instead of heat to the subject. But this much is beyond dispute: If Wallace lost the constitutional confrontation, he won the political war. True, at last count, approximately 300 Negroes were attending the University of Alabama as students. But at last poll, George Wallace, now governor by proxy, held the allegiance of his state's white majority as has no man before, not even his Populist predecessors, Bibb Graves in the 1920s and '30s, and Jim Folsom in the '40s and '50s.

In fact, much of the confusion regarding Wallace's true ideological bent—whether he is "conservative" or "liberal"—stems from a futile effort to translate the distinctive cast of Southern Populist tradition into national political terms.

Pointing up this semantic conflict, Wallace says he is a conservative "in the sense that I am against government regulations," although his administration in Alabama was undeniably marked by an expansion of centralized state power at the expense of local governments. His rationale: that "local governments" within a state are mere component subdivisions, while on the national level, the federal government, far from having created the states, was their creation.

This is a correct constitutional distinction, to be sure. But to a local or county school board in Alabama, elected by and for the citizens of the immediate area and threatened by overriding state authority out of Montgomery, "government regulation" is "government regulation"—and George Wallace's "conservatism" on the matter of local government is open to question.

Moreover, in a "Meet the Press" appearance last year, Wallace himself compounded that question when he explained that his well-known "segregation today . . . segregation tomorrow . . . segregation forever!" inaugural pledge wasn't meant to be taken literally, only symbolically. What is really meant, he told Lawrence Spivak, was "local government forever!"

But, Wallace's critics ask, if the word "segregation" uttered in 1963 can be redefined as "local government" in 1967, what might "local government" come to mean when fresh political "symbolism" is called for by "President" Wallace in the years ahead?

As Spivak and other experts at cross-examination have learned, however, there is no yardage to be gained by pursuing such semantic points with George Wallace. Second to no man on the contemporary political scene, he has proved himself a master at verbal counterattack, whether confronted by a Nicholas Katzenbach, a national correspondent—or a constitutional nicety not to his "conservative" liking. And this, too, is beyond dispute. For if it were not the case, Lurleen Burns Wallace would be a former First Lady today instead of governor of Alabama, having succeeded a governor constitutionally barred from succeeding himself.

Again, there is the question raised by traditional conservatives regarding the Wallace Administration's unprecedented borrow, tax, spend (and elect) philosophy. The gross disbursements of the State of Alabama, for example, were $963 million when Wallace came to office. Now they are $1.44 billion, an increase of 50 per cent. In five years under the Wallaces, the state's bonded indebtedness had tripled—$750 million in new borrowing.

Wallace "proudly" justifies and defends this spending on grounds that he is "for progress"; e.g., the most massive construction and biggest pension expenditures in the state's history, along with other government "benefits" financed only partially by the expanded borrowing, a 4 per cent sales tax, doubled drivers' license fees and additional levies on the fiscal resources and credit of the state and its three million citizens.

But by Wallace's "symbolic" definition, these programs are also "conservative," as opposed to "liberal," because, among other things in their favor, "at least we're not spending the money to build roads in Cuba or India."

Not since Louisiana's Sen. Huey P. Long and his "Share-Our-Wealth" third-party movement has any Deep Southern leader received such intense national media exposure. Yet the entire focus has been on the Governor Who Stood at the Schoolhouse Door, and the road he took from there—that is, the Wallace record from 1963 to the present.

Save for an "authorized" biography by his press secretary which gave a sanitized version of these early years, little detail has been furnished concerning the pre-Stand Wallace: the man on the rise who, before he could challenge the national Establishment, took on that of his own state—defeated it—then recreated it in his own image. (Thus, testifying to his final victory over the city boys, the "unofficial" Alabama auto plate today proclaims, This Is Wallace Country.)

Well, then, the question recurs, what exactly is George Wallace? "Conservative"? "Liberal"? "Populist"? An examination of the Alabama record, 1948-63, retracing the steps that led to the Schoolhouse Door, might provide the answers that have thus far evaded even the probes of Lawrence Spivak and other skilled inquisitors like him.

And certainly Wallace himself, by repeated attacks on California Gov. Ronald Reagan's "liberal" past, has invited a review of his own ideological origins.

Big Jim Folsom and other Alabamians remember George Wallace under another label—Folsomite. Like "Share-Our-Wealth," "Folsomism" was a regional political phenomenon that never fulfilled its national ambitions. There was a time in Alabama, however, when Folsomism was a label that young non-Establishment "outs" like George Wallace did not shun. And yet, how many people today—even in Alabama—remember the mayfly Folsom presidential candidacy of 20 years ago? It was announced in a political season (Jan. 27, 1948) when, as now, a poll-depressed Democratic President faced the prospect of a splintered party coalition. Anticipating a year when anything might happen at the polls, Folsom, still an ambitious young Alabama governor, asked for a popular mandate to lay siege to the Democratic convention at Philadelphia in July, there to "raise a banner we can fight for." And what kind of banner would that be? "Liberal"? "Conservative"? Like Wallace's unfurling banner of 1'68, it was both—and neither.

On the extreme left hand, despite the Alabama for Harry Truman's vice presidential candidacy, Folsom had been a *Henry* Wallace delegate at the 1944 Democratic convention ("because of personal convictions," he said). Further, according to the London *Economist*, Folsom had won the governorship in 1946 "on the most liberal platform ever offered in Alabama."

But, on the other hand, this Henry Wallace fan, this "liberal," told members of the tongue-clucking Eastern press that if elected President he would operate on the principle that "racial barriers is a states' right proposition, and that is a question that should be worked out by each individual state."

As for the direction in which he would take the country if elected President, the "liberal" Alabama aspirant of 1948 promised to "mop up the monopolists, the Wall Street lawyers"—so far, so "liberal," but wait—"and the State Department fancy pants." (At this verbal juncture, it may be imagined, Chester Bowles dropped his end of the fighting banner.)

On the economic front, Folsom's '48 platform promised to "cover the entire United States with TVAs," and otherwise to expand federal "benefits" by redirecting foreign aid moneys "slushed" around the world "at the expense of American roads, schools and buildings." Two decades later, Wallace—"for progress" and an enthusiastic TVA supporter in his own right—wants it clearly understood that he isn't one of those "ultras who is against everything," since, after all, it's not the federal spending programs that are wrong, only "the bureaucrats" who enforce them (and, besides, we're not "slushing" it "to build roads in Cuba or India," are we?).

But if the Folsom and Wallace presidential candidates bear similarity in philosophy and platform, the parallel ends abruptly at the point where the electoral skills of Wallace, the political heir, exceed those of Folsom, the progenitor. For, while Wallace is emerging as a national force in 1968, Big Jim's '48 campaign proved an ignominious fizzle.

In the hot, early July hours when Harry Truman accepted the nomination at Philadelphia, the governor of Alabama was far removed from the scene—as were a number of other Alabamians who, sent to the convention, took premature leave because of differences with the national party over racial segregation policies. In fact, the record shows it was the Alabama delegation, led by Folsom's '46 gubernatorial opponent, Handy Ellis, and then Birmingham Police Commissioner Eugene (Bull) Connor, that led the historic "Dixiecrat" walkout.

And here we come to another contradictory note in tracing the ideological claims of George Corley Wallace. For the record also shows that whatever Presidential Candidate Wallace now thinks about the need for an independent third-party states' rights movement, State Rep. Wallace, as a member of the Alabama delegation, failed to join the states' rights brigade that charged out of Convention Hall 20 years ago.

He concluded that, in Alabama, loyalty to the Democratic party was the best long-range policy, no doubt remembering the wreckage of the career of U.S. Sen. Thomas J. Heflin, who had bolted to Hoover in 1928. And sure enough, despite the success of the Thurmond-Wright ticket in Alabama and nearby states in '48, within two years the Hill-Sparkman political faction, loyal to the national Democratic party, had recaptured the Alabama state central committee machinery. The "Dixiecrats" were out of business. But State Rep. Wallace, having kept his seat while all about him were leaving theirs, was very much a going political concern.

Re-elected to the House in 1950, Wallace continued to advocate "liberal" Folsom programs during the early years of the administration of Big Jim's successor (and, as time would prove, his predecessor), Gordon Persons. As a member of the legislature, the representative from Barbour County distinguished himself by his fight against sales tax proposals (though he would approve a sales tax increase as governor) and otherwise made a significant legislative contribution by initiating the Wallace Act, a revenue bond measure enabling Alabama municipalities to grant tax exemptions to new industry moving into their area.

Still, Wallace was unknown in most parts of the state. Then, in 1952, when he plunged into the race against Circuit Judge Clayton, he attracted the attention of interested political observers throughout the state. The contest was closely watched by Montgomery professionals as a possible straw vote in the wind for the '54 governor's race.

It was not Wallace's gubernatorial possibilities that were being assessed, needless to say, but those of Big Jim Folsom.

Wallace's uphill victory over Clayton, therefore, signaled a Folsom resurgence. And two years later the "Little Judge," as he now styled himself, enthusiastically took over the south Alabama managership of Folsom's tornadic "Y'all Come" campaign for re-election.

If this is the fact, however, then observers of that '54 race can attest to the fact that a Wallace reluctant is worth any three campaign managers in full cry. The "Little Judge" was omnipresent, hyperactive. He organized. He buttonholed. He took a personal hand in the production of a television documentary extolling his candidate's past record and future promise. He introduced Big Jim at rallies, answering opposition charges that the first Folsom administration had been fast and loose with state moneys, by challenging—and the words came back to haunt him in the years that followed—"If that's Folsomism, then I'm for Folsomism!"

Folsom won the May primary election without a runoff. Then, three short weeks later, the U.S. Supreme Court delivered its first school desegregation decision, and small tremors—soon to reach seismographic proportions—shook Alabama's political structure. Six months after Big Jim was sworn in for his second term, his political stock was plummeting and the word was out that he and his erstwhile south Alabama campaign manager had "broken."

What came to be called "seg" politics, in the cynical vernacular of the state's professionals, was now the dominant theme of all campaigns for office, overshadowing every other issue. Thus, when Circuit Judge Wallace threatened to incarcerate any FBI "snoopers" who might come within his jurisdiction to examine voting records, he got his first statewide headlines. Now he was the "Fighting Little Judge."

Having broken with Folsom and taken a seemingly bold position in opposition to federal desegregation efforts, Wallace at age 37 was by now ready for his own run for the Mansion.

There were formidable obstacles in his path, however, the greatest being that the political atmosphere was so trenchantly anti-Folsom as to place any of the governor's former associates under a heavy campaign handicap. That Wallace was able to overcome the handicap of having supported Folsom—in fact, surfacing as a leading candidate to rescue the *state from "Folsomism"* after a few weeks—was tribute to his fast-developing political genius. And though this first gubernatorial race was a losing effort, national party leaders and candidates who might underestimate Wallace's potential would do well to contemplate what the "Fighting Little Judge" achieved during an intensive four months' campaigning: (1) he won the support of a large number of Folsom campaign leaders and followers, along with (2) the endorsement of several of Alabama's most vehement anti-Folsom dailies; and (3) a sizable number of conservative businessmen who were impressed by the Wallace Act and his repudiation of "Folsomism"; (4) but not so much as to exclude the state's AFL-CIO which also endorsed him because of his pro-labor legislative record and his past affiliation with Folsom!

Running against his former pupil, Folsom himself was the victim of his own advice. When the sorcerer opened his campaign with an $80 pension pledge, Wallace kicked off his campaign with a $100 bid. Within days Folsom, in a stump speech, increased his figure to equal Wallace's. But then the apprentice, announcing that he had restudied the state's revenue possibilities, declared he could do better than $100. Ten dollars better, in fact. There, at $110, the bidding stopped. (Footnote to history, for what it may reveal about Alabama political credibility: the average pension payment during the George Wallace Administration was $80.)

Wallace, carrying the old-age vote and the segregation vote, as well as most of the old Folsom branchheads vote, led the ticket, soundly defeating his run-off opponent, State Sen. Ryan DeGraffenried, to win the governorship. And Folsomism was dead . . . or perhaps it had only taken new shape and more formidable dimension.

But they were wrong. Along with others who contributed to the political advancement of George Corley Wallace, friends and opponents alike, they had misjudged their man and underestimated his potential.

During his four years in the governor's chair, George Wallace proved, at least through his expansive economic and fiscal policies, to be a true disciple of the Bibb Graves-Jim Folsom school of Alabama Populist politics—with a significant difference, however. Despite personal popularity, neither Graves nor Folsom was able to maintain consistent influence for any length of time with the traditionally conservative independent Alabama Legislature.

Thus, there was no precedent for the way in which Wallace, the disciple, successfully put his programs and favored projects through the legislature, by turns cajoling, threatening and arm-twisting, in a manner much like that used by Lyndon Johnson in his relations with Congress.

The governor's every speech might be lanced with withering references to the federal government—but he was nonetheless unabashed that a large percentage of funds used to create his "Wallace program" came down from Washington. In fact, Alabama receives $2.50 from the national government for every $1 in federal taxes it sends in.

"He stood for you!" proclaimed the Wallace campaign line in '64, when he sought Alabamians' support for his "independent elector" movement, and again in Lurleen Wallace's gubernatorial race.

That he stood is an irresistible fact of Alabama political life. Precisely what he stood for—that is, what he accomplished in the way of "raising constitutional issues," is not so clear. Nor is it clear what kind of America George Corley Wallace would "stand up" for, if he should become President of the United States. Is it the movement of the "liberal" Wallace, described by Drew Pearson and remembered by Alabamians who a decade ago watched him roar approval of his outsized candidate's castigation of the "Wall Street Gotrocks," "the damned decency crowd," and "them Hoover Republicans"?

Or is it the "conservative" Wallace now heard berating Bobby Kennedy, the beatniks and the draft-card burners?

The self-declared "states' righter" who not only opposed the States' Righters in '48 but who as governor publicly endorsed the principle of federal aid to education and other welfare and giveaway programs which move the federal government into areas previously controlled by states?

The "constitutionalist" who outdid even Folsom in shattering his own state's constitutional injunction against the establishment of a too-powerful central authority? Or the anti-LBJ Democrat whose presidential candidacy could help re-elect LBJ in a close '68 election?

Or is he none of these, not of a mold at all, but simply, as Huey P. Long once described himself, *sui generis?* As far as Wallace is concerned, let others argue their ideology and brandish their labels. George Wallace—who is nothing if not a realist—looks one election down the road and knows what the real question is. For him, it is not the meaning of the words that counts but simply who is to be master—that's all.

The Odyssey of Whittaker Chambers

By William Schlam   *(From the 14 March 1970 issue)*

Whittaker Chambers was constitutionally incapable of uttering or even writing an irrelevant sentence. There, if there ever were, was an American intellectual: a man irrevocably committed to words and ideas—and a man who accepts his limitations: that he is a witness rather than doer.

This, one will admit, is the only adequate definition of an intellectual; and I know of no more significant aspect of the scandal that was Whittaker Chambers than this: that the greatest native American intellectual this century has known was ostracized as a cave man by the lightweight megalomaniacs who form the Brotherhood of Licensed Intellectuals.

Any accidentally selected page of Whittaker Chambers' letters to a friend contains, I contend, more learned concern for words and ideas than Prof. J. K. Galbraith's collected works. And I am not even talking of Chambers' superior character—I am merely talking of the subtlety, the elegance, the professional acumen of a true intellectual's verbal undertakings.

Odyssey of a Friend (Chambers was a Quaker) reproduces the private letters W. C. wrote, over a period of seven years, to William F. Buckley Jr. (or, as it happens on a few pages of this volume, to me). Not one of these letters was written for posterity or even for publication, and yet Chambers was capable of scribbling a hasty personal vote without an overbearing responsibility for the words he was putting on paper.

This, true enough, was partly protectionism—a craftsman's proud demand on himself. But it was, above all, Whittaker Chambers' urgent and almost desperate need for clarification and authenticity. A true intellectual, he was so inescapably aware of the mystical, dangerous power of words that he wrote the simplest personal note with the kind of semantic prudence Messrs. Galbraith and Schlesinger Jr. would not waste on their *opera magna.* Significantly, *Odyssey of a Friend* mentions in a few places that Chambers, before he mailed a certain letter, had written and torn up a couple of drafts—drafts of a personal letter to a friend!

To enumerate the topics of Chambers' letters to this particular friend would be as impossible as it would be irrelevant. My advantage over most readers of *Odyssey of a Friend* is that I, too, was over a period of 10 years the recipient of Chambers' letters to friends (which, who knows, some day may be published too—but not before I get around to writing my memoirs).

In addition, throughout the '40s Chambers and I had the habit of lunching together across the street from the old Time-Life Building, often joined by John Chamberlain, the unforgettable Calvin Fixx and some other forlorn "counter-revolutionaries" in Harry Luce's "liberal" enterprise. On all such occasions, Chambers' capacity for cautious wisdom almost equaled his appetite, and even his faculty for shattering laughter. So I am in a rather special position to appreciate the gracious depth of the mind that produced *Odyssey of a Friend.*

It is of course perfectly true that Chambers could never overcome the fatal experience of his life—the experience of Revolution. But this was his strength, not his weakness. No man in our time could have a more meaningful, decisive, formative experience—if only he took it seriously, profoundly, with a historian's passion for discovering cause and effect.

It is entirely to Chamber's intellectual and moral credit that he never pretended his Communist years were but an accident, the irrelevant aberration of a spirited, but flirtatious youngster. Not for a second was he ashamed of his past—simply because he had not the slightest reason to be ashamed of it.

The moral reasons for which he had become a Communist in the '30s were exactly the moral reasons that made him a "counter-revolutionist" in the '40s and thereafter: his compassion with man who suffers from history.

A self-imposed rigid abstention from intellectual inquiry made it possible for Chambers to endure a few years inside the mental and moral ghetto of the party that had got hold of his need for indignation. But when his intellectual curiosity could no longer be tamed by such an emotional engagement, he changed, not his motivation (that remained his compassion for man *in extremis*), but the framework of perverted reference into which his compassion had been pressed.

It remains a measure of Chambers' intellectual consistency and his moral stamina that he never, not for a moment, minimized the earnestness of his Communist commitment. He had, on the contrary, in his own experience learned how powerful, persuasive, seductive the historical forces can be that push modern man into the heresy of Revolution.

He turned against Revolution, not because he had suddenly discovered its arrogant omnipotence and brutal optimism. What drove him to "the losing side" was his horrified recognition that Revolution may indeed be "the winning side."

He became a "counter-revolutionist," not because he had suddenly fallen in love with the corruptions of "bourgeois" existence, but because he had fully understood, and to his last day appreciated, the attractions of Lucifer.

Precisely because he had himself so completely submerged in the Revolution's conspirational underground (no man of Chambers' hunger for engagement would have settled for a less dangerous assignment), Whittaker Chambers never shared the anti-Communists' most common mistake: to consider communism fundamentally a conspiracy.

No one has better understood than Chambers that, on the contrary, Revolution has become the most visible, most public, most unmistakable fact of the age. For Chambers, the congenital historian, communism was the convergent sum total of all the heresies that had accumulated and finally merged throughout modernity.

Thus, to comprehend the Revolution, Chambers had to acquire an encyclopedic knowledge of history. No American of his generation read, studied and understood as much about Western literature; and it is significant for Chamber's need for authenticity that he taught himself to read Russian, German and French with the subtlest feelings for the complexities of these three decisive Continental languages.

It is this depth and width of knowledge that make every line in Chambers' letters an intellectual delight. Here is a mind operating that performs within a framework of informed reference. And, to repeat, it was a historian's sage mind, prudently analyzing and delightedly savoring every single fact against the complex pattern of its enmeshed relations to other facts.

So devoted to the complexity of fact was he that, despite his enchantingly impish sense of humor, Chambers was never afraid of sounding pompous. Sometimes even his friends could not help feeling embarrassed by the immense weight of a casual remark; for one is not always in the mood for having his mind improved, not even (or especially not) by a friend.

But Whittaker could not help it. He'd rather keep his mouth shut (and he could do it for painful hours) than say less than the whole and strenuous truth.

That made, as all his friends knew, life with Whittaker Chambers sometimes rather difficult: To live with him was as strenuous as to live history itself; only that he demanded from himself never less than the impossible—the ceaseless awareness of man's hopeless confrontation with history.

And yet I have never known a man more capable of tender loyalty to people he happened to love—in spite of their limitations, their laziness, their inadequate sense of tragedy. (He even loved, to his last day, Alger Hiss!)

No, Whittaker Chambers was no saint. He was not even a martyr. He was a man in deadly earnest. He was—and for this reason he will be forever rejected by the herd of educated asses who have constituted themselves as America's Academe—a true intellectual.

Conservatives Lose a Hero

(From the 20 October 1973 issue)

The humiliation and disgrace visited upon Spiro Agnew last week was not only a terrible blow to him personally, but a serious shock to those of us who championed him throughout his vice presidential career. Since he fired his verbal guns in 1968 on Baltimore Negro moderates for refusing to condemn black extremism—considered at the time a politically suicidal move—Agnew gradually became a symbol for courage, integrity and morality in a nation wallowing in permissiveness.

With an unusual gift of rhetoric, he resembled, like the prophet Amos in the Old Testament, a solid oak of probity. He condemned in this land what desperately needed condemning—lawlessness, the New Morality and those who openly sided with America's enemies. He emphasized what should have been emphasized: hard work, individualism, family loyalty, patriotism and strength of character. In a sea of timid politicians, who bend with every new wave, Agnew was a rock, an anchor.

While his own character turned out to be seriously flawed, he provided a magnificent service in speaking out as forcefully as he did. As Vice President, Agnew became the most effective opponent of the anti-war demonstrators, labeling them an "effete corps of impudent snobs" who were led by "hard-nosed dissidents and professional anarchists."

With his Des Moines speech in 1969, the Veep dramatically focused attention on the power and the bias of the media. A small group of men, he argued, decided the day's news for the networks. . . .

Through his forensic skills in the 1970 campaign, Agnew managed to have the Democratic candidates, many of whom had previously toadied to campus rioters, pro-Vietcong demonstrators and city revolutionaries, suddenly begin clasping American flag pins to their lapels and start acting is if they were running for local sheriff. The liberal chant that "law and order" was a code word for racism has never seriously surfaced since that time.

Because of his bluntness—few politicians have ever been so direct—and the values he championed, he carved out a constituency within the Republican party that was separate and more loyal than the constituency that supported the President. His popularity among Republicans was evidenced by the fact that he became its greatest fund-raiser. And even before his final fall, liberals came to respect him for his apparent candor—which stood in marked contrast to the President's waffling on Watergate and on other significant matters.

With his resignation and the admission of guilt to income tax evasion last week, coupled with the imposition of a $10,000 fine and suspended three-year sentence, Agnew's spectacular rise to power was dramatically ended. Not only was he out of office, but he had lost what he had carefully constructed his reputation on: his moral authority. He had built his following by fervently and eloquently voicing moral judgments and exhibiting a refreshing honesty. But his reputation evaporated when last week's events revealed he had been on the take.

Moreover, in the plea-bargaining agreement which Agnew voluntarily made, the Justice Department was allowed to release a 40-page document indicating that since 1967 Agnew had received over $100,000 in secret payments from Maryland engineering, architectural and building firms, some of those payments having been made as recently as last year.

But even the apparent extent of the payments to Agnew was not so upsetting to his supporters as his conduct since he was first notified he was under investigation in August.

Capitalizing on his reputation for candor and the sympathy that was bound to be aroused by the vicious leaks emanating from the Justice Department, the Vice President led much of the country, his staff, Republican friends, Sen. Barry Goldwater and such loyal partisans as his express secretary Vic Gold into believing he had been framed by the prosecutors—when he obviously knew this was not the case. This was a reprehensible action on his part. While he had a right to be powerfully infuriated at the leaks emanating from the Justice Department, his supporters have a right to be powerfully annoyed at his exploitation of them for his single purpose: to avoid a possible prison sentence. For it is now clear that his famed press conference after he was put on notice that he was under investigation by the Justice Department, his protestation of innocence and his pledges not to resign if indicted were given in large part to avoid federal prosecution.

The political demise of Agnew is by no means a small loss to the conservatives as well as to the country as a whole. Rep. John Ashbrook (R.-Ohio), who has attacked the President for his liberal policies asserted: "We have lost a star." Indeed, conservatives have. No longer do they have a probable presidential candidate in the vice presidential chair. No longer can Agnew have a major ideological impact on the central issues confronting the country.

But Agnew's behind-the-scenes role will also be lost. He was a major opponent of the Family Assistance Plan; he fought—and knocked down—an expensive national health insurance proposal and he went to bat against the excesses of the legal services program. Through a key political aide, David Keene, a bright, young lawyer who was once national chairman of the conservative youth group Young Americans for Freedom, the conservatives in Congress and outside managed to accomplish a great deal.

Until his felony conviction last week, he stood an excellent chance of succeeding President Nixon. But now that dream has gone up in smoke. Because he couldn't control the temptation to enrich himself illegally, because he lacked the moral fiber he rightfully believed America's leaders should have, his capacity to serve the Republic has come to an abrupt and unhappy end.

History's Vindication of Joe McCarthy

By M. Stanton Evans   *(From the 16 May 1987 issue)*

(Mr. Evans, columnist, radio commentator, and former editor of the Indianapolis News, *is a long-time student of internal security matters and of the controversy over Senator McCarthy.)*

This month marks the 30th anniversary of a sadly symbolic occasion in the history of the United States: The death of Sen. Joseph R. McCarthy of Wisconsin—who was then, and by a considerable margin still remains, the most vilified human being in the annals of our politics.

To an entire generation of Americans, the term "McCarthyism" signifies something not only distasteful, but dangerous to society; the reckless smearing of opponents in political debate, especially by lodging unfounded public charges of Communist allegiance. Such is the definition given to the term, and to the man, in Webster's dictionary.

Perhaps the most remarkable thing about this image of McCarthy is its universality. Books and articles defending him are microscopically few, and those that have been attempted were written many years ago. Even conservatives and anti-Communists nowadays who want to accuse their opponents of unfairness in debate speak of a "McCarthyism of the left."

The second most remarkable thing about this view of McCarthy is that it is supremely unfactual.

Most of the people who talk about "McCarthyism" so glibly would be hard put to tell you anything about him, of course, other than some generalizations for which they could offer no supporting evidence. But even the books and monographs that *claim* to be based on the historical record—including some revisionist works promoted for their alleged fairness—are rife with factual error.

Setting the record straight about these topics is a matter of great import, for three rather obvious reasons:

• First, as a matter of simple justice to the man himself, and to his memory.

• Second, in the interest of history, so that we may know with some degree of accuracy what happened to our country in the course of these intense disputes.

• Third, because the issues raised by McCarthy in the '50s—as witness the recent spate of arrests for espionage, the bugging of our Moscow embassy, and widespread charges of security laxness in the State Department—are all too clearly with us still.

In several respects, fortunately, assessment of such questions is easier now, at a remove of 30 years, than it was when McCarthy held the stage. Passions have cooled, personal vendettas have been forgotten, barriers to truth have been removed. Equally to the point, conventional perspectives on certain issues—most notably, perhaps, the majesty of "executive privilege"—have undergone enormous changes.

The paragraphs that follow are merely excerpts from a vast and burgeoning record on McCarthy. They do not pretend to cover every facet of his career or many collateral disputes in which he was involved. What is attempted, instead, is a brief survey of *the major public cases in which McCarthy was involved concerning charges of subversion or security dereliction.*

To understand the controversies in which McCarthy was engaged we need first recall the circumstances of the era—both in general and in particular. The fall of China to the Communists, the trials and ultimate conviction of Alger Hiss, the atom spy cases of the Rosenbergs and Fuchs, the Communist invasion of Korea in June of 1950. Such were the events contemporaneous with the original charges and major battles of McCarthy's career—engendering deep concern about suspected Communist penetration of our society.

Also intensely relevant is the specific background of the U.S. State Department, which had had a serious security problem thrust upon it in the aftermath of World War II. During the war, the Soviets had been our allies, and standards pertaining to Communist sympathizers working in the government were—in some departments—accordingly quite lax. At war's end, a number of special wartime agencies were abolished, and their personnel (an estimated 13,000 people) transferred *en masse* into the State Department.

At the time of this inundation, other changes were also occurring at State. Fairly tough-line anti-Communists such as Secretary of State J. Anthony Panuch, Under Secretary Joseph Grew, and others skeptical of the Soviets and/or in favor of strict enforcement of personnel security were being phased out of the department—replaced by people with very different views about both matters. Former Assistant Secretary of State Adolph Berle discussed this struggle when he testified before the House Committee on Un-American Activities in 1948 concerning Alger Hiss.

". . . In the fall of 1944," Berle said, "there was a difference of opinion in the State Department. I felt that the Russians were not going to be sympathetic and cooperative . . . I was pressing for a pretty clean-cut showdown then when our position was the strongest. The opposition group in the State Department was . . . Mr. Acheson's group, of course, with Mr. Hiss as his principal assistant in the matter. . . . Mr. Hiss did take what we would call today a pro-Russian point of view."

In matters of personnel security, this fight translated into a dispute about the standards used in assessing loyalty or security risks.

Hard-liners like Panuch wanted a reasonable-doubt standard, to be resolved in favor of the government. Their opponents wanted an innocent-until-proved guilty standard, in which a federal employee was treated like a defendant in a courtroom, holding his job until "convicted"—a laborious and often impossible task in the murky world of risk-assessment.

These matters had been bitterly fought out inside the Congress and the executive branch in the period 1946-50, with the lenient view prevailing in the State Department and its loyalty-review process. In late 1945, in the aftermath of the *Amerasia* case (see below), Under Secretary Grew was forced out of the department, and Dean Acheson replaced him. Thereafter, Panuch himself was forced out as well and his security program put out of operation. As he observed:

". . . We applied the reasonable-doubt test of loyalty. . . . In the new program of 1947 they put in what I call an overt-act test. They specified that in order to dismiss a man for disloyalty or to make him ineligible on loyalty grounds, there had to be reasonable grounds to show that there was present disloyalty. . . . [This was] absolutely ineffective. You can never get the evidence . . . *We tried to do something about it but in 1947 they put us out of business.*" (Emphasis added.)

Such was the prologue to Joe McCarthy's battle with the State Department.

*   *   *   *   *

McCarthy's first public charges concerning security problems in the State Department were made in a speech in Wheeling, W.Va., on Feb. 9, 1950. They were repeated on February 11 in another speech in Reno, Nev. In the Reno address (which was recorded), McCarthy said, "I have in my hand 57 cases of individuals who would appear to be either card-carrying members or certainly loyal to the Communist party, but who nevertheless are still helping to shape our foreign policy."

In making these charges, McCarthy was drawing on previous inquiries in Congress and the executive branch, but his insistent pounding on the issue in public forum served to focus new attention on the subject, prompting angry responses from President Truman and other Democratic spokesmen.

The upshot of these exchanges was that McCarthy took to the Senate floor on February 20 to spell out his accusations in detail—upping the ante to 81 cases of security-loyalty risks, or outright Communists, who had worked either for or with the State Department.

Naming the Names

A major accusation against McCarthy, as noted, is that he repeatedly made *public accusations* of Communist affinity, blackening the names of innocents who had no chance to defend themselves. Yet, as the record of his early speeches clearly indicates, nothing could be further from the truth.

In point of fact, McCarthy did *not* have a penchant for making public accusations against individuals. His initial and constantly repeated position in his Senate speeches was that the names of individuals he considered to be security or loyalty risks, or Communists, *shouldn't* be divulged.

This fact—so totally contrary to the public image of McCarthy—emerges repeatedly from his initial presentation in the Senate. Again and again, McCarthy stated that the naming of individuals would be neither fair nor to the point. Also again and again, the record reveals that it was his Democratic opponents who demanded that he "name the names." Here are a few excerpts from the debates:

Sen. Scott Lucas, Democratic majority leader: "I want him to name those Communists. . . . The senator is privileged to name them all in the Senate."

McCarthy: "The names are available. The senators may have them if they care for them. I think, however, it would be improper to make the names public until the appropriate Senate committee can meet in executive session and get them. If I were to give all the names involved, it might leave a wrong impression. *If we should label one man a Communist, when he is not a Communist, I think it would be too bad* . . . [Emphasis added.]

"The majority leader has been condemning me rather vigorously for not giving the names to the people. I have been making every effort possible to keep the information in such a form that no one can detect the names until a full hearing of each case has been held."

Sen. Withers (Democrat of Kentucky): "I should like to ask the senator what reason he has for not calling names? Does not the senator think it would be a fine thing to let the public know who the guilty are?"

   McCarthy: ". . . The matter is too important for me to use it as a utensil whereby I can satisfy someone's curiosity. . . ."

   Lucas: "The sooner the senator can name these persons, the better off we will all be. So far as I am concerned, it will not be in executive session."

I have quoted at length from these exchanges to show that the statements are in context and that the disagreement over "naming names" was not a casual matter. It was, instead, a bitter, persistent theme of the debate—with Democrats Lucas, Withers, and others baiting McCarthy and demanding that he name the names, and with McCarthy steadfastly refusing to comply.

The Numbers Game

Among the many disputes emerging from those speeches was the question of *how many* people McCarthy was discussing, as well as confusion as to what, exactly, he was accusing them of.

Examination of the record suggests that some confusion on this point is natural, since there is no definitive text of what McCarthy said at Wheeling, but that beyond this the dispute is contrived and beside the point. It's pretty plain, indeed, that the uproar about "how many" Communists or security-loyalty risks McCarthy was discussing was an effort to divert attention from the substantive merits of the issue.

Three numbers in particular are alluded to in such discussion (two of which have already been encountered): 205, 81, and 57. The existence of these three numbers in McCarthy's speeches is usually treated as a source of bafflement or indignation.

In point of fact, there was nothing absurd or mysterious about these numbers as they appear in McCarthy's speeches, and as he discussed them on the floor of the Senate, since they quite obviously referred to *three different things.*

In his initial speech at Wheeling, McCarthy made reference to the figure "205." He also alluded to it frequently in subsequent statements and speeches in the Senate. McCarthy's use of "205" referred to a letter written in 1946 by Secretary of State James Byrnes to Rep. Adolph Sabath of Illinois, a congressman concerned about security affairs. In this letter, Byrnes told Sabath that adverse security recommendations had been made against 284 employees of the State Department. Of these (as of July 1946) some 79 had been discharged from the department. The difference, between the 284 and 79 is—205, who, by an irresistible process of deduction, hadn't been dismissed from office.

The other two numbers—57 and 81—referred to individual cases McCarthy was putting together, obviously drawing on congressional hearings, sources inside the State Department (frequently saying that the data were all there in the department's files) and (unknown at the time) assistance from the FBI. Fifty-seven was the number of Communists or Communist sympathizers he cited in his remarks in Reno (reiterated on the Senate floor); 81, as we have seen, was the total number of cases he attempted to present before the Senate.

In all of this, even the change from 57 to 81, there is nothing at all mysterious. Since McCarthy was in the process of putting information together (and, as we now know, developing new sources for it), the expectable result would be a constantly *increasing* number of specific cases—which is exactly what occurred. (In fact, when he came before the Tydings Committee, he had 110 cases— although this number, for some reason, has not attained the celebrity status of the others.)

This doesn't address, of course, the *validity* of the cases McCarthy was presenting. It does suggest, however, the specious nature of "the numbers game" as it has been played by McCarthy's critics through the decades.

Smearing the Innocent

In the conventional view of things, McCarthy was the quintessential false accuser. In the typical McCarthy case, we are informed, he would accuse someone of being a Communist or Communist sympathizer—or of some grave delinquency in security matters—on the basis of dubious or nonexistent information. Subsequent inquiry would reveal that the person in question was not in fact a Communist. By then, however, it would be too late: The individual's reputation would be ruined, and McCarthy would have charged off somewhere else to ravage still other helpless innocents.

Examinations of particular cases shows almost no evidence to support this view. The hardest thing to find in the historical record is the case of someone whom McCarthy claimed on the factual record to be a Communist or security risk, who turned out on subsequent information *not* to be one.

The true situation on most of McCarthy's cases—and certainly on his most famous ones—was the very reverse of the typical image. Once McCarthy had "named the names"—almost irrespective of who they were—his victims would become the object of great solicitude. When the smoke had cleared and the evidence was in, however, it usually turned out that McCarthy was right, after all: The person McCarthy accused of Communist sympathy turned out to be guilty as charged.

The Institute of Pacific Relations

In tackling the China policy of the Truman State Department and in going after such people as John Stewart Service, Owen Lattimore, John Carter Vincent and Philip Jessup, McCarthy was also tackling a then-prestigious think tank called the Institute of Pacific Relations. Pro-Communist elements in and around the IPR, McCarthy alleged, had tilted our policy in China away from the anti-Communist Chiang Kai-Shek and in favor of the Communists. First and foremost of the pro-Communist luminaries of IPR, McCarthy said, was Lattimore.

These suggestions horrified the Democrats in the Senate. "Does the senator mean to convey the impression," asked Clinton Anderson of New Mexico, "that the Institute of Pacific Relations . . . was under Communist control?" The Tydings committee was supremely confident that it wasn't.

In 1951 and 1952, however, another committee of the Senate, headed by Democrat Pat McCarran of Nevada, examined back files of the IPR, called some 66 witnesses, sifted 20,000 documents, and compiled more than 5,000 pages of hearing record. In these hearings, the connections of the IPR with American Communists, Chinese Communists and Soviet Communists were documented at some length.

As the committee observed, "during the course of the hearings, 54 persons connected in various ways with IPR were identified by witnesses as participants in the Communist world conspiracy. . . ."

In like fashion, the connections of IPR into the U.S. government—and its influence on the conduct of our China policy—were fully documented. These connections were found to reach into the State Department and other branches of the executive, especially those that dealt with matters of Far Eastern policy, and in one notable case into the White House itself. Here are some of the committee's conclusions:

• "The IPR has been considered by the American Communist Party and by Soviet officials as an instrument of Communist policy, propaganda and military intelligence.

• "Members of the small core of officials and staff members who controlled IPR were either Communist or pro-Communist.

• "The IPR possessed close organic relations with the State Department through interchange of personnel, attendance of State Department officials at IPR conferences, constant exchange of information and social contacts.

• "The IPR was a vehicle used by the Communists to orientate American Far Eastern policies toward Communist objectives."

This was a verdict of a *Democratic*-controlled committee of the Senate, of which McCarthy himself was not a member, based on a vast amount of data painstakingly assembled over the course of a year's investigations.

Owen Lattimore

McCarthy's most important single case—on which he said he'd "stand or fall"—was that of Owen Lattimore, a scholarly-looking, tweedy professor from Johns Hopkins University. McCarthy told his colleagues, "I intend to give the Senate some documentation to show that he is a Soviet agent and also that he either is, or at least has been, a member of the Communist party." McCarthy asserted that, even though Lattimore was not a government official, he had a desk in the State Department, and wielded tremendous influence on China policy.

The Tydings committee examined Lattimore and found him a victim of "promiscuous and specious attacks on private citizens and their views." Lattimore himself denied everything, including Communist membership, pro-Communist sympathy, influence on U.S. foreign policy, and the desk in the State Department. On the Tydings performance, Lattimore was exonerated of all charges and McCarthy was judged an irresponsible scoundrel.

The IPR hearings, however, revealed a different story on Lattimore. The committee heard at length from the professor, as well as from others who knew of his activities, his writings, and his participation in government affairs. A sample of Lattimore's writings was read into the record, including, e.g., this treatment of Outer Mongolia, a well-known Soviet satellite, in his book, *Solution in Asia:*

"In Asia the most important example of the Soviet power of attraction beyond Soviet frontiers is in Outer Mongolia . . . Outer Mongolia may be called a satellite of Russia in the good sense . . . Soviet policy in Outer Mongolia cannot fairly be called Red imperialism . . . Russo-Mongol relations in Asia, like Russo-Czechoslovak relations in Europe, deserve careful and respectful study."

The theme of this book in general was summed up by Lattimore's publisher on the dust jacket:

"He shows that all the Asiatic peoples are far more interested in actual democratic practices such as the ones they can see in action across the Russian border, than they are in the fine theories of Anglo-Saxon democracies which come coupled with ruthless imperialism. . . ."

As for the "desk in the State Department," the McCarran Committee unearthed a letter Lattimore had written in 1942, in which he said: "I am in Washington about 4 days a week, and when there can always be reached at Lauchlin Currie's office, room 228, State Department Building." This was even more significant than it sounded, since Currie was executive assistant to the President and special adviser on Far Eastern Affairs.

It was Currie who gave Owen Lattimore one of his most important assignments during World War II—as adviser to Chiang Kai-shek! The McCarran Committee observed: "Lattimore made extensive efforts to conceal this relationship [with Currie] throughout his testimony before this subcommittee, as he had successfully done before the earlier Tydings Committee."

The committee's blunt conclusion: "Owen Lattimore was, from some time beginning in the 1930s, a conscious, articulate instrument of the Soviet conspiracy."

Against that backdrop, what was wrong with McCarthy's charges against Lattimore? Most obviously, his early statement—later modified—that Lattimore was an *espionage* agent, an unproven and unlikely one. What Lattimore was able to accomplish in behalf of communism, on the evidence of the IPR hearings, was far more important than pilfering documents.

John Stewart Service

Pilfering documents *did* occur in the world of IPR, however, as the tangled case of *Amerasia* and diplomat John Stewart Service—both frequent targets of McCarthy—amply illustrates. Service had been on duty in China throughout the early 1940s, sending back dispatches increasingly hostile to the anti-Communist cause and friendly to the Communists. On top of this, shortly after his return to the states in 1945, he was arrested on charges of passing official secrets to the pro-Communist (and IPR-connected) *Amerasia* magazine.

To McCarthy, the Service case summed up just about everything that was wrong in the State Department. "When Chiang Kai-Shek was fighting our war," McCarthy said, "the State Department had in China a young man named John S. Service. . . . He sent official reports back to the State Department urging that we torpedo our ally Chiang Kai-shek. Later this man . . . was picked up by the Federal Bureau of Investigation for turning over to the Communists secret State Department information. Strangely, however, he was never prosecuted. . . ."

The State Department emphatically disagreed with McCarthy about Service—and, as McCarthy noted, on no less than five occasions, "cleared" him of such charges.

As with Lattimore, a good way of assessing Service is to examine his writings—such as his famous dispatch No. 40, written in 1944. U.S. support of Chiang's party, Service said, "will only encourage it to continue sowing the seeds of future civil war by plotting with the present puppets for eventual consolidation of the occupied territories *against the Communist-led forces of popular resistance.*" (Emphasis added.)

Further, according to Service: "We need not fear the collapse of the Kuomintang government. . . ."

This and other dispatches by Service (and others) certainly supported McCarthy's version of what had been done to alter U.S. policy. Even more unsettling in McCarthy's view (expressed at length to the Tydings Committee) was the fact that Service, back in the United States, took to consorting with Philip Jaffe, editor of *Amerasia*, and also to sharing his official dispatches from China.

When the FBI moved in and arrested the *Amerasia* principals in June 1945, they harvested more than 1,000 documents in possession of the suspects and in the offices of the magazine—several bearing "top secret" classification. Among the documents were copies of some of Service's own dispatches. Also, he was overheard in wiretapped conversations telling Jaffe: "Well, what I said about the military plans is, of course, very secret."

The FBI, as McCarthy noted, thought it had an airtight case against Service and his fellow defendants. Yet, in a matter of weeks, the whole thing had collapsed. Service himself was released scot-free and restored to official duties in the State Department, and the remaining defendants escaped as well.

Defenders of Service argued that the failure to indict him proved that he hadn't done anything wrong. McCarthy saw the matter differently, suggesting that there had been a cover-up at the Department of Justice.

Thirty years later, we know that McCarthy's intimation of a fix in the handling of *Amerasia*, and the lenient treatment of John Service, was correct.

It turns out that, while the case was brewing, the FBI was tapping the telephone talk of various influentials in the Truman Administration, including well-known Democratic fixer Thomas (Tommy the Cork) Corcoran. Thanks to the Freedom of Information Act, we now have access to the logs of Corcoran's conversations concerning Service and *Amerasia*.

What these transcripts show us is Corcoran in constant touch with Lauchlin Currie, Service himself, officials at State, and higher-ups at Justice, moving heaven and earth to make sure that Service got off the hook. Here is an excerpt from the Corcoran phone calls:

Corcoran: "One of these fellows is a friend of mine—that fellow who was picked up in China—that fellow Service [Service was actually arrested in Washington] . . . My strategy would be to let the other fellows do the jumping up and down and let him slip out . . . I am not the slightest interested in the principle of the thing. I want to get my fellow and my friend out."

The State Department Files

Nor was the *Amerasia* case the only zone of McCarthy-State Department conflict in which a cover-up was occurring. A major source of friction between McCarthy and the Administration was a secrecy order handed down by President Truman in March 1948 which instructed all officials of the executive branch to withhold loyalty/security data from the Congress.

The Truman secrecy order said that "all reports, records, and files relative to the loyalty of employees or prospective employees . . . shall be maintained in confidence . . . There shall be no relaxation of the provisions of this directive except with my express authority."

Executive secrecy concerning alleged security risks and failure to take appropriate measures against them was a constant theme of McCarthy's struggles to the very end, as we shall see. In his confrontation with the Tydings committee, it resulted in his repeated demand that the State Department loyalty files be turned over to the senators, so that they could judge the matter for themselves. And, indeed, the committee, by resolution of the Senate on February 22, had been instructed to procure and examine these very files.

A month later, on March 29, the committee duly issued a subpoena—and the State Department, following Truman's order, duly ignored it. Sen. Tydings, who had been reluctant to issue the subpoena in the first place, did nothing to overcome this act of defiance. Finally, in June, the Administration turned over what it said were the security files of some 70 individuals referred to by McCarthy in his initial Senate speech. Sen. Tydings then announced that the files contained no evidence to sustain McCarthy.

Even before the files were so belatedly delivered, McCarthy alleged that they had been "stripped" of their derogatory data—basing his charges on affidavits from temporary employees of the Department.

As one affiant put it, "all of the clerks on this project were to pull out of the files all matters considered derogatory, either morally or politically."

McCarthy's charges about the stripping of the files were dismissed by Tydings, by the media at the time, and by most commentators since. But three years later, when the Republicans controlled the Senate and McCarthy chaired his own committee, he conducted an intriguing investigation of this subject. Among those called was Mrs. Helen Balog, supervisor of the State Department's Foreign Service file room.

The interrogation on this topic—conducted by McCarthy Counsel Roy Cohn—makes interesting, and dramatic, reading:

Cohn: "Now, Mrs. Balog, was there a time toward the end of 1948 or the beginning of 1949 when you were notified that a certain official of the State Department would be spending some time in the file room?"

Mrs. Balog: "Yes, sir."

Cohn: "Did this official actually, physically, appear in the file rooms?"

Mrs. Balog: "Yes, sir."

Cohn: "And, did he work on . . . the confidential files?"

Mrs. Balog: "Yes, sir."

Cohn: "For how long a period. . . ?"

Mrs. Balog: "I am quite sure he was there for the whole year of 1949."

Cohn: "Now, would you please tell the chairman and the members of the committee the name of this person in the State Department who worked on these confidential files at night. . . ?"

Mrs. Balog: "It was John Service."

*   *   *   *   *

The sequence of events that occurred between McCarthy's speeches in February 1950 and the Tydings report in the summer of that year constituted the first great crisis of McCarthy's campaign as a Communist fighter.

This pattern was more or less faithfully repeated in the second major trauma of his political career—his death struggle with the Eisenhower Administration that began in the summer of 1953 and concluded with his condemnation by the Senate in December 1954.

Despite the many political changes that had intervened—the protracted conflict of Korea, the election of a Republican President, McCarthy's own ascension to a committee chairmanship—the fundamental issues at stake were remarkably similar to those that surfaced with the Truman Administration. They were McCarthy's contentions:

(1) That security/loyalty risks, and outright Communists were slipping through the cracks of a jerry-built security system;

(2) That the responsible officials had been derelict in allowing this to happen; and

(3) That, rather than telling the American people the truth about such matters, or providing the necessary data to Congress, the Administration in power was dragging its feet or actively engaging in a cover-up.

Needless to remark, these were not assertions that a Republican Administration elected to "clean up the mess" in Washington—specifically including the internal security mess—enjoyed hearing from a Republican committee chairman. McCarthy's insistence on going his own way in such matters, and on proclaiming his independence of the Administration, made a showdown virtually inevitable. And in this conflict as well, we find a pattern in which McCarthy's allegations—supposedly invented out of whole cloth—turned out repeatedly to be correct.

Annie Lee Moss

In February 1954, looking into the security practices of the Army, McCarthy's committee called before it one Annie Lee Moss, an elderly-appearing black lady who worked in a code room of the Pentagon, handling secret messages in code form. According to testimony given to McCarthy's committee and the House Committee on Un-American Activities by an FBI informant (Mary Markward), Mrs. Moss had been a member of the Communist party.

When Mrs. Moss appeared before the committee to deny the charges, she seemed a dazed and pitiful figure. The Democrats leaped instantly to her defense, as did the media thereafter. She was not, she said, a Communist, she had never heard of Marx; it was a case of mistaken identity, since there were three people named Annie Lee Moss in the Washington phone book; she didn't know how to decode the messages she was handling, anyway. And so forth.

The stirring scene was duly conveyed to the American people by Edward R. Murrow the following week on "See It Now"—indelibly etching into the public mind the image of a poor black woman who wasn't a Communist being browbeaten by the McCarthy committee, which said she was. As one McCarthy critic writes, "the Moss case was a disaster for Cohn and McCarthy," a "triumph" for the Democrats. Thus the conventional image.

The only problem with this little morality play about the evils of McCarthyism was that, according to the records of the Communists themselves, Annie Lee Moss (this one, and not some other) *was* a member of the Communist party after all!

In her testimony, FBI informant Markward had given the address of Mrs. Moss as 72 R St., S.E., an address that Mrs. Moss herself confirmed. In reviewing certain Communist records in 1958, the Subversive Activities Control Board reported:

"The situation that has resulted on the Annie Lee Moss question is that copies of the Communist party's own records, the authenticity of which the party has at no time disputed, were produced to it . . . *and show that one Annie Lee Moss, 72 R St. S.W., Washington, D.C., was a party member in the mid-1940s.*"

Who Promoted Peress?

McCarthy achieved a similar vindication—after he had been condemned in the Senate, and after public interest in the matter had subsided—in the most famous of the Army-McCarthy cases, that of the "5th Amendment dentist," Irving Peress.

Dr. Peress had been called into the Korean War. In the course of his tour, he had occasion to sign various loyalty affidavits attesting to his non-subversive status. On one such form, he took a vow of non-Communist, and otherwise non-subversive, allegiance. But on three other occasions, confronted with similar questions, he responded, "Federal constitutional privilege claimed"—meaning the 5th Amendment privilege against self-incrimination. He similarly took the 5th when called before McCarthy's committee.

Despite the 5th Amendment plea (and apparent false swearing on the first response), Peress was promoted from captain to major—then given a hurry-up honorable discharge when McCarthy's committee pursued the matter too intensely. The discharge occurred, indeed, the day *after* McCarthy had written Army Secretary Robert Stevens urging that Peress not be honorably discharged but subject to court martial. The whole affair, in McCarthy's view, bespoke a dismal lack of concern about security.

A natural response to McCarthy's agitation on Peress was—why worry about a Communist *dentist?* McCarthy himself attributed limited significance to Peress as such. What was important, he thought, was what the case implied about procedures.

Even investigators *of the Democratic party* failed to find it very humorous that Peress had received a promotion and honorable discharge—despite false swearing, despite the 5th Amendment-taking, and despite the urgent request from a Senate chairman that the honorable discharge be held up.

In 1955, after the Democrats resumed control of the Senate, the permanent Subcommittee on Investigations, chaired by Sen. John McClellan of Arkansas, reviewed the tangled story of Peress, and came to these conclusions:

"I. The Secretary of the Army, or his superiors under whose direction he may have been acting, are to be criticized for the delay of almost one year before the facts of the Peress case were publicly released. . . .

"II. Mr. John Adams, Counselor, Department of the Army, showed disrespect for this subcommittee when he chose to disregard Sen. McCarthy's letter of Feb. 1, 1954, and allowed Peress to be honorably discharged on Feb. 2, 1954."

There is more in similar vein, but these comments from a Democratic committee make the essential points: That the Army security system in the Peress case had been derelict; that this betokened problems extending far beyond Peress himself; and that the Eisenhower Administration had withheld important data needed to resolve the problem. Sen. McCarthy, it would appear, could hardly have expressed it better.

No Personal Complaint

Bruising as they were, these encounters between McCarthy and the Eisenhower Administration were only warm-ups for the main event: the Army-McCarthy hearings, before the Mundt committee, that ran for 36 days in the spring of 1954.

These hearings revolved around the status of McCarthy aide G. David Schine, who had been drafted into the Army in the fall of '53. With a McCarthy staffer under the control of the Army, and with McCarthy conducting a series of investigations of the Army, the possibilities for reciprocal leverage and pressures both overt and subtle were readily apparent. Public charges to this effect—and countercharges—began to fly on March 10, 1954.

On that date, the Army issued a "Chronological Series of Events," compiled by Counselor John Adams, alleging that McCarthy, Committee Counsel Roy Cohn and Executive Director Francis Carr had brought pressures to bear to secure preferential treatment for Schine, and suggesting that McCarthy's investigations of the Army were efforts to induce such favors. McCarthy *et al.*, launched countercharges saying that the Army was using Schine as a "hostage" to force the cancellation of the hearings.

As it happened, the Army itself produced conclusive evidence that its charges were almost certainly false and brought for a tendentious reason—in the form of numerous monitored phone calls between the McCarthy committee and spokesmen for the Army, some of which became available in the course of the hearings.

Amazingly enough, when read into the record, these conversations showed quite clearly that Army Secretary Robert Stevens felt no pressure from or hostility toward McCarthy in the matter of David Schine, and freely expressed this view to those who called him.

Most revealing of all, perhaps, was a monitored conversation between Stevens and Sen. Stuart Symington, Missouri Democrat, who was trying mightily to get the Army secretary to deliver derogatory information on McCarthy. This was Stevens' statement to Symington, as recorded by the Army itself:

"I personally think that anything in that line would prove to be very much exaggerated.... *I am the secretary, and I have had some talks with the committee and the chairman, and so on, and by and large, as far as the treatment of me is concerned, I have no personal complaint....*" (Emphasis added.)

This private statement by the secretary of the Army was made two *days before the Army went public with its report alleging charges of improper pressure by McCarthy* (the report that Symington was trying to get).

The Mundt committee, Republicans and Democrats alike, affirmed that Cohn made numerous calls in Schine's behalf—which he should not have done, if for no other reason than the bind in which it put McCarthy. The evidence is that the Army saw this interest in Schine not as "pressure," but as a golden opportunity: By treating Schine well, the obvious assumption ran, we can get better treatment from McCarthy. As the committee Democrats observed:

"The record fully warrants the conclusion that Secretary Stevens and Mr. Adams did undertake to appease and placate Sen. McCarthy and Mr. Cohn. Unwarranted special privileges and preferential treatment were accorded Pvt. Schine."

The Army had charged that McCarthy was conducting his hearings to force special treatment for David Schine; the Mundt committee, in essence, found the mirror image of this: That special treatment was accorded Schine in the hope of getting the hearings, at least in part, called off.

The issues raised by McCarthy are with us still: Issues concerning Soviet penetration of our society, laxness (and worse) in maintaining safeguards against that penetration, and a woeful lack of information made available to the American people about the serious nature of the problem. All of these conditions exist right now, 30 years after McCarthy's death, and in some respects are worse today than they were in the 1950s. For that reason, as well as for vindication of the man himself and for the integrity of the historical record, the true, full story of Joe McCarthy (of which the foregoing is but an excerpt) must still be written.

William Casey: Forty Years in Defense of Freedom

By Lawrence W. Casey   *(From the 15 August 1987 issue)*

(Mr. Casey, nephew of William J. Casey, is an attorney, former congressional staffer of eight years, and served as an international business consultant with Casey and Co. in Washington, D.C.)

William J. Casey is still alive, the rumors say. I agree.

His mortal remains were interred on Long Island after funeral services in a church bulging at the seams with the great, near great and many average citizens. His life touched many thousands, and his commitment and spirit lives in each one of these special individuals.

This was truly an American life.

Fabricated reports still abound that Bill's death, like his life, is shrouded in controversy and mystery. But to the people who knew him well, Bill Casey was no mystery at all. His penetrating mind, patriotism, courage, shrewdness and devotion won him the confidence and admiration of countless world leaders, corporate giants and financial wizards of the past half-century. His generosity and interest in people and ideas won him the rest.

In the battle for freedom he "took no prisoners" because of his innate toughness and confidence in doing the best thing for America. It also won him the grudging respect, but outright animosity, of those who settle for political expediency and appeasement of America's adversaries.

In reviewing the career of Bill Casey it is very easy to focus only on his CIA years, particularly in light of conflicting news reports emerging each day. Overlooked is the splendid but unparalleled experience this man achieved in his 74 years.

It's time to set the record straight. And where better to start than with Hercules Mulligan, one of Bill Casey's favorite historical figures.

An unsung hero from the American Revolution and contemporary of executed spy Nathan Hale, Mulligan was different: he was not only successful, but survived to tell the tale.

Under deep cover as a New York clothing merchant, Mulligan slowly, quietly and effectively beat the drums for liberty, fermenting the fever pitch of revolution.

He was a confidant of Alexander Hamilton, and his sponsor for the secret society called the Sons of Liberty. Most importantly, he was an intelligence agent for the rebels. Known only to Gen. George Washington, Mulligan kept an eye on British troops and fleet movements, foiled a 10,000-man attack by Gen. Clinton on Rhode Island, and on two occasions in 1779 and 1781 prevented the seizure and kidnapping of Washington himself. He also advised him on the successful withdrawal of troops in the Battle of Long Island from Brooklyn to the high ground of Manhattan.

Later exposed and arrested by the now-British Gen. Benedict Arnold, Mulligan escaped. When later caught and tried, he was acquitted due to lack of evidence.

On Nov. 25, 1783, the first day of a free New York after the British evacuation, Gen. Washington entered on horseback. His very first event was to breakfast at the home of Hercules Mulligan—an honor that mystified his neighbors.

Mulligan did his job, escaped death time and again, and later died in relative obscurity at the age of 85. Nathan Hale, on the other hand, was executed and uttered the now famous "I regret that I have but one life to give to my country," and achieved posterity.

If Nathan Hale had one life, Hercules Mulligan had nine.

Bill Casey admired that in Mulligan, and felt that this great man deserved the honor of a statue or plaque at CIA headquarters. He was the epitome of a true intelligence officer: successful, accurate, kept his own counsel, and escaped with his life to serve his country again.

Bill Casey also had nine lives, literally and figuratively.

His career and contribution to uplifting the morale and work product at the CIA is well known. Equally important was his OSS service in World War II, coordinating the activities of agents behind enemy lines in Nazi Europe that earned him the status of war hero. The Nazi war machine was our clear enemy, and the nation was completely behind our effort. Many brave men and women sacrificed their lives in the OSS, and each was precious to Bill Casey.

The enemy faced today is different, but their goals are the same. Bill Casey stood firm 40 years later in defense of freedom from those who would take it all away.

Controversy first reared its head when he was selected to head the Securities and Exchange Commission. His appointment was compared to Joseph P. Kennedy, who was the controversial choice of FDR to head the SEC. Rough Senate confirmation hearings followed and charges flew back and forth. In the end Casey was confirmed, and confounded his critics when he took charge of the agency, overhauled it, and made it an activist institution.

He cracked down on fraud and misrepresentation in the marketplace, offered investors further protection through the SIPIC Act, began the process of permitting negotiated brokerage commission rates and eliminating fixed rates, and set up the fundamentals of the National Market System to better integrate capital markets domestically and internationally. He made his mark.

Bill then served as president of the Export-Import Bank, a lending institution that helps American business compete in the world marketplace. Bill Casey ran the bank in the black. Today, decimated by the Congress, it's in the red.

His experience setting up the Marshall Plan in Europe after World War II served him well in his Bank duties. It crystallized his view of the world as a free marketplace of ideas and opportunity, the best weapons in the arsenal of democracy.

Later, he assumed a diplomatic role as Under Secretary of State for Economic Affairs. He made people learn the lessons of history, think about the future, and not be afraid to dare new ideas. He was a man of dynamic action, not static passivity.

Government service was an important part of his contribution to our nation. In his private life, too, he made a significant mark.

A true renaissance man, he was interested in everything and everybody. He was famous among his friends for his reading habits and the volumes he consumed over the course of a day. His personal library overwhelmed many of the local public libraries.

The bibliophile in him led to his career as an author/editor. He published dozens of "How To" books, and reference guides for lawyers and businessmen, many of which are still used today. Tax books, estate planning texts, real estate guides and capital formation were among his areas of expertise. He also wrote a scholarly book on the American Revolution and was working on a volume on World War II at the time of his death.

He was a lawyer's lawyer and was sought after for his keen legal insight as well as his business acumen, a rare combination in the legal profession. He had the ability to set aside all the murk and sinew to find the very core of the issue. Bill Casey had little time for the collateral issues. It was the central issue that was important; the rest would fall into place. His respect for the law was immeasurable and his understanding of putting the proper pieces and words together to find the perfect argument to have his point prevail is well documented.

In business, his forte was capital formation to start up new businesses and help them grow and prosper. One such small business was Capital Cities Broadcasting, which later became strong enough to buy ABC.

Few excuses were accepted when working for Bill Casey. Either you got the point fast or he would refer it to someone who worked a little quicker. He was always three or four questions ahead of you at all times and you had to struggle to catch up.

If you were not on top of the issue or caught up on your reading, a brief but stormy encounter ensued with tough questioning. However, when he finished you knew you were in the company of a most unusual and brilliant human being. People came away from meeting Bill Casey with both awe and satisfaction of gaining knowledge and insight in a few precious moments.

Yet, there was the matter of understanding him and the famous "mumbling." It was not a mumble, but the reality that his brain moved so fast that his mouth could not keep up, particularly while he spoke in a soft voice.

As a politician Bill Casey was a strategic thinker and a prodigious writer of issue papers behind the scenes. He advised men and women running for every office from Town Supervisor to President of the United States. Every Republican presidential candidate since Wendell Wilkie turned to him as a key adviser. His law partner was Leonard Hall, a former Republican national chairman and manager of the Eisenhower, Nixon, Romney and Rockefeller presidential campaigns.

The fact that Casey was chosen to be the campaign manager for Ronald Reagan came as no surprise to Casey watchers. Gov. Reagan liked Bill's no-nonsense style and put him in charge.

He took the 1980 campaign that was in desperate shape, cut costs, devised a new strategy and put it on a winning track for November.

His one foray into elected office was for Congress in 1966. He primaried the GOP machine candidate, Steven B. Derounian, an arch-right-wing former congressman who had lost the previous term in the Goldwater debacle. Casey, running as a moderate Republican with quiet support from Rockefeller and Javits, branded Derounian as backward thinking and a loser. Bill Casey lost the primary, but he probably would have been frustrated in the "rarefied" air of Capitol Hill.

Personal campaigning was new to Bill Casey. He liked to tell the story of the time he met a father accompanied by his sons on a Long Island Railroad platform one crisp spring morning. Bill shook his hand, asked for his vote, and inquired of the two sons what they would do when they grew up. The man shot back, "If I raised them right, they won't vote for you."

Bill had a terrific sense of humor including self-depreciation and jokes at his own expense. **Which brings me to what is often lost in stories about Bill Casey. His humility and humanitarian efforts as a "people person" stand out in my memory.**

Aside from his great interest and helpfulness towards his immediate family, brother and sister, in-laws, assorted nieces and nephews, he was interested in providing opportunities for people who never got a crack at the American dream.

He took long shots on inventors who developed new technology, and business ventures with dynamic leadership and invested his time and money in both. Groups like the International Rescue Committee that cared for refugees fleeing Communist oppression occupied his free time. So too the various civic, religious and educational groups that constantly sought his leadership in raising funds and setting policy. He rarely refused, and once he accepted, the cause would overtake him and a whirl of activity would surround him and out of the blur would come a successful event.

He achieved great wealth, but he shared much of it in return for the opportunities he was fortunate to receive.

Perhaps the best example I can cite is the Sophia and William Casey Foundation, which was unusual in nature but monumental in scope. With his own money he created a fund to support 10 or more high school students each summer to work on a worthwhile project. The students would not have to take a summer job if they successfully competed in writing to receive summer grants judged by Mr. and Mrs. Casey and other trustees. The program was a success and many students found their first opportunities in a career in science, literature, politics or art.

Personally, I remember a man who was always going to the airport to some remote point of the globe on a mission for a client or his country with a few dozen books under his arm and a pocketful of ideas. I remember the lectures, the challenges, the opportunities he offered me.

To myself and to a host of other people there never will be another one like him.

And so, Bill Casey is indeed alive.

He is living and breathing in all those he touched directly or indirectly—whether they be the people of free Europe, grant recipients, refugees, or those brave souls who are fighting for their country in Nicaragua. He is among them, and his legacy, his example and standard of excellence lives in everyone who was fortunate enough to have basked in his sunlight.

Gore's Environmental Ignorance

By Julian Simon   *(From the 1 August 1992 issue)*

(Mr. Simon teaches business at the University of Maryland and is an adjunct scholar of The Cato Institute. His most recent book is Population Matters: People, Resources, Environment and Immigration.*)*

Democratic vice presidential candidate Albert Gore, Jr., recently published a book called *Earth in the Balance* about the supposed environmental and resource "crisis." The book is as ignorant a collection of clichés as anything ever published on the subject. It is truth that is in the balance, not our very durable planet.

Just about every assertion Gore makes points in the wrong direction—suggesting that conditions are getting worse rather than better, which they are.

His first example is soil erosion. After trotting out the obligatory scare words about how "eight acres worth of prime topsoil floats past Memphis every hour," Gore says that Iowa "used to have an average of 16 of the best topsoil in the world. Now it is down to 8."

The first footnote says only, "Conversations with the U.S. Army Corps of Engineers and the Iowa Department of Agriculture and Land Stewardship." One cannot use that vague reference to check the situation in Iowa. (Indeed, printed sources are generally scarce in the book.) But we do know the trend of increasing erosion for the country as a whole.

If Gore had done his homework, he would have examined the data in the publications of the U.S. Department of Agriculture's Economic Research Service. He would have talked to Bruce Gardner, assistant secretary of agriculture for economics, and to Gardner's teacher at the University of Chicago, Nobel laureate Theodore Schultz, and to Earl Heady of the University of Iowa.

Gore would then have learned that the average farm in the United States is becoming less rather than more eroded. That becomes clear from comparison of Soil Conservation Service surveys done at intervals since the 1930s.

Gore's treatment of soil erosion sets the pattern for the rest of the book. Gore alleges—in the first sentence—that there is a "global ecological crisis," that conditions have been worsening. But, in fact, all indicators of human welfare have been improving rather than deteriorating.

The second item Gore mentions is DDT, "which became for me a symbol of how carelessly our civilization could do harm to the world." He provides no data and cites no authorities, though he later adds that DDT "can be environmentally dangerous in tiny amounts."

A touch of research would have turned up writings such as *Mosquitoes, Malaria and Man* by Gordon Harrison, former director of the Ford Foundation's environmental program. Gore would have learned that with the aid of DDT, "India brought the number of malaria cases down from the estimated 75 million in 1951 to about 50,000 in 1961, and Sri Lanka reduced malaria from about three million cases after World War II to just 29 in 1964." As the use of DDT went down, however, by 1977 "the number of cases reached at least 30 million and perhaps 50 million."

Gradually, it became clear that DDT could be used quite safely. Rachel Carson's frightening scenarios, which Gore remembers troubling his mother, turned out to be without foundation. Commission after commission, top expert after top Nobel Prize-winning expert, have given DDT a clean bill of health.

The third item Gore mentions is Agent Orange (dioxin), which he describes as "the suspected cause of chromosomal damage and birth defects."

Again, Gore provides no documentation—this time with reason. There simply is no solid scientific evidence of any ill effects of dioxin. The Centers for Disease Control now admit that the evacuation of Times Beach, Mo., was unnecessary. But Sen. Gore has not gotten the word.

Love Canal is next. Gore seems unaware that the solid scientific consensus is that living near Love Canal did no observable damage to humans. And we are only up to page 3. The entire book is filled with environmental gossip, backed by no sources and contradicted by solid data.

Moreover, Gore questions other people's motives and behavior. He writes that "the statistics about forests can be deceptive too: although the United States, like several other developed nations, actually has more forested land now than it did a hundred years ago, many of the huge tracts . . . have been converted from diverse hardwoods to a monoculture of softwood."

But the same U.S. Forest Service statistics also show that the acreage in hardwoods is going up. Just who is deceiving whom?

Although the senator undoubtedly cares sincerely about the environment and natural resources, his ignorance is willed. He has been told in the past that his utterances do not correspond with the facts. But he has chosen to ignore the scientific literature.

To do so is not harmless, whether as a senator who has a large say in national policy on such matters or as Vice President of the United States—which Gore may well be.

Gore would (among other measures) tax the use of new raw materials to force more recycling, establish higher mileage requirements for cars, and require "efficiency standards throughout the economy"—all of which would raise costs and increase government intervention in people's lives. He would do those things on the basis of beliefs that are utterly contradicted by solid scientific facts. Is that any way for a potential Vice President to behave?

I.F. Stone Was Indeed a KGB Agent

By Herbert Romerstein   *(From the 15 August 1992 issue)*

The revelation in Human Events (June 6) that the investigative journalist and liberal icon, I. F. Stone, was a KGB agent, caused great consternation among his family, friends and comrades. I wrote the story based on discussions in Moscow and Washington with a retired high-ranking KGB officer who knew a great deal about Soviet intelligence operations in the United States.

The KGB officer, who asked to remain anonymous, commented on a statement made in a London speech by retired KGB Gen. Oleg Kalugin. Although he did not publicly name the agent, Kalugin said, "We had an agent—a well-known American journalist—with a good reputation, who severed his ties with us after 1956. I myself convinced him to resume them. But in 1968, after the invasion of Czechoslovakia . . . he said he would never again take any money from us."

According to my source, the agent referred to by Kalugin was I. F. Stone.

When my article appeared in Human Events, I was contacted by I. F. Stone's son, Jeremy, who tried to argue that his father would never have taken KGB money. I was also contacted by Don Guttenplan, who described himself as a biographer of Stone. Guttenplan tried to get me to identify the source, which I naturally refused to do.

Then the August 3/10 issue of the *Nation* came out with an article by D. D. Guttenplan in which he claimed that he phoned Gen. Kalugin, whose response to Romerstein's charges was unequivocal. It is not true, he said. I did not recruit him [Stone], and I did not pay him money.

I phoned Kalugin, who had read my Human Events article. He said that he had not contradicted anything I wrote. He has been speaking to Western journalists on this question but said that he didn't remember speaking to the *Nation* or to anyone named Guttenplan. It was possible, however, that he had done so, as he had spoken to a number of journalists.

Kalugin is an honest man. He tries not to deliberately lie. He is also an experienced intelligence officer and he tries to protect the identity of his agents. As he told the Western journalists, he will not publicly identify KGB agents.

As Kalugin explained it to me, he told the journalists that he had not recruited Stone. He did not comment on whether he recruited Stone after the KGB had lost him in 1956. He also said that he did not personally hand money to Stone. He did not comment on whether Stone received KGB money through another covert source.

Kalugin did tell the journalists, when asked, that he knew Stone well and had frequent meetings with him. When I asked Kalugin who first recruited Stone as a KGB agent, he answered, I believe truthfully, that he did not remember.

In Kalugin's speech in London, he made it clear that he did not originally recruit the agent but only re-recruited him. The reference to KGB money for the agent was that he said he would never again take any money from us.

In Guttenplan's *Nation* article, he quoted the Kalugin speech but left out the reference to the agent receiving KGB money.

That Kalugin and Stone were meeting was confirmed by a peculiar source. Jack Anderson, in a column critical of the FBI which appeared in the Washington *Post*, May 1, 1971, claimed to have obtained secret FBI files on Stone. He wrote:

"The most suspicious notation was placed in his file in 1966. On Feb. 11, 1966, at 1:00 p.m., states a surveillance report, the subject was observed to meet Oleg D. Kalugin in front of Harvey's Restaurant, 1107 Connecticut Avenue, N.W., Washington, D.C. Together, they subsequently entered Harvey's Restaurant.

"The FBI added darkly that Kalugin was the press secretary at the Soviet Embassy."

Kalugin was not only the Soviet Embassy press secretary, he was also a KGB officer in Line PR. This KGB section had the responsibility for collecting political information and covertly planting the KGB viewpoint and disinforming the press.

While Stone was sometimes critical of specific Soviet practices, he promoted their line on all major questions. During the Korean War, he wrote an entire disinformation book claiming to prove that the war was started by non-Communist South Korea. Recent writings by Russian researchers have proved that not only did Communist North Korea attack the South, but that they did it only after receiving permission from Stalin.

Confirmation that Stone was a KGB agent was also discovered by Reed Irvine of Accuracy in Media.

Irvine wrote in a July AIM Report that I learned about Stone's KGB connection when I showed a former KGB officer a list of about 20 journalists and asked if he recognized any of them as agents of influence. His answer was about a quarter of them. But the only ones he would name were Stone and the late Wilfred Burchett, an Australian Communist, who covered both the Korean and Vietnam wars mainly for Communist publications. Burchett had previously been identified as a KGB employee by a KGB defector named Yuri Krotkov.

I. F. Stone always presented himself as a publisher of a small newsletter struggling to make ends meet. Reed Irvine pointed out that Peter Osnos, Stone's research assistant from 1965 to 1966, wrote in an obituary tribute to Stone that he indulged in such luxuries as an annual trip across the Atlantic on the *Queen Elizabeth II*. Other former associates of Stone have remarked upon his expensive house and furnishings. Where he got the money for such extravagances has never been explained until now.

The KGB officers I talked to in Moscow were not defectors. Some were retired, but all were loyal to the KGB. In this current atmosphere of friendliness to the United States, some were prepared to talk a great deal about their experiences.

Additionally, interesting information is coming out of KGB files. This also bothers Guttenplan. He is clearly concerned that future revelations from KGB files will identify not only Stone but other American leftists as KGB agents. Guttenplan suggested in his *Nation* article that "the information—and disinformation—contained in the KGB files poses serious questions. . . ."

One of my jobs during my six years with the House Intelligence Committee was working on the problem of Soviet disinformation. All of my work at the U.S. Information Agency was on the same subject. I spent six years as head of the USIA Office to Counter Soviet Active Measures and Disinformation. Based on experience, I can tell you that the KGB frequently lied to the West in their covert media placements. They did not deliberately lie to their bosses. KGB files that we have seen recently have confirmed many things that we were told by KGB defectors in the past. Guttenplan's real concern is not disinformation but the truth about American leftists who collaborated or were agents of the KGB. Guttenplan wrote, "Why this attack, at this time, on this target? Communism may be dead, but Marxism, while hardly in vogue, is still breathing. And much of the credit for that must go to unrepentant radicals like I. F. Stone. Destroy his credibility and you effectively deny the possibility of an independent left position."

When Guttenplan phoned me after my HUMAN EVENTS article appeared, I was willing to speak to him. When I phoned Guttenplan after his article appeared, he never returned my call. Clearly, common standards of civil discourse are not a requirement for the left.

Guttenplan did make an interesting admission when he first phoned me. He revealed that I. F. Stone's family had destroyed all of his files after his death. Many lesser-known writers have their papers at university libraries all over the country. Why did Stone's family not want his papers available to future researchers? Clearly, the old saying is true, "The guilty flee where no man pursueth."

Prepping Anita for Sainthood

By L. Brent Bozell III   *(From the 31 October 1992 issue)*

I made a mistake. Recently, I congratulated NBC's "Today Show" Executive Producer Jeff Zucker for having a sudden outbreak of good taste in canceling an interview with Richard Burke, author of a new book of scurrilous charges against Sen. Ted Kennedy.

Zucker's good taste ended when "Today" aired two long interviews with Anita Hill, whose outrageous charges against Clarence Thomas are as unproven as Burke's against Kennedy.

By putting Anita Hill on the program October 6 and October 7, Zucker and his network have demonstrated their double standard remains: No tabloid trash, unless conservatives are the targets.

Of course, NBC didn't so much interview Anita Hill as give her a chance to promote herself and her $10,000-a-pop lecture tour. Katie Couric's questions were textbook softballs.

"You talked, Anita, about some of the very supportive letters you've gotten, and some of the letters that have touched you. Have you received any hate mail? . . . They find you offensive, most of all, because you are a black woman? . . . Twenty years from now, 50 years from now, when people look back at these hearings, how do you want them to think of you?"

Katie might have asked: "You said you had nothing to gain from testifying against Justice Thomas. But you're lecturing for $10,000 an appearance. You're writing a book, which you told the Senate you wouldn't do. Your witnesses claimed you were conservative and supported Robert Bork, which after the hearings, you emphatically denied. Doesn't this show you had something to gain, politically and financially, from testifying?"

Most journalists find such questions unnecessary, if not tasteless. Anita Hill is the media's patron saint of sexual harassment. *U.S. News & World Report* and the *Wall Street Journal* had the audacity to do polls announcing that more people now believe Hill. Can anyone be surprised, given the media's non-stop crusade on her behalf in the past year? That anyone still defends Justice Thomas after this propaganda campaign is a story in itself.

Do you remember Hill's accusations about Justice Thomas, the Coke cans and pubic hairs?

In the issue including its poll, *U.S. News & World Report* writer Gloria Borger reports for the first time the affidavit of Laurence Shiles, a student of Hill's who said he found black pubic hairs in his test papers. This damning affidavit clearly brings into question Hill's charges, not to mention her character.

Is the affidavit new? Well, no. It was available during the hearings, but the media ignored it then and for the past year.

The case against Anita Hill isn't just about Long Dong Silver and Coke cans. In the *American Spectator's* stunning March exposé of Anita Hill, writer David Brock detailed how Hill witness Susan Hoerchner, the only witness who claimed to know about Hill's charge against Justice Thomas at the time it supposedly occurred, may have lied to Congress.

According to Brooke, "In her [Senate] staff deposition and on another occasion, Hoerchner told interviewers that the call in which Hill said she was being sexually harassed occurred before September 1981, i.e., before Hill had gone to work for Thomas." After consulting with her lawyer, Hoerchner changed her story, telling senators she could not remember the precise date when Hill called. But nobody cared.

Nobody cared when independent counsel Peter Fleming released his report on how Hill's affidavit made its way to reporters Timothy Phelps and Nina Totenberg. Circumstantial evidence pointed convincingly to James Brudney, an aide to Sen. Howard Metzenbaum. NBC's Andrea Mitchell declared the Fleming probe "a waste of money."

That brings us back to the "Today Show," whose entire October 6 show was dedicated to the Thomas-Hill hearings. Amazingly, NBC brought on Phelps and Totenberg to defend Hill, but left out David Brock. NBC also did not invite Lally Weymouth of the Washington *Post* or Bob Cohn of *Newsweek*, the only other reporters who followed Hill's trail but who had their stories spiked.

NBC brought on three black leftist intellectuals (novelist Toni Morrison, law professor Patricia Williams, and Prof. Cornel West) but invited no black conservatives or any in-studio supporters of Justice Thomas.

In one question to Morrison, Couric openly suggested Justice Thomas lied by asking why blacks opposed Hill coming forward "regardless of the behavior."

But NBC set a record for audacity by having the whole sexual-harassment show co-hosted by Bryant Gumbel, himself charged with sexual harassment in a new book by former "Today Show" booker Judith Kessler:

"There were women unit managers [Gumbel] claimed to have slept with, and he would say things like, 'She's not even a good [deleted].' " Kessler also claimed Gumbel "got a kick out of scaring women" and "would give an assessment of everyone's bust size, and say, 'You know, I could sleep with that one if I wanted to.' "

Some of this sounds a lot like Hill's charges against Justice Thomas. Wouldn't it be fun to have Katie interview Bryant?

John Chamberlain, for many years the dean of the nation's conservative columnists, was a longtime contributor to HUMAN EVENTS.

Author M. Stanton Evans, who served as managing editor of HUMAN EVENTS from 1956-1959, has been a mainstay of HUMAN EVENTS ever since, penning more articles for HUMAN EVENTS than any other non-staff writer.

Thomas L. Phillips is the president of Phillips Publishing International, which is the leading newsletter publisher in the United States and the company that acquired majority ownership of HUMAN EVENTS in 1993.

The late Congressman John Ashbrook (R.-Ohio) served for many years as chairman of the American Conservative Union and was an avid reader and supporter of HUMAN EVENTS. In 1972, HUMAN EVENTS was the most influential force behind the Ashbrook challenge to President Nixon in the Republican primaries.

Chapter Eleven

Ronald Reagan

So closely have the fates of Ronald Reagan and HUMAN EVENTS been intertwined that an entire chapter has been devoted to articles by and about the president.

Reagan's first bylined piece in HUMAN EVENTS was a reprint of a speech he made to the Business Educational Institute of New Jersey. Titled "Encroaching Government Controls," it appeared in the 21 July 1961 issue.

His next article (28 November 1964), included in this collection, is the text of another speech—"A Time for Choosing"—that Reagan made on behalf of Sen. Barry Goldwater in the 1964 presidential campaign. This address has since become known as "The Speech." It brought the actor to national attention as a spokesman for conservatives and began his meteoric rise in American politics (28 November 1964).

The following November—a mere two years after the crushing defeat of Goldwater, which many pundits saw as the death blow for conservatism—Ronald Reagan was elected governor of California by a landslide majority of one million votes.

In August 1974, Gerald Ford assumed the presidency following the resignation of Richard Nixon and promptly began to disillusion conservatives with a string of policy and personnel decisions culminating in the selection of Nelson Rockefeller, the conservatives' nemesis, as his vice president. By 1975 the conservative wing of the GOP was on the verge of revolt and a debate raged in conservative ranks over whether to abandon the GOP altogether and start a new political party.

By the fall of 1975, Ronald Reagan was clearly preparing to run for president and on September 26 he gave a speech before the Executive Club in Chicago that laid out a program of "creative federalism for America's third century."

The speech, which advocated a "systematic transfer of authority and resources to the states," was written by Jeffrey Bell and M. Stanton Evans, both HUMAN EVENTS associates.

Its suggestion of a $90 billion federal spending cut later came back to dog Reagan in the New Hampshire primary because critics said the governor was not explicit in enumerating where the cuts would be made.

The speech ("$90 Billion Federal Cut," 4 October 1975) nevertheless presented a sweeping vision that Reagan was to continue to articulate in that and future campaigns.

Ronald Reagan left the White House in January 1989 with higher poll ratings than he had when he entered office. Nonetheless, since leaving office, Reagan has been subjected to a systematic effort by key figures in the liberal media who have sought to rewrite his record as one of failure.

James Roberts and HUMAN EVENTS editor Allan H. Ryskind rebutted this on-going campaign in the liberal media in "Liberal Media Rewrite History to Deny Success of Reagan Years" (18 April 1992).

'A Time for Choosing'

By Ronald Reagan   *(From the 28 November 1964 issue)*

(One of the highlights of the 1964 campaign was Ronald Reagan's television speech in support of Barry Goldwater's presidential candidacy. Widely acclaimed by both Republicans and Democrats, it was considered a brilliantly persuasive statement of conservative views. Following is the text of this speech.)

I have spent most of my life as a Democrat. I recently have seen fit to follow another course. I believe that the issues confronting us cross party lines. Now, one side in this campaign has been telling us that the issues of this election are the maintenance of peace and prosperity. The line has been used, "We've never had it so good!"

But, I have an uncomfortable feeling that this prosperity isn't something upon which we can base our hopes for the future. No nation in history has ever survived a tax burden that reached a third of its national income. Today 37 cents out of every dollar earned in this country is the tax collector's share, and yet our government continues to spend $17 million a day more than the government takes in.

We haven't balanced our budget 28 out of the last 34 years. We have raised our debt limit three times in the last 12 months, and now our national debt is one and a half times bigger than all the combined debts of all the nations of the world. We have $15 billion in gold in our treasury—but we don't own an ounce. Foreign dollar claims are $27.3 billion, and we have just had announced that the dollar of 1939 will now purchase 45 cents in its total value.

As for the peace that we would preserve, I wonder who among us would like to approach the wife or mother whose husband or son has died in Viet Nam and ask them if they think this is a peace that should be maintained indefinitely. Do they mean we just want to be left in peace? There can be no real peace while one American is dying some place in the world for the rest of us.

We are at war with the most dangerous enemy that has ever faced mankind in his long climb from the swamp to the stars, and it has been said if we lose that war, and in so doing lose this way of freedom of ours, history will record with the greatest astonishment that those who had the most to lose did the least to prevent its happening.

Well, I think it's time to ask ourselves if we still know the freedoms intended for us by the Founding Fathers.

Not too long ago two friends of mine were talking to a Cuban refugee, a businessman who had escaped from Castro, and in the midst of his story one of my friends turned to the other and said, "We don't know how lucky we are." And the Cuban stopped and said, "How lucky you are! I had some place to escape to."

In that sentence he told us the entire story. If we lose freedom here, there is no place to escape to. This is the last stand on Earth. . . .

This is the issue of this election, whether we believe in our capacity for self-government or whether we abandon the American Revolution and confess that a little intellectual elite in a far-distant capital can plan our lives for us better than we can plan them ourselves.

You and I are told increasingly that we have to choose between a left or right, but I would like to suggest that there is no such thing as a left or right. There is only an up or down— up to man's age-old dream—the ultimate in individual freedom consistent with law and order— or down to the ant heap of totalitarianism, and, regardless of their sincerity, their humanitarian motives, those who would trade our freedom for security have embarked on this downward course.

In this vote-harvesting time they use terms like "the Great Society," or, as we were told a short time ago by the President, we must accept a "greater government activity in the affairs of the people." But they have been a little more explicit in the past, and among themselves—and all of these things that I now will quote have appeared in print. These are not Republican accusations.

For example, they have voices that say "the cold war will end through our acceptance of a not undemocratic socialism." Another voice says that the profit motive has become outmoded; it must be replaced by the incentives of the welfare state, or is incapable of solving the complex problems of the 20th Century.

Sen. Fulbright has said at Stanford University that the Constitution is outmoded. He referred to the President as our moral teacher, and our leader, and he said he is hobbled in his task by the restrictions in power imposed on him by this antiquated document. He must be freed so that he can do for us what he knows is best.

And Sen. Clark of Pennsylvania, another articulate spokesman, defines liberalism as "meeting the material needs of the masses through the full power of centralized government." Well, I for one resent it when a representative of the people refers to you and me—the free men and women of this country—as "the masses." This is a term we haven't applied to ourselves in America.

Government Coercion

But beyond that, "the full power of centralized government"—this was the very thing the Founding Fathers sought to minimize. They knew that governments don't control things. A government can't control the economy without controlling people. And they know when a government sets out to do that, it must use force and coercion to achieve its purpose.

They also knew, those Founding Fathers, that outside of its legitimate functions, government does nothing as well or as economically as the private sector of the economy. Now, we have no better example of this than the government's involvement in the farm economy over the last 30 years. Since 1955 the cost of this program has nearly doubled. One-fourth of farming in America is responsible for 85 per cent of the farm surplus, three-fourths of farming is out on the free market and has shown a 21 per cent increase in the per capita consumption of all its produce. . . .

Sen. Humphrey last week charged that Barry Goldwater as President would seek to eliminate farmers. He should do his homework a little better, because he will find out that we have had a decline of 5 million in the farm population under these government programs.

He will also find that the Democratic Administration has sought to get from Congress an extension of the farm program to include that three-fourths that is now free. He will find that they have also asked for the right to imprison farmers who wouldn't keep books as prescribed by the federal government.

Every responsible farmer and farm organization has repeatedly asked the government to free the farm economy, but who are farmers to know what is best for them? The wheat farmers voted against a wheat program. The government passed it anyway. Now the price of bread goes up; the price of wheat to the farmer goes down.

Assault on Freedom

Meanwhile, back in the city, under urban renewal, the assault on freedom carries on. Private property rights are so diluted that public interest is almost anything that a few government planners decide it should be. In a program that takes from the needy and gives to the greedy, we see such spectacles as in Cleveland, Ohio, a million and a half dollar building, completed only three years ago, must be destroyed to make way for what government officials call a "more compatible use of the land."

Human Events

The President tells us he is now going to start building public housing units in the thousands where heretofore we have only built them in the hundreds. But [the Federal Housing Administration] and the Veterans Administration tell us that they have 120,000 units they've taken back through mortgage foreclosures.

For three decades we have sought to solve the problems of unemployment through government planning, and the more the plans fail, the more planners plan. The latest is the Area Redevelopment Agency. They have just declared Rice County, Kansas, a depressed area. Rice County, Kansas, has 200 wells, and the 14,000 people there have over $30 million on deposit in personal savings in their banks. When the government tells you you are depressed, lie down and be depressed!

We have so many people who can't see a fat man standing beside a thin one without coming to the conclusion that the fat man got that way by taking advantage of the thin one! So they are going to solve all the problems of human misery through government and government planning.

Well, now, if the government and welfare had the answer, and they've had almost 30 years of it, shouldn't we expect the government to read the score to us once in a while?

Shouldn't they be telling us about the decline each year in the number of people needing help? . . . . The reduction in the need for public housing? But the reverse is true. Each year the need grows greater, the problem grows greater. We were told four years ago that 17 million people went to bed hungry each night. Well, that was probably true. They were all on a diet!

But now we are told that 9.3 million families in this country are poverty stricken on the basis of earning less than $3,000 a year. Welfare spending is 10 times greater than in the dark depths of the depression. We are spending $45 billion on welfare. Now do a little arithmetic and you will find that if we divided $45 billion up equally among those 9 million poor families, we would be able to give each family $4,600 a year, and this, added to their present income, should eliminate poverty!

Direct aid to the poor, however, is running only about $600 per family. It seems that someplace there must be some overhead. So now we declare "War on Poverty," or "You, Too, Can Be A Bobby Baker!"

Now, do they honestly expect us to believe that if we add $1 billion to the $45 billion we are spending . . . one more program to the 30-odd we have (and remember, this new program doesn't replace any, it just duplicates existing programs). . . . Do they believe that poverty is suddenly going to disappear by magic?

Well, in all fairness I should explain that there is one part of the new program that isn't duplicated. This is the youth feature. We are now going to solve the dropout problem, juvenile delinquency, by re-instituting something like the old [Civilian Conservation Corps] camps, and we are going to put our young people in camps; but again we do some arithmetic, and we find that we are going to spend each year just on room and board for each young person that we help $4,700 a year!

We can send them to Harvard for $2,700! Don't get me wrong. I'm not suggesting that Harvard is the answer to juvenile delinquency.

Yet, any time you and I question the schemes of the do-gooders, we are denounced as being against their humanitarian goals. They say we are always "against" things, never "for" anything. Well, the trouble with our liberal friends is not that they are ignorant, but that they know so much that is not so!

We are for a provision that destitution should not follow unemployment by reason of old age, and to that end we have accepted Social Security as a step toward meeting the problem. But we are against those entrusted with this program when they practice deception regarding its fiscal shortcomings, when they charge that any criticism of the program means that we want to end payments to those people who depend on them for a livelihood.

They have called it insurance to us in a hundred million pieces of literature. But then they appeared before the Supreme Court and they testified that it was a welfare program. They only use the term "insurance" to sell it to the people. And they said Social Security dues are a tax for the general use of the government, and the government has used that tax.

There is no fund, because Robert Myers, the actuarial head, appeared before a congressional committee and admitted that Social Security as of this moment is $298 billion in the hole.

But he said there should be no cause for worry because as long as they have the power to tax, they could always take away from the people whatever they needed to bail them out of trouble! And they are doing just that.

Social Security Taxes

A young man, 21 years of age, working at an average salary . . . his Social Security contribution would, in the open market, buy him an insurance policy that would guarantee $220 a month at age 65. The government promises $127! He could live it up until he is 31 and then take out a policy that would pay more than Social Security.

Now, are we so lacking in business sense that we can't put this program on a sound basis so that people who do require those payments will find that they can get them when they are due . . . that the cupboard isn't bare? Barry Goldwater thinks we can.

At the same time, can't we introduce voluntary features that would permit a citizen to do better on his own, to be excused upon presentation of evidence that he had made provisions for the non-earning years?

Should we not allow a widow with children to work, and not lose the benefits supposedly paid for by her deceased husband? Shouldn't you and I be allowed to declare who our beneficiaries will be under these programs, which we cannot do?

I think we are for telling our senior citizens that no one in this country should be denied medical care, because of a lack of funds. But I think we are against forcing all citizens, regardless of need, into a compulsory government program, especially when we have such examples, as announced last week, when France admitted that their Medicare program was now bankrupt. They've come to the end of the road.

In addition, was Barry Goldwater so irresponsible when he suggested that our government give up its program of deliberate planned inflation so that when you do get your Social Security pension, a dollar will buy a dollar's worth, and not 45 cents worth?

I think we are for the international organization, where the nations of the world can seek peace. But I think we are against subordinating American interests to an organization that has become so structurally unsound that today you can muster a two-thirds vote on the floor of the General Assembly among nations that represent less than 10 per cent of the world's population.

I think we are against the hypocrisy of assailing our allies because here and there they cling to a colony, while we engage in a conspiracy of silence and never open our mouths about the millions of people enslaved in Soviet colonies in the satellite nations.

I think we are for aiding our allies by sharing of our material blessings with those nations which share in our fundamental beliefs, but we are against doling out money to governments, creating bureaucracy, if not socialism, all over the world. We set out to help 19 countries. We are helping 107.

Advance of Socialism

No government ever voluntarily reduces itself in size. Government programs, once launched, never disappear. Actually, a government bureau is the nearest thing to eternal life we'll ever see on this Earth!

Federal employees number 2.5 million. These proliferating bureaus with their thousands of regulations have cost us many of our constitutional safeguards. How many of us realize that today federal agents can invade a man's property without a formal hearing, let alone a trial by jury, and they can seize and sell his property in auction to enforce the payment of that fine?

In Chico County, Arkansas, James Wier overplanted his rice allotment. The government obtained a $17,000 judgment, and a U.S. marshal sold his 950-acre farm at auction. The government said it was necessary as a warning to others to make the system work!

Last February 19 at the University of Minnesota, Norman Thomas, six times candidate for President on the Socialist party ticket, said "if Barry Goldwater became President, he would stop the advance of socialism in the United States." I think that's exactly what he will do!

As a former Democrat, I can tell you Norman Thomas isn't the only man who has drawn this parallel to socialism with the present Administration. Back in 1936, Mr. Democrat himself, Al Smith, the great American, came before the American people and charged that the leadership of his party was taking the party of Jefferson, Jackson and Cleveland down the road under the banners of Marx, Lenin and Stalin.

And he walked away from his party, and he never returned to the day he died, because to this day the leadership of that party has been taking that party, that honorable party, down the road in the image of the Labor Socialist party of England.

Our Democratic opponents seem unwilling to debate these issues. They want to make you and I think that this is a contest between two men . . . that we are to choose just between two personalities. Well, what of this man they would destroy . . . and in destroying, they would destroy that which he represents, the ideas that you and I hold dear?

Is he the brash and shallow and trigger-happy man they say he is? Well, I have been privileged to know him "when." I knew him long before he ever dreamed of trying for high office, and I can tell you personally I have never known a man in my life I believe so incapable of doing a dishonest or dishonorable thing.

This is a man who in his own business, before he entered politics, instituted a profit-sharing plan, before unions had even thought of it. He put in health and medical insurance for all his employees. He took 50 per cent of the profits before taxes and set up a retirement plan, a pension plan for all his employees.

He sent monthly checks for life to an employee who was ill and couldn't work. He provides nursing care for the children of mothers who work in the stores. When Mexico was ravaged by the floods from the Rio Grande, he climbed into his airplane and flew medicine and supplies down there.

An ex-GI told me how he met him. It was the week before Christmas, during the Korean War, and he was at the Los Angeles airport trying to get a ride home to Arizona, and he said that there were a lot of servicemen there and no seats available on the planes. Then a voice came over the loudspeaker and said, "Any men in uniform wanting a ride to Arizona, go to runway such-and-such," and they went down there, and there was a fellow named Barry Goldwater sitting in his plane. Every day in the weeks before Christmas, all day long, he would load up the plane, fly to Arizona, fly them to their homes, then fly back over to get another load.

During the hectic split-second timing of a campaign, this is a man who took time out to sit beside an old friend who was dying of cancer. His campaign managers were understandably impatient, but he said, "There aren't many left who care what happens to her. I'd like her to know that I care." This is a man who said to his 19-year-old son, "There is no foundation like the rock of honesty and fairness, and when you begin to build your life upon that rock, with the cement of the faith in God that you have, then you have a real start!"

This is not a man who could carelessly send other people's sons to war. And that is the issue of this campaign that makes all of the other problems I have discussed academic, unless we realize that we are in a war that must be won. Those who would trade our freedom for

the soup kitchen of the welfare state have told us that they have a utopian solution of peace without victory. They call their policy "Accommodation." And they say if we only avoid any direct confrontation with the enemy, he will forget his evil ways and learn to love us. All who oppose them are indicted as warmongers.

They say we offer simple answers to complex problems. Well, perhaps there is a simple answer . . . not an easy one . . . but a simple one. If you and I have the courage to tell our elected officials that we want our national policy based upon what we know in our hearts is morally right, we cannot buy our security, our freedom from the threat of the bomb by committing an immorality so great as saying to a billion human beings now in slavery behind the Iron Curtain, "Give up your dreams of freedom, because, to save our own skin, we are willing to make a deal with your slave-master."

Alexander Hamilton said, "A nation which can prefer disgrace to danger is prepared for a master, and deserves one!" Let's set the record straight. There is no argument over the choice between peace and war, but there is only one guaranteed way you can have peace . . . and you can have it in the next second . . . surrender!

Admittedly there is a risk in any course we follow. Either course we follow other than this, but every lesson in history tells us that the greater risk lies in appeasement, and this is the specter our well-meaning liberal friends refuse to face . . . that their policy of accommodation is appeasement, and it gives no choice between peace and war, only between fight or surrender. If we continue to accommodate, continue to back and retreat, eventually we have to face the final demand—the ultimatum.

And what then, when Nikita Khrushchev has told his people he knows what our answer will be? He has told them that we are retreating under the pressure of the cold war and some day when the time comes to deliver the ultimatum, our surrender will be voluntary because by that time we will have been weakened from within spiritually, morally and economically.

He believes this because from our side he has heard voices pleading for a "peace at any price," or "better Red than dead." Or as one commentator put it, he would rather "Live on his knees than die on his feet."

And therein lies the road to war, because those voices don't speak for the rest of us. You and I know and do not believe that life is so dear and peace so sweet as to be purchased at the price of chains and slavery.

If nothing in life is worth dying for, when did this begin. . . . Just in the face of the enemy . . . or should Moses have told the children of Israel to live in slavery under the Pharaohs? Should Christ have refused the cross? Should the patriots at Concord Bridge have thrown down their guns and refused to fire the shot heard 'round the world?

The martyrs of history were not fools, and our honored dead who gave their lives to stop the advance of the Nazis didn't die in vain! Where, then, is the road to peace? Well, it's a simple answer after all. You and I have the courage to say to our enemies, "There is a price we will not pay." There is a point beyond which they must not advance! This is the meaning in the phrase of Barry Goldwater's "peace through strength!"

Winston Churchill said that the destiny of man is not measured by material computation. When great forces are on the move in the world, we learn we are spirits, not animals. And he said there is something going on in time and space, and beyond time and space, which, whether we like it or not, spells duty.

You and I have a rendezvous with destiny. We will preserve for our children this, the last best hope for man on Earth, or we will sentence them to take the last step into a thousand years of darkness.

We will keep this in mind and remember that Barry Goldwater has faith in us. He has faith that you and I have the ability and the dignity and the right to make our own decisions and determine our own destiny.

$90 Billion Federal Cut
Conservative Blueprint for the '70s

By Ronald Reagan   *(From the 4 October 1975 issue)*

(Following is the speech made by Governor Reagan before the Executive Club in Chicago, 25 September 1975.)

In his first Inaugural, nearly a century and three quarters ago, President Thomas Jefferson defined the aims of his Administration: "A wise and frugal government," he said, "which shall restrain men from injuring one another, shall leave them otherwise free to regulate their own pursuits of industry and improvement, and shall not take from the mouth of labor the bread it has earned. This is the sum of good government."

Jefferson believed the people were the best agents of their own destinies, and that the task of government was not to direct the people but to create an environment of ordered freedom in which the people could pursue those destinies in their own way. But he also knew that from the very beginning the tendency of government has been to be player as well as umpire. "What has destroyed liberty and the rights of man in every government that has ever existed under the sun?" Jefferson asked. "The generalizing and concentrating all cares and powers into one body."

If Jefferson could return today, I doubt that he would be surprised either at what has happened in America, or at the results. When a nation loses its desire and ability to restrain the growth or concentration of power, the floodgates are open and the results are predictable.

Fiscal Year 1976 ends four days before our Bicentennial. In this fiscal year government at all levels will absorb 37 per cent of the Gross National Product and 44 per cent of our total personal income. We destroy the value of our pensions and savings with an inflation rate that soars to 12 per cent a year. At the same time we suffer unemployment rates of 8 and 9 per cent.

Every minute I speak to you the federal government spends another $700,000. (I'd stop talking if they'd stop spending.) Washington is spending a *billion* dollars every day and goes into debt a billion-and-a-third dollars every week. I don't think it would surprise Jefferson to learn that the real spendable weekly income of the average American worker is lower than it was a decade ago—even though in these four years that same worker has increased his productivity 23 per cent. As Jefferson said, that is taking from the mouth of labor the bread it has earned.

If government continues to take that bread for the next 25 years at the same rate of increase it has in the last forty, the per cent of GNP government consumes will be 66 per cent— two-thirds of all our output by the end of this century. A single proposal now before Congress, Sen. Kennedy's national health insurance plan, would push the share of GNP consumed by government from 37 to more than 45 per cent, all by itself.

The absorption of revenue by all levels of government, the alarming rate of inflation, and the rising toll of unemployment all stem from a single source: The belief that government, particularly the federal government, has the answer to our ills, and that the proper method of dealing with social problems is to transfer power from the private to the public sector, and within the public sector from state and local governments to the ultimate power center in Washington.

This collectivist, centralizing approach, whatever name or party label it wears, has created our economic problems. By taxing and consuming an ever-greater share of the national wealth, it has imposed an intolerable burden of taxation on American citizens. By spending above and beyond even this level of taxation, it has created the horrendous inflation of the past decade. And by saddling our economy with an ever-greater burden of controls and regulations, it has generated countless economic problems, from the raising of consumer prices to the destruction of jobs to choking off vital supplies of food and energy.

As if that were not enough, the crushing weight of central government has distorted our federal system and altered the relationship between the levels of government, threatening the freedom of individuals and families. The states and local communities have been demeaned into little more than administrative districts, subdivisions of Big Brother government in Washington, with programs, spending priorities, and tax policies badly warped or dictated by federal over-seers.

Thousands of towns and neighborhoods have seen their peace disturbed by bureaucrats and social planners, through busing, questionable education programs, and attacks on family unity. Even so liberal an observer as Richard Goodwin could identify what he correctly called "the most troubling political fact of our age: that the growth in central power has been accompanied by a swift and continual diminution in the significance of the individual citizen, transforming him from a wielder into an object of authority."

It isn't good enough to approach this tangle of confusion by saying we will try to make it more efficient, or "responsive," or modify an aspect here or there, or do a little less of all these objectionable things than will the Washington bureaucrats and those who support them. This may have worked in the past, but not any longer. The problem must be attacked at its source. All Americans must be rallied to preserve the good things that remain in our society and to restore those good things that have been lost.

We can and we must *reverse* the flow of power to Washington; not simply slow it, or paper over the problem with attractive phrases or cosmetic tinkering. This would give the appearance of change but leaves the basic machinery untouched. In fact, it reminds me of a short fable of Tolstoy's: "I sit on a man's back, choking him and making him carry me, and yet assure myself and others that I am very sorry for him and wish to lighten his load by all possible means—except by getting off his back."

What I propose is nothing less than a systematic transfer of authority and resources to the states—a program of creative federalism for America's third century.

Federal authority has clearly failed to do the job. Indeed, it has created more problems in welfare, education, housing, food stamps, Medicaid, community and regional development, and revenue sharing, to name a few. The sums involved and the potential savings to the taxpayer are large. Transfer of authority in whole or part in all these areas would reduce the outlay of the federal government by more than $90 billion, using the spending levels of Fiscal 1976.

With such a savings, it would be possible to balance the federal budget, making an initial $5-billion payment on the national debt, and cut the federal personal income tax burden of every American by an average of 23 per cent. By taking such a step we could quickly liberate much of our economy and political system from the dead hand of federal interference, with beneficial impact on every aspect of our daily lives.

Not included in such a transfer would be those functions of government which are national rather than local in nature, and others which are handled through trust arrangements outside the general revenue structure. In addition to national defense and space, some of these areas are Social Security, Medicare, and other old-age programs; enforcement of federal law; veterans' affairs; some aspects of agriculture, energy transportation, and environment; TVA and other multi-state public-works projects; and certain types of research.

Few would want to end the federal government's role as a setter of national goals and standards. And no one would want to rule out a role for Washington in those few areas where its influence has been important and benign; crash efforts like the Manhattan and Apollo projects, and massive self-liquidating programs like the Homestead Act and the land grant colleges. Certainly, the federal government must take an active role in assuring this nation an adequate supply of energy.

Turning back these programs would not *end* the process of reform in Washington. In the immediate years ahead:

• In our regulatory agencies dealing with non-monopoly industries, we must set a date certain for an end to federal price-fixing and an end to all federal restrictions on entry.

• We must take steps to keep the spending and borrowing of off-budget agencies under control.

• We must reform our major trust funds to ensure solvency and accountability. Particularly important is the need to save Social Security from the colossal debt that threatens the future well-being of millions of Americans, even while it overtaxes our workers at a growing and exorbitant rate.

• We must put a statutory limit on the growth of our money supply, so that growth does not exceed the gain in productivity. Only in this way can we be sure of returning to a strong dollar.

• And we must radically simplify our method of tax collection, so that every American can fill out his return in a matter of minutes without legal help. Genuine tax reform would also make it more rewarding to save than to borrow, and encourage a wider diffusion of ownership to America's workers.

In the months ahead I will say more on each of these major areas of national policy. But for now, let me tell you what I think the massive transfer of federal programs to the states would mean.

It would mean a giant step toward solving the problem of inflation that is sapping the strength of our economy and cheating American wage-earners and pensioners. There is no mystery about inflation. It is caused by spending money that has not yet been earned. Without the enormous pressure of a $60-to-$80-billion deficit, the Federal Reserve System would have no mandate to pump too many dollars into the economy—which is the ultimate cause of inflation. The federal deficit provides the chief motive for the debauching of the dollar.

Add to this the gain in purchasing power that will accrue to all Americans from a sharp reduction in federal income taxes—the biggest spending burden the average family must absorb. Indeed, taxes of all kinds are a bigger family expense item than food, shelter, and clothing combined. Last year, according to a study by the Joint Economic Committee of Congress, income taxes at all levels rose by 26.5 per cent—the largest increase of any item in the family budget. By far the greatest part of this growing load of taxation is the federal personal income tax, whose bite gets sharper as inflation pushes taxpayers into higher surtax brackets. Government doesn't have to raise the tax rates to profit by inflation. The progressive income tax is based on the number of dollars earned, not their purchasing power, thus a cost-of-living pay increase results in a tax increase.

An immediate tax cut, some of which might have to be balanced by tax rises in the states, would be only the beginning of the savings that could be achieved. When we begin making payments on the national debt, we will also begin making further reductions in the tax burden. American taxpayers are currently being billed an average of $1 billion every 10 days just to pay interest on the debt. As the debt is retired, we can progressively reduce the level of taxation required for interest payments. Sen. Hubert Humphrey, excusing government spending, once said, "A billion here and a billion there—it adds up." Well, it can work the other way around.

With the spending reduction I propose, the federal government will no longer be crowding capital markets to finance its deficits. That will make available billions in new capital for private investments, housing starts, and job creation—and the interest rates will come down.

The transfer I propose does not mean that the specific programs in question are not worthwhile. Many are, though in my opinion many others are not. But the point is that *all* these programs are losing effectiveness because of the federal government's preemption of levels of government closer to the problems, coupled with Washington's ability to complicate everything it touches. The decision as to whether programs are or are not worthwhile— whether to continue on course—will be placed where it rightfully belongs: with the people of our states.

It is theoretically possible that local governments will simply duplicate programs as they now exist, and if that is what the people in the states desire, that is exactly what will and should occur. Certainly the bureaucrats who run them now will be available, for they will have no further work in Washington.

I think it likely, however, that some of the more worthwhile programs will be retained essentially as they are, many will be dropped, and others may be modified. But all the surviving programs will be run at much lower cost than is presently the case.

The present system is geared for maximum expenditure and minimum responsibility. There is no better way to promote the lavish outlay of tax money than to transfer program and funding authority away from state and local governments to the federal level. This ensures that recipients of aid will have every reason to spend and none to conserve. They can get political credit for spending freely, but don't have to take the heat for imposing the taxes. The French economist Bastiat, a hundred years ago, said: "Public funds seemingly belong to no one and the temptation to bestow them on someone is irresistible."

Spending Soaring Out of Sight

So long as the system continues to function on this basis, we are going to see expenditures at every level of government soar out of sight. The object is to reverse this: to tie spending and taxing functions together wherever feasible, so that those who have the pleasure of giving away tax dollars will also have the pain of raising them. At the same time we can sort out which functions of government are best performed at each level. And that process, I hope, would be going on between each state and its local governments at the same time.

The transfer of spending authority to Washington blurs the difference between wasteful states and prudent ones, and this too destroys incentives toward economy. If a state spends itself into bankruptcy on welfare, under the present system it is bailed out when Washington picks up the tab; indeed, many federal programs are geared toward encouraging this kind of behavior, bestowing greater aid in proportion to spending levels imposed by the states. The way to get more is to spend more.

By the same token, efforts at state economy are *punished* under the present system. A state that keeps its fiscal house in order and, for example, prevents the welfare problem from getting out of hand will find it derives no benefits from its action. It will discover, as we did in California, that efforts to impose some common sense in welfare will run afoul of federal bureaucrats and guidelines. Its citizens will be called upon to pay in federal taxes and inflation for other states that don't curb their spending.

Another benefit of localizing these programs is that state and local governments are more accessible to the local citizen, and in most cases prevented by statute from going in debt. When tax increases are proposed in state assemblies and city councils, the average citizen is better able to resist and to make his influence felt. This, plus the ban on local deficits, tends to put an effective lid on spending.

Federal financing is the spenders' method of getting around these restraints. Taxes are imposed at a level where the government is far and away inaccessible to the average citizen. The connection between big spending and high taxes is hidden, and the ability to run up deficits and print more money makes efforts to control the problem through the taxing side alone almost meaningless.

The proposals I have outlined will bring howls of pain from those who are benefiting from the present system, and from many more who think they are. Another Frenchman, Theirs, said, "For those who govern, the first thing required is indifference to newspapers."

We must turn a deaf ear to the screams of the outraged if this nation and this way of life are to survive. The simple fact is the producing class in this nation is being drained of its substance by the non-producers—the taxpayers are being victimized by the tax consumers. We may be sure that those in Washington and elsewhere whose life style depends on consuming other people's earnings while working people struggle to make ends meet, will fight to the last limousine and carpeted anteroom.

But if we ignore the taxers and the centralizers and do the things I know we can do, we'll do more than survive: we will inaugurate a new era of American diversity.

Take education. The United states built the greatest system of public education the world has ever known—not at the federal level, not even at the state level, but at the level of the local school district. Until a few years ago, the people had direct control over their schools—how much to spend, what kind of courses to offer, whom to hire. Is it an accident that as this local control gave way to funding and control at the federal and state level, that reading and other test scores have declined? It has just recently been announced that scores in college entrance exams have been nosediving for 10 years, and this year took the greatest plunge of all and yet spending on education in that same period has been skyrocketing. The truth is a good education depends far more on local school control than on the amount of money spent.

There is no question but that under local agencies certain abuses took place and certainly they needed to be cured, sometimes by federal intervention. This was certainly true of racial segregation in the South. But now that according to some estimates the South is the most *integrated* area of the country—now that there is an ongoing enforcement structure in the Department of Justice—is there any further reason to deny local control and funding of our schools?

Or take welfare. For years, the fashionable voices have been calling for a federal takeover of welfare. (Well, the old-age portions of welfare *have* been taken over—and in the first 18 months, more than a billion dollars have been paid out by mistake.) If there is one area of social policy that should be at the most local level of government possible, it is welfare. It should not be nationalized—it should be *localized*. If Joe Doaks is using his welfare money to go down to the pool hall and drink beer and gamble, and the people on his block are paying the bill, Joe is apt to undergo a change in his life style. This is an example of why our task force in California found that the smaller and more local government becomes, the less it costs. The more government is localized, the less you will see a situation like the one in Massachusetts, where a mother of six was receiving through cash and services the equivalent of a $20,000 earned income. That is twice the average family income of the state.

Unresponsiveness of Washington

The truth is that people all over America have been thinking about all of these problems for years. This country is bursting with ideas and creativity, but a government run by bureaucrats in Washington has no way to respond. If we send the power back to the states and localities, we'll find out how to improve education, because some districts are going to succeed with some ideas and other districts are going to fail with others, and the word will spread like wildfire.

The more we let people decide, the more we'll find out about what policies work and what policies don't work. Successful programs and good local governments will attract bright people like magnets, because the genius of federalism is that people can vote with their feet. If local or state governments grow tyrannical and costly, the people will move. If the federal government is the villain, there is no escape.

I am calling also for an end to giantism, for a return to the human scale—the scale that human beings can understand and cope with; the scale of the local fraternal lodge, the church congregation, the block club, the farm bureau. It is the locally owned factory, the small business-man who personally deals with his customers and stands behind his product, the farm and consumer cooperative, the town or neighborhood bank that invests in the community, the union local.

In government, the human scale is the town council, the board of selectmen, and the precinct captain.

It is this activity on a small, human scale that creates the fabric of community, a framework for the creation of abundance and liberty. The human scale nurtures standards of right behavior, a prevailing ethic of what is right and what is wrong, acceptable and unacceptable.

Three and a half centuries ago, peoples from across the sea began to cross to this great land, searching for freedom and a sense of community they were losing at home. The trickle became a flood, and we spread across a vast, virtually unpeopled continent and caused it to bloom with homesteads, villages, cities, great transportation systems, all the emblems of prosperity and success. And we did this without urban renewal or an area redevelopment plan. We became the most productive people in the history of the world.

Leadership by the People

Two hundred years ago, when this process was just beginning, we rebelled when, in our eyes, a mother country turned into a foreign power. We rebelled not to overturn but to preserve what we had, and to keep alive the chance of doing more. We established a republic, because the meaning of a republic is that real leadership comes not from the rulers but from the people, that more happens in a state where people are the sculptors and not the clay.

We are losing that chance today, and we know we are losing it. Two hundred years ago it was London that turned into a foreign power. Today, and it is a sad thing to say, it is Washington. The coils woven in that city are entrapping us all, and, as with the Gordian knot, we cannot untie it, we must cut it with one blow of the sword.

In one reference book, cutting the Gordian knot is defined as follows: "to solve a perplexing problem by a single bold action." The Gordian knot of antiquity was in Phrygia and it was Alexander the Great who cut it, thereby, according to the legend, assuring the conquest of Persia.

Today the Gordian knot is in Washington, and the stakes are even higher. But this is a republic, and we have no king to cut it, only we the people, and our sword has been beaten into ballot boxes. What applies to the role of government applies equally to the means of changing that role: leadership is necessary, but even more necessary is popular choice. The anonymous sage who defined leadership must have lived in a republic, for he said, "He is not the best statesman who is the greatest doer, but he who sets others doing with the greatest success."

Liberal Media Rewrite History to Deny Success of Reagan Years

By James C. Roberts and Allan H. Ryskind   *(From the 18 April 1992 issue)*

With the nationally televised proceedings of the opening of the Reagan Library in November 1991, millions of Americans had the opportunity to renew their acquaintance with the man who left the White House as one of the most popular Presidents in history. It was a vintage Reagan performance, a well-crafted speech, forcefully delivered, which reprised the Reagan record of accomplishments in a convincing way.

Yet there is now a massive effort underway on the part of the liberal media and academic elites to rewrite history to make the Reagan record one of failure and disgrace. Called the "Deconstruction of Reagan" by columnists Evans and Novak, this campaign theme tries to characterize Reagan as a failed President, too lazy and thick-headed for the White House.

Books, articles and television documentaries to this effect have been coming out in a growing stream.

The media vendetta is seen most clearly perhaps in the remarks of Bryant Gumbel of NBC's "Today Show." Gumbel rarely misses an opportunity to knock Reagan, frequently doing so by adding an anti-Reagan edge to a question.

Media Watch newsletter, which tracks Gumbel's anti-Reagan sputterings, reports that "Gumbel's Reagan bashing began soon after Reagan left the White House. For instance, on April 21, 1989, Gumbel told cartoonist Jeff MacNelly, 'The missteps, poor efforts and setbacks brought on by the Reagan years have made this a much more sober Earth Day. The task seems larger now.' "

Nearly three months later, in the seventh year of Reagan's economic expansion, Gumbel found disaster: "Poor in the U.S.A. Largely as a result of the policies and priorities of the Reagan Administration, more people are becoming poor and staying poor in this country than at any time since World War II."

In May 1990, with Reagan out of office for more than a year, he was blaming the ex-President for alleged economic havoc: "It's Wednesday morning, a day when the budget picture, frankly, seems gloomier than ever. It now seems the time has come to pay the fiddler for our costly dance of the Reagan years."

Five months later, Gumbel asked GOP consultant Roger Ailes, "Is this the legacy of Ronald Reagan politics—I mean, feel-good politics of the '80s about spending what we didn't have?"

Gumbel even refused to give Reagan credit for the U.S. success in the Persian Gulf war, noting in January 1991: "For that weaponry a lot of folks have been simplistically crediting Ronald Reagan, whose expensive procurements dominated government spending in the '80s. But as Capitol Hill correspondent Henry Champ reports, not everyone feels Reagan deserves the credit, or wants to return to Reagan-like levels of spending."

As might be expected, the Public Broadcasting Service and National Public Radio have been fountains of anti-Reagan commentary.

In January 1991, for instance, the Los Angeles *Times'* Jack Nelson was host of a PBS documentary on the life of former President Jimmy Carter which ended up as a shameless apologia for the politically exiled ex-President.

In the course of the interviews with Carter, the former President took the opportunity on numerous occasions to attack Ronald Reagan and his record, without challenge from Nelson, and to compare his own record favorably to that of his successors (again without challenge from Nelson).

The other networks have been equally hostile. Here, for instance, is Ed Bradley of CBS, election night, Nov. 6, 1990—nearly *two years* after Reagan had left office, five months after George Bush had entered into that disastrous summit with the Democrats and four months after he had publicly reversed his "no new taxes" pledge:

"If there's anything that we heard out there at the polls today, it was the sound of Reaganomics crashing all around us. If there's anything left of Reagan's trickle-down theory, Dan, it seems to be anxiety which seems to be trickling down through just about every segment of our society."

A month later Bradley's colleague Leslie Stahl took another swipe at the Reagan economic program when she accosted HUD Secretary Jack Kemp on "Face the Nation":

"There's a new analysis that says the American family is worse off today than it was in 1973. After 10 years of Reaganite, supply-side economics that you so passionately advocate, and that old question that Reagan used to ask about Carter—are we better off—apparently families are worse off. Do you really think the American people buy supply-side anymore? Don't they just think it was debt accumulation?"

Back at NBC, Reagan was responsible for the homeless problem: "In the 1980s—the Reagan years—the amount of government money spent to build low-income housing was cut drastically. Then the homeless began to appear on the streets and in doorsteps and housing became a visible, human problem," according to Garrick Utley.

Meanwhile, *Newsweek's* Eleanor Clift gave Kitty Kelley's sleazy, scantily documented "biography" of Nancy Reagan a generally favorable review.

Newsweek was joined in this disreputable exercise by the New York *Times*, which published an uncritical front-page story on the book on April 7, 1991, as did the Los Angeles *Times* which noted, "It adds to the already blistering historical record of President Reagan's many failures to fully take command of his own Administration and deals another blow to his place in history."

Lou Cannon and Haynes Johnson were joining the fray with books on the subject. Cannon's *Reagan: The Role of a Lifetime*, while more high-minded in tone than Kelley's bio, expresses the conclusion, as Evans and Novak put it that the "... bottom line is a lazy, ignorant President pursuing errant policies."

Over at *U.S. News & World Report*, Editor Roger Rosenblatt wrote off the Reagan legacy as "A dangerous failure. . . . A mess in Central America, neglect of the poor, corruption in government. . . . And the worst legacy of all, the budget deficit, the impoverishing of our children."

With the media still engaged in an orgy of Reagan-bashing, it might be well to consider the major charges. First off, you would think that the media would acknowledge, even if they didn't agree, that a legitimate case can be made that the Reagan presidency was an enormous triumph.

For many objective observers, Reagan rescued a country burdened by the policies of the Carter Administration, rejuvenated the nation's morale and stored the reputation of the presidency. He turned around the U.S. economy, wracked by skyrocketing interest rates and inflation, with major tax and spending cuts and an energetic deregulatory program.

He filled the federal judiciary with strict constructionists and tough-on-crime judges, restored America's standing in the world and rebuilt America's defenses, launching the weapons system that many believe finally forced Mikhail Gorbachev to cry "uncle" in the Cold War, the Strategic Defense Initiative.

Indeed, his spectacular military buildup, coupled with his financing of anti-Communist guerrilla movements on four continents, not only brought an end to the Cold War, but the *defeat* of the Soviet Empire and the rebirth of liberty in a score of nations previously under the heel of Moscow.

Yet the major media cannot bring itself to credit Ronald Reagan for any of these remarkable achievements.

Perhaps the most frequently voiced allegation is that Ronald Reagan's economic policies launched this country on a "decade of greed," and while the rich got richer—and greedier—the poor and minorities suffered.

Reagan's policies, in truth, gave us a decade of unparalleled prosperity and generosity, not greed. When the President was leaving office in January 1989, the economy was in its record 74th month of a peacetime recovery whose average GNP growth was close to four per cent a year. The economy had created over 17 million jobs, while cutting the Carter inflation by two-thirds and Carter interest rates by more than half.

The U.S. unemployment rate had dropped to its lowest rate in 16 years—5.3 per cent. Top marginal income tax rates, as high as 70 per cent when Reagan took office, had dropped to 33 per cent, and, best of all, Americans through a device known as "indexing," could no longer be pushed into higher federal income tax brackets because of inflation.

The late, brilliant economics writer Warren Brookes, a numbers cruncher par excellence, revealed how well Reaganomics was working in the Sept. 2, 1988, issue of HUMAN EVENTS, pointing out that every segment of the population benefited—black and white, poor and rich, families and single individuals.

From 1981 through 1986, wrote Brookes, "real per capita disposable income rose 12.3 per cent, or a little over 2.3 per cent per year, more than double the one per cent a year during the Carter budget years."

Brookes noted that Census Bureau data on family income and poverty showed not only a 4.2 per cent rise in median family income in 1986 (the largest rise since 1972), but also that since 1981 median family income in real dollars had risen by 9.1 per cent.

While the percentage of families with income under $12,500 rose in constant dollars, both for blacks and whites, from 1977-1981, the percentage of these low-income families *fell* during the Reagan era. And even as these low-income families were moving into the middle class, the middle class was losing even larger numbers to the income brackets above $50,000. As Brookes noted:

"From 1981 to 1986, white families with incomes over $50,000 shot up from 16.6 per cent to 22 per cent, a huge 33 per cent rise—offsetting a seven per cent drop from 1977-1981.

"But the most striking progress was made by blacks, whose share of families making over $50,000 rose from seven-and-one-tenth per cent to 12 per cent, an impressive 69 per cent rise, after a 12.3 per cent loss during 1977-1981. What is happening, then, is that even as the low incomes are moving up, the middle is also 'vanishing' upwards."

But were Americans getting greedier as they were climbing the ladder of prosperity? Richard B. McKenzie, in a comprehensive survey on charitable contributions for the Center for the Study of American Business at Washington University, put the lie to those who charge that gross self-indulgence was the signature of the Reagan years. Quite the contrary. McKenzie's conclusions:

"Between 1955 and 1980, total charitable contributions by living individuals, bequests, corporations and foundations more than doubled in 1990 dollars, increasing from $34.5 billion to $77.5 billion, or at a compound annual growth rate of 3.3 per cent.

"Between 1980 and 1989, total giving in real dollars expanded 56 per cent to $121 billion, or by a compound annual growth rate of 5.1 per cent. The yearly rate of growth in total giving in the 1980s was nearly 55 per cent higher than in the previous 25 years.

"Private charitable contributions by individuals grew at a 68 per cent faster pace in the 1980s (5.2 per cent a year) than in the late 1970s and earlier years (3.1 per cent a year between 1955 and 1980). And it should be noted that in the 1980s individuals increased their purchases of consumer goods in general and on a wide range of goods and services that might be considered extravagances."

Lifting the poor out of poverty, making the middle class better off, lowering unemployment, giving more to charity—since when have we labeled programs that made this all possible "policies of greed"?

But what about the savings and loan scandals, considered the epitome of excess under Reagan, according to liberal mythology? The S&L scandals, it turns out, were created by a *Democratic* President and a *Democratic* Congress.

First off, it was the high money market rates under Jimmy Carter—rates caused by inflation—that triggered a massive outflow of deposits from the thrifts in 1979 and 1980.

In order to staunch the hemorrhaging, the Democratic Congress in 1980 not only decided, wisely, to allow the S&L institutions to raise interest rates for depositors, but then, disastrously, paved the way for the scandals by guaranteeing S&L depositors up to $100,000 of their money.

So the looters and gamblers in the S&L business—realizing that Uncle Sam was willing to pick up the tab if any S&L went under—began offering outrageously high interest rates backed by enormously risky loans. And the depositors, aware that the Feds would reimburse them if the S&Ls went bellyup, were eager to put their money with the high rollers. That, in truth, is how the S&L scandal began.

And when Reagan appointee, regulator Ed Gray, tried to clean up what he perceived as a growing mess, congressional Democrats, who had become so cozy with the S&L boys, turned out to be the biggest obstacles to reform.

Four of the "Keating 5," after all, were Democrats, and House Speaker Jim Wright and his No. 2 man, Tony Coelho—both Democrats who had intervened heavily on behalf of the S&Ls and raised big bucks for the Democratic Party from their top officials—felt compelled to resign their seats in Congress as House probers began snooping into their financial activities.

So the "biggest and greediest" scandal during the Reagan era was produced by the Democrats, not Ronald Reagan or the Republican Party. But you'd never understand that listening to Gumbel and his fellow anti-Reaganites.

What about the charge that homelessness escalated because Ronald Reagan drastically cut federal housing aid? Columnist M. Stanton Evans scotched that canard neatly in the Dec. 2, 1989, issue of HUMAN EVENTS:

"In fact," he noted, "spending for housing assistance programs, and the number of people aided, both rose dramatically in the Reagan era. Annual outlays for such purposes have *tripled* over the past decade (from about $5 billion in 1977 to $15.3 billion in 1987), while the number of households aided went from 3.2 million to 5.4 million."

So the prosperity was all due to mounting red ink then? That's not true either, although President Reagan's critics have a point that he did not do nearly enough to combat the deficits. But because of his efforts to reduce domestic discretionary spending, lower taxes, and, finally, embrace the Gramm-Rudman anti-deficit legislation, the deficit in total terms and as a per cent of gross national product began falling dramatically in his second term.

In 1986, the deficit had risen to $220 billion, but it was slashed $70 billion the following year. Moreover, as Brookes wrote in our Sept. 24, 1988, issue, "Indeed, it may come as a shock that the nation's total government debt (at all levels combined) this last year was less than $108 billion, or about 2.4 per cent of GNP—well below most of the major nations in the world."

Nothing seems more sophomoric than the media pretense that President Reagan had nothing to do with the collapse of communism. Just think about this absurd proposition for a moment.

When Jimmy Carter was in office, lecturing us about the "inordinate fear of communism" and emasculating our defenses, the Soviet Union was building the most deadly military force in the world; aggressively arming foreign Communist governments, anti-Western guerrilla movements and terrorists on three different continents, toppling existing governments in Africa and Latin America, and launching a brutal invasion of Afghanistan.

When Ronald Reagan took office, the Soviets suddenly hit steel. We rebuilt our military, took the Communists on directly by supplying weapons to anti-Communist guerrilla groups—including those indispensable Stingers to guerrilla fighters in Afghanistan—put nuclear-tipped Pershing missiles into Europe (defeating the Soviet-sponsored "peace movement" in the process) and decided to go ahead with the Strategic Defense Initiative.

Further corroboration of Reagan's role in helping to effect communism's collapse has come from an unlikely source—*Time* magazine.

In a recent cover story, Carl Bernstein writes that the President and Pope John Paul II entered into a secret agreement to keep the Solidarity movement alive in Poland. In an effort that lasted for several years, the White House and the Vatican, according to Bernstein, funneled millions of dollars worth of funds and equipment to Solidarity forces throughout Poland.

Reagan and the pope were convinced that if Solidarity could survive, the Soviet hold on Poland could be broken and with it, eventually their hold over Eastern Europe as well. Clearly, that plan was effective.

In addition, Reagan's successful economic policies showed the Soviets they could never compete with capitalism. And only after all these policies were put into effect did Mikhail Gorbachev decide to call it quits. Surely, even Gumbel & Co. should be able to see the correlation between our policies and the Soviets tossing in the towel.

And whose military policy do the illustrious figures of the Fourth Estate think forced Saddam Hussein to be humbled? Not Jimmy Carter's. Former Under Secretary of State William Schneider, who recently headed the U.S. government's General Advisory Committee on Arms Control and Disarmament, tells HUMAN EVENTS that "The spare parts situation, the ammunition situation and the training situation were in such desperate shape [under President Carter] that 10 of the 16 Army divisions and half the Navy and air tactical wings were rated as non-combat ready."

Frank Gaffney, a defense expert who served in the Reagan Administration, says that Jimmy Carter did provide funding for research and development for some of the technology used in the gulf war.

But unlike Jimmy Carter, Gaffney tells us, President Reagan made the "hard decision" to put real money into the systems we used to make them operational, and to take on the U.S. Congress to ensure their survival.

The *Wall Street Journal's* Pentagon correspondent, Walter Mossberg, acknowledged that the Reagan years were crucial to the success we achieved in the gulf. Said Mossberg while the war was in its initial phase (Jan. 22, 1991):

". . . The Reagan buildup provided the quantities of weapons, depth of training and spare parts that were in short supply when President Carter left office. It's doubtful, for instance, that President Bush today could have marshaled the six modern aircraft carriers now in the war if Mr. Carter's faint support for carriers had continued.

"Even former [Carter defense] Secretary Harold Brown concedes, 'When it comes to the size of the force and putting the money in to buy the weapons and train the forces, the Reagan Administration deserves credit.'

"And the Patriot missile, which has been dazzling in knocking down the Iraqi Scud missiles, is Mr. Reagan's baby, not Mr. Carter's. The Patriot limped along with technical glitches during the Carter years, and didn't really get going until the Reagan era, when it was brought on line in quantity and given the capability to attack incoming missiles as well as attacking planes."

Reagan's critics have distorted the record of his defense buildup—like the distortion of his record in general—in part to settle a score with their old adversary.

As President, Reagan got the best of them again and again. This is a key aspect of his present difficulties with people like Bryant Gumbel because they were opponents of his philosophy and his programs and incredulous of his ability to prevail with the voters.

While in office, Ronald Reagan was a living reproof to everything they stood for—and they couldn't do anything about it while he controlled the airwaves as President. Now that he is gone they are getting their revenge.

It is likely that in the fullness of time truth will prevail, the Reagan presidency will be judged fairly on its merits, and that history will accord Ronald Reagan his proper place as one of our best Presidents. If that is so, however, it will be in spite of perhaps the most determined assault in history on the record of a former President.

At 81 and in retirement, Ronald Reagan is in no position to combat this onslaught. His many supporters are not, however, and it is time they spoke up.